125580

Population Growth Estimation

POPULATION GROWTH ESTIMATION

A Handbook of Vital Statistics Measurement

Eli S. Marks

William Seltzer

Karol J. Krótki

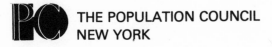
THE POPULATION COUNCIL
NEW YORK

The Population Council
245 Park Avenue
New York, New York

The Population Council is an organization established in 1952 for scientific training and study in the field of population. It endeavors to advance knowledge in the broad field of population by fostering research, training, and technical consultation and assistance in the social and biomedical sciences.

The Council acknowledges, with thanks, the funds received from the Ford Foundation, the United Nations Fund for Population Activities, the United States Agency for International Development, the World Bank, and other donors for the publication program of the Population Council.

Distributed for The Population Council by Key Book Service, Inc.

425 Asylum Street

Bridgeport, Connecticut 06610

Contents

List of Tables

List of Figures

Preface

In 1967 the Population Council embarked upon a program to develop a series of manuals that would be useful to evaluators of family planning programs. The first of these, entitled *A Handbook for Service Statistics in Family Planning Programs,* published in 1968, recommends the kinds of data that should be collected by the family planning program itself and suggests how these data should be analyzed. The second, *A Manual for Surveys of Fertility and Family Planning: Knowledge, Attitudes and Practice,* published in 1970, outlines procedures for collecting data on fertility and information about knowledge of, attitudes toward, and practice of family planning, both within family planning programs and in the private sector.

Together these manuals provide a guide to the most needed program-related research. An evaluation program is not complete, however, unless one knows on a current basis what is happening to the rates of population growth and the fertility of the entire population. This information is lacking for many countries in the developing world because their national civil registration systems function poorly: too often the geographic coverage is incomplete, a substantial (but unknown) proportion of events go unregistered, and the system is a number of years behind in processing of those events that are registered. Moreover, these statistical deficiencies have considerable impact in areas other than family planning evaluation. Reasonably accurate information about current levels of population growth and likely future trends is required for effective development planning in such diverse areas as labor force, agriculture, health, and education planning. The present manual is concerned with clarifying these problems of demographic measurement and providing procedures for dealing with them.

Because of the long time period involved in bringing about meaningful improvements in a civil registration system, a number of alternative methods of obtaining this information have been investigated in many developing countries over the past 20 years. For example, sample surveys have often included questions relating to fertility, although for the most part these have been add-on questions rather than being the focus of the survey. And, although relatively little attention was given to the methodological issues posed by the need for reliable and up-to-date surveys until the early 1960s, considerable progress has been made in this area during the past ten years. This manual reviews that progress, contributes to it, and points to the further development work that needs to be done. Indeed, it should be clear from this Handbook that the methodological problems we face do not always have simple or unique answers and that our knowledge is evolving.

Work on this manual was begun with the organization of a series of Population Council seminars on the topic "Problems of Population Growth Estimation." These seminars were held in New York during 1969 and 1970, and we are deeply indebted to the some 30 experts who participated in one or more of them. In particular, we should like to express our appreciation to Morris Hansen, who chaired the first seminar, "The Chandrasekaran-Deming Technique: Theory and Application"; to Philip M. Hauser, who chaired the second session, "Optimum Procedures for Matching Two Lists of Vital Events"; to Ansley J. Coale and the late Frederick F. Stephan, the co-chairmen of the third seminar, "Alternate Techniques for the Collection of Data on Population

Growth"; and to Forrest E. Linder, who chaired the last session, "Designs for Estimating Population Growth." The issues raised at the first three meetings did much to guide the thinking of the authors in the initial phases of preparing this Handbook. An early draft of the Handbook served as the working document for the final seminar of the series, and the present text benefited greatly from this exposure to critical review.

Much of the work relating to this Handbook was accomplished through financing provided to the Council by the United States Agency for International Development under contract No. AID/csd-1185. We are appreciative of this support from USAID and particularly to James W. Brackett and the late Harald Frederiksen of that organization.

<table>
<tr><td>New York, N.Y.
February 1974</td><td>W. Parker Mauldin
Vice President
The Population Council</td></tr>
</table>

Acknowledgments

The first drafts of Chapters 3, 5, and 7 were prepared by Eli S. Marks, of Chapters 1, 2, and 6 by William Seltzer, and of Chapter 4 and the Glossary by Karol J. Krotki. Final responsibility for coordinating revisions rested with Mr. Seltzer. However, all three authors made substantial contributions to each chapter as the manuscript went through successive revisions, and the final work is the result of a genuinely collaborative process.

Numerous individuals aided in the preparation of this book by reading and commenting upon earlier versions of the text. Ivan Fellegi, Christopher Scott, and H. Bradley Wells deserve particular thanks for the very careful reading they gave the full text and the detailed comments they provided. At various stages helpful suggestions and criticisms were also received from C. Chandrasekaran, Ansley Coale, W. Edwards Deming, Nusret H. Fisek, Bernard Greenberg, Thomas Jabine, Francis Madigan, John Rumford, Walt Simmons, Monroe Sirken, R. Som, Jorge Somoza, and Benjamin Tepping. Collectively, these comments have improved the accuracy and the clarity of the text substantially. Needless to say, none of these persons bears any responsibility for any of the specific recommendations made in this Handbook.

A number of other individuals played important roles in the preparation and production of this work. Ilze Hobin and Wayne W. McVey, Jr., of the University of Alberta developed the six maps reproduced in Chapter 4. Rita Fand, Peter Miller, and Carol Smith of the Population Council assembled most of the basic data used throughout the Handbook. Mr. Miller was also responsible for the technical editing of an earlier version of the work and redrafting substantial portions of Chapter 7. In addition, Ms. Fand reviewed the entire manuscript for accuracy and consistency and assisted in the final preparation of the book for publication. Overall responsibility for the production of this volume was in the hands of Ethel Churchill, and the book was designed by Larry Alexander. The contributions made by all these individuals are acknowledged with thanks.

Population Growth Estimation

Introduction 1

A. The Nature of the Problem

A country striving to achieve a variety of social and economic development goals in the face of critical shortages of skilled administrators, technically trained personnel, and foreign-exchange reserves must consider carefully the proper allocation of these resources. For this reason, quantitative techniques of development planning have come to play an increasing role in the formulation and implementation of policy in many countries of Africa, Asia, and Latin America. The value of such techniques depends largely upon the quality of the data employed. Unfortunately, the fact that national statistical systems are an important part of a country's infrastructure is often ignored, and a wide gulf frequently exists between the data required for effective planning and the information available.

Many kinds of statistics are needed for knowledgeable social and economic decision making. Among these are data on population growth, fertility, and mortality that serve as the starting point for population projections. Such projections are required in many parts of the planning process: for example, in forecasting the demand for agricultural production, in estimating the number of classrooms or medical facilities needed in the future, in developing social security and social welfare plans on a sound footing, and in preparing for future trends in the size and composition of the labor force. In addition, an adequate evaluation of a number of programs in the health sector, including family planning programs, is dependent upon the availability of accurate, up-to-date fertility and mortality data.

Data on population growth and its components may be obtained from a variety of sources: periodic national censuses, special censuses of local areas, a national vital events registration system, a population registration system, sample vital registration schemes, and various types of sample household surveys. Each of these sources has advantages and limitations in terms of the kind and quality of data produced and the effort required to employ it successfully.

In general, a population census receives first priority in the development of a comprehensive program for obtaining demographic data. A national population census conducted at regular five- or ten-year intervals provides a valuable series of statistical profiles, as well as a useful frame for sample studies during the years following each census. In addition, since it provides roughly comparable data for an entire nation, the census can be a unique source of tabulations for individual local areas, cities, or other subnational units. Despite these important features, however, a population census alone cannot supply the full range of demographic data a nation requires. It is, therefore, important for each country to plan for the timely development of other sources of demographic statistics appropriate for its needs.

Any realistic examination of the demographic data available in the world today indicates the seriousness of the problem confronting development planners. To meet the full range of planning needs most efficiently, up-to-date population estimates and projections are required for small local areas as well as at the national and regional level. Unfortunately, this ideal is rarely achieved except in the very few economically developed countries that go to the expense of maintaining an up-to-date population registration system. Local-area population statistics for most countries of the world—developed or developing—are markedly deficient, except in the period immediately following a well-conducted and speedily tabulated national census.

Even with respect to the more basic needs for data on population growth and size at the national level, the situation is very poor. For example, in 1967 for the world as a whole, current data on population growth, fertility, and mortality were available for only 40–50 percent of the world's population (U.N. Economic and Social Council, 1969). Moreover, where current data at the national level are available, the quality often ranges from uncertain to poor and is usually least adequate in those countries where population growth and its social and economic consequences are greatest. All too frequently, planners have discovered that the population estimates that served as the basis for many crucial parts of their work were grossly deficient.

Perhaps the most important cause of this situation is the almost universal tendency to underestimate the difficulty of obtaining an accurate count of the births and deaths occurring in a country. A national vital registration system—probably the best method in the long run for obtaining basic current data on fertility and mortality—is one of the most difficult types of statistical systems to establish and maintain. This is because such a system, if it is to produce reliable national data, must function continuously throughout the year in each village and city in every part of the country. In addition, a vital registration system cannot by itself provide vital rates; some other source is needed to give the population base—for example, a recent census.

If each vital event cannot be registered as it occurs, events must be enquired about retrospectively—for example, by asking each household in a census or survey about births and deaths that occurred in the past 12 months. Although this approach is relatively simple, it cannot routinely be depended upon to produce reliable estimates. In general, such retrospective questions about vital events produce erratic results because they are dependent upon both the repondents' memories and the interviewers' skill and persistence. The difficulties inherent in the retrospective approach to fertility and mortality measurement are such that efforts to use this method, without some system of calibration or adjustment, have produced unusable or misleading estimates in country after country.

B. *The Scope of the Handbook*

A variety of approaches have been used to overcome the limitations of registration and retrospective survey data. This handbook concentrates on one method of preparing adjusted estimates of basic demographic rates. The method involves the use of two collection systems to obtain independent reports of vital events for the same population, the matching of these two sets of reports with each other on a case-by-case basis, and the use of the match rates obtained to estimate the total number of events or the completeness of either collection system. The technique itself does not require that either method of data collection be of any specific type. Reports of vital events may be obtained from the official civil registration system, various kinds of special registration systems, one-time or multiple-visit household surveys, or, on occasion, population censuses.

In recent years such dual collection systems, regardless of the details of their design, have been frequently referred to as "Population Growth Estimation" studies, or "PGE" studies. (The expression "Population Growth Estimation" comes from the name of a particular study carried out in Pakistan from 1962 through 1965.[1] For more details of this study, see Chapter 2.) In general, we continue this practice and use the terms "dual collection system," "Population Growth Estimation," or "PGE study" interchangeably. Moreover, by extension, we often use the letters "PGE" to refer to the procedure itself or to some particular aspect of such a study (for example, "PGE technique," "PGE estimate," "PGE areas"). Any exceptions to this generic usage of PGE, as in referring to Pakistan's experiment, will be specifically indicated.

The purpose of this handbook is to provide: (1) an explanation of what the PGE technique is; (2) some information on experiences around the world in its use; (3) guidance on the general planning and the detailed design of a PGE study, including questions of cost; (4) examples of procedures that may serve as models (even though imperfect ones) for the preparation of actual procedures; and (5) a methodology for dealing with the inevitable weaknesses in the procedures used and in the estimates prepared. Essentially, then, this handbook deals with the problem of establishing appropriate procedures for the calibration of registration or survey estimates of population growth and vital rates.

Given these objectives, the question then arises of what material should be included in such a handbook and what it is safe and advisable to omit. Initially we viewed our assignment as solely one of making a "state-of-the-art" presentation of the PGE approach. However, we quickly discovered that, although a considerable body of experience in the use of the technique existed, little systematic thought had been given to many important aspects of PGE design and operation. In the end the Handbook has turned out to be a mixture of state-of-the-art wisdom and some new material. Actually the new material usually represents the application of a well-tested principle or procedure from another field to one of the problems presented by the PGE approach.

In writing this handbook we have tried to strike a rough balance between the general and the specific in our recommendations. On the one hand, vague generalities, although always true, are not very helpful in carrying out a study. On the other hand, specific rules, although easy to follow, are almost always inappropriate in any given situation. Undoubtedly, too much of the uselessly general and the uselessly specific has been included. However, since we are not quite sure what the best mix of the general and the specific is, we have been relatively tolerant of both tendencies.

Needless to say, even in our narrow field of PGE studies, this handbook is not a definitive work. Such a work could only be attempted after many of the design alternatives discussed had been systematically tested. We consider the Handbook to be a provisional guide to an important technique; hopefully our readers will also.

In order to keep this work from becoming prohibitively long, the discussion of certain subjects has been kept to a minimum. The procedure we have followed is to refer readers to standard texts whenever possible for advice and instructions on technical matters that are not specific to the PGE approach. For that reason, no attempt has been made in the Handbook to cover the basics of sampling, survey design and methodology, civil registration methods, data processing, or demographic analysis. In effect, this assumes that personnel with general competence in these technical fields will be available whenever an actual PGE study is to be attempted. Except in Chapters 3 and 7 (where some knowledge of sampling is helpful), no specialized knowledge or training beyond an elementary statistics course is needed to read the Handbook.

C. Other Methods of Dealing with the Problem

The dual collection system approach is not the only method available either for adjusting deficient data or for providing useful estimates of basic demographic variables. Certainly no single technique is appropriate for all situations. In choosing among the various possible alternatives, a careful review should be made of the specific kinds of data needed, how they are to be used, and the consequences of serious errors in them. In addition, the problems involved in obtaining the data needed and the resources available for this task must be realistically considered.

One valuable approach not covered in detail in this handbook involves the use of model life tables and stable population techniques. An excellent description of these techniques and their limitations, together with examples illustrating their use, is given in the United Nations manual prepared by Ansley Coale and Paul Demeny, *Methods of Estimating Basic Demographic Measures from Incomplete Data* (United Nations, 1967). In certain circumstances one or another of these techniques can be used to estimate the levels of most basic demographic measures from any two population parameters. Because they are analytical techniques, they can often be employed without going to the expense of gathering new data. On the other hand, these techniques may give quite erroneous results if they are used in situations that represent a marked departure from the assumptions underlying these methods. Moreover, where the quality of the data is poor, where questions exist about the appropriateness of the model used, or where the validity of any required assumptions of stability is uncertain, real caution is needed in interpreting the resultant estimates. Furthermore, the uncertainty introduced by the assumptions generally precludes the use of these techniques to identify short-run changes in fertility or mortality or to examine regional variations in levels.

A number of other techniques rely on the systematic nature of certain types of reporting errors to provide adjustment factors to correct deficiencies in the data. One major example of this kind of approach is William Brass's use of census or household survey data on children ever born and surviving children—data known to be in error—to provide corrected estimates of total fertility and recent childhood mortality. The basic Brass technique and a number of extensions of it are discussed in the United Nations manual referred to in the preceding paragraph. Another approach, developed by R. K. Som, consists of adjusting the number of events reported in a retrospective period to compensate for an assumed pattern of increased forgetting as the period becomes longer. This technique is described in detail in his monograph *Recall Lapse in Demographic Enquiries* (1973).

Finally, a number of methods have been suggested for approaching the problem of poor data directly, by insisting that careful training and supervision of field work and the proper analysis of results can hold errors down to acceptable levels. For example, it has been asserted that a detailed pregnancy history will yield useful fertility estimates (Bogue and Bogue, 1967); evidence of good results from a simple retrospective mortality study in Turkey has been presented (Goldberg and Adlakha, 1968); census and survey data on the age of own children by age of mother have been used to reconstruct past fertility (Grabill and Cho, 1965); and Wishik (1968) has tested a five-year retrospective fertility history in Pakistan.

The one overriding shortcoming that we find in all the alternative methods discussed is that they do not provide any built-in measure of reliability. Although a number of these approaches use powerful analytical techniques and brilliant dodges to overcome weaknesses in the data, the best they can come up with is an internally consistent set of estimates—which may or may not be correct. Certainly demographic analysis can and should be used to set limits on the plausible values for fertility and mortality. However, these limits are usually very wide, so that questions about the correctness of any given estimate very quickly become a matter of judging whether the estimate appears "reasonable." This judgment, in turn, depends largely upon the training and experience of the person deciding what is reasonable. The routine acceptance of a particular fertility or mortality estimate as "reasonable" because it agrees with a number of other apparently independent estimates ignores the fact that the same error processes may be affecting all the estimates. To put the matter somewhat colloquially, the alternative approaches discussed in this section do not go looking for trouble in the data. The value of the dual collection approach, as we see it, is that it has a built-in "trouble detector." At its worst, the PGE approach, like all the other approaches, can produce unusable results. However, the very nature of the dual collection method usually makes its failures self-evident. Unfortunately, this is often not the case when the other approaches are used.

D. *The Principles Underlying the Handbook*

At this point let us state some of the principles that guided us in the preparation of this book. Seven principles seem to form the basic rationale for most of our recommendations: (1) no one design is optimal, either theoretically or practically, for all situations; (2) certain underlying principles of good design exist and can be specified; (3) a theoretically sound design is worthless if it is either impractical to implement or likely to be implemented improperly; (4) no matter how carefully a study is designed, its execution will be flawed—in other words, no set of data will be error-free; (5) producers of statistical data have an obligation to investigate and report on the amount of error that may be present in the data they collect; (6) any given design, good or bad, can be improved on the basis of administrative experience and the statistical evaluation of results; and (7) any given study is a system of interrelated parts, and an improvement of one feature of the design without considering its effect on the balance of the design is wasteful and undesirable.

These principles are general in nature; that is, they are equally applicable to the design of any system used to obtain statistical data. This handbook is simply an effort to apply these principles to the particular problem of measuring basic demographic variables in countries lacking reliable birth and death registration data. We hope that users of this handbook will keep these basic principles in mind while reading the book and considering our specific recommendations.

E. *An Outline of the Chapters*

The Handbook is divided into seven chapters followed by a bibliography and a technical glossary. Chapter 2 contains a review of the use of the PGE technique in vital statistics measurement in various parts of the world over the past 40 years, as well as the use of the technique in other fields. Chapter 3 is a detailed exposition of how one goes about designing a PGE study. Emphasis is placed on the process of choosing between explicit alternatives at each stage of the design, and particular attention is given to the problem of deciding upon reasonably accurate and efficient rules.

In Chapter 4 we present three sets of model procedures that can be used as guidelines in preparing the full range of field and office materials needed for a PGE study. The three designs envisioned by these model procedures were chosen because among them they cover most of the situations commonly seen. Nevertheless, it is our expectation that any specific PGE study will differ from these models, in varying degrees, to accommodate specific local conditions. Almost certainly the unthinking implementation of those procedures will produce less than optimum results. It is our hope, however, that a thoughtful implementation of those procedures deemed important will produce better results than those that would have been obtained if this handbook were not available. Chapter 5 presents a case study of the design of a PGE study in a fictional country. It is intended to illustrate and clarify principles and procedures described in Chapters 3 and 4.

Chapter 6 deals with the evaluation of PGE study results. The alternatives of adjusting study results, modifying the present study design, or moving to a completely new design are examined as possible consequences of the process of evaluation. Finally, in Chapter 7 we take up a number of important, but diverse, issues omitted for the sake of clarity from earlier chapters.

We are aware that the various chapters overlap to some extent. (This is particularly true with respect to Chapters 3, 4, and 5.) Because most of those who will be using this book will have neither the time nor the technical background to read it from cover to cover, we thought it safe to assume that each chapter would have a somewhat different audience. Accordingly, the topics basic to a properly designed and executed PGE study have been discussed from a different perspective in each chapter. We hope that those who do read major portions of this work will find that the overlap clarifies the text more than it dulls or annoys the reader. Indeed, some effort was made to introduce quite different examples into each treatment of a given topic.

F. *Our Intended Audience*

The primary audience we had in mind while writing the Handbook was the personnel of a government statistical office. We envisioned an overburdened director trying to balance the conflicting demands of many programs, with inadequate resources to carry them out; a trusted division chief charged with drawing up the plans for the study, working with the field staff to ensure that the procedures are properly implemented, designing and supervising the matching operations, and assigned the responsibility for writing the final report; a junior statistical officer instructed to prepare drafts of field manuals, training materials, schedules, and coding instructions; and a sampling expert unfamiliar with some of the particular problems that may come up in the design of samples appropriate for PGE studies. In some offices, there may be additional personnel involved, while in others one or two persons may carry the entire administrative and technical burden. But regardless of the details, the personnel filling these roles are the primary group for whom this handbook is intended.

Statistical consultants working in countries with deficient vital statistics may also find the Handbook useful. Such consultants may be asked by the director of the statistical office whether a PGE study should be undertaken, and if they recommend one, to prepare a broad outline of the study. Like the trusted division chief mentioned above, a consultant may be asked to play a variety of roles in the design and implementation of a PGE study.

Many parts of the Handbook are also suitable for the users of demographic data—for example, public health physicians and biostatisticians in the health ministry concerned with assessing the quality of the civil registration system for which they are responsible; members of the planning commission staff concerned with monitoring current development progress and planning future programs; and others in and out of government interested in the quality of demographic data.

Finally, those concerned with questions of survey design in general may find the Handbook of interest, if not provocative. The need for a dual collection system approach arose primarily because of the inability of traditional survey or registration procedures to handle the job on a consistent basis in many parts of the world. Because of this, many aspects of PGE design and implementation represent attempts to take into account large fixed and variable nonsampling errors.

G. *How to Use this Handbook*

If sufficient time is available, the Handbook can be read from beginning to end. In this way, one will receive a balanced picture of the general methodological problems of PGE design, on the one hand, and a great deal of information about the details of PGE operations, on the other. Of course, such a reading alone cannot provide all the technical information needed to assure a satisfactory PGE study design. As we indicated earlier, the guidance provided by the Handbook must be supplemented by the knowledge of skilled technicians such as sampling and data processing experts. There is a real danger that valuable resources will be wasted if a PGE study or any similar data gathering operation is undertaken without the assistance of such experts.

Depending on the interest and background of the reader, the following abbreviated reading programs are suggested if time does not permit reading the entire Handbook. (Those who will be reading only limited portions of the Handbook are reminded that a glossary of techical terms can be found at the back of the book.)

(1) *Administrators interested in getting a quick, basically nonstatistical impression of the PGE approach.* Read Chapters 1 and 2 and Sections A and B of Chapter 3; in addition, Chapter 5 and Sections D, H, and L of Chapter 3 are recommended if the decision has been made to go ahead with a PGE approach.

(2) *Sampling experts.* Read Chapters 2, 3, 5, and parts of 7.

(3) *Personnel directly responsible for dealing with the day-to-day problems of design and implementation.* Read Chapters 1 and 4 and Sections F, I, and K of Chapter 3. They will also find useful background material in Chapters 2 and 5 and Sections A, B, C, and L of Chapter 3.

(4) *Personnel responsible for the analysis and publication of data from the study.* Read Chapters 2, 3, and 6.

(5) *Users of demographic data.* Read Chapters 1, 2, and 6.

Despite the value of these abbreviated reading programs, it is recommended that at least one responsible official in any statistical office undertaking a PGE study read all seven chapters. This will help ensure proper coordination between all parts of the study.

Footnote

[1] Subsequent to this study, East Pakistan became an independent nation, Bangladesh. References to Pakistan dealing with the period prior to 1971 refer to the then-current boundaries of Pakistan, including Bangladesh.

The PGE Approach: Some Background 2

A. Introduction

This chapter provides a description of the PGE technique and a review of the procedures and results of PGE studies conducted in various parts of the world over the past 40 years. Our purpose is threefold: first, to provide a relatively nontechnical introduction to the PGE approach; second, to illustrate the wide variety of circumstances in which this approach has been used; and third, to provide, in relatively compact form, a body of experience on which statistical administrators, survey statisticians, and demographers can draw in planning new PGE studies.

Essentially, the PGE approach as used in the measurement or evaluation of vital statistics has three distinct features: the collection of reports of vital events by two quasi-independent data gathering procedures;[1] the case-by-case matching of the reports in the two systems to determine which events are reported by both systems; and the preparation of an estimate of the number of events adjusted for omissions, or an estimate of the relative completeness of either system, on the basis of the match rates obtained. All three factors must be present for the study to be classified as one using the PGE approach. This definition is broad enough to include both traditional studies of civil registration completeness (for example, the 1950 U.S. birth registration test) and such efforts at basic demographic measurement as the Pakistan PGE study and the Turkish Demographic Survey. However, supervisory rechecks and reinterviews of the type frequently employed in census or survey work are not PGE studies by this definition. Supervision in this form is not "dual collection" as the term is used in this handbook, since it involves the use of data collection procedures that are highly *dependent*. Moreover, the overriding purpose of supervision is to limit and correct the mistakes of individual field workers rather than to provide statistical adjustments by which the estimates of an entire measurement process can be corrected for omissions.

11

Dual collection, by itself or in conjunction with case-by-case matching, may also be used in various kinds of analytical or methodological studies. Two or more records for the same individual or event, each containing somewhat different kinds of information, may be linked with each other to provide a larger number of variables for analysis than that present in any one record alone. For example, in order to study the relationship between infant mortality and the weight of a baby at birth it may be necessary to match death certificates for infants with the corresponding birth certificates because the death certificates do not contain information on birth weight (U.S. National Center for Health Statistics, 1970). Similar matching operations have been conducted to permit the study of the incidence of certain kinds of inherited diseases (Newcombe, 1966), or, to cite an example in the industrial sector, to enable the cross-tabulation of data collected on an establishment basis with that obtained from individual company reports (U.S. Bureau of the Census, 1964e).

Another large group of studies involving dual collection and matching, which again are not PGE studies as the term is used in this handbook, are those undertaken to evaluate the quality of the responses to one or more of the items contained in a census, survey, or registration system. Thus, death certificates for the period after a population census may be matched with census reports for the same individuals in order to evaluate the quality of the information reported on the death record (U.S. National Center for Health Statistics, 1969). In a similar way, the quality of census data on labor force status or age can be measured by comparing the responses obtained in the census for these items with those obtained for the same individuals in a post-enumeration quality check survey (U.S. Bureau of the Census, 1960). In studies of household financial characteristics, wealth, and savings, comparisons between survey reports on individual savings account balances and corporate stock holdings and the relevant institutional records can be used to evaluate survey responses for these items (Ferber, 1965).[2]

Dual collection itself, without case-by-case matching, is implicit in any comparison of totals—for example, when the total number of registered births is compared with the enumerated census population under one year of age adjusted for estimated underenumeration and mortality (Whelpton, 1934), or when the population of a particular birth cohort is followed through successive censuses (Barclay, 1958). However, as we have already indicated, the PGE approach goes beyond the comparison of totals to the case-by-case comparison of individual reports to obtain a statistical estimate adjusted for omitted events.

B. A Statistical Introduction

The principle underlying the PGE adjustment for omitted events is one of the basic propositions of probability—namely, if two events, A and B, occur independently of each other, then the probability of

A and B jointly occurring is equal to the probability of A occurring times the probability of B occurring. For example, since the probability of drawing the three of spades from a standard deck of 52 playing cards is one out of 52, or about .0192, and the probability of rolling a three with a standard six-sided die is one out of six, or about .1667, the probability of *both* drawing the three of spades *and* rolling a three is .0192 times .1667, or approximately .0032.

In algebraic notation,[3]

$$\Pr(A \text{ and } B) = \Pr(A) \cdot \Pr(B) \quad,$$

where

$$\Pr(A) = \frac{A}{A + \text{not } A} \quad \text{and}$$

$$\Pr(B) = \frac{B}{B + \text{not } B}$$

Alternatively, the same relationship can be expressed by

$$P(AB) = P(A) \cdot P(B)$$

or by

$$P_{12} = P_1 P_2 \qquad\qquad\qquad\qquad [2.1]$$

where

$$\Pr(A) = P(A) = P_1 \quad \text{and}$$

$$\Pr(B) = P(B) = P_2$$

It is important to remember that one condition *must* be met for equation 2.1 to be true: The occurrence of A can have no effect on the occurrence of B, and *vice versa*. This condition is called "statistical independence."

The principle stated in equation 2.1 has applications to the problem of vital statistics measurement. Any method of collecting reports of births and deaths will obtain information about some events but miss others. (A very good collection system will omit relatively few events, whereas a very poor system may omit more than half the events that occur.) If the system functioned with unvarying efficiency, the proportion of vital events recorded would remain constant; and if this proportion were once determined, it would be a simple matter to come up with the true number of events occurring in, say, a year, given the number reported for that year.

If the proportion of live births or deaths recorded by the collection method is equated with the probability, P_1, that an event will be reported by the method in question, and if N_1 events are reported for a given period,[4] then the estimate of the total number of events for that period will be

$$\hat{N} = \frac{N_1}{P_1} \quad, \qquad\qquad\qquad\qquad [2.2]$$

where

$\hat{N}$ = estimate of the total number of live births or deaths,

N_1 = number of live births or deaths reported by method 1, and

P_1 = probability that any given birth or death will be recorded using method 1.

For example, if a civil registration system was known (or believed) to obtain reports for 94 percent of the live births actually taking place and 500 births were recorded for a given month, the number of births actually occurring during the month would be estimated from equation 2.2 as

$$\hat{N} = \frac{500}{.94} = 532 \quad .$$

In other words, if we know the number of events recorded (500) and the completeness, or efficiency, of the data gathering procedure (94 percent), it is a simple matter to estimate the total number of events occurring (532).

Unfortunately, the value of P_1 is not constant. In fact, it may vary widely for different parts of the population, for different types of collection systems, and for different time periods within any given collection system. Furthermore, even an appropriate average value for P_1 is usually not available. The PGE approach, by means of dual collection and matching, provides a way of making a satisfactory estimate of P_1 as long as certain basic conditions are not violated too seriously.[5] If these conditions are met, the estimate of P_1 is as precise as any other sample estimate of a percentage or a proportion.

How do we estimate P_1 so that we can obtain a value for $\hat{N}$ using equation 2.2? First, assuming statistical independence between the two systems or sources, we can say, on the basis of equation 2.1, that

$$P_1 = \frac{P_{12}}{P_2} \quad . \tag{2.3}$$

Next, we define P_1, P_2, and P_{12} in terms of our particular problem[6]:

$$P_1 = \frac{N_1}{N} \quad , \tag{2.4a}$$

$$P_2 = \frac{N_2}{N} \quad , \quad \text{and} \tag{2.4b}$$

$$P_{12} = \frac{M}{N} \quad , \tag{2.4c}$$

where

N = true total number of events, regardless of whether they were reported or missed,

N_1 = number of events reported by source 1,
N_2 = number of events reported by source 2, and
M = number of events reported in both sources.

We then substitute N_2/N for P_2 and M/N for P_{12} in equation 2.3. Finally, noting that both the numerator and the denominator of the right side of this equation have a common factor, N, that can be "cancelled out," we have

$$P_1 = \frac{M/N}{N_2/N} = \frac{M}{N_2} \quad . \qquad [2.5]$$

The accuracy of this estimate depends in part upon the degree to which statistical independence is achieved. It also depends upon the accuracy of M and N_2, which in turn depend upon the accuracy of the matching and the elimination of out-of-scope reports, respectively.

Equation 2.5 provides us with a method of estimating the efficiency, or completeness, of source 1. This can be clearly seen when we use N_1/N in place of P_1 in equation 2.5. Thus,

$$\frac{N_1}{N} = \frac{M}{N_2} \quad , \qquad [2.6]$$

which leads to the general proposition that *the match rate of either source in a dual collection system is the estimated coverage rate of the other source.*

In addition to providing a coverage, or completeness, estimate, this technique also provides a method of estimating the total number of events adjusted for omitted events in either or both systems. The estimated total can be found by simply transposing the terms of equation 2.6 or substituting the right side of equation 2.5 into the denominator of the right side of equation 2.2 and reducing the fraction. Either method yields the result

$$\hat{N} = \frac{N_1 N_2}{M} \quad , \qquad [2.7]$$

where

$\hat{N}$ = estimated total number of events,
N_1 = number of events reported by source 1,
N_2 = number of events reported by source 2, and
M = number of events reported both in source 1 and in source 2.

In other words,

$$\hat{N} = \frac{N_1}{W_1} = \frac{N_2}{W_2} \quad ,$$

where

$$W_1 = \frac{M}{N_2} = \text{estimated completeness of reporting for source 1, and}$$

$$W_2 = \frac{M}{N_1} = \text{estimated completeness of reporting for source 2.}$$

The estimate of N given by equation 2.7 has many uses beyond the field of vital statistics estimation—for example, in measuring the size of various kinds of wildlife populations (see Section E of this chapter). The fact that it is not a unique or special kind of statistical adjustment should be apparent from the simplicity of its derivation and the relatively modest amount of data needed to use it.

If we let

$$U_1 = N_1 - M = \text{number of events reported in source 1 only,}$$

$$U_2 = N_2 - M = \text{number of events reported in source 2 only,}$$

and substitute $M+U_1$ for N_1 and $M+U_2$ for N_2 in equation 2.7, we can express the PGE estimate of the total number of events, $\hat{N}$, in terms of the number of events reported in both sources, the number of events reported in either source alone, and the estimate of events missed by both sources. This alternative form of the PGE estimate can be expressed as

$$\hat{N} = M + U_1 + U_2 + \frac{U_1 U_2}{M} \quad . \tag{2.8}$$

Although PGE estimates using equation 2.7 had been made previously, it was not until the 1940's that the use of equation 2.8 in connection with vital statistics estimation was proposed, by C. Chandrasekaran and W. E. Deming (1949). In the years since their paper appeared, this general approach, the specific technique, and the estimate itself have frequently been identified by their names. In a way this identification has been a mixed blessing. Because their paper was written in terms of the specific problem of estimating vital statistics from inadequate data, it facilitated the use of this approach in a number of countries with very inadequate vital registration data. On the other hand, the technique was presented as a specialized one, and because the form of the estimate obscured its identity with the estimate of equation 2.7, doubts about its validity tended to arise.[7]

We have already shown how equation 2.8 can be derived from equation 2.7. The four components of equation 2.8 can also be restated in terms of the basic probabilities of collection by each source. In definition equation 2.4c above, we established that the proportion of events covered by both systems is equal to

$$\frac{M}{N} = P_{12} = P_1 P_2 \quad . \tag{2.4c}$$

Analogously, the proportion of events caught by source 1 but missed by source 2 equals

$$\frac{U_1}{N} = (P_1)(1 - P_2) \quad , \qquad\qquad\qquad\qquad [2.9a]$$

and the proportion of events omitted by source 1 but caught by source 2 equals

$$\frac{U_2}{N} = (P_2)(1 - P_1) \quad . \qquad\qquad\qquad\qquad [2.9b]$$

Finally, the proportion of events missed by both source 1 and source 2 can be expressed as

$$\frac{X}{N} = (1 - P_1)(1 - P_2) \quad , \qquad\qquad\qquad [2.9c]$$

where

X = number of births or deaths missed by both source 1 and source 2.

In comparing equation 2.7 with equation 2.8, three points are particularly worth noting. First, the two equations emphasize two different ways of analyzing the reporting errors of the two systems. Equation 2.8 focuses on the absolute or relative number of true events covered by both systems (M), covered by either system alone (U_1 and U_2), or missed by both systems (X), with the last term estimated by $(U_1 U_2)/M$. On the other hand, equation 2.7 emphasizes the relative completeness of reporting of the two sources (P_1 and P_2), with the former estimated by $M/(M + U_2)$ and the latter by $M/(M + U_1)$.

Second, equation 2.8 requires that three numbers (M, U_1, and U_2) be known or estimated in order to obtain the PGE estimate $\hat{N}$. To date, in all PGE studies using equation 2.8 the reports of *both* sources were searched to determine the match status of each report so that the number of unmatched reports in each source could be found directly. This type of design is frequently referred to as a "two-way match."[8] To use equation 2.7 one need know only one number (N_1 or N_2) and one ratio (N_1/M or N_2/M); thus it is necessary to determine the match status of the reported events in only one of the two systems. Such a design, often referred to as a "one-way match," has been widely used in registration coverage checks. Although the distinction between a "one-way" and a "two-way" match is a valid and useful one, there is no necessary link between either design and the PGE estimating equation used. In particular, one can use equation 2.8 regardless of whether U_1 and U_2 are determined directly from a two-way match or $U_1 = N_1 - M$ and $U_2 = N_2 - M$ are determined from a one-way match.

Third, despite the emphasis on the Chandrasekaran-Deming "fourth category" (that is, events missed by both sources) in the literature, it is the sum of the "third" and "fourth" categories that provides the relevant statistical adjustment to an estimate prepared from a single source. In other words, given N_1 as the number of events reported by one system, one must add $U_2 + [(U_1 U_2)/M]$ to obtain the proper estimate of the total number of events adjusted for omission N. Only if the adjustment used takes into account both categories will it be numerically equal to the adjustment of N_1 implicit in equation 2.7.

C. A Historical Review

Since about 1930 the PGE approach, involving dual collection, matching, and statistical estimation, has been used in a variety of circumstances related to the measurement or evaluation of vital statistics. Estimates based on this technique are available from a dozen countries and for a much larger number of subnational areas. These applications range in size and purpose from isolated pilot studies to official checks of the civil registration system and to large-scale studies of population growth, fertility, and mortality conducted in national probability samples.

C.1   STUDIES IN CANADA, THE UNITED STATES, AND THE SOVIET UNION

The PGE technique has been used in three countries that are today classified as economically developed—Canada, the United States, and the Union of Soviet Socialist Republics—to study the coverage of the civil registration system. The Canadian study, the earliest we have any adequate knowledge of, was conducted in the early 1930s to assess the completeness of civil registration of births in the several provinces of Canada. At that time Canada was a relatively small country (total population about 11 million in 1931), sparsely populated (less than three persons per square mile), and predominantly rural (only one-third of the population lived in towns or cities with over 5,000 inhabitants). Although its overall literacy rate was high (over 92 percent) and its per capita income was above average (about $360 in 1931 dollars), large population subgroups—for example, the French-speaking and Indian populations—were considerably "less developed." This early study of birth registration completeness, reported in a monograph (Tracey, 1941) published in connection with the 1931 Census of Canada, was apparently lost sight of until relatively recently.[9]

The Canadian study involved a one-way match consisting of a search of civil registration birth records for infants enumerated as under one year of age in the 1931 Census. The proportion of Census enumeration reports for which a registration report could be found—the match rate for the Census source—was taken as an estimate of civil registration completeness. Somewhat different sampling and matching procedures were used in the various provinces, and precise details of certain aspects of the study are not available. For example, the monograph makes no mention of the specific matching criteria used. Undoubtedly, this is because no precise criteria were formulated and the matching was done on the basis of a subjective assessment of the reported information on such items as name of infant, parents' names, sex of infant, and address. However, the sampling and basic matching operation was carried out under the control of the Dominion Bureau of Statistics; hence despite some regional variations it is probable that at least roughly comparable procedures were used throughout the study. A summary of the procedures and results of the Canadian study are given in Table 2.1.

We saw from equation 2.6 that the match rate of one source is the PGE estimated completeness rate for the other source. Thus when we find, in the province of Prince Edward Island, that the civil registration birth record was found for 80 percent of the infants under age one enumerated in the 1931 Census it means that the PGE estimate of birth registration completeness is 80 percent. As Table 2.1 shows, the match rates among the nine provinces ranged from 80 to 91 percent for the population not living on Indian Reserves and from 57 to 74 percent for the Indian population.

As Tracey indicates, these completeness estimates are subject to various sorts of errors. Some kinds of births were likely to be missed both in the Census and in the registration system; for example, few babies that died shortly after birth survived to be enumerated in the 1931 Census, and these babies also had a higher than average probability of not being registered. In other words, the reporting of births in the two sources was not statistically independent, or, to put it in even more technical terms, "response correlation bias" existed. This form of bias almost always tends to raise the match rate and the PGE estimate of completeness above the true completeness rate. However, on the basis of external evidence Tracey rejects this source of bias as a serious problem in the Canadian data.

More crucial, in Tracey's view, were the problems created by what today we would refer to as "out-of-scope" reports; that is, events reported in either or both sources that are outside the geographic, temporal, or conceptual dimensions of the demographic parameter being measured. For example, Tracey notes that families who had recently moved from one province to another sometimes reported their infant children as being born in the province in which they were enumerated in the 1931 Census, when in fact these infants were born in some other province. Registration reports for such infants were not in the registration files for the province in which the infant was enumerated, although a registration report might exist in some other province. This meant that these Census reports would remain unmatched, biasing both the match rate and the PGE completeness estimate downward.[10] In this handbook the bias arising from out-of-scope reports is referred to as "coverage bias" or "out-of-scope bias."

Another source of error that Tracey recognized as affecting his estimates of birth registration completeness was related to deficiencies in the matching procedures. In Quebec and Ontario matching was

Table 2.1 Procedures and Results of the 1931 Canadian Birth Registration Study, for Each Province

(Study limited to infants enumerated in their province of birth; for other qualifications, see footnotes and text.)

Province	Population subgroup	Approximate sampling fraction	Number of enumerated infants in study	Matching procedures used[1]	Final match rate (percentage)
Prince Edward Island	Total population	One	1,764	Standard	80
Nova Scotia	Total population	One-fifth	2,067	Standard	86
New Brunswick	Total population	One-fifth	1,865	Standard	89
Quebec	Non-Indian	One-twelfth	5,473	Stage I only[2]	91[3]
Quebec	Indian	One[4]	227	Unspecified	57
Ontario	City non-Indian[5]	One-fifth }	5,763	Stage I only	89[6]
Ontario	Other non-Indian	One-tenth }			
Ontario	Indian	One[4]	453	Unspecified	57
Manitoba	Non-Indian	One-fifth	2,402	Standard	90
Manitoba	Indian	One[4]	366	Unspecified	66
Saskatchewan	City non-Indian	One-fifth }	2,806	Standard	87[8]
Saskatchewan	Other non-Indian	One-seventh[7] }			
Saskatchewan	Indian	One[4]	239	Unspecified	68
Alberta	City non-Indian[9]	One-fifth }	2,203	Standard	90[8]
Alberta	Other non-Indian	One-seventh }			
Alberta	Indian	One[4]	310	Unspecified	74
British Columbia	City non-Indian[10]	One-fifth }	1,862	Standard	87[8]
British Columbia	Other non-Indian	[11] }			
British Columbia	Indian	One[4]	424	Unspecified	62

[1] The standard matching procedure conducted by the staff of the Dominion Bureau of Statistics involved two stages. First, a search was made of the civil registration records for the county in which the enumerated infant resided at the time of the 1931 Census to determine the match status of each infant reported in the census. Second, reports for enumerated infants not matched after the first stage were compared with the reports for the balance of the province. Departures from this standard procedure are noted below.

[2] Except for the Montreal and Jesus Islands, where the search was conducted throughout the whole of the islands.

[3] A subsequent application of the second stage matching procedure by the provincial authorities raised the match rate from 91 to 94 percent.

[4] Sample confined to census records for Indian Reserves.

[5] Hamilton, Ottawa, London, and Windsor.

[6] Match rate weighted to allow for different sampling fractions. It was estimated that if an allowance had been made for births registered outside the county of residence the match rate would have risen from 89 to 92 percent.

[7] The sampling rate given in the text for Saskatchewan towns appears to be in error.

[8] Match rate adjusted to allow for different sampling fractions.

[9] Calgary, Edmonton, Lethbridge, Medicine Hat, Drumheller, Red Deer, and Wetaskiwin.

[10] Vancouver, Victoria, and New Westminster.

[11] In part a purposively selected sample stratified by racial origin and in part a systematic sample of every fifth census book not included in the purposive sample.

SOURCE: Tracey, 1941.

confined to comparing Census infant reports with the civil registration birth records only for the county in which the infant was enumerated in the 1931 Census. In the other provinces the estimates were made on the basis of a provincewide search of registration records. Subsequent studies conducted by provincial registration authorities indicate that provincewide matching would have raised the match rate from 91 to 94 percent for Quebec and from 89 to an estimated 92 percent for Ontario. Although the existence of errors arising from deficiencies in the matching process was recognized by Tracey, no detailed study of matching error was carried out.

A number of advances in the technique of PGE estimation have been made since the 1931 Canadian birth registration test. The various sources of error touched upon by Tracey have been subjected to more thorough analysis, including in some cases empirical investigation, and their nature and importance have been clarified. In particular, the study of matching errors has received substantial help in recent years from the practice of employing precise and explicit matching rules. In the early studies using matching the fact of a match was considered intuitively obvious; hence no precise operational definition was given for the degree of agreement between two reports necessary for such reports to be classified as matched.

Another major series of developments relates to the use of a special registration system as one of the methods of data collection in place of the official civil registration system and a corresponding shift in the motivation for conducting PGE studies from administrative evaluation to demographic estimation. The use of sampling in both sources, two-way matching, and the extension of the technique to the study of death reporting are all associated with this line of development.

The balance of this review will be concerned with tracing the threads of these developments that are common to many studies, as well as noting some of the distinctive features of individual studies that represent specific solutions to the design problems appropriate to a particular time and place. We have used modern terminology in describing the procedures and results of earlier studies that used the PGE approach. Although those conducting such studies often recognized many of the concepts and problems that are basic to PGE estimation, the language they used is sometimes quite different from what we would use today. Moreover, issues that were unrecognized or only vaguely understood sometimes resulted in silence or cloudy language. It is hoped that this use of modern terminology will help to clarify the historical experience for those who today must deal with many of these same problems.

Initial attempts at the evaluation of civil registration completeness in the United States did not involve matching and PGE estimation (Gutman, 1959, and Shapiro, 1950a). In the latter half of the nineteenth century, attempts were made to estimate birth registration coverage by comparing the aggregate number of infants aged less than one year enumerated in the decennial census with the number of births registered in the preceding year. Even after a correction was made in the census count for infants that failed to survive to the date of enumeration, this technique was found to overestimate the completeness of birth registration because of the underenumeration of infants in the census and errors in the reported age for enumerated infants (U.S. Census Office, 1872).

In an effort to improve the census count of births, direct questions about births and infant deaths in the preceding year were added to schedules in the Censuses of 1880, 1890, and 1900. However, the attempt met with little success, and after the Census of 1900 "all attempts to obtain vital statistics through the enumeration method were completely abandoned" (Shapiro, 1950a, p. 89). As Shapiro observed, "Lack of confidence in the reliability and completeness of vital statistics collected through the enumeration procedure had been expressed by census statisticians as early as 1850. The method was used as the alternative to having no data at all." (*Ibid.*, footnote 3)

The earliest U.S. studies using case-by-case matching to measure birth registration coverage were conducted by compiling lists of births from public sources (for example, birth announcements in newspapers, baptismal lists, and infant death records) and then searching for these births in the civil registration records (Shapiro, 1950a, p. 93). The proportion of these births found in the civil registration files—the match rate for the list compiled from secondary sources—was used as the estimated completeness rate for the birth registration system. Although the procedure had the advantage of almost no field costs, the match rates and the PGE completeness estimates obtained were biased sharply upward due to a lack of independence between the two sources (response correlation bias). A list of births obtained from newspaper announcements and similar indirect sources would generally contain a very low proportion of unregistered births.

Beginning in the early 1920s a technique was employed which attempted to increase the independence between the two sources by directly canvassing the general population for birth reports. Post offices were supplied with large numbers of postal reply cards and instructed to deliver them to all families in the area. Typically, the card requested that if a birth had occurred in the family in the past 12 months the card be completed and returned to the agency conducting the study. The information requested included the full name and race of the baby, the date and place of birth, and the name and address of the parents. Each postal card returned represented a birth report that could then be used in a one-way match with the civil registration records.

This design represented a considerable improvement over earlier studies, in that birth reports were obtained directly from the population and not from secondary sources such as newspapers. Moreover, the procedure remained relatively inexpensive, since the only data collection costs were for printing and postage.[11] However, the approach was still subject to considerable response correlation bias; registration completeness was higher for the births mentioned on the returned postal cards than for other births. Although the post office was supposed to deliver cards to all families, there is no doubt that postal delivery was particularly deficient among those groups least likely to register births: secondary families and individuals, illiterates, recently arrived migrants, and persons with no fixed residence. Also, among families that received cards, the mail-back rates were generally lower for parents with unregistered births than for those with registered births. As a result, these studies rather consistently overestimated the completeness of birth registration; and since little or no control was exercised over either the mail-out or the mail-back phases of data collection, it was very difficult to approximate even roughly the amount of bias involved.[12]

A major purpose of most birth registration tests conducted in the United States between 1915 and 1933 was to certify that individual state systems had achieved 90-percent completeness and hence could be considered part of the national birth registration reporting system. This administrative use of birth registration tests left many census statisticians with mixed minds about these biases. On the one hand, they wanted to be able to supply correction factors to adjust the published birth registration statistics for underregistration; and, on the other hand, they wanted to avoid offending the state registration authorities and to ensure that all the states would be brought into the registration reporting system as rapidly as possible.

By 1933, all the states had been included in the registration system. Undivided attention could now be given to the issues of data quality and accuracy, and the Chief Statistician of the Vital Statistics Division of the Bureau of the Census could write

> The future policy of the Division will be that the object of such checks will be to help the state in its problems of registration, rather than to threaten its removal from the registration area. Regardless of . . . registration completeness, all data should be published for scientific investigators, and the users of vital statistics may then correct the data for each state according to the relative completeness of the registration. (Dunn, 1936, p. 349)

Although matching studies were conducted in many states during the 1930s, published results appear to be available only for two studies. It is not clear whether this restrictive publication policy was due to dissatisfaction with the quality of the matching studies or to a lingering reluctance to face up to their results. Dunn (1936) cites the former problem as the cause, whereas Whelpton (1938, p. 31) remarks, "[The] policy of withholding results may be necessary from the standpoint of relations with the states, but if the tests are sound statistically it imposes a serious handicap on users of vital statistics data." Whatever the reason for not publishing information about the procedures and the results of these studies was, the international statistical community has been the loser in the long run by our present inability to benefit from the lessons of these studies.

As part of an effort to improve procedures for testing registration completeness, the Bureau of the Census conducted a birth registration test in 26 counties of Georgia in 1934. The results of this study, and a subsequent 1937 study in Maryland, were published by the Bureau of the Census (Hedrich, Collinson, and Rhoads, 1939) and present an important insight into the development of the PGE approach. These studies were designed to permit a comparative assessment of different methods of measuring the completeness of civil registration, including the postal reply card procedures.

A distinctive feature of the Georgia and Maryland studies is that one method used to obtain birth reports was a one-time retrospective household survey. There is no reason to believe that the completeness of birth reporting in this one-time canvass was any better than that achieved in comparable areas by retrospective questions on births asked in the U.S. Censuses of 1880 to 1900. However, unlike the earlier census results, the Georgia survey results were not used to provide a single-source estimate of the number of births. In order for the aggregate number of retrospective birth reports to provide an accurate estimate of completeness of birth registration, one must assume that retrospective birth reporting involves no omissions. If such reports are used for matching and PGE estimation it is assumed only that the omissions in the two sources are statistically independent.

Published details of field procedures for the Georgia study are vague, but the broad outlines are clear. The postal authorities were supplied with large numbers of conventional registration test cards for distribution to all families in the study area. About two weeks after the test cards had been distributed, 38 university students started a house-to-house canvass for births in the 26 Georgia counties. Apparently, these enumerators completed a schedule for each live birth occurring in the preceding year, giving identification information for the baby and its parents for matching purposes, some data on the socioeconomic status of the family, information on whether the baby was still alive at the time of the interview, and information about whether the test card had been received and returned. The enumerators were able to work only 21 days because of budgetary constraints, so that only a portion of the households in the 26 counties were canvassed and the study was confined to births reported by these households. Although efforts were made to ensure the "representativeness" of the resulting sample, the 6,805 usable birth schedules obtained by the household survey procedure could not be considered to be a probability sample of births occurring in the study area. However, the survey sample of births was certainly less biased with respect to registration coverage than the births reported by the postal reply card procedure.

The survey birth reports were matched "against the birth register, and all names not found registered were rechecked by experienced members of the regular staffs. . . . Searches were made both in the index and in the certificate files, and [nonmatched reports] were followed up with letters to parents and to health officers for verification of the data." (Hedrich, Collinson, and Rhoads, 1939, p. 683) The authors stressed the importance of follow-up with local health officers, noting that "names and other data in the birth record [were] so frequently changed or given inaccurately" that additional information available locally could sometimes reduce the proportion of reports classified as nonmatched by as much as one-half for some population subgroups. On the other hand, departing from former Census Bureau practice, the birth reports relating to "follow-up inquiries [which] were unanswered or returned as 'unclaimed' were . . . retained in the sample since to reject them would probably throw out an undue proportion of unregistered births."

Final match rates for the survey birth reports indicated an overall estimated birth registration completeness of 87 percent, ranging from

Table 2.2 **Match Rates Obtained in Selected Studies of Birth Registration Completeness Conducted in the United States: 1934 to 1970**

(Percent of birth reports obtained by specified collection procedure matched with civil registration reports. All studies based on one-way matching.)

Subgroup	Georgia, 1934[1]		United States, 1940[2] (Infants under 4 months enumerated in 1940 Census)	United States, 1950[2] (Infants under 3 months enumerated in 1950 Census)	United States, 1964–68[3] (Children under 5 years enumerated in CPS and HIS household surveys, June 1969– March 1970[4]).
	Household survey	Mail-out/ mail-back postal survey			
All groups					
Number of reports	6,173	3,375	663,000	780,000	14,632
Percent matched	87	91	93	98	99
Match rate					
Urban[5]	93	94	96	99	u
Rural	81	87	87	93[7]	u
White	90	92	94	99	99
Nonwhite[6]	84	89	82	94	98
Hospitalized	98	u	99	99	99
Nonhospitalized	83	u	86	88	94[8]
Survived 12 months	87	u	u	u	u
Did not survive 12 months	76	u	u	u	u

u = unavailable.
[1] Sample covered an unspecified number of households in 26 counties of Georgia.
[2] Covers 48 states and the District of Columbia.
[3] Sample universe consisted of 50 states and the District of Columbia.
[4] Current Population Survey (CPS) and Health Interview Survey (HIS)
[5] Urban, in the Georgia study, apparently refers to cities of 25,000 and over, with the balance of the sample included under rural. In the other studies the current census definition was employed.
[6] Apparently limited to Negro only, for the 1934 Georgia study.
[7] For residents of area, completeness estimate (match rate) is 97 percent.
[8] Includes place of birth not known.
SOURCE: Hedrich, Collinson, and Rhoads (1939, table F) for the Georgia study; Shapiro (1950a, table 2) for the 1940 Birth Registration Test; Shapiro and Schachter (1952, table 2) and Shapiro and Schachter (1954, table B) for the 1950 Birth Registration Test; and Koons (1971, tables A and B) for the 1970 Birth Registration Test.

75 percent for rural blacks to 94 percent for urban whites (Hedrich, Collinson, and Rhoads, 1939, Table 4). Birth registration completeness estimates for various population subgroups obtained in this and other major matching studies conducted in the United States are shown in Table 2.2. As was to be expected, the Georgia study showed that the match rates and completeness estimates based on the mail-out/mail-back registration test cards were biased upward relative to those based on the survey approach—by 4 percent for all births in the sample and by 15 percent for rural black births.

In commenting on the small differences between the PGE completeness estimates based on the two procedures for population subgroups with relatively complete registration, Hedrich, Collinson, and

Rhoads recognized the interrelationship between the true completeness rate and the biasing effects of response correlation. In their words,

> When birth registration is very nearly complete—say, 99 percent—even the most violent overselection of registered births can at best raise the calculated completeness ratio by only 1 percent [-age point] . . ., however, . . . as the completeness ratio declines from the 100 percent ceiling . . . the effect of biased sampling [that is, response correlation] becomes decidedly more pronounced. (Hedrich, Collinson, and Rhoads, 1939, p. 685)

The next major study that used matching to estimate registration completeness in the United States was the 1940 birth registration test. The overall design of the 1940 study closely paralleled the 1931 Canadian study: Reports of infants enumerated in the 1940 Census were matched against the civil registration files and the final match rate for the census birth reports was used as the estimate of completeness of birth registration. However, in various ways the study represented a notable advance over its predecessors. It was confined to census reports of infants less than four months old as of the census date. Since this increased the proportion of infants born during the reference period who survived to be enumerated in the census, it effectively reduced response correlation bias to some extent. The four-month age cutoff also helped to reduce the size of the collection and matching operations. An extensive follow-up of nonmatched reports was carried out, involving letters to parents and institutions, searches in state and city registration files, and, in some cases, personal interviews or additional correspondence with concerned families. The basic study design and the procedures used are summarized in Figure 2.1. For a summary of the substantive results, see Table 2.2.

From a methodological point of view, the most notable achievement of the 1940 registration test was in the area of matching. This was the first study in which an attempt was made to formulate and write out explicit matching rules, to recognize that both erroneous matches and erroneous nonmatches can occur, and to point out that the bias in the overall PGE estimate attributable to matching error is determined solely by the size of net matching error (the difference between the numbers of erroneously matched and erroneously unmatched reports in a given source) (Grove, 1943). No doubt the sheer size of the matching operation in the 1940 study was a major impetus for handling the matching more systematically. The commitment of the Bureau of the Census to the efficient production of statistics of high quality was also a crucial factor. Without such a commitment, this large matching operation would merely have produced confusion and unidentifiable errors rather than methodological advances.

Some 650,000 infant cards completed in the 1940 Census had to be compared with registration records in files of comparable size.[13] (By comparison, the 1931 Canadian test involved only some 30,000 infant reports.) A matching operation of this size could no longer be completed in one or two months by a small group of experienced

Fig. 2.1   A Summary of the Design and Procedures of the 1940 U.S. Birth Registration Test

A. Data sources

1. System 1: Special copies of the birth certificates filed in state offices prior to 1 August 1940 for births occurring during the period 1 December 1939 to 31 March 1940, inclusive.

2. System 2: (a) Infant cards prepared by the 1940 Census enumerator for all infants who were stated to have been born during the period 1 December 1939 to 31 March 1940, inclusive, and who were alive on 1 April 1940. (b) Special copies of death certificates filed for infants born during the period 1 December 1939 to 31 March 1940, inclusive, but dying prior to 1 April 1940.

B. Matching and field follow-up procedures

1. All system 2 reports were completely alphabetized by the last, first, and middle name of child, by state of birth. All system 1 reports were alphabetized in the same way. The two sets of records for each state were then matched by hand.

2. The remaining nonmatched reports from each system were realphabetized by maiden name of mother and the matching operation was repeated.

3. The remaining nonmatched reports from each system were again realphabetized by name of father and the matching operation was repeated.

4. The remaining nonmatched reports from each system were then sorted by county of birth within each state and matched by hand.

5. Form letters were mailed to the parents of each child named on the remaining system 2 nonmatched reports in order to verify the correctness of the information on the reports or obtain missing information. In some cases, a letter was also sent to the hospital or institution where the birth occurred. On the basis of any new or corrected information obtained, another match with the system 1 reports was carried out. In addition, a number of system 2 reports could be eliminated as out-of-scope.

6. The remaining system 2 nonmatched reports were sent to the appropriate state or city bureaus of vital statistics for direct matching with the original birth certificates (system 1 reports) filed in these offices.

7. About one-third of the states carried out a complete, or nearly complete, field investigation of the residual nonmatched census reports by either correspondence or personal interview. Another one third of the state completed a substantial part, but not all, of their field investigation. About one third of the states did practically no field work.

C. Matching criteria

1. Six items were used in deciding whether two reports referred to the same birth: name of child, name of father, maiden name of mother, date of birth, place of birth, and sex of child.

2. If any four of these items, two of which involving names, were essentially identical, the records were considered matched, subject to verification.

3. Cases not meeting these standards but considered to be true matches were referred to a supervisor. Supervisors were authorized to liberalize the rule and to consider the records in terms of the overall probability that they did or did not refer to the same infant.

SOURCE: Based on data from Grove, 1943; and Shapiro, 1950a.

clerks working under close professional supervision. A manual matching operation of this size would require, say, five clerks working steadily for a little over two years or 25 clerks working for about half a year.[14] However, with either staffing pattern, inconsistencies in the handling

Fig. 2.2   A Summary of the Design and Procedures of the 1950 U.S. Birth Registration Test

A. *Data sources*
  1. System 1:   Copies of birth records filed in state offices prior to 1 January 1951 for births occurring during the period 1 January 1950 to 31 March 1950, inclusive.
  2. System 2:   Infant cards prepared by the 1950 Census enumerators for all enumerated infants reported to have been born during the period 1 January 1950 to 31 March 1950, inclusive.

B. *Matching and field follow-up procedures*
  1. Punchcards were prepared for each system 1 and system 2 report. Cards were compared mechanically according to combinations of primary items specified in the matching criteria. Pairs of cards matching on primary items were listed. Secondary items and any primary items that had not been matched by machine were examined manually for similarity.
  2. The remaining nonmatched reports from each system were sorted and listed by various primary and secondary items to facilitate manual matching. If the information in the listing was too inadequate to permit a conclusive decision but a match seemed likely, copies of the original records were reviewed for confirming evidence.
  3. Letters were mailed to the parents of each child named on the remaining system 2 nonmatched reports in order to verify the correctness of the information on the reports or to obtain missing information. In some cases, a letter was also sent to the hospital or institution where the birth occurred. On the basis of the new or corrected information obtained, about 7,700 additional matches were made and about 8,100 system 2 reports were eliminated as out-of-scope or duplicate reports.
  4. The remaining system 2 nonmatched reports were sent to the appropriate state and city registration offices for direct matching with the original birth certificates (system 1 reports) filed there. About 7,300 additional matches were made in the state office searches, and about 5,300 system 2 reports were eliminated as out-of-scope or duplicate reports at this stage.
  5. Although local registration officials and, in the case of adopted infants, local welfare agencies were sometimes contacted during the state search, no house-to-house field investigation of system 2 nonmatched reports was carried out.

C. *Matching criteria*
  1. Twelve items were used in deciding whether two reports referred to the same birth. These items were classified as either primary or secondary. The six primary items were first four letters of child's last name, first four letters of mother's maiden name, date of birth, race, sex, and place of birth. The six secondary items were first four letters of child's first name, first four letters of mother's first name, age of mother, age of father, birth order, and type of attendance at birth. In making comparisons, a one-day difference in the date of birth was not considered significant. Similar tolerance limits were established for a number of other items.
  2. Six sets of matching criteria were established, based on various combinations of the primary and secondary items appearing on the punchcard records. Set 1 required agreement within the tolerance limits on all six primary items and on either the child's or the mother's first name. In sets 2 to 6 conditions regarding primary items were relaxed with compensating increases in the number of secondary items on which agreement was needed.
  3. A seventh set of criteria used information appearing on the original records. Considerable weight was given to the fact that the street address of the child's residence was the same on the infant card as it was on the birth record. Information on the full spelling of names, mother's usual residence, father's occupation and industry, and name and size of the hospital or community in which the birth occurred were also taken into account in determining whether a pair of records

represented the same child. Agreement on items carried more weight if the
information involved was unusual (for example, an odd name or occupation).

SOURCE: Based on data from Shapiro and Schachter, 1952.

of similar situations were certain to occur unless the matching procedure
was held in control by explicit, written rules.

Although the size of the entire work load clarified the need
for explicit matching rules in the 1940 test, the size of the units in
which the initial matching was done (that is, the states; see Figure
2.1) was undoubtedly one reason erroneous matches were at last clearly
recognized as a form of matching error. With areas as large as states,
it is likely that a number of events were not uniquely identified by
the matching criteria used, so that some infant cards for unregistered
births were erroneously linked to the registration record for a different
infant.[15] Other things being equal, the use of smaller areas for matching
means a larger proportion of events that are uniquely identified by
the matching criteria, and consequently fewer erroneous matches. Not
only were erroneous matches probably more common in the 1940 test
than in many of the earlier studies, but more matching errors were
identified because more effort went into quality control and evaluation
than in earlier studies. In any case, Shapiro (1950a, p. 102) indicates
estimates of roughly 2,000 erroneous nonmatches and 7,000 erroneous
matches among the infant cards at the end of the 1940 study, yielding
a net upward bias in the match rate and the PGE estimate of registration
completeness of about 0.5 percent.

Other potential sources of error were either minimized by the
study procedures employed (such as field follow-up) or an estimate
of their effect on the completeness estimate was prepared. For example,
Shapiro (1950b) attempted to identify the extent to which response
correlation bias affected the overall completeness estimate by estimating
the number of births adjusted for underregistration separately for minor
civil divisions by color, summing these subgroup estimates, computing
a new completeness estimate on the basis of the sum, and comparing
the original completeness estimate with the new one. This procedure
lowered the completeness estimate by less than one percentage point
for the country as a whole, and by a maximum of two to three points
in the five states with the lowest registration completeness. On the
other hand, it was estimated that the completeness rate for the United
States as a whole would have been raised by about the same amount
without the 31 July cutoff that effectively treated as unregistered all
births registered more than four months after the close of the reference
period (Shapiro, 1950a, p. 102).

Another birth registration matching study was conducted in
conjunction with the 1950 Population Census. The planning for the
study benefited greatly from the detailed evaluation of the 1940 test
conducted by statisticians at the Bureau of the Census and the National
Office of Vital Statistics. Indeed, the 1950 registration test employed
essentially the same overall design as the earlier study (see Figure 2.2).

There were, however, some differences in procedure between the two studies. The 1950 test was limited to infants born within three months of the Census enumeration date (1 January to 31 March 1950), whereas the 1940 test used a four-month reference period (1 December 1939 to 31 March 1940).[16] It was thought that confining coverage to three months in one calendar year would reduce the number of out-of-scope errors and simplify the matching. Other modifications included extending the cutoff date for the receipt of delayed registration records from four to nine months,[17] abandoning completely the use of death registration reports to estimate the completeness of birth registration for infants not surviving to 1 April, and switching the matching from a manual operation to a largely mechanical one (Shapiro, 1954).

The mechanical matching procedure used in the 1950 test employed standard 80-column punchcards and conventional punchcard equipment (not digital computers). Machine matching appeared attractive because of the size of the job (both files were larger than in 1940), and because the data from both files would have to be punched for tabulation purposes eventually. However as Shapiro (1954, p. 7) noted,

> Machine matching called for rigid control of many relatively small groups of punched cards. Without such control at every step and exercise of high level skill in scheduling the operation, the test could bog down badly. Another problem posed by the machines was the fact that comparisons of items on the two sets of punched cards could result only in a designation of "agreement" or "disagreement." Slight variations in name spelling were treated by the machine in the same way as entirely different names.

Fortunately a well-trained and experienced processing staff was available and experimental evidence on the adequacy of the matching rules being formulated could be obtained from census pretests in 1948 and 1949.

In the 1950 study machines were used to perform two kinds of tasks: (a) the identification of "easy" matches (that is, cases where two reports were clearly and unambiguously in agreement), so as to reduce the pool of unmatched reports in subsequent stages of matching; and (b) the preparation of machine listings of unmatched reports that had the same information for any given matching criterion, so as to simplify the work involved in the subsequent clerical matching. These two tasks correspond to Step B.1 and Step B.2, respectively, in Figure 2.2. Rather than doing away with the need for clerks, mechanical matching enabled the matching clerks to concentrate on the more difficult cases. However, the value of such a division of labor could easily have been negated by poor matching rules.

The complex interrelationship between matching rules, matching error, and other aspects of study design is well illustrated by the 1950 birth registration test. Because the punchcards contained only 80 columns, the full name of the infant and its parents could not be used in the mechanical match.[18] Only the first four letters of the baby's first name, the first four letters of the baby's family name, the first four letters of the mother's family name, and the first four letters of the mother's given name were punched. Although using only the first four letters of a name meant that some possibly relevant information was ignored in matching (for example, reports with names such as Shapiro and Shapley were classified as agreeing on name), the information not used might have differed only because of a minor spelling error (for example, an entry of Shaply instead of Shapley). Thus, the net effect of ignoring all letters after the fourth would depend upon the distribution of the population by name and the accuracy with which names were recorded in both sources, as well as the impact of the other matching rules.

One of the major topics dealt with in later chapters of the Handbook is the construction of matching rules that should minimize matching error. The rules used in the 1950 study and summarized in Part C of Figure 2.2 were apparently well chosen. Shapiro (1954, p. 10) concludes, on the basis of a review of various quality control checks used in the 1950 study, that erroneous matches were probably a lesser problem in 1950 than in 1940 and, since erroneous nonmatches were very low in both studies because of the exhaustive follow-up procedures used, net matching error was probably lower in 1950 also.

A new registration test was conducted in 1970 to confirm that overall registration remained virtually complete and to update the 1950 results for subgroups then estimated to have relatively poorer registration completeness. The 1970 study used household surveys rather than the census to obtain birth reports for matching purposes. Interviewers completed a birth report form for children under five years of age enumerated in the Current Population Survey and the Health Interview Survey, and these reports were manually matched with the civil registration birth records for the 1965–1970 period.[19] Follow-up interviews were conducted for survey households reporting unmatched births, and additional matching was attempted on the basis of the supplementary information obtained. Only a brief report covering substantive findings has been released to date (Koons, 1971). These results and those for the 1950 test are summarized in Table 2.2.

In concluding this discussion of the use of matching to estimate registration completeness in the United States, it is appropriate to mention two studies in which matching went in the other direction, providing estimates of completeness of the reporting of infants and vital events by household enumeration procedures. As part of the evaluation program for the 1950 Census, the completeness of the enumeration of infants under three months of age was estimated from the proportion of birth registration records for the period from January to March 1950 that were found enumerated in the 1950 Census (U.S. Bureau of the Census, 1953).

This study, the 1950 Infant Enumeration Study, was a complement to the 1950 birth registration test. Both studies used the same collection sources and birth reports, and the initial stages of matching were the same for both (see Figure 2.2). However, the follow-up work on nonmatched reports in the Infant Enumeration Study was limited to a sample of the unmatched registration reports, and there were some differences between the two studies in the procedures used in preparing the final estimates of completeness.[20] The adjusted estimate of enumeration completeness for infants under three months of age was 96 percent for the United States as a whole, 98 percent for urban whites, and 90 percent for rural farm nonwhites (U.S. Bureau of the Census, 1953, Table 1). This adjusted estimate was based essentially on a weighted average of the proportion of birth registration records in each of six match status categories weighted by a rough estimate of the likelihood that records with a given match status had been enumerated in the Census.

Some care must be taken in trying to apply the results of the 1950 Infant Enumeration Study to the coverage of infants in other countries. The study excluded births known to be illegitimate and births that occurred in a state other than the usual state of residence of the mother. Note also that this study estimated the completeness of the enumeration of infants under three months of age and did not deal directly with the question of the completeness of birth reporting in the Census. Even if the number of infants were correctly enumerated this figure would be smaller than the number of births that actually occurred during the corresponding period because some babies did not survive to be enumerated.[21] The accurate estimation of annual births on the basis of the number of enumerated surviving infants is considerably more problematical in many parts of Asia and Africa, as infant mortality in such areas may be four to six times as high as it was in the United States in 1950.

A study that dealt more directly with the problem of fertility estimation and the accuracy of retrospective questions on births and deaths was conducted in 1965 in seven North Carolina counties by the Research Triangle Institute (Horvitz, 1966). In this study interviewers gathered reports of vital events by means of retrospective questions about births and deaths in about 3,000 households known to have had a birth or death on the basis of registration records. In order to hold down response correlation bias—in this instance to prevent the field workers from knowing that all the households had events to report—each interviewer's assignment also included some addresses at which registered events had not occurred.[22] Study questionnaires used either of two kinds of retrospective questions: (a) questions that referred to the past 12 months or (b) questions that referred to the period since 1 January 1965. The latter questions involved a recall period of about ten months.

Only a brief summary of results from this study has been published to date (Horvitz, 1966), but even these limited findings provide valuable insights into the performance of retrospective questions. The published results indicate that little difference was found between the two types of retrospective questions in the completeness of reporting, except that "telescoping" seemed to occur somewhat more frequently with the second type of question than with the first. For both types of retrospective questions combined, the survey obtained 92 percent of the births and 82 percent of the deaths known to have occurred on the basis of the registration records. The completeness of birth reporting varied sharply with the legitimacy status of the infant among whites (94 percent of the legitimate white births were reported, whereas only 50 percent of the illegitimate ones were) and was somewhat less for births reported by neighbors for households that moved away (74 percent) than for births reported by the household itself (92 percent). Reporting of deaths was particularly poor for infant deaths, and even poorer when the baby failed to live more than one day or when the respondent was someone other than the baby's mother (see Table 2.3).

Because of the possible nonrepresentativeness of the seven counties and the small number of cases in some subgroups, one can generalize from these results only with caution. Nevertheless, the carefully designed and executed North Carolina study does provide rather strong evidence that, in the United States, a well-run one-time household survey gathering information on vital events by means of retrospective questions can substantially undercount both births and deaths. The conclusion is strongly supported by the results of a recent study in Los Angeles, California (Sirken and Royston, 1971) and by global comparisons between estimates from the Census Bureau's Quarterly Household Survey for October 1962 and civil registration data (Mauldin, 1966).

Dual collection and case-by-case matching have also been used extensively in the Soviet Union in assessing the completeness of civil registration. The Central Statistical Board of the U.S.S.R. matched reports for infants under one year enumerated in the 1959 Census of Population with birth registration records for a 10-percent systematic sample of village Soviets. (The population of a village Soviet was then about 3,000 persons.)[23] A similar study was conducted in connection with the 1939 Census (Vostrikova, 1963), and Dmitrieva (1969) announced that the procedure would also be employed in connection with the 1970 Census.

Table 2.3 Completeness of Death Reporting in a One-Time Retrospective Survey, by Age at Death and Type of Respondent, for Sample Households with Known Death, North Carolina: 1965

(For details of the study see text and source.)

Characterstic	Percentage of registered deaths reported by retrospective survey questions	
All deaths	82	
Infant deaths	53	
Mother respondent		67
Other respondent		37
Baby lived at least one day		57
Baby did not live one day		46
Other deaths	84	

SOURCE: Horvitz, 1966.

Retrospective survey questions on births and deaths have also been used in the Soviet Union to obtain reports of vital events for matching with civil registration records (Vostrikova, 1963). During the 1960s the procedure was employed in the rural areas of a number of Central Asian Republics, for example, the Tadjik and Kirghiz S.S.R.s, to study the completeness of civil registration (Dmitrieva, 1969). Matching between civil registration records and lists of reported events obtained from other sources (for example, population registers, medical records of hospitals, clinics, or maternity centers) has also been attempted at various times in the Soviet Union (Vostrikova, 1963).

Some uncertainty remains as to the extent to which these matching studies were used to adjust registration statistics for incompleteness. Vincent (1955), at the 1954 World Population Conference, reported on the use of matching studies in the Soviet Union and cited a work by Boyarski and Shusherin (1951) in which an adjustment based on the results of matching, comparable to that in equation 2.7, was used to correct birth registration statistics for underregistration. It is not clear from Vincent's report whether the procedure had been used or was proposed for future use. Dmitrieva (1969) implies that adjustments are sometimes made, but does not spell out their exact nature.[24]

Regardless of the nature of the statistical adjustments made, it is clear that a large amount of matching work involving reports of vital events has been carried out in the Soviet Union. Regretfully, details of the matching procedures used, details of other aspects of design and implementation, and methodological results from these studies do not seem to be available outside the Soviet Union. Because of the many similarities in culture and geography between the central Asian republics of the Soviet Union and the nations of southwest Asia (that is, from Turkey eastward to Pakistan), statisticians in these countries faced with the problems of designing and implementing a PGE study might be able to make almost direct use of Soviet experience in the Asian republics. It would be particularly helpful if details of the matching procedures used were released together with quantitative measures of matching error (including information on the discriminating power of various identification items used in matching) based on any methodological studies conducted in these republics.

The substantive results of the Soviet matching studies are also of considerable interest to all those who must measure vital statistics on the basis of a not wholly adequate civil registration system. For example, Vostrikova (1963, p. 4) observes,

> When undertaking a sample verification of the completeness of the registration of births and deaths special emphasis is laid on the completeness of the registration of children who died when less than 1 year of age and particularly of those who died at the age of 1 month, the omission of which is most probable, as well as the registration of children who died during the first days of their life and who might not have been registered neither among the dead nor among the born ones.

It would be invaluable for those in other countries trying to collect basic demographic data to have the empirical estimates of error that underlie this statement. Similarly, Bystrova (1967), in the course of describing the use of the fertility history approach in Soviet household surveys, reported on an evaluation employing case-by-case matching between two household surveys conducted seven years apart.[25] She noted (pp. 136–37) that

> The comparison revealed omissions in information supplied by the women regarding children who had died, especially in the case of children under one year of age. Such omissions, as might be expected, were especially frequent in relation to events which had occurred many years before the date of the survey.

This nonquantitative summary of findings provides a helpful insight into errors that are likely to occur when very long recall periods are used. Demographers and statisticians in the many nations who employ retrospective procedures to study fertility would be given even greater assistance if the quantitative data on response variation from this study could also be made available to the international scientific community.[26]

C.2   PGE STUDIES IN ASIA

As indicated earlier, the PGE approach had two largely independent origins: civil registration completeness studies in the more developed countries and studies aimed at demographic estimation, first in India, then in other Asian nations, and more recently in a number of countries in Africa and the western hemisphere. Along with their different purposes, PGE studies in these two traditions typically employed quite different designs. Studies in the developing world have tended to cover deaths as well as births, employ sampling in both sources, and use two-way matching. In contrast, civil registration completeness studies in the developed world usually have covered only birth registration, have been conducted on a complete-count basis in one or both sources, and have used one-way matching.[27]

The first of the Asian studies was conducted in 1947 in a health demonstration area, the Singur Health Center, near Calcutta, India. It was reported on in the 1949 paper cited earlier in which the PGE estimate was first presented in the form of equation 2.8 (Chandrasekaran and Deming, 1949). This study involved a two-way match between retrospective reports of live births and deaths for a two-year period obtained in a one-time household survey and vital events reported by the traditional civil registration system over the same period. The survey, which covered all the approximately 12,000 households in the Singur Health Center and also obtained information on the number and characteristics of the base population, was completed by 16 locally recruited interviewers in about two and one-half months. Four persons were employed as investigators to do the matching and subsequent verification of the nonmatched reports.

In general, the address information obtained in the survey was found to be adequate for matching and verification, whereas the address information on the registration reports frequently was not. The study excluded a number of registration reports that could not be verified because they were illegible or incomplete and a smaller number that could be verified as out-of-scope, as well as all reports of nonresident institutional events.

The Singur Health Center study obtained the following final completeness estimates (expressed as percentages):

	Live births	Deaths
Civil registration		
1945 events	52	48
1946 events	60	51
Retrospective survey		
1945 events (approximately a 2-year recall)	53	32
1946 events (approximately a 1-year recall)	67	51

The improvement in estimated completeness in civil registration between 1945 and 1946 can be at least partially attributed to a program for improving the registration system in the study area that became operational in January 1946. The improvement in the PGE estimate of survey completeness, which was even more marked, can almost certainly be attributed to the shorter recall period used to obtain the 1946 data.[28]

The Singur Health Center study was conceived as a demonstration project for a procedure that could be extended by means of appropriately designed samples to estimate needed demographic data for India and other countries lacking reliable vital statistics. Chandrasekaran and Deming, in their 1949 article, presented a wide variety of information that would be helpful to those trying to design such studies in the future, including estimates of response correlation bias, coverage bias, and sampling error, and data on the costs of such a study.

In order to overcome anticipated response correlation bias the authors developed and applied a technique of preparing PGE estimates separately for population subgroups in which collection probabilities are relatively homogeneous. The PGE estimates for individual subgroups are then summed to obtain an improved estimate of the total number of events. Using this technique, with subgroups based on age and sex of deceased, they obtained a PGE estimate for 1945 about 8 percent larger than the PGE estimate based on the aggregate match rate. (The comparable gain for 1946 was about 4 percent.) No gains of this magnitude were found for births, or in subsequent PGE studies (see Tables 2.13 and 2.14 in Section D of this chapter), indicating either that response correlation was not a major problem or that the subgroups used were not actually homogeneous with respect to coverage.

Two attempts were made to apply the PGE technique in the Mysore Population Study (United Nations, 1961). This study, carried out in 1951–52 in south India, was a joint undertaking of the Government of India and the United Nations as a large-scale experiment in the use of sample survey methods to measure demographic trends and characteristics and to investigate the interrelationships between population and economic and social change. Chapter 16 of the study report deals with the completeness of reporting of vital events by survey and registration procedures and presents the results of the two applications of the PGE approach in this study.

In the rural areas of Mysore state a two-way match was conducted between the birth and death reports obtained retrospectively in the one-time household survey and those obtained by the civil registration system. (No matching with the civil registration system was attempted in urban areas because of pretest results indicating that information on the civil registration reports was inadequate for allocating reports to households sampled in the survey without an expensive field follow-up operation.) The household survey covered about 4,900 households in 191 villages and used a recall period that ranged between one to two years, depending upon the actual date of interview. Unfortunately, civil registration records were available for only about three-fourths of the 191 sampled villages, so that the PGE estimates of survey and registration completeness were based on the necessarily biased sample of villages for which reports of both sources were available for matching.

Matching was done locally while the survey staff remained in the village (but after the interviewing was completed), and the non-matched reports of both sources were promptly investigated to determine whether they referred to bona fide in-scope events. The final completeness rates for the three rural zones of the state combined (expressed as percentages) were as follows (United Nations, 1961, Tables 16.2 and 16.5):

	Live births	Deaths
Civil registration—total	43	44
Retrospective survey—total	93	90
12 months or less between occurrence and interview	96	94
More than 12 months between occurrence and interview	90	83

The second use of matching in the Mysore study involved a two-way match between the reports obtained by simple retrospective questions in the household survey and those obtained in a KAP-type survey of a subsample of married women conducted by female interviewers using a detailed pregnancy history. The comparison was based only on events reported as occurring after 15 September 1950 (the cutoff date for the retrospective survey and the registration reports), and results were given only for Bangalore City because the sample for the rural strata was too small to produce reliable estimates.

The following completeness estimates were obtained for Bangalore City (United Nations, 1961, Tables 16.6 and 16.7):

	Live births	Deaths
Retrospective survey with 1–2 year recall period	96	88
Pregnancy history in fertility and attitude survey	92	88

The relatively high completeness rates for both sources must be interpreted cautiously, as they may be an artifact of response correlation bias. As the study report notes:

> Although the interviews were held at different times and by different interviewers, and although the questions asked in the Fertility and Attitude Survey called for more detailed information, it was only to be expected that some of the same [types of] births and deaths which were overlooked in one interview would also escape attention in the other. Hence, the results of the cross-check would tend to exaggerate the completeness of reporting. (United Nations, 1961, p. 226)

Despite these and other limitations, the report of the Mysore Population Study is a valuable document containing much important information for a PGE study designer. In addition to the detailed results of the matching studies summarized there, the report contains, for example, data on interviewing time and variance estimates. Some of the latter information is reproduced in Section D of this chapter.

After the initial matching experiences in the Singur and Mysore studies, no further work was done in India on PGE studies until the early 1960s.[29] In 1964, the Office of the Registrar General in India initiated a program of sample registration, first on a pilot basis in the rural areas of a few states and then on an expanding basis (Wells and Agrawal, 1967; Agrawal, 1969; India, 1970). At present, most of the Indian population is included in the frame of the Indian Sample Registration Scheme (SRS).[30]

The Indian SRS uses dual collection and case-by-case matching of reports, but does not use PGE estimates in the form of equations 2.7 or 2.8. In rural areas a part-time registrar, typically a schoolteacher, serves as the collection agent for the first source, preparing reports for all events occurring to the resident population of the sample area with the help of leads provided by local informants. Each sample area is a village as defined in the Census of India, or a portion of a village if the population of the village is in excess of 2,000 persons. Each six months the registrar's supervisor, who also serves as the collection agent for the second source, conducts a house-to-house canvass of the area, updating information on the base population and inquiring about vital events that occurred after the last enumeration.

At least initially, the matching was also done by the supervisor, who, in any case, was working part-time on the SRS. Quite properly, this created doubts about the effectiveness and independence of the second source in the SRS; and, as a consequence, the Registrar General's Office decided that the use of the PGE estimate was not warranted. Instead, the unduplicated count of events reported by the special registrar and the supervisor was used as the basis of the SRS estimate (Ramabhadran, 1971).

Whatever one thinks about the choice of estimator used, the SRS must be acknowledged to be a formidable statistical and administrative accomplishment.[31] Moreover, in the course of developing the SRS procedures, a number of well-documented pilot studies were carried out from which it is possible to prepare PGE estimates and to obtain much useful guidance on matching and other aspects of PGE design. One important group of studies was conducted in Gujarat state under the direction of D. C. Mehta. The rural pilot study (Mehta and Shah, 1966) identified a long list of practical problems that adversely affected the quality of the data collection. For example, administrative arrangements for paying field staff salaries were unsatisfactory and personnel were only paid after considerable delay; a one-day training session for field workers was too short; the existing village system of house numbering was not complete; registrars found it difficult to complete schedules printed in English accurately; the failure to keep study records confidential adversely affected respondent cooperation; unless they were closely supervised, the registrars tended to accumulate a backlog of events known but not yet entered on the registration forms; inadequate supervision and guidance were given to the supervisors themselves; and part-time supervisors did not have sufficient time to do their supervisory work adequately.

In support of the last point, Mehta and Shah (1966, p. 7) supplied data indicating that the registrars in the 14 sample areas with routine supervision by personnel working part-time on the project reported about 7 percent fewer births and 14 percent fewer deaths than the registrars in six sample areas that received relatively more intensive supervision. Mehta and Shah also presented data showing that the estimated completeness of vital events reporting for both the registrars and the supervisors was substantially higher for sample areas with a population of under 1,000 than for areas with a population of 2,000 and over (see Table 2.4). Subsequent reports by Mehta and Shah (1968) and Mehta (1969) covered the full-scale implementation of the SRS design in 166 sample areas in Gujarat as well as presenting PGE estimates for the state sample.

In addition to testing and implementing a design appropriate for the rural areas of the state, an attempt was also made to test procedures in urban areas (Mehta, 1967a). To this end, a pilot study was conducted on a sample basis in Vaso, a town of approximately

Table 2.4 **PGE Estimates of the Completeness of Vital Events Reporting, by Size of Sample Area and Type of Collection Procedure, Pilot SRS Study for Rural Gujarat: 1964**

(Completeness expressed as a percentage of PGE estimate of true number of events.)

Sample area population	Live births		Deaths	
	Registrar	Supervisor	Registrar	Supervisor
All areas	**92**	**89**	**91**	**89**
Under 1,000	98	98	96	97
1,000–1,999	91	88	97	95
2,000 and over	89	87	84	82

SOURCE:　Mehta and Shah, 1966, p. 10.

10,000 population, using local civil registration records as one source and a one-time retrospective survey with a recall period of somewhat over two years as the second source. Estimated completeness rates for these two sources are shown in Table 2.5, along with the completeness estimates for three time intervals in the study's 28-month reference period. Registration completeness varied little over the full period except for a slight dip in the most recent interval, a consequence of the fact that many events were not registered promptly. On the other hand, estimated survey completeness rose consistently as the recall period was shortened.

A major problem in using the civil registration system records in matching was the adequacy of the identification information on the registration reports. In order to establish a satisfactory procedure, a number of different matching rules were applied to the Vaso data and the resulting match rates tabulated (Mehta, 1967b). This analysis focused on five identifying characteristics for matching purposes: name of baby's mother or name of deceased, sex of baby or deceased, residential status of vital event, house number, and date or month of vital event.

Table 2.5 **PGE Estimates of the Completeness of Reporting of Live Births and Deaths, by Type of Collection Procedure and Time Period, Pilot SRS Study, for Vaso, Gujarat: 1964–66**

(Completeness expressed as a percentage of PGE estimate of true number of events.)

Time period	Live births		Deaths	
	Registration	Survey	Registration	Survey
All periods	**86**	**65**	**82**	**51**
Feb. 1964–Mar. 1965	86	58	83	45
Mar. 1965–Feb. 1966	87	71	84	53
Mar. 1966–May 1966	84	73	70	70

SOURCE:　Mehta, 1967a, table 2.

Reports agreeing on all five characteristics were classified as matched, and those agreeing on one to four items were classified as partially matched. The partially matched reports, together with the nonmatches, were sent back for independent field follow-up. The results tended to support the importance of a good system of house numbering and the value of independent field follow-up, but the analysis was hampered by the small number of common items in the two sources and the relatively small number of reports available for matching. An additional limitation of the study was that the results were presented in such a form that one cannot ascertain the extent of erroneous matches and erroneous nonmatches associated with any given matching rule. A study conducted in the Punjab area of Pakistan suffered from a similar limitation (Naeem, 1969). In other words, showing that the obtained match rate varies with the matching rules used does not provide guidance as to which set of rules produces minimum matching error.

An Indian study that focused more sharply on the issues underlying a good matching procedure was conducted by the staff of the Institute of Rural Health and Family Planning at Gandhigram in Tamil Nadu (Srinivasan and Muthiah, 1968). The approach used by Srinivasan and Muthiah was to tabulate separately the number of erroneous matches and erroneous nonmatches obtained from the application of alternative matching criteria. The number of matching errors was found by examining the differences between the actual results of the matching and the "correct" match status of each report. The latter was determined on the basis of the results of a field follow-up procedure. Moreover, Srinivasan and Muthiah gave specific tolerance limits for each item so that it was possible to understand what was meant by a phrase such as "agreeing on an item." Details of the procedures and results of this study are presented in Section F.4 of Chapter 3.

Various other studies conducted at Gandhigram (Wells, 1971, pp. 18–19) suggest that "results for females interviewing females were better than for females interviewing males, which in turn were better than for males interviewing males," and that "married women in *new* dwelling units added after the baseline had higher fertility levels than women already in the study." Additional Indian matching studies of special interest include a long-term pilot study carried out in the Mehrauli block near New Delhi (Murty and Jain, 1967); a series of investigations carried out in Kerala state in connection with the SRS (Kerala, 1967 and 1968); and an attempt to evaluate the completeness of vital events reporting in the states of West Bengal and Tamil Nadu by matching reports obtained by National Sample Survey interviewers with those gathered by personnel affiliated with the SRS and using SRS procedures (U.N. Advisory Mission to India, 1969).

Major Asian efforts at dual collection and matching of reports of vital events outside India included the Pakistan Population Growth Estimation Experiment, the Thai Survey of Population Change, and the Turkish Demographic Survey. These three studies employed national probability samples, and, unlike the Indian SRS, each prepared estimates of vital rates adjusted for omissions on the basis of the PGE technique, though they differed from one another in a number of other respects (see Table 2.6). Collectively, they provided benchmark demographic estimates covering somewhat over 4 percent of the world's population; in addition they provided an important impetus toward the refinement of PGE study procedures and the clarification of the underlying measurement problems. In subsequent chapters of the Handbook, we shall make extensive use of this experience, and some of the methodological findings from these studies are included in the tabular materials of Section D.

Table 2.6 Summary of Sampling, Data Collection, and Matching Procedures Used in National PGE Studies Conducted in Pakistan, Thailand, and Turkey: 1962–67

Procedure	Pakistan—Population Growth Estimation Experiment (PGE)	Thailand—Survey of Population Change (SPC)	Turkey—Turkish Demographic Survey (TDS)
I. Sample and Period of Coverage			
A. Areas for which estimates were prepared	Pakistan, East Pakistan, West Pakistan	Whole kingdom	Five regions (urban and rural) and three largest cities
B. Sample size (persons)	120,000	170,000	235,000
C. Number and type of sample areas	24 compact clusters, averaging 5,000 persons each[1]	302 villages in rural areas and 17 blocks in municipal areas, averaging about 530 persons per cluster; Bangkok excluded	30 villages per region for rural areas; 30 blocks of about 100 households each for the urban areas and each large city[2]
D. Period of coverage	January 1962 to December 1965	July 1964 to June 1967	Phased start between October 1965 and June 1967; continuing
II. Data Collection			
A. Registration 1. Staff used	Full-time employees of study assigned to live in area (typically, high school graduates with rural background)	Civil registration personnel (village headmen or other local officials)	Part-time employees (local residents)
2. Source of reports	Registrar made regular rounds visiting "neighborhood contacts" to obtain information about events; visited household and completed registration form for each event	Relatives had to go to commune level (a group of villages) to report an event; register maintained at district level	Monthly visit to each household by registrar to update list of household members and record vital events
3. Transmittal procedure	Originals of all reports mailed directly to national headquarters each month; copies withdrawn prior to quarterly survey	Clerks from study headquarters visited district registration offices and transcribed information from civil registration records	Copies of newly updated household schedules mailed to national headquarters each month
4. Field supervision	Six full-time supervisors for 20 registrars, plus visits by senior staff	Full-time study staff for the clerks; unknown for civil registration personnel	Full-time study staff often twice yearly at the time of field verification
5. Special features	*Unofficial* birth and death certificates given to families	Efforts to get reports directly from commune level in later years	Unknown

Table 2.6 (continued)

Procedure	Pakistan—PGE	Thailand—SPC	Turkey—TDS
B. Household survey			
1. Staff used	Full-time nonresident enumerators on the regular staff of the government statistical organization	Originally, part-time local personnel; subsequently, full-time employees of the government statistical organization	Full-time nonresident "professional survey staff supervisor"
2. Frequency	Fresh household enumeration annually; quarterly visits between annual full enumerations used household list from preceding visit	Full household enumeration in first round; thereafter, quarterly visits to household, with changes entered on household schedule	Full household enumeration in first round; thereafter, visits to household twice yearly, with changes entered on household schedule
3. Reference period	12 months; four overlapping periods each year	Since last enumeration (approximately three months); no overlap	Alternately, six months and 12 months; overlap for only half the year
4. Transmittal procedure	Copy of original household schedule completed in annual full enumeration sent to headquarters; original schedule used by enumerator for one year mailed to headquarters from regional offices of government statistical office; quarterly change reports and reports of vital events mailed to headquarters after each survey round	Copy of original household schedule completed in first round sent to headquarters; all changes and events found in subsequent rounds recorded on special form and sent to headquarters after the round	Original sent to central office after each survey round
5. Supervision	Regular field supervisors of government statistical office; occasional visits by senior study staff	Rounds 1 to 5, nine recent graduates of Bangkok universities; round 6, 14 recent graduates; thereafter, regular field supervisors of government statistical office; occasional visits by senior staff throughout the study	Occasional visits by senior study staff
6. Information recorded	Live births, stillbirths and deaths; characteristics of household members and visitors; pregnancy status of married women	Live births and deaths; characteristics of household members and visitors; pregnancy status of women and information on seriously ill persons	Live births, stillbirths, and deaths; characteristics of household members; details on in- and out-migration
C. Counting rule used	*De facto* in both sources for population and events; in 1965, survey used both *de facto* and *de jure* rules	*De jure*; visitors recorded as "present" for four or more rounds also included	*De jure*

	III. Matching		
A. Frequency and place	Annually at headquarters[3]	Semiannually or quarterly at district level	Semiannually at headquarters
B. Type and mode	Two-way machine match (punchcard equipment) with manual checks; similar to that used in 1950 U.S. birth registration test	Two-way manual match	Two-way manual match

Table 2.6   (continued)

Procedure	Pakistan—PGE	Thailand—SPC	Turkey—TDS
C. Reports used	Cards punched from vital events reports; machine listings and original schedules used in manual checks	Events reported on survey household schedule and those on registration transcription form	Events reported on most recent household survey schedule and cumulative information reported by registrar
D. Items specifically used in matching			
1. Births	Dwelling number, sex, baby's name, father's name, caste, relationship, parity	Name, parents' names, sex, age of mother, place of occurrence and residence, address	Unknown
2. Deaths	Dwelling number, sex, name, father's name, caste, relationship, age group	Name, sex, age, place of occurrence and residence, address	Unknown
E. Field follow-up			
1. Scope	Unmatched reports of both sources not otherwise confirmed by information in the office	Unmatched registration reports[4]	Unmatched reports of both sources
2. Method	Field visits	Field visits	Letter or field visits
3. Staff	Registration system supervisors[5]	Unknown	Staff supervisor not responsible for enumeration of the area

[1] Both the survey and registration sources were operative in 16 sample areas, the survey alone was operative in four areas, and the registration system alone was operative in four areas. A minimum of 20 areas was necessary for a national sample.

[2] The sample originally totaled 450,000, with 60 villages per region for the rural areas and 30 to 60 blocks per region for the urban areas and for each of the large cities.

[3] In one year (1964), matching was done semiannually.

[4] A special study of unmatched survey reports was conducted in 1966 as part of a KAP study of civil registration practices; see Thailand, 1969b.

[5] In one year (1965), field follow-up was carried out by persons completely unconnected with field operations.

SOURCE: Data from Population Growth Estimation, 1968 and 1971; Rumford, Heperkan, and Fincancioglu, 1968; Thailand, 1969a; and Wells, 1971.

The estimated completeness rates obtained in these national PGE studies are given in Table 2.7. These completeness rates indicate clearly that no one collection procedure is inherently best. For example, in the Pakistan study the "registration" system had a higher estimated completeness than the "survey" system, whereas in Thailand and Turkey the estimated "survey" completeness was almost always higher. This difference also reflects differences between the studies in the nature of the registration or the survey procedures employed (see Table 2.6 and footnote 1 to Table 2.7).

Some of the difference also reflects the different levels of effort expended on each source. In Pakistan, the registration system was implemented by a temporary field staff under the direct control of the project director and principal investigator of the study, whereas the survey was carried out by the regular field staff of the government's Central Statistical Office. Almost of necessity, a multipurpose, permanent government statistical office has a broader set of technical priorities and is subject to more restrictive bureaucratic controls than a temporary organization dedicated solely to the task of demographic measurement. In Thailand the registration system was under the overall control of the Interior Ministry, which had a minimal interest in the technical problems involved, and the actual registration work was a minor duty of the village headman or other local officials. The Thai survey, on the other hand, was carried out by a special unit of the National Statistical Office that was very competent and dedicated and had strong administrative backing. Considering the relative inputs to each source, it is not surprising that the registration system in the Pakistan study apparently covered more events than the survey, whereas the reverse was true in Thailand. In PGE studies, as in other types of statistical data gathering, there is usually a strong relationship between the quality of the data and the effort and expertise that goes into their collection.

More detailed descriptions of these studies can be found in Population Growth Estimation (1968 and 1971) for the Pakistan study, Thailand (1969a) for the Thai study, and Turkish Demographic Survey (1967) for the Turkish study. In addition, Mauldin (1966), Lauriat (1966), Seltzer (1969), Abernathy and Lunde (1970), and Wells (1971) have described and analyzed these studies from a comparative viewpoint.[32]

Table 2.7 PGE Estimates of Completeness of Reporting for Live Births and Deaths, by Type of Collection Procedure Used, for National PGE Studies Conducted in Pakistan, Thailand, and Turkey: 1962–67

(Completeness expressed as a percentage of PGE estimate of true number of events.)

Area and year	Live births		Deaths	
	Registration[1]	Household survey	Registration[1]	Household survey
Pakistan, 1962–65				
East	83	75	84	61
West	76	71	77	56
Thailand, 1964–65	84	87	63	80
Turkey, 1965–67				
Region 1 (Urban)	67	86	61	82
Region 1 (Rural)	67	82	61	70
Region 2 (Urban)	70	83	62	75
Region 2 (Rural)	67	82	64	72
Ankara	62	66	50	50
Istanbul	76	77	68	70
Izmir	66	86	58	72

[1] Full-time special registrar in Pakistan, civil registration in Thailand, and a monthly household canvass for vital events by part-time special registrar in Turkey.

SOURCE: Seltzer, 1969.

C.3 PGE STUDIES IN AFRICA, LATIN AMERICA, AND THE CARIBBEAN

Building upon the experience of the three national PGE studies in Asia, a PGE study was begun in May 1969 in Liberia (Rumford, 1970). To date, this study has been a model of a carefully executed and efficiently administered national PGE study. The primary purpose of the study is to obtain basic demographic estimates for Liberia as a whole and separately for the urban and rural sectors of the country. In the rural areas the sample consists of 100 villages (averaging about 500 persons each); in urban areas 100 "blocks" (averaging about 200 persons each) were selected. The total sample thus comprises about 70,000 persons.

The two collection procedures employed in the Liberian study are similar in design to those employed in the Turkish study. One source uses a local resident as a part-time "registrar" to canvass all households in a sample area each month to obtain information on vital events and migrations, primarily as reflected in month-to-month changes in household composition. The other source involves a twice-yearly household survey conducted by staff supervisors. This survey employs the same schedules as the monthly canvass, but alternates in obtaining information about household changes, events, and migrations over six- and 12-month periods. Like the Thai and Turkish studies, the Liberian study uses a two-way manual match. After the match, a field follow-up procedure is carried out and estimates of vital rates adjusted for estimated omissions on the basis of the PGE technique are published. Estimated completeness rates for each source are given in Table 2.8.

The Liberian study departs from its Turkish prototype in a number of innovative ways. Letters of congratulations (for births) and

Table 2.8 PGE Estimates of the Completeness of Birth and Death Reporting, by Type of Collection Procedure, for Liberia (May 1969–April 1970) and for Tunisia (January 1967–May 1969)

(Completeness expressed as a percentage of PGE estimate of true number of events.)

Study	Live births		Deaths	
	Registration[1]	Survey	Registration[1]	Survey
Liberia—total[2]	**59**	**60**	**66**	**65**
Urban	57	55	64	56
Rural	59	62	68	68
Tunisian study[3]	**78**	**97**	**60**	**88**

[1]In Liberia, a monthly canvass of each household in the sample area by a part-time resident field worker; in Tunisia, the civil registration system.
[2]Study based on a national probability sample.
[3]Study based on data collection and matching in two small, nonrandomly designated, rural *cheikhats;* completeness estimates based on combined results from three survey rounds.

SOURCE: Rumford, 1971, Table 20; and Vallin, 1971, Table 5.

condolence (for deaths) are issued to respondents. These letters contain information about the event and are printed on heavy-stock paper to facilitate safekeeping. Even though literacy rates are low, these documents are valued by the respondents and helpful in conducting field operations. Better control is obtained over the twice-yearly survey by having a team of staff supervisors do the interviewing in each sample area rather than assigning the responsibility for a given area to one supervisor. In order to control the cost of field follow-up of nonmatched reports, rules have been developed limiting follow-up to situations about which there is genuine uncertainty. As Rumford notes, "although it is possible that by using . . . these procedures an occasional event may be included or lost, field tests have indicated that this rarely happens. For unmatched [reports] other than those mentioned, however, field verification is necessary." (Rumford, 1970, p. 970)

Many of these features have been used in one form or another in some earlier PGE study; however, the Liberian procedure of giving incentive payments to individual members of the field staff on the basis of the valid events reported seems to be a novel development. Under the Liberian incentive scheme the part-time "registrar" is paid one dollar for each verified live birth or death recorded in the monthly canvass, while the supervisor is paid an equal amount for each verified vital event he records in the semiannual survey that was omitted in the monthly canvass. The procedure is designed to reward the field staff of both sources for diligence in obtaining reports of vital events. Although there are no explicit penalties for inventing reports, incentive payments are made only if all disagreements are verified by a third party in the presence of the respondent.

One unfortunate possible consequence of the incentive payment scheme is that it may introduce a negative response correlation bias into the reporting of births and deaths. That is, the supervisor may tend to be less diligent in recording events that were already reported in the monthly canvass, and for which the respondents have letters of congratulations or condolence, than in reporting events missed in the monthly canvass, because he receives an incentive payment only for reporting events *missed* in the monthly canvass. However, Rumford concludes that "although there are obvious dangers in the incentive system, field verification . . . reduces them to a minimum. Thus far the incentive system has worked well in Liberia, and the number of reported and verified events is encouraging." (*Ibid.*, p. 967)

One aspect of the Liberian study about which there can be no reservations is the rapidity with which the processing has been completed and reports issued. Field work commenced in May 1969; a preliminary report covering the period from November 1969 to October 1970, and containing basic PGE estimates, was issued in February 1971 (Liberia, 1971a); and final reports on fertility (Liberia, 1971b) and mortality (Liberia, 1971c) for the same period were issued in August 1971 and October 1971, respectively. The standard of prompt publication set by the Liberian study is very high relative to both PGE studies and single-source procedures. (See Table 2.16, Section D.)

In addition to promptly developing and releasing substantive demographic estimates, the Liberian study undertook a major methodological investigation of response correlation bias. A preliminary report of this study was prepared by Rumford (1971). It will be recalled that Chandrasekaran and Deming (1949) suggested that the effects of response correlation bias could be reduced by grouping events into strata that were reasonably homogeneous with respect to their probability of collection, preparing PGE estimates separately for each stratum, and summing the stratum estimates. Rumford attempted to expand the list of characteristics used to form such strata from variables that referred essentially to characteristics of the event (for example, age of mother, sex of deceased) to those that referred to the collection procedure (for example, size of sample area or education of field worker). He first examined whether a given method of stratification produced subgroups with markedly different match rates (that is, completeness estimates), and found that omission rates for births, deaths, and infant deaths rose as the size of the sample area increased; that younger workers had higher omission rates than their older counterparts; that omission rates were higher for female births than male births and for male deaths than female deaths; and that neonatal deaths and deaths among urban infants had higher omission rates than post-neonatal deaths and infant deaths in rural areas, respectively. Of course, these findings must be interpreted in light of the specific procedures employed in the Liberian study; one should not assume that they are universally valid.

Rumford also compared the PGE estimates obtained by using a number of stratifying variables. Some results of the second type of analysis are included in Tables 2.13 and 2.14 in Section D. In general, he found, as did those before him, that preparing PGE estimates separately for subgroups did not noticeably change the result.

A number of smaller studies in Africa also made use of the PGE approach. As part of the Tunisian Demographic Survey, a two-way match was conducted for two rural *cheikhats* (primary-level administrative units) with a combined population of somewhat over 5,000 persons between the civil registration records and the events reported in a three-round demographic household survey carried out between January 1968 and May 1969 (Vallin, 1971). No subsampling was done within the *cheikhats* for either source, and all unmatched reports were sent for field follow-up. PGE completeness estimates for the survey and the civil registration system are given in Table 2.8 for the two *cheikhats* combined.

Dual collection was also attempted in the 1969–70 Algerian multiround demographic survey (Bahri, 1969), in the Malawi population change survey, and in a small demographic study in rural Tanzania. In the Algerian study, field staff for the second source were functional in only nine out of a planned 27 sample areas. It is not clear whether any matching will be attempted for these nine areas. The studies in Malawi and Tanzania would seem to illustrate the point that the PGE approach is not immune to poor study design or perfunctory execution. The Malawi study, in particular, which used a questionnaire borrowed from Turkey and Liberia and a sample design inappropriate to local conditions is an unfortunate example of the costs that may be incurred by an inappropriate study design (Blacker, n.d.). In any case, no matching results from these three studies have been released as yet.

In conjunction with the Poplab program of the University of North Carolina, the government statistical office in Morocco began a PGE study in the latter part of 1971. The study was designed to provide basic demographic estimates for two major regions of Morocco as well as to test various hypotheses about data gathering procedures (Fellegi, 1971). For a preliminary report of results from the Moroccan study, see Rachidi (1973).

The Latin American and Caribbean region has been the site of three studies employing the PGE approach: a 1967–68 pilot study of civil registration completeness conducted in the Valdivia *comuna* in Chile (Tacla, 1969), a full-scale study of birth registration completeness in the Commonwealth Caribbean conducted in association with the 1960 Eastern Caribbean Population Census (Byrne, 1966), and an experimental PGE study now being conducted by the government statistical office in Colombia as part of the University of North Carolina Poplab program (Colombia, 1971).

The Valdivia study involved a one-way match of birth and death reports obtained in a multiround household survey with the civil registration records for events occuring in the Valdivia *comuna* between May 1967 and April 1968. The survey was conducted at approximately four-month intervals during this period. Registration completeness estimates from this study are presented in Table 2.9. An estimate of completeness based on the experience of one *comuna* (with a population of approximately 7,000 persons) cannot be used to infer anything about overall registration completeness in Chile. Nevertheless, the Valdivia study does provide direct evidence that, at least in some parts of the country, a nontrivial proportion of vital events go unregistered and that it is feasible to employ a PGE study to estimate the completeness of registration in Chile.

Such a study of civil registration completeness was conducted in 1960 in the Commonwealth Caribbean territories of Barbados, Dominica, St. Lucia, and Trinidad.[33] This study followed, in broad outline, the design used in the 1931 Canadian registration study and the 1940 and 1950 birth registration tests in the United States. In the Commonwealth Caribbean study a special schedule was prepared for all infants aged three months or less enumerated in the 1960 Population Census. In addition to general household identification information, the infant schedule contained items on name, sex, and race of infant; date and place of birth; date and place of registration; institution (if any) where birth occurred; single or multiple birth; name and age of mother; name, age, and occupation of father; place of usual residence of parents; and place of infant's baptism (if already

Table 2.9 PGE Estimates of the Completeness of Birth and Death Reporting in the Civil Registration System, for the Commonwealth Caribbean (January 1960–April 1960) and for Valdivia, Chile (May 1967–April 1968)

(Completeness expressed as a percentage of PGE estimate of true number of events.)

Study and area	Live births	Deaths
Commonwealth Caribbean [1]		
Trinidad	89	u
Barbados	98	u
St. Lucia	74	u
Dominica	94	u
Valdivia study [2]	80	85

u = unavailable.

[1] Based on a match of infant schedules from the 1960 Census with the civil register.

[2] Based on a match of vital events reports from a household survey with the civil register for a sample of 85 out of 1,065 enumeration zones in the Valdivia *Comuna*.

SOURCE: Byrne, 1966; and Tacla, 1969.

baptised). Infant schedules were matched against the civil registration birth records on file in the central registration offices for all births registered prior to the end of 1960.

Matching was done manually in each of the four territories, using explicit matching rules. The process was described by Byrne as follows (1966, pp. 7–8):

> Of the seventeen items of information requested on the infant schedule, fourteen could be matched directly against information in the birth registers. A match was considered made when the name and sex of the child, date and place of birth, name of father, and maiden name of mother were identical in both records. Where at least three of the above mentioned [six] items and at least five of the remaining eight items coincided in both records a match was considered made. Cases of doubtful matches were referred to a supervisor who decided each case on its own merit. The operation consisted of first arranging the infant schedules by week of occurrence of birth and geographical location (county or parish). Each week's batch was then separated into male and female births before being matched against the corresponding week's entries in the birth register. . . . Schedules not matched in this first phase were then compared with births registered outside the range of supposed occurrence, with the period of comparison ever widening in order to maximize the number of matches.

In addition, remaining unmatched reports were carefully reviewed

> with special attention being paid to certain factors which might have created problems of identification, for example, illegible entries in the registers, matching of some criteria and not others, clerical errors, registration of still births as live births, name changes due to the legitimization of illegitimate births. (*Ibid.*, p. 9)

Completeness estimates for the birth registration system in each of the four territories are given in Table 2.9. Byrne noted a variety of problems that could lead to matching errors. (The fact that these problems were recognized as such was certainly attributable to the use of explicit matching rules.) In Trinidad, frequent repetition of a few popular names and the abbreviation of names, particularly among the population of East Indian origin, gave rise to considerable uncertainty in matching. In St. Lucia, the variability in the reporting of infants' names probably gave rise to many erroneous nonmatches, and Byrne ascribes the low completeness estimate for St. Lucia to this cause. On the other hand, in Barbados and Dominica the lack of house numbers, registration of illegitimate births in the name of the father, and the common practice of registering births before naming the baby probably gave rise to a large number of erroneous matches. In Byrne's words, "Where at first glance two sets of records would appear to refer to the same birth, closer inspection with respect to the other criteria invariably revealed that the records referred to two different infants." (*Ibid.,* p. 11)

The Colombian Poplab project involves dual collection and matching in a probability sample of two of Colombia's 16 *departmentos.* One source is based on a twice-yearly retrospective survey; the other source uses a monthly household canvass in some areas (following the Turkish and Liberian procedure) and a special registrar who obtains leads about vital events from neighborhood informants in other areas (following the Indian sample registration scheme and the Pakistan PGE procedure). The sample is so designed that it should be possible to test the relative effectiveness of the various procedures (Losee, 1970).

The design was implemented on a trial basis in one *departmento,* and in November 1971 the birth and death reports obtained in the retrospective survey for the period from 1 July to 1 October 1971 were matched against the reports obtained from the continuous observation procedures covering the same period. It appears from this preliminary experience that the identification information that can be collected (names, addresses, special house numbers assigned by the study field staff, identity card numbers, and so on) will permit accurate matching (Seltzer, 1971b). If the initial promise of this study is realized, its results will provide important guidance to those designing both single-source and dual collection procedures for demographic measurement. Some early results are presented in Wells and Horvitz (1973).

Two major conclusions can be drawn from this review of the history of the use of the PGE approach in various parts of the world. First, because all PGE studies must deal with certain basic issues relating to sampling, data collection, matching, field follow-up, study administration, and so on, a number of common elements run through many studies. Thus, regardless of whether a particular study is considered "a success" or "a failure," a careful review of the procedures employed and the results obtained can provide guidance to others faced with these decisions. Second, despite the fact that there are many common technical and administrative problems, each study must be designed to conform to the unique factors present in a particular situation. Almost by definition, an optimum study design is not an exportable commodity, and the information about specific studies presented in this section should be interpreted in this light. It is our hope that by bringing together the results of a large number of PGE studies employing a variety of design features we will facilitate the task of developing new designs appropriate to the conditions at hand.

D. *A Summary of Data on Design Parameters*

This section contains, in tabular form, selected methodological findings from various PGE studies based primarily on the experience reviewed in Section C. A data gathering endeavor such as a PGE study necessarily has many interacting features, and to be able to examine any particular aspect of such a study one frequently needs quantitative estimates relating to other aspects of the study. This section is designed to meet that need. At the same time these tables, by providing at least a rough indication of the observed magnitudes of various design parameters, can help to place some of the discussion of PGE design in subsequent chapters in a realistic context.

Unfortunately, a number of important topics relating to the design and execution of PGE studies are not covered in the tables in this section. Basically, these omissions are due either to a lack of quantifiable information on a topic (for example, data on the costs of demographic measurement are almost nonexistent) or to the fact that the limited data available (for example, information on matching problems) are not readily expressible in summary form without distortion. Although some of the topics omitted were covered in Section C, adequate coverage of other topics depends upon the collection of methodological information not now available (see Chapter 6, Section D.4).

In using the tables in this section, one must be aware that there is no guarantee that the appropriate parameter value for some specific PGE study will not differ substantially from those experienced in the past. Indeed it is entirely possible that some feature of the country or of the contemplated design will result in values quite different from those presented here. These tables are only a starting point for making preliminary design decisions; it is also important to identify and take into account any previous local experience that is relevant. Furthermore, once preliminary decisions have been made, there should be some effort to test the correctness of these decisions by conducting pilot studies; and even after the substantive study is underway, some modification of procedures may be necessitated by the information obtained while carrying out the study itself.

This section consists of nine tables. Tables 2.10 and 2.11 provide an indication of the variations in the data collection procedures used and completeness estimates obtained in a substantial number of Asian PGE studies using two-way matching. Table 2.12 provides a similar summary of worldwide experience with PGE studies of civil registration completeness. Tables 2.13 and 2.14 present data based on the procedure suggested by Chandrasekaran and Deming (1949) for minimizing the effect of response correlation bias. (See the discussion of the Singur Health Center Study in Section C.2 and Chapter 3, Section E.) Table 2.13 shows the relative gain obtained by preparing PGE estimates on the basis of subgroups formed by using a single stratifying variable. In contrast, Table 2.14 indicates, for each PGE study that used the procedure of homogeneous subgroups, the maximum gain achieved and the combination of variables employed to achieve it. The results of three follow-up studies of nonmatched birth reports are summarized in Table 2.15. The last three tables treat more general design questions. Table 2.16 presents data on the duration of time between field work and the publication of results, for a variety of studies in the developed and developing worlds. Table 2.17 provides estimates of sampling errors for crude birth and death rates obtained from three Asian sample

Table 2.10 PGE Estimates of the Completeness of Birth and Death Reporting, for Each Collection System, Selected Asian PGE Studies Using Two-way Matching: 1945–67

(Coverage of each system expressed as a percentage of the PGE estimated total for each study.)

Study number[1]	System 1			System 2		
	Type of system	Estimated coverage		Type of system	Estimated coverage	
		Births	Deaths		Births	Deaths
1	Civil registration	52	48	One-time survey	53	32
2	Civil registration	60	51	One-time survey	67	51
3	Civil registration	43	44	One-time survey	93	90
4	One-time survey	96	88	One-time survey	92	88
5	Special registration	92	91	Multiple-visit survey	89	89
6	Civil registration	86	82	One-time survey	65	51
7	Special registration	89	74	Multiple-visit survey	91	81
8	Special registration	83	85	Multiple-visit survey	92	89
9	Civil registration	43	33	One-time survey	28	23
10	Special registration	83	84	Multiple-visit survey	75	61
11	Special registration	76	77	Multiple-visit survey	71	56
12	Civil registration	84	63	Multiple-visit survey	87	80
13	Special registration	67	61	Multiple-visit survey	86	82
14	Special registration	67	61	Multiple-visit survey	82	70
15	Special registration	70	62	Multiple-visit survey	83	75
16	Special registration	67	64	Multiple-visit survey	82	72
17	Special registration	62	50	Multiple-visit survey	66	50
18	Special registration	76	68	Multiple-visit survey	77	70
19	Special registration	66	58	Multiple-visit survey	86	72

[1] Key to study numbers:

Studies 1–2	Singur Health Center Study for 1945 and 1946, respectively.
Study 3	Mysore Population Study, 1950–52, three rural zones.
Study 4	Mysore Population Study, 1950–52, Bangalore city.
Study 5	Gujarat SRS, 1964, rural pilot study.
Study 6	Gujarat SRS, 1964–66, urban (Vaso) pilot study.
Study 7	Mehrauli Block, South Delhi, 1963–66.
Study 8	Kerala SRS, 1965–67.
Study 9	Taeduk Gun Matching Project, South Korea, 1963–66
Studies 10–11	Pakistan PGE, 1962–65, for East and West Pakistan, respectively.
Study 12	Thailand SPC, 1964–65.
Studies 13–19	Turkish Demographic Survey, 1965–67, for region 1 (urban), region 1 (rural), region 2 (urban), region 2 (rural), Ankara, Istanbul, and Izmir, respectively.

For further details of individual studies and appropriate citations, see Section C.2.

SOURCE: Seltzer, 1969.

Table 2.11 Median and Range of PGE Completeness Estimates for Birth and Death Reporting by Type of Collection System, for Selected Asian PGE Studies Using Two-way Matching: 1945–67

(Coverage of each system expressed as a percentage of the PGE estimated total for each study.)

Type of system	Number of systems	Estimated proportion of births covered		Estimated proportion of deaths covered	
		Median	Range	Median	Range
All types	**38**	**77**	**28–96**	**69**	**23–91**
Civil registration	6	56	43–86	49.5	33–82
Special registration	12	73	62–92	66	50–91
One-time household survey	7	67	28–96	51	23–90
Multiple-visit household survey	13	83	66–92	72	50–89

SOURCE: Table 2.10.

Table 2.12 A Summary of Procedures and Results for PGE Studies of Civil Registration Completeness, for the World: 1931–70

Place and year of study	Information about second source					Type of match	Estimated completeness[3]	
	Type of collection procedure	Type of sample[1]	Size of sample (in 1,000s)[2]				Live births	Deaths
			Persons	Birth reports	Death reports			
Canada, 1931[4]	Census	B	u	26.2	0	One-way	88	u
Georgia, 1934	One-time survey	E	1,181	6.2	0	One-way	87	u
United States, 1940	Census	A	132,594	662.8	0	One-way	93	u
Singur, 1945	One-time survey	C	64	1.5	0.7	Two-way	52	48
Singur, 1946	One-time survey	C	64	2.5	0.9	Two-way	60	51
United States, 1950	Census	A	152,271	780.1	0	One-way	98	u
Mysore, 1950–52[5]	One-time survey	D	23	0.3	0.1	Two-way	43	44
Ceylon, 1953	One-time survey	B	85	0.6	0.1	One-way	88	89
Trinidad, 1960[6]	Census	A	828	u	0	One-way	89	u
Barbados, 1960	Census	A	232	u	0	One-way	98	u
St. Lucia, 1960	Census	A	86	u	0	One-way	74	u
Dominica, 1960	Census	A	60	u	0	One-way	94	u
South Korea, 1963–65	One-time survey	C	100	3.8	0.6	Two-way	43	33
Gujarat, 1964–66	One-time survey	C	9	0.5	0.2	Two-way	86	82
Thailand, 1964–65	Multi-round survey	B	172	6.4	1.5	Two-way	84	63
Tunisia, 1967–69	Multi-round survey	C	5	0.6	0.2	Two-way	78	60
Chile, 1967–68	Multi-round survey	D	7	0.2	0.1	One-way	80	85
United States, 1970	One-time survey	B	218	14.6	0	One-way	99	u

u = information unavailable.

[1]Type-of-sample code: A = national complete count; B = national probability sample; C = local complete count; D = local probability sample; and E = local nonprobability sample. Classification is based on the overall sample design of second source, ignoring minor frame exclusions and errors of execution.

[2]Approximate coverage of second source sample; in the case of birth and death reports this refers to the number of events reported by the second source. In a number of cases such reports were compiled for a period other than a year, so that meaningful vital rates cannot be computed from the data presented here.

[3]PGE estimate of registration completeness expressed as a percentage.

[4]Data in this table exclude the experience of the Indian population.

[5]Combined experience in three rural zones.

[6]Apparently includes Tobago.

SOURCES: Same as Tables 2.1 and 2.2; Chandrasekaran and Deming, 1949; United Nations, 1961; Ceylon, 1953; Byrne, 1966; Choe, 1967; Seltzer, 1969; Mehta, 1967a; Thailand, 1969a; Tacla, 1969; and Vallin, 1971.

Table 2.13 Percentage Gain in PGE Estimates Achieved Through Stratification on a Single Variable, by Variable Used and Type of Event, for Selected PGE Studies: 1940–70

Type of event and stratifying variable	Number of studies using each variable	Number of studies with specified percentage gain[1]					Median percentage gain[1]
		Less than 0	0.0	0.1–0.4	0.5–1.4	1.5 or more[2]	
Live births							
Geographic area[3]	5	0	0	1	3	1	0.8
Sex of baby	2	0	2	0	0	0	0
Age of mother	2	1	1	0	0	0	0
Parity	1	0	1	0	0	0	0
Deaths							
Age	5	0	0	1	2	2	1.0
Geographic area[3]	3	1	0	1	0	1	0.2
Sex	5	0	2	3	0	0	0.1

[1] The stratified PGE estimate less the unstratified PGE estimate divided by the latter, expressed as a percentage.

[2] The maximum gains achieved were 1.9 percent for geographic area for live births, and 8.2 percent for age and 2.9 percent for geographic area for deaths.

[3] Varies with study; see original sources and Table 2.14, footnotes 2–5 for further information on the geographic units used.

SOURCE: Derived from data in Chandrasekaran and Deming, 1949; Shapiro, 1950b; Shapiro and Schachter, 1954; Thailand, 1969a; Population Growth Estimation, 1971; and Rumford, 1971.

Table 2.14 Stratification Yielding Maximum Gain in PGE Estimates, by Type of Event, for Selected PGE Studies: 1940–70

Area	Study	Stratification used	Percentage gain from stratification[1]
Live births			
Liberia	PGS, 1969–70	Sex, mother's age, and parity	3.1
Pakistan	PGE, 1963	Sex and geographic area[2]	2.3
India	Singur Health Center, 1946	Geographic area[3]	0.8
Arkansas	Birth Registration Test, 1950	Attendant at birth and geographic area[4]	0.8
United States	Birth Registration Test, 1940	Race and geographic area[5]	0.8
India	Singur Health Center, 1945	Geographic area[3]	0.2
Thailand	SPC, 1964–65	Mother's age	−0.0
Deaths			
India	Singur Health Center, 1945	Age and sex	8.2
India	Singur Health Center, 1946	Age and sex	4.1
Pakistan	PGE, 1963	Sex and geographic area[2]	3.1
Liberia	PGS, 1969–70	Age and sex	2.0
Thailand	SPC, 1964–65	Age and sex	0.6

[1] The stratified PGE estimate less the unstratified PGE estimate divided by the latter, expressed as a percentage.

[2] Sample clusters of approximately 5,000 persons each. To correct for possible ratio bias, the percentage gain for deaths was calculated using equation 7.93 for subgroups with less than ten matched death reports. If these subgroups are excluded altogether, the gain from grouped estimates based on sex and geographic area drops to 1.6 percent and the greatest gain (2.9 percent) is achieved by geographic stratification alone. For births, all available subgroups contained more than ten matched reports.

[3] Union Board.

[4] Cities over 10,000 population and balance of county; race may also have been used as a stratifying variable.

[5] Cities over 10,000 population and balance of county; race used only in states with 10 percent or more nonwhite population.

SOURCE: Same as Table 2.13.

studies, and Table 2.18 presents rough estimates of the intraclass correlation coefficients for the crude birth and death rates in a number of African and Asian sample studies.

Because of differences between studies in design, in execution, and in the populations under study, small variations in the tabled values must be interpreted with great caution and, in most cases, disregarded.

Table 2.15 Results of Follow-up Studies of Nonmatched Birth Reports for the United States Birth Registration Tests, 1940 and 1950, and for the Pakistan PGE Study, 1962–65

(Based on birth reports obtained in census or survey household interviews.)

Category	U.S. Birth Registration Tests		Pakistan PGE, 1962–65[3]	
	1940[1]	1950[2]	East Pakistan	West Pakistan
Number of reports				
Nonmatched reports prior to follow-up—total	125,000[4]	45,000	1,571	2,034
Excluded as out-of-scope	36,000[5]	13,400[6]	311	270
In central office	u	8,100	2	3
In local offices or field	u	5,300	309	267
Reclassified as matched	39,000	15,000	171	202
In central office	u	7,700	141	182
In local offices or field	u	7,300	30	20
Remaining nonmatches after follow-up[7]	50,000[8]	16,600	1,089	1,562
Percentage				
Nonmatched prior to follow-up—total	100	100	100	100
Excluded as out-of-scope	29	30	20	13
Reclassified as matched	31	33	11	10
Remaining nonmatches after follow-up	40	37	69	77
Percentage of follow-up changes done in local offices or field:				
Exclusions	u	39	99	99
Matches	u	49	18	10

u = unavailable.

[1] Unmatched census reports of infants under four months after a one-way match with civil registration birth reports. Follow-up consisted initially of letters to parents and institutions, followed by searches in local registration offices and, in some cases, by further investigation with letters or personal interviews. See Figure 2.1, and Shapiro, 1950a. The numbers shown are approximate and rounded.

[2] Unmatched census reports of infants under three months after a one-way mechanical match with civil registration reports. Follow-up consisted initially of letters to parents and institutions, subsequently of searches in local registration offices and contacts with adoption agencies. See Figure 2.2, and Shapiro and Schachter, 1952, Table 1. Numbers shown are independently rounded and figures for subgroups may not add to totals.

[3] Unmatched survey reports of births in the last 12 months after a two-way mechanical match with special registration reports. Follow-up consisted initially of an intensive search of unmatched registration reports by special staff and subsequently of household interviews by field supervisor of registrar and by senior members of study staff. See Population Growth Estimation, 1971, Tables III.3 and III.4.

[4] Shapiro, 1950a, p. 96.

[5] Estimated from the statement by Shapiro, 1950a, p. 96, that "between one-quarter and one-third of the 125,000 unmatched infant cards were eliminated from the test because replies from the parents clearly indicated that the children were born outside the test period."

[6] Includes a number of duplicate reports in addition to temporal out-of-scope reports.

[7] Includes both verified in-scope nonmatched reports and those unverified reports for which there were no positive grounds for excluding or reclassifying as matched.

[8] Tuthill, 1945, p. 106.

SOURCE: See individual footnotes.

On the other hand, wide ranges based on a substantial number of studies do *suggest* bounds within which the values for most studies can be expected to fall. Since in many cases even an approximate range for a particular parameter is adequate for design purposes, these data from previous PGE studies comprise a useful resource in planning any new study.

Table 2.16 Alternative Measures of the Time Lag Between Field Work and the Publication of Results, for Specified PGE Studies and Other Estimation Procedures

Country	Study and reference period	Date field work began (a)	Date field work ended[1] (b)	Date of preliminary or first report[2] (c)	Date of final report (d)	Elapsed time in months			
						(a) to (c)	(b) to (c)	(b) to (d)	(a) to (d)
Dual system studies									
United States	Birth Registration Test, 1940	Dec. 1939	Apr. 1940	Apr. 1943	Aug. 1946	40	36	76	80
United States	Birth Registration Test, 1950	Jan. 1950	Apr. 1950	Dec. 1952	Sept. 1954	35	32	53	56
United States	Birth Registration Test, 1964–68	June 1969[3]	Mar. 1970	Apr. 1971	u	22	13	u	u
India	Singur Health Center Study, 1945–46	Feb. 1947	Apr. 1947	u	Mar. 1949	u	u	23	25
Pakistan	Population Growth Estimation Study, 1962	Jan. 1962	Mar. 1963	Dec. 1964	Dec. 1968	35	21	69	83
Pakistan	Population Growth Estimation Study, 1963	Jan. 1963	Mar. 1964	Sept. 1965	Dec. 1968	32	18	57	71
Pakistan	Population Growth Estimation Study, 1964	Jan. 1964	Mar. 1965	Mar. 1968	July 1971	50	36	76	90
Pakistan	Population Growth Estimation Study, 1965	Jan. 1965	Feb. 1966	Mar. 1968	July 1971	38	25	65	78
Thailand	Survey of Population Change, 1964–65	July 1964	June 1965	Aug. 1966	Mar. 1969	25	14	45	56
Turkey	Turkish Demographic Survey, 1966–68	May 1966	May 1968	Jan. 1969	1970[4]	32	8	25	49
Liberia	Population Growth Survey, 1969–70	Oct. 1969	Oct. 1970	Feb. 1971	Aug.–Oct. 1971[5]	16	4	11	23
Single system procedures									
United States	Civil Registration System, 1968	Jan. 1968	Dec. 1968	Mar. 1969	Jan. 1970	14	3	13	24
Pakistan	Intercensal Growth Rate, 1951–61	Feb. 1951	Feb. 1961	Mar. 1961	June 1964	121	1	40	160
India	National Sample Survey, 1960–61	July 1960	June 1961	Apr. 1963– Feb. 1964[6]	1967[4]	38	27	72	83
Brazil	Guanabara Demographic Pilot Survey, 1961	Jan. 1961	Dec. 1961	u	1964[4]	u	u	30	41
Republic of Korea	Korean Fertility Survey, 1968	Sept. 1968	Oct. 1968	Sept. 1969	Dec. 1970	12	11	26	27

u = unavailable
[1] Excluding field follow-up, if any.
[2] Providing estimates of vital events adjusted for omissions.
[3] Refers to the beginning of data collection in the Current Population Survey.
[4] Where the month of publication was unavailable, June was used for the calculations.
[5] Natality results published in August 1971, and mortality rates in October 1971. Mean (September) used for table.
[6] Draft reports submitted to the Government of India in April 1963, and February 1964. Mean (September) used for table.

Table 2.16 (continued) SOURCES:

For United States, 1940
  Grove, 1943; and Tuthill, 1946.
For United States, 1950
  Shapiro and Schachter, 1952; and Shapiro and Schachter, 1954.
For United States, 1964–68
  Koons, 1971; final report not yet available.
For India, 1945–46
  Chandrasekaran and Deming, 1949.
For Pakistan, 1962
  Krotki and Ahmed, 1964; and Population Growth Estimation, 1968.
For Pakistan, 1963
  Krotki, 1967; and Population Growth Estimation, 1968.
For Pakistan, 1964
  Seltzer, 1968; and Population Growth Estimation, 1971.
For Pakistan, 1965
  Seltzer, 1968; and Population Growth Estimation, 1971.
For Thailand, 1964–65

Lauriat, 1966; and Thailand, 1969a.
For Turkey, 1966–68
  Turkish Demographic Survey, *Bulletin*, vol. II, no. 4 (Jan. 1969); and Turkish Demographic Survey, 1970.
For Liberia, 1969–70
  Liberia, 1971a, 1971b, and 1971c.
For United States, 1968
  U.S. National Center for Health Statistics, *Monthly Vital Statistics Reports*, vol. 17, no. 12 (March 12, 1969); and U.S. National Center for Health Statistics, *Monthly Vital Statistics Reports*, vol. 18, no. 11 Supplement (Jan. 30, 1970).
For Pakistan, 1951–61
  Government of Pakistan, *Census of Pakistan, 1961*, "Bulletin Number 1" (March 1, 1961); and Government of Pakistan, *Census of Pakistan, 1961*, vol. I (Karachi: Ministry of Home and Kashmir Affairs, 1964).
For India, 1960–61

Government of India, National Sample Survey, draft reports no. D116/1 and D116/2, submitted to the Government of India in April 1963 and February 1964, respectively (preliminary reports); and Government of India, *The National Sample Survey: Sixteenth Round, July, 1960–June, 1961* (Calcutta, the Cabinet Secretariat 1967).
For Brazil, 1961
  United Nations, 1964a.
For Korea, 1968
  Ross and Koh, "The Korean 1968 Fertility and Family Planning Survey," paper given at meetings of the International Union for the Scientific Study of Population, London, Sept. 3–11, 1969; and Koh and Smith, *The Korean 1968 Fertility and Family Planning Survey* (Seoul, National Family Planning Center: 1970).

Table 2.17 Some Sample Design Parameters and Approximate Sampling Errors for Estimated Crude Birth and Death Rates for Three Specified Studies: 1950–66

Study name, area, and year	Number of clusters in sample	Mean population per cluster[4]	Sampling rate within cluster (percent)	Total sample size[5]	Births			Deaths		
					CBR[6]	σ_B [7]	CV_B (%) [8]	CDR[6]	σ_D [7]	CV_D (%) [8]
Mysore Population Study Household Survey[1]										
Rural zone I, 1950–52	48	320	33	5,100	40	2.7	7	13	1.9	14
Rural zone II, 1950–52	67	320	33	7,100	42	2.6	6	16	1.8	12
Rural zone III, 1950–52	76	440	33	11,100	38	2.4	6	18	1.3	7
Bangalore city, 1950–52	200	740	17	24,500	30	1.3	4	8	0.8	9
Pakistan Population Growth Estimation Project[2]										
East Pakistan										
1964 Registration	10	5,000	100	50,000	43	3.6	8	17	1.2	7
1965 Registration	10	5,000	100	50,000	40	2.1	5	16	1.5	10
1964 Survey	10	5,000	100	50,000	43	1.9	4	17	1.3	8
1965 Survey	10	5,000	100	50,000	35	2.5	7	9	1.8	19
West Pakistan										
1964 Registration	10	5,000	100	50,000	39	3.6	9	14	1.5	10
1965 Registration	10	5,000	100	50,000	38	2.4	6	12	1.3	11
1964 Survey	10	5,000	100	50,000	41	3.1	8	12	1.5	12
1965 Survey	10	5,000	100	50,000	35	2.5	7	8	0.6	7
Turkish Demographic Survey[3]										
Region I (Central Anatolian Provinces)										
1965–66 Urban	60	500	100	32,500	36	1.3	4	12	0.8	7
1965–66 Rural	60	630	100	38,100	51	1.8	4	18	1.3	7
Region II (Black Sea Provinces)										
1965–66 Urban	60	500	100	29,700	29	1.4	5	9	0.8	9
1965–66 Rural	60	625	100	37,600	40	2.0	5	13	0.8	6
Ankara, 1965–66	60	400	100	24,900	32	1.7	5	8	0.5	6
Istanbul, 1966	40	400	100	15,600	27	2.1	8	9	0.8	9
Izmir, 1966	30	450	100	13,400	23	1.5	7	9	0.8	9

Table 2.17   (continued)

[1] United Nations, 1961, Tables 2.1, 2.2, 2.4, 6.1, 6.2, and 6.5.

[2] Yusuf, 1968b, Table 9; and Seltzer, 1968, Appendix Table C1.

[3] Rumford, Heperkan, and Fincancioglu, 1968, Table 1; and Turkish Demographic Survey, 1967, Appendix Table 1 and Appendix E. After the period covered by these estimates, the samples for the urban and rural parts of Regions I and II and for Ankara were reduced to approximately one-half their former size. The number of clusters shown for these areas is the number prior to the reduction in sample size.

[4] Approximate cluster size before further sampling, if any.

[5] Approximate total population included in sample.

[6] Crude birth rates (CBR) and crude death rates (CDR) per 1,000 population shown in this table are those to which the estimated standard errors and coefficients of variation refer. These rates may differ somewhat from other estimates available from the same studies because of special tabulation procedures introduced to facilitate the estimation of standard errors.

[7] The estimated standard error of the crude birth rate (σ_B) or death rate (σ_D). The standard errors are those shown in the source indicated and are expressed in terms of the rate per 1,000 population.

[8] The estimated coefficient of variation of the crude birth rate (CV_B) or death rate (CV_D) expressed as a percentage of the estimated rate. The coefficients of variation were calculated from the unrounded standard errors and rates shown in the sources indicated.

SOURCE: See individual footnotes.

Table 2.18 Mean and Range of Approximate Intraclass Correlation Coefficients for Crude Birth and Death Rates, by Type of Cluster, for Six Specified Studies: 1950–66

(For full qualifications, see sources cited. Values of δ are approximate and are rounded to 3 places.)

Type of cluster	Number of domains[1]	Mean population per cluster[2]	Crude birth rate			Crude death rate		
			Mean[3] δ	Range of δ		Mean[3] δ	Range of δ	
				Low	High		Low	High
All types	46	572	+.002	−.001	+.008	+.003	−.001	+.013
Region and country								
Africa—total	33	333	+.002	−.001	+.008	+.003	−.001	+.013
Cameroon, 1960–65	23	356	+.001	−.001	+.005	+.002	−.001	+.010
Chad, 1964	7	300	+.001	−.001	+.005	+.005	+.000	+.013
Nigeria, 1965–66	3	235	+.005	+.004	+.008	+.005	+.002	+.012
Asia—total	13	1,179	+.002	+.000	+.005	+.002	−.001	+.006
India, 1950–52	4	455	+.002	+.000	+.004	+.004	+.000	+.006
Pakistan, 1964–65	2[4]	5,000	+.002	+.001	+.002	+.001	+.001	+.002
Turkey, 1965–66	7	501	+.003	+.001	+.005	+.001	−.001	+.002
Type of residence								
Urban	6	498	+.002	+.001	+.005	+.001	−.001	+.005
Rural	38	351	+.002	−.001	+.008	+.003	−.001	+.013
Mixed	2	5,000	+.002	+.001	+.002	+.001	+.001	+.002
Cluster size[5]								
Under 300	11	275	+.001	−.001	+.008	+.005	+.001	+.013
300–349	19	323	+.002	−.001	+.005	+.003	−.001	+.009
350–649	12	457	+.003	+.000	+.005	+.001	−.001	+.010
650 and over	4	2,917	+.002	+.001	+.002	+.002	+.001	+.005

[1] A "domain" is a group of clusters for which the intraclass correlation coefficient is available separately. Domains often correspond to sample strata.

[2] Mean of the average cluster size reported for each domain in the original source. The cluster size shown is that prior to additional within-cluster sampling, if any.

[3] Mean of the unrounded intraclass correlation coefficients for the specified number of domains.

[4] Each province is treated as a domain, with the intraclass correlation coefficient based on the average survey and registration values for 1964 and 1965.

[5] The reported mean population per cluster of each domain.

SOURCES:

For Cameroon: Scott, 1968, Table 1, pages 164–65.

For Chad and Nigeria: Scott and Coker, 1969, Tables 1 and 2. (Nigerian estimates are based on artificially constructed clusters of 50 consecutive household questionnaires completed by the same interviewer.)

For India, Pakistan, and Turkey: Intraclass correlation coefficients are calculated from data presented in Table 2.17 using, Scott and Coker's binomial approximation.

E. *Related Techniques and Applications*

Nearly all the work on the PGE approach has proceeded as if it were a statistical technique that is unique to demography. Actually, as Som (United Nations, 1971) has noted, it is closely related to the "capture-tag-recapture" technique commonly used in estimating the abundance of animal populations (Andrewartha, 1961, pp. 24–34; Feller, 1968, pp. 45–46). This approach has been used to estimate, for example, the number of wild ducks in North America (Lincoln, 1930), tsetse flies (Jackson, 1933), fish in a lake (Schnabel, 1938), and butterflies on an island (Dowdeswell, Fisher, and Ford, 1940).

In its most elementary form, the capture-tag-recapture (CTR) procedure involves selecting a sample of individuals from a closed population of unknown size (capture), marking these individuals in some manner (tag), and then returning them to the population from which they were selected. After sufficient time has elapsed for the tagged individuals to become mixed among the general population, a second sample is drawn (recapture), and the proportion of individuals in the second sample with tags is noted. The total population can be estimated from the product of the reciprocal of this proportion and the size of the initial sample; that is,

$$\hat{N} = \left(\frac{N_2}{T_2} \right) N_1, \qquad\qquad\qquad [2.10]$$

where

N_1 = number of individuals initially sampled and tagged,
N_2 = number of individuals in the second (recapture) sample, and
T_2 = number of tagged individuals in the second sample.

The similarity between this expression and the PGE estimate given in equation 2.7 is obvious.

Biases may arise in this estimate if the population under study is not closed (that is, if births, deaths, or migration occurred between the capture and recapture operations); if some individuals tend to be captured more readily, if the mixing of tagged individuals prior to recapture is incomplete, or if the probabilities of recapture are altered by the tagging procedure; and if the size of the capture or recapture samples is very small. These sources of bias in CTR estimation correspond roughly to the problems in PGE estimation that produce, respectively, coverage bias, response correlation bias, and ratio bias.[34]

Despite these similarities, there is an important difference between the basic objectives of the PGE and CTR techniques. While the CTR procedure is used to estimate population size, the PGE technique is used to estimate the two components (live births and deaths) of natural increase. In the case of human populations, population size is measured either by some form of direct enumeration or by measuring the components of change since a previous enumeration. However, Deming and Keyfitz (1967) have suggested using the PGE technique to estimate the total human population in a region. In addition, the completeness of the census enumeration in a number of countries has been estimated by conducting an independent post-enumeration survey, matching one-way from the survey to the census, and using the survey match rate as the estimate of census completeness.

The somewhat different objectives of PGE and CTR estimation are also reflected in the procedural details of each approach and in the different lines of methodological development associated with each technique. For example, in most wildlife censuses only a relatively small fraction of all individuals in the population are captured in each round, while with the dual collection approach to vital statistics estimation the proportion of vital events reported in each source in a PGE study is typically between .75 and .99. In other words, although it is unusual for "events missed by both sources" in a PGE estimate (that is, the fourth-category estimate of equation 2.8) to amount to more than 15 percent of the true number of events (Seltzer, 1969, Tables 4 and 5), it is common to find over half the population not included in either sample of a simple CTR study. For this reason the literature on the CTR technique has given relatively more attention to questions related to ratio bias and variance than has the PGE literature. (See, for example, Bailey, 1951, and Chapman, 1954, who present modified estimating equations designed to correct for ratio bias.)

Another line of development that has evolved from the simple CTR technique is the use of multiple rounds of sampling, tagging, and resampling to improve the accuracy and precision of the CTR estimate of population size (Chapman, 1954; Andrewartha, 1961, pp. 26–34). Multiround CTR designs have been used to identify and adjust for biases arising from the occurrence of births, deaths, and migration between the capture and recapture rounds of a simple two-round CTR study (Dowdeswell, Fisher, and Ford, 1940; Bailey, 1951). They have also been used to ensure that a sufficient number of tagged individuals will be recaptured to control ratio bias and variance (Goodman, 1953). Note that a CTR estimate based on a multiple recapture design is similar in concept to a PGE estimate based on the matching of reports from more than two collection systems.[35] However, while CTR studies with multiple rounds of sampling are widely used, PGE studies with three or more collection systems are very rare. This type of PGE design is discussed in Section D.1 of Chapter 7.

There has also been a wide divergence between most CTR and PGE studies in how matching is viewed. Largely because the original PGE studies were concerned with determining whether or not a specific event was registered, the matching process in these studies focused on whether or not two reports referred to the same specific event. In contrast, in CTR studies the focus has almost always been on determining whether an individual is a member of one or another class of individuals—the previously captured or the previously uncaptured—and rarely on identifying a specific animal. Indeed Goodman (1953, pp. 58–59) has shown that, assuming a closed population, undifferentiated tags are a sufficient basis for estimation even in a multiround design. (In some multiround CTR estimation procedures, it may be necessary for the tags to specifically indicate the date of release.)

An analogous conclusion holds for PGE estimation. In theory, all one need know to prepare an estimate adjusted for estimated omissions is whether an event reported by one source was among the *group* of events reported by the other source. Although one cannot usually "tag" individual births and deaths except on the basis of their individual characteristics, so that case-by-case matching is necessary for PGE estimation, one need not consider a report in one source linked to the wrong report in the second source erroneously matched if its true counterpart exists in the second source. In this handbook, such a match is termed a "mismatch" (see Chapter 3, Section F.1).

It should be clear from this brief review of the capture-tag-recapture approach that, despite its basic similarity to the PGE technique, it has developed along different methodological lines. In many cases the differences in methodology stem from practical differences in the measurement problem. However, at least part of this divergent development can be attributed to the fact that there has been almost no interaction between those working on the two approaches. A few possible applications of CTR methodology to PGE studies are given in Chapter 7 (see Sections B.4 and D.1). Additional examples of the use of statistical theory developed for CTR studies in PGE estimation can be found in Choi (1970). However, the considerable literature of both techniques should be reviewed more thoroughly to determine the possible benefits that users of each approach may derive from the past work on the other approach.[36]

We shall close this chapter, which has been devoted largely to a review of the history of the PGE technique, with a novel application of the procedure to a historical topic. All the uses of the PGE approach cited so far have related to attempts to prepare *current* estimates of some demographic parameter. The arbitrariness of such a time horizon is demonstrated by a study of Charbonneau, Lavoie, and Légaré (1970) in which a two-way match was carried out between parish registration birth reports and the reports of infants enumerated in the Canadian Population Censuses of 1666 and 1667. The authors conclude on the basis of the obtained match rates that the parish registration of births was about 89-percent complete.

Clearly, there are few situations in which dual sets of records with sufficient detail to permit matching are preserved for 300 years. However, the situation is probably not unique, and those working in the field of historical demography may want to review the materials available to them to determine if a matching effort is feasible. Of course, as in any situation in which PGE estimation is used, one must be on the alert for out-of-scope errors, response correlation, matching errors, ratio bias, and so on. (In the case of the Canadian estimates for 1665–66, the authors state that migration is negligible and that there is complete independence in the working of the two collection systems.) In practice, the uncertainties associated with the other types of estimates made for these periods are such that even relatively weak PGE estimates will often be able to provide an additional and useful piece of evidence about the completeness of a statistical system in the historical past.

Footnotes

1. The restriction of the number of collection systems used to two is arbitrary. In Chapter 7, Section D.1, the use of three or more collection systems in a PGE study is discussed and the possible advantages and problems of such an approach are reviewed. Clearly the simplest case of a multiple collection system is that involving two methods (that is, a dual collection system). For reasons discussed in Chapter 7, it appears that the use of two collection systems rather than a larger number usually results in a more efficient use of resources in vital statistics measurement. Consequently, this handbook, except in Chapter 7, deals exclusively with designs using a dual collection system.

2. Most response error studies attempt to evaluate the quality of responses to specific items either by counting and classifying the variations in responses obtained from the two sources or by constructing a summary index of erroneous or inconsistent responses (U.S. Bureau of the Census, 1964a, b, c). Other response error studies use the match results to derive correction factors that reduce or eliminate the effect of response error in the specific substantive variables being measured. Studies of this type (the Ferber study cited is one) have an objective similar to that of PGE matching studies and frequently are similar in design.

3. In this notation, "Pr (__)" or "P(__)" is read as "the probability of outcome __ occurring." For example, "Pr(A)" is read as "the probability of outcome A occurring" and "P(AB)" as the probability of outcomes A and B occurring jointly. Similarly, "P_1" can be read as "the probability of outcome 1 occurring" and "P_{12}" as "the probability of outcomes 1 and 2 occurring jointly."

4. The notation used in this handbook differs in some respects from that used in the past by others dealing with topics related to PGE studies.

5. Briefly, one assumes that the two collection procedures will be reasonably independent, that net matching error will be low, and that few out-of-scope events will be reported. Much of this handbook is concerned with methods of controlling departures from these assumptions.

6. A rigorous proof would involve the use of an additional concept—the expected value of a random variable. This concept allows us to move from the probability that an event is caught by source 1 to the number or proportion of events that are caught. For simplicity, the expected value concept is omitted from this chapter.

7. These doubts arose in part from problems encountered in carrying out the technique, in part from a general disbelief in the estimates of fertility or mortality produced, and in part from a lingering uncertainty about the orthodoxy of the technique. Whatever their cause, these doubts have often led to statements implying that the technique itself was invalid or inappropriate; see, for example, Brass (1971a) and Ramabhadran (1971).

8. Because of the effort involved in conducting a two-way match, studies employing this approach generally confine all the data gathering and matching operations to a scientifically selected set of sample areas. Such studies also usually involve an effort to search for and eliminate out-of-scope reports in both sources.

9. We are grateful to Nora Powell of the United Nations Population Division for providing the lead that enabled us to locate this pioneering Canadian effort.

10. Matching was limited to the province in which the infant was residing at the time of the 1931 Census, probably for reasons of cost. Infants whose province of birth was reported in the 1931 Census to be different from their province of residence were excluded from the study; thus it was only when the province of birth was misreported in the Census that this problem arose.

11. There was, of course, the cost of the civil registration system itself. However, we are concerned here with expenditures directly chargeable to the budget of a PGE study.

12. Despite this initial lack of success with postal enumeration, the U.S. Bureau of the Census conducted a major portion of the 1970 Census of Population and Housing on the basis of a mail-out/mail-back procedure. However, there are two major differences between the use of this approach in the 1920s and in the 1970s. First, literacy rates and the average level of education have risen markedly in the United States over the last 50 years. Second, both the mail-out and mail-back phases of the 1970 Census were tightly controlled by the use of an address register for the mailings and a thorough follow-up of nonresponses.

13. As indicated in Figure 2.1, the study design was somewhat more complex and also involved a match from infant death registrations to birth registration records. For simplicity, this aspect of the study will be ignored.

14. The estimate is based on an arbitrary guess that the clerical staff will average no more than 30 matching decisions an hour or 5,160 decisions per month (that is, 30 decisions per hour times 40 hours per week times 4.3 weeks per month). With a file containing 650,000 reports, roughly 126 clerk-months (that is, 650,000 divided by 5,160) or 10.5 clerk-years are needed for the matching work. This estimate almost certainly underestimates the size of the job.

15. In some of the literature—for example, Shapiro and Schachter (1952, 1954)—such erroneous linkages are referred to as mismatches. In this handbook, they would be called "erroneous matches," since the term "mismatch" has quite a different meaning (see Chapter 3, Section F.1, and the Glossary).

16. If seasonal variations in the completeness of reporting had been significant, shortening the reference period could have adversely affected the usefulness of the study. However, this was not the case (Shapiro and Schachter, 1954, p. 51). The shorter reference period did not reduce the number of births in the 1950 study, primarily because the birth rate had risen since the earlier study.

17. This change was made at the insistence of some state registration authorities, despite the delay it would cause in matching and field follow-up. It had a negligible effect on the completeness estimate. However, since the cooperation of the state authorities was essential and the Bureau staff was heavily engaged in processing the 1950 Census during this period, the extension of the cutoff date may not have been as poor a design decision as it might at first appear.

18. In theory two or more cards per infant could have been used. In practice, because of the kind of equipment available and the nature and the size of the operation, such a procedure would have been unworkable.

19. Such a design, although acceptable in a country with an l_5 approaching unity, would almost certainly be inappropriate for countries with markedly higher childhood mortality.

20. It is probably least confusing to consider these studies as two distinct one-way matching studies going in opposite directions, rather than as a single study employing a two-way matching operation.

21. Global comparisons between estimates of infants under one year of age from the Current Population Survey and birth registration statistics adjusted for underregistration for the period 1960–63 indicate a median undercount by the survey of about 8 percent. During the same period, the median survey undercount of infants was about 5 percent for whites and about 20 percent for nonwhites (Mauldin, 1966).

22. Strictly speaking, there is some doubt as to whether the North Carolina study is properly a PGE study. Assuming that the admixture of addresses without events served its intended purpose, the proportion of registered events reported in the survey corresponds to a PGE estimate of the survey coverage rate. However, without a survey estimate of events for households both with and without registered events, the PGE estimate of the total number of events adjusted for omissions, N, cannot be made. Regardless of the PGE status of the North Carolina study, however, the research design was excellent, since the objective of the study was to measure the completeness of survey reporting for various categories of vital events in a situation where the registration system provided a nearly complete sampling frame.

23. In regions where registration errors and omissions were known to be particularly frequent, a 20-percent sample was used.

24. Some of the field procedures described by Vostrikova and Dmitrieva are disquieting from the standpoint of response correlation bias. The publication of lists of unmatched reports, in particular, would seem to be a powerful incentive for collusion between the field workers of the two sources. In remote rural areas, such collaboration between field workers might be difficult to control.

25. The survey was conducted in the rural areas of Soviet Georgia, the first round in 1940 and the reinterview in 1947. It is rare that survey reports by individuals so distant in time can be compared. Hopefully, a more comprehensive report of this important study of response error will be made.

26. See, for example, the study by Hashmi and Alam (1969), which reported on response variation in age reporting among a panel of women over a four-year period.

27. There were exceptions, as there are to any generalization about history. Chandrasekaran and Deming (1949) discussed both demographic estimation and the estimation of registration completeness, Shapiro (1950b) applied a procedure suggested by Chandrasekaran and Deming in an effort to assess the accuracy of the 1940 registration completeness estimate for the United States. Coale (1961) noted the basic identity between the Chandrasekaran-Deming technique and the approach used in the U.S. birth registration tests. Match rates have been used to estimate registration completeness in such developing countries as Chile, South Korea, Sri Lanka, Thailand, and Tunisia. Nevertheless, the distinction is valid, and until recently there was little attempt to relate the international experience with registration completeness studies to the problem of demographic estimation.

28. There is some evidence from other Indian survey data (Mauldin, 1966) that if the February 1947 Singur survey had inquired about events in 1946 only (that is, had used only a one-year recall period), but been identical in all other respects to the survey actually carried out that the completeness rates for 1946 would have been lower. In other words, some of the observed difference in survey completeness rates for 1945 and 1946 events was due to the fact that the shorter recall period used to obtain events for 1946 was contained within a longer recall period.

29. During this period, demographic estimation in India was based almost exclusively on the analysis and adjustment of single-source data from the 1951 and 1961 Censuses of India, the National Sample Survey, and the civil registration system.

30. Various data gathering procedures have been tested in the urban areas for possible use in the SRS, with only limited success (India, 1969). In addition, Sarma (1964) reported on an attempt to measure civil registration completeness for births

in the Bombay area using one-way match and a small probability sample.

31. See Chapter 7, Section D.1, for our assessment of the estimator used in the SRS.

32. For a further treatment of the practical and theoretical issues raised by these Asian studies, see also Ahmed and Krotki (1963); Mauldin, Sagen, and Stephan (1964); Hansen (1965); Jabine and Bershad (1968); Seltzer and Adlakha (1969); and Tepping (1971). An important study of PGE methods is being conducted in the Philippines by the Mindano Center for Population Studies as part of the University of North Carolina's Poplab program. For further information, see Madigan (1973) and Wells and Horvitz (1973). For data on birth registration tests conducted in Ceylon (Sri Lanka), Korea, and Indonesia, see Ceylon (1953), Choe (1967), and Indonesia (1968).

33. We are grateful to Mr. Jack Harewood for providing us with the information that enabled us to locate the Byrne paper describing this study and its results.

34. Ratio bias is a potential source of upward bias in both PGE and CTR estimation. It is defined briefly in the Glossary and discussed at greater length in Chapter 3, Sections E.2 and K.3; in Chapter 6, Section C.2; and in Chapter 7, Section B.4.

35. Goodman (1953, pp. 56–57) suggests the following demographic application of a CTR design involving sequential sampling:

> It is well known that the decennial census is not complete. One would, therefore, like to estimate the total number actually living in the United States; that is, consider the problem of finding out how many people were not enumerated in the census. We would draw a sample of people and investigate how many people in this sample had been enumerated. We would then list the nonenumerated people in this sample, draw another sample and investigate how many people in this second sample had been enumerated in the census or had been listed in the first sample . . . ; this procedure is discontinued when a total of at least L people have been found who had been enumerated in the census or listed in one of the preceding samples.

Although Goodman presents estimates of N given L as well as the variance of the estimates, he does not discuss problems of implementation. In particular, he specifically excludes any consideration of coverage bias and response correlation bias.

36. References to some of the more recent work on the CTR technique can be found in Seber (1970) and Samuel (1969).

Choosing
Appropriate Techniques 3

This chapter deals with the design of efficient PGE studies, focusing particularly on the achievement of a proper balance between quality and cost. In order to explore these issues adequately, we have tried to make the discussion of individual topics as widely applicable as possible. Consequently, various issues explored in some sections may seem irrelevant to those interested in designing a PGE study for a specific country. In large part what is relevant depends upon what is taken for granted, and we have tried in this chapter to take very little for granted. In our view, this is the appropriate attitude to have when making basic design choices. Once these choices have been made and the implementation phase is reached, a shift in emphasis is in order. The presentation in Chapter 4 of model procedures for three basic PGE designs reflects this change in emphasis.

As indicated in Chapter 1, the reader should consult more specialized texts for detailed instructions on sampling (for example, Hansen, Hurwitz, and Madow, 1953, or Kish, 1965); interviewing (for example, Kahn and Cannell, 1957, or Richardson *et al.,* 1965); questionnaire and schedule design (for example, Lininger and Warwick, 1967, U.N. Economic Commission for Africa, 1971, or Sirken, 1972); and administration and control (for example, U.S. Bureau of the Census, 1965–67, or Simmons, 1972). Nevertheless, it is our hope that, despite the need for references to these outside sources, this chapter will serve as a useful introduction to all aspects of PGE study design. One topic, "matching," is covered in particular detail because the required references are in widely scattered sources, some of which are difficult to come by.

A. *Net Value and Optimal Procedures*

The design of a PGE study involves balancing the costs of obtaining the estimates against their "value." The "value" of the estimates depends in turn upon the uses they can serve and the confidence that can be placed in them. Ideally, the estimation procedure should be set up in such a way as to maximize the "net value" of the study—"net value" being defined as the value of the information produced less the cost of doing the estimation. The cost includes the cost of data collection, data processing (including matching, error correction, and tabulation), and overhead (for planning, sampling, questionnaire design, supervision, and so on).

The value of information is difficult to define and even more difficult to measure once it has been defined. Of course, people are quick to say "that will cost too much" or "that information is not good enough," but few are prepared to say how much the data *should* cost (that is, how much they are worth) or how good is "good enough."

The net value of information on population growth, fertility, and mortality is a function of the detail of data provided, the timeliness of the estimates, the errors of the estimates, and the costs of preparing them. Although theoretically it may be possible to handle these factors simultaneously, the practical difficulties of doing so are too great given the present state of the art. We shall therefore follow the more usual procedure of treating three of the four factors as given and optimizing with respect to the remaining one (in this case, the level of error). Actually, we consider the process as an iterative one in which, after having first obtained a solution by optimizing with respect to error for specified levels of detail, timeliness, and cost, we then consider whether a better solution could be achieved by a change in the variables previously specified as fixed—usually whether increased expenditures would yield more satisfactory net values, but also (implicitly at least) whether greater or less detail or timeliness would improve the net value of the estimates.

A certain arbitrariness is involved in this procedure, as in any complex optimization process. For example, we could have considered finding the minimum cost for achieving prespecified levels of detail, timeliness, and accuracy. In general, this approach tends to give a much slower convergence to a satisfactory solution than does trying to minimize error when the level of detail, the timeliness, and the cost are fixed.

Although, on the basis of our present knowledge, we cannot resolve each design question explicitly on the basis of a determinable maximum net value, much can be done to improve the design of PGE or other demographic studies—that is, to move in the direction of increased net value. Usually, in designing a procedure for estimating vital statistics, one starts with a tentative budget request. This budget usually represents a "historical accident"—that is, the amount budgeted in past years adjusted (slightly) upward or downward depending upon the demands of competing projects, the feeling of satisfaction or dissatisfaction with past results, and the *immediate* pressures for improved results (for example, the need to know whether existing development programs should be stepped up or maintained or can be reduced to "more manageable" levels).

Given this tentative budget, one attempts to produce results of maximum quality. Sometimes, the best one can do with the tentative budget is so bad as not to be worth doing.[1] And sometimes, this leads to pressure for a larger budget or a new design to do the best one can within these budgetary limits. In the long run, repetition of the process leads to something like an optimization of net value.

Aggravating (and possibly wasteful) as the procedure above is, we recommend it here because the alternative is to do *nothing* to optimize procedures. As a measure of "quality," we recommend the "mean square error" (MSE) of an estimate. Briefly, the mean square error is the sum of the variable error (variance) and constant error (bias) of an estimate. (The concept is defined more rigorously in Section C of this chapter.) We begin the process of optimization by determining which of the procedures permissible with the available budget will minimize the mean square error. If the minimum mean square error obtainable with this budget is "too large," then it will be necessary to see whether increasing the budget to reduce the mean square error is warranted—that is, whether a reduced mean square error will provide enough "additional value" to justify the additional expenditure.

Although some components of error (the variances) can be estimated with reasonable precision, for other components (the biases) we usually have only "order-of-magnitude" estimates. Crude as these estimates are, they make possible a much more efficient use of limited funds than does the procedure of either ignoring errors we cannot estimate precisely or estimating them as "extremely large"—whichever course seems best given the "hunches" and motivations of the moment.

Seltzer and Adlakha (1969) define three components of bias in PGE estimates:

(1) response correlation effects,
(2) matching error bias, and
(3) out-of-scope bias.

The variance component of the mean square error can also be separated into three components:

(1) sampling variance,
(2) response error variance, and
(3) matching error variance.

This description of the components of bias and variance relates only to PGE estimates of the overall number of births or deaths (or rates based on these overall estimates). With respect to age-specific rates or estimates by such variables as father's occupation, family income, or education, there is also a "classification bias" (or "response bias") arising from biases in reporting the characteristic used in the classification. In single system estimates, response correlation bias and matching error bias would be replaced by the net undercoverage error of such systems (also frequently referred to as "response bias"), and this might be further broken down into errors due to missed households and errors due to missed events in covered households.

The separation of error into its variance and bias components is primarily in terms of the difference in techniques used for controlling the specified component. Actually, the components interact and the effect of a reduction or an increase in one component of error on the total mean square error (MSE) may be quite different in magnitude, and even in direction, from the effect on the component itself. For example, the direction of the response correlation bias is usually different from that of the out-of-scope bias. (The former tends to produce underestimates and the latter overestimates of events.) Under these conditions, if the absolute magnitude of the response correlation bias is less than that of the out-of-scope bias and opposite in sign, reducing the response correlation bias will actually increase the MSE.

Although it is theoretically possible to achieve a small overall bias by balancing off large bias components with opposite signs, in practice such a strategy is extremely dangerous. As noted above, one rarely has more than an order-of-magnitude estimate of any bias component. Thus, if one has an out-of-scope bias that may range from +5 to +15 percent, a matching bias somewhere between +5 and +40 percent, and a response correlation bias of at least −5 percent and not more than −50 percent, one may very well have an overall bias of between −5 and +5 percent. But one could also have an upward bias of as much as +50 percent and an underestimate of as much as −40 percent. Furthermore, biases, unlike variances, are *not* more likely to fall near the middle of their estimated range than at one of the extremes.

In general, the strategy for controlling bias is to try to minimize the absolute values of all the components, giving priority to those areas where the largest reductions in bias can be achieved for a given expenditure of effort, time, and money. However, if a given expenditure is likely to have about the same effect on all the components of bias, it is desirable to consider the effect on the net error in selecting the component(s) to receive attention first.

Even more important than these numerical relationships is the fact that the reduction of one form of error is usually accompanied by an increase in another form of error. Some of these interactions operate through the medium of cost. For example, we can reduce the coverage (out-of-scope) bias by doing special checks on cases near the time boundaries. In obtaining births for a year, for instance, we can check particularly on children reported as born in the first three months and on late registrations for the last three months. But doing such special checks will entail extra costs, which will have to be met by cuts elsewhere—for example, by cutting the sample size and thus increasing the sample variance.

There are also direct trade-offs among types of error. In PGE studies, matching error (in terms of both bias and variance) can be reduced by checking to verify or correct discrepancies (unmatched reports of events). But such checks tend to increase the response correlation bias; usually, in fact, the most effective methods of checking on matching errors also have the greatest effect on response correlation bias. For example, it has been suggested that matching be done "in the field" so that the sample areas can be revisited and discrepancies "reconciled" more promptly. But this increases the likelihood of contact between the two sources (and thus of response correlation bias), particularly if the field matching involves personnel (usually supervisors) connected with one or both of the sources. Thus, one must consider whether the reductions in matching and out-of-scope errors achieved by prompter revisiting and reconciliation are greater or less than the increase in response correlation bias likely to result from field matching. One must also consider whether savings in cost from field matching and prompter revisits could be used to lower error in some other phases of the operation.

B. *Alternative Methods of Measurement*

B.1   A LIST OF ALTERNATIVES

Estimates of population growth and vital rates have been based on a variety of data collection and estimation procedures. A partial listing of the major alternatives, grouped under six headings, is given in Figure 3.1. These alternatives are listed here to help identify the total range of options available to those trying to collect basic demographic data and to emphasize that there is no single solution to the design problems presented in this chapter and in the next three chapters. The listing also makes clear the importance of examining alternatives rather than assuming that the procedures with which one is familiar are the only usable ones. Unfortunately, in study design one frequently becomes obsessed with the difficulties of adapting some known technique that may have been used very successfully in other circumstances to the realities of the current situation; consequently one fails to ask whether there are other alternatives that may be better suited to the problem at hand. Since the decision on the type of collection system (registration, survey, or census) to be used is both critical in itself and a determining factor in decisions about other aspects of the design, we shall review some of the considerations involved in this choice in the next three subsections.

B.2   REGISTRATION APPROACHES

Registration systems, whether they operate on a complete count or sample basis, permit only limited variations in the method of data collection. The goal of all registration endeavors is to obtain information about births and deaths on a current basis. Ideally, the registration report should be prepared within a few days of the occurrence of

Fig. 3.1   Major Design Alternatives for Measuring Basic Demographic Variables

A.   Type of report
   1. Continuous (registration)
   2. Periodic (multiround survey)
   3. One-time (one-time survey or census)

B.   Type of reporter (person paid to "register" or "enumerate" events)
   1. Local
   2. Outside but from the same background
   3. Outside and from a different background

C.   Type of reporting activity
   1. Passive (receives reports of vital events)
   2. Active (solicits reports of vital events)
   3. Full canvass of all households

D.   Source of report
   1. Household (parents, spouse, survivors)
   2. Doctor, midwife, undertaker, hospital, etc.
   3. Neighborhood source (village chief, neighbors, school children, local school teacher, landlord or his agent, shopkeepers, etc.)
   4. Other sources (health workers, clinics, police, or other government officials not specifically employed as registrars or enumerators)

E.   What is collected
   1. Reports of vital events in "defined reference" period
   2. Data for demographic analysis (number of children ever born, children surviving, children dead, etc.)
   3. Data on the base population (age, date of birth, sex, relationship, etc.)
   4. Other types of data for fertility measurement (pregnancy status, pregnancy history, date of last live birth, etc.)
   5. Information on changes in household composition since last survey round (births, deaths, in-migration, and out-migration)
   6. Field control information and identification information for matching (names, addresses, dates, etc.)

F.   Methods of estimation
   1. Direct estimates based on the reported numbers of births or deaths or people adjusted only for sampling (if a sample was used) and not for coverage or reporting errors
   2. "Derivative" estimates based on demographic or statistical analysis without matching[1]
   3. "Simple" estimates based on matching
   4. Derivative estimates with matching

---

[1] Generally, derivative estimates use information in addition to that on vital events listed under E.1. For example, data on children born (E.2) or age (E.3) may be used to estimate vital rates on the basis of assumptions about the nature of the population or the reporting errors for individual respondents. Some examples of the preparation of such derivative estimates are contained in Coale and Zelnik (1963), United Nations (1967), Brass and Coale (1968), Brass (1969), and Som (1973).

an event. The major design choice is between "active" and "passive" registration—that is, between having the registrar canvas his territory regularly, looking for vital events to register, or having him wait at a designated registration office for events to be reported to him. In general, civil registration systems involve "passive" data collection on a complete count basis, while special registration systems usually involve "active" collection on a sample basis. Since most countries already have a civil registration system of some sort, and these are almost universally passive, there is generally little point in setting up a passive special registration system.

Civil registration systems are usually based on some legal requirement for reporting births and deaths imposed upon relatives, doctors, midwives, undertakers, and the like. Despite the fact that registration is obligatory under the law, most births and deaths in some countries are not reported to the civil registration authorities. In other countries, burial practices, religious customs (baptism, rites for the dead), the rigorous enforcement of legal requirements, and a widespread need to produce a registration certificate as legal proof of an event operate to produce registration of relatively high (70 percent or more) completeness. In these countries, PGE studies will often be oriented toward estimating the completeness of civil registration and locating and correcting the weaknesses of the registration system.

In the less developed countries, it is difficult to achieve good coverage in a civil registration system in the face of disinterest in registration by the public, as well as, sometimes, by the local officials responsible for registration. For this reason, the legal registration requirements need to be supplemented by publicity and educational campaigns designed to convince people of the importance of registration, to encourage them to register vital events, and to explain the registration procedures.

In some cases, the publicity and educational campaigns take the form of regular visits to the towns and villages in the registrar's district with formal and informal talks to doctors, midwives, undertakers, priests, school teachers, mayors or village chiefs, and other local officials. Such local visits are sometimes accompanied by a certain amount of "active" registration. Frequently, however, a registrar must cover such a large area that visits are necessarily infrequent and "active" civil registration is restricted to inducing local officials to round up people to come in during the campaign to register births, deaths, and marriages. Moreover, if the person responsible for receiving birth and death reports in the civil registration has many other responsibilities, the civil registration may be so "passive" that persons who wish to register a vital event have to expend a considerable amount of time and effort to do so.

Special registration systems, as mentioned earlier, usually involve "active" canvassing for vital events. The canvassing may involve visits by the registrar to each household, but visits to selected households, to neighborhood contacts, and to specific local functionaries (for example, midwives, religious officials, and the police) are more common. On learning about the occurrence of a birth or death, the special registrar customarily visits the family involved, prepares a reporting form for each event, and often gives a copy of this unofficial form to the family.

Special registration systems are usually set up primarily for the purpose of collecting statistical data. This means that the constraints on the civil registration system arising from its legal uses do not apply. Because of statutory requirements, a civil registration system must often operate uniformly throughout the nation, while a special registration system can limit its operations to a relatively small number of sample areas. Since only a sample of areas is involved, there can be greater flexibility in the size of the registrars' assignments, in whether the registrars are employed full-time or part-time, in whether they are exclusively engaged in birth and death registration work or have other duties, and so on. In addition, the registration documents used in special registration systems are usually more closely tailored to the requirements of a statistical reporting system and the needs of data users than are the civil registration documents, since the latter must also serve as legal records. A number of these points are discussed in more detail in Sections C and D of Chapter 4.

Offsetting these advantages of special registration are some major cost and administrative disadvantages. In general, civil registration systems can be considered a "free" resource, while special registration systems have to be approved and financed as a new item in the statistical budget. However, the decision as to the relative net value of using an existing civil registration system rather than establishing a special registration system in a particular situation depends upon a number of factors. The issues involved here are one of the major themes of Chapter 5.

B.3 HOUSEHOLD SURVEY AND CENSUS APPROACHES

Household surveys offer greater possibilities of variation in data collection techniques than registration systems. A survey may involve a one-time interview with a sample of households or periodic interviews. One-time surveys and censuses must obtain reports of vital events by retrospective questions, while multiround surveys either can use the retrospective approach or can obtain information about most births and deaths by observing changes in the household composition recorded in successive survey rounds. This last approach, "the household-change technique" is described more fully in Section B.3, "Periodic Household Surveys," of Chapter 4.

By their nature, household surveys involve active canvassing for vital events. Usually, the survey interviewer is assigned several sample areas; he or she sometimes lives in or near one of the assigned areas but is generally not personally familiar with the residents of any of them. Some surveys use part-time interviewers, in some cases housewives or retired persons. If full-time interviewers are employed, they may be assigned to work on a number of other household surveys in a variety of fields. These variations in household surveys are usually decided, sometimes unwisely, on administrative grounds.

More important in the design of household data collection

procedures are other alternatives involving primarily attempts to overcome the lack of the principal advantage and distinguishing feature of a registration system—the fact that registration is (at least in theory) "continuous." Basically, household surveys try to approximate "continuous" reporting by shortening the reference period for a given interview. Thus, vital events for a year may be covered by four interviews taken three months apart, each covering the three months preceding the interview.

Such a short reference period tends to increase the reporting of vital events. Part of this increase may be the result of a reduction in omissions due to "memory loss," since more recent events are less likely to be forgotten in answering the retrospective survey questions than events more distant in time. However, at least as important is the reduction in omissions attributable to changes in household composition, particularly the dissolution of old households and the creation of new ones as a result of deaths, marriages, and changes of residence.

A short reference period for reporting vital events does not, in itself, have another advantage of continuous reporting, that of precise temporal location of the event. In fact, when retrospective questioning is used, short reference periods tend to increase the inclusion of temporal out-of-scope events—that is, some events that actually occurred prior to the reference period are reported as occurring during the reference period, a phenomenon known as "telescoping." The time location advantage of registration can be obtained by repeated interviews with the same household, covering only events that occurred during the period between two successive interviews. Information about events can then be obtained either by the household-change technique or by retrospective questions whose scope is bounded by the preceding interview. In either case, there are two disadvantages to such a procedure: (1) an additional interview may be required to cover the same time period (for example, five quarterly interviews to cover a year) if the events prior to the first visit are not used in the estimates and (2) as with any procedure involving reinterviews with the same households, some method must be found to compensate for the loss of households that cannot be reinterviewed because they have been dissolved by death, marriage, or migration or have moved to a location which is unknown or where an interview is not feasible for cost reasons.

There are other drawbacks to frequently reinterviewing the same households. For one thing, repeated interviews at short intervals may be irritating and ultimately generate negative reactions. In this connection, it is necessary to consider as one of the "costs" of any data collection system the burden imposed upon the public. In general, registration systems tend to impose less of a burden on the mass of the population. The burden may, however, be concentrated on a few individuals (the village chiefs, the local health officers, and so on), to the point where resentment builds up. Usually, however, this can be offset easily by payment either in money or prestige, or by granting reciprocal favors.

The burden on respondents of household surveys cannot be offset in this manner. Within limits, a short and stimulating interview on topics in which the respondent is interested has its own compensations. What should be avoided is repetitive and duplicating inquiries and questions that call for information not readily available to the respondent. Even these questions, however, can be made interesting and challenging if phrased properly.

While the number of negative respondent reactions attributable to repeated survey interviews is usually small, the monetary cost of shortening the reference period for reporting can be substantial. For example, if the reference period is three months, a household must be interviewed four times to cover births and deaths for a year, as opposed to once if the reference period is a year. Thus, survey interviewing costs for the three-month reference period will, for the same size sample, be nearly four times those for a 12-month reference period. This difference in costs is quite substantial, so that frequent reinterviews should be considered only where the biases associated with long reference periods are very large—for example, where a survey is used by itself as the basis of a single-source estimate, and mobility or infant mortality is high. In these circumstances, the extra cost of more frequent survey rounds may well be justified. However, rather than employing the same collection procedure—the household survey—at very frequent intervals, one should consider the advantages of combining the survey approach with a quite different collection procedure.

B.4   ASSESSING TRADE-OFFS BETWEEN ALTERNATIVES

In general, a "good" estimate of population growth (that is, one with a relatively small error) will require some combination of the methods listed in Figure 3.1. For example, most studies collect, at minimum, vital events (births and deaths) for some fixed time period (Category E.1 in Figure 3.1) plus data on the population base (Category E.3). Birth or death rates are then computed by dividing the estimated number of births or deaths by the estimated population. The base population can also be estimated by "updating" a previous census, using births and deaths and net migration in the interim. However, using the same sample to supply population age-sex data and reports of vital events usually contributes to the quality of the demographic estimates; and the value of these gains may considerably outweigh the (marginal) costs of obtaining the added data.

Similarly, substantial improvements in quality can be obtained at a relatively small extra cost by adding to the household reports (D.1 in Figure 3.1) information obtained from some (or all) of the sources listed in D.2, D.3, and D.4. Affirmative decisions to collect routine data on the base population or to employ other reporting sources are usually made fairly easily on the basis of the relatively small costs involved. In many cases, in fact, the decision-makers are not even aware that these activities entail any additional costs; they consider listing such information as the age, sex, and relationship to head of each member of each household and making routine inquiries of the village chief, neighbors, police, as part of the process of locating and recording vital events. In reality, of course, it is quite possible to ask about vital events without listing anyone other than infants, their parents, and decedents, and most civil registration systems do just that.

Although information about the basic characteristics of all household members will almost invariably be routinely obtained in a survey, information on children ever born and surviving children (Category E.2 in Figure 3.1) required for some types of demographic analysis will usually not be, unless a special effort is made to have questions on these topics included. Those without demographic training are often unaware of the importance of these items so that they may have to be convinced of their usefulness before they will add them to the survey questionnaire. Fortunately, an extensive literature now exists that describes both the questions needed and the methods of analysis (see, for example, United Nations, 1967; Demeny, 1967; United Nations, 1971). For the present, it is enough to note that the marginal cost of adding these questions is usually small and the potential value of including them is large.

In addition to those combinations of techniques that produce appreciable advantages at a trivial cost, there are some combinations of techniques implied by Category F.2, F.3, or F.4 in Figure 3.1 that may produce very important gains in quality, but at a considerable cost. For example, one form of derivative estimate, Bogue's "pregnancy history" approach (Bogue and Bogue, 1967) involves collecting, for each woman of childbearing age, a complete history of all the pregnancies she has experienced. In addition to the fact of the pregnancy itself, one determines the outcome (live birth, stillbirth, spontaneous abortion, induced abortion), months of gestation, sex of live-born children, whether single or multiple birth, survival of live-born children, and age at death of deceased children. It is also useful to probe any period of two or more years for which no pregnancy was reported to determine whether a pregnancy has been missed and/or whether contraceptives were being used. Bogue and Bogue indicate that the data thus collected are used "as a substitute for vital registration. In fact, when completed, the pregnancy history may be looked upon as a set of certificates for the pregnancies of a particular group of women. By a few calculations it is possible to transform these data into bonafide statistics" (Bogue and Bogue, 1967, p. 213).

Actually, the calculations (and prior editing and computer processing) required to produce the fertility rates and birth rates are fairly complex; but more to the point, obtaining pregnancy history data adds considerably to the cost of collection and processing in a survey. Nevertheless, within the context of a single-visit household survey, this expenditure may be justified by gains in the reporting of both current and cumulative fertility. The approach would appear to be of direct value in improving the reporting of births for women in the immediate family of the household head. At the same time, it does nothing to improve reporting for unlisted women. Indeed, the use of the pregnancy history approach does not guarantee the sought-for improvement in the completeness of birth reporting. For example, in the Mysore Population Study a special survey using a full pregnancy history recorded somewhat fewer current births than the regular survey canvassing the same households with a retrospective question on births (United Nations, 1961).

PGE estimation, or more precisely the dual collection and matching it necessitates, is also more costly than a single-visit household survey. How much additional cost is involved depends in large part upon the particular PGE study (for example, whether one source is a "free" civil registration system or both sources must be financed from the study budget) and to a lesser extent on the cost of the single-visit survey with which it is compared. In our view, the added costs associated with the PGE approach can often be justified by commensurate increases in the quality of the estimates produced and the confidence that can be placed in them.

In this connection we would stress four principal advantages of the PGE approach. First, the major assumptions of the PGE approach, as distinct from most analytical approaches, are statistical rather than demographic in nature, and relate to the characteristics of the data collection procedures rather than the characteristics of the population under study. Second, the dual collection and matching features of PGE estimation provide considerably more information about the quality and character of the data gathering operations than does any single-source procedure; thus if major defects exist one has substantially more assurance that they will become manifest. It follows that if no major defects are identified one is justified in placing more confidence in this finding than in a comparable one for a single-source study. Third, in many situations dual collection is the most effective way of devoting more resources to the reduction of the major sources of nonsampling error associated with vital statistics measurement. Fourth, the PGE estimate is relatively robust to variations in the conditions of observation or the quality of either source; in any case, it is more so than the estimates based on a single-source procedure.

Others would differ with these assessments in whole or in part. For example, Brass (1971a, p. 409) has concluded that "the independent matching vital events surveys [that is, PGE studies] are costly and it is not established that they can achieve reasonably accurate measures of population growth," although he also notes that "the interpretation of the evidence . . . depends on personal judgements about the value of demographic measures of varying degrees of accuracy and detail and the possibility of improvements in the design, organization, and control of surveys."

For the reasons indicated above, we strongly believe that the best results can be obtained by a study that combines the PGE approach with the analytical techniques recommended by Brass (Category F.4 in Figure 3.1). However, we agree that the PGE approach is neither free from error nor free from cost. The issue is how much error it entails, how much it costs, and what alternatives are available. These considerations underscore the need for efficient study designs, a careful choice of design alternatives, rigorous control of study operations, and a thorough analysis and evaluation of study estimates, regardless of the basic approach employed.

Reasoning along the same lines, the First Population Growth Estimation Seminar (held at the Population Council offices in New York on 23 January 1969) concluded that "a single system is unsatisfactory in the present state of the art in under-developed countries; a balanced dual system is essential" (Mauldin and Bean, 1969). The seminar participants also stressed that the "balanced dual system" must be continued "at least until a national registration system, with monitoring, has demonstrated that it serves these needs."

A key word in this recommendation is "balanced." The participants listed six tasks that must be accomplished:

(a) development and careful scrutiny of System 1;
(b) development and careful scrutiny of System 2;
(c) careful matching of events collected by the two systems;
(d) reconciliation of unmatched cases, including doubtful matched cases, in the field;
(e) attaining a low level of correlation between the occurrence of errors of omission in the two systems;[2]
(f) careful determination of the total population base (the denominator of the estimated vital rates).

The summary goes on to note that "it is essential to do each of the steps (a–f) carefully, on a small enough scale (sample) to do them with high standards." However, it stresses that there must be "some hope" of *ultimately* doing things on a large enough scale "to produce useful results." That is, although it will usually be necessary, in the initial phases of a study, to devote considerable time and money to each of these steps *separately*, eventually the errors and costs involved in each step must be weighed against each other and against the sampling errors and costs. This balancing process can be complex, because many factors are involved in a PGE study. It is, however, necessary if the PGE approach is to be used effectively.

C. *Variance, Bias, and Mean Square Error*

C.1 VARIANCE AND EXPECTED VALUE

In discussing the precision of statistical estimates it is convenient to distinguish two types of error—variance and bias. Variance is error resulting from the operation of random factors. For example, in selecting areas for inclusion in a sample one may, through the process of random selection, get areas with high, low, or intermediate birth rates. Since it is most unlikely that any two samples will include exactly the same areas, the estimated birth rate will differ from sample to sample. Other factors than the sample selection may also cause variations from sample to sample and contribute to variance. For example, even if a given area were to be included in all samples, different interviewers might do work of different quality and so obtain different numbers of birth reports.

As a matter of fact, the correctly measured birth rate or death rate in a given year for any area can be thought of as a value that varies around some average ("expected") value determined by the underlying conditions of fertility, health, mortality, and so on in the area. That is, the actual birth rate for any given area in any given year can be viewed as the outcome of an underlying "true" rate operating in the face of a multitude of diverse factors, such as the death or illness of women, or their husbands, who otherwise would have had babies; the number of weddings over the past year or so; and fights or reconciliations between individual couples. If the period of observation is short or the area observed is small, the effect of these individual factors may be large enough to produce a birth rate that is not a good measure of underlying fertility in the population. As the observation period lengthens and the area covered is enlarged, the extraneous factors tend to cancel out and the actual rate becomes an increasingly better approximation of the underlying "true" birth rate.

The concept of a birth or death rate resulting from the underlying conditions of fertility, health, mortality, and so on in an area is of particular importance in studies of trends, seasonal variations, and the like. In such studies, one may assume that age-specific vital rates are constant or vary in accordance with some continuous time curve that can be estimated by regression techniques. Except for very small populations or very short time periods, the differences between the actual birth or death rates and the theoretical rates postulated in regression analysis tend to be small compared to the other sources of variation—sampling and measurement errors. For most purposes, then, one can assume the simpler problem of estimating a fixed (but unknown) actual number of births or deaths (and/or the corresponding vital rates) for a given period.

The discussion of vital rates in this handbook applies primarily to the problem of estimating the actual birth or death rate for a given time period—for example, for a given year. Where it is desirable to use some type of "smoothing" to estimate individual rates for a series of short time periods (for example, monthly rates), the concept of an underlying birth or death rate that changes in a continuous manner may be convenient.

With either concept, an estimated x actually obtained in a study can be thought of as a "random variable" that has a probability of occurring of P_x. That is, because of sampling and reporting variation, the particular estimate made is one of many values that could occur. Multiplying each possible x by its probability and summing gives us the average or expected value, $\bar{x}$ or $E(x)$. The variance of x is a measure of the amount of variation of the x values around their average $E(x)$ and is defined as

$$\sigma_x^2 = \Sigma P_x [x - E(x)]^2 \quad , \tag{3.1}$$

where

$$E(x) = \Sigma P_x x \quad , \tag{3.2}$$

and where the summations are taken over all possible values of x.

The square root of the variance, or "standard error," σ_x, is also used as a measure of the variation of x around $E(x)$. Under somewhat general conditions, the variation of x around $E(x)$ will tend to follow the "normal distribution." Thus there is a probability of about .95 that x will not differ from $E(x)$ by more than $2\sigma_x$.

C.2 BIAS AND MEAN SQUARE ERROR

The difference between the expected value, $E(x)$, and the (unknown) "true" value, X, that we are trying to estimate is called the bias (β_x). If $E(x) = X$ (that is, $\beta_x = 0$), the estimate x is said to be unbiased. Bias is that portion of total error which is *not* the result of random factors, and, unlike variance, it cannot be reduced by increasing the sample size.

Bias may arise from deficiencies in the sample design or its implementation or from the data collection or estimation procedure used. Sometimes small biases are accepted in the estimation procedure to achieve a substantial reduction in variance—for example, in the use of ratio estimates. Specific collection procedures can also be thought of as biased. For example, survey data on children ever born by age of mother frequently provide underestimates of cumulative fertility for women above ages 30–35 (United Nations, 1967, p. 31), and one-time retrospective surveys tend to be particularly deficient in obtaining reports of deaths (Seltzer, 1969).

Bias may arise from any factor in the collection process—the respondent, the enumerator or registrar, the concepts and definitions used, the survey or registration documents, and the editing or processing procedures. It is difficult to measure bias in any particular study because the true value is usually unknown (though it may be approximately known or estimated by some other method) and because of the fact that the demarcation between response bias and response variance is necessarily somewhat arbitrary.

An estimate is likely to be a good estimate (that is, to be close to the true value, X) if both the variance (or standard error) and the bias are small. Conversely, an estimate will be of poor quality (that is, have a low probability of being near the true value, X) if *either* the variance *or* the bias is large. As a measure of the combined effects of the variance and bias, we use the mean square error (MSE), which is equal to the variance plus the square of the bias—that is,

$$MSE(x) = \sigma_x^2 + \beta_x^2 \quad . \tag{3.3}$$

The square root of this measure, or "root mean square error," defined as

$$RMSE(x) = \sqrt{\sigma_x^2 + \beta_x^2} \quad , \tag{3.4}$$

is also frequently used as a measure of the error of x. In general, there is a high probability that the value x will lie within two or three times $RMSE(x)$ away from the true value X. In comparing two techniques for estimating the same true value X, the estimate with the smaller RMSE is likely to be subject to a lower error and is therefore preferable—provided the cost of obtaining it is equal to or less than that of obtaining the less accurate estimate.

It should be noted that both β_x and σ_x^2 are unknown for a given study—although, with many designs, it is possible to estimate σ_x^2 from the results. In addition, it is often feasible to obtain estimates of the bias β_x of a proposed procedure by carrying out pilot tests of other small exploratory studies with high unit costs (see, for example, the studies of matching error described in Section F.4). Where data from some previous experience with a given procedure are available, they may supply "order-of-magnitude" estimates of biases and will usually give somewhat more precise estimates of variance. Poor as the data on bias may be, using them is preferable to ignoring the bias or assuming equal biases for all proposed procedures.

D. Dual System Estimates

D.1 THE PGE ESTIMATE

As indicated in Sections A and B of Chapter 2, "PGE" or "dual system" estimates are prepared by using two different sources to obtain reports of vital events in the same population and matching the events reported in the two sources. Usually, one source is a registration system (either the official civil registration system or a special registration system of some sort) and the other is a household survey or a census. Less often, both sources will use the survey approach.

The formula for the PGE estimate is

$$\hat{n} = \frac{n_1 n_2}{m} = m + u_1 + u_2 + \frac{u_1 u_2}{m} \quad , \tag{3.5}$$

where

$\hat{n}$ = PGE estimate of the number of events (births or deaths),
n_1 = $u_1 + m$ = number of events (births or deaths) based on source 1 data only,

$n_2 =$ $u_2 + m =$ number of events (births or deaths) based on source 2 data only,

$m =$ number of reports of births or deaths from source 1 also found, by matching, to be in source 2,

$u_1 =$ number of events reported in source 1 but not reported in source 2, and

$u_2 =$ number of events reported in source 2 but not reported in source 1.

Usually, n_1, n_2, m, u_1, and u_2 are themselves estimates, obtained by multiplying the events reported in a sample by the appropriate sampling raising factors.

As noted previously, $\hat{n}$, and its components (n_1 or u_1, n_2 or u_2, and m) vary because of both sampling *and* reporting variations. That is, the particular sampling process used will give different results depending upon the particular sample areas selected. Similarly, for a specified sample area the events *reported* by a given method of data collection will vary depending upon a number of randomly determined factors such as which of several qualified interviewers or registrars is actually hired to do the job, the order in which the area happens to be canvassed on a particular occasion, which respondent(s) the field worker talks to for a given household, and even the time of day or the mood of the respondent and the field worker. In addition, many nonrandom factors such as the general attitude of the population toward field studies, the wording of the questionnaire, and the availability of qualified field workers may affect the number of events reported.

To understand the essential feature of PGE estimates, namely the handling of *reporting* variance and bias, it will be convenient to consider a situation where no sampling is involved—that is, a situation in which efforts are made to obtain reports of all the N events (births or deaths) occurring in a population during some specified time period. If two methods of data collection are used, the first source obtaining reports of N_1 events and the second source of N_2 events, the N events occurring in the entire population can be divided into the M events reported by both sources, the U_1 and U_2 events reported in only one source, and the Z events not reported by either source. This situation is illustrated by the two-by-two table in Figure 3.2, where the following relationships hold:

Fig. 3.2 Basic Dual Collection Model

Source 2	Source 1		
	Reported	Not reported	Total
Reported	M	U_2	N_2
Not reported	U_1	Z	V_2
Total	N_1	V_1	N

$$N_1 \; = \; M + U_1 \; = \; \text{number of events (births or deaths)}$$
$$\text{reported in source 1,}$$
$$N_2 \; = \; M + U_2 \; = \; \text{number of events reported in source 2,}$$
$$V_1 \; = \; U_2 + Z \; = \; \text{number of events omitted by source 1,}$$
$$V_2 \; = \; U_1 + Z \; = \; \text{number of events omitted by source 2,}$$
$$\text{and}$$
$$N \; = \; M + U_1 + U_2 + Z = \text{total number of events.}$$

Since no *sampling* variation is involved, N (the total number of events) is fixed; but the numbers of events reported or not reported by one or both sources (N_1, N_2, M, U_1, U_2, and Z) vary. Their expected values and variances will be determined by the probabilities resulting from the nature of the reporting process, as distinct from the actual reporting that occurs on a given occasion. These probabilities can be defined as

$P_1 \;\; = \;$ probability of a vital event (birth or death) being reported in source 1,

$P_2 \;\; = \;$ probability of a vital event being reported in source 2, and

$P_{12} \; = \;$ probability of a vital event being reported in *both* sources.

These definitions refer to the average, or expected, probability of an event being reported in either or both sources, given that the event took place. Such average probabilities are a function of both the nature of the specific events that occur and the collection processes used in their measurement. For example, births occurring in hospitals or to the family of a village chief are more likely to be covered by a civil registration system than unattended births occurring among recently arrived migrants living in urban slums or among itinerant agricultural laborers. On the other hand, the use of the household-change technique (see Chapter 4, Section B.3) in a multiround survey may well lead to lower probabilities of inclusion for births occurring in the head of the household's family when the infants do not survive to the time of the interview than when they do survive, lower even than those for births occurring to servants or minor relatives.

More explicitly, $P_1 = \mathrm{E}(P_{1j})$ where P_{1j} refers to the probability of source 1 reporting event j in the population. This latter probability may be regarded as the proportion of times event j is reported by source 1 in a large number of conceived repetitions of the particular source 1 collection process operating under the same general study conditions (Hansen, Hurwitz, and Bershad, 1961). Analogous definitions can be made for P_{2j} and P_{12j}. The values of P_{1j}, P_{2j}, and P_{12j} will vary from event to event depending upon the characteristics of each event and data source.

P_{1j} and P_{2j} will differ for a particular event because of differences in the data collection processes used. The differences (if any) between P_1 and P_2 and the value of P_{12} reflect the expected value of these differences in the two data collection processes taken over all events.

The probabilities P_1, P_2, and P_{12}, in turn, determine the expected number of events reported by source 1, by source 2, and by both sources. That is,

$$E(N_1) = P_1 N ,$$
$$E(N_2) = P_2 N , \text{ and}$$
$$E(M) = P_{12} N .$$

Also, if we let

$$W_1 = \frac{M}{N_2} = \text{ proportion of all events reported in source 2 that are also reported in source 1 (= estimated completeness of source 1), and}$$

$$W_2 = \frac{M}{N_1} = \text{ proportion of all events reported in source 1 that are also reported in source 2 (= estimated completeness of source 2),}$$

then

$$E(W_1) = \frac{E(M)}{E(N_2)} = \frac{P_{12} N}{P_2 N} = P_{1.2} \quad \text{and}$$

$$E(W_2) = \frac{E(M)}{E(N_1)} = \frac{P_{12} N}{P_1 N} = P_{2.1} ,$$

where

$$P_{1.2} = \frac{P_{12}}{P_2} = \text{ probability of an event being reported in source 1, } conditional \text{ upon its being reported in source 2, and}$$

$$P_{2.1} = \frac{P_{12}}{P_1} = \text{ probability of an event being reported in source 2, } conditional \text{ upon its being reported in source 1.}$$

From the values N_1, N_2, and M, one can obtain the PGE estimate of N:

$$\hat{N} = \frac{N_1 N_2}{M} .$$

This is a special case of the estimate $\hat{n}$ of equation 3.5. Because of reporting error, $\hat{N}$ will differ from N. The PGE estimate $\hat{N}$ is based on the assumption that the N_1 events reported in source 1 and the N_2 events reported in source 2 are *independent* selections from the total of N events. In other words, one assumes that there is a probability P_1 of an event being reported in source 1 and a probability P_2 (which may be greater than, less than, or equal to P_1) of the same event being reported in source 2; and *the probability of an event being included in one source is the same whether or not the event is included in the other source.* This basic assumption of independence means that the probability P_{12} of an event being included in both sources is equal to $P_1 P_2$.

Furthermore, P_1 will be equal to the expected value of the completeness estimate W_1 and also to the expected value of M/N_2, of N_1/N, and of U_1/V_2, while P_2 will be equal to the expected value of W_2 which, in turn, will be the same as the expected value of M/N_1, of N_2/N, and of U_2/V_1.

With sampling, there is, in addition to the reporting variation, a variation in the number and characteristics of the events that happened to be selected in the sample. Therefore, corresponding to the values of Figure 3.2, a sample would result in the values shown in Figure 3.3.

Although n_1, n_2, m, u_1, and u_2 can be obtained directly from the sample, the values of the other cells of Figure 3.3 cannot. They are

n = total number of sample events,
v_1 = number of events not reported in source 1,
v_2 = number of events not reported in source 2, and
z = number of events not reported in either source.

Equation 3.5 can be used to obtain estimates of n and z and, by subtraction, of v_1 and v_2.

Regardless of whether they are estimated directly from the sample or by equation 3.5, the values in Figure 3.3 may, because of sampling variation, differ from those in Figure 3.2. However, given unbiased sampling and estimation procedures, the expected values of the sample estimates shown in Figure 3.3 will be equal to the expected values of the corresponding statistics in Figure 3.2. That is, $E(n_1) = E(N_1)$, $E(n_2) = E(N_2)$, $E(m) = E(M)$, $E(u_1) = E(U_1)$, $E(u_2) = E(U_2)$, $E(z) = E(Z)$. Also, the expected value of n will be equal to N and $E(\hat{n}) \doteq E(\hat{N})$.[3] Of course, the sample value n will be subject to a sampling variance, but not to a reporting variance. The other sample values in Figure 3.3 will be subject to variances which are greater than those of Figure 3.2, since the variance of the sample values includes the reporting variance of the Figure 3.2 results *plus* the sampling variance. Similarly, the variance of $\hat{n}$ will be greater than that of $\hat{N}$ since it, too, is subject to sampling variance as well as reporting variance.

The assumption of independence for N_1 and N_2 corresponds to a similar assumption for n_1 and n_2, expressed by the equations

Fig. 3.3   Sample Values for a Dual Collection Model

Source 2	Source 1		
	Reported	*Not reported*	*Total*
Reported	m	u_2	n_2
Not reported	u_1	z	v_2
Total	n_1	v_1	n

$$P_1 = E\left(\frac{n_1}{n}\right) = E\left(\frac{u_1}{v_2}\right) = E\left(\frac{m}{n_2}\right) = P_{1.2} \quad \text{, and} \qquad [3.6]$$

$$P_2 = E\left(\frac{n_2}{n}\right) = E\left(\frac{u_2}{v_1}\right) = E\left(\frac{m}{n_1}\right) = P_{2.1} \quad . \qquad [3.7]$$

Equation 3.6 states that P_1, the probability of inclusion in source 1, is the same whether one talks about all n events, the n_2 events reported by source 2, or the v_2 events omitted by source 2. Equation 3.7 makes a similar statement about all n events, the n_1 events reported by source 1, and the v_1 events omitted by source 1.

D.2   SOURCES OF BIAS AND VARIANCE

The assumption of independence has been stressed because one source of bias associated with the PGE technique is the failure to fulfill that assumption in practice. Other basic assumptions of PGE estimates are (a) that all events reported either in source 1 or source 2 properly belong in the universe and in the sample, and (b) that it is possible to identify accurately events that were reported by both sources by matching the two sets of events. The failure to meet these three requirements results in the three major biases of the PGE estimate of the number of events or of the completeness rate listed by Seltzer and Adlakha (1969):

1. Response Correlation Bias. On the average, events *included* in source 1 do not have the same probability of inclusion in source 2 as events *not included* in source 1, due to lack of independence of the two sources.

2. Matching Bias. The number of erroneous nonmatches is not equal to the number of erroneous matches, that is, net matching error is not equal to zero. In this Handbook "erroneous matches" are defined as those reports in a given source that are classified as matched, yet refer to events omitted by the other source. Similarly, "erroneous nonmatches" are defined as those reports in a given source that are classified as nonmatched, yet refer to events reported by both sources. Other definitions of erroneous matches and erroneous nonmatches are possible (see Section F.1) but have no particular advantage for PGE estimation.

3. Coverage Bias. The bias arising from the erroneous inclusion of "out-of-scope" vital events among the reports of either source, that is, by the inclusion of vital events which should not have been listed because either (a) they did not occur within the specified time period or region (and hence were not properly "in the universe") or (b) they were not properly in the sample.

The last source of bias operates much as it does for estimates based on a single source. That is, inclusion of events which occurred outside the specified time or geographic limits will bias the estimate upward. However, in PGE estimation the bias will be increased by the fact that out-of-scope cases will ordinarily be reported in only one of the two sources, ending up in one of the "unmatched" categories, u_1 or u_2, and will thus lower the match rate and the estimated completeness rate.

Geographic out-of-scope errors will usually be trivial where both sources cover the entire country.[4] However, many PGE estimates use samples—usually a sample defined in terms of relatively small areas, each of which is supposed to be covered completely by *each* source. Here, geographic out-of-scope errors (that is, the inclusion of births or deaths that did not occur in any sample area) are quite common.

Estimates of vital rates are also subject to errors affecting the denominator of the rate; that is, those affecting the estimate of the base population. Other things being equal, these errors—most frequently underestimates of the base population—have a greater impact on vital rates using PGE adjustments than on estimates using alternative procedures. Because the biases of single-source estimates of the base population tend to be smaller than those affecting the number of events, the use of single-source population estimates in calculating PGE vital rates usually leads to more accurate estimates than vital rates obtained directly from a single source.

In addition to bias, the PGE estimate is subject to variances from the following sources.

1. Sampling. The PGE estimate is subject to the usual variance in using a sample to estimate a population parameter. Of course, if both sources cover the entire population (for example, in a census–civil registration match) there is no sampling variance.

2. Response Error. The values of m, n_1, n_2, and therefore $\hat{n}$, are subject to a nonsampling variance since, even if sampling were not involved, the number of vital events *reported* by each source from among the n events occurring during some well-defined time period would vary about some *expected* number.

3. Matching Error. Errors in matching do not result in a bias if the expected number of erroneous matches is equal to the expected number of erroneous nonmatches for a given set of matching rules. The *actual* difference between erroneous matches and erroneous nonmatches in any particular application of these rules will vary around the *expected* difference.

Actually, both response error and matching error have a sampling variance component. That is, in addition to the variance in the level of response error and matching error that would occur in a 100-percent sample (for example, in a census or a civil registration system), there is variation in the response error and matching error due to sampling.

The response error variance and matching error variance of a 100-percent sample are closely associated with the corresponding biases (response correlation bias and matching bias), so that the nonsampling variance and the bias will be considered jointly for response correlation errors (in Section E of this chapter) and for matching errors (in Section F).

The sampling variance of a PGE estimate $\hat{n}$ is a function of the variances and intercorrelations of the number of events reported (n_1 and n_2) and the number of events treated as matched (m). These variances in turn reflect the variation among sample areas of four factors: (a) the true number of vital events for each area; (b) the correlation between sources within each area, in the completeness of reporting; (c) the out-of-scope bias for each area; and (d) the *net* matching error for each area. The correlations among these factors may be positive or negative. For example, the correlation between the true number of events and the *net* matching error can be positive, negative, or zero. The sign of this correlation will depend upon whether the matching procedures are such that erroneous matches or erroneous nonmatches predominate for most sample areas. This is true even though the correlation between the true number of events and the *gross* matching error (erroneous matches plus erroneous nonmatches) tends to be positive. (Positive because, where there is a larger number of events to be matched one may also expect a larger number of matching errors.)

In any case, in this Handbook the term "sampling variance" will be used to refer to the total variance resulting from sampling areas. Sampling variance can be reduced by the conventional techniques of increasing the sample size, improving the stratification, and reducing the cluster size. Reductions in sampling variance will usually be accompanied by increases in cost, but these increases may not be proportional to the decrease in variance. Unfortunately, a reduction of sampling variance is often accompanied by an increase in bias—for example, when the reduction in variance is due to an increase in sample size purchased at the cost of skimping on the quality of the enumeration or registration.

In estimating the effects of bias and variance, one must consider not only the separate components, but also their joint effect. As Seltzer and Adlakha (1969) have observed, "the net bias of $\hat{n}$ may not be substantial even if the biases due to each of the three factors by themselves are large, since the effects of the individual biases are not necessarily in the same direction." The reverse situation may also be true—that is, we can have three small biases in the same direction[5] which combine to produce a large net bias.

Furthermore, a small bias combined with a large variance is as undesirable as a large bias combined with a small variance. The objective must be to control the *total* error at an acceptable level. (What constitutes "an acceptable level" will depend upon how the resulting vital statistics are to be used.) In general, however, every reduction in error has a price tag. A critical question is, then, how to get the greatest reduction in the *total* error for a given expenditure.

D.3   SINGLE VERSUS DUAL COLLECTION SYSTEMS

The objections that have been raised to the use of a dual system are primarily in terms of cost and bias. With respect to costs, these are frequently exaggerated. Many countries in which there has been strong opposition to PGE methods have a civil registration system and a household sample survey (usually for labor force estimation). Where the civil registration system is satisfactory for PGE purposes, the main additional costs would be for matching, because the costs of adding vital statistics questions to the household survey are usually minor. Even if the civil registration cannot be made usable for PGE purposes without very large expenditures, some of the money and resources being put into a household survey might profitably be devoted to establishing a dual system using a smaller sample of households or, in the case of a multiround survey, reducing the frequency of interviewing. Using a smaller sample will mean higher variances, but this disadvantage may be largely offset by the reduction in bias. Of course, the reduction in bias will apply only to vital statistics, while the variance increase will apply to all statistics furnished by the survey. Thus, the main question is whether the reduction in bias for the vital statistics justifies the costs in terms of money and increases in variance. The answer to this question depends in large part upon the uses planned for the demographic information.

With respect to bias, the most *frequent* objections to the PGE approach are directed to the correlation bias (Ramabhadran, 1971; Brass, 1971a), although the most pertinent objections in our view relate to matching bias, and particularly to a high level of erroneous nonmatches. The presence of correlation cannot increase the coverage bias over that of using a single source. That is, even if the correlation is +1.00[6] (which is almost never the case), the completeness rate for each of the two sources will be estimated (erroneously) as 100 percent and the PGE estimate will be identical with those obtained from each source alone. Thus, the objections to the PGE techniques based on the correlation bias argument effectively come down to the statement that because the technique does not remove *all* the undercoverage one should not bother to remove *any* of it. Alternatively, the objections to correlation bias may be based on the advantages of some other technique for correcting the bias of single-source estimates—for example, the use of a base population estimate subject to incompleteness to balance an assumed similar incompleteness in the estimate of the number of events, or an analytical technique that, in the hands of different users, yields widely different vital rates (Robinson, Seltzer, and Hashmi, 1965). This argument ignores the question of whether, given the same expenditure, the proposed technique would give better results with a dual system estimate than with a single system estimate. It particularly overlooks the fact that adjustments applied to very poor data may amplify rather than reduce the level of error.

On the other hand, a high rate of erroneous nonmatches will

result in a small value of m, and thus an underestimation of the completeness rates of the two sources. This can mean biases toward overestimation in a dual system just as serious as the underestimations of a single system. Actually, if reasonable care is taken in the design of PGE procedures, this will not be the case. Furthermore, work on improving matching techniques in a PGE system will frequently have a much faster and much bigger "payoff" than an equivalent expenditure of money and effort to improve the completeness of a single system.

In any case, matching bias and high matching costs are the most serious problems of the PGE technique. The most valid reason for rejecting a civil registration system as one of the PGE sources is the inability to match vital events from the other source that are actually in the civil register. Low completeness of the civil registration system in conjunction with a high proportion of *correctly* unmatched reports in the other source usually means only a slightly higher variance for a PGE estimate. However, inability to locate the events that are actually included in the civil register because of poor identification in the register is a more important problem and should, in most cases, be the main consideration in deciding whether to use the civil registration system as one of the sources in a PGE system. There are, as already noted, considerable cost advantages to using the civil registration system, since its cost will be incurred in any case. If satisfactory matching against the civil register can be achieved without expensive modifications of the registration system, the advantages of using the civil registration system as one source will be clear-cut. (As discussed later, using the civil registration system ordinarily means using "one-way matching," and the consequent reduction in out-of-scope bias associated with one-way matching would be an added attraction.)

One important use for improved fertility statistics in a number of developing countries is in the evaluation of national family planning programs. It has been argued that, for this purpose, measuring the absolute level of fertility is frequently secondary to measuring the amount of change. Furthermore, it is held that one can treat the low coverage of, say, a civil registration system as a fixed bias and thus make a reasonably good (that is, accurate) estimate of the year-to-year change in fertility on the basis of data from a single system.

Unfortunately for the single system proponents, the year-to-year variation in the completeness of most of the civil registration systems involved appears to be greater than the yearly variation in actual birth and death rates. What is more important, for any short period (two or three years or less) the year-to-year variation in the completeness of civil registration exceeds the reduction in the birth rate expected to be achieved by most family planning programs. Moreover, although the use of special registrars, or of a periodic household survey aimed specifically at detecting vital events, would probably improve the *expected value* of the completeness of reporting relative to the civil registration data, the use of an improved single system tends to have little effect upon the amount of *variation* in the completeness of reporting. As a matter of fact, successful attempts to improve the completeness of reporting would probably increase the short-run year-to-year variability in completeness of reporting.

The difficulties of attempting to keep the level of reporting completeness in a single system constant are particularly acute in periods of high internal migration. Vital events of migrants, particularly those moving into the low-income areas of large metropolitan centers, are often missed. The reporting of deaths among such migrants tends to be particularly poor, since these persons often live alone and have no friends or relatives in the area where they die. Moreover, because large-scale rural-urban migration often precedes the construction of adequate low-cost housing, recent migrants often live in unplanned conglomerations of shacks or huts, or in nonresidential structures such as stores or warehouses. Maps for such areas tend to be inadequate for controlling census or survey work, particularly with respect to defining assignment boundaries and identifying those households to which return visits are necessary because no information could be obtained on the first visit. In fact, the overall quality (of interviewing, supervision, sampling, and so on) of a census or a periodic household survey may improve over time while the completeness of reporting declines because there has been an increase in the proportion of the population living in areas that are difficult to enumerate.

It has been argued that a superior multiround household survey conducted at reasonably frequent intervals and with a built-in but exceedingly slow system of rotation might well overcome all the problems reported here. This is, of course, the case if the system of household surveys is truly "superior" and remains truly superior over time. In general, however, to assure oneself that a purportedly superior system is really doing what its supporters claim one must resort to some independent method of verification. If this verification consists merely of comparing the household survey estimate with an "independent" estimate of the same total, the question again arises of how good the independent estimate is and whether it may be subject to as much error as the figure one is trying to "verify." Of course, it can be argued that if the two estimates agree very well from year to year, one has solved the problem of variation in year-to-year completeness of reporting. But is this so, or is it merely that the so-called "independence" of the aggregates is illusory and the same error processes affect both sources? This happened, for example, in the Pakistan PGE study, where both the special registration system and the household survey showed a spurious decline in fertility and mortality between 1964 and 1965 that was at least partially due to the disruption of routine training and supervisory activities caused by the India-Pakistan conflict of 1965 (Seltzer, 1968).

Essentially, dual systems using the PGE approach attempt, through matching, to estimate the completeness of reporting of one or both systems and to correct for the estimated omissions. In any single system, there are changes from year to year in the completeness of reporting even of the nonmigrant population, largely because of variations in the quality of the field work. For example, over time, originally conscientious interviewers or registrars tend to become bored and careless; and new interviewers, hired as replacements, initially lack the experience of the older ones and only gradually learn the techniques of good field work such as checking to see whether anyone sleeps in what looks like a woodshed behind the main house.

In short, the completeness of reporting will vary with the average experience of the field staff and with many other factors. This affects the single-source estimates (n_1 or n_2) but not the PGE estimate $\hat{n}$, since if n_1 or n_2 decreases or increases m will tend to decrease or increase proportionately, provided the correlation of the sources remains constant. For example, suppose that in a given year source 2 had an unusually high turnover of personnel and the level of completeness for source 2 dropped 10 percent, while that for source 1 remained the same or increased slightly. If the correlation between the sources remained low and constant, the expected value of the match rate of source 1 (m/n_1), which is the estimated completeness of source 2, would also drop 10 percent and the expected value of $\hat{n}$ would remain the same.

Even if the completeness of reporting of *both* systems varies considerably over time, *the effect of this variation on estimates of changes in birth and death rates is much less with a dual system than with a single system.* Certainly, dual systems are subject to biases and variances in the estimation of completeness of reporting. But since the dual system estimate is based on measuring the completeness rate and correcting for incompleteness, it is usually easier to maintain approximately constant completeness in dual system estimates than in single system estimates. Even so, the completeness rate will rarely, if ever, be absolutely constant over time.

E. *Response Correlation and Response Error*

E.1　RESPONSE CORRELATION BIAS

As noted above, the PGE technique assumes that the probability of omission of reports from source 2 is the same whether or not the same vital event is included among source 1 reports—that is, "response correlation" equals zero. Response correlation bias occurs when the basic assumption of statistical independence between the two collection systems is not met, and the probability of an event being reported by one source *is* related to whether it was covered or omitted by the other source.

Response correlation is of two types:[7]

1. Correlation due to the nature of the events and the collection systems—The probabilities of collection in the two sources are likely to be similar for certain types of events. In particular, the same events are likely to be omitted by both sources because they occur in population

subgroups that are difficult to enumerate and register. For example, households of very low economic status are often omitted from surveys of any type, are more likely to fail to register births or deaths, and are more likely to have unattended births or deaths, with no doctor, midwife, or undertaker to report the events.

2. Correlation due to communication between the collection systems—Communication may be either planned or unplanned and includes any interaction between the procedures or field workers of one source and those of the other that effects the coverage or omission of events in either or both sources. Unplanned communication between sources may take the form of collusion between an interviewer and a registrar to "share" their data and thus reduce their work load but not their compensation. Planned communication between sources may take the form of common maps, a common system of structure numbers, common definitions of basic concepts, and so on. An extreme case of planned communication occurs when the personnel of the second source are given the list of events reported in the first source and instructed to search for any vital events missed by the first source.

Correlations of both types are usually positive and lead to overestimates of the completeness rates (m/n_2 and m/n_1); as a result, $\hat{n}$ is an underestimate. It is, of course, possible to have a situation in which inclusion in one source tends to be associated with exclusion from the other. For example, the registrar for an area may, because he is friendly with the village chief and the police, spend much of his time in the center of the village and get particularly good coverage there while the survey interviewer may stay at a house near the outskirts of the village and get particularly good coverage there. Such negative correlations are, however, unusual.

The formula for response correlation *rho* (ρ) is

$$\rho = \frac{P_{12} - P_1 P_2}{\sqrt{P_1 Q_1 P_2 Q_2}}$$

[3.8]

where

$$Q_1 = 1 - P_1 \text{ and}$$

$$Q_2 = 1 - P_2 \quad .$$

As mentioned earlier, bias is defined as the difference between the expected value of an estimate and the underlying "true" value. For the PGE estimate ($\hat{n}$), this becomes

$$\beta = E(\hat{n}) - N \quad .$$

[3.9]

Thus the relative bias (the bias relative to the true value, N) is

$$B = \frac{E(\hat{n}) - N}{N} = \frac{E(\hat{n})}{N} - 1 \quad .$$

[3.10]

If there is no matching or out-of-scope bias, relative bias consists only of its response correlation component and is equal to

$$B = \frac{P_1 P_2 - P_{12}}{P_{12}} \quad . \qquad [3.11]$$

Using equations 3.8 and 3.11, we can derive, in terms of ρ, the relative bias due to response correlation, which is

$$B = \frac{-\rho \sqrt{Q_1 Q_2}}{\rho \sqrt{Q_1 Q_2} + \sqrt{P_1 P_2}} \quad . \qquad [3.12]$$

If the reporting in the two sources is independent ($P_{12} = P_1 P_2$), both B and ρ will be zero. In general, P_{12} is greater than $P_1 P_2$; so that ρ will be greater than zero and B will be less than zero—that is, the correlation will be positive and the bias negative, so that $\hat{n}$ will be an underestimate of N. Note that β is not a linear function of ρ; as ρ increases from zero to 1, the absolute value of the bias increases but at a decreasing rate.

E.2 STRATIFYING TO REDUCE CORRELATION BIAS

To deal with the first type of response correlation bias mentioned above (correlation due to the nature of the population), Chandrasekaran and Deming (1949) suggest classifying the vital events into homogeneous groups on the basis of age, sex, and other characteristics; estimating $\hat{n}$ separately for each group; and summing to get the estimated total number of vital events. Their report presents some examples of the use of this approach.

Jabine and Bershad (1968) give a hypothetical illustration of the reduction in bias achieved by making separate PGE estimates for strata and then summing. Their illustration involves a population that contains two strata, with zero correlation between sources within each stratum. The true contingency tables for the two separate strata are shown in Table 3.1, and Table 3.2 presents comparable data for the whole population (that is, the sum of the two strata). Although

Table 3.1 True Number of Events Caught and Missed, by Source and Stratum: Hypothetical Data

First source	Second source		
	Observed	Not observed	Total
Stratum I			
Observed	36	24	60
Not observed	24	16	40
Total	60	40	100
Stratum II			
Observed	98	42	140
Not observed	42	18	60
Total	140	60	200

SOURCE: Hypothetical data from Jabine and Bershad, 1968.

Table 3.2   True Number of Events Caught and Missed, by Source, for Strata I and II Combined: Hypothetical Data

First source	Second source		
	Observed	Not observed	Total
Observed	134	66	200
Not observed	66	34	100
Total	200	100	300

SOURCE: Same as Table 3.1.

there is zero correlation for each stratum, there is positive correlation in the completeness if stratification is ignored and the two strata are combined. Thus the PGE estimate has a zero bias if estimates are made for each stratum and then summed and a negative bias (an underestimate of the number of events) if it is based on the data without stratification. Jabine and Bershad indicate that the "example is for illustrative purposes and is not intended to show the size of the negative bias."

In order to examine the possible reduction in response correlation bias achievable through stratification, let us consider a situation in which there are K strata, with independence between source 1 and source 2 for each stratum, and a probability $P_{1i} = P_{2i} = P_i$ of an event being reported in source 1 or source 2 for stratum i. Under these conditions the relative response correlation bias will be

$$B = \frac{- \sigma^2_{p_i}}{P^2 + \sigma^2_{p_i}} \quad , \qquad\qquad [3.13]$$

where

$$P = \frac{\sum\limits_{i}^{K} N_i P_i}{N} = \begin{array}{l}\text{overall probability that an event} \\ \text{will be reported in source 1 or} \\ \text{source 2,}\end{array}$$

$$\sigma^2_{p_i} = \frac{\sum\limits_{i}^{K} N_i (P_i - P)^2}{N} = \text{variance of } P_i \text{ over the } K \text{ strata,}$$

$$N_i = \text{number of events in stratum } i, \text{ and}$$

$$N = \sum\limits_{i}^{K} N_i \quad .$$

If the values of P_i vary from zero to .95 with a mean P of .7 and a standard deviation σ_{p_i} of .2, the relative bias (B) will be about 8 percent. This is, of course, a large bias even if it is also a substantial improvement over the 30-percent bias associated with a single system estimate based on either of the two sources alone. It would not be too unusual to have different probabilities of being reported for different types of events with about the same probability of reporting the event in either source, nor would an average probability of .7 be too unusual. Ranges of P_i as great as zero to .95 and standard deviations as large as .2 would, in general, *not* be encountered, except where data collection was very difficult or field control was very poor.

Thus there is, in theory, a possibility of appreciable gains from making separate estimates for different types of events and summing them. Unfortunately, examples of substantial gains from making separate estimates for population subgroups are few. Estimates that use a summation of subgroup PGE estimates were prepared for the United States' 1940 and 1950 birth registration tests, for India's Singur Health Center Study, for Thailand's Survey of Population Change, for Pakistan's Population Growth Estimation Experiment, and for Liberia's Population Growth Study. Only in the Singur Health Center Study was there a substantial difference between the single, global PGE estimate and one obtained by summing the separate subgroup estimates. Even in this case, although separate geographic, sex, and age-sex subgroups were studied, only the age-sex breakdown for deaths showed a major gain from stratification (see Chapter 2, Tables 2.13 and 2.14).

The main difficulty with trying to correct for correlation bias by making separate estimates for subgroups is that it is very difficult to define subgroups which are homogeneous with respect to the probabilities of coverage. As a result, the correlation between sources within groups is not much different from the overall correlation.

Studies preparing separate PGE estimates for individual subgroups or strata have, in the past, used demographic variables (for example, age, sex, parity) or geographic variables (for example, county, Union Board, sample cluster of 1,000 households) to form the strata. Apparently, in the former case the variables were only indirectly related to the coverage probabilities, while in the latter, the areas used were so heterogeneous with respect to average probability that within-area correlation was high. Clearly, it would be desirable to use characteristics more directly related to completeness than those used in the past.

In order to make separate subgroup estimates one must be able to classify all events in *either* source by subgroup (see Section K). Unfortunately, most of the characteristics *directly* related to completeness are not ordinarily entered on vital events reports. For example, proximity to a major street or highway may have a considerable effect on the probability of inclusion for both collection sources, yet not be recorded on the documents of either. Nevertheless, at a cost, some relevant characteristic(s) might be identified and included on the survey or special registration vital events documents. Obtaining satisfactory reporting of such characteristics in civil registration systems is usually not feasible. Alternatively, one might try to use more homogeneous geographic units than has been done in the past.

It should be noted that if the sample is divided into *very small* subgroups to prepare stratified estimates, considerable "ratio bias" may be introduced. Ratio bias occurs when (a) one divides by a random variate and (b) the ratio is not independent of its denominator.[8] The bias is due to the fact that the distribution of $1/x$ can be badly skewed (toward very high values) even if the distribution of x is symmetric; thus $E(1/x)$ is always greater than $1/E(x)$. In particular, if x is near zero the value of $1/x$ will be extremely large.

In the case of PGE estimates, the ratio bias will be small if $E(m)$ is large relative to σ_m. In this case, m is constrained to lie near $E(m)$ and $E(1/m)$ will be approximately equal to $1/E(m)$. The difference can be seen by comparing $\sigma_m = .02\ E(m)$ with $\sigma_m = .45\ E(m)$. In the former case, most values of m will be between $.96\ E(m)$ and $1.04\ E(m)$ (that is, $\pm 2\sigma$ of $E(m)$) and, therefore, most values of $1/m$ will be between $.96^2/E(m)$ and $1.04^2/E(m)$. In the latter case, m will generally be between $.1\ E(m)$ and $1.9\ E(m)$, while the corresponding range of $1/m$ will be $.526/E(m)$ to $10/E(m)$.[9] Since $1/m$ is used in PGE estimation (see equation 3.5), one must be alert to the possibility of ratio bias whenever estimates are made for population subgroups. The problem is discussed at greater length in Section K of this chapter.

Both types of response correlation bias can also be minimized by making the personnel (including the supervisors) and the work of the two collection systems as different as possible. This will reduce the opportunity and motivation for collaboration, and make unplanned communication both difficult and unrewarding. It will also tend to result in different probabilities of reporting in the two sources for various types of events. These considerations were important in selecting the procedures presented in Chapter 4.

E.3   RESPONSE ERROR VARIANCE

In addition to bias components, response error also has a variance component. Response error variance is due to the fact that, although a given event is assumed to have a fixed probability of being reported in a given source, the actual reporting of events is stochastic (that is, subject to random variation). Thus, the estimates n_1, n_2, m, and therefore $\hat{n}$ will vary from their expected values N_1, N_2, M, and N even with a 100-percent sample.

Response error variance is a function of the fact that, while the expected values of the completeness rates are fixed (at P_1 and P_2), the actual completeness rates obtained in a particular sample will vary around these expected values. Usually, this does not affect the total variance very much. That is, if the sampling units in the population have birth rates varying from 10 per 1,000 to 70 per 1,000, introducing a variation among sampling units in the completeness of reporting of from 50 to 100 percent will, at worst, extend the range of obtained birth rates to from 5 per 1,000 to 70 per 1,000. However, the response error variance does increase as the completeness of reporting decreases.

Moreover, the increase in response error variance is usually proportionately greater than the decrease in completeness because the completeness tends to be much poorer for some sampling units than for others. That is, differences in such factors as the competence and conscientiousness of the field workers, the educational and economic level of the population in the sample areas, and the accessibility and ease of interviewing in the areas result in a very uneven distribution of the reporting errors between segments. Thus, with an overall completeness rate of 90 percent, the completeness may range from 80 to 100 percent, but if the overall completeness goes down to 70 percent, one may well get a range of from 40- to 100-percent completeness among the sample areas.

E.4 CORRELATION BIAS AND RESPONSE VARIANCE CONSIDERED JOINTLY

Response variance in PGE studies reflects primarily sampling considerations (that is, the size and the design of the sample) and completeness rates. As usual, the effect of response variance increases as the size of the sample decreases, the clustering increases, stratification decreases, and so on. With respect to completeness rates, response variance increases as completeness decreases. Correlation bias and the sampling component of variance are independent. However, although there is no necessary connection between correlation bias and the completeness rate, it is more difficult to control correlation bias with the high variances associated with low completeness. To illustrate this point, Jabine and Bershad compute the relative bias, B, of the estimated total for various completeness rates and levels of correlation (see Table 3.3). In this exercise they assumed that the underlying probabilities of collection were the same for both sources—that is, $P_1 = P_2 = P$, so that $E(N_1) = E(N_2)$ and $E(U_1) = E(U_2) = U$. The columns of Table 3.3 are expressed in terms of $M/(U + M)$, the expected value of which is equal to both $P_{1.2}$ and $P_{2.1}$ in the notation used earlier.

Table 3.3 tends to emphasize the danger of a substantial bias

Table 3.3 Relative Bias of $\hat{n}$ for Selected Values of ρ and $M/(U + M)$

ρ	$M/(U + M)$				
	.5	.6	.7	.8	.9
.00	.000	.000	.000	.000	.000
.05	.053	.035	.023	.013	.006
.10	.111	.074	.048	.028	.012
.15	.176	.118	.076	.044	.020
.20	.250	.167	.107	.063	.028
.30	.429	.286	.184	.107	.048
.40	.667	.444	.286	.167	.074

SOURCE: Jabine and Bershad, 1968.

for lower values of $M/(U + M)$ (that is, values less than 0.8). Actually, the situation is not as bad as one might infer from the table. High values of *rho* (ρ) in association with low match rates $M/(U + M)$ are most unlikely because of the very low values of P_1 and P_2 this implies. This can be seen by substituting P for P_1 and P_2, and $PP_{1.2}$ for P_{12} in equation 3.8, and obtaining

$$P = \frac{P_{1.2} - \rho}{1 - \rho} .$$

[3.14]

Thus, for ρ to be .4 with $P_{1.2} = M/(U + M) = .5$, P would have to be .167. This would mean that while half the cases reported in one source were also reported in the other source, only one-tenth of the cases missed by one source would be reported by the other source. It would also mean that three-fourths of all births or deaths were missed by both sources and that each system was obtaining reports for only one out of six events. Such situations can occur, but only in extremely poor systems where no real attempt is made to control the quality of either source. Since as equation 3.14 shows, P cannot be negative, ρ can never be greater than $P_{1.2} = M/(U + M)$. In actual practice, as shown above, ρ will almost necessarily be considerably lower than $M/(U + M)$, so that high values of ρ (say, values greater than .4) will occur only in combination with high values of $M/(U + M)$. Actually, the relative bias is directly related to the ratios $P_1/P_{1.2}$ and $P_2/P_{2.1}$ and can be determined from the following equation:

$$B = \frac{P_1}{P_{1.2}} - 1 = \frac{P_2}{P_{2.1}} - 1 .$$

[3.15]

Although high values of $P_{1.2}$ and $P_{2.1}$ can (and do) occur when the data from the two sources are independent, it is always well to be suspicious of such values (that is, of high estimated completeness rates, m/n_2 and m/n_1) and to check very carefully for response correlation bias. On the other hand, with low estimates of $P_{1.2}$ or $P_{2.1}$ response correlation bias is likely to be less of a problem than response variance. Correlation will tend to be reduced by the fact that, where the completeness of one or both sources is very low, the completeness of the poorer source will tend to be low even in those areas where the other source happens to get relatively good reporting. On the other hand, as noted previously, with low completeness the coverage rate tends to be much worse in some segments than in others and the response variance rises disproportionately.

In any case *both* the completeness rate and the correlation bias depend heavily upon the competence and integrity of the field staff. The first goal of a PGE study should be to recruit competent field personnel and to pay, train, and supervise them in such a way that they will be motivated toward high-quality data collection with stress on getting as complete coverage as possible. *High actual* coverage (rather than merely high estimated coverage) will reduce both response variance and the first type of response correlation bias—that due to differences within the population in the probability of events being reported in either source.

Although improvements in completeness can reduce response correlation bias, this will occur only if the improvement in coverage is primarily in those sectors of the population which initially were poorly covered in both sources. Correlation bias will not be reduced by improving completeness in a given source uniformly over the whole range—for example, by increasing the probability of reporting for every type of event by .05. The correlation bias can actually be increased if improvements in coverage are limited to those cases where it is already good—for example, by increasing registration completeness from 80 to 90 percent in the better-educated sectors of the population, for which survey reports of vital events will also be quite complete.

Therefore, the most effective way to improve completeness is to concentrate funds and manpower in the areas where coverage tends to be poorest—for example, slum areas of cities and the more remote rural areas. As previously noted, the use of PGE estimates based on stratified subgroups for these areas may not reduce the effects of correlation bias if the correlation within the areas is high enough to inflate the completeness rate estimates to the level of that for groups with high coverage.

F. *Matching Error*

There are two types of matching errors, erroneous matches and erroneous nonmatches. If the expected value of the difference of these two types of errors is zero, matching errors have no effect on the bias of the PGE estimate. Similarly, the variance of the PGE estimate is affected only by net matching error. "Matching error variance" is, in fact, largely a result of the "intraclass correlation" resulting from the fact that net matching error is not independently distributed among the sampling units. That is, erroneous matches will predominate within some sampling units because of similarities of names and duplications or other inadequacies of the address identification. Within other sampling units, erroneous nonmatches may predominate because of a poor interviewer or a careless registrar who makes errors in recording names, addresses, and other identification data. The magnitude as well as the sign of net matching error will vary between sampling units depending upon the severity of the factors cited.

F.1 MISMATCHES

At first, the definitions of "erroneous match" and "erroneous nonmatch" seem simple. An "erroneous match" means treating as matched two reports that *do not* correspond to the same event; an "erroneous nonmatch" means a failure to treat as matched two reports that *do* correspond to the same event. Unfortunately, the definitions are complicated by "mismatches"—cases where a report in one source that corresponds to a report in the other source is correctly treated as matched but is paired with the *wrong* report in the other source. For some purposes a mismatch can be considered as generating *both* an erroneous match and an erroneous nonmatch. That is, two records which do not correspond to the same event are matched; at the same time, either or both of these records may remain unmatched to their proper partners.

For PGE purposes, however, it is preferable to treat a mismatch as *neither* an erroneous match *nor* an erroneous nonmatch since each mismatched report has been correctly classified as a match, regardless of whether the report to which it is wrongly linked is properly a match or a nonmatch. The definitions of "erroneous match" and "erroneous nonmatch" are important primarily during the process of trying to determine matching rules that will minimize bias and variance.

To minimize matching bias we need only be concerned with the net matching error, that is, the *difference* between the number of erroneous matches and erroneous nonmatches. Regardless of how mismatches are handled—whether they are included or excluded from the erroneous matches and erroneous nonmatches—the matching bias remains unchanged. Furthermore, since matching error variance is a function of the level of net matching errors in the *individual* sample areas and mismatches do not affect net matching error either on an overall basis or for individual sample areas, it again makes no difference how the mismatches are handled.

Although mismatches do not affect either the bias or the variance of the PGE estimate for the entire population or for an individual area, they may create a problem when estimates for population sub-groups—for example, estimates of age-specific fertility or mortality—are made if there is a discrepancy between the two matched reports in the characteristic being tabulated. However, this problem is not unique to mismatches. The reported characteristics of correctly matched reports may also differ. Methods of handling discrepancies in the characteristics of matched reports are discussed at the end of this chapter, in Section K.

Of course, the presence of a large number of mismatches is undesirable since, if the number of mismatches is high, one is likely to have a large number of erroneous matches. (That is, not all the reports matched to mismatches will be mismatches themselves.) Such a situation will be reflected adequately by "gross matching error," which is the *sum* of the number of erroneous matches and erroneous nonmatches.[10] It is therefore possible, and also preferable, to consider all mismatched reports correctly matched and to ignore mismatches in determining both the number of erroneous matches and the number of erroneous nonmatches. Given this exclusion of mismatches, the precise definitions of "erroneous match" and "erroneous nonmatch" are as follows:

(1) Erroneous match—A report that is classified as a match but does not correspond to *any* report in the other system; and

(2) Erroneous nonmatch—A report that is classified as a nonmatch and does correspond to a report in the other system.

F.2 MATCHING BIAS

On the basis of the definitions of matching error given in the preceding section, we can proceed to a more rigorous examination of matching bias. First, let us establish the following notation:

n_{1a} = number of erroneous matches among source 1 reports using some specific set of matching rules; that is, the number of source 1 reports classified as matched for which no true counterpart exists among any of the source 2 reports;

n_{2a} = number of erroneous matches among source 2 reports under the same matching rules;

n_{1b} = number of erroneous nonmatches among source 1 reports under the same matching rules; that is, the number of source 1 reports classified as nonmatched for which a true counterpart does exist among the source 2 reports;

n_{2b} = number of erroneous nonmatches among source 2 reports;

n_c = $n_{1a} - n_{1b} = n_{2a} - n_{2b}$ = net matching error;

n_{1d} = $n_{1a} + n_{1b}$ = gross matching error for source 1; and

n_{2d} = $n_{2a} + n_{2b}$ = gross matching error for source 2.

The probabilities P_{1a}, P_{2a}, P_{1b}, and P_{2b} and the expected net and gross error rates P_c, P_{1d}, and P_{2d} are obtained by dividing the appropriate expected values of the variables defined above by the true total number of births or deaths. That is,

$$P_{1a} = \frac{E(n_{1a})}{N} \quad ,$$

$$P_{2a} = \frac{E(n_{2a})}{N} \quad ,$$

$$P_{1b} = \frac{E(n_{1b})}{N} \quad ,$$

$$P_{2b} = \frac{E(n_{2b})}{N} \quad ,$$

$$P_c = \frac{E(n_c)}{N} \quad ,$$

$$P_{1d} = \frac{E(n_{1d})}{N} \text{ , and}$$

$$P_{2d} = \frac{E(n_{2d})}{N} \quad .$$

In addition,

m_t = number of reports in source 1 or source 2 that should match in the absence of matching error, given P_1, P_2, and P_{12} (That is, the number of vital events which are reported by *both* sources) and

$$P_{12} = \frac{E(m_t)}{N} \quad .$$

As before, n_1 and n_2 are the number of events reported by source 1 and source 2, respectively, in a given study, m of which from each source are classified as matched by the matching procedure.

Since the number of matched reports in source 1 is identical to that in source 2, we have

$$m = m_t + n_{1a} - n_{1b} = m_t + n_{2a} - n_{2b} = m_t + n_c \quad , \qquad [3.16]$$

where m_t, n_{1a}, n_{1b}, n_{2a}, n_{2b}, and n_c are the sample estimates whose expected values were defined above. In other words, for either system, the number of matched reports, m, is equal to the number of reports that should match, plus the erroneous matches, less the erroneous nonmatches. Substituting $m_t + n_c$ for m in equation 3.5 shows that only the net matching error affects the PGE estimate. That is,

$$\hat{n} = \frac{n_1 n_2}{m} = \frac{n_1 n_2}{m_t + n_c} \quad . \qquad [3.17]$$

The relative bias of the PGE estimate due to matching error (B_m) is

$$B_m = -\frac{E(n_c)}{E(m)} = -\frac{E(n_c)}{E(m_t) + E(n_c)} \quad . \qquad [3.18]$$

In other words, the relative bias is equal to the expected value of the true net matching error divided by the expected number of matches. The relative bias due to matching error can also be expressed as

$$B_m = -\frac{P_c}{P_{12} + P_c} \quad . \qquad [3.19]$$

In any specific situation B_m can be estimated by

$$b_m = -\frac{n_c}{m} = \frac{m_t - m}{m} \quad , \qquad [3.20]$$

where

m = number of matches obtained in a particular study,

m_t = estimated number of events that should match (that is, the number of "true matches"), and

n_c = estimated net matching error.

That is, the relative matching bias is estimated by the ratio of net matching error to the observed number of matches. Of course, in ordinary circumstances, m_t and n_c are unknown. It is, however, possible to make a reasonably good approximation of m_t for a (small) sample of cases by very thorough (and very expensive) checking of all cases that are not clearly matched. This procedure would ordinarily be too expensive to use as a regular operating procedure, but the expenditure would be justified to obtain an initial (and probably one-time) estimate of m_t and n_c.

F.3 MATCHING PROCEDURES

Several models have been developed for determining "optimum" matching procedures, that is, for establishing procedures that minimize n_c subject to given costs and other constraints—see Nathan (1967), Newcombe (1965), Sunter and Fellegi (1967), and Tepping (1960, 1968). (For a comprehensive bibliography on matching methodology and applications, see Wagner and Newcombe, 1970.) All these models contribute valuable concepts to the theory and practice of matching, even though no one of them is completely satisfactory for our present purposes. In the following discussion of matching we shall use only those elements of these models that can be applied directly to the requirements of a PGE study. We recognize that much additional work on both theory and practice is needed before matching models fully applicable to PGE studies can be developed. Hopefully, this discussion will suggest profitable lines of research. However, anyone contemplating such research is urged to study carefully the original articles from which the concepts presented here were taken, in addition to the material in this Handbook.

One fundamental concept, used by Sunter and Fellegi and by Tepping, is a "comparison pair" that consists of a record from one source and one of the possible matches from the other source. The operation "matching" is then conceived of as involving a "comparison function" that measures the degree of agreement between the records in a comparison pair, a set of possible actions (a_1, a_2, a_3 . . .), and "decision rules" that determine the action to be taken for each comparison pair. The comparison function uses a set of identifying characteristics (for example, name, father's name, mother's name, sex, date of birth, place of birth) to divide the comparison pairs into "comparison classes" varying according to the degree to which two reports of vital events resemble each other with respect to these identifying characteristics. The same action is assigned to all pairs in any given comparison class. Of course the same action may and usually will be assigned to more than one comparison class.

The action set in a PGE study can contain only two final actions: treat the comparison pair as matched (a_1) or treat the comparison pair as unmatched (a_2). However, one may want to take some intermediate actions. For example, Tepping (1968) suggests the following:

a_3 = Temporarily treat the pair as matched; but review and if necessary, correct the temporary action if additional information can be obtained.

a_4 = Take no action immediately, but try to obtain additional information on which to base a decision.

a_5 = Similar to a_3, but the temporary action is to treat the pair as unmatched.

One form of comparison function is the vector obtained by giving each characteristic of a comparison pair one of the following values:

(1) reports agree on the characteristic,
(2) reports contradict each other on the characteristic, or
(3) no entry for the characteristic for one or both reports.

The terms "agreement" and "contradiction" are defined with reference to "tolerance limits" set up to allow for some variability in the reporting of characteristics. For example, as Table 3.5 (p. 113) shows, Srinivasan and Muthiah (1968) required exact agreement on place of birth, religion and caste, sex, permanent address, and attendant at delivery but allowed for some discrepancies on other characteristics.

Some matching studies have used more than three comparison function values (that is, more than three comparison classes) for some or all of the identifying characteristics. The additional values represent various degrees of correspondence of the entries—for example, (1) date of birth identical; (2) same year and day of birth but different month; (3) same month and year but different day; (4) other, but within one month; (5) other, within a year; (6) discrepancy of more than one year between the dates of birth.

In order to be able to sequence comparison pairs according to the extent to which they agree, it is convenient to work with a measure of agreement of the identifying characteristics of a comparison pair expressed in scalar rather than vector terms. One method of converting the comparison function values to scalar terms is to assign weights based on agreement or disagreement on a given characteristic. These weights can reflect "presumptive evidence" for or against a match. For example, if weights from +5 to −5 were used, the value given for agreement on name might be +5 if the name was unusual and there was exact agreement on all the letters; +2 if the name was somewhat common and there was exact agreement on the spelling; +3 if the name was unusual and there was agreement on the sound but not the spelling (Chibichev versus Tchybytchef); zero if the name was very common and there was exact agreement or agreement on the sound (Li versus Li or Li versus Lee); −2 if there was disagreement on both the sound and spelling but the disagreement could have been the result of an error by the interviewer or the registrar (for example, Cho versus Choi); or −5 if there was no resemblance at all between the names. Similarly, agreement on sex might receive a weight of zero and disagreement on sex a weight of −5. One could then add the weights, classify those above a specified positive value as matched and those below a specified negative value as unmatched, and try to investigate the other cases further. If one wanted to classify all cases on the basis of the data already available, one could classify cases with positive total weights as matched, classify those with negative total weights as unmatched, and randomly classify half the zeros as matched and half as unmatched. Weighting is discussed in fuller detail in Fellegi and Sunter (1969).

A weighting system, based either on explicit weighting rules or on implicit rules embodied in the judgment of the matcher, has the advantage of using an expanded body of evidence to determine matching status. There may be, for example, pertinent information in the subsequent letters of a name which is disregarded by a tolerance rule that uses only the first four letters. However, to use the additional information we need some method of offsetting the effects of errors in it; and this means a more complex system or one more dependent upon the judgment of the matcher. Thus the decision to use or not to use a weighting system will depend heavily upon the availability and cost of clerical personnel competent enough to make a weighting system operate effectively.

The assigning of scalar match scores to the comparison classes is an attempt to do explicitly what the use of a vector does implicitly—that is, assess the "weight of the evidence" for and against treating the comparison pair as matched. In evaluating evidence, it should be remembered that agreement on some characteristics has a different "probative value" as evidence for a match than as evidence for a nonmatch. For these characteristics, agreement is a necessary but not a sufficient condition for a match. For example, agreement between two records on some common name (such as Smith in the United States or Kim in Korea) is not much evidence of a match, whereas disagreement (Smith vs. Jones or Kim vs. Park) is very powerful evidence of a nonmatch.

For other characteristics, agreement is a sufficient but not a necessary condition for a match. For example, exact agreement on something like social security number or identity card number (of a decedent or of the father or mother of a newborn infant) is very strong evidence of a match, since these numbers are assigned in such a way that chance agreement because of an error in one or two digits is unlikely. On the other hand, records that disagree on social security or identity card number may still be matches because of the high probability of error when entries are based on verbal reports made without consulting the social security or identity card. Most items fall in between—possibly "leaning" one way more than the other. Of course, the usefulness of any particular characteristic as identification in matching, and the possible weight given to agreement or disagreement in the characteristic, can only be determined in relation to the conditions in a specific country.

The method outlined above for expressing the comparison function in scalar form assigns weights to each value of each of the comparison function components (the identifying characteristics) and sums them for a given comparison class over all characteristics. Other methods of assigning weights can be used. Fellegi and Sunter (1969) suggest two methods based on knowledge about the probability of erroneous agreement on the characteristic for a randomly selected pair of records corresponding to different events and the probability of erroneous disagreement on the characteristic for a randomly selected pair of records corresponding to the same event.

Whether the comparison classes are assigned a vector or a scalar value, the objective is to determine which action to assign to comparison pairs having a given level of agreement or disagreement. Although, as noted above, intermediate actions may be assigned temporarily, the ultimate action must be to treat the pair as matched or to treat it as unmatched. The goal is, using the available resources, to assign the final actions in such a manner as to minimize matching error—basically to minimize net matching error for some low level of gross matching error. For this purpose, we suggest the procedure below, which is a modification of that developed by Tepping (1968).

The first step in determining the linkage rule is to estimate the values of $P(M)$, defined as the probability that both records of a comparison pair randomly selected from all pairs in the same comparison class will correspond to the same event. In doing this, we may encounter two problems. First, some comparison classes may have been defined so narrowly that there are too few pairs in them to permit a meaningful estimate of $P(M)$. For example, if only five pairs were available, it could happen that three were really nonmatches although they happened to agree on the specific characteristics involved. In this case, it is necessary to merge classes with similar $P(M)$ values to obtain new classes with more pairs. In deciding which classes have similar $P(M)$ values, one should estimate what the $P(M)$ for the comparison class would be if a large sample of pairs with this comparison function value was available on the basis of past experience or a pilot study. Ideally, all comparison classes should give high or low $P(M)$ values (that is, values near 1.0 or 0.0) and should contain at least 30 comparison pairs to give some stability to the estimate of $P(M)$.

The second problem one may encounter is that of comparison classes for which the estimate of the "underlying" $P(M)$ value—that is, the $P(M)$ value which would obtain in a very large sample of pairs with this comparison function value—is not near 0.0 or 1.0. Here it is desirable, if possible, to redefine the comparison class and split it into two or more new classes for some of which the $P(M)$ estimates will be near 0.0 or 1.0. If this results in new classes that are too small, they will have to be merged with other classes with similar $P(M)$ values.

In some cases, splitting a class will require additional data and one must take the "intermediate action" of trying to obtain more information about the pairs in this comparison class. In other cases, there may be additional information that was not used in defining the original comparison classes. For example, the original class may have grouped some pairs that agreed on very common family names with others that agreed on very rare family names. If the comparison class is redefined to separate pairs with common family names from those with unusual family names, the $P(M)$ for the latter group may become nearly 1.0. On the other hand, the $P(M)$ for the pairs that agree on common family names may move nearer to 0.5 (for example, from 0.6 to 0.5), but this will not change the cost of obtaining additional information (or the probability of an erroneous match if one acts without obtaining additional information) for common name pairs in the original comparison class.

An example of a set of comparison classes might be

A. two reports from different villages—with very small $P(M)$;
B. both reports from the same village; names of mother, father, and infant *all* different—with $P(M)$ also small;
C. both reports from the same village, all names agree, dates of birth agree within two months, age of mother agrees within four years—with $P(M)$ near 1; and
D. both reports from the same village, names of mother and father the same, name of infant missing in source 2, dates of births differ by two months, age of mother differs by five years, and neither event gives a Class C pairing with any other event—with $P(M)$ about 0.6.

Each comparison pair is then assigned a specific matching status or a specific indeterminate outcome that depends upon its class. For example, the set of possible outcomes—the "action set"—might consist of

a_1 = classify the comparison pair as a match,
a_2 = classify the comparison pair as a nonmatch, and
a_3 = do a field check to verify and complete the data.

The linkage rule might assign outcome a_1 to comparison classes with high $P(M)$ values (say, values of .7 or more), outcome a_2 to classes with low $P(M)$ values (say, 0.3 or less), and outcome a_3 to classes with $P(M)$ values between 0.3 and 0.7. Thus, pairs of reports in Class C, above, would be considered matched (outcome a_1), pairs of reports in Classes A and B would be considered unmatched (outcome a_2), and pairs of reports in Class D would be sent to the field for further investigation (outcome a_3). Outcome a_3 would ultimately result in placement of the pair in a new comparison class (A, B, or C), and hence in outcome a_1 or a_2. For example, investigation of a Class D pair of reports might indicate that there were two couples, both with the same very common name, living in the same village. If one couple had had a baby girl on the date indicated in source 1, the other couple had moved away and could not be traced (though the neighbors thought they had a baby girl prior to their departure), and the mother's age and parity given in the source 2 report were not inconsistent with the neighbors' recollection of the family, these reports might be assigned to a comparison class with a low $P(M)$ value and be considered unmatched.

The probability of an erroneous match or an erroneous nonmatch will, of course, depend upon the comparison function, the action set $\{a_i\}$, and the linkage rule. The possible meaningful values of a_i are limited (that is, one could not usefully add more than four other actions to the set listed above), and the appropriate linkage rule will pretty much follow directly from the value of $P(M)$ for the comparison class and from the "costs" and probable gains associated with such actions as a_3 above.

In some matching problems, it is permissible to have multiple matches, either in both directions or in only one direction. In PGE studies, it is usually desirable to impose the restriction that no report in one source can be matched to more than one event reported in the other source.

Several methods of deciding among multiple pairings of the same record are discussed by Nathan (1964, 1967). Which method should be used depends upon the costs and probable "gains" associated with each one. In the case of PGE matching the decision is simplified by the fact that the "utility" of a given procedure is determined by the number of matches and is not affected in any major way by mismatches. Thus, the critical question is whether a record (in, say, source 1) is treated as matched, not whether it is matched to the correct record in the other source. In general, then, we need make a decision about a given (source 1) record only with respect to that pair (or pairs) containing it which has the highest $P(M)$ value. That is, if we decide that the $P(M)$ for this pair is such that we can classify the pair as unmatched, (action a_2) without further investigation, we will certainly classify the other pairs with lower $P(M)$ values as unmatched. If we decide on the basis of the $P(M)$ value for this pair that we should do a field check or examine other data (action a_3), we can also consider other matches for this record in the course of this further investigation. If we decide that the $P(M)$ for this pair is high enough to justify calling it a match, (action a_1) without further examination, we can treat the other pairs as unmatched (action a_2). However, in classifying the pair with the highest $P(M)$ value as matched, we are deciding that the probability of our finding that it is not matched is so low that further investigation is not warranted from a cost or utility standpoint.

Thus, to "resolve" multiple linkages for a given record, we first classify as a nonmatch all pairs involving that record except the pair with the highest $P(M)$ value. (If there are two or more pairs with the same $P(M)$ for any record, we can select one of them at random for further consideration and classify the others as unmatched.) This leaves at most, one unclassified pair for each record. That is, there will be at most one pair unclassified for each record in the source with fewer total records. These unclassified pairs can then be grouped into comparison classes for which new $P(M)$ values can be estimated and the appropriate action determined. If the linkage rule specifies further investigation, the comparison classes and $P(M)$ values can be revised again.

Ultimately, then, action a_1 or a_2 will be assigned to each comparison pair in such a way that no report will be in more than one comparison pair to which action a_1 is assigned—that is, which is classified as matched.

It should be noted that after multiple pairings have been eliminated, $P(M)$ is equal to the probability of an erroneous nonmatch if action a_2 is assigned to all pairs in a comparison class, and $1.0 - P(M)$ is equal to the probability of an erroneous match if action a_1 is assigned. Thus if $P(M)$ is high for the final comparison class, the linkage rule should specify action a_1; if $P(M)$ is low, the linkage rule should specify action a_2. If the value of $P(M)$ is neither high nor low, one can try to obtain more information and eventually specify action a_1 if the revised $P(M)$ estimate is more than some cutoff value P_0 or action a_2 if $P(M)$ is less than P_0. The amount of additional effort to be put in will depend upon costs and upon the probability of getting information which will substantially reduce the probability of matching error—that is, which will move $P(M)$ near 1.0 or 0.0.

The cutoff value, P_0, should be determined with a view to minimizing the expected net matching error. However, the proportions of erroneous matches and erroneous nonmatches obtained in a test to determine the matching rules will only be estimates of the probabilities P_{1a}, P_{2a}, P_{1b}, and P_{2b} for an ongoing system using these matching rules. Thus it is desirable to make sure that we do not have too high a variance for our estimated net matching error. That is, we need to maintain low levels of the gross matching error (which is nearly proportional to the variance of the net matching error), but not at the cost of substantial increases in net matching error. For example, if the choice is between a cutoff value, P_0, that gives an estimated net error of .02 and a gross error of .22 ($P_{1a} = .12$, $P_{1b} = .10$) and another, P_0', that gives a net error of .04 and gross error of .06 ($P_{1a} = .05$ and $P_{1b} = .01$), one should chose the latter, assuming that P_0' is not prohibitively expensive to apply. However, if the choice is between a P_0 value that gives a net error of .02 and a gross error of .10 ($P_{1a} = .06$ and $P_{1b} = .04$) and a P_0' that gives a net error of .04 and a gross error of .06 ($P_{1a} = .05$ and $P_{1b} = .01$), one should probably chose the former, assuming that both P_0 and P_0' will cost approximately the same to apply.

F.4   MATCHING CHARACTERISTICS

Initially, trial values of $P(M)$ can be assigned on the basis of whatever past experience is available. Frequently, it is desirable to do some studies with intensive field checks to try to determine what the probability of an erroneous match or an erroneous nonmatch is. Once a working system for matching has been set up, the initial period of operation should include additional field work to determine matching status more definitively for doubtful cases—that is, to improve the estimates of $P(M)$ and the determination of comparison functions and linkage rules. There should also be periodic checks in a working system to determine whether probabilities have changed in such a manner as to require a change in the matching rules.

Errors in matching occur because (a) the identification used in matching the birth or death reports is insufficient to identify each event uniquely or (b) errors occur in the identification material. These two sources of error interact. That is, one can usually obtain enough identifying information to obtain a unique identification of every vital event, but if one uses this identification without making allowances for errors in the data the incidence of "erroneous nonmatches" will

Table 3.4   Estimated Matching Error, by Type, for Specified Combinations of Matching Characteristics: Gandhigram, India, 1966

Matching characteristics used[1]	Erroneous match probability (P_a)	Erroneous nonmatch probability (P_b)	Gross matching error $(P_a + P_b)$	Net matching error $(P_a - P_b)$	σ of gross matching error[2]	σ of net matching error[3]
1	.119	.000	.119	.119	.013	.013
1,2	.110	.000	.110	.110	.013	.013
1,2,3	.100	.015	.115	.085	.013	.014
1,2,3,4	.064	.024	.088	.040	.012	.012
1,2,3,4,5	.054	.046	.100	.008	.012	.013
1,2,3,4,5,6	.029	.068	.097	−.039	.012	.013
1,2,3,4,5,6,7	.008	.135	.143	−.127	.014	.015
1,2,3,4,5,6,7,8	.007	.176	.183	−.169	.016	.016
1,2,3,4,5,6,7,8,9	.000	.220	.220	−.220	.017	.017

[1] See Table 3.5 for a description of each characteristic.

[2] Estimated standard deviation of the estimated gross matching error, calculated, assuming simple random sampling, from the expression

$$\sigma = \sqrt{\frac{P_d - P_d^2}{n}}.$$

where P_d is the gross matching error $(P_a + P_b)$ and n is the true number of vital events in the sample.

[3] Estimated standard deviation of the estimated net matching error, calculated, assuming simple random sampling, from the expression

$$\sigma = \sqrt{\frac{P_d - P_c^2}{n}},$$

where P_c is the net matching error, and P_d and n are as defined in footnote 2.

SOURCE: Based on data in Srinivasan and Muthiah, 1968, and personal communication with the authors.

be very high. For this reason, it is usual in matching to provide tolerance limits within which discrepancies in the identification may be ignored. For example, one may consider two birth reports to be matches if the name of the village, infant, and mother are the same, and the birth dates do not differ by more than one month. One may specify a narrower tolerance limit, such as, that the birth dates must agree on year and month (considering 31 March 1971 and 1 April 1971 to be nonmatches); or, one may provide a broader tolerance limit, such as considering up to three months difference in birth date acceptable.

As one increases the amount of independent identification material needed to classify a pair of reports as matched, each report will be more uniquely identified and the number of erroneous matches will decrease. On the other hand, an increase in the amount of identification material used also increases the likelihood of an accidental discrepancy that exceeds the tolerance limit occurring in the identification material of a pair of reports referring to the same event. Thus, if tolerance limits are held constant the number of erroneous nonmatches will increase as more identifying material is used. This can be seen by examining the data in Table 3.4, which are from a study of matching error by Srinivasan and Muthiah (1968). The characteristics used for matching and the tolerance limits adopted for each characteristic appear in Table 3.5.

Table 3.5 Matching Characteristics, Criteria, and Tolerance Limits Used in Srinivasan and Muthiah Matching Study: Gandhigram, India, 1966

Reference number[1]	Characteristic	Criteria and tolerance limits for matches
1	Name of the parents	In both the mother's and father's name, the first or last four letters agree and the remaining part does not disagree
2	Place of birth	Identical in both
3	Religion and caste	Identical in both
4	Sex	Identical in both
5	Permanent address	Identical in both
6	Parity of the mother	Parity in one source is within ±1 of parity in the other
7	Date of birth	The date of birth in one source is within ±15 days of the date of birth in the other
8	Age of the mother	The age in one source is within ±4 years of the age in the other
9	Attendant at delivery	Identical in both

[1] See Table 3.4 for reference number.

SOURCE: Same as Table 3.4.

In this study the procedure used to determine the true number of matched reports (m_t in the notation used in Section F.2) and the components of matching error were described by Srinivasan and Muthiah (1968) in the following terms:

> For the sake of reaching a most probable decision regarding the "match-status," of every event in the Gandhigram data, it was decided that if an event in the Survey list agrees in all the nine characteristics (within the predetermined criteria and tolerance level) it is considered "matched" with another event in the register; if there is disagreement in three or more characteristics it is considered "unmatched." If there is disagreement in only one or two characteristics the matching status was considered "doubtful." These "doubtful" cases were reinvestigated in the field with regard to the characteristics (one or two) in which there is disagreement and on the basis of this investigation every "doubtful" event was reclassified either as "matched" or "not matched." Thus for each event, the most probable matching status was obtained by an arbitrary procedure as defined above. Once this is done, it is obvious that for any given sequence of characteristics, the two types of errors can be estimated.

The probabilities of an erroneous match and an erroneous nonmatch can also be varied by changing either the linkage rule or the action set. In the Srinivasan and Muthiah study two reports were classified as "matched" if they agreed on all characteristics within the tolerance limits specified in Table 3.5. They were classified as unmatched if they disagreed by more than the specified tolerance limit on *any* characteristic. The action set in the Srinivasan-Muthiah study consisted of only two possible actions—classify the comparison pair as matched or classify the comparison pair as unmatched.

More complex systems allow for more values of the comparison function and may use weights to express the comparison function in scalar form. Nevertheless, these systems have to specify some value of the comparison function such that pairs of records with this value or with a value indicating the same or greater "agreement"—that is, the same or a higher value of $P(M)$—would be considered matched and other pairs would be considered unmatched. If we adjusted the characteristics considered and the tolerance limits, the very simple system used by Srinivasan and Muthiah could be made to give essentially the same results as most of the more complex systems.

To reproduce the results of other complex systems (for example, some of the weighting systems), one could examine additional characteristics for *some* comparison pairs. For example, one might match all pairs on Characteristics 1, 2, 3, and 4 and classify as unmatched any case that disagreed by more than the tolerance limit on any of the four characteristics. However, for cases that agreed on all four characteristics, one might specify a list of common names; then, if *both* the mother's name and the father's name were on this list, one would also examine Characteristics 5 and 6. This procedure would produce fewer erroneous matches than examining only four characteristics. It would produce fewer erroneous nonmatches than examining six characteristics but probably more than examining four, and it could produce fewer errors of either type than examining five characteristics for all cases.

As noted above, the use of a different action set or a different linkage rule changes the level of both erroneous matches and erroneous nonmatches and may affect one type of error more than another. However, for a *fixed* linkage rule and action set, the number of erroneous matches tends to decrease as more information is considered and the number of erroneous nonmatches tends to increase. This would, for example, be true for the weighting system described above. With fixed weights for a given characteristic and a breaking point of zero, the use of additional matching characteristics tends to decrease the number of erroneous matches and increase the number of erroneous nonmatches. Here again, varying the weights is equivalent to varying the tolerance limits and can be used to balance the increased number of characteristics.

We can see from Table 3.4 that the absolute value of net matching error is least when the first five characteristics are used. This also happens to be in the region (the use of four to six characteristics) where the sum of the two types of error is least. There is no *necessary* connection between minimizing total matching error and minimizing net matching error. However, *in practice minimum net error is rarely obtained for an alternative with large total error.*

Even though both the bias and variance of a PGE estimate are a function of net matching error, it is extremely dangerous to try to obtain a small net error by using a large erroneous match probability to offset an equally large erroneous nonmatch probability. Although in theory this can be done, it should be remembered that an experimental procedure to determine the minimum net error (like that in Table 3.4) produces only *estimates* of net error and these are subject to a variance that is very sensitive to the size of the *gross* matching error. The formulae for the σ's of the estimated gross and net matching errors are given in footnotes 2 and 3, respectively, to Table 3.4. Note that the variance of net matching error is an increasing function of the gross matching error and a decreasing function of the absolute value of net matching error. Thus, a very small estimated net matching error is subject to a large variance if there is a very large gross matching error.

In other words, the estimate of net matching error is itself based on a sample, and the variability from sample to sample will usually be large enough to make the estimate of net matching error unreliable when gross matching error is large. However, if the choice is among gross errors of about the same magnitude (for example, the use of four, five, or six characteristics for matching in Table 3.4), it will be satisfactory to select the alternative with the lowest net matching error. Although it is desirable, then, to try to make the gross error small, one should keep an eye on the costs and not introduce large expenditures to reduce gross error when the probable effect on net error is small. For example, given the situation shown in Table 3.4, it would be desirable to use Permanent address (Characteristic 5) as this would mean a substantial improvement in net error at little or no extra cost.

F.5 TOLERANCE LIMITS

In addition to studying the effects of increasing the number of characteristics, it is important to consider the consequences of varying the error "tolerances" of individual characteristics and the effects of using alternative characteristics. As indicated above, narrowing the tolerance limits has the same effect as increasing the number of matching characteristics; that is, it increases the amount of identifying information. The truth of this statement can be seen by looking at the results in Table 3.6, which are from a study by Nitzberg and Sardy (1965) of matching death certificates with health insurance records. The table shows the total number of matches—both correct and erroneous—obtained by using one of five tolerance limits for agreement on name in conjunction with either of two different tolerance limits for agreement on age.

One can see from Table 3.6 that widening the tolerance limits for age from ±1 year to ±5 years for those cases with agreement on Soundex code (ignoring agreements or disagreements on all other aspects of name) more than tripled the number of matches. Some of this increase was due to a reduction in the number of erroneous nonmatches (that is, an increase in the number of correct matches); but, probably, a larger part was due to erroneous matches where different

Table 3.6 Number of Matches Obtained Using Various Tolerance Limits for Agreement on Name and Age: New York City, United States, 1961–63

Tolerance limit for name of deceased	Tolerance limit for age of deceased	
	± 5 years	± 1 year
Soundex code[1]	89,306	26,075
Soundex code and first or last name[2]	69,265	20,460
Soundex code and first name	63,461	18,808
Soundex code and last name	26,675	8,680
Exact first and last names	20,871	7,036

[1]Soundex code based on both first and last name. For a fuller description of the Soundex system, see Chapter 4, Section B.6. Briefly, it is a system of coding names designed to minimize the effects of mispronunciation (and mishearing) and of alternative spellings. In Soundex, vowels are omitted (except for the initial vowel of a name) and combinations of letters having the same sound or very similar sounds are treated as the same. For example, Marx, Marks, Moreks, Marsh, Mars, and Mears might be given the same Soundex code (M620 using the code scheme shown in Chapter 4).

[2]"First name" refers to the given name of the individual, and "last name" refers to the person's family name.

SOURCE: Nitzberg and Sardy, 1965.

people with the same or similar names who died in different years were considered matched using the ±5-year age tolerance and not using the ±1-year tolerance. Similarly, the number of matched reports also increases as the tolerance limit for name is widened from insistence on exact agreement on both first and last name to exact agreement on first *or* last name along with Soundex code agreement.

One can also consider Soundex code, first name, and last name as three separate characteristics. The bottom four lines of Table 3.6 show the effect of alternative selections of two of these characteristics; for example, using the Soundex code with first name produces more matches (more erroneous matches and/or fewer erroneous nonmatches) than using the Soundex code with last name, regardless of which age tolerance is used.

The fact that broadening the tolerance limits has the same effect as reducing the number of characteristics is not a mere coincidence. As Tepping (1955, 1968) and Nathan (1967) have pointed out, the probability of an erroneous match is a function of the number of population elements (in this case, reports of vital events) per "identification code class."[11] Eliminating a matching characteristic tends to increase the number of elements per identification code class—that is, it tends to reduce the "discriminating power"[12] of the identification code. This is illustrated in Table 3.7.[13] Increasing the tolerance limits also tends to increase the number of elements per identification code class—for example, by considering as the same those names which sound alike, even though the spelling may differ (for example, Jones, Johns, and Janis).

Although erroneous matches result from the low discriminating power of the characteristics used to identify individual reports, erroneous nonmatches are due to errors that cause reports which should match to differ (by more than the tolerance limits) on one or more of the matching characteristics. In other words, erroneous nonmatches generally arise from errors in the data used as identification in matching. This type of matching error can be reduced by improving the accuracy of the data, widening the tolerance limits, modifying the weights, or eliminating the characteristic as a matching item. Improvements in the accuracy of the identifying information may be achieved by improved collection or processing procedures (for example, by better training, supervision, questionnaire design, and so on).

An optimal set of matching characteristics can be arrived at by a process similar to that used by Srinivasan and Muthiah (1968), or by any of several other procedures. Of course, the definition of a "matching characteristic" includes the specification of tolerance limits for the characteristic. One method of arriving at the "optimal tolerance limits" for any characteristic is to start with zero tolerance and gradually increase the limits, recording the number of erroneous matches and erroneous nonmatches (with respect to this characteristic) at each step. Tolerance limits can then be set at the step where the increase in erroneous matches begins to be greater than the decrease in erroneous

Table 3.7   Measures of Discriminating Power and Matching Error Obtained Using Alternate Identification Codes in Three Geographic Areas: United States, 1955

Composition of identification code			Percent of units with unique codes	Average number of units per identification code class	Percent of erroneous matches[2]	Percent of erroneous non-matches[3]
Post office name	Additional address data[1]	Letters of family name included				
Delaware						
Not used	Not used	First 4	21.7	2.76		
Used	Not used	First 2	17.6	3.40		
Used	Not used	First 3	33.4	2.08		
Used	Not used	First 4	50.7	1.54	33.5	0.2
Used	Not used	First 6	61.5	1.36		
Used	Used	First 4	98.5	1.008	0.5	2.3
Used	Used	First 6	98.7	1.007	0.3	2.8
Vermont						
Not used	Not used	First 4	14.4	3.54		
Used	Not used	First 4	81.1	1.12	12.7	0.9
Used	Used	First 4	99.1	1.004	0.2	4.4
Denver						
[4]	Not used	First 4	24.7	2.59	45.6	0.5
[4]	Used	First 4	98.9	1.005	0.6	1.3

[1] Additional address data limited to four characters.

[2] Erroneous matches as a percent of the number of cases in the smaller file. No precise determination of erroneous matches was made for empty cells; however, the percentage is certainly large.

[3] Erroneous nonmatches as a percent of the number of cases in the smaller file. No precise determination of erroneous nonmatches was made for empty cells; however, the percentage is certainly near zero.

[4] Not applicable, since matching confined to the area covered by the Denver post office.

SOURCE: Tepping, 1955.

nonmatches; that is to say, where the gross matching error is minimized for the characteristic.

Given fixed tolerance limits and linkage rules, we would apply the procedure of Srinivasan and Muthiah, starting with the characteristic having the smallest net error. This will usually be the characteristic with the lowest probability of erroneous matches since, with a single matching characteristic, erroneous matches will ordinarily have a larger probability than erroneous nonmatches. As suggested earlier, the lowest probability of erroneous matches will be associated with the characteristic having the smallest average number of elements per identification code class. One would next select the remaining characteristic that would yield the greatest reduction in net error. And this process would be repeated until the sign of the net error changed.

In the example in Table 3.4 the absolute value of the last positive net error (.008) was significantly less than that of the first negative net error (−.039). In many cases, however, one has two small values that do *not* differ significantly. In such situations, to determine whether to include or exclude the last characteristic, one should consider the absolute size of the net error with and without this characteristic, the probable magnitudes of the other (correlation and coverage) biases, the size of the gross error, and the cost of applying either alternative. Usually, gross error will be about the same on either side of the point of zero net error. It is important to note that coverage bias leads to an overestimate, and correlation bias usually leads to an underestimate. Similarly, an excess of erroneous matches over erroneous nonmatches causes underestimation, while an excess of erroneous nonmatches causes overestimation. Thus, if one has reason to believe that the coverage bias is greater than the correlation bias, one should favor the method that gives a *small* excess of erroneous matches. If the reverse is true (if correlation bias exceeds coverage bias), it will be desirable to have a *small* excess of erroneous nonmatches. However, these considerations do *not* apply where there is a *clear-cut* minimum for the net matching error.

Note that the emphasis is on getting the *minimum absolute* net matching error but permitting some small increase over this level to partially offset nonmatching biases. However, as noted previously, it is very risky to permit substantial increases in matching bias in order to counterbalance other biases. The measurement of biases is, by its very nature, subject to unknown biases of its own. The sign of a bias estimate is frequently correct, but estimates of bias magnitude are usually questionable. Even where the bias estimates appear to be reliable, balancing large biases may increase the variance.

Just as dangerous as trying to balance biases of opposite sign is unconditional reliance upon net matching error as a criterion for determining the optimal matching procedure. However, as we have already noted, procedures with relatively small (absolute) net errors tend to have relatively small gross errors. Where this is not the case, it may be desirable to see whether it is possible *at a moderate cost* to reduce the gross error for some alternative with small net error or to reduce net error (by, for example, a change in tolerance limits) for some alternative with small gross error.

To simplify the discussion in this chapter, we have covered in detail only those matching rules where a single set of identification characteristics is used for all reports; that is, procedures in which a source 1 report is compared with a source 2 report with respect to a set of characteristics which is the same for every comparison pair. If the two reports that make up the comparison pair agree within tolerance limits on this set of characteristics, they are considered matched; otherwise, they are classified as unmatched.

Another approach is to use distinctly different or partially overlapping sets of identification characteristics for different groups of events. For example, infant's name, parents' first names, parents' ages, and address may be the identification set for those comparison pairs where both a house number and street are shown for the address. For other cases, one may use mother's maiden name, parents' birthplaces, and father's occupation in place of the address. Alternatively, one might not bother to consider addresses at all for rural areas or places where the address does not provide a very precise identification of a particular household.

One example of a matching system using more than one set of identification characteristics is illustrated in Chapter 4, Section B.6. (A similar approach is used in the Pakistan PGE study, Population Growth Estimation, 1968, pp. 44–51.) After matching is attempted on the basis of an initial set of identification characteristics, the remaining nonmatched reports are compared using a new set of identification characteristics. This operation can be repeated a number of times, each time using the new set of identification characteristics and comparing only those reports remaining unmatched after the previous set of characteristics has been used. Such a matching system can yield better results than when a single set of characteristics is applied to all cases, *if* the personnel available are capable of applying the more complex rules objectively and in a properly controlled manner.

This type of matching procedure is appropriate when the quality of the identification is poor and highly variable in one or both sources— for example, when names have low discriminating power or may contain considerable recording errors and when addresses and other characteristics are recorded poorly or are frequently omitted. In such a situation, wide tolerance limits are required for the identifying data to be usable at all. To offset this, it is necessary to use more characteristics and to specify some *minimum* amount of agreement for a match. However, the variable nature of what information is available makes it necessary to specify alternative minima. That is, for any given set of characteristics, there will be a substantial number of pairs of records that do not meet the agreement criteria because of omissions but cannot be reliably classified as unmatched on the basis of these characteristics only.

Setting up such a matching operation would involve design principles similar to those for the simpler procedure. In general, one would try to select a given set of matching characteristics from identification items (with appropriate tolerance limits) that produce a negligible number of erroneous matches. The number of erroneous nonmatches (and net and gross matching error) can then be reduced to as close to zero as costs and the data available for identification permit, by applying successive sets of characteristics. However, great care must be exercised to keep the matching (and classification) errors under control, since with each successive set of matching characteristics employed the possibility of confusion and mistakes on the part of the matching staff increases.

F.6   IMPLICIT VERSUS EXPLICIT MATCHING RULES

The matching procedures described so far have been based on explicitly formulated criteria of what constitutes a match, whether expressed in terms of "tolerance limits" or of rules for "weighing" evidence. An alternative to this is matching based on implicit rules; that is, on a subjective assessment by the person doing the matching of whether a particular pair of reports refers to the same event. For example, a clerk, after examining a pair of birth reports, may consider whether there is more evidence for a match than there is against one. Each particular decision is left to the judgment of the clerk, although some general instructions or guidelines may be given in the form of specific examples.

Weighing the evidence for or against a match on the basis of implicit rules has the advantages of greater flexibility and of using all the available information. There are complex situations where it is almost impossible to phrase satisfactory explicit matching rules, but where a well-informed person—an intelligent and conscientious clerk or a junior professional—can make the subtle distinctions needed to classify one pair of reports as a match and another pair that is almost identical as a nonmatch.

On the other hand, implicit weighting, or any other procedure whose rules are not clearly defined, is almost impossible to control over time, even if one can secure satisfactory personnel for the initial period. Moreover, although *in theory* a matching procedure with implicit rules uses all the available information, there is no way of knowing if, *in fact,* this is the case. Are the matching clerks really using *all* the available evidence or merely some unknown portion of the information on the documents? Finally, with implicit rules it is difficult to set up experiments or other procedures for improving matching techniques. That is, one cannot pinpoint the features to be tested and cannot, therefore, determine which procedures, if any, should be improved.

In general, the drawbacks of implicit rules outweigh their advantages. Thus matching should usually be based on explicit criteria. One possible exception to this principle is the use of implicit rules in the professional review of doubtful cases turned up by an explicitly defined matching procedure. Such a review should be done by a very small number of highly qualified persons; and their decision, *along with the reasons for it,* should be recorded in every case where the explicit determination is reversed. The records of these special decisions should be reviewed in making new implicit rulings and should be continually studied with the aim of developing an explicit rule to replace them.

The continual review of any decisions based on implicit rules is particularly important in order to guard against the tendency for a trend, once started, to accelerate without any consideration being given to its effects on net matching error. That is, having made a decision in a borderline case, there is a tendency for the person who has made the decision to treat subsequent cases in the same way, even though many of them would have been decided differently if there had been no "precedent." In part, this results from a need to justify the wisdom of one's original decision and the tendency for a personal judgment to be reinforced rather than weakened by the need to defend it against opposing evidence. The development of a decision trend is also partly a result of inertia and "taking the course of least resistance"—that is, routinely following precedent rather than going through the effort of weighing all the evidence and reaching a conclusion.

The need for special decisions arises (a) when there is complex evidence which it may be unwise to have evaluated by a clerk (that is, the evidence may well confuse the clerk or increase the time and costs of matching) and (b) in very borderline situations where the decision depends upon the exact assessment of a small and possibly ambiguous piece of evidence. The first group of cases may be resolved by having professional reviewers apply an explicit rule or a general principle. The second group may be resolved by formulating an explicit rule to be applied by the regular clerical personnel. In both situations, it will be desirable, pending the formulation of an explicit rule, (1) to rotate the person(s) deciding particular types of cases at frequent intervals if competent substitutes are available and (2) to make sure special decisions tend to go one way about as often as they go the other way. In these cases, $P(M)$ must be so near .5 that treating half the cases as matched and half as unmatched produces a very small net matching error over all such decisions.

G. *Coverage Bias*

Basically, the PGE estimation procedure is a method of correcting one form of coverage error—erroneous omissions. The other form of coverage error is erroneous inclusions—the counting of births or deaths outside the scope of the inquiry. Such "out-of-scope" reports most often refer to events occurring outside either the time period or the geographic area to be covered by the estimate. In addition, a few out-of-scope reports may refer to events that did not take place at all or events that were misclassified as to type (for example, a stillbirth reported as a live birth and an early infant death).

Time period ("temporal") out-of-scope errors arise from the erroneous reporting of the date of occurrence of the vital event. Geographic out-of-scope errors have relatively little effect on the estimates of vital rates for an entire country, if sampling is not involved. Once sampling is introduced, geographic out-of-scope errors can become more common because of boundary problems and questions about the *de facto* versus the *de jure* location of the event. Moreover, the problem of boundary definitions becomes more acute as the size of the sample areas becomes smaller.

Out-of-scope reports, if present, will tend to bias both single-source and PGE estimates upward, although they usually make a greater contribution to net error in the case of PGE studies. As Seltzer and Adlakha (1969) have noted, there are two main approaches to controlling out-of-scope errors: (1) designing procedures to minimize the occurrence of out-of-scope reports and (2) using field follow-up to detect and correct such errors. This use of field follow-up as a control device is discussed in Section I.1 of this chapter. A variety of procedures to reduce the incidence of out-of-scope reports can be employed. Of course, each procedure has its associated costs; but before a specific technique is rejected as "too expensive," the costs of *not* using it (for example, an increase in bias or the subsequent cost of extensive field follow-up) also must be taken into account. Five methods of reducing coverage bias are described below.

1. The Use of "Check" Questions. If a few dates of local significance (for example, religious holidays, the start of the rainy season, the visit of some prominent person) can be determined, they can be used as "anchor points," by asking whether the birth or death occurred before or after one of the events. In this way one may be able to place a proportion of vital events as definitely in-scope or definitely out-of-scope with respect to the time period. As an aid in preventing geographic out-of-scope errors one can obtain reports for both *de jure* and *de facto* vital events and then attempt, by supplementary questions, to determine where each event reported actually occurred.

2. The Improvement of Boundary Definitions. Sometimes a religious or national holiday falls very near the date when the retrospective reference period should start. In this situation it is often desirable to use this well-known date in the questions about vital events rather than some unmemorable but proper starting date. (For example, "Since Christmas, did your aunt have a baby?" would be preferable to "Since January 1st, did your aunt have a baby?") Similarly, one may employ geographic boundaries that are easily identifiable (for example, rivers, major highways, or power lines) even at the sacrifice of sampling efficiency. If the use of these boundaries will make the resulting sample areas far too large, artificial but recognizable boundaries may be created by means of special signposts or marked stakes, boulders, or trees.

3. The Use of Statistical Procedures. The Brass procedure is essentially a method of correcting temporal out-of-scope errors by the use of information on the number of children ever born and the number of children dead. The technique of overlapping reference periods used by Som (1959) and by Neter and Waksberg (1965) has also been suggested as a direct method of correcting for temporal out-of-scope errors. With this method, interviews for two samples are taken six months apart, but the interviewer asks about all events in the preceding twelve months. The first (earlier) half of the reference period for the later interviews corresponds to the second (later) half of the reference period for the earlier interviews, and the estimated number of events for this six-month period should be the same (except for sampling error) for the two periods. If the estimated number of events for the overlapping six-month period is greater for the second interviews than it is for the first, the excess reflects the inclusion of out-of-scope events in the second interview. Unfortunately, the number of events during the period of overlap, as reported in the second interview, is usually less than the number reported in the first period because of memory loss. The inclusion of temporal out-of-scope events is a common form of memory loss—in this case, of the exact date of the event—and this increases over time as the suggested techniques assume. However, memory loss can just as easily lead to the omission of in-scope events (because the date is moved back before the time period) as it can to the inclusion of out-of-scope events (because the date is moved forward within the year).

4. The Adjustment of Work Loads. The work loads of the field workers can be modified so that they spend a greater proportion of their time on out-of-scope problems. This might involve more work in mapping areas, in specifying "landmarks" to aid in defining geographic boundaries, in maintaining house numbers, or in marking the boundaries by painting marks on trees, and so on. It might also involve additional work on clarifying time limits—for example, by listing names and dates of birth of siblings of the infant.

5. The Use of the Household-Change Technique. This technique involves interviewing the same sample households several times over a period of one to two years, observing any changes in the household (including changes in pregnancy status), and accounting for these changes in terms of births, deaths, in-migration and out-migration. Since this technique permits the fixing of many of the births and deaths between two known points in time, it is useful in reducing temporal out-of-scope errors. However, its potential value extends beyond reducing out-of-scope errors, and for this reason it is discussed more fully in Chapter 4, Section B.3.

H. Sampling and Sampling Error

H.1 THE SAMPLING FRAME

A "sampling frame" is a representation of the elements in a universe in a manner that facilitates sampling. The major purpose of a sampling frame is to ensure that each element of the universe has a known probability of being included in the sample. An excellent discussion of the various considerations involved in sampling-frame design can be found in Kish, *Survey Sampling* (1965).

In PGE estimation, the source 1 and source 2 samples must normally be the same, or one must be a subsample of the other. That is, for matching purposes any event that is properly included in the sample for one source must also be included in the sample for the other source; or, if one sample is a subsample of the other, the events to be included in the subsample must be the same for both sources. The reference here is to *events,* not to *reports;* an event is "included in the sample" for a given source if it should be reported in that source. For example, *all* events occurring within a given sample area during a specified time period (say, the year 1971) might be "in the sample" for both sources, even though neither source actually reported all such events.

Since the actual sample in a PGE study consists of geographic areas, the sampling frame must assign each vital event in the universe[14] to one and only one sample area. The problem here is similar to the problem of sampling in a household survey using an area sample, where some unique method must be found for assigning each household and person to one and only one sample area. Offhand, the problem of establishing a unique "location rule" looks fairly simple—one simply assigns each event, household, or person to the area in which it is physically located. However, although the physical location (that is, place of occurrence) of an event is unique, the location of a person varies from time to time, even within the same day. For example, a person may leave home to go to work, to market, or to visit relatives or friends and may or may not return home later that day. At a given instant in time, a household may have several possible "locations" depending upon the location of its various members. Even for vital events, which do have a unique "actual location," determining that location and getting a report of the event there may be difficult or impossible. For example, if a woman gives birth along the road on her way to a clinic or hospital, neither she nor those who helped her may be able to report the exact location to the registrar or enumerator.

Because of these difficulties, some systems have required that vital events be reported at the location where the person (the decedent or the parent of the infant) resides. This requirement is particularly likely to be useful in surveys where one can expect an appreciable lapse of time between the occurrence of an event and the survey interview.

The problems of defining where a person, household, or event should be reported are not confined to PGE or sample reporting. Civil registration systems must designate where a birth or death is to be registered; place of occurrence, place of usual residence, and place of legal residence have all been used for this purpose.

In counting people, the term "*de jure*" is usually applied in censuses when persons are to be reported where they live (at their "usual residence") and the term "*de facto*" when persons are to be reported wherever they happen to be staying at the time of the census (at their "actual location"). Similarly, in counting vital events, it is customary to refer to reporting at the place of "usual residence" of the decedent or infant as *de jure* reporting and to reporting at the place of occurrence of the event as *de facto* reporting.

The main restriction on a sampling frame is that there be a *unique and operational* manner of associating every element of the universe with one and only one "ultimate" sampling unit. Failure to associate a vital event with any sampling area will result in neither source including it, and thus in its erroneous omission. If the frame is defined in such a way that some events can be included in more than one place or different definitions are used by the two sources, the result may be the equivalent of an out-of-scope error if one source includes the event at one location and the other includes it at another location.

The rule used to associate a person or an event with the same unique sample area in both collection systems must be operationally functional as well as theoretically correct. Thus, a special registration system and a household survey may both define inclusion on a *de facto* basis—that is, on the basis of where the event occurred; and, in general, such a definition is to be preferred to the *de jure* definition for events. However, it is not sufficient merely to depend upon the phrase *"de facto"* and the simplicity of this definition to secure an identical sampling frame for both systems. It may be simple for the special registration system to apply the definition rigorously, but it will usually be more difficult for the household survey to do so; and many events occurring outside the sample area to usual residents of the area may be recorded by the survey interviewers. Of course, field follow-up may disclose such errors, but it may not. To make the *de facto* definition operational in the survey, interviewers must be instructed to check carefully that the birth or death actually occurred in the area, and not merely assume that this was the case because the mother was reported to be there in interviews both before and after the birth. The requirement that any definition used must be made operational has implications for questionnaire design, the training and supervision of interviewers, the frequency of enumeration, and the editing of completed questionnaires (see Section B.4 of Chapter 4).

Regardless of which general definition is used for determining where to report households, persons, or events, there will have to be special rules to take care of cases where the general definition is inapplicable. For example, there are persons with no usual place of residence (that is, persons who sleep wherever they can find temporary shelter), persons with multiple residences, and events for which place of occurrence cannot be determined.

In selecting the sampling frame for a PGE study—both the general definition of it and the special rules—one must consider the probabilities of undercoverage due to omitted events and correlation bias, as well as the probabilities of overcoverage due to the double-counting of events and out-of-scope errors. In addition, some attention should be given to the simplicity and ease of application of the rules—not for their own sake, but because complex and difficult rules are likely to be misapplied, leading to increased bias and variance. (Note, incidentally, that simplicity and ease of application are not the same thing. For example, the simple, but absolute, rule that all births and deaths must be reported at their *actual* place of occurrence is, as we have already noted, very difficult to apply.)

Although the same sampling frame should be used for both sources, it may be that a rule which is simple, is easy to apply, and gives good results for one source gives less satisfactory results for the other source. For example, *de facto* reporting tends to be better than *de jure* reporting for registration systems, provided registration is restricted to reporting within a few days after the event. The reverse tends to be true for surveys. Thus, it may be necessary to sacrifice some efficiency in the registration system for the sake of the survey or *vice versa*. Alternatively, it may be feasible in some situations to modify the matching procedures in order to be able to use *de facto* reporting for the registration source and *de jure* reporting for the survey. The problems associated with such special designs are discussed in Chapter 7, Section D.2. In general, however, the losses to registration through the use of *de jure* reporting and the losses to the survey through the use of *de facto* reporting are minor. For the bulk of vital events, the two locations are the same; and, in any case, one can usually work out an acceptable system on either basis.

Although the rule for associating vital events with sampling units will almost always have to be the same for both sources in a PGE study, there is no requirement that the rule for linking the "base population" to sampling units be the same as the rule for linking events. Actually, it is impossible to have such a requirement, since no matter what rule is used for vital events, it cannot be strictly applied to persons. This is because persons are necessarily counted at a fixed instant in time, whereas vital events must be counted over an interval of time. Unfortunately, this distinction is often not recognized and an attempt is made to make the counting rules for the population and for events "consistent." In fact, if the rules used for each are correct, they will produce consistent national estimates regardless of the label applied. Moreover, there are cases where it is difficult to produce consistent local estimates without using different definitions for the base population and the number of vital events. For these reasons, in designing PGE studies, it is best to consider the rules for persons and events separately and judge them on their own merits.

In any case, for most births and deaths, the variations in counting rules will make no difference because the event occurred where the decedent or mother was living at the time and where the family was living both before and after the event. It is important not to invest so much time and energy in dealing with the rare and complex exceptions that inadequate attention is given to the more common and simpler cases.

H.2   SAMPLE SIZE AND INTRACLASS CORRELATION

Early work in sample surveys tended to concentrate on sampling error. More recently, work on nonsampling error has begun to monopolize the attention of statisticians to the point where there is now a tendency to ignore sampling error. As Scott (1967, footnote 2, pp. 157–58) notes:

Sampling statisticians often have to face the argument from field work specialists that "sampling error is unimportant compared with observational errors," so that efficient sample design is a mere luxury. While it is true that sampling and observational errors have to be considered together and appropriately balanced, the above argument condemning sampling efficiency in absolute terms is nonsensical. If sampling error is unimportant in any survey the sample should be reduced until it begins to become important, otherwise money is being wasted. A useful dodge for sidestepping this kind of argument is to speak always in terms of *cost for a given sampling error* rather than *sampling error for a given cost.* . . . That one sample involves a 40 percent higher sampling error for given cost than another may not sound very serious, but when we point out that the former costs twice as much for given error, the practical man begins to listen.

The current overemphasis on nonsampling error is, in a sense, a reaction to the earlier notion that only 100-percent coverage could give adequate figures for the entire population. The advance of statistical science has demonstrated that complete coverage is neither necessary *nor* sufficient for accurate measurement in the field of population or in any other field. Thus, to measure population growth accurately, it is necessary to consider *both* sampling *and* nonsampling error and to balance the two in order to minimize the *total* error.

The major trade-offs between sampling and nonsampling error relate to size of the sample and the size of the sampling units. The trade-offs between an increased sample size and other forms of error reduction can be summarized simply. On the one hand, as the sample size increases, sampling error tends, other things being equal, to decrease. On the other hand, an increase in the size of the sample means that any given data collection or data processing expenditure is spread more thinly, which in turn tends, other things being equal, to increase nonsampling errors.

With respect to size of the sampling units, larger units are desirable in order to decrease costs per household and to reduce boundary errors. Small sampling units may make resident registrars infeasible or very expensive since no single area would be a full-time job for a registrar. With sufficiently large units, resident interviewers or registrars can be used and this may improve coverage. More important, if the use of resident registrars is coupled with use of nonresident interviewers for a household survey, correlation bias will tend to be reduced because of the marked differences in the sources of information about vital events that such an arrangement entails.

Counterbalancing these advantages of large sampling units are the disadvantages in terms of increased errors or costs associated with both matching and sampling. Where the blocking unit used in matching is the sampling unit, the difficulty of a matching operation tends to increase roughly with the square of the number of true events in the unit and thus with the size of the unit. The sampling variance of an estimated mean is related to the number of sampling units (k) and the mean number of elements per unit $(\bar{h})^{15}$ by the following approximate expression:

$$\sigma_{\bar{x}}^2 = \frac{\sigma^2}{k\bar{h}}\left[1 + \delta\,(\bar{h} - 1)\right] = \frac{\sigma^2(1 - \delta)}{h} + \frac{\sigma^2\delta}{k} \quad , \qquad\qquad [3.21]$$

where

$\sigma_{\bar{x}}^2$ = variance of the estimate of a mean or vital rate;

σ^2 = variance between sampling units in the frame for the characteristic being estimated (that is, σ^2 is a parameter of the frame not affected by $\bar{h}$ or k);

δ = intraclass correlation between elements within sampling units;

k = number of sampling units;

h = number of elements (persons) in the sample; and

$\bar{h}$ = h/k = average number of elements per sampling unit.

The intraclass correlation δ is a measure of the degree of "internal homogeneity" of the sampling units. If all the elements in each sampling unit were identical (for example, if either all or none of the individuals in a PGE area died during the year, or all or none of the women aged 20–24 in an area had a baby), the intraclass correlation would be 1. If the resemblance between two elements from the same area is the same as that of two elements from different areas, then $\delta = 0$. For example, if the difference in the probability of death during the year for two randomly selected persons is the same whether they are selected from the same area or from two different areas, then $\delta = 0$ for estimates of the number of deaths.

The value of $\sigma_{\bar{x}}^2$ depends on the mean size of the sampling unit, $\bar{h}$, both directly and through δ. A very small δ may still have considerable importance for a large $\bar{h}$. For example, with $\delta = .001$ and $\bar{h} = 5{,}000$, the variance would be six times that of a simple random sample of the same size. If the homogeneity measure δ were to stay the same as the size of sampling unit $\bar{h}$ increased, and if $h(= k\bar{h})$ were also kept fixed (that is, if the number of sampling units k were reduced as $\bar{h}$ increased), it is clear from equation 3.21 that the variance, $\sigma_{\bar{x}}^2$ (or $\sigma_{\hat{n}}^2$) would increase.

Actually, δ tends to get smaller as $\bar{h}$ increases; that is, for most characteristics, larger areas tend to be more heterogeneous. This also tends to be true of births and deaths for units larger than a household.[16] For example, households in the same village may tend to be similar with respect to age composition, and therefore with respect to probabilities of birth or death; but within the same district there will be less resemblance between randomly selected households in birth and death probabilities; and within a province, still less resemblance. In general, also, some unit costs decrease as $\bar{h}$ increases. Thus, with larger sample units one can usually cover a larger number of elements for the same total expenditure, with a resultant reduction in the variance of the PGE estimate.

H.3   ADMINISTRATIVE AND COST CONSIDERATIONS

The advantages of large sampling units in terms of reduced coverage error have already been mentioned. However, the major reasons for using large units are administrative (because of the desire to have sample areas large enough to permit full-time, resident field personnel) and financial. Furthermore, the cost and administrative considerations are related. With small sampling units, either one must use part-time interviewers and/or registrars, or the interviewers and the registrars must cover more than one sample area. If the sampling units are independently selected, as is assumed in the case of the k units in equation 3.21, there will be substantial travel costs, which will increase the total cost.

Various cost functions have been used to represent the cost picture with clustered samples. The simplest of these assumes that there are some costs, c_1, that increase with the number of sample areas, k (that is, costs for travel, mapping, sample selection, and so on), and other costs, c_2, that increase with the total number of elements, h. Although some of the relations are nonlinear (for example, travel costs are more likely to increase proportionally to $\sqrt{k}$ rather than proportionately to k), a linear cost function like the following is frequently a useful approximation:

$$C = c_1 k + c_2 k \bar{h} \quad , \qquad\qquad [3.22]$$

where

C = total cost of data collection;
c_1 = unit cost per sampling unit for those costs which vary proportionally to k, the number of sampling units, independently of the size of the sampling unit; and
c_2 = unit cost per element for those costs which vary proportionately to h, the number of elements, regardless of the number of sampling units.

In other words, the total cost is equal to the sum of the costs that vary proportionately to the number of units and the costs that vary proportionately to the number of elements. Costs that vary with the number of sampling units regardless of the number of elements per sampling unit include mapping costs, sample selection costs, and the costs of interviewer and supervisor travel between sampling units. Costs per element include such items as interviewing time per household, travel between households within sampling units, calls to locate a satisfactory respondent, and editing, coding, and punching the data collected. Some costs may vary both with the number of elements and with the number of sampling units, as, for example, do costs for matching, field follow-up, and interviewer recruitment. These latter costs must be allocated, at least approximately, between c_1 and c_2. In addition, there are costs that vary with k or $k\bar{h}$, but not in a linear manner. However, equation 3.22, although far from exact, is a simple and useful approximation.

Given a fixed budget of C for data collection, the average size of the sampling unit that will result in the minimum sampling variance (derived from equations 3.21 and 3.22) is

$$\bar{h}_{opt} = \sqrt{\frac{c_1(1-\delta)}{c_2\delta}} \quad . \tag{3.23}$$

Thus when $\delta = .002$ (see Chapter 2, Section D), $\bar{h} \doteq 20\sqrt{c_1/c_2}$. The corresponding value for the number of sampling units can be found by substituting the value of $\bar{h}_{opt}$ obtained from equation 3.23 in the cost equation (3.22) and then solving for k.

A rough indication of the increase in variance due to departures from the optimum cluster size can be seen in Table 3.8, which shows, for various ratios of c_1 to c_2, the ratio of the variance obtained by using specified cluster sizes to the variance obtained using the optimum cluster size for a given cost ratio. It is evident that very large clusters can only be justified by either major gains in the control of nonsampling errors or very important administrative advantages.

These issues are explored more fully in *Sample Survey Methods and Theory* (Hansen, Hurwitz, and Madow, 1953), which gives formulae for more complex sample designs (designs involving stratification and multistage sampling appropriate to PGE studies), presents and discusses

Table 3.8   Relative Increase in Variance of Specified Sample Design Compared with Variance of Optimum Design, by Cluster Size and Ratio of c_1/c_2, Given a Fixed Total Budget

Cost ratio used[1] c_1/c_2	Optimum cluster size for the given cost ratio[2] $(\bar{h}_{opt})$	Cluster size used[3]			
		100	500	1,000	5,000
1	20	1.1	1.8	2.8	10.1
5	50	1.0	1.7	2.5	9.1
10	70	1.0	1.6	2.3	8.5
50	160	1.0	1.3	1.8	6.4
100	225	1.1	1.1	1.6	5.4

[1] See equation 3.22 for definitions of c_1 and c_2.

[2] Approximate values of $\bar{h}_{opt}$ obtained from equation 3.23, assuming $\delta = .002$ and the specified cost ratio.

[3] Approximate values of $\sigma^2_{\bar{h}}/\sigma^2_{\bar{h}_{opt}}$ derived from equation 3.21, equation 3.22, and $\bar{h}_{opt}$ as calculated; and assuming a fixed total budget, $\delta = .002$, and the specified cost ratio and cluster size.

more complex cost functions, and provides detailed procedures for estimating sampling errors, determining costs and intraclass correlations, and determining optimal sample designs. Chapter 7 of this handbook also contains more exact formulae for estimating the variance of the PGE estimate, $\sigma_{\hat{n}}^2$.

I. Field Follow-up and Additional Matching Topics

I.1   FIELD FOLLOW-UP

The amount, type, and timing of field follow-up is an important aspect of study design. Those making decisions in this area should weigh the anticipated costs against the anticipated gains. The gains and costs of the "optimum" field follow-up plan must be assessed in light of the gains and costs of alternative techniques for improving quality. Some ongoing field follow-up that continues throughout the collection phase of the study is certainly essential, if only to prevent field workers from "relaxing" and permitting the quality of their output to deteriorate. However, greater emphasis should be placed on follow-up in the early phases, in order to refine the procedures and techniques to be used throughout the study. Funds properly spent in this area will have a substantial effect on the quality of the results for the duration of the study.

Broadly speaking, field follow-up has three major functions, though the distinctions between them are often ignored: first, it is a quality control procedure; second, it is a method of improving the design of the data collection and matching operations; and third, it is a method of detecting and correcting individual matching, coverage, and content errors.

In practice, field follow-up is often used where there is considerable concern about the quality of the matching operation. Some or all nonmatched events may be sent to the field where there is concern about the low match rates achieved in the office, doubtful matches may be sent for follow-up when there is concern about the adequacy of the matching criteria used to distinguish between events, and virtually all reports—matched or nonmatched—may be sent to the field to guard against defects in a newly instituted set of office matching procedures.

Another major use of field follow-up is to identify out-of-scope reports present in one or both sources. As discussed in Section G, such reports introduce an upward bias in the PGE estimate. They arise because events for the wrong time period or the wrong place are included along with the correctly reported events. Since these out-of-scope events are most often found among the nonmatched reports, the use of field follow-up in connection with out-of-scope reports is related to its use in resolving matching problems.

Unfortunately, field follow-up has often been employed without a considered review of its likely costs and benefits, with regard to both the particular problem at issue and total error. For example, if one sends only the unmatched reports for field investigation, the number of erroneous nonmatches may be reduced; but the number of erroneous matches is usually left unchanged. The result may be an increase in net matching error and, even more serious, the addition to response correlation bias of another bias in the same direction (toward underestimation). Moreover, although it is reasonable to assume that the unmatched cases will contain a larger proportion of out-of-scope events than the matched cases (since the failure to match may be due to the cases being out-of-scope), it is not true that *all* matched cases are in-scope. That is, there may well be some out-of-scope cases that are included in *both* sources.

Several of the problems relating to field follow-up can be effectively illustrated by citing the experience of the Pakistan Population Growth Estimation Experiment. In Pakistan, "unconfirmed nonmatched events were sent to field inspectors concerned for field investigation" (Population Growth Estimation, 1968, p. 50). Thus, according to Yusuf (1968a), 200 out of 2,283 birth registrations and 391 out of 1,823 births reported in the survey were sent back for field investigation. As a result of this field follow-up, it was determined that ten of the reports investigated actually matched, while seven of the registration births and 135 of the survey births were out-of-scope.

The ten reports determined to be matches by field investigation in the Pakistan PGE for 1962 represented less than 1 percent of the total of 1,313 matches. Thus, not correcting them would have had a trivial effect on the PGE estimate (compared to the effects of other sources of error). The seven out-of-scope registration reports also would have had no appreciable effect on the PGE estimate. Consequently, the value of the field investigation rested almost entirely upon the elimination of the bias (possibly substantial) caused by the 135 out-of-scope survey births, and this reduction in bias was obtained at a substantial cost. It is important to compare this kind of gain with those achievable by equivalent expenditures on some other phases of the study. For example, one could spend an equivalent amount to improve the quality of the *original* data collection through improved training and/or better supervision of interviewers, the addition of special procedures to better define the date of the vital event, checking *de jure* against *de facto* reports of vital events, and improved mapping to provide better definitions of sampling unit boundaries.

It will be noted that in Pakistan only nonmatched cases were sent to the field for follow-up. As we have stated before, the exclusion of matched reports from the follow-up involves the risk of increasing net matching error and failing to detect some out-of-scope reports among the matches. However, in the Pakistan study, almost all the gain from field follow-up was in the detection of out-of-scope events. There was no appreciable change in the number of erroneous nonmatches and no great change in net matching error. It also seems probable that there were relatively few matched out-of-scope events;

only seven out-of-scope reports were found among the nonmatched registrations in Pakistan, and there would presumably be even fewer out-of-scopes among the matched registrations. Thus, the restriction of field follow-up to unmatched cases was, *for Pakistan,* an efficient use of resources. That is, it permitted the study personnel to concentrate on those cases (the unmatched ones) most likely to contain the kind of error (out-of-scope error) efficiently detected by field follow-up.

However, the Pakistan experience does not necessarily apply elsewhere. In other countries—for example, where there *is* more matching error—field follow-up may detect more matching error than out-of-scope error. Since the initial stage of a PGE study is likely to (and *should*) entail extensive field follow-up anyway, checking on a few "confirmed matches" will not increase field costs greatly. It is advisable, therefore, to check some matched reports in addition to the unmatched cases during this stage—both for matching errors and for out-of-scope errors (even though the latter are much more likely among the unmatched cases). The objective should be to determine where an equivalent reduction in error can be achieved at a lower cost by field follow-up than by other means. Once the areas where field follow-up is more efficient have been determined, the investigation should concentrate on these areas and deemphasize those where costs are high and/or the "yield" in terms of error reduction is low.

The timing of field follow-up is particularly sensitive since it may affect the entire design of the survey and the registration source. Here the problem is to balance the accuracy gained by prompt follow-up against the almost inevitable deterioration of independence it causes, keeping in mind cost and administrative constraints. A field investigation long after the fact may do little to improve data quality, since much of the relevant information may be lost or forgotten. In other words, increasing the time between collection and follow-up decreases the ability of the follow-up interviewer to get accurate information. On the other hand, reducing the time between the original data collection and the field follow-up may mean increased correlation bias because of the impact of three persons checking on vital events within a relatively short time period.

The discussion in this section deals primarily with detecting and correcting matching error and controlling out-of-scope error; other uses of field follow-up—particularly quality control and the improvement of study techniques—are discussed in Chapter 4. The following general points, however, deserve repeating: (1) a substantial part of the effort and expense of field follow-up should be concentrated in the initial stages to develop techniques and procedures, and some matched cases as well as nonmatched and doubtful ones should be sent to the field during this phase of the study; (2) in spite of the costs and difficulties involved, a modest level of continuous follow-up should be maintained throughout the study; and (3) decisions concerning the amount, type, and timing of follow-up should be made only after a careful review of the costs, the effects on total error, and the possible alternatives.

I.2 MATCHING MODES

The physical process of comparing the reports of vital events from the two sources to determine whether or not they match can be carried out by human beings, by mechanical punchcard equipment, or by an electronic computer. However, the fact that human clerks, punchcard equipment, and electronic computers can all do the job does not imply they can do it in the same way or that they can do it with equal efficiency (Marks, 1958).

In choosing one of these matching modes, one must consider the nature of the matching job and the type of personnel and machines available. This assessment must go beyond such generalities as "computers are fast" or "human matchers are flexible and can exercise common sense"; for, although each mode has a number of theoretical advantages, these are often negated in practice. Computers may turn out to be very slow after the time required to develop and test programs and to code and keypunch the two files of vital events reports is taken into account. On the other hand, the flexibility and common sense of matching clerks may, in practice, amount to little more than uncontrolled carelessness and prejudice.

More positively, one can overcome various disadvantages of a particular mode by appropriate planning and by allocating sufficient resources. For example, the time needed for the clerks to do the matching can be reduced by assigning more clerks to the task, and a computer matching operation can be made more flexible by making the computer program more complex. Here again, as in other aspects of design, we must balance the anticipated costs and gains of alternate courses of action.

The major advantage of using machines in matching (either punchcard equipment or electronic computers) is that one is assured, whatever the explicit matching rules are, that they will be applied uniformly and rapidly throughout the matching operation. Because the rules are applied consistently from report to report, the quality of the matching operation will be maintained throughout the study, unless the nature of the vital events reports or the quality of identifying information changes sufficiently to reduce the applicability of the original matching rules. Machines, unlike humans, will not grow bored and develop short-cuts as the matching operation continues; nor do they tend to function more erratically before lunch or at the end of the day. Moreover, the very fact that machines (particularly computers) force one to develop very explicit matching rules can be counted as a gain (see section F.6, "Implicit versus explicit matching rules").

An additional advantage of electronic computers is that very complicated matching rules (for example, those involving multiple sets of matching criteria) can be used without the danger of matching clerks being confused or frustrated by their complexity. With conventional punchcard equipment, complex matching rules may necessitate the manual shifting of large numbers of card stacks, which can easily lead to confusion and error. Of course, the computer programmer also can be confused by complicated matching rules, but the programmer's mistakes (unlike those of the machine operators) can be corrected before the matching operation starts.

These advantages of machine matching should be weighed against the costs and time of preparing the computer programs (or wiring the necessary boards) and preparing the vital events reports for machine input. Systems analysis and programming takes time; debugging the matching program takes even longer. Even after these operations are completed, there are often delays because various specialists are working on other assignments. The availability of an underutilized computer (a fairly common situation in developing countries) does not mean that qualified programmers and systems analysts are underutilized.

A major disadvantage of machine matching compared to manual matching is that birth and death reports of both sources received from the field have to be transformed into suitable machine-readable input. Usually, this involves at least some editing and coding of source 1 and 2 event reports and extensive keypunching and verification. (If the quality of the identification data collected is poor, considerable editing and coding may also be involved.) Since punching errors contribute directly to matching error by increasing the number of erroneous nonmatches, very strict quality-control standards must be maintained for the punching operation. Moreover, control measures adequate to the task (such as checking card or tape listings against the original source documents) may, along with the required coding and punching, add significantly to the time needed to carry out the matching.

The punchcards themselves can be a source of difficulty if they are lost or damaged in the course of the matching operation. Although this problem arises most often when the matching is done with sorters and collators, it may also occur when card input is used with some small computers. In the case of matching on a computer with tape drives, most of the problems of card loss or damage can be avoided by immediately converting the cards to tape or by using some of the newer devices that permit direct key-to-tape input.

Manual matching has two important advantages compared with either of the machine modes: flexibility and low start-up costs. "Flexibility" here does not mean just the absence of rigid matching rules. Some rigid matching rules must be part of any matching operation. It refers to both administrative flexibility and the ability of the matching staff to recognize and handle special cases easily. Especially when a study is just getting under way, it may be difficult to foresee what problems will arise in the matching operation. Here again, the flexibility of manual matching is an advantage. A related advantage is the relatively low start-up cost of a manual matching operation. Whatever matching mode is used, time will be required to frame the matching rules; but once these have been decided, manual matching can be started with relatively little effort compared to either of the machine modes.

Manual matching is particularly easy to do where the blocking units within which matching is attempted are small. For example, with ultimate clusters averaging 100 households one might expect no more than about 20–25 birth reports a year from each source. In such a situation the examination and comparison of all the relevant documents from both sources will be a simple task.

On the cost side, manual matching is slow and there is little assurance that the matching rules will be followed consistently (either between clerks or by an individual clerk) as time goes on. Matching is a repetitive task and requires great attention to detail. If the study continues for some time, the clerks may become bored and careless. Alternatively, they may resign, and new clerks will have to be recruited and trained. Thus, if manual matching is used, considerable resources must be devoted to the continuous supervision and training of the matching staff.

Another problem arises with regard to manual matching when the blocking units are quite large: The physical wear and tear on the source documents necessitated by frequent comparisons among the large number of reports can result in the destruction of the reports prior to the conclusion of the matching operation. If copies of the event reports are made in order to deal with this problem, this will add to the costs of manual matching.

In many situations, particularly in developing countries, manual matching is chosen largely by default; that is, the facilities and personnel needed to conduct a successful machine match cannot be obtained within the PGE study budget. In any case, because of the difficulty and cost involved in starting a computer matching operation, this mode is generally not justified unless the matching operation is quite large. Other requirements for computer matching include the availability of appropriate programming staff, computer time, and high-quality keypunching. The requirements for mechanical matching with conventional punchcard equipment are not as rigorous as those for computer matching, but one does need experienced machine operators and high-quality keypunching. In brief, one should think carefully about assigning the matching task to a data processing unit unless it is a strong organization and is accustomed to meeting performance standards.

Over the long run, there is room for considerable research into the use of mixed modes for matching. Clearly, the "best" matching mode is one that uses machines to do the jobs they do well (large-scale rapid collation based on invariant and explicit rules) and uses clerks to do the kind of matching they do well (intelligent evaluation of matching evidence on the basis of loosely defined rules). This is, in fact, essentially the procedure adopted in many successful matching operations. An excellent example of the efficient use of clerks in matching is described by Perkins and Jones (1965). The clerks entered a supplementary matching code based on evidence other than that used in the main matching identification code. For example, they entered "++" to indicate that "excluding information used in the address-name coding, the remaining evidence is *very strong* that the sample person is included in the Census household being compared."

The supplementary matching codes described by Perkins and Jones could have been determined by machine by defining a large number of additional matching characteristics with very elaborate tolerances. However, the additional programming needed would have been enormous. A solution was found by combining all the other identifying information into a single "matching characteristic," but having clerks make a decision based on broadly defined "tolerances."

A good starting point for experimentation with mixed matching modes would be to use a machine match to determine which cases clearly match and which clearly do *not* match. The remaining cases can then be evaluated manually, placing a premium on human flexibility and judgment. Finally, some (hopefully, very small) proportion of "totally ambiguous" cases may be returned to the field for further investigation.

I.3   ONE-WAY MATCHING

Most of the discussion of matching and PGE estimation in this chapter has focused on situations in which "two-way matching" is employed; that is, where the matching status of all the vital events reports from both sources is determined. One may also prepare a PGE estimate on the basis of a "one-way match." A one-way match involves going through the list of reports for one of the two sources and determining, for each report in that source, whether or not a match exists among the reports of the other system. It does not involve determining explicitly the match status of each report in the second source.

In principle, both a one-way match and a two-way match can provide the information needed to make a PGE estimate. Furthermore, either procedure can be used when both sources employ sampling, when only one does, or when neither does (that is, when both sources attempt to obtain reports for all events in the sample frame). Although there is no necessary relationship between the matching and the sampling designs employed, practically all studies with sampling in both sources have used two-way matching and practically all studies with sampling in one source have used one-way matching. In the former case—where sampling is used in both sources—two-way matching is generally preferred because geographic out-of-scope reports can be detected more readily. If either or both sources do not employ sampling, one-way matching is usually a necessity for reasons of cost. Because of the apparent drawbacks of other design combinations, the following discussion is limited to the two combinations usually encountered. Indeed, unless otherwise specified, it should be assumed that if two-way matching is mentioned both sources use sampling and if one-way matching is mentioned only one does.

The choice between one-way matching (and sampling in one source) and two-way matching (and sampling in both sources) usually depends upon considerations of cost and feasibility, rather than on explicit considerations of bias and variance. If one of the sources already provides reports for the *entire* population—for example, if a civil registration system exists prior to the design of the PGE study—a one-way match can often be used to provide a PGE estimate economically. Unfortunately, because of the quality of the data or because of administrative problems, it is not always possible to utilize this economic alternative.

The most common use of one-way matching in vital statistics estimation is in completeness studies of a civil registration system. Such a study typically obtains reports of vital events in a sample household survey and matches these reports against the reports in the civil registration system. The unregistered reports included in the sample survey are identified, but no attempt is made to identify registered reports that should be included in the sample survey but were not. The resulting PGE estimate is

$$\hat{N} = \frac{N_1 n_2}{m} = \frac{N_1}{w_1} \, ,$$

[3.24]

where

$\hat{N}$ = PGE estimate of number of vital events,

N_1 = number of vital events reported in source 1 for the entire population,

n_2 = estimated number of vital events reported by source 2 for the entire population,

m = estimated number of matched vital events for the entire population, and

$w_1 = \dfrac{m}{n_2}$ = estimated completeness of source 1.

Note that the sole difference between equation 3.24 and equation 3.5 is that equation 3.24 uses the universe value N_1 in place of the sample estimate n_1 used in equation 3.5. Since n_1 is an estimate of N_1, the PGE estimates, $\hat{n}$ and $\hat{N}$, are the same, except for the sampling variation of n_1 around N_1 and the correlation between n_1 and m. If the true completeness rate of source 1 is greater than .5, $\hat{N}$ will almost always have a lower variance than $\hat{n}$. This is one advantage of using one-way matching or, rather, of using N_1 instead of n_1.[17]

Another advantage of one-way matching is that geographic out-of-scope errors (coverage bias) will have a negligible effect on the estimate of $\hat{N}$—provided enough of the source 1 file (that is, the source without sampling) is searched so that vital events erroneously included in the source 2 sample will be matched if they were (properly) included in source 1. For example, one may compare all source 2 reports that do not match in the source 2 sample areas with the source 1 reports for adjacent areas, place of recent residence, place of mother's parents' residence, and so on. If the completeness of source 1 tends to be different near the boundaries of the sample areas than at their center, some coverage bias may remain; but this will usually be a "second order effect" that can safely be ignored.

Although designs employing one-way matching can be used to minimize the effects of coverage bias, they have their own bias problems. These include miscounting error, misfiling error, and "conditioning" of the population residing in the sample areas to reporting vital events.

"Miscounting" occurs when the value of N_1 available does not accurately reflect the true number of source 1 reports. Of course, miscounting can lead to either an overcount or an undercount in the number of reports. Clearly, if N_1, for whatever reason, is a net overcount, the PGE estimate $\hat{N}$ will also be overestimated, whereas if N_1 is an undercount, $\hat{N}$ will be underestimated. Moreover, both the direction and the extent of miscounting will vary between PGE areas and will therefore contribute to the variance of a PGE estimate based on a one-way match.

A major source of bias attributable to miscounting error is the use of a value for N_1 based on a count made at a different level from that at which the matching is done. This may happen if matching is done centrally, based on copies of individual registrations sent to some provincial or national office, while N_1 is based on the sum of the counts made in the local registration offices. In such a situation, N_1 will tend to be an overcount of the number of source 1 reports actually used for matching because of "slippage"; that is, because of losses that occur in transmitting copies of individual registration certificates from the local registration offices to the correct central office. On the other hand, if matching is based on the individual reports on file at the local registration offices, while N_1 is based on a tabulation of the individual reports reaching the central office, N_1 will be an undercount.

Miscounting bias can be avoided or corrected by making sure that N_1 actually reflects *a physical count of the file used for matching*. For example, if matching is done in the local office, N_1 should be a count of certificates filed in the local offices. Periodic recounts should be made of the certificates in the files used for matching in the sample areas. These recounts should be checked against the original counts for the sample areas. If major discrepancies develop, steps should be taken either to correct N_1 for *all* areas or to substitute an estimate based on the (corrected) counts for the sample areas only. Equivalent measures can be adopted to prevent miscounting bias where matching is done against a central office file.

Misfiling, which causes erroneous nonmatches and thus leads to an upward bias in the PGE estimate, can occur in designs using one-way or two-way matching. Generally misfiling is easier to control with a two-way match because both sources, being limited to samples, are of a more manageable size and because all the reports of both sources are examined.

With one-way matching, if a registered event is included among the reports of another geographic area there is practically no chance of finding the certificate when the event is reported in source 2, unless the entire file for source 1 is searched. With central office matching, reports may be placed in the wrong file by accident or punchcards may be punched with the wrong area identification. Another very common source of misfiling error is events registered at the wrong local office. This will affect the matching results—whether done at the local level or at the central office—unless the registration reports (or punchcards) are correctly rearranged in the central office.

The most frequent reason for filing certificates in the wrong office is a difference between the place of occurrence of an event and the place of residence of the decedent or the newborn infant. Although many registration systems have some arrangements for the transmission of the registration record from the place where the registration formalities happened to have been completed to the place(s) where the record is supposed to be filed, the process tends to be slow and is often unreliable.

Misfiling bias can be reduced by searching for events in source 1 files at the place of occurrence *and* at the (actual and/or legal) place of residence. This technique is, however, limited by the extent to which accurate information about the place of residence can be obtained for events reported on a place of occurrence basis or by the accuracy of information about the place of occurrence (or place of legal residence) for events reported on a place of current residence basis.

A simpler technique may be to select a sample from the source 1 file and, from this sample, estimate the proportion of certificates in the file that are misfiled, regardless of the cause. This estimate can be used to correct N_1—that is, to estimate the number of source 1 events with *correctly filed certificates*. The corrected value of N_1 can then be used in equation 3.24. The estimate of misfiled source 1 certificates can be made by using source 2 sample areas and checking there for misfiled certificates.[18] For example, in a household survey, one might try to list all events that involved residents of the area as well as those that occurred in the area. If the civil register was set up on a *de facto* basis, one could see whether any events reported by the survey as occurring outside the area to residents of the area were erroneously included in the civil registration for the area. One could also gather reports of events occurring near ambiguous segment boundaries in the household survey, and those reported by the survey as occurring *outside* the sample area could be checked to determine whether the registration reports were filed *inside* the area.

Conditioning bias may arise because the population in the sample areas covered by source 2 becomes "sensitized" to the reporting of vital events or because the registration authorities in these areas become more attentive to their registration duties, so that the completeness of source 1 improves there. When this occurs, a higher proportion of vital events will be registered for the sample areas than for the rest of the country. Thus, w_1 will be a valid measure of registration completeness only for the sample areas covered by source 2, while, for the country as a whole, w_1 will provide an overestimate of the completeness of the number of registered events.

The conditioning of source 2 sample households (or sample areas as a whole) can be made negligible by frequent changes in the sample, so that neither the population nor the registration officials have much chance to become "sensitized." Unfortunately, frequent rotation of the source 2 sample generally adds to the costs of data collection as well as placing additional administrative burdens on those directing the field work. Additional aspects of conditioning bias are discussed in Section C of Chapter 7.

Over and above the bias problems just discussed are issues related to the variances, costs, and feasibility of carrying out a one-way or a two-way match in any particular situation. Since it is more expensive to collect and analyze data for the entire population than for a (small) sample, the use of a design with one-way matching is usually limited to situations where the source 1 data are being collected independently of the PGE study (for example, the civil registration system) or are low-cost supplementary data about vital events obtained in a population census (for example, from a census question on births in the last three months).

Ideally, the money saved by doing a one-way match to the "free" source (the census or civil registration system) should more than pay for the costs of the matching operation. If this is in fact the case, PGE estimates can be prepared with a minimum of cost and effort. However, a number of factors may make it difficult or impossible to use such a "free" source in PGE estimation. The quality of identification information in the census or civil registration vital events reports may be so poor that the matching is subject to very large errors. The registration or census files may be so organized that searching them to determine whether they contain a specific report is expensive and prone to error. In some situations it may be impossible to obtain sufficient cooperation from the registration or census authorities to make a matching operation feasible. Whether the civil registration system can be used is an important issue in the design of a PGE study, and one we shall return to in Chapters 4 and 5. In addition, Chapter 7 contains an extended discussion of the costs and variances of designs with one-way matching and subsampling.

J. *Estimating the Base Population*

In addition to estimating the number of vital events, a PGE study must provide estimates of birth and death rates, which means that an estimate of the current population must be available. This base population estimate may be derived either from one of the two sources or from an independent estimate. If the population estimate is supplied by either of the two sources, it will almost always be the population enumerated in a household survey. Independent estimates, on the other hand, are usually based on the most recent census updated to take into account population growth.

For PGE studies, either method will usually lead to satisfactory results unless the survey or independent estimate is clearly deficient. Since how the population base is derived has, in general, only a minor effect on the PGE estimates of vital rates, one should *not* devote much of the planning effort to this decision.

The relative robustness of dual system estimates under different ways of deriving the base population is in marked contrast to the situation of a single system. For single system estimates, a base population figure derived from the same sample as the estimate of the number of events may have considerable advantages over an independent estimate for reducing the variance or the bias or both, even where there has been a satisfactory recent census and there are adequate independent data for estimating growth since the census.[19] Because of the undoubted advantage of using survey-based population estimates in single system estimation, one must guard against assuming that the same bias and variance considerations apply with equal force to PGE estimation.

J.1 BIAS CONSIDERATIONS

In theory, a modest bias in the base population can be used to offset an equivalent bias in the number of births or deaths, yielding an unbiased vital rate. Thus, from the point of view of bias, there may be an advantage in using the lower of two population estimates, if the estimate of the number of events is believed to be particularly deficient (for example, if it is based on retrospective survey questions only).[20] If, on the other hand, the number of events has been estimated without substantial bias (for example, in a PGE study), one will wish to use the best population estimate available in calculating the vital rates.

Actually, the available estimates of the base population are often biased downward, regardless of whether they are derived from a survey enumeration or from a census count adjusted for population growth. However, independent estimates of the total population based on a recent census are usually more accurate (that is, larger) than those based on a recent sample survey because surveys tend to be inferior to censuses with respect to overall population coverage.[21] If the census is known to have been particularly poor or is long out of date (and as time passes the independent estimate is increasingly a function of the adjustments used to correct for population growth subsequent to the census), then the survey estimate will usually be closer to the true population figure and hence preferable.

One argument sometimes advanced against using a survey as the source for the base population estimate in a PGE study is that it leads to overcorrection and an upward bias in the vital rates. The problem arises because one group of omitted events—those occurring in households omitted by the survey—are subject to a form of "double correction." That is, the reduction of the base population due to the erroneous omission of households in the survey tends to correct for the omission of vital events for these households. Moreover, the PGE estimate of births and deaths includes a correction for missed vital events, in *omitted* as well as covered households.

Although this overcorrection is a potential source of bias, a number of factors work to minimize its consequences. First, the magnitude of the "double correction" bias itself is usually small because the count of persons enumerated in a household survey tends to be a modest undercount, unless the survey field work is particularly inadequate. Note that relatively high population coverage and relatively poor coverage of events are logically consistent. In an enumeration of persons in a census or survey one attempts to count the population of a household (using a *de jure* or a *de facto* counting rule) at one point in time, usually at the time of interview. On the other hand, since vital events take place over time, one has to obtain reports of occurrences (births and deaths), usually retrospectively, over a period of time. The introduction of the time dimension into the enumeration of vital events almost inevitably leads to poorer coverage of events than of population for any given level of effort in a census or survey. Thus, the net population undercoverage usually ranges from 3 to 10 percent for a census conducted by a reasonably competent statistical office and from 5 to 15 percent for a comparatively well-run labor force or demographic survey. In contrast, net undercoverage for retrospective reports of vital events averages about 10 to 25 percent in fairly good demographic surveys.[22]

Another factor that may reduce the effect of the double correction bias is that the bias due to geographic out-of-scope error will often be reduced if the base population estimate used is derived from a survey. The very same inadequate maps and collection procedures that lead to omission of in-scope households near the sample area boundaries (and hence to double correction bias) also lead to the inclusion of out-of-scope households. If an independent estimate of the base population is used, the double correction bias affecting the PGE estimate of the vital rate is reduced, while the out-of-scope bias remains. If the household survey supplies the base population estimate, the double correction bias remains but the geographic out-of-scope bias is reduced.

In algebraic terms, the PGE estimate of a vital rate ($\hat{r}$) is

$$\hat{r} = \frac{\hat{n}}{b} = \frac{n_1 n_2}{mb} = \frac{r_1}{w_1} = \frac{r_2}{w_2} \;, \qquad\qquad [3.25]$$

where

b = estimated population base,

$w_1 = \dfrac{m}{n_2} =$ estimate of completeness of source 1 reporting of vital events,

$w_2 = \dfrac{m}{n_1} =$ estimate of completeness of source 2 reporting,

$$r_1 = \frac{n_1}{b} = \text{estimated vital rate for a single system estimate using source 1,}$$

$$r_2 = \frac{n_2}{b} = \text{estimated vital rate for a single system estimate using source 2, and}$$

$\hat{n}$, n_1, n_2, and m are defined as in equation 3.5.

The inclusion of out-of-scope events in source 1 will increase r_1 and reduce w_2. The inclusion of out-of-scope events in source 2 will increase r_2 and reduce w_1. If both source 1 and source 2 contain out-of-scope errors, the biasing effect on $\hat{r}$ will be approximately the sum of the upward biases introduced into r_1 and r_2. If source 1 is the household survey and the base population is estimated from the household survey (that is, if $b = b_1$), b_1 will include the people in households erroneously included in the survey, and this will partially correct r_1 and $\hat{r} = r_1/w_1$ for geographic out-of-scope error in source 1.

J.2   VARIANCE CONSIDERATIONS

As equation 3.25 indicates, the PGE estimate of a vital rate is the ratio of two values—the single system rate using a given source and the completeness of that source as estimated by matching with the other source. Using the form $\hat{r} = r_1/w_1$, the variance of the estimated vital rate is

$$\sigma_{\hat{r}}^2 = \frac{1}{w_1^2} (\sigma_{r_1}^2 + R^2 \sigma_{w_1}^2 - 2R\rho_{r_1 w_1} \sigma_{r_1} \sigma_{w_1}) \quad , \qquad [3.26]$$

where R, W_1, and R_1 and $\sigma_{\hat{r}}^2$, $\sigma_{w_1}^2$, and $\sigma_{r_1}^2$ are, respectively, the expected values and variances of $\hat{r}$, w_1, and r_1; and $\rho_{r_1 w_1}$ is the correlation of r_1 and w_1.[23]

In general, $\rho_{r_1 w_1}$ will be small.[24] Also, the choice between a base population of $b = b_1$ derived from source 1 and a base population of $b = B'$ independent of the sample but having the same bias (that is, having $E(B') = E(b_1) = B$) will not affect R, R_1, W_1, or $\sigma_{w_1}^2$. Whether b_1 or B' yields a higher variance for the PGE estimate $\hat{r}$ depends upon which yields the higher value of $\sigma_{r_1}^2$. The variance of r_1 is given by

$$\sigma_{r_1}^2 = \frac{1}{B^2} (\sigma_{n_1}^2 + R_1^2 \sigma_b^2 - 2R_1 \rho_{n_1 b} \sigma_{n_1} \sigma_b) \quad . \qquad [3.27]$$

If an independent base population, B', is used, the variance of the estimate $r_{11} = n_1/B'$ is

$$\sigma_{r_{11}}^2 = \frac{1}{B^2} (\sigma_{n_1}^2 + R_1^2 \sigma_{B'}^2) \quad , \qquad [3.28]$$

compared with a variance for $r_{12} = n_1/b_1$ of

$$\sigma_{r_{12}}^2 = \frac{1}{B^2} (\sigma_{n_1}^2 + R_1^2 \sigma_{b_1}^2 - 2R_1 \rho_{n_1 b_1} \sigma_{n_1} \sigma_{b_1}) \quad . \qquad [3.29]$$

By comparing equations 3.28 and 3.29, we can see that $\sigma^2_{r_{11}}$ is always greater than $\sigma^2_{n_1}/B^2$, whereas $\sigma^2_{r_{12}}$ can be less than $\sigma^2_{n_1}/B^2$ if

$$V_{b_1} < 2\rho V_{n_1} \quad , \tag{3.30}$$

where

$$V_{b_1} = \frac{\sigma_{b_1}}{B} = \text{ coefficient of variation of } b_1,$$

$$V_{n_1} = \frac{\sigma_{n_1}}{N_1} = \text{ coefficient of variation of } n_1, \text{ and}$$

$$\rho = \rho_{n_1 b_1} = \text{ correlation coefficient between } b_1 \text{ and } n_1.$$

As V_{b_1} is almost always less than V_{n_1}, $\sigma^2_{r_{11}}$ will be greater than $\sigma^2_{r_{12}}$ if ρ is moderately high. In other words, if the correlation between the number of events and the number of persons reported in a sample area is moderately high, the survey population estimate will yield a rate with a smaller variance than one that uses an independent population estimate in the denominator. On the other hand, if the correlation is negligible there is no *a priori* reason, from a variance standpoint, to prefer any specific type of population estimate.

The major source of such a correlation is variation in the size of sample areas (that is, in the number of households or persons in the areas). For areas of nearly equal size, $\rho_{n_1 b_1}$ will be near zero; but the correlation increases rapidly as the variation in the size of the sample areas increases. For large clusters (averaging 1,000 or more persons) variations in size of 20 to 30 percent may result in a fairly substantial correlation between the number of vital events and the number of persons in the sample areas.

The main factors that lead to a high bias from the use of an independent estimate of the base population also tend to produce large variations in cluster size and a variance differential unfavorable to the independent estimate. Both the independent estimate and the measures of size used in forming and selecting sample areas are usually derived from the most recent census. If the census coverage is poor, the definition of boundaries inadequate, or the census so old that extensive population changes have occurred, the independent estimate will suffer and the actual populations of the sample areas reported in a household survey will differ greatly and unevenly from the measures of segment size used in sampling. Similarly, if there is no census satisfactory for sampling purposes, economically feasible alternative methods of defining cluster boundaries will also result in segments of highly variable population size.

J.3   THE USE OF RATIO ESTIMATES

If the household survey estimate of the base population is significantly smaller than the independent estimate and w_1 (the estimated completeness of n_1) is relatively low, the low values of both b_1 and w_1 are likely to reflect a substantial number of erroneously omitted households. In these circumstances, if both are used in the PGE estimate $\hat{r}$, the birth and death rates may be overestimated. For this reason, it may be advisable to use the independent estimate of the base population and the ratio estimate of n_1,

$$n_1 = \frac{Cn_1'}{c'} \quad , \qquad\qquad [3.31]$$

where

$n_1' =$ number of vital events reported by source 1 for the sample areas,

$C =$ population of the country according to the most recent census, and

$c' =$ population of the sample areas according to the most recent census.

If the sample areas are not drawn with equal probabilities, n_1' and c' (the number of vital events and the population of the sample areas) should be weighted proportionately to the reciprocals of their probabilities of selection.[25]

Using the survey estimate of the number of events provided by equation 3.31 and an independent estimate of the base population, the PGE estimate of the vital rate is

$$\hat{r}_1 = \frac{r_{11}}{w_1} = \frac{n_1'}{w_1 t_1 c'} \quad , \qquad\qquad [3.32]$$

where

$\hat{r}_1 =$ PGE estimate of the vital rate using a ratio estimate for events reported in the survey and an independent estimate for the base population,

$r_{11} =$ comparable single system estimate of the vital rate,

$w_1 =$ estimated completeness rate of the survey's vital events reporting,

$n_1' =$ number of vital events in the sample areas as reported by the survey,

$c' =$ population of the sample areas in the most recent census, and

$t_1 = \dfrac{B'}{C} =$ ratio of the independent estimate of the current population (B') to the census population (C) for the country as a whole.

Using ratio estimates, as in equation 3.31, to estimate both n_1 and b_1, and using $b_1 = Cb_1'/c'$ for the survey estimate of the base population, the PGE estimate of the vital rate can be written as

$$\hat{r}_2 = \frac{r_{12}}{w_1} = \frac{n_1'}{w_1 t_2 c'} \quad , \qquad\qquad [3.33]$$

where

b'_1 = current population of the sample areas as reported by the survey,

$\hat{r}_2$ = PGE estimate of the vital rate using a ratio estimate for events reported in the survey and a survey-derived ratio estimate for the base population,

r_{12} = comparable single system estimate of the vital rate,

$t_2 = \dfrac{b_1}{C} = \dfrac{b'_1}{c'}$ = ratio of the current population of the sample areas as reported by the survey (b'_1) to the census population of the areas (c'), and

w_1 and n'_1 are defined as before.

It is clear from equations 3.32 and 3.33 that the only difference between the PGE estimates $\hat{r}_1$ and $\hat{r}_2$ is that the former uses t_1 and the latter t_2 to adjust for population change since the most recent census. Essentially, t_1 represents the change in population for the country as a whole since the last census, and t_2 the comparable change for the sample areas only. Although both t_1 and t_2 may have the same expected value for any specific set of sample areas, the value of t_2 may differ from the average postcensal growth rate for the nation as a whole. Such differences may reflect the differential fertility and mortality of the areas. In general, however, the major cause of differences between the postcensal population change of the country as a whole and that of the sample areas is internal migration. In other words, internal migration is the major reason for differences between t_1 and t_2, except those attributable to the quality of the population estimates (for example, survey underenumeration or a long out-of-date census).

Particularly in samples based on a relatively small number of clusters, population shifts attributable to housing construction or industrial development in or near a few sample areas may cause t_2 to differ markedly from t_1. Errors in identifying the PGE area boundaries in the census materials can have the same effect. In these situations it may be better to use $\hat{r}_2$ (the PGE estimate based on the survey population) because the correlation between n'_1 and $t_2 c'$ generally exceeds that between n_1 and $t_1 c'$; that is, the correlation between the numerator and denominator of equation 3.33 generally exceeds the correlation between the numerator and denominator of equation 3.32.

On the other hand, with large samples, if the survey population estimate for the nation (b_1) is considerably less than the independent estimate (B') and the completeness estimate of the survey vital events reporting (w_1) is substantially less than one, the PGE estimate based on the independent estimate is probably preferable from a bias standpoint. In such cases the difference between t_1 and t_2 is likely to be attributable largely to survey underenumeration. However, regardless of whether the population estimate used is b_1 or B', one should consider whether using the ratio estimate of equation 3.31 would be advantageous.

K. *Estimates for Subgroups*

So far in this chapter we have concentrated on the problems of estimating overall fertility or mortality for the entire nation. In this section we shall deal specifically with cases in which the objective is to prepare estimates for one or more population subgroups in addition to the aggregate national estimate. The term "population subgroup" refers to any division of the population (or the sample) that has analytical or methodological significance. A wide range of characteristics may be used to form subgroups—biological (age, sex, number of previous live births), socioeconomic (education, literacy, occupation), geographic (place of residence, size of place, place of birth), and so on. Although this section will use examples involving age and geographic areas in most of the discussion, the principles described are equally applicable to subgroups based on other characteristics.

The interest in subgroup estimates arises (1) because of the analytical insight into aggregate national trends such estimates can provide, (2) from concern about demographic developments in specific population subgroups, and (3) because if match rates are available for individual subgroups it may be possible to reduce the correlation bias of the PGE estimates. The use of age- and sex-specific fertility and mortality rates in preparing population projections is a common example of the analytical applications of subgroup estimates. Concern about demographic developments in certain population subgroups is illustrated by the frequent interest in preparing individual population estimates for each province and major city in a country. The use of subgroup estimates in connection with correlation bias has already been described in Section E.2 of this chapter.

If subgroup estimates are to be prepared, additional statistical problems relating to "classification bias" and increased sampling variance in the estimates are introduced. There is also a problem, peculiar to PGE studies, involved in selecting the "completeness rate" to be used for a specific subgroup.

K.1 CLASSIFICATION BIAS

"Classification bias" refers to errors arising from the failure to classify a specific vital event or member of the base population as belonging to the correct subgroup. These errors may arise because the information supplied by the respondent is not correct, because the field worker records the information wrongly, or because of subsequent processing or tabulation errors.

In estimating the total number of births or deaths, the issue of classification bias does not arise. Any reported live birth, for example, counts in the crude birth rate whether or not the age of mother is correctly recorded. (Note, however, that the same error processes that lead to classification bias also lead to omitted events, matching errors, and out-of-scope reports.) On the other hand, if the age of the mother is recorded incorrectly on a birth report, two age-specific fertility rates may be affected.

It is frequently assumed that classification biases affect the information reported for the base population and the vital events equally, leaving the fertility and mortality estimates for the subgroups unbiased. This assumption, however, cannot always be relied upon. For example, in the case of mortality estimates using civil registration data, the information on the death certificate is usually obtained from a different respondent than the comparable information for the base population. Obviously, the dead person himself cannot furnish information for a death certificate, and frequently this information will be furnished by other family members, who are also likely to be respondents in a census or household survey. Neighbors will more often be the source of data for a census or survey than for a death certificate; however, an undertaker, a physician, or a religious official may be the source for many "estimated" (that is, guessed) entries on death certificates. Although neighbors and undertakers may have similar biases, or may even be unbiased in estimating some characteristics, on one important characteristic—age—they are likely to differ. Undertakers, using the appearance of the corpse as a basis, will probably tend to estimate the person's age as higher than the neighbors, who base their judgment on the decedent's appearance while alive.

To a lesser extent, the classification biases of reported characteristics will also differ between birth reports and census or household survey reports. However, for birth certificates or other birth reports, characteristics of parents will tend to be reported more accurately than the characteristics of the corresponding base population groups in a census or household survey, whereas for death reports the reverse will be true. That is, if the birth is reported at all, the source of the data will usually be a parent, who is both better informed and better motivated to supply correct information than many respondents in a census or a household survey. The person best-informed about the characteristics of the decedent, the dead person himself, is never available to provide information to a registration system or single-visit household survey.

Apart from relying upon classification bias in the base population to compensate for classification bias in the number of vital events, one can (1) analyze the base population and the vital events for evidence of classification bias and (2) use regression techniques and combinations of adjacent groups to reduce the effects of identified classification biases. For example, analysis might disclose a higher fertility rate for women 30–34 years of age or 20–24 years of age than for women 25–29 years old. Further analysis might suggest that there was a much larger age classification bias for the women enumerated in the base population than for the number of births reported—that is, a greater tendency among women aged 20–24 and 30–34 in general to report themselves as aged 25–29 than among mothers. Assuming that fertility should show a continuous rise until some age in the middle 20s (23–27) and then a continuous decline, one could fit the age-specific fertility rates with a regression curve constrained to reflect this assumption. Alternatively, one might decide to use larger groups (for example, ages 19–26, 27–33, 34–40, and so on) or cumulative age groups (for example, under 30 or under 35) to reduce the effects of errors of misclassification across the 25- and 30-year lines.

The use of regression or of larger or cumulative groups will not, of course, remove all the classification bias; but it will, frequently, greatly reduce the error and therefore greatly improve the utility of the estimates. The use of cumulative age groups, in particular, has been a valuable tool in demographic analysis (see United Nations, 1967).

K.2 VARIANCE

Subgroup estimates inevitably have larger sampling variances than comparable aggregate estimates because of the smaller number of sample cases involved in a subgroup estimate. Often the increases in variance associated with the use of subgroup estimates are substantial. However, the use of regression techniques and large subgroups (both of which are helpful in controlling classification bias) may also be helpful in reducing somewhat the higher variances associated with subgroup estimates. Moreover, except for subgroups based on geographic areas, the increase in variance is generally not as rapid as the decrease in the number of sample cases.

One can understand the reasoning behind this statement and its implications for making subgroup estimates, by recalling equation 3.21. As indicated by that expression, the variance of a mean or vital rate estimated from a sample of areas has two components:

(1) the "within-segment variance," $\dfrac{\sigma^2 (1 - \delta)}{h}$, and

(2) the "between-segment variance," $\dfrac{\sigma^2 \delta}{k}$,

where k is the number of sample segments (sample areas) and h is the number of sample elements (persons). In the case of subgroup estimates, h can be taken as the number of sample persons in the subgroup and k as the number of sample areas used in making the subgroup estimate.

When the subgroup is based on some geographic classification (for example, the "urban" population), the estimate will be based only on the sample areas involved (for example, all "urban" areas). In this situation, k will be reduced proportionately to h and both the "within" and "between" components of variance will increase. Thus, if one-half the population is urban and the sample areas are sampled at the same rate throughout the country, both k and h will be approximately halved and the variance of the urban (and rural) estimate can be expected to be about twice that of the national estimate. On the other hand, if only 10 percent of the country is urban, both k and h will be reduced to about one-tenth of their original size and the variance will increase by a factor of ten. Of course, the sample can be designed to increase the number of segments included for geographic subgroups of particular interest. However, an increase in the number of such areas can be achieved only by increasing total expenditures, reducing expenditures per area, or increasing the variance of some other subgroup estimate.

In practice, these variance considerations lead to the following loose guidelines for making subgroup estimates formed along geographic lines. For national samples of 30 to 100 independently selected primary sampling units, estimates for more than three to five geographic regions are inadvisable. Urban or rural estimates will be satisfactory if either category comprises between 20 and 80 percent of the total population, but beyond that point the publication of estimates for the smaller category may be undesirable.

Certain types of subgroups, although not based on geographic classifications, have so localized a geographic distribution that they can be considered equivalent to a geographic subgroup from a variance viewpoint. For example, estimates for a particular ethnic or linguistic community living in one part of the country will be subject to variances involving a sharply reduced k. In any case, it is advisable to avoid publishing rates for any subgroup based on fewer than ten sample segments.

For many other kinds of subgroups—for example, age categories—the cases in the subgroup are spread over all the sample areas. Thus, although the within-segment variance increases in inverse proportion to the number of cases in the subgroup (h), there is little or no change in the between-segment variance. In fact, because the intraclass (intrasegment) correlation (δ) may be lower for some subgroups than for the population as a whole, the between-segment variance may actually decrease as a result of using a smaller subgroup, although this decrease is always less than the increase in the within-segment variance. In any case, the within-segment variance increases without limit as h decreases and, for small groups, will make the estimates of vital rates unusable.

If it is necessary to publish vital rates for groups of very small size, regression techniques can be employed, using information about vital rates in adjacent subgroups plus knowledge of the form of the regression (for example, the fact that mortality is a nondecreasing function of age for persons over about age ten years) to improve the estimate for a given category.

K.3   CONSIDERATIONS RELATING
TO THE PGE ESTIMATE AND MATCHING

In preparing PGE estimates for subgroups, the question arises whether to use an estimated completeness rate (the match rate of the other source) based on the subgroup or one based on the entire sample.

Where there are substantial differences among subgroups in the completeness of birth or death reporting—as, for example, the differences found by Chandrasekaran and Deming (1949) in death reporting among age-sex groups—using the overall completeness rate may introduce very substantial biases into the subgroup estimates.

On the other hand, the use of separate completeness rates for subgroups will increase the variance of the subgroup estimates. If some of the subgroups are very small, the use of separate estimates of completeness may also result in large "ratio biases." Therefore, if the completeness rates for the subgroups are not very different from the rate for the entire population, considerations of variance and ratio bias would dictate using the overall completeness rate. However, if the completeness rate for a subgroup can be estimated with acceptable accuracy and also differs substantially from the overall completeness rate, it will be best to use the subgroup completeness rate (unless the subgroup is so small and the completeness rate so near zero that doing so will introduce a large ratio bias).

Often, however, we find a situation where the subgroup completeness rate is clearly different from the overall rate but the precision of the subgroup rate is too low to be used as the basis for a PGE estimate. For example, we may have an overall estimated completeness rate for the nation of .8 and an estimated subgroup completeness rate for a particular province of .4. If the standard deviation of the subgroup completeness rate estimate is, say, about .08 and that of the overall completeness rate is about .01, the subgroup clearly has a lower completeness rate than the general population; but the true rate could well be as high as .55 or as low as .25, and using the subgroup estimated completeness rate of .4 will substantially increase the variance of the estimated birth or death rate for the group.

It is necessary, then, to balance the possible increase in bias involved in using an overall estimate of completeness against the increase in variance and ratio bias involved in estimating separate completeness rates for the subgroups. It is advisable to use subgroup estimates if *both* of the following conditions are met: (1) the subgroups are important and reasonably large (involving 30 or more sample events), *and* (2) the difference between the vital rate estimate using the overall completeness estimate and one prepared on the basis of separate completeness estimates for subgroups is at least twice as great as the estimated standard deviation of the latter vital rate estimate.

If the subgroups are too small to meet these criteria individually, one can try using a completeness rate based on an intermediate grouping—for example, applying the estimated rate of completeness of reporting for all persons 65 and over to reports of deaths of males and females aged 65–69, 70–74, and 75 and over. These groups may not differ too much in coverage among themselves but still have a very different completeness of reporting from that of the population as a whole. Alternatively, one might use the overall rate but warn users that the subgroup estimate is an underestimate; use some intermediate value between the completeness rates for the subgroup and the total; present a range of estimates based on the overall and subgroup completeness rates; or "avoid" the problem by suppressing estimates for small subgroups. In any case, the question of using a uniform completeness rate or separate rates for individual subgroups should be given careful thought and decided consciously rather than by default.

One condition that must be met if subgroup completeness rates rather than the overall completeness rate are to be used is that the characteristic used to subdivide the population must be reported in both sources. If the characteristic is recorded in only one of the two sources, an estimate can be made for the subgroup based on the reports in the source that contains the characteristic. For example, birth rates by mother's literacy status can be estimated on the basis of literacy reports in the household survey only. However, since the classification of unmatched events in the source without the characteristic is unknown, a separate estimate of the completeness rate of the other source for the subgroup cannot be made. Moreover, even if both sources report the characteristic used to define the subgroup, there may be differences between the sources with respect to which *matched* reports belong in the subgroup, since two reports may be considered matched but differ with respect to the characteristic for which subgroup estimates are being made.

A number of different procedures can be used to prepare estimates in the face of these difficulties. We begin by establishing the following definitions:

m = estimate of all matched events,

n_1 = estimate of total number of events reported in source 1,

n_2 = estimate of total number of events reported in source 2,

$w_1 = \dfrac{m}{n_2}$ = estimated overall completeness rate for source 1,

$w_2 = \dfrac{m}{n_1}$ = estimated overall completeness rate for source 2,

m_{1g} = estimate of matched events in subgroup g as determined from source 1 reporting of characteristics,[26]

m_{2g} = estimate of matched events in subgroup g as determined from source 2 reporting of characteristics,[26]

n_{1g} = estimate from source 1 of the number of vital events in subgroup g,

n_{2g} = estimate from source 2 of the number of vital events in subgroup g,

$w_{1g} = \dfrac{m_{2g}}{n_{2g}}$ = estimated completeness rate of subgroup g in source 1,

$$w_{2g} = \frac{m_{1g}}{n_{1g}} = \text{estimated completeness rate of subgroup } g$$
$$\text{in source 2, and}$$

$$m_{12g} = \text{estimate of matched events reported as in}$$
$$\text{subgroup } g \text{ by both source 1 and source 2.}$$

We cannot compute a completeness rate for subgroup g using m_{12g} since there is no comparable value for the denominator of such a rate. However, we may use w_{1g} and w_{2g} to obtain two different PGE estimates of events for the subgroup. That is,

$$\hat{n}_{1g} = \frac{n_{1g}}{w_{1g}} = \frac{n_{1g}n_{2g}}{m_{2g}} \quad , \text{ and} \qquad\qquad [3.34]$$

$$\hat{n}_{2g} = \frac{n_{2g}}{w_{2g}} = \frac{n_{1g}n_{2g}}{m_{1g}} \quad . \qquad\qquad\qquad [3.35]$$

If $\hat{n}_{1g}$ and $\hat{n}_{2g}$ are nearly equal, either estimate will be satisfactory. Alternatively, one can use the mean of these two estimates,

$$\hat{n}_{g} = \frac{(\hat{n}_{1g} + \hat{n}_{2g})}{2} \quad . \qquad\qquad\qquad [3.36]$$

If $\hat{n}_{1g}$ and $\hat{n}_{2g}$ differ appreciably, there is sometimes a reason to prefer one source as being uniformly more accurate with respect to the classification characteristic. This situation is relatively rare. However, a large difference between $\hat{n}_{1g}$ and $\hat{n}_{2g}$ is often due to extensive item nonresponse involving the characteristic on which the subgroup is based—that is, to the presence of a substantial proportion of reports in either source that cannot be definitely classified as belonging in or outside subgroup g. It is best, then, to choose the estimating equation (3.34 or 3.35) that uses the subgroup completeness rate for the source with the smaller proportion of unclassified reports. For example, if the proportion of reports lacking information on the subgroup characteristic is smaller for source 2 than for source 1, it is preferable to make the PGE estimate for the subgroup on the basis of the subgroup completeness estimate for source 2. (Note, however, that this completeness estimate is based on the match rate of the source with the *larger* proportion of unclassified reports.)

Estimating equations 3.34 and 3.35 (and hence $\hat{n}_{1g}$ and $\hat{n}_{2g}$) implicitly assume that (1) if the unclassified reports were properly classified they would not alter the completeness estimate for the subgroup and (2) none of the unclassified reports properly belongs in the subgroup. Although the first of these assumptions is generally quite reasonable, the second is not. Using the completeness estimate for the source with the smaller proportion of unclassified reports is one way of minimizing this problem. In addition, one may want to adjust n_{1g} or n_{2g} in order to distribute the unclassified reports to the subgroup in the same proportion as the reports that could be classified. If source 1 contained the smaller proportion of unclassified reports, the adjusted estimate would be[27]

$$\hat{n}_g = \frac{n_1 n_{1g}}{(n_{1g} + n_{1\bar{g}}) w_{1g}} = \frac{n_1 n_{1g} n_{2g}}{(n_{1g} + n_{1\bar{g}}) m_{2g}} = \frac{\hat{n}_{1g}}{p_{1g}} \quad , \qquad [3.37]$$

where

$$n_{1\bar{g}} = \text{estimate from source 1 of the number of reports definitely not in subgroup } g,$$

$$n_{1g} + n_{1\bar{g}} = \text{estimate of number of source 1 reports that can be definitely classified as in or not in subgroup } g, \text{ and}$$

$$p_{1g} = n_{1g} + n_{1\bar{g}} = \text{proportion of all source 1 reports that can be definitely classified as in or not in subgroup } g.$$

If only one source has information for determining the subgroup classification, one must use the overall completeness rate, w_1 or w_2, to make the subgroup estimate. In such a situation, one usually will also want to adjust the estimate for any unclassified reports in the source that reports the subgroup characteristics. If source 1 provides information on the subgroup characteristic, the PGE estimate for the subgroup using the overall completeness rate with such an adjustment will be

$$\hat{n}_g = \frac{n_{1g}}{p_{1g} w_1} = \frac{n_1 n_2 n_{1g}}{m(n_{1g} + n_{1\bar{g}})} \quad . \qquad [3.38]$$

Equation 3.38 should also be used to estimate $\hat{n}_g$ if the accuracy of the classification data in one of the sources is doubtful.[28] One can usually assume that one or both sources have dubious classification entries if $(w_1 - w_{1g})$ differs very drastically from $(w_2 - w_{2g})$, particularly if they are opposite in sign.

To illustrate the use of estimating equations 3.34 through 3.38, let us consider the problem of making a PGE estimate of the number of births occurring to women aged 25–29. Table 3.9 presents data from a hypothetical PGE study on the number of birth reports by matching status and type of age data available (for example, age not reported, age reported as 25–29, some other age reported) for source 1 and source 2. These data are typical of those one might expect to find for a wide range of subgroups in many countries. To facilitate the correct substitution of data in equations 3.34 through 3.38, the table also shows, for each category, the notation used in these equations.

In this example, 120 births to mothers aged 25–29 were reported in source 1 and 128 were reported in source 2. Of the 120 source 1 reports for this subgroup, 96 were matched to a source 2 report (regardless of whether the source 2 report was counted as definitely in the subgroup or definitely outside the subgroup, or was unclassifiable); of the 128 births to mothers aged 25–29 recorded in source 2, 72 were found to match a source 1 report. However, only 56 of the matched birth reports had mother's age recorded as 25–29 in both sources.

The estimated completeness rate for births to mothers aged 25–29 in source 1 is

$$w_{1g} = \frac{m_{2g}}{n_{2g}} = \frac{72}{128} = .56 \quad ,$$

and the corresponding source 2 completeness estimate is

$$w_{2g} = \frac{m_{1g}}{n_{1g}} = \frac{96}{120} = .80 \quad .$$

Substituting these completeness estimates in equations 3.34 and 3.35, respectively, gives us the PGE subgroup estimates

$$\hat{n}_{1g} = \frac{n_{1g}}{w_{1g}} = 120 \div \frac{72}{128} = 213 \text{ and}$$

$$\hat{n}_{2g} = \frac{n_{2g}}{w_{2g}} = 128 \div \frac{96}{120} = 160 \quad .$$

Using equation 3.36, we can average n_{1g} and n_{2g} to obtain another estimate of births in the subgroup,

$$\hat{n}_g = \frac{213 + 160}{2} = 187 \quad .$$

Table 3.9   Number of Birth Reports, by Source of Report, Type of Age Data Available, and Matching Status: Hypothetical Example

Type of age data and matching status	Source 1		Source 2	
	Notation used	Number of reports	Notation used	Number of reports
All birth reports	n_1	480	n_2	400
Mother's age reported	$n_{1g} + n_{1\bar{g}}$	440	$n_{2g} + n_{2\bar{g}}$	279
Age reported as 25–29	n_{1g}	120	n_{2g}	128
Other age reported	$n_{1\bar{g}}$	320	$n_{2\bar{g}}$	151
Mother's age not reported	$n_1 - (n_{1g} + n_{1\bar{g}})$	40	$n_2 - (n_{2g} + n_{2\bar{g}})$	121
All matched birth reports	m	280	m	280
Mother's age reported as 25–29	m_{1g}	96	m_{2g}	72
Matched to report with mother's age 25–29	m_{12g}	56	m_{12g}	56
Matched to other report[1]	$m_{1g} - m_{12g}$	40	$m_{2g} - m_{12g}$	16
Mother's age not reported as 25–29[1]	$m - m_{1g}$	184	$m - m_{2g}$	208
Matched to report with mother's age 25–29	$m_{2g} - m_{12g}$	16	$m_{1g} - m_{12g}$	40
Matched to other report[1]	$m - m_{1g} - m_{2g} + m_{12g}$	168	$m - m_{1g} - m_{2g} + m_{12g}$	168
All nonmatched birth reports	u_1	200	u_2	120

[1] Reports with mother's age not reported or reported as other than 25–29.
SOURCE: Hypothetical data.

However, because $\hat{n}_{1g}$ and $\hat{n}_{2g}$ differ so markedly, it is probably best in this instance not to rely on the estimates produced by equations 3.34 through 3.36. As an alternative, we can consider an estimate from equation 3.37 or equation 3.38.

As discussed earlier, a principal cause of large differences between $\hat{n}_{1g}$ and $\hat{n}_{2g}$ is extensive item nonresponse for the characteristic used to form the subgroup. Because all the terms in equations 3.34 and 3.35 involve only reports definitely belonging to the subgroup, these equations make no provision for including any of the 40 birth reports in source 1 with mother's age not known in the estimate $\hat{n}_{1g}$ or any of the 121 corresponding source 2 reports in $\hat{n}_{2g}$. We can take these unclassified reports into account by using equation 3.37. In our example, 8 percent of all source 1 reports and about 30 percent of all source 2 reports lack usable information on age of mother (see Table 3.10). That is,

$$p_{1g} = \frac{440}{480} = .92 \quad \text{, and}$$

$$p_{2g} = \frac{279}{400} = .70 \quad .$$

Because source 1 contains a smaller proportion of unclassified reports, we want to adjust n_{1g} rather than n_{2g} for the reports whose subgroup status is unknown. Thus, we use equation 3.37 to obtain the adjusted PGE estimate for the subgroup:

$$\hat{n}_g = \frac{\hat{n}_{1g}}{p_{1g}} = 213 \div \frac{440}{480} = 232 \quad .$$

Except for differences due to rounding, this is the equivalent of adding to the 120 source 1 subgroup reports a proportion of the 40 unclassified reports equal to 120/440 and applying the subgroup completeness estimate of 72/128 based on the reports in source 2.

In this case there is considerable evidence that the data on age of mother in source 2 is quite unreliable. For example, the relative contribution of mothers aged 25–29 to the total number of births with age of mother known based on source 1 data is quite plausible (27

Table 3.10 Estimated Overall and Subgroup Completeness Rates, by Source, for Birth Reporting: Hypothetical Example

	Source 1		Source 2	
Type of statistic	Notation used	Proportion	Notation used	Proportion
Estimated overall completeness rate	w_1	.70	w_2	.58
Estimated completeness rate for subgroup "mother's age 25–29"	w_{1g}	.56	w_{2g}	.80
Proportion with mother's age reported	p_{1g}	.92	p_{2g}	.70

SOURCE: Hypothetical data from Table 3.9.

percent), whereas the comparable proportion based on source 2 reports (46 percent) seems very unlikely. The substantial proportion (30 percent) of source 2 birth reports with age of mother not known has already been mentioned. Finally, there is the sharp divergence in sign and magnitude between $w_1 - w_{1g}$ and $w_2 - w_{2g}$ (.14 versus $-.22$). Thus, the use of equations 3.34 and 3.37, which are based on the source 1 subgroup completeness estimate ($w_{1g} = 72/128$), derived from the reports classified in the 25–29 age group in source 2, is not recommended. Instead, it is advisable to apply the overall completeness estimate to the number of subgroup reports adjusted for unclassified reports. This is the estimate embodied in equation 3.38. Substituting the appropriate values from Tables 3.8 and 3.9 gives us the PGE estimate, with w_1 $= 280/400$,

$$\hat{n}_g = \frac{120}{\left(\dfrac{440}{480}\right)\left(\dfrac{280}{400}\right)} = 187 \quad .$$

The fact that this estimate equals the estimate produced by equation 3.36 is coincidental. Another numerical example could have produced a quite different result.

The various subgroup estimates based on the data for this example are presented in summary form in Table 3.11. These estimates range from 160 to 233 births; thus if the lowest estimates corresponded to an age-specific fertility rate of .250, the highest would imply a rate of .364. This example clearly illustrates the problems frequently encountered in subgroup estimation and the care that must be exercised in interpreting the estimates. Some further suggestions for analyzing and dealing with data problems of this type are given in Chapter 6.

Table 3.11 Alternative PGE Subgroup Estimates of the Number of Births Occurring to Mothers Aged 25–29: Hypothetical Example

Basis of subgroup estimation	Equation number[1]	Estimated number of births
Estimated subgroup completeness rate for source 1 ($\hat{n}_{1g}$)	3.34	213
Estimated subgroup completeness rate for source 2 ($\hat{n}_{2g}$)	3.35	160
Mean of $\hat{n}_{1g}$ and $\hat{n}_{2g}$	3.36	187[2]
Estimated subgroup completeness rate for source with smaller number of unclassified reports, adjusted for unclassified reports	3.37	233
Estimated overall completeness rate for source with smaller number of unclassified reports, adjusted for unclassified reports	3.38	187[2]

[1] See the text for details of the estimating equations.
[2] The agreement of estimates based on equations 3.36 and 3.38 is coincidental.

SOURCE: Hypothetical data from Tables 3.9 and 3.10.

L. *Concluding Remarks*

In this chapter we have discussed a number of key aspects of design related to the planning and execution of a PGE study. Basically our approach has been one of weighing alternatives rather than stating rigid rules. Because a discussion of the gains and costs of alternative solutions to various design problems is necessarily complex, the chapter has been a lengthy one.

In any particular situation, the number of options available will probably not be as extensive as the discussion in the chapter might imply. Nevertheless, the existence of design constraints should not be used as an excuse to avoid careful planning. Even when there are a considerable number of constraints, time spent in rationally assessing alternative design features can result in major improvements in a PGE study and its statistical output.

On the other hand, one must remember that the ultimate objective of a PGE study is the measurement of population growth and not the creation of a perfect design. As in any other endeavor, after a certain point the discussion of design alternatives yields diminishing returns. Beyond this point, only the experience of actually operating a PGE system will yield enough information to permit improvements that justify their cost. Although it is desirable to set up a system that provides for changes as *new* information is developed, continued debate about the "finishing touches" of a study can sap energy that would be more usefully spent in supervising the collection and processing of data. At some point leadership must be exercised, decisions made, and the study commenced. The purpose of this chapter has been to help ensure that such decisions will be as informed as possible.

Footnotes

1. Occasionally, one runs into the opposite situation, where eliminating waste and inefficiency yields unnecessarily precise results and it is appropriate to reduce the budget. (This is, however, unusual, at least as far as official records go.)

2. One strives, of course, for complete independence of the systems but "settles" for a low correlation between them.

3. The symbol "$\doteq$" should be read as "is approximately equal to."

4. If only one source covers the entire country, the bias attributable to geographic out-of-scope reports will also be trivial, provided matching of the sample is not restricted geographically.

5. However, as indicated later, bias due to lack of independence usually has an opposite sign from the bias due to including out-of-scope events, while the sign of the matching error bias depends upon whether the matching rules are "loose" or "strict."

6. In theory, of course, the correlation can be negative. However, the factors leading to a positive correlation are more definite and more common; and, in fact, where correlation bias has been identified or suspected in the past, the correlation has been positive.

7. This division is somewhat arbitrary, and we acknowledge that some forms of response correlation could, without too much difficulty, be classified as in either category. Nevertheless, the distinction is useful.

8. For example, the percentage of all sample births that are first births is *not* subject to ratio bias even though both the numerator and denominator are random variables. This is true, in general, of a percentage whose denominator is a subgroup of the population, since the numerator tends also to vary up or down with the denominator and the expected percentage for a fixed size of denominator is the same regardless of the denominator's size.

9. In the limit, where there is an appreciable chance that m will equal zero, the value of $E(1/m)$ can in theory become infinite.

10. As discussed later, large gross matching errors, although they do not contribute to bias or variance directly, should be viewed with concern.

11. An "identification code class" consists of all units in the universe (vital events) having the same matching identification. For example, if the matching identification were name of Post Office and first four letters of surname, surnames in Montpelier, Vermont beginning with "JOHN" (John, Johns, Johnson, etc.) would be one identification code class; surnames in Montpelier, Vermont beginning with "BART" would be another identification code class; and surnames in Denver, Colorado beginning with "JOHN" would be a third identification code class. The last identification code class would tend to have more items in it than the first two (since Denver is a larger city than Montpelier, and the first class would probably have more items than the second).

12. "Discriminating power" is the ability of an identification code to distinguish items that are actually distinct—that is, to prevent erroneous matches. Thus if there is only one event in the population with a given identification code (for example, one decedent with a family name beginning "LITZ" in Montpelier), this code provides complete discriminating power for that event. However, if there are several events with the same code (for example, several decedents with surnames beginning "SMIT" in Wilmington, Delaware), the discriminating power of the code is low. The "percentage of unique codes" and "average number of entries per identification code class" are used as measures of discriminating power.

13. The records matched in this study were a "master file" of magazine subscriptions and a much smaller "transaction file" of subscription renewals, changes of address, and new subscriptions. Each renewal or change of address should have matched a master file record. The new subscriptions should not have matched any master file record. The match was a "one-way match" of transactions against the master file. The base for calculating the percentage of units with unique codes and the average number of units per identification code class was the master file. The base for calculating the percentage of erroneous matches and the percentage of erroneous nonmatches was the number of records in the transaction file. Incidentally, this example illustrates that experience from a wide variety of matching operations can be helpful in developing PGE procedures.

14. The vital events "in the universe" consist of all events that occurred in the specified geographic area during the designated time period.

15. Usually the sampling units will be geographic areas (for example, groups of households, villages, or townships), and the elements will be individual persons. The occurrence of a vital event (dying or giving birth to a child) during a time period can be treated as a characteristic whose value for a given person is zero or 1.

16. Within a household there will usually be a *negative* δ for births—that is, the probability of two persons from the same household being born within the past quarter (or past year) will be less than the probability of two persons from different households both being newborn. For deaths, the δ within households will be zero for the large, "extended family" type of household or positive for households containing primarily nuclear families.

17. Conversely, the variance of $\hat{n}$ is likely to be less than that of $\hat{N}$ if N_1 includes less than half the total number of events. For a more extended discussion of the variances of $\hat{n}$ and $\hat{N}$ and their likely differences, see Section A of Chapter 7.

18. Note that this technique could also be helpful in identifying reports erroneously included for this reason in a special or civil registration system with two-way matching.

19. In fact, one advantage that single system surveys have over comparable registration efforts is that the latter must almost always employ independent population estimates in forming vital rate estimates.

20. A caution is necessary against overreliance upon a population base derived from the same sample as the reported events to correct for deficiencies in coverage. For example, a method developed by the United Nations Demographic Center for Latin America attempts to correct for undercoverage by using as the population base the "exposure to risk" only for the individuals included in the survey. The technique has been used thus far in studies of Guanabara (Brazil) and Cauqenes (Chile). This is a very promising technique that should certainly be explored further. However, it certainly does not remove *all* the (usual) tendency to underestimate birth and death rates distinctive of single source systems. For one thing, it does not correct for failure to report a birth or death in correctly enumerated households. Moreover, the assumption that birth and death rates for missed households are the same as those for enumerated households is frequently not borne out. For example, the Guanabara study showed deficiencies in the enumeration of persons who changed residences during the survey period. That is, the study lost considerably more people due to migration from the sample segments (but within the general area of the study) than it picked up due to migration into the sample segments from elsewhere in the study area. One fairly common cause of households changing residence is the death or birth of family members. Deaths, in particular, may break up a household and *force* the survivors to move to another dwelling unit. Thus birth and death rates may be higher for households that move than for those that do not, and an underrepresentation of migrants in the sample would lead to underestimates of birth and death rates. The degree of underestimation would, of course, depend upon the number of migrants and the households actually enumerated.

21. A reasonably successful census will tend to be superior in coverage to a sample survey taken by the same personnel, although there may be larger errors in reporting the characteristics of enumerated people. For example, erroneous inclusions in a census are either duplications, which tend to be rare, or enumerations of diplomatic personnel (or other out-of-scope persons), which tend to be rarer. There are also some features of a census that tend to reduce omissions which are not operative in a sample survey. For one thing, boundary problems are less critical in a census enumeration than in a survey; the population on both sides of the boundary is to be included, and a census field supervisor can usually ensure that any disputed area is included in one of the enumeration districts under his control. Moreover, people are usually aware that a census is going on, they are willing to be enumerated (even if they object to some of the census questions), and they even tend to insist on being included. In any case, it is quite common for sample surveys taken simultaneously with a census to come up with substantially lower estimates of the population.

22. The completeness estimates cited are not based on any specific study; rather, they represent a synthesis of the authors' experience and the results of various evaluative studies. They are presented as ranges to reflect conditions in the statistically developed regions of the world. The values cited are, of course, only approximate, and numerous contrary examples exist.

23. For a fuller discussion of sampling and of the variance formula in this chapter, see Section A of Chapter 7 and Hansen, Hurwitz, and Madow (1953). The terms in equation 3.26 refer to the expected values, variances, and correlations that would be obtained by repeatedly drawing different samples and repeating the data collection, estimation, and so on using the same procedures as for the original sample.

24. Some of the variation in the estimated vital rate r_1 will be due to selecting sample areas with high or low completeness of reporting, w_1. However, the bulk of the variance of r_1 will be due to variation of the actual vital rates. In the case of a sample which happens to have a birth or death rate higher or lower than that which would be obtained from a complete canvass of the entire country, there will usually be no reason to expect a completeness rate correspondingly higher or lower than that obtained by covering the entire country using the same procedures as for the sample areas.

25. The number of vital events or the population of each sample area would be divided by the probability of selecting the area for the sample, and these ratios would be summed over all sample areas to give the values n_1' and c'. Similar weighting would be necessary to obtain the values of b_1 and of m and n_2 (used to estimate w_1).

26. A report is counted in m_{1g} if source 1 classifies it there and if it matches a source 2 report, whether or not the source 2 report belongs in subgroup g. A report is counted in m_{2g} if source 2 classifies it there and it matches a source 1 report, whether or not the source 1 report belongs in subgroup g.

27. Basically, this estimate involves adding to n_{1g}, the number of source 1 reports for the subgroup, a proportion of the source 1 unclassified reports equal to $[n_1 - (n_{1g} + n_{1\bar{g}})] \cdot [n_{1g}/(n_{1g} + n_{1\bar{g}})]$; that is, a proportion equal to the number of source 1 reports for the subgroup divided by all source 1 reports whose subgroup status is known. Equation 3.37 can be derived by substituting this adjusted number of source 1 reports in equation 3.34 and simplifying.

28. If the accuracy of the classification data for *both* sources is doubtful, one should avoid making any estimate for the subgroup.

Procedures for Three Alternative Approaches 4

A. *Introduction*

In this chapter we attempt to provide the operating personnel of a PGE study with model procedures that embody the principles of study design presented in Chapter 3. In addition, specific guidance is given about methods of overcoming administrative and technical problems often encountered in PGE studies. To minimize vagueness, the bulk of the chapter (Sections C, D, and E) is organized around three alternative approaches to a dual system design. These are

(1) a civil registration system combined with a periodic household survey (Section C),

(2) a special registration system combined with a periodic household survey (Section D), and

(3) a periodic household survey with substantial overlaps in the periods of recall and independent enumeration in successive rounds (Section E).

These alternatives represent a wide range of possible combinations of collection systems. Together, they illustrate most of the basic problems faced by those running a PGE study.

Users of this Handbook should consider the chapter as providing material that will aid in the development of the detailed procedures suitable for use in a specific country, rather than inflexible rules to be applied in all countries. In practice, actual study procedures will probably be pieced together from material in different parts of this chapter, from any pilot study results available, and from previous survey research experience, after an assessment of the probable gains or losses associated with alternative procedures. As described in Chapter 3, this assessment should be made with the overall objective of producing statistics on basic demographic variables with "maximum net value."

Much of the material presented here overlaps with that in Chapter 3. However, the purposes and the intended audiences of the two chapters are somewhat different. The emphasis in the present chapter is on supplying the operating staff with satisfactory procedural models rather than describing a method of achieving an optimal design. Thus, although the subject matter of the two chapters necessarily overlaps, the emphasis and level of the material differs. For example, we have tried in Chapter 4 to avoid extended theoretical justifications—particularly those dependent upon complex statistical arguments. (Instead, the reader is referred to the appropriate sections of Chapters 3 or 7 for a fuller treatment of the statistical issues involved.) Moreover, topics already covered in the technical literature available in the libraries of most statistical offices are dealt with in a very abbreviated fashion. Hence such matters as questionnaire design, sampling methods, interviewing techniques, the conduct of pilot studies, the design of tables for methodological and substantive purposes, timetables and scheduling, training, management, and report writing, all critical to the successful design and execution of a PGE study, are not covered in detail in this chapter.

B. Procedures Common to All Three Alternatives

Before sketching procedures for each approach separately, we shall describe a number of features common to all three. These include methods of ensuring adequate geographic control of the field work (Sections B.1 and B.2), details of the household survey (Section B.3), procedures for establishing a common *de facto* definition for vital events reporting in both collection systems (Section B.4), the content of the field documents (Section B.5), basic information about the matching operation (Section B.6), and a summary of standard tabulations (Section B.7). In addition, portions of the text in Sections C, D, and E also describe procedures that are generally applicable. For example, the discussion in Section D.3 of the organization of the central staff of the study and the control of operations may be helpful regardless of the study design used. Cross-references have been inserted into the text at appropriate points to alert readers to such general discussions.

B.1 MAPPING

Good maps contribute directly to the reduction of sampling biases and costs, and to the efficient administration and control of the field work. In a PGE study, maps have the following major functions:

(1) They show the location of each sample area, as well as the travel routes to and from each area.
(2) They provide a record of the boundaries of each sample area and thus help to define the geographic scope of the study.

(3) They aid the allocation and control of work assignments within each sample area by showing landmarks, boundaries of internal subdivisions, and convenient travel paths within the area.

(4) They enable each individual structure within the sample areas to be identified and located, thus facilitating better coverage of isolated households, house numbering, supervisory callbacks, matching, and field follow-up.

Because of the very important role maps can play in ensuring operational efficiency and the validity of estimates, PGE study managers are justified in devoting considerable resources to developing and maintaining an adequate system of maps.

The mapping system used depends, in part, upon how the PGE sample areas are subdivided for administrative and control purposes. The amount of subdivision required depends, in turn, upon the extent of clustering, the density and dimensions of the areas, and the difficulty of the terrain. In the discussion that follows, we assume a three-layered system of organizing the field work and maps: PGE area, chunk, and block. A *block* corresponds roughly to a small census enumeration district in size (that is, a conveniently bounded area containing about 50 to 100 structures or 200 to 500 persons). A *chunk* consists of some two to five blocks and may also correspond to a local administrative unit (for example, a village or subward); each sample area may contain two or three chunks. This system of organization is applicable over a wide range of PGE cluster sizes.[1]

A map should be prepared for each sample area and for each subdivision created for the purposes of the study. If the standard three-layered organization is used, one map is prepared for each block, chunk, and PGE area in the sample. For convenience, we shall refer to the PGE sample area maps as Map No. 1, the chunk maps as Map No. 2, and the block maps as Map No. 3. The major function of Map No. 1 is to indicate the location of one sample area. Map No. 2 serves as a link between Map No. 1 and the many Map No. 3s that may be needed to cover one PGE area, as well as helping to demarcate boundaries of assignments within the sample areas. Each Map No. 3 shows individual structures and structure numbers for one block, pathways, and the details of block, chunk, and PGE area boundaries. In order to ensure that all block maps are both legible and of a convenient physical size, it is best to organize the system of chunks and blocks in such a way that no block contains more than 100 structures.

As important as mapping is, the employment of a professional cartographer by the PGE study is neither a necessary nor a sufficient condition of success. It is vital, however, that existing maps prepared by professional mapmakers be used as skeletons for the production of whatever maps may be required by the field workers. The mapping, and particularly the construction of Map No. 1, must not commence with pencil scribbling by enumerators or registrars. It should, if at all possible, be based on available maps that field workers (whether special registrars or survey enumerators) can readily use for PGE purposes.[2]

The system of mapping described above and the means by which the maps can be developed by the study staff from existing maps of professional quality are illustrated in Figures 4.1(a), 4.1(b), 4.2(a), 4.2(b), 4.3(a), and 4.3(b). Each type of map (area, chunk, and block) is shown first without and then with the additions made by the PGE staff. Conceptually, Figures 4.2(a) and 4.3(a) represent Figure 4.1(a) blown-up in scale. However, it is usually unwise to accomplish this change of scale by reproducing an optical enlargement of Figure 4.1(a). Such enlargements are usually difficult to read, and ordinarily there will be insufficient space to enter the structure numbers on Map No. 3 legibly. The preferred procedure is to draw the outlines and major features of the chunk and block maps on the basis of the information shown in Map No. 1, with the detailed information entered at the time of house numbering.

Figure 4.1(a) shows the original map that serves as the basis for Map No. 1 for one PGE area (referred to as the Showak PGE Area after the largest settlement within it), and Figure 4.1(b) shows the same map after the boundaries of the PGE area and its three chunks have been added. Map No. 1 also shows the means of access to the area (in the present case, a road usable in the dry season leading to the District headquarters some 40 kilometers to the west, and a railroad from the Provincial capital 85 kilometers to the north). The residences and offices of local PGE workers, and any other relevant offices, should be at least approximately indicated. (Note that in Figure 4.1(b) the government rest house and the quarters of the PGE special registrar are shown.) A typical scale for Map No. 1 might be from 1:100,000 to 1:50,000, although very great departures from this range might be required.

Figure 4.2(a) illustrates Map No. 2 for Chunk No. 3 of the Showak PGE Area without the block boundaries, and Figure 4.2(b) shows the same map after the block boundaries have been added. In order to fit this map on one page of the Handbook only part of it is reproduced in these figures. Omitted is that portion of this chunk that includes the hamlet of Abbuda and runs southeasterly through the hamlets of Aradeiba and Umm Ali, see Figure 4.1(b). As another space-conserving measure, the basic scale used in Figures 4.2(a) and 4.2(b) is 1:20,000, and the uninhabited region in the northwest corner of the chunk is shown in about the same scale as is used in the figures illustrating Map No. 1.

One Map No. 2 should be prepared for each chunk in the PGE area. In practice, each chunk map will be at least as large as two facing pages of this book and typically will use a scale of 1:10,000 but, again, considerable variation in this figure is likely. These maps should indicate block boundaries, areas of settlement, travel paths within the sample area, and major topographical features. In the present example, Figure 4.2(b) shows the boundaries of Blocks 11, 12, and 13 as well as the

**Fig. 4.1(a) Map No. 1: Showak PGE Area and Surrounding Territory
No Boundaries Shown**

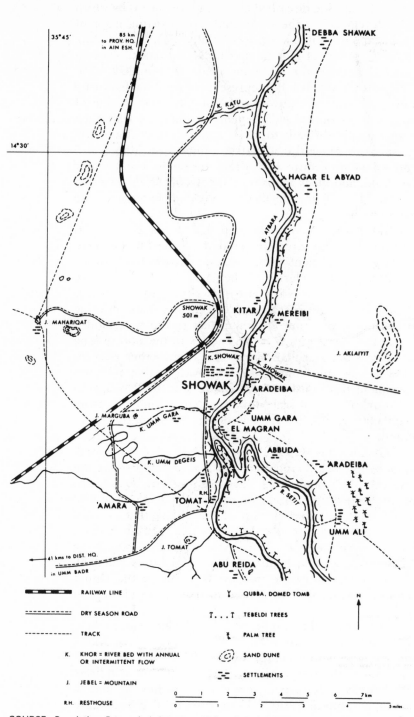

SOURCE: Population Research Laboratory, University of Alberta, Edmonton.

**Fig. 4.1(b) Map No. 1: Showak PGE Area and Surrounding Territory
Boundaries of PGE Area and Three Chunks Added**

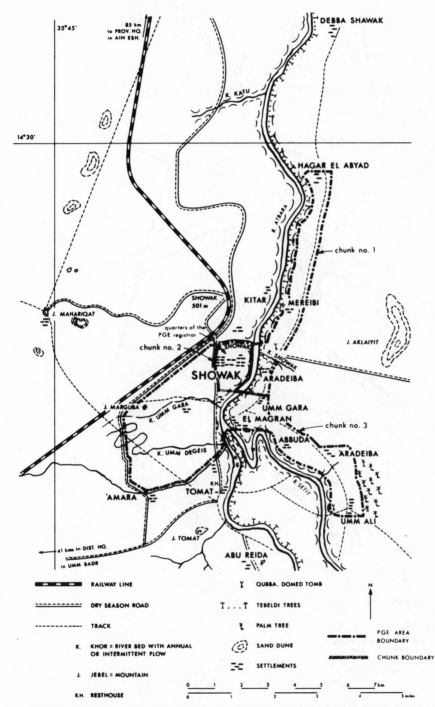

SOURCE: Population Research Laboratory, University of Alberta, Edmonton.

**Fig. 4.2(a) Map No. 2(part): Western Part of Chunk No. 3 in Showak PGE Area
No Block Boundaries Shown**

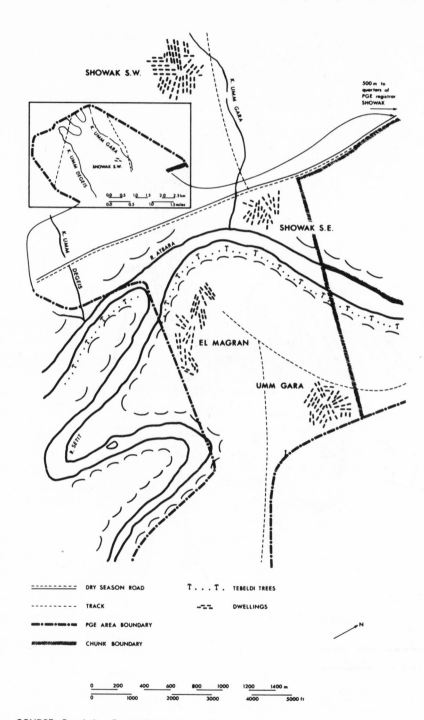

SOURCE: Population Research Laboratory, University of Alberta, Edmonton.

Fig. 4.2(b) Map No. 2(part): Western Part of Chunk No. 3 in Showak PGE Area Boundaries of Blocks 11, 12, and 13 Added

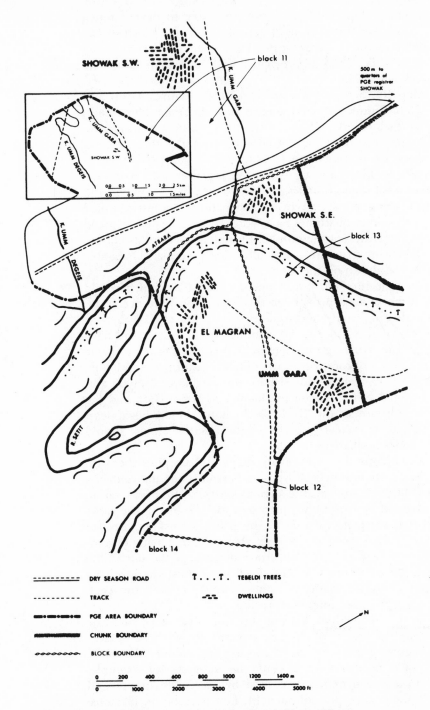

SOURCE: Population Research Laboratory, University of Alberta, Edmonton.

western boundary of Block 14 for Chunk No. 3. The locations of South East and South West Showak, both of which were too small to identify by name in Map No. 1 are also shown in Figures 4.2(a) and 4.2(b). In adding detail to Map No. 2 it is not necessary to devote much effort to the addition of further topographical details, for which special training would be required.[3] As indicated earlier, the primary function of Map No. 2 is to be a link between the PGE area map (Map No. 1) and the block maps (Map No. 3).

Each Map No. 3 represents one block. (In Figures 4.3(a) and 4.3(b), Block 13 of Chunk No. 3 of the Showak PGE Area is illustrated.) Each block, like each chunk and each PGE area, requires its own map. Thus, if we have, for example, a PGE area consisting of three chunks with five blocks each, there will be 15 Maps No. 3. Map No. 3 shows the approximate location of each structure, together with a unique identification number for each structure. We would advocate, in general, the use of a numbering system that covers *all* structures, not just occupied ones, although a number of studies have assigned numbers to occupied structures only. Regardless of the numbering system used, all dwellings, all temporarily vacant structures, and all other potentially habitable structures are to be shown on the map.

A typical scale for Map No. 3 might be 1:2,000, and it would be surprising if major departures from this suggestion were necessary. With such a scale one could comfortably fit six miles (10 kilometers) on one piece of paper 20 inches (50 centimeters) in length and have room to display 100 structure numbers individually. In order to make Figures 4.3(a) and 4.3(b) conform to the dimensions of this handbook, the maps of Block 13 as reproduced here use a scale of 1:5,000 and omit an uninhabited zone between the hamlet of Umm Gara and the Alabara River. For use in the field, block maps should be at least twice as large and, particularly at the edge of settled areas, should avoid omitted zones or changes in scale.

The task of constantly improving maps and keeping them up to date requires a routine procedure, cumbersome but unavoidable, to ensure that all maps used in the various parts of the organization are always corrected and brought up to date swiftly and in the same manner, and that adequate records of the process are kept. Record keeping is particularly important because, obviously, in a living organization it will never be possible to withdraw all maps at the same time and have them all corrected together. Each copy must therefore be numbered and a record made in some central register for each amendment when the given map is corrected.

The vigilance of field workers in checking their maps could be enhanced through a system of modest rewards for each acceptable new finding requiring a correction of the existing edition of a map. The reward could be direct, or it could be indirect—for example, incorporated in a system of points earned by the field workers and accumulated toward some periodic benefit. Let there be no illusions, however, as to the amount of time and effort the operation of such a system would require. It is considerable, and unless the investment necessary to administer a "rewards" system properly can be afforded it would be better not to adopt one at all.

In some cases, it may be possible to use sources from outside the organization to update maps. For example, highway department reports of road construction, building permit records, tax records, and other official sources may provide regular data and, occasionally, new maps. In some countries special programs such as the WHO Malaria Eradication Program may be a useful source of maps and changes therein. The use of outside sources for updating maps has the advantage of keeping the two collection systems as independent as possible. Unfortunately, it is often quite difficult to obtain usable and timely reports from outside agencies, so that in updating the maps one often has to rely only on the reports of the field staff and visits of senior project officials.

Regardless of the methods used, adequate time should be allowed for the production and correction of maps in order to ensure adequate geographic control of field operations. For a more detailed discussion of the establishment of geographic control in PGE studies, see Cooke (1971).

B.2   ADDRESSES OR NUMBERING OF STRUCTURES

A basic requirement in most PGE studies is that every structure carry a unique and unambiguous identifying number. It is best if a generally recognized address system is used. Then, even if some isolated structures are without numbers, a survey carried out under the supervision of the PGE organization can be used to identify and number these structures in accordance with the original address system. In fact, an offer by the PGE organization to the proper office of the municipal government in larger cities to keep the official system of house numbers freshly painted on placards in front of every structure in the city's PGE sample areas will usually be worth the expense and effort, as it can result in rapid access to municipal maps. A system of numbering may also exist as a result of a recent field activity, such as a national census or a Malaria Eradication Program. Provided the updating required is modest and the old numbers are still legible, it is often advantageous to use such an existing system. One possible drawback to this, however, is that a recoding system may be necessary if the matching is not done by hand. If no usable prior numbering system exists, the PGE organization must do its own numbering, preferably in conjunction with the mapping of the area. In some cases, an existing numbering system can be used in the larger urban areas, even though the PGE organization has to number structures in smaller towns and in rural areas itself.

If a numbering system is to be established specifically for PGE purposes, one error to be avoided is the numbering of structures consecutively, following the haphazard path of the mapper over the area. It is always advisable to begin with a plan. For example, assume

**Fig. 4.3(a) Map No. 3: Block 13, Chunk No. 3, Showak PGE Area
No Structures Shown**

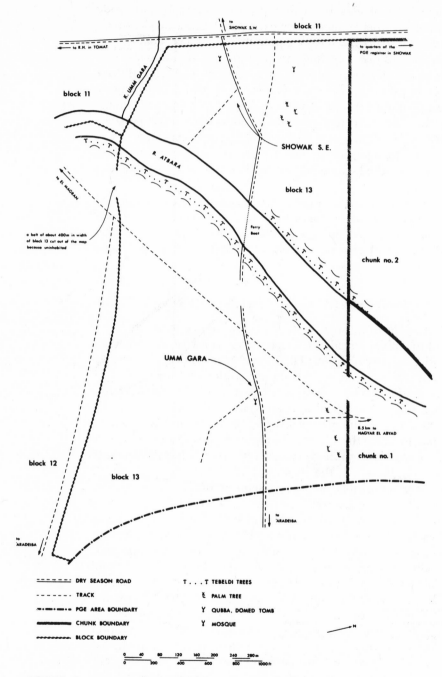

SOURCE: Population Research Laboratory, University of Alberta, Edmonton.

Fig. 4.3(b) Map No. 3: Block 13, Chunk No. 3, Showak PGE Area
Structures and Structure Numbers Added

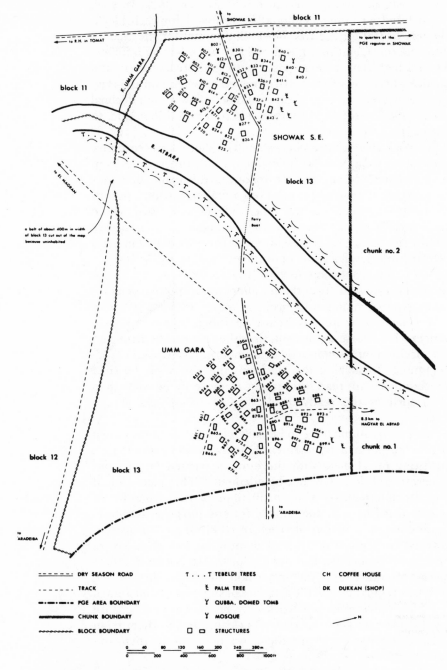

SOURCE: Population Research Laboratory, University of Alberta, Edmonton.

that the sample area contains some 6,000 persons, or 1,400 households, and 1,200 occupied structures. Assume further such density and transportation facilities that the whole area can be divided into two chunks and ten blocks, with an average of 120 dwellings per block. In such a situation two hundred numbers should be reserved for each block; for example, 001 to 199 for the first block, 200 to 399 for the second, 400 to 599 for the third, and so on, with the last block having numbers from 1,800 to 1,999. To make it possible to add structures in the correct sequence when new structures are erected or when unnumbered structures are discovered, each number should be followed by a decimal point and a (smaller) zero; for example, 157.0, 158.0, 159.0, and so on.[4]

Within a block, structure numbers should be allotted in accordance with some obvious system, such as following a road, proceeding from one group of dwellings to another, or following the main directions (N, E, S, and W). A system of having even numbers on one side of a road and uneven numbers on the other side may be used where this is appropriate. The exact details of the arrangement of structure numbers within the block are of less importance, provided there has already been an orderly allocation of numbers to blocks. A block is small enough for any confusion to be easily sorted out, if its own group of numbers is isolated from the numbers used in other blocks.

Another type of numbering problem arises when more than one script or system of writing is in use in the country, especially if some numbers have close equivalents in other scripts. A firm and unambiguous decision on a single style of numbering is necessary from the very beginning. In making this decision, the ability of the field staff and respondents to read the script is more important than considerations such as the ready availability of typewriters with a particular script.

In order for the numbering to be fully effective, numbers must be affixed in some permanent manner. Usually nothing less than a sturdy, nonrusting metal plate with the number written in oil paint will do; whitewash will definitely not be adequate.[5] This plate should be affixed (preferably nailed) to the main door of the structure, or to a nearby tree if the door is not suitable for the purpose. It should be placed high enough to be out of reach of children and to prevent its being covered by a growing heap of manure or harvested crops, or being overgrown by plants. The upkeep of the structure numbers requires special attention, and the inspection of the quality of the numbers must be a regular part of the activities of supervisory personnel. In addition, some public relations work may be necessary to ensure that the respondents help keep the numbers clean, prevent them from being overgrown, do not overpaint them, do not remove them, do not deface them, etc.

When changes take place or when errors are discovered, maps have to be corrected and new numbers allocated. Unnumbered structures may be detected by the regular field staff while they are working in the sample areas, by the supervisory staff during routine inspections, or in special periodic efforts to update the maps and numbers. In general, the assignment of numbers to new or otherwise unnumbered structures should be done in such a way as to be independent of whether or not any vital events are reported by either collection system for such structures. If this is not the case, there is likely to be some reduction in the independence between the two systems in the reporting of vital events because, other things being equal, events in numbered structures are more likely to be covered than those in unnumbered structures. Thus if the enumerator or registrar is expected to report unnumbered structures, his responsibility should explicitly extend to *all* unnumbered structures, not just those associated with vital events. With a special registration system, the registrar might be given responsibility for reporting, and even numbering, unnumbered structures so long as he is properly supervised and his instructions clearly indicate that he is responsible for all structures in the sample area. With similar instructions and supervision the survey enumerator could also be given this responsibility. However, a passive civil registrar is *not* a good source of information on unnumbered structures, since his information about such structures generally refers only to those with vital events.

An alternate method of updating structure numbers, and a better one from the viewpoint of maintaining independence, involves a periodic field review of the maps and structure numbers for the specific purpose of assigning numbers to all unnumbered structures and repairing or repainting existing numbers. This review can be separated from the actual enumeration or registration work and performed once or twice a year by the supervisor of either the enumerator or the registrar, or by one or more persons specifically assigned to move from sample area to sample area doing the review work on an essentially full-time basis.

Regardless of how unnumbered or erroneously numbered structures are discovered, the responsibility for allotting and correcting numbers in any one area must remain with one person. If other personnel discover structures without numbers, they should mark them in the enumeration or registration records with an X, followed by the number of the nearest structure (for example, X278), and see that the person responsible for numbering is informed.

B.3   PERIODIC HOUSEHOLD SURVEYS

The household surveys called for in each of the three alternative designs described in this chapter have enough features in common to make a general, introductory section on surveys valuable. As a preliminary step, the area to be surveyed must be well defined and described on high quality maps, as discussed in Section B.1. In general, the sample area of the two systems will be coterminous.[6]

In a household survey, information on individual vital events can be obtained by asking whether any births or deaths occurred in the past (the "retrospective question" approach) or by questions linked to changes in the household membership enumerated in successive survey rounds (the "accounting for household changes" approach). Neither approach is totally satisfactory.

The retrospective approach is subject to errors due to failure to find a relevant respondent for each birth and death, failure of respondents to recall the date of events correctly, or failure of respondents to report some events at all. A relevant respondent may be lacking either because of the migration or death of the "best" respondent, or because the interview is conducted with an easily available household member or neighbor rather than a less accessible but more knowledgeable family member. At the cost of more frequent interviews, problems attributable to the migration or death of the "best" respondent can be reduced, but not eliminated. Clearly, for a death in a one-person household there is no best respondent. Although neighbors may be able to provide some information about the dead person, the quality of the information will deteriorate very rapidly over time, particularly in urban areas. At the cost of more time per survey round, enumerators can be instructed to interview only those household members deemed most knowledgeable about births and deaths. In large households, particularly those with more than one married woman of reproductive age, one might want to try to obtain interviews with a number of different family members. However, if carried beyond a certain point, this tactic can be very costly in terms of both the survey budget and the respondents' goodwill.

The inability of respondents to recall accurately the date of a vital event may result in a number of distinct problems. Births and deaths occurring before the start or after the end of the survey reference period may be reported by the respondent as having occurred in the reference period. This phenomenon, termed "telescoping" (Hansen and Waksberg, 1970), is a very common problem in survey research and affects the reporting of such topics as physicians' visits, household repairs, and the purchase of consumer durables. It may well arise from an effort of respondents to help the work of the survey as much as possible. In vital statistics estimation, telescoping is the source of temporal out-of-scope reports. Typically, such out-of-scope reports tend to be clustered near the far end of the recall period; that is, in January for a recall period running from January to June. Of course, respondents may also fail to report some events that occurred during the reference period because they remember them as having occurred prior to it. In practice it is not possible to distinguish this source of omission from other reasons events are not reported (for example, a poor choice of respondent, forgetting, or uncertainty about whose births and deaths should be reported). The various sources of omission are frequently referred to, somewhat inaccurately, as "memory loss." As with the case of telescoping, "memory loss" problems are not unique to demographic surveys. Finally, reports of events with errors in the time of occurrence can be the source of erroneous nonmatches if the date of the event is used as a matching criterion and the "tolerance limits" are not sufficiently wide.

Because of the confounding of the "memory loss" and telescoping phenomena, it is difficult to make simple rules for dealing with these two problems. The effects of telescoping can be reduced by using a reference period shorter than the recall period (for example, asking about the 12-month period from January to December 1968 in January 1969, but using that survey round to provide results for the July–December period only).

In a multiround survey, the effects of both telescoping and omissions due to wrongly dated reports of vital events can be reduced by using overlapping recall periods. The amount of overlap is a function of the length of the recall period and the frequency of enumeration. With a 12-month recall period and quarterly enumerations, there will be an overlap of nine months in the recall periods of successive survey rounds and each event should be reported four times. With semiannual enumerations and a 12-month recall period the overlap will be six months and each event will be reported twice. Annual enumeration and a 12-month recall period will provide no overlap. Since overlap can be achieved for any frequency of enumeration merely by choosing a recall period of the appropriate length, the out-of-pocket expense involved is small. There will be a slight increase in the average time spent per household, for households associated with events, in both collection and processing.

Shortening the period of recall, which can only be accomplished at the cost of increasing the frequency of enumeration in multiround surveys or of increasing the variance in both types of surveys, often reduces most of the types of errors attributable to "memory loss." However, the effect of shorter recall periods on telescoping is more complex. Although a respondent's ability to date events accurately tends to improve as the recall period is shortened, the proportion of the total recall period that is near (say, within one month of) the beginning of the period increases. Neter and Waksberg (1965), in a carefully designed study, attempted to sort out the differential effects of telescoping, memory loss, and the other components of response error affecting the reporting of expenditures for home repairs. The results of this study give weight to the view that the effects of telescoping are more pronounced when short recall periods are used. However, it is evident from their data and the literature generally that telescoping effects are quite dependent upon the subject matter of the investigation and the specific questions asked. In any case, in vital events reporting, unless the recall period is markedly longer than the reference period, it is difficult to be sure how much telescoping will be affected by changing the length of the recall period.

Although the use of a shorter recall period may improve the bias of reporting, this gain often will not balance the increase in variance due to a smaller sample size or the increase in cost due to taking more interviews if the original sample size is maintained. However, coupling a short recall period with the method of accounting for household changes may reduce the bias enough to compensate for the increase in variance or costs involved.

The method of accounting for household changes referred to here is the one recommended by Jabine (1969) for use as part of the Atlantida program (U.S. Bureau of the Census, 1965–67) for training in household survey work. In the Atlantida program, the household survey is conceived as a general purpose survey. It can, however, be limited to measuring population changes. On the first visit to any household, persons resident there are listed in the usual manner. On subsequent visits, the listing is updated. People who have moved in or been born since the preceding visit are added, and people who have moved away or died are deleted. In each interview, the current household composition is checked against the composition of the household at the time of the immediately preceding visit. If a person listed as a household member at the time of the first visit is not with the household on the second visit, the cause of absence (dead, moved elsewhere, temporarily absent) is determined. If the dwelling unit is empty (or demolished, converted to nonresidential use, etc.) or occupied by another family, the reasons for the absence of the former household members are also explored. Similarly, if a person (or an entire household) not listed on the first visit is present on the second visit, the cause of the addition (birth, moved from another address, temporarily present) is determined. The same procedure has also been referred to as the "follow-up" technique or the "multiround survey" approach (U.N. Economic Commission for Africa, 1971).

The important feature of this technique is that the household sample is based on the population as it existed prior to the reported events rather than on an attempt to reconstruct this population *ex post facto*. This is particularly important in the case of deaths. One of the most frustrating experiences in trying to obtain death reports by means of a household survey is trying to find a method of sampling that gives some promise of the death being reported five or six months after it occurs. Of course, one can ask about deaths that occurred in a given building or area, but whom does one ask? Frequently (particularly in urban areas), the occupants of the building know nothing about persons outside their own households—particularly neighbors who no longer exist—and the local authorities may be equally uninformed.

However, not all births and deaths will appear as changes in the listed household population. For example, the procedure misses the birth of an infant who was born after any given visit but died or moved away before the next visit and the death of a person who moved in after the first visit and died before the second visit. To detect these cases one must ask retrospective questions about any other births or deaths that occurred between the two visits. Also, since infants who were born and died between the two visits may be particularly hard to trace, it may be useful to supplement questions about changes in household membership with inquiries about the pregnancy status of each woman in the household in each round and ask about the outcome of each pregnancy in the next round.

Two other kinds of problems may be particularly troublesome in applying the household-change technique. First, there is some danger that enumerators or respondents will fall into the habit of reporting "no change" or "everything is the same as last visit." This type of response largely nullifies the advantages of the household-change technique and will result in an undercount of births and deaths. The problem can be minimized by providing one set of questions to be completed for each person reported as "present" and another set for each person reported as "no longer present" and by asking each present household member at least one question to which the response can be reasonably expected to vary from round to round for one or more family members.

Second, since the household-change technique focuses on changes in the membership of each household enumerated in a previous survey round, surveys using this approach sometimes concentrate on existing households and cover newly formed households inadequately. New households may be created when a family moves into the sample area, when grown-up children marry and form a household of their own, or when an existing household splits into two or more households for some other reason. A tendency to concentrate on existing households at the expense of newly formed households would introduce a serious bias into any single system estimate of vital rates. Although this problem is less crucial in a dual system, survey procedures, questionnaires, instructions, and supervision should be designed to provide explicit coverage of newly formed households.

Other aspects of household surveys, in addition to the method of obtaining birth and death reports, also offer great possibilities for variation. Usually, but not always, the survey interviewer is assigned several sample areas. He or she sometimes lives in or near one of the assigned areas but is usually not personally familiar with the residents of any of them. Surveys may employ either full-time or part-time interviewers. If full-time interviewers are used, they may be assigned other duties such as interviewing on other types of household surveys.

Another important choice to be made is whether each sample area should be covered by one enumerator or by a team of enumerators. Enumeration by a team may increase the independence between the two systems by ensuring different geographic assignments for the workers of the two systems. In addition, by making it possible to enumerate the area swiftly (optimistically, in a day or two), use of a team decreases the number of temporal out-of-scope cases. Moreover, it may be possible to exercise greater supervisory control by assigning one supervisor to each enumeration team. On the other hand, the cost of enumerating by a team can be higher, additional boundary problems arise, and problems occur in defining individual responsibility within each sample area.

The choice between enumeration by a team or by one enumerator depends partly upon the actual number of household questionnaires an enumerator can handle. This can be ascertained, at least approximately, during the first pilot survey. In particularly trying circumstances and with a particularly involved questionnaire, a PGE enumerator might be limited to as few as five completed household interviews daily; on the other hand, in very densely populated areas and with a simple household questionnaire, he might complete as many as 25 household interviews per day. The question of whether to use individual or team enumeration should be decided largely by the actual circumstances in this regard.

All the periodic surveys discussed in this chapter (except in Section E) assume the use of the technique of accounting for household changes, with enumerations every six or 12 months. For events not covered by the household-change method (infant mortality between rounds and events occurring to persons moving in and out between rounds), the recall period is assumed to be 12 months in the case of enumerations conducted every six months or 15 months in the case of annual enumerations. Semiannual survey rounds are particularly useful in areas where infant mortality is high; however, they are considerably more expensive.

Familiarity on the part of a high proportion of the population with a fixed date in a year, such as an important religious holiday, can help in lessening the uncertainties and ambiguities concerning the exact meaning of the recall period. If such dates are being used to pinpoint the beginning of the recall period, the enumerators must be adequately instructed in their use. In particular, instructions may have to be developed to deal with delayed surveys or religious holidays that do not fall on a fixed date in the (Gregorian) solar calendar.

The timing of the household survey also depends upon seasonal variations in factors affecting survey administration and the seasonality of migration. Seasons of heavy rainfall or excessive heat or cold, as well as religious holidays, should be avoided if possible. Scheduling enumerations for periods when large numbers of people are absent from their usual residence only aggravates reporting problems regardless of whether a *de facto* or a *de jure* definition is used. Such absences may be caused by pilgrimages, cultivation, fish and forest harvesting, seasonal work in towns and on plantations, traditional holidaying, etc.

B.4   IMPLEMENTING A *DE FACTO* APPROACH

The survey and registration procedures for collecting reports of vital events described in this chapter are assumed to be on an essentially *de facto* basis; that is, only vital events that occur in the sample areas are covered. As discussed in Section H.1 of Chapter 3, one needs to have some rule to insure that each vital event and each member of the base population is counted only once. Considered from the viewpoint of field operations, the *de facto* and *de jure* approaches (the latter counts events and persons at the place of usual residence) are simply two different ways of determining which events and persons should be associated with a particular sample area and thus counted by a given member of the field staff.

At the national level, *de facto* and *de jure* estimates should be approximately equal, whether data are collected on a complete count basis or by sampling. Estimates for subnational areas, particularly urban areas, may differ substantially depending upon which approach is used, if many vital events take place away from the usual residence of the mother or dead person. If most births and deaths occur at the place of usual residence, *de jure* and *de facto* estimates will not vary much, even at subnational levels.

As indicated in Chapter 3, in certain circumstances and with certain types of collection systems it is easier to use the *de facto* approach, whereas in other situations the *de jure* rule is easier to apply.[7] For example, household surveys usually (but not always) use a *de jure* concept for counting most persons and events, whereas registration systems usually (but not always) use a *de facto* concept for counting events. In the case of population censuses there is no fixed tradition—some countries use a *de facto* rule and others a *de jure* one. Moreover, either rule can be modified to facilitate its use in a particular situation so long as the modified rule provides that each person and event in the universe is counted only once or, if sampling is employed, can be associated with one, and only one, sample area.

An additional constraint arises in the case of most PGE studies: Both collection systems must use the same rule for counting vital events. The major exception involves PGE studies in which one source does not employ sampling and it is operationally and financially feasible to search the entire national file of this source for each event reported in the other source. These conditions may be met in some tests of civil registration completeness, see Chapter 7, Section D.2. For another possible exception, see the as yet untried design described in Chapter 7, Section B.2. In all other situations, the two systems must use a common rule for gathering information about births and deaths.

Whatever rule is used, it must provide for the handling of three broad classes of events: those that occur in the sample area to usual residents, those that occur to usual residents when they are away from the sample area, and those that occur to visitors to the sample area. In addition, some events are associated with persons without any usual residence or whose usual residence is not known, and a decision must also be made on the handling of these events. Table 4.1 indicates which of these classes of vital events should be associated with a given sample area using two different counting rules—one based on a *de facto* concept and one based on a *de jure* concept. The rules given in this table assume that the determination of physical presence or usual residence is based on the status at the time the event took place. In the case of a single-source collection system, this determination can refer to the status at either the time of occurrence or the time of collection. The latter method

Table 4.1 ***De Facto*** **and** ***De Jure*** **Counting Rules for Vital Events Using Status at Time Event Occurred**[1]

Description of situation	De facto *concept*	De jure *concept*
1. Mother[2] or dead person a usual resident and physically present in sample area	Count	Count
2. Mother[2] or dead person a usual resident, but temporarily absent from sample area	Ignore	Count
3. Mother[2] or dead person a usual resident elsewhere, but a temporary visitor to the sample area	Count	Ignore
4. Mother[2] or dead person has no usual residence, but physically present in the sample area	Count	Count

[1] "Status at time event occurred" refers to the usual residence (*de jure*) or the physical presence (*de facto*) of the mother at the time of the birth or of the deceased at the time of death. "Status at time of collection" is not suitable for PGE studies, since the dates of collection in the two systems usually involved—registration and survey—are different and therefore violate the requirement of a common counting rule. Time of collection can, however, be used as the reference point for classifying vital events in single-source methods, as well as in the enumeration of the base population.

[2] Regardless of the legal requirements, it is almost always easier to classify births in terms of the mother's residence rather than the father's.

of determining the status of vital events is not suitable in a PGE study because, typically, there is a difference between the registration system and the survey with respect to the date of collection for a given event.

As Table 4.1 indicates, a central issue in choosing between a *de facto* and *de jure* approach is the relative difficulty of obtaining reports of events occurring to short-term visitors in the sample area (which must be included in a *de facto* count) as opposed to the difficulty of obtaining reports of events occurring to usual residents who are temporarily away from the sample area (which must be included in a *de jure* count). Both approaches count the events occurring to usual residents who are physically present in the sample area. Thus, in deciding between alternative concepts we are concerned both with the potential of each for minimizing bias due to double-counting and omissions and with the difficulty and cost of making the chosen concept operational. This latter aspect includes the inability of respondents to provide the information required to apply the rule accurately, as well as the training and supervision of the field staff needed to implement the rule properly.

Although Table 4.1 is helpful in clarifying the differences between alternative concepts, the instructions to the field staff should be more direct. The rule for counting vital events used in the PGE study procedures described in this chapter is as follows: "Count births and deaths at the place where they occur." Put this way, the rule is easy to explain to the field staff, tends to avoid ambiguity, and meets the need for a counting rule that is common to both systems. It is also a correct rule, corresponding to the *de facto* concept in Table 4.1. Under this rule the following factors are *not* relevant in determining whether a birth or death should be included in the survey or registration system: (1) the place of residence of the mother (or the dead person) at the time the event took place, (2) the place of residence at the time of registration, (3) the place of residence at the time of enumeration, or (4) the physical presence of the mother in a household at enumeration time.

The implementation of the *de facto* concept poses no real problems in the case of a special registration system and few in the case of a civil registration system. In both cases the registration documents will ask for information about where the event took place. This information must be as specific as possible, and in the case of a special registration system the registrar should certainly provide the structure number where the event occurred in all but exceptional circumstances. If the structure number is not known or no system of structure numbers exists, then sufficient identifying information must be reported so that the office staff can determine whether the event occurred in the sample area.

Information other than the structure number useful for this purpose includes the name of the head of household where the event took place; a description of the structure and its location (for example, "third hut back from road on footpath leading from 'Victory' tea stall"); and the name of the village, urban ward, section of a town or village, etc. in which the structure is located. Generally, in order to be reasonably certain whether any given event in the civil register took place in the sample area, it is necessary to have information on more than one of these points. As we have pointed out, one reason for taking on the cost of establishing a special registration system is that it is sometimes impossible, using the information recorded, to associate large numbers of civil registration reports with specific sample areas.

A different set of problems arises in using a *de facto* counting rule for vital events in the household survey. First, as indicated earlier, household surveys are usually carried out on a *de jure* basis, so that senior staff members may feel more comfortable with this approach than with a *de facto* rule. Second, some events, particularly deaths, may occur in places (for example, nonresidential structures, rivers, or streets) that are not associated with any specific household. Third, infrequent survey rounds and long recall periods may cause some real problems in obtaining complete and accurate reports of births and infant deaths associated with visitors to the sample area or with households that have dissolved. Fourth, some uncomplicated procedure must be employed to relate the *de facto* collection of vital events reports in the survey to the enumeration of the base population, which may be on either a *de facto* or a *de jure* basis.

Let us deal with these topics in turn. Although many surveys are said to be carried out on a *de jure* basis, this expression usually refers to the method used in enumerating the base population. There is an important distinction between enumerating vital events (which occur over time) and enumerating the base population (which is counted as of one point in time), so that neither the *de facto* nor the *de jure* concept means quite the same thing with reference to events as it does with reference to people. For example, the usual residents at the time of the survey may not be identical with the usual residents to whom vital events occur during the course of the year. Thus, the use of a *de facto* counting rule for vital events does not imply that a *de facto* rule need be used in enumerating the base population. It is quite possible, and in many cases desirable, to combine a *de jure* concept in the enumeration of the base population with a *de facto* concept for vital events.

Because the survey method is based on interviews with each household in the sample area, vital events occurring in public places may not be reported by any household when a *de facto* rule is used in counting vital events. The problem arises most clearly with respect to deaths in nonresidential structures, streets, and so on; but may also arise because of births and deaths occurring to nomads or other transient populations who live in temporary camps, stay in the area briefly, and are not associated with any currently extant household. Coverage of these types of events can be improved somewhat by asking specifically whether any births and deaths occurred in the street or footpaths near each dwelling and by instructing the enumerator to contact local police officials to obtain reports of deaths in public places in the sample area. Coverage by a household survey of deaths in public places is somewhat improved when a *de jure* approach is used, but this gain generally does not outweigh the overall advantages of a *de facto* rule for events in a PGE study.

As the recall period lengthens, the likelihood that visitors (usually relatives of regular residents) will have entered and subsequently left the sample area increases. Some of these visitors will have been mothers who had babies while in the area or persons, including mothers and babies, who died. The reporting of these events tends to be less complete than the reporting of events involving usual residents. One way to improve the reporting of such events is to include specific questions about them on the survey schedule. A question such as "Since my last visit, did a daughter, or anyone else, visit you and have her baby here?" would be very helpful in countries where women tend to give birth in their mothers' homes. The reporting of deaths may be improved by asking, "Did any other deaths take place in or near your dwelling since my last visit, for example, to someone visiting with you?" The routine question "Is the baby still living?" asked about all live births, can improve the reporting of mortality among very young infants whose mothers came from outside the sample area to give birth. Of course, one must also determine, for each such death, whether it occurred inside or outside the area so that the latter deaths can be excluded in editing.

Another type of problem associated with the *de facto* rule, and intensified by long recall periods, is the possible loss by the survey of events that occurred in the sample area to members of dissolved households or households that moved from the area. Some provision has to be made for making a thorough inquiry into whether any births or deaths occurred in such households during the reference period but prior to their dissolution or departure. This may be done on the regular household enumeration schedule or on a special form to be used when no member of a previously enumerated household remains. Of course, more frequent enumeration rounds can lessen the problems associated with obtaining reports of events involving either visitors or dissolved or departed households.

Regardless of whether a *de facto* or *de jure* rule is used in counting events, a discontinuity will exist between the enumeration of vital events and of persons. The time reference of the rules illustrated in Table 4.1 is the time of occurrence of the event. However, for the purpose of enumerating the population, the only realistic rules are those that use a specific time reference close to the moment of enumeration. This means that whatever rule is used for enumerating the base population, some births and deaths can occur to persons not listed in the roster of household members. To avoid missing these events, specific questions about them must be included in the household survey schedule. The interviewer can start by asking about the births to each listed woman, but one must eventually ask about births to women not on the list. An example of questions about births and deaths suitable for use with a *de facto* counting rule for events and either a *de jure* or *de facto* rule for enumerating the population was given above.

Furthermore, since there is not a full correspondence between events and population regardless of the concept used, the reduction of the sampling error of the estimated vital rates due to the covariance of the numerator and denominator will be about the same whether the population is counted on a *de jure* or a *de facto* basis. For these reasons, although a *de facto* rule will usually be more suitable for counting events, we suggest that the counting rule used in enumerating the population be the one the field staff and supervisors are most comfortable with.

If a *de facto* approach is used, the question "Did _____ spend last night in this household?" can be used to ascertain the status of previously listed persons and the question "Did anyone else spend last night in this household?" to ascertain the status of unlisted persons. One advantage of these questions is that the enumerator has a clear set of items for which he is expected to obtain "yes" or "no" replies at each household. If a *de jure* rule is used to enumerate the population, much debate can be avoided if the words "usual resident" are *not* used in the questionnaires, in manuals, or in training. Instead, one can ask "Who lives here?" and then "Do they usually live here or somewhere else?" in more complicated situations. In other words, rather than devising a complicated definition of a "usual resident" and making the enumerator memorize it, one should use a question that is directly meaningful to the respondent in most situations and base the *de jure* definition of usual residence on it.

In addition to these general considerations and recommendations, there are a host of specific details that have to be worked out in the light of the actual situation in each country. If special population subgroups (for example, nomads, military personnel and their families, persons in institutions, families living on houseboats, and seasonal labor camps) pose unique problems with respect to the counting of either events or people, specific instructions should be given on how these problems are to be handled. (Although it is generally recognized that nomadic tribal groups are difficult to enumerate, individual families and unattached persons with no usual residence often pose an even greater challenge to those concerned with complete coverage of the study area.) Methods for dealing with a few of the major problems associated with covering some of these groups are discussed in appropriate sections of Chapter 7. However, since all problems cannot be anticipated, interviewers and registrars should be instructed that "when in doubt, record a doubtful event and describe the circumstances that give rise to the doubt on the schedule." The office staff can then take the responsibility for resolving doubtful cases and for the preparation of improved field instructions.

Although enumerators and registrars should be informed of this method of handling doubtful cases, they should not consider it a procedure to be used routinely. The reporting rules we describe are simple, and in the vast majority of cases they will permit respondents and the field staff to reach the correct decision with a minimum of thought on whether specific events or persons are to be covered.

The part-time lawyers among the field staff will inevitably find a host of hypothetical circumstances in which these rules appear to fail or seem inadequate. Some of these queries reveal misunderstandings about the rules, and the majority relate to situations so rare that almost any solution is satisfactory. Occasionally, most often near the start of a study, they point up the need for a clarification of the field instructions. In general, however, clarifications should arise not from the hypothetical problems posed in training sessions but from the actual problems encountered in field work.

To conclude, let us restate the simple set of counting rules that have been discussed in this section and that will be suitable for most PGE studies. In listing vital events, the rule is count "the events at the place where they occurred." In enumerating the base population, the rule is count either "those who live here" (*de jure* base population) or "those who spent last night here" (*de facto* base population).

B.5   THE CONTENT OF THE SURVEY QUESTIONNAIRES AND REGISTRATION DOCUMENTS

The content and design of the PGE questionnaires and documents should be based on a blend of the experience of other countries, the social and cultural circumstances of the country in which the PGE study will be undertaken, and the objectives and limitations of the particular study. For the first of these factors, the rich and helpful literature on the subject should be consulted, both for principles and examples (U.S. Bureau of the Census, 1965a; United Nations, 1955; United Nations, 1964b) and for possible sources of error (Kahn and Cannell, 1957; Oppenheim, 1966). The purpose of this section is to provide guidelines for constructing field documents and to give a concrete example of how such documents can actually be designed.

A list of items to be considered for inclusion in the survey and registration documents is given in Table 4.2. This listing was developed as a working model for a proposed PGE study in a particular country. The final determination of items to be used was to be decided on the basis of small-scale pilot tests conducted prior to the actual PGE study and a careful review of the questionnaires and results of other studies conducted in the country. The items listed in Table 4.2 should be considered suggestive rather than definitive; modifications in the items and in their relative importance will be necessary in any particular application. For example, in the context of the country concerned, marital status was considered neither analytically significant nor helpful in the collection of data. Thus this item was not even listed. In some other country, an item on marital status would be included.

Each item being considered for inclusion in the data collection documents of the study should be assessed in relation to: (a) field control needs—that is, the information needed to facilitate supervision, documents control, and follow-up; (b) the data needed in the preparation of basic estimates by means of demographic analysis;[8] (c) the need for sufficient items common to both collection systems to permit accurate matching; (d) substantive tabulation needs—that is, the information to be used in preparing the basic PGE estimates of fertility, mortality, and population characteristics;[9] and (e) the items needed for methodological studies—that is, information required for the study of the demographic measurement process itself. In addition, certain special items may be required on the civil registration documents for legal purposes.

In terms of any one of these factors, some items are essential, some are quite useful but not essential, some are only marginally useful and others are of no particular use. In the end, these sometimes conflicting requirements must be balanced. In order to provide some guidelines to those responsible for designing the field documents, each item listed in Table 4.2 for possible inclusion in the survey and the civil registration forms was provisionally ranked in terms of its usefulness in relation to each of the five factors listed above. The ranking used was 1 = essential, 2 = useful, 3 = marginal, and 4 = irrelevant.

The survey questionnaire (Part A of Table 4.2) contains both birth and death information on the same form, whereas the registration document for births (Part B.1) is separate from that for deaths (Part B.2). In part this reflects the fact that information for all vital events

Table 4.2   Possible Items for Inclusion in PGE Survey and Registration Documents, by Reason for Inclusion

A.   Items for the survey questionnaire

Item	Field control	Demographic analysis	Matching	Substantive tabulations	Methodological studies
1. For each household interview:					
District	1	4	4	4	4
Chiefdom section	1	4	2	4	2
Enumeration Area (E.A.)	1	4	1	1	1
Village	1	4	2	4	2
Structure number	1	4	1	4	2
Date of interview	2	4	1–2	4	2
Enumerator's name	1	4	4	4	1
Enumerator's signature	2	4	4	4	4
Supervisor's name	1	4	4	4	2
Supervisor's signature	2	4	4	4	2
Length of interview	4	4	4	4	2
Language of interview	4	4	3	4	2
Name of principal respondent	2	4	4	4	2
Sex of respondent	4	4	4	4	2
Relationship to household head	3	4	4	4	2
No. of adult household members talked with	4	4	4	4	2
Remarks	2	4	2	2	2
Special report if entire household moved away	1	4	1	2	1
2. For each de facto person:					
Full name	1	4	2	4	2
Relationship	2	4	2	3	2
Usual place of residence (here or elsewhere)	1	2	1	1	2
If residence elsewhere, give place	2	4	3	3	2
Sex	2	1	3	1	1
Age	2	1	3	1	1
Father alive	3	1–2	4	3	1
Mother alive	3	1–2	4	3	1
Was person present last night?	1	4	2	1	2
If absent, why (dead, moved away, etc.)	1	4	2	3	2
If previously unlisted, give reason	1	4	3	3	2
For birth, give place of birth	3	4	2	2	2
For new arrival, give place of previous residence	1	4	4	3	2
Was the person present at interview?	2	4	4	4	2
3. For each woman aged 13 and over:					
How many children ever borne by this woman					
—are now living at home?	2	1	4	1	2
by sex	3	1–2	4	3	2
—are now living elsewhere?	3	1	4	1	2
by sex	4	1–2	4	3	2
—are now dead?	3	1	4	1	2
by sex	4	1–2	4	3	2
For first round:					
Date of most recent live birth	3	1	2	3	2
For subsequent rounds:					
Has this woman given birth to a child since the previous round?	3	2	1	1	2
4. For each live birth:					
Name and line number of baby	2	4	1	4	2
Name and line number of mother	2	4	1	4	2

Table 4.2 (Continued)

A. Items for the survey questionnaire (continued)

Item	Field control	Demographic analysis	Matching	Substantive tabulations	Methodological studies
Name and line number of father	2	4	1	4	2
Date of birth	2	2	1	1	1
Place of birth	2	2	1	1	1
Sex of baby	2	3	1	2	1
Place of usual residence of mother . . .	3	3	1	2	1
Age of father	4	4	3	2	2
Age of mother	3	2	2	1	2
Birth order	2	2	3	1	2
Multiple birth	2	4	2	2	3
Is the baby still alive?	2	4	3	3	2
Name of village midwife or other person attending birth	2	4	2	2	2
5. For each death:					
Name and line number of dead person	2	4	1	4	2
Date of death	2	2	1	1	1
Usual residence	3	3	1	2	1
Place of death	2	2	1	1	1
Sex of dead person	2	2	1	1	1
Age at death	3	2	2	1	2
If ever married, name of spouse	2	4	2	4	3
If child or infant:					
—name of mother	2	4	1	4	2
—age of mother	4	4	3	2	3
6. Check questions for each household:					
Births to unlisted women	1	4	4	4	2
Deaths of unlisted persons	1	4	4	4	2
Any other births	2	4	4	4	2
Any other deaths	2	4	4	4	2

B. Items for the registration documents

Item	Field control	Demographic analysis	Matching	Substantive tabulations	Methodological studies
1. For each live birth:					
Province	2	4	4	1	4
District	1	4	4	2	4
Chiefdom	1	4	2	2	2
Chiefdom section	1	4	2	1	2
Village	1	4	1	1	1
Date of birth	2	4	1	1	1
Name of baby	1	4	1	4	2
Sex of baby	2	4	1	2	1
Place of birth					
If institutional:					
—name of institution	1	4	1	4	2
—type of institution	2	4	3	1	2
If noninstitutional:					
—village name	1	4	1	2	2
—structure number	1	4	1	4	2
Father's name	2	4	2	4	2
Mother's name	2	4	1	4	2
Place of mother's usual residence	2	4	1	2	2
Mother's age	3	4	2	1	2
Mother's parity	4	4	3	1	2
Multiple birth	1	4	2	2	2

Table 4.2   (Continued)

B. Items for the registration documents (continued)					
Item	Field control	Demographic analysis	Matching	Substantive tabulations	Methodological studies
Name and title of person attending birth	1	4	2	2	1
Name of person reporting birth	1	4	3	4	1
Relationship to baby	2	4	3	4	1
Signature of person reporting	2	4	4	4	4
Date of report	2	4	3	3	1
Name of registrar	1	4	3	4	1
Date of registration	1	4	2	2	1
Signature of registrar	1	4	4	4	4
2. For each death:					
Province	2	4	4	1	4
District	1	4	4	2	4
Chiefdom	1	4	2	2	2
Chiefdom section	1	4	2	1	2
Village	1	4	1	1	1
Date of death	2	4	1	1	1
Name of deceased	1	4	1	4	2
Place of death					
If institutional:					
—name of institution	1	4	1	4	2
—type of institution	2	4	3	1	2
If noninstitutional:					
—village name	1	4	1	2	2
—structure number	1	4	1	4	2
Usual residence	2	4	1	2	2
Sex of dead person	2	4	1	1	1
Age of dead person	2	4	2	1	1
If under 5 years:					
—mother's name	2	4	1	4	2
—mother's age	4	4	3	2	3
If under 1 year, birth registration number	2	4	2	4	2
If married, name of spouse	2	4	2	4	3
Cause of death	4	4	4	1	2
Name of certifier	2	4	4	4	2
Title of certifier	3	4	4	2	2
Name of person reporting death	1	4	3	4	1
Relationship to dead person	2	4	3	4	1
Signature of reporting person	2	4	4	4	4
Date of report	2	4	3	3	1
Name of registrar	1	4	3	4	1
Date of registration	1	4	2	2	1
Signature of registrar	1	4	4	4	4

is collected at once in a household survey, whereas the nature of a registration system requires a separate document for each event. Differences in format, order of items, and even wording increase the difficulty for the field workers of one system in consulting documents of the other system. Such variations also make the interviews somewhat less repetitive for the population of the sample areas. However, the use of different forms in the two sources may increase the difficulty of the work at the matching stage. In order to ensure that the cost of these differences is not too high, some practice matching should be tried before the forms are printed.

With regard to the actual design of the forms, a compromise must be struck between subject-matter and processing requirements on the one hand, and those of the field staff and the public on the other. Features of records that are attractive and understandable in the field may pose problems for the office processing work. Moreover, small and lightweight documents, although convenient for the field workers to carry, may not provide enough room for making legible entries and may lack sufficient durability. It is assumed that except where there are particularly strong arguments for not doing so, a copy of the PGE registration document will be left with the respondents whenever a special PGE registration is part of the study.

Some items, particularly names and addresses, are subject to considerable national and local variation. In societies where naming follows some established pattern, it is advisable to allow for that pattern. For example, in Arabic countries where surnames are not in general use, the pattern might be own name, father's name, grandfather's name. In Latin America one should allow space for the mother's maiden name and other *appellidos*. In societies that include a proportion of Chinese, the first name must be clearly distinguished from the last name. Other peculiarities such as the wife's unwillingness to mention the husband's name, males' reluctance to talk about their unmarried daughters at home, delay in giving names to the newborn, or changes in names with the rites of passage or because parents or godparents (or their equivalents) change their minds must also be allowed for.

The address is likely, in the great majority of cases, to be the structure number specially allotted for the PGE study. In most cases the existing addresses will not be adequate for matching purposes. However, should they be, more space for recording should be provided.

In addition to the substantive items on the registration and enumeration records, there will be several entries to be used for processing purposes, for which space should be provided. Some of these have been included in Table 4.2 (for example, the name of the official making the entry). In other studies space might also be required for such entries as the code for the type of assumed information (when reference back to the field is avoided by making reasonable assumptions about missing or inconsistent data during office processing) and cross-references to other documents pertaining to the same household (when more than one birth or death occurred in the same household). If possible, space for coding entries should be provided on the field documents to avoid the creation of separate coding sheets and the consequent inconvenience of checking codes against entries on a different piece of paper.

In designing the survey questionnaire one should keep clearly in mind that data on births and deaths is obtained as a byproduct of the enumeration of all households in the sample and such periodic updating of these enumerations as may be decided upon. The main responsibility of the field personnel during enumeration is to list each household with all its members and to record all the required characteristics of the households and their members.

Some questions may be included that are not directly relevant to the estimation of vital rates. With relatively little effort, the PGE enumeration can provide important substantive data about the social and economic characteristics of the population. However, care should be taken that the central purpose, vital events collection, is not undermined by the inclusion of too many additional topics. For example, the effort in terms of questionnaire space, training time, and interviewer work load needed to obtain high quality data on consumer income or expenditures, labor force characteristics, or detailed migration histories may be such that the questions on vital events are given insufficient emphasis by both interviewers and respondents. In contrast, as an example of the kind of data that can be easily and usefully collected, the suggestions made by Demeny (1967) for countries lacking adequate standard demographic data should be seriously considered. These items are shown in Part A.3 of Table 4.2.

If in multiround surveys the "household-change technique" is used, the survey questionnaire will ask for answers to a number of items in terms of changes since the preceding visit. However, it must be remembered that special questions must be included to detect vital events associated with persons who are not listed as household members in any survey round; for example, the live birth and early infant death occurring between survey rounds or the death of an unlisted visitor or elderly relative who recently joined the household.

It will be clear to readers with some field experience that not all questions can be asked with an equal degree of ease. For example, in many societies questions about the pregnancy status of female household members or about a pregnancy's outcome should be asked only of married women whose husbands are present, although in some situations such questions would cause no offense if asked of any woman of reproductive age. Accordingly, a serious effort should be made, before any PGE study is begun, to anticipate difficulties that may be caused by the wording of the various questionnaires and make adjustments as appropriate. However, in general, government officials and the field staff are more troubled by so-called "sensitive" questions than are respondents. This is another reason for conducting field tests of survey documents and procedures.

Several of the questions will require specific definitions. In the case of most definitions, it is not the precise accuracy of the wording that matters, but the consistency with which the definitions are applied and the care taken with the instructions given during training and in the instruction manuals. For example, a working definition of a live birth that refers to the "first cry" of an infant is very much preferable to a complex and medically sound definition that involves concepts and terminology unfamiliar to both the field staff and the respondents.[10] Whenever possible, however, internationally recognized concepts and definitions should be used, as long as they are commonly understood and relevant to the purposes of the inquiry. Some of these definitions will be found in the glossary to this manual.

In some parts of the world it is common practice to insist on a questionnaire that specifies the exact wording to be used for each item. This undoubtedly simplifies the task of the enumerator and, if fully implemented, results in a more standardized collection instrument. However, in other parts of the world "austere," or abbreviated, questionnaires that provide only a list of the items to be collected are used. The enumerator in this situation is forced to put each question to the respondents in his own words. In multilanguage countries, or where the spoken language is markedly different from its written form, this latter approach is often the only feasible way of conducting surveys. In the event that the items are shown only in abbreviated form on the questionnaire, the training of field staff and the enumeration manuals must place increased emphasis on the problem of standardized approaches. For example, the enumeration manual should provide examples of the words to be used in asking each item, and the training should include a number of taped or live interviews conducted by someone well acquainted with the questionnaire. These interviews can serve as models for the trainees.

B.6   THE MATCHING OPERATION

A discussion of matching theory relevant to the design and conduct of a PGE study was presented in Chapter 3, along with a method for arriving at a set of objective matching criteria. In this section, we suggest some specific procedures for establishing and carrying out the matching operations in a PGE study. Later, in Chapter 5, some of the stages in the development of a matching operation will be illustrated by means of a hypothetical case study.

The matching operations described in this section assume that the match will be done manually, by a relatively inexperienced clerical staff supported by one or two senior professionals. In general it will be safer, faster, and cheaper to do the matching by hand, even if one has relatively easy access to a computer or mechanical punchcard equipment. As indicated in the section "Matching modes" in Chapter 3, an idle computer does not mean that programmers and systems analysts will be available to work on the matching. Furthermore, the need to convert the information contained on the survey and registration documents into machine readable form—most commonly by keypunching—both lengthens the matching operation and contributes to matching error. Certainly, the physical task of manually comparing the two piles of records for a given PGE area is easily managed for the cluster sizes used by most PGE studies. On the other hand, the use of manual matching deprives the matching operation of the consistency imposed by mechanical matching. Therefore, when manual matching is used, the senior personnel of the PGE study assume the responsibility for ensuring that the matching rules are applied as consistently and objectively as possible.

The matching operation has two basic phases. In the first, establishing matching procedures, one is concerned with determining the items on the field documents that will be used in comparing records, formulating the rules for classifying pairs of reports as matched or nonmatched, and devising the initial methods of implementing these matching rules. The second, or maintenance, phase of the process involves making practical arrangements for ensuring that reasonable standards of speed and quality are maintained and that information obtained from the matching and field follow-up of one year can be used to improve the matching operations in subsequent years.

Work associated with the establishment of a matching procedure should be considered a capital investment in the PGE study. Thus, one is justified in devoting considerably more effort to the planning and development phases of the matching operation than the study can routinely afford to spend on matching. On the other hand, the procedures that will be used routinely must be simple enough so that the matching clerks can apply them consistently and correctly.

As we saw in Chapter 3, Section F, erroneous matches arise when the discriminating power of the matching characteristics and tolerance limits used is low; that is, when many reports in effect carry the same identification label. Erroneous nonmatches, on the other hand, arise because there are errors in the data recorded for a given characteristic beyond that specified by the tolerance limit; that is, there are errors in the information used to identify individual reports such that the two reports for the same given event are assigned a comparison code class with a low probability of containing truly matched reports. The difference between these two types of matching error is called "net matching error," while the sum of the number of erroneous matches and erroneous nonmatches is called "gross matching error." The matching bias of the PGE estimate is based on net matching error and is unaffected by the size of gross matching error. However, gross matching error is the major determinant of the variance of the estimate of net matching error and hence is involved in determining minimum net matching error.

If matching bias is to be minimized (through a reduction in net and gross matching error), the choice of matching characteristics and the tolerance limits to be used for each characteristic must be made in some systematic fashion. To do this, one must have some objective measures of matching error associated with different tolerance limits and characteristics. How one obtains this necessary information depends largely upon whether previous relevant matching experience exists and on the operations timetable for the study.

Experience of previous matching studies conducted in the same population, if it exists in the proper form, can aid the development of matching rules by indicating the effect of alternative rules (that is, different combinations of characteristics and tolerance limits) on net and gross matching error. Of course, if major changes have occurred since the earlier studies, such as the introduction of a new system of house numbering, the earlier matching experience may give only a rough idea of what will happen in any new matching study. Similarly, if the quality of the field work in the new study is likely to be substantially different from that in the old, one cannot expect that a rigid application of the old matching rules will yield the same results in the new study. Nevertheless, previous matching experience is very helpful. At the very least, it can supply some objective way of identifying, in the population under study, those items that tend to have high (or low) discriminating power and those that tend to be reported consistently (or inconsistently) by two independent sources.

Ideally, the earlier matching studies available should involve the matching of birth or death reports. Often this is not the case and the only relevant previous experience comes from matching persons—for example, in a census post-enumeration quality check, in a health study in which clinic records are linked to household survey data for the same individuals, or in an administrative study that matches lists of ration card holders with persons on the electoral rolls. Again, such experience should not be ignored, as it can give some guidance about the relative discriminating power of possible matching items.

A more serious problem arises if only summary results of earlier matching studies are available. Frequently, all that is known about a previous study is the final match rates obtained, the subjective assessment of the success or failure of the matching operation, and, possibly, the matching rules employed. This kind of experience is *not* very helpful in making the detailed decisions necessary to establish a matching procedure, because it tells us little about the effect of various combinations of matching criteria and tolerance limits on matching error in the population under study.

If relevant previous experience is not available, the matching rules will have to be developed on the basis of a pilot study or early results of the main study. Generally, the operations timetable determines which of these two approaches is used. If the decision to conduct a PGE study is made in a relatively short time and the study must be begun as quickly as possible thereafter, then there is no choice but to use the early results of the main study in formulating the matching rules.

In such a situation it will be necessary to decide upon the items to be included in the survey questionnaire and registration forms without the guidance provided by the results of an actual matching study. In these circumstances it would be advisable to include, initially, as many potentially useful matching items as possible on the field documents. Once the final set of matching characteristics is determined, it may be possible to discontinue the collection of some identification items that are not used in matching.

Provision must also be made for the rapid processing of vital event reports from both sources so that a supply of completed documents will be available for experimental matching well in advance of the first main matching operation. A special survey enumeration can be conducted in some of the PGE areas a few months (say, three or four) after registration work has begun to generate survey reports for experimental matching. No special effort will be required to obtain the registration documents if the registrars are routinely sending copies of the completed registration certificates to headquarters at the end of each month. If they are not, supervisors or senior members of the headquarters staff must themselves pick up copies of any outstanding certificates about four to six weeks after the special survey round has been completed.

In assembling vital events reports from the main study for advance matching, it is best to use all available reports from a purposive sample of PGE areas rather than attempt to obtain a systematic or other type of probability sample of reports from all the PGE areas. (Indeed, if, for some reason, it is possible to obtain reports from the two sources for areas outside the main study sample these should also be quite adequate.) Insofar as possible, the purposive sample should be built from PGE areas that include the major linguistic, cultural, and socioeconomic groups of the population, particularly insofar as living arrangements, family structure, and patterns of naming are concerned. In addition, it is desirable to have the full range of field work quality exemplified by the areas in the sample.

Alternatively, and preferably, the operations timetable should permit a pilot study. Such a study can help determine which items should be included for matching purposes in the data collection documents of both sources. It can also supply the information needed to formulate the initial matching rules on an objective basis, provide experience in the conduct of an ongoing matching operation, and provide a mechanism for testing data collection procedures and generally familiarizing study managers and staff with many of the practical problems of running a PGE study. In particular, if the main study will involve a substantial expenditure of funds and the office conducting it has had little experience with demographic surveys, registration, or matching, many costly mistakes can be avoided by conducting a pilot study and acting upon the experience gained from it.

The pilot study need not involve a probability sample. Any convenient purposive sample will provide some useful information, though it is preferable that the pilot study sample be as broad as possible in its coverage of major population subgroups. However, there are two major constraints on a pilot study with regard to matching. First, a pilot study should be completed early enough so that its results will be available prior to the deadline for deciding which items are to be included in the field documents of the main study. Second, the pilot study must be able to supply enough birth and death reports to ensure that the matching rules developed on the basis of pilot study experience will, within reason, apply to the main matching operation. Unfortunately, these two objectives may conflict to some extent. Often, it will be necessary to strike a balance between them, bearing in mind the limited amount of funds that can profitably be spent on the pilot study.

If one of the data collection sources uses active special registrars, it is possible to accumulate a sizable number of vital event reports rapidly by introducing some retrospective data gathering into the pilot study registration system.[11] This can be achieved by instructing the pilot study's special registrars to obtain information about all events occurring in the area during the past six or 12 months during their initial rounds and thereafter to proceed with registration on a current basis. A pilot study so conducted might, for example, have ten special registrars, each covering 400 households for an average of four months, with the first month devoted primarily to obtaining retrospective reports for the preceding 12 months. In addition, from the beginning of month four, an equal number of interviewers would conduct a household survey in the same areas, asking retrospective questions about vital events over the past two years. An interviewing force of this size should be expected to complete the pilot study enumeration before the end of month five, ensuring that matching will be well underway within six months after the start of the pilot study registration work. Depending upon the actual level of fertility and mortality and the coverage rates of the two sources, such a pilot study might yield about 800 to 1,100 live-birth reports for the average 15-month reference period common to both sources and about one-third to one-half this number of death reports.

At the price of an additional survey round in the pilot study sample areas, it is possible to meet the deadline for finalizing the field documents on the basis of an analysis of the match results of, say, 500 birth and 250 death reports in each system and to select the final matching characteristics and tolerance limits on the basis of a substantially larger number of reports. If this approach is used, it may be possible to have the pilot study work overlap with that of the main study.

Finally, one should remember that the purpose of a pilot study is to provide guidance in designing the main study. If there is reason to believe that a pilot study is unrepresentative of the main study in some major respect—because of differences in either the population studied or the procedures used—the pilot study results should be interpreted in the light of these suspected differences.

Regardless of whether the matching rules will be developed using the experience of previous studies, advance data from the main study, or pilot study results, the basic tasks facing the managers of the PGE study are the same. One must obtain information about the number of erroneous matches and nonmatches that arise when various matching characteristics and tolerance limits are used. On the basis of this information one must select the combination of matching characteristics and tolerance limits that minimizes net matching error for some low level of gross matching error, within the constraints of cost and operational feasibility. These initial matching rules must then be closely monitored (particularly in the early phases of the study), using field follow-up to determine the correctness of the matching decisions and to refine further the rules for handling doubtful matches.

Implicit in this line of action is the assumption that the "true" matching status of each report can be known with certainty—in other words, that we can know accurately the number of erroneous matches and erroneous nonmatches that any given matching procedure yields. Clearly this is not the case. Even with very intensive field follow-up, some uncertainty about the correct match status of certain reports will remain. Further uncertainty is introduced into the matching operation by the fact that the matching rules were developed from a body of data that necessarily differed from the full group of vital events reports generated in the main study. Although complete certainty is impossible, a combination of experienced professional judgment and careful field follow-up can determine the match status of most reports unambiguously and correctly. For this reason, relatively large inputs of professional time and extensive field follow-up are needed while the matching rules are being developed and when the initial rules are first applied in the main study.

The field follow-up procedure was described in Chapter 3, Section I.1. Let us now examine how experienced professional judgment can best be used to determine the "true" match status, particularly of the group of reports from which the initial matching rules will be developed. It is suggested that three members of the professional or junior professional staff with extensive field experience (and preferably somewhat diverse cultural or socioeconomic backgrounds) work *independently* at classifying the available vital events reports from the two sources according to their matching status. In most situations the following three categories will be sufficient: (a) definitely matches with a report in the other system; (b) definitely does not match with a report in the other system; and (c) some uncertainty as to correct match status.

The three persons doing this special matching should be instructed by the project manager on the nature of their assignment. The instructions should stress that the matchers are to assign reports to the three match categories on the basis of all the information on the reports; that in making these determinations they are to use their common sense, their field experience, and any special knowledge they have about the populations under study and the behavior of field workers; and, finally, that they are to work completely independently of each other. In line with this last instruction, the matchers must be provided with private working space and forms on which their matching decisions can be entered so that no entries need be made on the field documents themselves. The reason for stressing that the three matchers must work independently is that there is substantial evidence that pooling independent judgments will yield a more accurate result than a jointly reached consensus judgment (Dalkey, 1971). As a very loose rule of thumb, one would want to carry out such a procedure for between 300 and 600 birth reports from each source and for an equal number of death reports. The lower limit is imposed out of concern for the reliability of the results obtained, whereas the upper limit arises from the fact that as special matching is extended indefinitely its quality inevitably deteriorates while its cost rises.

A suggested method for pooling the independent classifications made by the three special matchers for each report into a final decision on match status is shown in Table 4.3. This procedure is not foolproof, but it does provide a controlled method of obtaining the benefits of common sense and expert judgment in developing the matching procedures. If the number of reports designated for field follow-up by this procedure is too large for the available resources, it can be reduced by a suitable modification of the pooling rules. For example, category III (any two matchers agree) can be further divided into two subcategories. The first group would consist of situations where the lone dissenter assigned a match status consistent with, though different from, the majority view (for example, if there were two definite matches and one uncertain one or two uncertain matches and one definite nonmatch). The second subcategory would consist of disagreements in which the match statuses assigned were inconsistent with each other (that is, if there were two definite matches and one definite nonmatch or two definite nonmatches and one definite match). To reduce the volume of field follow-up, one might send out only the second group of category III reports—those where the dissenting judgment was inconsistent with the majority judgment—for field investigation and assign the remaining category III reports the matched status given them by the majority.

Once the "correct" matching status of a sizable number of birth and death reports from each source has been established, the tolerance limits and matching characteristics are selected. The selection process

Table 4.3 One Procedure for Combining Independent Judgments of Three Special Matchers into a Final Determination of Match Status

Category	Result of independent judgments on a given report	Final decision or other action on a given report
I	All three matchers agree	Unanimous definite match or definite nonmatch judgments accepted as final; send unanimous uncertain judgments for field follow-up.
II	All three matchers disagree[1]	Send report for field follow-up.
III	Any two matchers agree	Matchers should be informed of disagreement and be given an opportunity to reclassify the report[2]; if unanimity achieved, treat as category I above; if disagreement persists, send report for field follow-up.

[1] It is recommended that if all three matchers disagree on more than one-fourth of the reports, the matchers should be brought together with the study manager to discuss the implicit matching criteria used; thereafter the matchers should independently reevaluate their original classifications, changing any they think appropriate.

[2] If the matchers are approximately equal in seniority and status, this process can be carried out in a conference between the three matchers and the study manager. In other situations, it will be better to keep the procedure entirely anonymous.

has three stages: first, the formation of a list of feasible matching characteristics; second, the determination of the optimum tolerance limit for each characteristic on the list of feasibles; and, finally, the selection of a combination of characteristics, using the previously determined tolerance limits, that produce acceptably low levels of matching error.

The list of feasible matching characteristics includes items on the field documents of both sources that can help to identify individual events accurately. The final set of matching characteristics will be drawn from this group of feasible characteristics. A variety of names and addresses should almost always be included on the list of feasibles. For births, this might mean name of infant, name of mother, name of father, name of maternal or paternal grandfather, name of attendant at birth, address where birth took place, and address of usual residence of mother. A comparable list of feasible name and address items for deaths would include name of dead person, name of spouse or mother, name of father, address where death took place, and address of usual residence of dead person.

Depending upon local conditions and the content of the field documents, various other items could be included on a list of feasible matching characteristics. To cite a few examples, for both births and deaths, date of event, relationship to head of household, and sex could be included; for births, age of mother and mother's village of birth could be used; and for deaths, age, marital status, number of living sons, and village of birth could be used. A number of other candidates for the list of feasibles can be found in Tables 4.2 and 5.2 and in Figures 4.5 and 4.6. However, some of the items listed in these tables and figures would certainly not be feasible matching characteristics in some countries, whereas other, unlisted items might be quite suitable for particular studies.

Items that, though inquired about in both systems, have high nonresponse rates should not be included in the list of feasibles. Similarly, items that, both alone and in combination with other items, have very low discriminating power for the amount of "blocking" used in the study would not be listed as feasible characteristics. For example, occupation would not help to distinguish between events in a predominantly agrarian society, tribal group or mother tongue would not be helpful where there was little intermixing of the population along tribal or linguistic lines, and citizenship seldom provides any help.

In summary, to be listed as a feasible characteristic for matching purposes, an item must be included on the questionnaires or registration certificates of both sources. It should have low rates of nonresponse and, in the case of agreements, help to identify particular events from among other events in the same general area. (That is, it should have high discrimination, as, for example, does address.) In the case of disagreements, it should present a strong indication that the two compared reports refer to different events. (That is, there should be low rates of reporting error in both sources, as, for example, with sex.)

After the list of feasible matching characteristics has been developed one attempts to determine the optimum tolerance limit for each such characteristic considered by itself. A very strict tolerance limit for a particular characteristic implies that the information in the two reports being compared must correspond exactly for the two reports to be considered to agree on that characteristic. For example, with a very tight tolerance limit on name of father, mispronunciations, spelling errors, careless handwriting, and other minor mistakes associated with data collection might result in two reports that referred to the same event being considered as not in agreement on name of father. When tolerance limits are relaxed (for example, when names that "sound alike" are considered to be in agreement regardless of how they are spelled), errors of this type (erroneous nonmatches) are reduced. Roughly paralleling this decrease in erroneous nonmatches as tolerance limits are widened is an increase in the likelihood that two reports classified as agreeing on father's name refer to two events with different father's names. In setting tolerance limits the task is to balance these opposing sources of error so as to minimize their sum.

To find the tolerance limit for a particular characteristic that produces minimum gross matching error, one first draws up a list of possible tolerance limits for the characteristic. Some possible tolerance limits for name of father, date of event, and mother's parity are shown in Figure 4.4. These illustrative tolerance limits are listed more or less in order of decreasing rigor; that is, the first tolerance limit listed corresponds to zero tolerance and calls for exact agreement between reports on the characteristic, the next tolerance limit permits some variation in the information recorded, the next somewhat more, and so on. However, the order of listing is approximate, and one need not waste time trying to decide the order of the intermediate listings.

The terms "consistent" and "inconsistent" used in Figure 4.4 refer to whether or not the entries in the two reports being compared are logically compatible with each other—that is, whether both entries, though different from one another, can be true simultaneously. For example, nonresponses, illegible responses, "don't knows," or blanks are all consistent with any entry in the other source; similarly, an entry such as M. Hansen is consistent with Morris Hansen, whereas M. Hansen and John Hansen are inconsistent entries for given name (that is, personal forename).

The process of specifying possible tolerance limits is repeated until sets of possible tolerance limits have been developed for all the feasible matching characteristics, except for a few items, such as sex, where zero tolerance is adopted without testing. At this stage, the only constraint on the nature of the tolerance limits specified is that they have some possibility of being made operational. It follows that tolerance limits which require greater detail than the field documents contain should not be listed (for example, the hour of the day would not generally be a possible tolerance limit for date of event), nor would one want to specify tolerance limits that required the matching clerks to engage in complex recoding or arithmetic.

Fig. 4.4   **Examples of Possible Tolerance Limits for Three Specified Matching Characteristics**
(For each characteristic, tolerance limits are ordered, approximately, by decreasing rigor. For a further explanation, see text.)

A. Father's name
1. Exact agreement on full name.
2. Exact agreement on family name; consistency on all other names.
3. Exact agreement on family name.
4. Agreement on first six letters of family name; consistency on all other names.
5. Agreement on first four letters of family name; consistency on all other names.
6. Agreement on Soundex code of family name; agreement on initial letter of given name.
7. Agreement on Soundex code of family name; consistency on given name.
8. Agreement on Soundex code of family name.

B. Date of event
1. Exact agreement on day of month, month, and year.
2. Consistent agreement on day of month, month, and year.
3. Exact agreement on month and year.
4. Agreement within 30 days.
5. Agreement on month, ± one month.
6. Agreement on month, ± two months.
7. Agreement on month, ± two months, or exact agreement on date in January with different years.

C. Mother's parity
1. Exact agreement.
2. Agreement, ± 1 child.
3. Agreement, ± 2 children.
4. Agreement within two broad categories: 1–3 children, 4 or more.

The next step is to determine the optimum tolerance limit for each characteristic by comparing the results of a matching operation using various tolerance limits for each characteristic with the previously determined "correct" matching result. This is done by going through the reports of one system, classifying each report that agrees with a report in the other system on the basis of a single characteristic and tolerance limit as a match. As soon as two reports have been classified as a match, both reports are withdrawn from the pool of potentially matchable reports, at least until all comparisons for a given tolerance limit have been made. This process is repeated for all specified tolerance limits of all feasible characteristics. If the possible tolerance limits for a given characteristic are clearly ordered by decreasing rigor, only the nonmatches remaining after any given tolerance limit has been applied need be compared on the basis of the next, less rigorous tolerance limit. However, if the number of reports available for experimental matching is small or the order of tolerance limits is uncertain, it will be wiser to ignore the match status assigned on the basis of any previously used tolerance limit; that is, to return all reports to the pool of potentially matchable reports whenever a new tolerance limit is applied.

On the basis of this single-characteristic matching and the previously determined "correct" match status of each report, one can tally the number of erroneous matches and erroneous nonmatches that each tolerance limit and characteristic considered alone will produce.[12] For any given characteristic, the specified tolerance limit with the lowest gross matching error is accepted as the provisional tolerance limit to be used. For an example of this procedure based on hypothetical data, see Section D.3 of Chapter 5.

Although gross error is the most important factor in the selection of tolerance limits, other considerations should not be ignored. Some tolerance limits are easier than others for matching clerks to apply rapidly and accurately. Similarly, there are variations among tolerance limits in the number of supervisory referrals needed to resolve doubtful situations. Other things being equal, it is preferable to select a tolerance limit that involves the lowest cost and the fewest clerical mistakes. Thus, if differences in gross matching error between two tolerance limits are minor, the tolerance limit that will be simpler for the matching clerks to apply should be selected.

It may also be necessary to depart somewhat from the criterion of minimum gross error in situations where one has strong reason to believe that the group of reports used in the experimental matching differs in some important respect from those that will be encountered in the regular matching operation. Moreover, if the final matching rules are to be applied sequentially, it will be necessary to select a tolerance limit considerably stricter than the optimum implied by minimum gross error.

After the tolerance limits have been established for each characteristic on the list of feasibles, it is then necessary to select a few of these characteristics (together with their already determined tolerance limits) as the criteria to be used in the actual matching operation. This selection should be made on the basis of net and gross matching error and operational efficiency.

Ultimately, matching bias is solely a function of net matching error. Thus one should, so far as other constraints permit, strive in the selection of matching criteria to minimize net matching error. However, the net matching error produced by any set of characteristics is subject to variance, as is the estimate of which set gives the minimum net matching error; and the size of this variance largely depends upon the amount of gross matching error. A set of matching characteristics that produces both low net matching error and high gross matching error is of as little value as a set that produces low gross error and high net error.

It is also undesirable to purchase low net and gross matching error at the price of excessive operational inefficiency. For example, if low net and gross error are obtained by using a very large number of characteristics as matching criteria, the matching clerks may work so slowly and in such an unreliable manner that the set is far from optimal. Although net and gross matching error can be defined and estimated with relative ease, operational efficiency is considerably more difficult to define and quantify.

Among the factors to be considered in assessing the operational efficiency of any set of characteristics are:

(1) the length of time needed to do the matching,
(2) the clerical error rate,
(3) the supervisory referral rate and the net value of supervisory interventions, and
(4) the field follow-up referral rate and the net value of field investigations.

Fortunately, because of the special role that supervisory referrals and field follow-up play at the beginning of a PGE study, for the purposes of designating an initial set of matching characteristics, operational efficiency can be assessed primarily in terms of the first two factors.[13] Even then, however, operational efficiency remains a difficult concept to use directly in any process of optimization. (For example, in any such use the relative importance of the two remaining components of operational efficiency—the time needed and the clerical error rate— needs to be fixed, and a comparable determination has to be made of the relative importance of operational efficiency, however defined, and matching error.)

For this reason, we recommend that operational efficiency be introduced into the process of choosing a set of characteristics only implicitly, through the judgment of the study managers. Their judgment is exercised chiefly by avoiding the selection of sets with many characteristics and those with particularly difficult to apply characteristics and tolerance limits. Such a policy is likely to hold down the time needed to do the matching and the rate of clerical errors and, to a lesser extent, the need for supervisory referrals.

Given that this policy is reasonably successful in preventing the designation of an unacceptably inefficient set of characteristics, the problem of selecting a set that is satisfactory in terms of both net and gross matching error remains. The achievement of this twin goal is less difficult than it may appear at first. Both net and gross matching error tend to behave similarly in situations where tolerance limits can be treated as fixed: First, as one adds matching characteristics, they both decline, and then, as one continues to add characteristics, they both rise in absolute terms. While the minima for net and gross matching error need not be reached with the same number of matching characteristics, it is likely that the minima for both will occur in the same general region. It is also likely that the level of either net or gross matching error or both will be relatively constant in the region of these minima so that one can, at little cost in terms of one measure of error, vary the *number* of characteristics used to reduce the other measure of matching error. Furthermore, different *combinations* of characteristics, all yielding the same amount of net matching error, may produce different levels of gross matching error. Taken together, these factors provide considerable flexibility in selecting, from a list of matching characteristics with predetermined tolerance limits, a set that meets the goal of having low net and gross matching error.

The basic method of selecting a combination of characteristics that produces minimum error is first to rank the feasible matching characteristics in terms of decreasing discriminating power, and then to determine the match status of all the reports available for experimental matching using the series of cumulative combinations of these ranked characteristics (that is, first using the characteristic ranked first in terms of discriminating power; next using the first- and second-ranked characteristics jointly; next using the first-, second-, and third-ranked characteristics jointly; and so on). Because the correct match status of all such reports has already been determined, it is possible to tally the number of erroneous matches and erroneous nonmatches, and hence the number of net and gross matching errors, that each combination of characteristics produces. The procedure is quite similar to that described earlier for establishing optimum tolerance limits for individual characteristics, with two major exceptions. First, match status in the present instance is determined on the basis of whether the two reports agree on several characteristics simultaneously; and second, minimum error is defined primarily in terms of net matching error.

The ranking of characteristics by discriminating power can be roughly achieved by examining the number of erroneous matches produced by each characteristic in the study of tolerance limits. In general, the smaller the number of erroneous matches produced by a characteristic the higher the discriminating power of the characteristic is. (Of course, one would want to make this comparison and ranking on the basis of the tolerance limits to be used in the final matching operation, since the number of erroneous matches is in part a function of the tolerance limit adopted.) If there are marked differences between characteristics with respect to nonresponse rates, the absolute level of erroneous matches observed may be a misleading index of discriminating power. In such a situation an erroneous match rate obtained by dividing the number of erroneous matches by the number of correct matches with usable responses for the characteristic in both reports would be a better guide to discriminating power.

A special problem arises in the case of a small group of very accurately reported characteristics with only low or moderate discriminating power when considered singly. (Sex of infant and sex of decedent are the primary examples of characteristics of this type.) Such a characteristic might usefully be included in many sets of matching characteristics, but it would never be tested because it would be far down on the list of characteristics ranked by increasing number of erroneous matches. However, the ranking should be viewed as providing guidance on the orderly expansion of the set of characteristics and not as establishing an unbreakable rule for expansion. Sex of infant or sex of decedent, if added to a set of characteristics yielding more erroneous matches than erroneous nonmatches, can often, though not invariably, reduce both net and gross error. We therefore recommend that these two characteristics[14] be routinely tested for their effect on matching error. This can be accomplished by adding the characteristic (usually on the basis of zero tolerance) to the set near the point at which gross error is at a minimum and net error still positive and observing whether net and gross error decline sufficiently to warrant the use of the expanded set. An example of this procedure, based on hypothetical data, may be found in Table 5.8.

A number of examples of sets of matching characteristics for live births and deaths are shown in Figures 4.5 and 4.6, respectively. These illustrative sets—six for births and six for deaths—are provided to give some idea of the range of possible solutions to the problem of selecting matching characteristics. In any given matching operation some of these sets, or perhaps all of them, are likely to yield very

Fig. 4.5   Six Illustrative Sets of Matching Characteristics for Live Births
(See text for discussion of individual characteristics.)

Set B.1
    Structure number
    Sex of baby
    Father's name

Set B.2
    Structure number
    Sex of baby
    Mother's name

Set B.3
    Structure number
    Date of birth
    Baby's name

Set B.4
    Name of village[1]
    Sex of baby
    Father's name
    Mother's name

Set B.5
    Name of village[1]
    Date of birth
    Relationship to head of household
    Father's name
    Grandfather's name[2]

Set B.6
    Baby's name
    Sex of baby
    Date of birth
    Mother's name
    Mother's village of birth[3]

[1] In urban areas, urban ward can be used in place of village.
[2] Name of father's father.
[3] As appropriate, religion, linguistic group, or tribe may be used in place of village of birth.

Fig. 4.6   Six Illustrative Sets of Matching Characteristics for Deaths
(See text for discussion of individual characteristics.)

Set D.1
    Structure number
    Sex of deceased
    Name of deceased

Set D.2
    Structure number
    Sex of deceased
    Name of dead person's father

Set D.3
    Structure number
    Sex of deceased
    Age group of deceased
    Date of death

Set D.4
    Name of village[1]
    Name of deceased
    Age group of deceased
    Name of dead person's mother

Set D.5
    Name of village[1]
    Sex of deceased
    Age group of deceased
    Dead person's relationship to head of household
    Name of dead person's father

Set D.6
    Name of deceased
    Dead person's village of birth[2]
    Dead person's relationship to head of household
    Date of death
    Attendant at death

[1] In urban areas, urban wards can be used in place of village.
[2] As appropriate, religion, mother tongue, or tribe of dead person may be used in place of dead person's village of birth.

high error rates. The effectiveness, in terms of expected error rates, of the combinations of characteristics listed (or any other combinations) will depend upon the nature of the population under study, the size and type of blocking employed in the matching, the tolerance limits used, and the quality of the field work in both sources.

It may be helpful to describe the circumstances in which these various illustrative sets might be used and then to discuss a few of the major characteristics in detail. The sets involve from three to five characteristics. In a typical PGE study in which matching is confined to the sample clusters and the clusters contain less than 1,000 households, one will seldom need to use as many as six characteristics. However, when a very large file must be searched, as may be necessary in matching to some civil registration systems, a larger number of characteristics may be appropriate. In general, the larger the blocking unit is, the greater the proportion of erroneous matches for a given set of characteristics and tolerance limits will be, since a given report in one source has more possibilities for being coincidentally similar to some report in the other source. Hence larger files may require more matching characteristics. On the other hand, the number of characteristics needed to achieve minimum matching error is also partly a function of the tolerance limits used for each characteristic: Wide tolerance limits imply more characteristics if matching error is to be held constant.

In general, the three-characteristic sets (such as B.1, B.2, and B.3 in Figure 4.5 and D.1 and D.2 in Figure 4.6) are adequate only if matching is confined to relatively small clusters, if structure numbers identify most households uniquely, and if the list of commonly used names is long and diverse. In some cultures, infants do not always receive a distinctive name for weeks or even months after birth; thus Sets B.3 or D.1 may produce an unacceptable number of erroneous matches unless nearly all dwelling units contain a single nuclear family. Sets B.3 and D.1 also illustrate the interaction between the tolerance limits used and the value of additional matching characteristics. In many languages, the full given name (personal forename) of an individual reveals that person's sex, so that the use of sex as a matching characteristic contributes almost nothing to the reduction of erroneous matches when the tolerance limit on name calls for exact agreement on given name.[15] On the other hand, a less rigorous tolerance limit on given name often means that the features of a name that identify sex are lost, and there is then a definite gain in discriminating power from including the sex of the baby or of the deceased as one of the characteristics in the set.

When structure number—which often has quite high discriminating power—cannot be used as a matching characteristic, one will generally need additional characteristics to make up for the lost discriminating power. This situation is reflected in Sets B.4, B.5, B.6, D.4, D.5, and D.6. However, except in Sets B.6 and D.6, it is assumed that village name, urban ward, or some other general "neighborhood" address is available. Where such a neighborhood identification is not available, more characteristics generally have to be used if the number of erroneous matches is to be held down.

Sets of matching characteristics may strongly reflect the cultural background of a country. For example, sets such as B.1, B.5, D.2, or D.5 might produce minimum error in societies strongly dominated by males, sets such as B.2, B.6, or D.4 might be selected in societies that are largely matriarchal, and sets such as B.4 or D.3 would probably be used in countries where stable nuclear families are common.

Turning now to some of the specific matching characteristics mentioned in Figures 4.5 and 4.6, it is clear that characteristics involving addresses or names of individuals play a crucial role in the PGE matching operation. Procedures for assuring that adequate address information will be available were described in Section B.2 of this chapter. In the illustrative examples in Figures 4.5 and 4.6, there is some intentional ambiguity as to whether the address item listed (structure number or village name) refers to the place of usual residence or to the place where the event took place. In practice, it may be that either one alone or both together must be used to produce minimum error. In establishing the tolerance limits for village name, one must remember that most rural events occur in the village of usual residence. As a result, the field documents of both sources frequently have entries such as "this village" or "here" for this item; alternatively, the same place may be indicated by spelling out or abbreviating the name of the village. One must be sure that one constructs and tests a tolerance limit that adequately reflects the diversity of entries which mean "this village," regardless of what tolerance limits are used for entries referring to other villages.

Characteristics involving the names of individuals have high discriminating power; but if the tolerance limits used are too strict, a high proportion of erroneous nonmatches will result. The use of some standard method of coding names can control many sources of recording errors that give rise to erroneous nonmatches. One system in general use is called Soundex. Several variations of Soundex are available, and adaptations will be required, particularly for names transcribed from writing systems other than Latin script. Alternatively, and often preferably, Soundex equivalents for each language and script can be experimented with separately. A set of Soundex rules, taken from Hubbard and Fisher (1968; see, generally, Acheson, 1968), is illustrated in Figure 4.7. In this particular application of the Soundex system, Alvarez would be coded as A416, Kim as K500, Mohammad as M530, and Smith as S530.

Various difficulties may be encountered if this system is employed without modification to suit the language in use. For example, Mohammad and Mahmud, two distinct names in common use in most Islamic countries, will both normally have the same Soundex code (M530). However, even with an unmodified Soundex code, it is possible that the gains in terms of reduced erroneous nonmatches may substantially outweigh the disadvantages in terms of reduced discriminating power and increased erroneous matches. That is, while code M530 lumps all Mohammads and Mahmuds into one identification code class, it also assures that entries such as Mohammed, Muhammad, Mohamad, and Mhmd will be in the same class. Nevertheless, the usefulness of the Soundex system can be enhanced considerably by introducing minor modifications that preserve important distinctions in very common names, such as between Mohammad and Mahmud, while ignoring nonsignificant differences, such as between Mohammad and Mohammed.

With manual matching, as recommended in this Handbook for PGE studies, the system of coding names, through a Soundex system or any other method, may appear somewhat cumbersome.[16] One may think that the matching clerks can make all the necessary decisions

Fig. 4.7   An Example of Soundex Rules for Coding Names

1. The code consists of a single alphabetic character followed by three digits.

2. The initial letter of the family name forms the first character of the code.

3. Subsequent characters of the family name are coded according to the following table:

Letters								Code
B	F	P	V					1
C	G	J	K	Q	S	X	Z	2
D	T							3
L								4
M	N							5
R								6

4. The coding continues until three digits of code have been obtained or until the characters of the name have been exhausted, whichever occurs first. One, two, or three zeros, as needed, shall be added to the right of the initial alphabetic character or last numeric code to ensure that all codes consist of three digits.

   The letters A, E, I, O, U, and Y are not coded, but may act as separators (see 5 below).

   W and H are ignored.

   Hyphens are ignored.

5. Letters which follow letters having the same code are not coded unless preceded by a separator.

6. 'TCH' is coded as 'C'.

SOURCE: Adapted from Hubbard and Fisher, 1968.

mentally. However, to avoid ambiguities, errors, and subjectiveness, and to routinize as much of the procedure as possible, complete coding seems to be advisable, at least in the first year or two of the study. It is usually best if this coding is done by one or two coding clerks rather than by the matching clerks at the time of matching. A separate coding operation usually makes both the coding and the matching faster and more accurate than they would have been if the two operations had been combined.

Not all matching characteristics with high discriminating power are equally useful. In general, names of distant relatives or places will be subject to greater response variances than the names of immediate family members or nearby places. Thus the former will tend to produce very many erroneous nonmatches unless tolerance limits are loosely set. Similarly, items that may involve long recall periods, such as a survey report of the date of an event, are often subject to large response variances.

The appropriateness of characteristics such as religion, mother tongue, tribal group, or village of birth is very closely tied to the cultural background of the population under study.[17] In many countries one or more of these items has little relevance. (For example, there are no tribes in Korea, no linguistic differences in Cuba, and no religious diversity in Saudi Arabia.) Even in countries where such characteristics are relevant, they often have poor discriminating power. This is because these same characteristics frequently determine where people live; that is, people with the same background tend to live in the same areas. Occasionally, particularly in urban areas where persons with diverse backgrounds live very near to one another, such items will be very effective in matching.

The procedure described earlier in this section for determining tolerance limits and selecting matching characteristics may not always produce a combination of characteristics yielding acceptably low levels of both net and gross matching error. A number of techniques are available for dealing with this situation. First, one can try adjusting the tolerance limits slightly for one or two characteristics from a set that produces low, but not low enough, matching error. Using the same set of characteristics, but with the modified tolerance limits, the match status of the reports available for experimental matching can be redetermined, and one can observe whether the change in tolerance limit has reduced matching error. Alternatively, one can depart from the ranking of characteristics by discriminating power, which, after all, is somewhat arbitrary in that it ignores interaction between the characteristics, and test different combinations of characteristics. Again, the match status of the experimental reports is then redetermined, and the effect of the new combinations of characteristics on net and gross matching error is ascertained.

A somewhat different approach is to accept a particular set of characteristics, even though it produces unacceptable levels of matching error, because one is reasonably certain that improvements in specific field procedures can be introduced in the main study to deal with the problem. For example, if, in some matching study, most erroneous matches are due to a failure to identify separate living units in large compounds and most erroneous nonmatches are due to the fact that the field workers in the two collection systems use different procedures for assigning numbers to unnumbered structures, more frequent and complete structure numbering can be expected to reduce matching error substantially.

These and other methods can be used to "fine tune" the matching operation in terms of anticipated matching error. As long as the modifications tested continue to substantially reduce net or gross matching error, with little or no reduction in operational efficiency, efforts of this type are usually justified. However, one must stop tinkering when operational efficiency begins to reach unacceptably low levels, when gains in both error measures become slight, or when a reduction in one error measure is offset by an increase in the other. After all, initial tolerance limits and matching characteristics are chosen on the basis of estimates of anticipated matching error. It would seem wisest, then, when the experimental matching results indicate that a number of mixes of tolerance limits and characteristics yield about the same low levels of matching error, to choose the set of characteristics from among such roughly equal alternatives that is easiest for the matching clerks to apply, has the lowest item-nonresponse rates, and produces the smallest number of cases needing field follow-up. Only after the results of the first round of full-scale matching and field follow-up have been completed will it be possible to estimate more exactly the error rates for the tolerance limits and characteristics used and, on this basis, to explore ways of achieving further reductions in the errors and costs associated with matching and field follow-up.

Before concluding our discussion of how initial matching criteria are established, we shall describe briefly two radical alternatives to the procedures already outlined—the use of multiple sets of matching criteria and the use of criteria designed for individual population subgroups. The use of multiple sets of matching criteria involves the successive application of sets of characteristics, each set having high discriminating power and yielding a negligible number of erroneous matches, to the "residual nonmatched reports," (that is, the reports left over after the application of the previous sets). This technique enables one to achieve the previously stated objective of "minimum net matching error for some low level of gross matching error" because the individual sets, by explicit design, produce few erroneous matches and the number of erroneous nonmatches is reduced through the use of successive sets.

In effect, this is the procedure that was used in the Pakistan PGE study (Population Growth Estimation, 1968, Chapter 6). In Pakistan, the sequential matching was done mechanically on conventional punch-card sorters and collators. If a sequential matching procedure is done manually, one must be careful that the clerks do not depart from the designated sequential steps either because of confusion or because of a desire to "simplify" things.

Although sequential matching, properly used, can produce low net and gross matching error, one must not combine a sequential matching operation with the basic approach described earlier. An essential feature of sequential matching is that each set of characteristics is designed to produce a minimum number of erroneous matches. In the basic matching procedure, the set of characteristics used is designed in terms of net and gross matching error. The application of successive sets of characteristics of the latter type to all the residual nonmatches could certainly decrease the number of erroneous non-matches after each application, but it would not reduce the number of erroneous matches that arose in the earlier runs. Indeed, the successive application of combinations of characteristics that were originally de-signed in terms of net and gross matching error could only add slightly to the number of erroneous matches each run. As a result, net error may be increased.

Another alternative is to design procedures that are optimal for various major population subgroups. For example, if a country has two or three major linguistic groups, one may establish characteristics and tolerance limits separately for each group. Separate sets may also be considered when the same matching criteria seem inappropriate for use in both rural and urban areas because of differences in the two types of address information. Either a basic matching procedure or a sequential procedure can be developed for specific population subgroups, and it may well result in lower matching error and less of a need for field follow-up. However, there are a number of disadvantages in terms of operational efficiency to using separate matching criteria for individual population subgroups, and these must be balanced against any anticipated gains from the procedure.

If separate tolerance limits and matching characteristics are to be selected for a number of subgroups, the results of the experimental matching must be analyzed in terms of the same subgroups. Because the total number of reports available for this purpose is limited, one must design the criteria for each subgroup on the basis of a very small group of birth and death reports, thus creating considerable uncertainty about the correctness of the matching procedures so developed. It is quite possible that all the reduction in errors and costs that one hoped to achieve by individual subgroup matching rules will be negated if the rules developed for each subgroup are far from optimal.

Moreover, it is much harder to control a manual matching operation if different criteria are being applied to different groups of reports. Either individual matching clerks become specialists in working on the reports of particular subgroups and in using specific rules, or the matching clerks are considered to be generalists and are assigned as needed to work with the reports of any subgroup. If the matchers are subgroup specialists, the final estimates of fertility and mortality for individual subgroups may be subject to considerable error because of the idiosyncrasies of the individual matching clerks. On the other hand, if clerks are shifted among subgroups, it is doubtful whether they will be able to apply the proper matching rules, consistently, to the reports of each subgroup. To put it simply, if everyone always has the same job to do it is easier to make sure they are doing it than it is to make sure that the same group of people are doing a number of different jobs.

A proposal for individual subgroup matching rules may produce the suggestion that the matching for each subgroup be done at separate locations. Such a proposal is often advanced on the grounds of administrative efficiency (because, for example, "there will be less movement of documents," "the staff in a particular region ought to be able to deal with the reports for that region," "a number of matching teams at separate locations can do the job more quickly and cheaply"). Unfortunately, decentralized matching may easily lead to a situation where the matching operations actually carried out at each location are quite different from one another. Whether the initial matching rules were developed for individual subgroups or a single set of rules was developed for the whole population, there is a very strong tendency for the staff at each location to implement the written rules differently.

As time goes on minor differences in early interpretations multiply into major differences in terms of how the matching operation is conducted and in terms of the results produced. This problem can be overcome by shifting the staff between matching locations, but such a policy would negate the administrative advantages of doing the matching at separate locations cited earlier.

In general, we strongly recommend against any decentralized matching operation. If decentralized matching is used, we urge that staff and supervisors be rotated between locations. Furthermore, at least in the initial stages of matching, one senior member of the professional staff must be in continuous travel status visiting each location to keep the various matching operations moving along common lines. Somewhat less vigorously, we recommend that individual matching rules not be used for population subgroups. If this procedure is used, we suggest that it be introduced only after the results of the first round of matching and field follow-up from the main study have become available. In this way one will have a substantial number of reports from which to develop the subgroup matching rules, and at least some of the idiosyncrasies of the matching clerks will have been detected and corrected.

Underlying the recommendation that neither decentralized matching nor individual subgroup rules be used is the concern that anything which tends to fragment the matching process can easily lead to a situation in which the study managers have lost control of the matching operation. With manual matching such a development is disastrous in terms of accuracy and, sometimes, in terms of costs. Therefore, if one must do something that tends to fragment the matching operation, one should accompany this decision by actions that lead to more effective unified control of the matching staff and their work.

Once the initial matching criteria have been adopted one must see to it that these rules will be implemented properly. A number of suggestions as to how this may be done are given later in the chapter, in Sections C.3, D.3, and E.1. At this point we shall cover only a few aspects of implementation that are applicable to the major design alternatives discussed in this chapter: training, the physical process of matching, the classification of reports by match status, and the handling of doubtful cases.

Matching clerks should be given one week of largely practical training before they are certified as qualified to work on "live data" from the main study. (If the clerks have had previous experience in a study with high-level statistical standards, this requirement can be relaxed, but to no less than two days.) The lecture part of training (covering the objectives of the PGE study, the purposes of matching, the matching rules, the procedures for recording match status, and the procedures needed to assure proper documents control) can be completed in two hours at the most, and the balance of the training time should be devoted to practical matching work. The matching decisions made in this practice matching work must be evaluated periodically and problems discussed with the clerks. The objective here is to detect and correct poor procedures before the clerks learn wrong ways of doing the matching. A test can be given on the last morning of the training period, graded by early afternoon of the same day, and "graduation" ceremonies held later in the day for those passing the test. Failure to pass the test should not automatically bar a clerk from ever doing matching work, but it is an indication of possible trouble that cannot be ignored. In addition, the work of all the matching staff must continue to be carefully supervised after graduation, so that both the accuracy of their matching decisions and the rate at which they work can be controlled.

The easiest way for the clerks to make the many comparisons that a matching operation involves is first to arrange the two sets of reports in order by structure number, find the definite matches according to the rules adopted, and set these matched reports aside. They can then order the two files of as yet unmatched reports by some other characteristic in the set (say, the Soundex code for mother's name) and repeat the process just described. In two-way matching one proceeds until all reports in both sources have been assigned a match status. (In one-way matching, match status is determined for each report in one source only.) The instructions for the ordering of reports by address, name of dead person, name of midwife, and so on should not be confused with the rules used to determine matching status, which remain unchanged however the reports are arranged physically. The reason for arranging the vital events reports in this manner is to facilitate the prompt identification of the "easy matches" (pairs of reports that agree exactly on many characteristics with high discriminating power) and thus reduce the number of reports involved in the more time-consuming search for pairs of reports that barely agree within the established tolerance limits. Note that no distinction is made between "easy-to-find" and "hard-to-find" matches in assigning match status.

In PGE studies with more than about 100 birth reports in either source involved in the matching for one PGE area, there may be a real danger that the physical process of sorting and re-sorting documents may lead to the loss or destruction of individual reports.[18] In such a situation it may be best if the birth and death reports for a given PGE area, source, and time period are bound separately in books or files with heavy cardboard covers. Although binding eliminates the possibility of easy re-sorting on the basis of different characteristics, it does help to protect the reports from loss and damage during office processing.

If possible, each book or file should be thin enough, and so bound, that it will lie flat and remain open at any report. In addition, the binding used should permit the addition or deletion of reports in case mistakes are discovered after the initial binding. It will greatly facilitate matching if the reports in each book, when bound, are arranged by structure number (or some other basic characteristic) so that the easy matches can be found quickly. With bound reports, one should not try to physically remove the matched pairs. Instead, the words, "MATCH: Paired with report no. _____ in source _____" should be prominently stamped on both reports in red ink. One can then easily ignore such reports when searching for additional matches. (Clerks should be cautioned against using the red stamp too quickly, however, since once a document has been stamped the mark is difficult to erase. As a minimum, they must look at all the reports from both sources for a given structure number before stamping pairs of reports as matched.) After all the easy-to-find matches have been found and stamped, the clerks must proceed systematically through the reports of one file, comparing each report without a stamp with all the unstamped reports in the other system. Because the number of comparisons involved in such a procedure can be large, identifying the easy matches first can reduce the size of the matching job considerably.

Regardless of the method of filing the reports, the clerks must assign some match status to each report in both sources if two-way matching is used. In theory, numerous match status categories could be used, each reflecting a somewhat different probability that reports so categorized truly match with a report in the other source. In practice, it is recommended that the clerks employ a scheme with either two categories (that is, match/nonmatch) or three categories (that is, definite match/definite nonmatch/possible match). Initially, it is safest for the clerks to use a two-category scheme based on a rigid application of the matching criteria developed in accordance with the principles already described. At the same time, the matching supervisor should verify a sizable number of these initial assignments to identify both the mistakes being made by the clerks and instances in which the rules fail to deal adequately with new or special situations.

With time, however, the clerks can be entrusted with the added responsibility of classifying as "possible matches" some reports that would otherwise have been classified as nonmatches, had the matching criteria been rigidly applied. For example, a possible match might arise, if Set B.1 of Figure 4.5 was used, when two reports agreed within tolerance on sex of baby and father's name and almost agreed on structure number, except for a reversal of the last two digits. Any report not classified as a "definite match" or a "possible match" should be classified as a "definite nonmatch."

In thinking about match status, it is important to keep in mind the distinction between the outcome of the comparison of some given pair of reports and the outcome after a given report has been compared with all relevant reports in the other source. Here, the term is used in the latter sense. However, in the case of definite matches, we do not search among reports associated with different structure numbers for a better match. On the other hand, if a definite match is not found in reports associated with the same structure, reports associated with other structure numbers should be examined. In addition, note that the three match categories are defined in terms of reports rather than pairs of reports, though in the case of definite and possible matches two reports (one in each source) will be assigned to the same category.

The final match status assignments made by the matching clerks should be clearly entered on the documents, using rubber stamps similar to the one described earlier for definite matches. Alternatively, one stamp could be used for all information on match status. For example, one might use a stamp, the top half of which looks like this:

```
Match status:      DM   DN   PM
(circle one)

If DM or PM, paired
with report no. ____

Matcher's initial ____ Date _____
```

The space below the dotted line could be used for equivalent information based on supervisory verification or the results of field follow-up.

The supervisors of the matching clerks have five main duties: handling totally unanticipated situations; verifying some of the work of each clerk from time to time to ensure that there has been no decrease in quality; maintaining control of the administrative aspects of matching so that documents do not get lost and the work does not proceed too slowly; dealing with reports classified as possible matches; and assigning a final match status to reports sent for field follow-up. The matching clerks should be encouraged to refer to their supervisors problems that the instructions do not appear to cover. Unless the supervisors welcome and encourage questions, the clerks will find it easier to discuss the matter among themselves, and a major decision about the matching operation may be taken without the professional staff hearing about it. Even if the clerks are willing to refer problems, they may not always recognize them. One of the characteristics of unanticipated situations is that they are not recognized as such, so that the matching supervisors must spend some time each day actively looking for problems. Verifying some of the work of the clerks will facilitate the search for problems to some extent; in addition, the supervisors should spend part of the day just watching the clerks at work.

How the supervisors resolve doubtful cases can be a major variable in the process of fine tuning the matching operation, at least in terms of cost. Two extremes are possible. The supervisors can be ordered to resolve all uncertainties so that each report is classified either as a definite match or a definite nonmatch, or they can be told to do nothing and all the possible matches can be sent out for field follow-up. Toward the beginning of a PGE study, many of these uncertain cases should be sent to the field. However, as experience and costs increase, one would want to develop more complete rules for resolving doubtful cases in the office.

Even initially, some of the possible matches can be resolved in the office. Indeed, some of the possible matches so obviously refer to the same event (for example, those that agree in great detail on many characteristics with very high discriminating power but have a blank or a simple error beyond tolerance in one characteristic of the set) that the clerks would undoubtedly handle the situation correctly. However, as indicated earlier, the burden of handling those situations for which the basic matching rules do not work properly should initially be shifted to the supervisors. Eventually, as the clerks become more experienced, rules for handling some of the most frequently occurring special situations can be codified so that the clerks can handle these situations directly.

The varied uses of field follow-up were described in Section I.1 of Chapter 3. In accordance with the recommendations given in that section, it is assumed that field follow-up for initial matching rounds will involve many reports: some definite matches to confirm that the matching procedures are working properly and that there are few out-of-scope reports among the matches; many definite nonmatches, some to confirm the adequacy of the matching procedures, but more to help identify the extent of the out-of-scope problem and to suggest measures for dealing with it; and many possible matches so that rules can be developed for resolving such cases in the office. Office procedures based on the experience gained from extensive field follow-up in the early matching rounds can be developed to handle many of the possible matches and to reduce the coverage bias by identifying some of the out-of-scope reports. Nevertheless, some field follow-up should still be done, if only to check on the quality of the matching process.

B.7 STANDARD TABULATIONS

In specifying the tabulations to be produced from a PGE study, it is necessary to find a middle way between the requirements of timeliness in the release of estimates and the need for extensive and detailed results. On the one hand, excessive zeal to bring out quick results may compromise confidence in the entire study through the release of estimates with large or obvious errors. More commonly, however, the publication of results is delayed for months (or years) because of tabulation plans that were much too elaborate in the first place. The development of lengthy tabulation plans requires lengthy discussions and debates among the study managers and data processing administrators that take them from more important duties. Another likely consequence of overly ambitious tabulation plans is hasty and sloppy systems analysis for each of the specified tabulations. Inadequate systems analysis leads, in turn, to the expense, delay, and frustration of frequent retabulations.

After the production of the high-priority, core tabulation program has become routine, it is possible to consider the requests and demands for an expanded tabulation program. However, a firm decision must be made at the start to resist trying to do the "interesting" and even "important" tabulations until the essential core tabulation program has been completed.

Some data processing personnel may resist this line of reasoning, arguing that it is easier and speedier to run off all tabulations from the same file at one time. We suggest that, in general, the time "saved" by such an approach is not worth the risk of long delays in completing the central tasks of the study. If the tabulations are to be done by electronic computer, the extra time spent in repeatedly loading the same tape or card file is a small price to pay for accurate and timely tabulations of basic statistics. If the files are long and the tabulations are to be done on mechanical punchcard sorters or tabulators, the additional sorting time involved may be substantial. In this event the PGE study managers must be prepared either to pay the additional costs or to drop the second- and lower-priority tabulations.

One aspect of detail is the number of variables tabulated; another is the number of geographic areas for which tabulations and estimates are to be prepared. The constraint on the production of estimates for subnational areas generally arises not because of data processing considerations but because of limitations in the quality of the estimates for such areas. Sampling errors and the effects of some kinds of nonsampling errors become more pronounced as one moves down from national to regional to local area estimates. The critical issues involved in determining what subnational estimates should be produced are discussed in Chapter 3, Section K. Usually, the sampling errors and the quality of the field and matching work will not justify estimates for geographic or administrative divisions smaller than the first order below the national level. If the first-level administrative units are too numerous, it may be safer to combine them into some significant groupings (coastal, interior, and mountainous regions, for example) and provide tabulations for these geographic groupings rather than for each administrative unit. Estimates for specific cities are usually subject to such large errors that one should not try to provide them, unless individual cities contain a substantial proportion of the total population of a country or the sample has been designed specifically to permit such estimates.

Taking into account both the number of variables and the number of areas involved, we would suggest an initial core tabulation program for a PGE study that provides the data needed to produce estimates of the crude birth rate, age-specific fertility rates, the crude death rate, age- and sex-specific mortality rates, and the infant mortality rate. These estimates should be prepared for the nation as a whole and for geographic or administrative regions containing at least a third of the country's total population.

Given this core program, the exact tabulations to be run will depend in part upon how the estimated rates are to be derived. On the one hand, rates for individual sample areas may be computed directly from the unweighted sample observations of events and population, and the needed national and subnational estimates can be produced by weighting these rates appropriately. Alternatively, separate estimates of the aggregate numbers of events and population can be made from the sample data and the rates computed from the estimated national and subnational aggregates. For the purposes of this chapter, we assume that the latter method will be used. One advantage of this method is that it produces estimates of rates and aggregates that are internally consistent without further adjustment; for example, estimates of both aggregate deaths and population, by age, are additive to their respective all-age totals, and the crude and age-specific rates can be calculated from these aggregates.

Three different types of standard tabulations have to be produced routinely: methodological, vital events, and base population. The purpose of methodological tabulations is to obtain information to help ensure that the various phases of the PGE study function properly and to help identify and measure operational and design errors. Methodological tabulations may refer to either vital events or the base population and are generally based on the unraised sample counts. In contrast, the vital events and base population tabulations are usually in terms of the raised or weighted estimates. An initial set of method-ological tabulations for a PGE study might include the following six tabulations (abbreviated M.1, M.2, etc.).

M.1—*Vital events control totals.* The number of birth and death reports by stage of operation (collection, prior to office matching, after field investigation, during tabulation) and disposition (not a live birth, temporal out-of-scope, geographic out-of-scope, definite nonmatch, etc.) for each sample area and stratum, and for the nation. In studies using a two-way match, tabulation M.1 should be prepared separately for each collection system. It should be prepared annually on a year-of-oc-currence basis and should refer to the concept—*de jure* or *de facto*—on which the final estimates will be based. Some parts of M.1 will be prepared by hand, others on the basis of machine counts of card or tape records. Since one purpose of these control totals is to account for each record from collection to final tabulation, it is important that discrepancies from stage to stage be explained satisfactorily. The information in M.1 on the number of in-scope reports by final match status for each collection system serves as the basis for the PGE adjustments of omitted events. Finally, tabulation M.1 supplies the control totals for the substantive vital events tabulations.

M.2—*Base population control totals.* The number of persons enumerated in each survey round by final disposition (in-scope member of base population or person wrongly enumerated) for each sample area and stratum, and for the nation. Detailed editing and coding of the enumerated base population should usually not be done more than once a year. However, regardless of the frequency of enumeration, it is important for control purposes to obtain a reasonably accurate tally of the number of persons enumerated for each sample area in each survey round. This tally can be made by hand at the time of the original receipt of the survey documents from the field. Since such hand tallies can easily produce inaccurate totals, they should be verified on a sample basis, at least for those rounds in which the additional check provided by detailed editing and coding is not available. It may also be helpful to prepare properly raised national estimates on the basis of these control totals. In some countries, such estimates can be usefully compared with independent estimates based on an updated census count, to give a rough indication of the quality of survey enumeration.

M.3—*Matching operation summary.* The number of reports of live births and deaths by detailed matching status for each sample area and stratum, and for the nation. If the matching is done on an electronic computer, the M.3 tabulations can be a direct byproduct of the matching operation. If the entire match, or a substantial part of it, is done by hand, this tabulation may have to be done on a selective basis—for example, using a systematic sample of reports or a sample of areas or matching clerks. In addition to providing information on the results of the particular set of matching rules currently in effect, this tabulation may be modified to show the outcome using alternative matching criteria.

M.4—*Field follow-up summary.* The number of reports of live births and deaths sent for field follow-up, by system reporting the event, reason for sending for field follow-up, and result of follow-up, for each sample area and stratum, and for the nation.

M.5—*Raising factors to be used in tabulations.* This is simply a listing of the factors by which sample results must be multiplied to obtain estimates of events and population. Depending upon the sample design, a unique raising factor will be associated with each sample area, with each stratum, or with groups of strata. Tabulations are often facilitated by adjusting the basic sampling raising factor to take into account the PGE estimate of omitted events. If this procedure is used, tabulation M.5 should indicate the basic sampling raising factors, the PGE adjustments, and the final raising factor that takes both sampling and the estimate of missed events into account. The two components of the final raising factor—the sample weight and the PGE adjustment—need not necessarily be calculated separately for the lowest level for which the other is available; for example, a unique sampling raising factor for each primary sampling unit may be used with a PGE adjustment factor that has been determined separately for each stratum. In general, final raising factors can be shown as whole numbers, since the substantive vital events and base population estimates will be presented rounded to the nearest hundred or thousand.

M.6—*Variance estimates.* The estimated variance and relative variance of the crude birth rate, crude death rate, and rate of natural increase, for each subnational area for which separate estimates of these rates are shown, and for the nation. In preparing these estimates of sampling variance, it may be necessary or desirable to introduce a number of simplifying assumptions to make these estimates available more rapidly, to reduce the cost of preparing them, or to minimize the number of calculation errors. In general, one should be willing to accept small or even moderate biases in the estimated variances as the price for the prompt release of basic study estimates accompanied by estimates of sampling variability. Section A of Chapter 7 contains a number of equations for estimating the sample variance of the PGE estimate. Much time can be saved in preparing estimates of sampling error, and many serious blunders avoided, if a recognized expert in survey sampling is consulted before the specifications for the M.6 tabulation are prepared. To maximize the understandability of estimates of sampling variability, such estimates should be presented (regardless of how they are tabulated) in terms of the same unit of measure as the substantive estimates to which they refer. For example, an estimated sampling variance of .000000518 for a crude birth rate estimate of 48 per 1,000 should be presented as a standard error of 0.7 per 1,000, or a two-sigma confidence interval of 46.6 to 49.4, rather than as an uninformative nine-digit decimal.

As indicated earlier, vital events tabulations present the substantive raised estimates of live births and deaths. For the core tabulation program described above, only two tabulations will be needed:

V.1—Estimated live births by age of mother and
V.2—Estimated deaths by sex and age of deceased. Both tabulations will be for the nation and, possibly, for a limited number of subnational areas. If a two-way match is used, the tabulations may show the estimated number of events based on the reports of either system alone as well as the PGE estimate.

Vital events tabulations should rarely be based on vital events reports for a period of less than 12 months. Since strong seasonal patterns in the occurrence of vital events are common, the extrapolation of three, six, and even nine months' worth of events to annual figures is a very speculative undertaking. This is particularly true in the first year or two of a study, when the seasonal patterns are unknown and the pressure for estimates is the greatest. However, the pressure for first estimates can sometimes be met by using analytical techniques in conjunction with the base population tabulations.

Frequently, the systems analysis of vital events tabulations is faulty because of inadequate communication between the staff of the PGE organization and the data processing staff. To avoid error, the events being tabulated in each vital event tabulation must be defined in terms of three characteristics, namely:

(1) type of event (live birth or death; if stillbirth reports are also keypunched they must be excluded from all live birth tabulations),
(2) year of occurrence (that is, the year the event took place, *not* the year the event was registered or enumerated), and
(3) place of occurrence (if a *de facto* definition is used) or place of residence (if a *de jure* definition is used).

Both the requests by the PGE staff for tabulations (which should be in writing) and the detailed tabulation specifications prepared by the data processing staff (which should be submitted to the PGE staff for review) must be specific on each of these three points if errors are to be avoided.

The classification of events by characteristics (such as age) was discussed in Chapter 3, Section K. A decision must be made as to whether the registration or survey data should provide the information on the characteristics of the individual event in preparing the PGE tabulations. (Of course, if separate estimates are shown for each reporting system, the characteristics used are those reported in the individual system.) If a special registration system or a reasonably good civil registration system is available, the information therein is likely to be of higher quality than the survey data. Thus one will want to maximize the use of this information in preparing the PGE estimates. To do this, one uses the registration characteristics for all events—matched or unmatched—reported by the registration system. The remaining events can be handled in either of two ways.

First, the characteristics of events that have not been registered can be assumed to be like those registered. If this method is used, the PGE estimates are made by multiplying the registration reports by a raising factor equal to the product of the sampling weight and the reciprocal of the overall survey match rate.

Alternatively, one may use the characteristics reported in the survey for events that were obtained only by that method, while the characteristics of the events estimated as omitted from both systems (that is, the fourth category events) can be assumed to be like those of the combined group of registration reports and nonmatched survey reports (that is, like the total of the first three categories).[19] An easy way of using this approach is to create a new computer file or card deck by merging a copy of the registration file with copies of the nonmatched records from the survey file. PGE estimates can then be prepared by multiplying each record in the new file by a raising factor equal to the product of the sampling weight times a ratio equal to the sum of the four PGE categories divided by the sum of the first three.

If the overall quality of the information about events in the survey reports is thought to be better than that in the registration reports, the entire process described in the last three paragraphs can be reversed. In addition, as described in Chapter 3, Section K, other procedures may be appropriate in specific situations.

The base population tabulations needed for the core program are:

B.1—Population, by age and sex, for the nation, and for a limited number of subnational areas;

B.2—Women aged 15 to 54, by age and number of children ever born, for the nation, and for a limited number of subnational areas; and

B.3—Women aged 15 to 54, by age and number of surviving children, for the nation, and for a limited number of subnational areas.

The latter two tabulations are needed to prepare fertility and mortality estimates using some of the techniques of demographic analysis (United Nations, 1967). These tabulations (B.2 and B.3) should not, as a rule, be run annually, since the analytical techniques available are not precise enough to permit detection of year-to-year variations in fertility or mortality. However, if they are run from the data obtained in an early enumeration round, perhaps the first round, they can help fill the gap until the PGE estimates become available.

In general, it is sufficient to present most tabulations by age in terms of standard five-year age groups (under 5, 5–9, 10–14, 15–19, and so on). However, since tabulations by single years of age are quite useful in assessing data quality, the additional effort involved in obtaining single-year data at the national level for all tabulations involving age should be discussed with the data processing staff. As a minimum, the base population under age 10 and the deaths occurring to children under age 5 should be tabulated by single years of age.

A number of tables of derived statistics—principally rates—must also be produced. It is usually quicker to calculate these rates on a desk calculator than on a computer. These tables are based on the vital events and base population tabulations and include the crude rates, age-specific fertility, age- and sex-specific mortality, and the infant mortality rate. In general, rates should be expressed to two, or at most three, significant digits (for example, a crude birth rate of 46 per 1,000 population; an infant mortality rate of 115 per 1,000 live births; an age-specific fertility rate of .147 births per woman 30 to 34 years).

The final tabulation plans must be prepared and reviewed by both the subject-matter specialists and data processing staff each year, at about the time the matching operation begins. A set of basic tabulations should be produced each year in a substantially identical format to facilitate year-to-year comparisons. Once the production of these basic tabulations becomes routine, additional tabulations can be considered. A few of the supplementary tabulations can be run on an annual basis, some once every two or three years, and some on a one-time basis. However, great care must be taken that the expansion of the tabulation program does not progressively slow down the release of basic data. Systems analysis work on the new tabulations must be as thorough as on the core tabulations. Moreover, one should be alert to the possibility that an attempt to produce some new tabulation, by changing programming, may have the effect of introducing errors into a previously checked-out tabulation.

Information about tabulations that might be included in an expanded tabulation program can be found in various handbooks, manuals, and reports prepared by both the Statistical Office and the Population Division of the United Nations. Another source of possible tabulations for an expanded program, which also contains an excellent description of the detailed procedures involved in producing tabulations from survey data, is the booklet *Tabulation Processes,* Unit VIII of the Atlantida case study (U.S. Bureau of the Census, 1967).

C. *Civil Registration Combined with a Periodic Household Survey*

This combination of systems makes use of information on births and deaths collected by the official system of registration. Clearly, this may give rise to a great variety of possibilities, depending upon the actual circumstances in a given country, particularly the organizational situation and the personalities of the government officials concerned. If the civil registration system is under the same department, or at least under the same political head, as the organization charged with carrying out the survey and the matching operations, the situation is a tenable one. If, in addition, the personalities concerned are high-caliber officials with a tradition of cooperation, the situation is still better. On the other hand, if the management of the civil registration system is isolated from the mainstream of modernizing influences, if its interests are limited to the legal or clerical aspects of civil registration, the situation is less promising.

Apart from the organizational framework within which the work must be done, there are, of course, many other features of any given country that determine the actual details of a PGE study. There are too many special and unforeseeable factors to enable us to make firm generalizations, but such suggestions as can reasonably be attempted will be made in the next few paragraphs.

There are certain basic conditions that must exist before a PGE study based on the civil registration can be considered a realistic possibility. To begin with, data available from the civil registration system must be manageable, which means that at least one of the following three conditions must be fulfilled:

(1) the registration units must be small enough so that the matching task for each sample area involves no more than about 200 births per year, which at 40 births per 1,000 would mean an area of 5,000 persons; or

(2) the filing system in the civil registration office must be such that vital events referring to any reasonably defined sample area (smaller than the smallest official area recognized by the registration system) can be swiftly, inexpensively, and relatively unambiguously isolated; or

(3) the quality of addresses must be high enough so that reports can be categorized with certainty according to dwellings.

It is, of course, better if a combination of these conditions exists, but the unconditional and unqualified existence of at least one of them will suffice.

We have already drawn attention to the problems arising when the top management of the civil registration system is different from the top management of the household survey. However, if there is too much cooperation, particularly at the lower levels, between the registration system and the survey organization, there is considerable danger that the independence of the two systems will be threatened. For these reasons, it is unwise to give the responsibility for the survey to the personnel already supervising the registration system.

A further complication may arise if the local official responsible for registration of births and deaths is an important local personage such as a village chief. Such an official may consider the discovery of unregistered events or any systematic investigation of his work a threat to his position in the community. In such a case, therefore, personnel involved in the survey, and particularly those following up the nonmatched or doubtful cases in the field, must have sufficient stature so that, with a combination of tact, respect, and persistence, the required field work can be carried out.

Various procedures for obtaining copies of the civil registration reports are possible. One can make photocopies of the actual registration documents on file with the agency responsible for registration, copy the information needed from the registration documents onto transcription sheets, or provide for an additional official copy of the certificate to be prepared at the time of filing. Any one of these alternatives may be preferable to taking the survey schedule to the registration office and attempting to do the matching there.

One should never combine the survey and the matching into one interviewing job—for example, by providing the interviewer with a copy of each registration form or by relying solely on the responses to a survey question such as "Was this event registered?" The major objection to the use of either of these approaches, from the point of view of PGE estimation, is that they both compromise the independence of the two collection systems. In addition, the results of the first approach are often very difficult to assess because of the great variability among survey personnel in how the copy of the registration document is used. Ascertaining the completeness of registration simply on the basis of which survey-reported events are said to be registered by the respondent is inadvisable for two reasons. First, these responses may be wrong. Second, even though the response is correct, and even if a copy of a registration document is produced by the respondent, there is no guarantee that the registration report has actually been included in the national vital statistics data.

C.1   THE SAMPLE

Before selecting the sample a decision must be reached about three major aspects of the sample design: the number of sample areas, their size, and the possible benefits of systematically rotating the sample areas. As noted in Chapter 3, several conflicting factors must be balanced:

the work load for the registrar and the enumerator, the size of the matching task, the boundary problem, and the sampling error of the estimates and other statistical sampling issues.

The work load consideration is less important when civil registration is combined with a household survey than for other PGE designs. Since the civil registration system is already functioning, one need only worry about the work of the enumerator, and here the requirements of efficiency are quite flexible. The enumerator is usually in travel status anyway, so that staying in the area a bit longer or traveling a bit farther requires no special arrangements. Even doubling the enumerator's assignment from three weeks to six may cause no insurmountable difficulties.

In designing a sample for a PGE system, explicit regard must be given to the cost and quality of the matching operation. In matching to the civil registration system, the size and organization of the civil registration files is usually a major constraint. If a two-way match is being used, it is necessary to design a sample that permits one to locate all the registration reports in the civil registration files for each sample area, whether or not the event was reported by the survey. Thus all the registration reports for some identifiable geographic area have to be distinguishable in the registration files. There is no great loss of accuracy and efficiency if the registration files are organized so that the geographic unit within which the matching is done is slightly larger than the sample area, so long as one can unambiguously determine, on the basis of the information on the registration reports, which of them belong to the sample area and which do not. If the registration files are stored alphabetically or numerically for geographic units of over 15,000 to 20,000 population, the matching effort for a two-way match will be prohibitively expensive in most instances. However, if the registration records are filed separately for smaller geographic units, then a two-way match can be considered.

In order to hold down erroneous nonmatches and out-of-scope reports, accurately recorded identifying details are required in both the registration and the survey documents. Out-of-scope reports can be identified unmistakably only when entries are clear with regard to both space and time, since events can be out-of-scope with respect to either space *or* time (or both). However, in the case of a one-way match, geographic out-of-scope reports need not be a source of bias if one has access to the full civil registration file.

With regard to the boundary problem, one is in this case entirely in the hands of the civil registration system. Whatever boundaries it uses have to be accepted, unless the registration documents are filed in such a way that one can identify exact locations with certainty. On the other hand, the boundary problem is also likely to be less severe than it would be if the civil register were not used, inasmuch as the boundaries of civil registration units are usually well known and well established. If the boundaries are not well defined and the houses not well numbered, a field force may be necessary to map and number the structures in the area so as to provide adequate geographic control for the household survey and sufficient identification for the matching operation.

The choice between a fixed and a rotating sample depends primarily upon three considerations: the intended duration of the study, the type of estimates to be derived, and the cost of establishing a system of rotation.[20] If the costs of sampling, mapping, and numbering an initial set of sample areas is large and if the study is meant to be short-lived, then the arguments for rotation are weak. On the other hand, if the study is designed primarily to measure the completeness of the civil registration, it is possible that, as time goes on, the sample areas in which the study is conducted will cease to be representative of registration practices in the country at large. Regardless of the purpose of the study, the strongest argument for rotation is that it tends to increase the independence of the two collection systems by reducing the opportunity for communication between them.

C.2 COLLECTION OF DATA

Three types of data will be collected: reports of vital events from the civil registration system, reports of vital events from the household survey, and information on the base population. The nature of the task of collecting data from the civil registration system will be determined, to a large extent, by the administrative and statistical characteristics of the civil registration system and will be, to that extent, outside the influence of the PGE study managers. For example, it will be necessary to accept the prevailing *de facto–de jure* definitions. If the registration documents are filed both at the *de jure* place of residence and at the *de facto* place of occurrence, care must be taken to extract the *de facto* occurrences and not the *de jure* registrations, if the *de facto* concept is used in the household survey and in matching. If a one-way match is involved, either the *de jure* or *de facto* filing system can be used. For a further discussion of some of the issues involved here, see Chapter 7, Sections D.2 and D.3.

In some registration systems a distinction is made between the legal and the statistical parts of the report. Generally, one will need to have access to both parts unless names and other identifying information are on the statistical part. If there is a problem because of the confidentiality of part of the records, most civil registration authorities will arrange for PGE officials to be sworn in under the legislation operating the system. Alternatively, officers of the civil registration system can be designated to carry out selected aspects of the PGE operation. However, for a variety of reasons, this is likely to be a less satisfactory arrangement.

One key issue in design is the level within the civil registration system at which the registration documents will be extracted for matching. There are often long delays and some losses of documents ("slippage") at each stage between the original report of a birth or death at the village level and the final receipt of the report in the national registration office. To cite a hypothetical, but probably not atypical, example, suppose that in a given area, out of 100 live births actually occurring in a year, 80 are registered at the village registration office. This office, during the course of the year, transmits about 75 birth registration documents to the district health board, which in turn sends 70 to the provincial registration office. Of these 70 reports, 60 are properly filed at the provincial office, five are improperly filed, and five are irretrievably lost. To complicate matters, a statistical summary showing 63 births is transmitted to the national registration office.

If the results of a one-way match (from survey to civil registration) are to be used to adjust national vital statistics data for incompleteness, the problem of slippage can become critical. This problem can be reduced or eliminated by extracting the returns at any convenient level and preparing estimates of the extent of slippage up to the national level, or by doing two-way matching so as to be able to prepare an independent PGE estimate of the total. Generally, there are advantages, in the form of reduced transcription errors, to extracting the data at the lowest level possible. The lower levels will also have access to detailed information on boundaries, addresses, practices, and other special circumstances. In our judgment, these advantages counterbalance the risk of loss of independence, which increases as the level at which documents are extracted becomes lower. At any rate, the risk of loss of independence when civil registration and a household survey are used is small compared to the risk when special registration and a survey are combined (although, of course, communication between civil registration personnel and the survey field staff can occur and should be guarded against).

Before large-scale extractions of data are begun, full information about the civil registration system and its detailed procedures must be obtained through a pilot, or trial, survey. Unfortunately, the information required is generally *not* available from registration authorities in the central office, and almost certainly not obtainable from personnel in other government offices. Part of the problem is that there are many in the bureaucracy who confuse the formal registration system as it exists in the legal code or among an urban elite with the system as it actually functions, both administratively and statistically. It is, therefore, important to supplement the impressions of registration officials by observing directly through a pilot survey how the system functions. Such a study must be large enough to cover several parts of the country if there is any indication that practices vary significantly in different areas. If the responsibility for civil registration is divided among several jurisdictions (for example, provinces, municipalities, and counties), the variety of alternative procedures may be so great that the use of civil registration data would require a large amount of work in liaison with local government agencies. An element of parochialism and possessiveness sometimes associated with provincial organizations, as distinct from central governments, may make it necessary to give up the idea of using civil registration data in such circumstances. However, the idea should not be abandoned without a realistic appraisal of its feasibility. Matching studies involving a large number of separate jurisdictions are possible. For example, in the United States at least 48 state registration offices, as well as a number of municipal offices, cooperated in the 1940 and 1950 birth registration tests.

Even in the best registration system there will always be some lag between the date of occurrence and date of registration of an event. In poorer systems this delay can become quite extended. In fact, one measure of the quality of a civil or special registration system is the average number of days between occurrence and registration for each type of event. This item is an important one to be investigated by any pilot study.

Because registrations do tend to be delayed, it is necessary to allow for this lag in planning for the extraction of the registration documents and for the matching operation. The recommended course of action is to do the survey field work first and then make use of the registration system files. By the time the survey field work is completed, the bulk of the registration records will usually have been filed. In any event, one should allow at least two or three months between the near end of the survey recall period and the start of anything but preliminary work in the registration files. The lag will have to be longer if delayed registration is common.

At some point, however, a cutoff date will have to be established, after which the registration system files will be considered closed for the purposes of the study. (That is, registration reports arriving after this date will not be eligible for matching.) Although this cutoff date will vary greatly from country to country, a reasonable rule might be to use a cutoff of between six and nine months from the near end of the survey recall period. In terms of estimating the coverage of the civil registration system, a cutoff can be justified on the grounds that one is measuring the completeness of "timely" registrations only. If very few registrations are "timely," then it may pay to establish a special PGE registration system.

Having examined the basic considerations involved, one must then decide the actual details of area size, boundaries, and the means of extraction of data. Often the critical problem is to carve out smaller areas from one book of records, which usually covers areas much too large for PGE treatment. The actual operational details of this procedure depend too much upon a large number of national and local factors to permit detailed suggestions in this regard. However, many problems associated with using the civil registration system's jurisdictional areas and boundaries can be eliminated by doing a one-way match.

The collection of data by means of a household survey was described in Section B.3. Special arrangements will have to be made to provide the high quality maps and structure numbers needed for effective enumeration and matching. Although the enumeration staff may well be assigned the task of mapping and numbering prior to the survey round, the same staff should not be used either to extract the registration reports from the civil registration system or to do the matching.

The base population can be obtained either from the household survey or from census data brought up to date by a suitable adjustment as described in Chapter 3, Section J. In practice, the latter alternative often proves inadequate in those countries doing PGE studies. Consequently, it is usually preferable to use household survey data to estimate the base population, and use adjusted census totals only in special circumstances.

C.3   PROCESSING OF DATA

The nature of the data processing operations will depend first upon whether it is possible to associate individual records in the civil registration system accurately with specific PGE sample areas. If this is not possible, a one-way match must be used. In such a case, an administrative unit of the civil registration system may cover, say, a population of 25,000 persons, or 750 births and 350 deaths in a given year. The household survey covering a sample of, say, 5,000 persons from within the larger civil registration area may obtain reports of 180 births and 75 deaths in the same year. The task then is to match the 180 births and 75 deaths from the survey with the corresponding events among the 750 birth registrations and 350 death registrations. Such a match will permit an estimate of the extent of underregistration in the civil registration system, but it will not allow the identification of events reported to the civil registration organization but omitted from the enumeration. Only when it is possible to carve out of the books of the civil registration system those events that refer to the PGE area and to the time period in question does two-way matching become feasible. Since there is little difference in processing between civil and special registration in a two-way match, the balance of this subsection will be concerned with handling one-way matches. For a larger discussion of processing considerations appropriate to a two-way match, see Section D.3 of this chapter.

Basically, matching should be done in accordance with the principles described in Chapter 3 and Section B.6 of this chapter. Remember that it should be done area by area rather than at the national level—that is, with blocking on the basis of small batches specific to each area with no national processing. Similarly, the initial recording, scrutiny, and coding should be undertaken area by area.

It is assumed in this discussion that there will be a minimum of temporal and geographic out-of-scope reports. Strict enforcement of the *de facto* definitions used in this chapter will help very much to prevent geographic out-of-scope errors. (A one-way match tends to reduce this problem anyway, since out-of-scope reports in the civil register are relevant only if they are also included—erroneously—in the household survey.) Furthermore, geographic out-of-scope problems are much less likely to arise in PGE areas that do not have a common boundary with the civil registration area. If there are temporal out-of-scope reports, hopefully they will be weeded out during the matching operations or in subsequent field follow-up.

In general, the matching should be done by hand because of the small numbers involved and the likelihood of clerical errors in the original documents (see Chapter 3, Section I.2). Nevertheless, data for each event reported in the survey should be put routinely onto punched cards whenever possible to facilitate subsequent tabulation. Cards should carry all the relevant identifying items and codes for each substantive characteristic discussed in Section B.5. Space should also be provided for punching the final match status.

The value of the appropriate raising factor can either be gang-punched onto each card or stored in the computer and accessed by a table look-up instruction. Typically, there will be a separate raising factor for each stratum (or for each PGE area, if the PGE areas in any one stratum are selected with unequal probability or if a separate completeness estimate is prepared for each PGE area) and for each type of vital event. With each record carrying its own raising factor, the production of tabulations becomes only a matter of clerical and machine programming and execution. A table look-up procedure, although initially more economical, can be a source of much confusion if the table or the look-up procedure is lost or misunderstood during the course of staff turnover. If no mechanical or electronic processing equipment is available, useful estimates of the extent of completeness of the civil registration system can be made by hand.

A national coverage estimate is best prepared by weighting the matched cases in each sample area, weighting the total number of events reported, and then taking the ratio of the two—that is, by using

$$w_1 = \frac{\sum_i f_i m_i}{\sum_i f_i n_{2i}} = \frac{\sum_i n'_{2i} \dfrac{m_i}{n_{2i}}}{\sum_i n'_{2i}} \quad , \qquad\qquad [4.1]$$

rather than the weighted average of the survey match rates for each sample area,

$$w_1 = \frac{\sum_i f_i \dfrac{m_i}{n_{2i}}}{\sum_i f_i} \quad , \qquad\qquad [4.2]$$

where

f_i = sampling raising factor for area i,
m_i = number of matched cases for area i,
n_{2i} = number of events reported by household survey for area i,

$$n'_{2i} = f_i n_{2i}, \text{ and}$$

w_1 = PGE estimate of the completeness of the civil registration system.

C.4   ANALYSIS AND EVALUATION OF DATA

The analysis of match results depends to a large extent upon whether a one- or a two-way match is undertaken. In the case of a one-way match, the analysis is generally presented in terms of coverage, or completeness, estimates for the civil registration system and, frequently, vital statistics (both absolute figures and rates) adjusted for under-registration. As indicated earlier, if the matching is carried out at an administrative level different from the level at which the official registration statistics are compiled, then the problem of the loss of civil registration documents between the two levels can result in errone-ous completeness estimates. One-way match estimates are subject to most of the same kinds of errors as two-way match estimates.

One-way match results are often shown separately for major subgroups of the population—for example, by residence, medical attendance at the birth or death, geographic area, age, socioeconomic group, and educational attainment or literacy. Although the sample size frequently limits the detail of cross-tabulations, thoughtful analysis can often provide both administrative guidance to the civil registration authorities and statistical procedures for making improved estimates of vital rates. Thus, if a matching study indicates that poor completeness rates are confined to certain parts of the population, registration authorities may be able to take specific remedial action to deal with the problem. Any remedial action should be carried out on a mass basis, rather than by focusing on individual omissions.

On the statistical side, the preparation of separate civil registration completeness estimates (survey match rates) for population subgroups permits the adjustment of major subgroups for underregistration. These subgroup-adjusted estimates then can be combined into a new adjusted national estimate that, as Chandrasekaran and Deming (1949) have noted, may have some of the biases arising from the lack of independence between the two systems removed.

Sometimes it is possible to establish, from the analysis of com-pleteness estimates for population subgroups, that some other variable is so clearly related to coverage that it can be used to estimate registration completeness in the interval between matching studies. For example, Moriyama (1946) assumed that registration levels for births occurring in and outside hospitals in the United States remained constant from 1935 to 1944 and used changes in the proportion of births occurring in hospitals (routinely available from civil registration tabulations) to prepare annual estimates of the completeness of birth registration and of births adjusted for underregistration.

In the event that a two-way match is used in the study, a number of additional lines of investigation open up.[21] These are covered in detail in Section D.4 of this chapter. One analytical implication of the use of two-way matching in conjunction with a civil registration system is that if the matching operation has been successful, the slippage problem can usually be ignored.

C.5 THE PROBLEM OF LOW COVERAGE IN CIVIL REGISTRATION

Use of the civil registration system as one source in a dual collection procedure has, of course, substantial cost advantages for any given sample size. If coverage in the civil registration system is fairly good, there will also be variance advantages to using a one-way match between the sample source and the entire civil register, due to the absence of sampling variance for N_1, the number of events counted in the civil register. However, there is also a variance of the civil registration-estimated completeness rate, w_1, and as registration coverage declines, this variance increases more rapidly for $\hat{N}$ (the PGE estimate based on a one-way match from a sample survey to the full civil registration file of events), than for $\hat{n}$ (the PGE estimate based on a two-way match between a sample survey and the registration reports in the same sample areas). For civil registration systems that cover about 50 percent or less of vital events, the one-way match estimate, $\hat{N}$, will have a higher variance than the comparable two-way match estimate, $\hat{n}$. The explanation of this phenomenon is given in mathematical terms in Section A of Chapter 7.

It is possible to overcome the higher variances of $\hat{N}$ associated with very low civil registration completeness rates by increasing the sample size of the other source used in the one-way match. However, lower total costs for a given level of variance may be achieved by substituting for the civil registration system a special registration with a higher completeness rate, since this allows a smaller sample to be used. A simple example will illustrate the point.

Let us assume, for simplicity, a self-weighting sample with zero intraclass correlation for both the true number of vital events and the completeness rates, and independence between sources. In this case the relvariance of the PGE estimate $\hat{N}$, based on one-way matching, is

$$V_{\hat{N}}^2 = \frac{1 - P_1}{P_1 N} \left(\frac{1}{P_2 f} - 1 \right) \, , \qquad [4.3]$$

where

N = total number of vital events for the country,
f = sampling rate for the sample source (survey),
P_1 = completeness of the 100-percent source (the civil registration system), and
P_2 = completeness of the sample source.

For two-way matching the relvariance is

$$V_{\hat{n}}^2 = \frac{1 - R}{fN} + \frac{(1 - P_1)(1 - P_2)}{P_1 P_2 fN} \, , \qquad [4.4]$$

where

R = vital events rate.

Equations 4.3 and 4.4 also give the relvariances of the comparable vital rate estimates if the base population is estimated independently of the sample. We can consider three alternatives:

(1) a household survey with a one-way match to civil registration,
(2) a two-way match between a household survey and civil registration, and
(3) a two-way match between a household survey and special registration.

We shall compare the cases of civil registration systems varying in completeness from 20 to 80 percent. For this purpose, we assume that both the household survey and the special registration system will pick up 80 percent of the vital events. Suppose that the true death rate is 20 per 1,000 and the country can be divided into 50,000 sampling areas of 1,000 population each. Assuming that all the alternatives give unbiased (or equally biased) estimates, the choice among them depends upon the cost and variance. Suppose the household survey costs per year are $4,000 per sample area and special registration costs are $3,000 per sample area. These are inclusive cost figures covering all aspects of the survey and special registration work, except matching. Assume also that costs per year per sample area are $1,000 for one-way matching with the civil register, $1,500 for two-way matching of the survey and civil registration, and $800 for two-way matching of the survey and special registration.

On the basis of these assumptions it is possible to determine the number of sample areas needed and the costs involved in achieving a PGE estimate with a specified sampling error. Table 4.4 shows the number of sample areas and the budget needed to achieve a 5 percent coefficient of variation for the PGE estimate of the number of deaths for three alternate designs and various true completeness rates for the civil registration system.

In the example in the table, both a one-way and a two-way match with the civil registration system cost less than using a special registration system if the civil register is as much as 60-percent complete, and there is a small savings from a two-way match with the civil registration system even when the registration is only 40-percent complete. It should also be noted that, for reasons previously explained, the variance and costs of a one-way match with the civil registration system are much more sensitive to the completeness of the civil register than are the variance and costs of two-way matching.

The results in Table 4.4 depend upon the cost relationships assumed, particularly the relationships between matching and other costs. The gain from using civil registration rather than special registration is primarily attributable to the fact that the extra matching costs per sample area for civil registration are assumed to be considerably less than the costs of doing a special registration. Although the cost

Table 4.4   Sample Size and Cost Requirements for Preparing PGE Estimates with a Specified Sampling Error, by Type of Design and True Completeness of Civil Registration System: Hypothetical Data

(Based on assumptions of 20 deaths per sample area of 1,000 people, 80-percent completeness of household survey reporting, and 80-percent completeness of special registration. For other qualifications, see text.)

Procedure	True completeness rate of civil registration system (percentages)			
	20	40	60	80
One-way match of household survey and civil registration				
Number of sampling areas needed[1]	100	38	17	7
Estimated annual costs ($000)	500	190	85	35
Two-way match of household survey and civil registration				
Number of sampling areas needed[1]	40	28	23	21
Estimated annual costs ($000)	220	154	127	116
Two-way match of household survey and special registration				
Number of sampling areas needed[1]	21	21	21	21
Estimated annual costs ($000)	164	164	164	164

[1] Calculated in order to achieve a 5 percent coefficient of variation and assuming zero intraclass correlation.

relationships indicated are in line with what may be expected in many countries, there will be situations where the civil registration system cannot be used at all because there is inadequate identification information for matching[22] or cannot be used for two-way matching because individual birth and death certificates cannot be associated with specific sample areas. In other cases, the problems of matching with the civil registration may not be insuperable, but the costs of overcoming the matching difficulties may exceed the costs of doing a special registration.

D.   *Special Registration Combined with a Periodic Household Survey*

The most important difference between this approach and the use of the civil registration system combined with a household survey is that the special registration system is not an ongoing system like the civil registration system described in Section C, but is explicitly designed for use in a PGE study. Because of this it has a number of very distinct advantages: First, its primary function is to collect statistical information. Second, the registrar actively circulates through an area attempting to find births and deaths. Third, matching operations are facilitated by ensuring that the registration documents contain an adequate number of accurately recorded items with high discriminating power. In contrast, a civil registration system (1) has as its primary task the legal documentation of vital events; (2) in general, passively receives reports of births and deaths; and (3) makes no special provision for the possibility of matching. In addition, special registration areas can be made to correspond with household survey areas, thus making possible—or at least greatly facilitating—the use of two-way matching.

As previously discussed, a special registration system is more "expensive" than civil registration (at least as reckoned by identifiable line items in a budget) and may be somewhat less independent of the household survey. Regardless of the differences between special and civil registration, however, there are many similarities. To avoid unnecessary repetition of descriptions of these common features, readers will be referred to the relevant parts of Section C as appropriate.

D.1 THE SAMPLE

In Section C.1, we discussed some considerations relevant to the selection of sample areas for a dual collection system that uses records from the civil registration system. With our own special registration system the constraints arising from the use of the files of another agency no longer apply. On the other hand, a new constraint is introduced by the need to use the special PGE registrars economically.

The work load of a special registrar, of course, depends to a considerable degree upon the size of the PGE sample area. The choice of an optimum size for a PGE area is a complicated one, involving a balance among sampling error, various sources of nonsampling error, and costs (see Section H.2 of Chapter 3).

From the viewpoint of sampling error, a large number of small clusters almost always yields a lower variance than a small number of large clusters, and to the extent that persons with similar fertility and mortality characteristics are found living in the same areas, the variance advantage of a design involving more and smaller clusters becomes more pronounced. However, both cost considerations and those relating to many types of nonsampling error argue against fragmenting the sample into very many small clusters.

As explained in Chapter 3, a major issue in any sample design is the proper allocation of fixed resources between the costs associated with the number of clusters (k) and those associated with the average size of each cluster ($\bar{h}$). A design with numerous small clusters generally involves a large field staff (which means high salary and training costs), high supervisory costs, and the allocation of substantial portions of the data collection budget to travel and communication between sample areas. In addition, as the number of clusters increases and their average size declines, it becomes more difficult to control the quality of the field work adequately and problems related to geographic out-of-scope errors generally increase. On the other hand, small clusters make the matching operation simpler and more accurate.

Within these overall considerations much depends upon the nature of the special registration system and how the PGE registrars' jobs are defined. There are many possible ways of employing special registrars, three of which have been used frequently in the past. The registrar may be a full-time employee resident in or near one compact cluster, a part-time employee resident in or near a compact cluster, or a full-time employee working in a number of neighboring clusters. In the case of a resident, full-time special registrar, the decisive consideration is how often it is thought that he (or she) should visit each part of the sample area. One must weigh the advantage of catching births early—particularly those occurring to transients (for example, daughters coming to the houses of their mothers for confinement) and those resulting in neonatal mortality—against the risk of straining the respondents' patience and possibly appearing ridiculous.

From the standpoint of work load consideration, a preliminary population size of 3,000–6,000 or 600–1,200 households per registrar is suggested.[23] With "daily rations" covering about 50 to 100 households by visits to a smaller number of contacts each day, and assuming that the registrar has to spend up to a quarter of his time traveling within the area of his daily assignment (and up to another quarter of his time walking to and from these daily assignments), then PGE areas of this size will permit return visits to each part of the sample area every two to five weeks. Naturally, much of the arithmetic will have to be adapted to suit local circumstances, because density, travel costs, and the like will vary greatly. For example, some urban areas, with their lower community cohesion, will have to be canvassed more intensely. In some cases, visits may have to be made to each household. On the other hand, less time will be needed for travel within urban areas.

With a resident, part-time special registrar, the cluster size can be reduced sharply, as the registrar need only be paid in proportion to the time spent on PGE registration work. Unfortunately there are many difficulties involved in the use of part-time employees that at least partially offset the variance and matching advantages of small clusters. The basic problem with a part-time registrar is that he is employed full time doing something else and his primary allegiance is to this other activity. For example, in some countries village school teachers or university students have been used as part-time PGE registrars. Not only is it difficult to supervise such employees adequately, but they may have to give up their registration activities suddenly when the demands of their full-time activity require it.

Another possibility is to have one registrar cover a number of distinct but neighboring subclusters. The advantage of having such a "traveling" registrar is that it enables the planners of the PGE scheme to cover several clusters with the same special registrar. Assuming that the clusters are different from one another, variance can be reduced because of the larger number of clusters that can be used in the sample. If, however, the dispersion of the clusters is limited by the distance that can be traveled in one day, then the variance reduction may well be small, unless the clusters are markedly different.

It is erroneous to argue that there is no great expense involved in letting the registrar wander among the components of his far-flung empire. The factors that must be considered include the direct costs of extra time and travel, as well as the psychological effects on the registrar of such a loose routine and of having insufficient contact with the population of individual clusters. In addition, there is the possible loss of efficiency due to less attention being given to mapping details when the registrar's area consists of several small subclusters. We strongly recommend, therefore, that before resorting to a design with a "roving" registrar one obtain empirical data on the amount of variance reduction achievable and on the probable costs of the proposed scheme.

Regardless of the type of registrar used, one aspect of the work is equally applicable. To the extent that the special registrars in a PGE organization are charged with maintaining accurate maps, clearly marked boundaries, and a comprehensive system of structure numbers, these responsibilities will make an important claim on their time and on the registration work load; hence the average cluster size should be appropriately reduced.

D.2   COLLECTION OF DATA

The first decision to be made with respect to data collection is whether the PGE registrar should be a full-time or part-time employee. Again, we strongly recommend that the PGE registrar be hired as a full-time employee of the organization, if possible. When one person is given multiple responsibilities, one of which is birth and death registration, little attention is usually given to the registration work. However, in some circumstances and for some designs the use of part-time registrars may be the only answer. If part-time employees have to be used, more intensive supervision will be required. In many instances the only realistic way of structuring the work, in fact if not by job title, is to consider the part-time registrars as assistants to the full-time supervisor and give the supervisor specific responsibility for the registration of vital events.

The work of a PGE registrar is quite different from that of the registrar in a civil registration system in that he actively solicits information on vital events. Although the registrar need not come from the sample area to which he is assigned, he should come from a similar area; for example, in rural sample areas, one should hire personnel used to village life. The characteristics of a good special registrar are literacy, responsibility, some initiative, good health, good character, an ability to deal with people, and an interest in them. The possession of diplomas or certificates from the formal educational system should not be a condition of employment.

The area under any one registrar can be conveniently divided into chunks, and chunks can be divided into blocks, which in turn are made up of structures. Ordinarily, a chunk is equivalent to a "weekly ration," while a block is equivalent to a "daily ration." Daily and weekly rations are specific groups of structures that the registrar is expected to cover on a specific day or week. The use of daily rations facilitates supervision and ensures a full canvass of the sample area. Commonly, under any one registrar there may be two to four chunks and ten to 20 blocks.[24]

In rural areas, the registrar's routine search for vital events among the inhabitants of his area of responsibility generally need not involve a visit to every structure. It is usually sufficient to have one or two local contacts for every six to 18 households, who will be able to tell the registrar about recent vital events in their "neighborhood." In urban areas, depending upon the character of the sample area, more attention may have to be given to contacting individual households.

On hearing of an event associated with one of the households in the daily ration, the registrar should visit the household concerned, verify the report, and complete the appropriate registration documents. Each registration document should be made out in triplicate so that there is one copy for the respondents (except possibly in the case of a stillbirth), one for headquarters, and one for the registrar's own records. In order to avoid jurisdictional disputes with the civil registration authorities, it is recommended that the PGE birth registration form contain the following notice:

> This document is issued in acknowledgment of PGE registration. Parents, and other persons responsible, are strongly urged to carry out their registration responsibilities with the official registration authorities.

The comparable notice on the PGE death record should read:

> This document is issued in acknowledgment of PGE registration. Persons responsible are strongly urged to carry out their registration responsibilities with the official registration authorities.

In general, families are not reluctant to accept their copy of either the PGE birth or death registration form. Obviously the document should not be forced on an unwilling family, but reluctance need not be assumed. Actually, the practice of distributing copies of registration records to respondents may go a long way to ensure their cooperation with the PGE study; see also the discussion on special incentives in Section B of Chapter 3.

The PGE registrar should not keep his copy of the registration forms indefinitely. There should be a rule that a book of copies of registration documents, when completed, is to be sent to headquarters within about two weeks or after the registrar has completed the next full canvass of the area. With perhaps 30 vital events per month (20 births and 10 deaths) and three certificates per event, a book of birth forms would have to have about 120 pages to last two months, and a book of death forms would have to have about 60 pages to ensure that, on the average, one book was used up after about two months. Allowing another two to four weeks before the completed books are sent to headquarters, the registrar would never have data for more than the last three months on his hands. Even with quarterly enumerations, the registrar would have, on the average, only six weeks of reports on hand at one time, and the occasions for collusion between the field workers of the two systems would be limited.

Typically, at the end of a weekly ration, the registrar will make out his weekly report and send it to headquarters with copies of the registration documents completed during the period. The sixth day of the week can perhaps be set aside for this purpose. He should also send a copy of the weekly report, but without the registration documents, to his regional supervisor.[25]

In addition to the ordinary PGE registration procedure involving daily rations and neighborhood contacts, the registrar may contact a number of informal sources to obtain leads on births and deaths. These, along with the neighborhood sources, are called, in the glossary, "sources of first intelligence." All sources of first intelligence must be investigated by visiting the households concerned, and registration forms should be completed as appropriate.

The number of informal sources of information about births and deaths is extensive. Included among these sources are those persons such as village midwives, local religious officials, traditional healers, barbers, and fortune-tellers whose routine activities are likely to make them knowledgeable about vital events; as well as those places such as coffee and tea houses, shops, police stations, and local administrative offices where knowledgeable persons gather. Anyone may turn out to be a good source of information about a vital event—the shoeshine boy in front of the tea shop, an old lady selling beads, or the village night watchman. It is not someone's formal job, social status, or education that is important, but whether the person is interested in the affairs of other people, hears about births and deaths, and can remember them reasonably well. In other words, a good informal source of information has some of the characteristics of a busybody and gossip. However, there are also disadvantages to using such persons: Nonroutine contacts tend to sit together, drink tea together, and intimidate one another. The information gleaned from them may sometimes seem certain and self-corroborating, and yet be wrong. They are, after all, reinforcing one another with the same stories for hours and days. Their information will also be limited by their range of contacts, so that those segments of the population not of interest to the gossipmongers will be ignored. In one study regular tea parties given by the registrar were suggested as sources of leads on births and deaths. We do not think such an approach very productive. A registration system is not a tea party, and an active PGE registrar must not allow himself to be burdened by passive duties, however pleasant. In any case, there will be time for tea or tobacco after the work is done.

Schools do not prove to be very efficient "sources of first intelligence," especially in countries with long vacations, but school children do. Often, children quickly become acquainted with the registrar on his rounds; and if he remains their friend, they will collect the latest news for him with great zeal and thoroughness. On his daily round, long before he comes to a group of dwellings, little bands of children will run ahead to greet him and tell him the "latest" happenings since his last round. One advantage children have over other sources is that they can be used to supplement the daily rounds; with other informal sources there is a risk that they will soon be used instead of the daily rounds.

The absence of hospitals and dispensaries, as well as cemeteries, from the lists of potential sources of informal news in the previous paragraphs is deliberate. Although they may appear to be the obvious and first sources, in practice they prove unsatisfactory. The leads they give often turn out to be difficult to follow up, much happens outside their purview, and they frequently cater to a population very far out of scope from the standpoint of a *de facto* sample. Records kept in local offices are often of even less value. There is seldom, if ever, very great similarity between the boundaries of the PGE areas and the boundaries of the jurisdiction of the local authorities. Relying on the books of hospitals, cemeteries, or local authorities is likely to result in many out-of-scope reports. Moreover, possible gains in coverage from such sources must be weighed against the possibility that the registrars, relying on these official sources, will become less thorough in canvassing the routine round contacts.

There is probably one group of events on which more adequate information can be obtained from official channels than from routine round contacts and informal sources: vital events, particularly deaths, occurring to transients and strangers. If events are being enumerated on a *de facto* basis, all such events should be recorded; but often they will not be discovered during the course of a routine round. For this reason, a periodic visit to the local official responsible for handling such deaths should be included in the registrar's program.

Although informal sources can be helpful to the registration process, the psychology of the field work is such that if the registrar believes too greatly in the alleged efficacy of informal sources he may fail to exercise the vigilance necessary for the observation of all households. The registrar receives no daily support from association with colleagues. He is alone. He depends primarily on the moral strength and feeling of duty inside him, but also on the rules and routines of the PGE study, in the following of which—he knows—he will be supervised. Unfortunately, no effective method of supervision can be devised for a collection process based largely on informal sources.

Whatever the importance of informal sources, on one point there can be no doubt: The informal sources, and such official channels as can be used, must not be compensated. No system of rewards could be designed that would be worth the trouble of administering it; furthermore, the risk of biases arising through rewards would never be worth the resultant meager improvement in net coverage.

The household survey has been described in Section B.3, and only a few comments need to be made here. A particular difficulty with a dual collection system involving special registration and a household survey is keeping the work of the enumerator and registrar independent while preventing them as individuals from becoming antagonistic to each other. In urban areas there is little difficulty, because there is little contact. In rural areas, however, the enumerator and the registrar are likely to be working near each other. After all, they are both collecting statistical data, and the accommodations available for strangers in a village are very limited. If collusion develops, it usually can be detected in the matching operation by the large numbers of perfect matches, or even earlier by good field supervision. (For some procedures to help prevent collusion, see Section F in Chapter 7 on the independence problem.) Antagonism between the personnel of the two sources is also a possibility. Disputes about prestige, house rent, personal matters, and boundaries can all be the cause of friction between the two systems at the lowest level, reducing morale and, possibly, independence. In general, an attitude of tolerant indifference toward the personnel of the "other" system should be the goal.

One additional point should be made here. As discussed in Section B.2 earlier in this chapter, the enumerators must be instructed to visit every structure in the sample area, not just occupied dwellings or numbered structures. Only if the enumerator visits unnumbered structures as well as the numbered ones can the full power of the dual collection system be realized. Enumeration manuals, training materials, and supervision should all be specific on the point that structure numbers must be recorded and used if available, but that all structures in the sample area are to be included in the enumeration. This places the burden of ensuring that the house numbering is complete and legible on the registrar's supervisor. If a large proportion of unnumbered structures are identified in the survey, one should determine whether the enumerator wandered outside the PGE area or whether the structure numbering was neglected. Appropriate remedial action can then be taken on a mass basis. If only a few unnumbered structures are found in the survey no specific remedial action is necessary, as it is clear that the structure numbering is reasonably up to date.

D.3 PROCESSING OF DATA

With a dual system involving special registration and a household survey, the processing task facing the headquarters' staff of the PGE organization is large. First, there is the routine flow of registration forms arriving each month from the special registrars. Assuming a national sample of about 20,000 households (100,000 population), approximately 300 to 400 birth registrations and 100 to 200 death registrations can be expected each month. The reports from each registrar must be logged in promptly and then given a quick review by someone assigned overall supervisory responsibility for the PGE registration system.

During this review, the registration documents should be checked for evidence of sloppiness, long delays in registration, consecutiveness of serial numbers, and so on. The registration forms should also be checked against the weekly and monthly reports of the registrar for consistency. Problems should be immediately referred back to the field for action by the registrar's field supervisor or to the registrar directly.

However, the registration documents themselves should not be sent back to the field. If the registration forms for a particular area have not arrived by the established deadline, a telegram should be sent. It is very important for the morale of all concerned that no registration documents be permitted to fall in arrears. Delayed submission of registration forms should be considered grounds for dismissal of a registrar. This should be clearly explained to the registrar candidates during their training.

After review, the registration documents can be sent to the editing and coding section for further processing. It may be efficient to group registration documents for two or three months together to make work assignments ("batches") of a reasonable size. Since the matching cannot begin until the survey reports are available, it may also be possible to send some of the coded registration batches for keypunching before these documents are needed for matching.

It will be recalled from Section C above that when the civil register is used, sufficient time has to be allowed for delayed registration. With an active PGE special registration system much less time is needed, so that matching can begin more promptly. However, enough time must be allowed for the PGE registrar to make this routine canvass at least once after the near end of the survey recall period. Generally two or three months is sufficient to allow the registrar time to do the necessary field work and to get the documents to headquarters.

The arrangements for processing the survey vital events reports will depend upon the frequency of the survey and the length of recall period. Unless a monthly survey with a monthly recall period is used, reports of vital events from the survey will arrive at PGE headquarters for processing in much larger batches than registration reports. In the illustrative sample of 100,000 described in the first paragraph of this subsection, the registration system produced 300 to 400 birth reports and 100 to 200 death reports each month. In contrast, a household survey of the same sample using a 12-month recall period with interviews every six months might yield from 4,000 to 5,000 birth reports and 1,000 to 2,000 death reports each survey round. (However, if only data for the most recent six-month period were used for matching and tabulation purposes, only about half this number of reports would need to be processed each round.) If the same survey was conducted annually with a 15-month recall period, approximately 5,000 to 6,000 birth reports and 1,200 to 2,500 death reports would be generated. The difficulty facing the headquarters staff is that these reports all arrive at one time.

At the same time that the PGE staff is inundated with this flood of documents, 20,000 household schedules containing information on the enumerated base population (approximately 100,000 persons in our illustration) will also arrive at headquarters. The issue of whether to use the survey base population or an external population estimate in determining the vital rates has been covered elsewhere (in Section J of Chapter 3 and Section F.1 of this chapter). Assuming that the decision is made to use the enumerated base population, it will be necessary to process the household schedules. We strongly recommend that in the first year of operations only a minimum amount of data from these be processed. The varied processing jobs associated with a two-way match are so great that plans for full exploitation of the information on the household schedules can be carried out only at the expense of other processing operations. Specifically, we recommend that the initial processing be limited to the coding, keypunching, and tabulation of age and sex for the *de facto* population.

Because of the variety of tasks involved in a full dual system approach, the work of the headquarters staff must be well organized. We suggest that the PGE headquarters be organized into a number of small sections: (1) Documents Control; (2) Vital Events; (3) Matching; (4) Base Population; (5) Administration; and (6) Operations Control.[26] If a relatively small sample is involved, say 10,000 to 20,000 persons, then a number of these functions can be combined and the actual organization by section may be considerably modified. (Needless to say, the same functions will exist however the work is distributed.) In a large sample, say 50,000 or more persons, some sort of explicit organizational recognition of the different parts of the complex processing operation is necessary to avoid chaos.

The functional division of the work involved in a large PGE study can be illustrated best by describing briefly the responsibilities of each section.

a. The Documents Control Section

The objective of the Documents Control Section is to help the other sections by keeping track of the registration and survey vital events reports for each sample area and of the household survey schedules. This involves binding documents into convenient semipermanent work units called "batches," keeping a record of the whereabouts of each batch, repairing damaged documents, and protecting all the documents stored in the section against rain, mildew, mice, white ants (termites), and the like. As time goes on the Documents Control Section will also be given the responsibility for the safekeeping of transcription sheets, punchcard listings, and tabulation printouts. The section often can be handled by one person, but he must be given additional help at peak periods and plenty of accessible shelf space.

b. The Vital Events Section

This section is responsible for editing and coding the vital events reported both in the survey and in the special registration system. Editing and coding should be done internally within each system; that is, doubtful coding situations should not be resolved by referring to the reports of the other system. Since the reports for each system, area, and type of event are in separate batches, it is unlikely that such comparisons will arise casually. The decision as to whether to enter the codes onto the document or onto a special transcription sheet has to be made in consultation with the staff of the data processing unit. If the field documents were designed to facilitate processing operations, transcription sheets should not be required. In processing vital events, it is important that each reported event be assigned a unique identification number that is entered onto the punchcard for that report. For registration reports, the PGE registration certificate number can be used. In the case of survey reports, a unique numbering system will have to be established.

If the matching is to be done with mechanical equipment or with a digital computer, then this section must be given all the help it needs in editing and coding the survey reports when they arrive, since keypunching and data processing operations take much less time per document than editing and coding. In these circumstances, and given that all the survey reports will arrive at one time, the Vital Events Section will become the narrow funnel through which all inputs to the matching operations flow. In addition, the punchcards representing the events reported in each system should be listed and the listings checked (proofread) against the documents. This is necessary because any errors in the data used in matching will result in erroneous nonmatches. If matching is to be done manually—which we recommend—the coding and keypunching for the bulk of the registration reports can precede the matching work, whereas that for the bulk of the survey events reports will follow the matching operations.

c. The Matching Section

The job of this section is to do the matching; keep careful records of the match results by sample area; prepare the forms for the field investigation of nonmatched reports; and, on the basis of the results of the investigation, prepare the final raising factors that will be gang-punched into the cards. A more detailed description of the matching operation can be found in Section B.6, above. In addition, readers may wish to refer to Chapter 6 of the *1962–63 Report of the Population Growth Estimation Experiment* (Population Growth Estimation, 1968) for the details of the procedures used in one particular mechanical matching operation. It is desirable to organize the work within the section so that one or two persons *not* involved in the earlier phases of the matching operation give all the nonmatched reports a "fresh look" and then prepare the forms to be used in the field investigation— the object being to identify probable matches on the basis of more relaxed tolerance limits than those used in the routine clerical matching operation. Also, at least one responsible member of the professional staff should be assigned to work with the matching clerks. During the initial phases of the matching this should be a full-time assignment.

d. The Base Population Section

This section should edit and code data on the enumerated base population from the household survey and supervise the tabulations arising from these data. As indicated earlier, only a minimum amount of data (specifically, the population by age and sex) should be processed in the first year. Once the matching has been established as a going operation, it will be possible to allocate somewhat more resources to the exploitation of the household enumeration data. A number of different types of data processing records can be extracted from the enumeration data: (1) a record for each person in the population, (2) a record for each household, and (3) a record for each married woman of reproductive age. Whether either of these latter two files should be established depends upon the staff time available and the quality of the data.

e. The Administration Section

The Administration Section sees that field and office staff are paid on time, receive timely reimbursement for allowable expenses, and are provided with the supplies they need. For effective administration, records will have to be kept and rules made. However, prior to their implementation, the record systems and rules should be reviewed to determine what effect they may have on the quality of the statistics being produced.

f. The Operations Control Section

The goal of the Operations Control Section is to manage the work of the organization in such a way that a high quality statistical product is achieved swiftly and at minimum cost. The section must have access to timely information about all phases of study operations, professional competence in the collection of statistical data, and the authority to resolve operational problems. In practice, the section may consist of one person. However, if a large national sample is involved, some aspects of the job must be shared by others. The Operations Control Section will be responsible for (1) maintaining ultimate supervision of the collection systems, or liaison with them if they are external to the organization; (2) interweaving the flow of work and staff among the various sections so as to avoid wasteful processing backlogs; (3) planning for the orderly build-up of staff in the early stages of the project; and (4) ensuring that all operations are carried out in a manner consistent with the theory of PGE studies. For a description of the kinds of activities involved in the work of this section, see Simmons (1972).

One person in each section should be designated as the section chief and given general responsibility for the work of the section. There should be regular meetings of all the section chiefs so that misunderstandings can be cleared up, bottlenecks unclogged, and crises anticipated. Care should be taken that the organizational structure does not in itself become an obstacle to efficiency. In particular, it should be understood that individuals will be shifted about between sections to accommodate the ebb and flow of processing jobs.

D.4   ANALYSIS AND EVALUATION OF DATA

The processing work of a PGE study generally takes much longer than anticipated. Consequently, there may be some frustration among prospective users of demographic estimates and those who believe that sampling should provide quicker results than a full census. To meet this problem, some quick provisional results based mainly on hand tabulations should be circulated in a series of interim reports.

The final analysis and evaluation can be carried out along a number of parallel lines, in accord with the basic philosophy of the dual system method. Although the evaluation of study results is discussed at some length in Chapter 6, it will be useful to summarize the various approaches here. The first part of this evaluation involves an examination of the PGE growth rate, vital rates, and age-specific fertility and mortality in comparison with the results of demographic analysis, including the "Brass technique," and the growth rates observed in the enumerated base population between survey rounds. The next step involves the preparation of variance estimates and a review of the crude and age-specific rates for each collection system separately. Finally, various methodological studies should be done to provide a clearer understanding of the process of PGE data collection and estimation. These may involve attempts to isolate the extent to which the PGE estimates are affected by response correlation bias and matching error, variations in the performance of different groups of field personnel, the accuracy of age and parity data, and so on. At this stage, one may also examine additional substantive tabulations covering the detailed characteristics of births, deaths, persons, households, married couples, and women of reproductive age.

In general, the PGE staff should concentrate their analytical efforts on an assessment of the quality of the data they are producing and leave the preparation of population projections and life tables for a later date or to others. Certainly, a clear summary of substantive findings, covering basic estimates of population growth and fertility and mortality by age, is in order and should be released by the PGE organization as promptly as possible. However, by and large, the reports of the PGE study should consist mostly of tables of substantive results, long and detailed descriptions of the procedures followed, and some methodological analysis.

E.   *Periodic Household Surveys with Substantial Overlaps in the Periods of Recall*

In this section, we describe a dual system—overlapping household surveys—with which we have very little experience, and which is relatively untested in practice.[27] Therefore, the presentation will be much sketchier than that of the other two approaches covered in this chapter. With the present alternative, dual collection is achieved through a succession of overlapping recall periods and the matching of events in the common (overlapping) recall period carried out between each successive pair of survey rounds. In other words, the pairs of successive survey rounds are the two systems. The events occurring in the overlapping portion of the recall periods may be reported in either or both reporting systems. Assuming that the probability of an event being reported in each survey round is independent, an estimate of events adjusted for omissions can be prepared.

The main advantage of this approach is that it can fit relatively easily into the current field programs of a national statistical office. Enumerators from other programs can be periodically assigned to the PGE surveys and then return to work on, say, the labor force survey or the collection of price data. The approach has two main drawbacks. First, since both systems involve a survey, the level of independence between the two systems is likely to be considerably reduced. Each step taken to increase independence will raise costs; thus, the apparent savings in administrative costs associated with this approach is largely offset by the effort necessary to provide results of comparable quality. Second, since there is very limited experience with this approach on which to draw, the PGE study personnel will be largely on their own.

E.1   COLLECTION AND PROCESSING OF DATA

The major design questions with a dual system based on overlapping recall periods are those of any household survey—the frequency of the survey rounds and the length of the recall period. A secondary consideration is the extent to which the PGE administrators are able to meet the costs of maintaining and using two largely independent field staffs for successive survey rounds.

In planning the survey, one should be sure that the survey rounds are frequent enough and the recall periods long enough for a complete overlap in recall periods; that is, events for each month must have a chance to be reported in at least two different survey rounds. Figures 4.8 and 4.9 are concrete examples of recall periods and survey intervals

Fig. 4.8   Overlapping Recall Periods for Semiannual Surveys with 12-Month Recall Periods

Survey round number	Survey date	Recall period	Common (overlapping) period
1	1 January 1970	January–December 1969	—
2	1 July 1970	July 1969–June 1970	July–December 1969
3	1 January 1971	January–December 1970	January–June 1970
4	1 July 1971	July 1970–June 1971	July–December 1970
5	1 January 1972	January–December 1971	January–June 1971

Fig. 4.9   Overlapping Recall Periods for Semiannual Surveys with 18-Month Recall Periods

Survey round number	Survey date	Recall period	Common (overlapping) period
1	1 January 1970	July 1968–December 1969	—
2	1 July 1970	January 1969–June 1970	January–December 1969
3	1 January 1971	July 1969–December 1970	July 1969–June 1970
4	1 July 1971	January 1970–June 1971	January–December 1970

that meet the basic requirement of full overlap. Figure 4.10 illustrates a design combination (annual surveys with 18-month recall periods) that does *not* provide complete overlap. The general rule is simple: To achieve complete overlap, the recall period must be at least twice as long as the interval between successive survey rounds. Particularly in countries still experiencing high infant mortality rates, there is a strong case for using this approach with relatively frequent survey rounds—for example, three-month intervals with six-month recall periods. Note also in Figure 4.9 that when the recall period is more than twice the survey interval, data will be available from more than two sources for at least part of the year. In this case, each vital event occurring from July 1969 to June 1970 is part of the recall periods of three successive survey rounds, thus making possible, in theory, a three-way match for this period. However, an analysis of the complexities of a three-way, or greater, match are beyond the scope of this chapter. (For a brief discussion of some of the issues involved, see Chapter 7, Section D.1.)

Insofar as possible, successive survey rounds should be conducted by different enumerators with different supervisors, to maximize independence. In any event, a separate interviewing questionnaire should be used and a real attempt made to assign different enumerators to any given household on successive survey rounds. Money "saved" here will almost certainly have a detrimental effect on the quality of the final estimates.

It will be possible to use smaller clusters in this approach than

Fig. 4.10   Overlapping Recall Periods for Annual Surveys with 18-Month Recall Periods

Survey round number	Survey date	Recall period	Common (overlapping) period
1	1 July 1970	January 1969–June 1970	—
2	1 July 1971	January 1970–June 1971	January–June 1970
3	1 July 1972	January 1971–June 1972	January–June 1971
4	1 July 1973	January 1972–June 1973	January–June 1972

in either of the others, because the sample can be designed without having to accommodate the constraints imposed by the organization of the civil registration system or the work load of a special registrar. In fact, it may be possible to make use of a well-designed existing national probability sample. However, one would have to consider whether the additional burden placed on respondents by the double-interviewing implied by the overlapping recall periods would adversely affect the quality of response in the basic study for which the sample was selected. Almost certainly some system for rotating the sample would need to be incorporated into the design.

Particular emphasis must be placed on accurate dating of events in the survey field work. Unless this is done, serious matching and out-of-scope problems will arise. One method of reducing the effect of dating errors on the matching operation is to have a large enough number of other identification items with high discriminating power so that one can exclude the date of the event from the items used in matching. This means that structure numbers must be present on the maps, the structures, and the field documents for each survey round. This, again, is not the place to "save" money.

The processing operations involved in the overlapping recall period approach do not appear to present any unique problems. However, without real field experience one cannot be sure. It is unclear whether a one-way or a two-way match is more appropriate. In either case, each survey round will be involved twice in the matching operations—first with the round preceding it and then with the subsequent round. The number of files of vital events cards the processing operation will yield depends upon the length of the overlap, upon whether a one- or two-way match is done, and upon the analytic needs of the PGE study. At least one file will be produced for the events occurring in one calendar year. There is certainly no need to code, keypunch, and tabulate data on the enumerated base population at intervals more frequently than once a year.

E.2   ANALYSIS AND EVALUATION OF DATA

There is a real cause for concern that the use of overlapping recall periods in successive survey rounds to form a dual system will yield seriously biased estimates because the same kinds of events are likely to be missed in both survey rounds. Therefore, both analysis and evaluation should focus on the problem of independence. The preparation of separate PGE estimates for population subgroups as suggested by Chandrasekaran and Deming (1949) and discussed earlier, in Section C.4, seems particularly appropriate in this instance.

In addition to using substantive demographic variables such as sex, age of mother, age of deceased, and so on to form subgroups, using a few methodological items would be important. In particular, if there is some variation in the study as to whether the same or different enumerators interviewed a given household in successive rounds, this fact, if entered on the events cards, would enable estimates to be prepared separately for each group. A careful review of survey procedures may uncover other potentially powerful classifying variables. If so, they should be keypunched so that they can be tested.

Since this approach is based entirely on retrospective reports of vital events, recall lapse and telescoping of reports may occur. The latter phenomenon will probably be controlled by the overlapping recall periods and field investigations of nonmatched reports. The problem of recall lapse appears more substantial. One method of dealing with it may be to prepare estimates adjusted for omissions separately by month of occurrence and then to sum these monthly estimates to obtain a new annual figure. The usefulness of this method will, in part, be dependent upon the timing of the survey rounds and the length of the recall period. In addition, it may be possible to apply, in this instance, some of the procedures developed by R. K. Som (1973) for dealing with recall lapse.

F. Further Advice on Some Topics Related to Study Design

F.1   THE UNDERESTIMATION OF THE DENOMINATOR

This section deals with the problem of estimating the denominator, an obvious necessity for the estimation of vital rates. It also deals with some of the ways of obtaining the base population most relevant to the vital events collected during a PGE study. The narrow and somewhat misleading title of the section is meant to draw attention to the central fact that in most empirical exercises the base population is underestimated.

As discussed in Chapter 3, Section J, there are essentially two ways of obtaining the base population: from either or both of the PGE collection systems or from sources external to the PGE study. In practice, there are usually two choices at best—the PGE household survey and an independent estimate based on a recent census. Available census data are often unusable because they are long out of date or of doubtful quality, or because there is no reliable way of estimating population change in the years since the census. Thus, in most situations, the base population obtained from the household survey is the only reliable source.

A base population can be derived from the household survey because the enumerator, in order to establish all the changes in the household over the recall period, must first list all the members and determine their relation to one another (usually, and more strictly, to the head of the household). Thus the base population becomes a byproduct of the main activity of the enumerator, though it is admittedly somewhat silly to call nine-tenths of his work a mere "byproduct." Using the enumerator to obtain the base population can also be justified on the grounds that this helps to preserve the independence of the two systems by ensuring that a major part of his work is different from that of the registrar.

If an adequate census-based estimate of the base population is available as well as the survey-derived estimate, the more accurate of the two should be used. (See Chapter 3, Section J, for a discussion of the considerations involved.) Data from a census year can be used if the census coincides with the enumeration undertaken for PGE purposes. Even if the census date is a few years removed, census data can be used if they are suitably adjusted using the latest available estimate of the growth rate of the population. However, there must be some assurance that the populations of the PGE sample areas were not subject to differential migration. With an independent estimate of the population, observed changes in estimated vital rates may be due merely to events attributable to substantial migration in one or more sample areas rather than to any change in the fertility and mortality of the population. With small areas particularly, an enumeration of the base population at least once a year may be a necessity because the independent estimates may not be adequate.

The PGE approach as described in this handbook is a method of adjusting survey or registration reports of vital events for omissions. In circumstances in which the vital rate numerator is adjusted for omissions while the denominator remains underestimated, we may find ourselves with vital rates that are overestimated. However, since survey or census counts of the base population are likely to be much closer to the correct figure than the comparable counts of events, the PGE estimates of vital rates are likely to be much closer to the true rates than those of a single-source household survey. The reason estimates of the base population are much closer to reality than counts of events is that counting the base population is a one-time operation to obtain current data, whereas enumerating vital events is either a one-time retrospective endeavor (survey) or an operation conducted continuously throughout a year (registration).

Although the typical underestimation of the denominator need not be considered a bar to the PGE approach, it clearly is a problem and requires some action. Five ways of meeting this situation, at least partially, can be distinguished. The first and most orthodox is to undertake a traditional post-enumeration survey (PES) in order to correct the estimates arising from the original enumeration. There is a rich literature on the ways of conducting a PES and on the benefits accruing from one. When considering a PES, it is essential to keep in mind the need to separate errors arising from the omission of whole households from those arising from the omission of individual members of households. Different procedures are required to detect errors caused by these two types of omissions, and different procedures are required to correct them.

The second method of dealing with base population problems is to make an arbitrary upward revision of the estimate of the total population, based possibly on demographic analysis, on a hunch, or on a reasonable figure based on the experience or practice of another country. A third possibility is to apply the Chandrasekaran-Deming solution to the denominator (see Deming and Keyfitz, 1967). This procedure, however, creates some problems. There is danger of a loss of independence if the jobs of collecting field data become too much alike; there would certainly be a horrendous amount of work involved in matching all persons, not just the infants and deceased; and finally, there is no certainty that the expense and effort will be justified by the results.

The fourth alternative, and the one we recommend here, is a long-term approach: Improve the enumeration process over time to obtain a better count of the base population. Obtain a grip on the population and your field force, and do a high quality job. Evaluate the enumeration work, primarily by means of tests of internal consistency and variability, with a view to identifying specific problem areas. Through periodic surveys improve your coverage each round in several obvious ways, some of which were explained in Section B.3. There are reports suggesting that this approach can be effective (United Nations, 1964a).

A fifth approach is to live with one's biases and do nothing. This alternative is recommended until such time as the study organization becomes strong enough to switch its attention away from teething troubles. Biases caused by an underestimated denominator need not destroy the value of the PGE estimates. As indicated earlier, the question comes down to whether an adjusted PGE estimate with a small bias is more useful than an unadjusted survey or registration rate with a large bias. For a further discussion of the implications of this alternative, see Chapter 6.

F.2 ON THE FALLACY OF BEING TOO CLEVER BY HALF, ON THE CHESS PRINCIPLE, AND ON THE TENDENCY TO OVERELABORATION AND OVERSOPHISTICATION

Any system of operations leading first to the collection of two sets of data under conditions requiring maximum independence and then to the analysis of these data through case-by-case matching is a complicated affair, even in its simplest form. Since PGE studies are conducted as a rule in conditions of at least some administrative, transportation, communication, literacy, financial and organizational deficiencies,[28] it becomes a matter of serious concern when elaborations are contemplated. Such elaborations are typically suggested by planners in an attempt to reach levels of sophistication beyond those of the simplest designs. It is difficult to argue against endeavors so highly motivated. Yet, at the beginning of a study, this rule should be proposed: The virtues of features beyond what is required by the main purposes of the system, narrowly conceived, must be thrashed out before they can be accepted into the system. This is an instance where the best is the enemy of the good, due to overloading of the organization with avoidable additions. The burden of proof should always be on the advocates of any avoidable feature.

Basically, the attitude toward avoidable features will be largely dictated by the purposes of the study. Should it be purely experimental, many more questionable and untried features can be considered than when a study has a substantive purpose. However, given a substantive assignment, the PGE system is too expensive, its potential results are too valuable for the national planners, and its gestation takes too much time for it to be left at the mercy of a series of short-lived "novel approaches." For example, the problem of recall is central to many questions in demographic and social survey analysis, but it cannot be claimed that the success of any one PGE study depends upon the ability to use varying recall periods. This should, therefore, be avoided, at least in the initial phases of the field and analysis work. In Chapter 3, Section H.1, and in Section B.4 of this chapter we discussed the use of the *de facto* and *de jure* concepts. Using the evidence available from pilot studies or other relevant sources, one of these two concepts must be chosen for each source. In general one should resist the suggestion, often made, that the survey should collect data on vital events on both a *de facto* and *de jure* basis in any substantive study. Of course, such a dual concept approach to data collection permits the analyst to postpone his choice between a *de facto* and *de jure* concept until some preliminary results are available. (If he still cannot make up his mind, he can insist that all tabulations be produced both ways.) However, this attitude offends against another basic rule: No matter how difficult the work becomes at headquarters, it should be made as easy as possible in the field. It would be a poor argument to burden the field staff in order to add to the comforts of the already comfortably settled and desk-bound analyst. In short, the call of analysts for excessive and elaborate data should be answered by the field man with skeptical questions about the uses of these data. And his voice, emanating from under the heaps of his burdens, should not be a weak squeak.

There is a group of features that performs a useful and probably essential function when used minimally but becomes a cumbersome burden when organizers try to be "too clever by half." An example is the use of overlapping recall periods in obtaining data on vital events. Experience has shown that this approach has two uses: First, the grip of the enumeration on the population tightens progressively with each round. Second, it is useful to have the same event enumerated more than once when doubts arise during the matching process. Such doubts can often be resolved by referring to other entries (Yusuf, 1968a), without the expense and delay involved in a field follow-up. It is, however, overly optimistic to hope that the multiple entries will give rise to some other and new methods of analysis. Such means of analysis have still to be invented, and they are not likely to be discovered in the midst of the conflicting demands of a large and complicated organization such as that of a PGE study. Anyway, much of the gain in terms of control of response error resulting from the use of overlapping recall periods can be obtained by using the simpler household-change procedure.

The examples of avoidable features are many, and organizers

of PGE systems may do well to remember the rhyme "when in doubt, leave it out." Even when a feature is acceptable to the field staff and does not jeopardize the main mission, doubt may remain as to whether it is worthwhile. The analyst may be quick to ask for a frill, without having made up his mind what he will do with the results when they are presented to him. Consider, for example, the "registration only" and "survey only" areas in the Pakistan PGE. These were areas where only one of the two collection systems was used. The idea behind this limitation was the interest in the difference between the effects of using two collection systems jointly, as opposed to using either one alone. In spite of its simplicity, the arrangement produced neither useful findings nor suggestions as to how the data could be used.

This line of reasoning can be pushed a bit further. In Chapter 6 much is made of the need for and advantages of building opportunities for periodic changes, revisions, and improvements into the study as a matter of routine, that is, in a manner that does not produce a crisis every time a change is made. Such a procedure must above all be orderly, because otherwise the study may become either prematurely rigid or easy prey to off-the-cuff novel approaches to data collection and ill-considered attempts to meet highly specialized data needs. The requirement of orderliness in change, however, is not by itself enough to protect the PGE study from special-interest requests and the possible damage that may follow from trying to meet such requests. Proposed changes, no matter how well intentioned, may well be inconsistent with the basic PGE task of vital statistics measurement and must be assessed in terms of this task. Moreover, outside researchers eager to obtain data for their analyses should think more than twice before they make their recommendations and requests, particularly when they are unfamiliar with all the relevant dimensions of the local scene, including the personalities involved.

A word of caution is in order even with respect to the basic study features. One should recognize that there are alternative ways of achieving the same goal, and the simplest is usually the best. The principle is easy to enunciate: The procedures must never be too difficult for the personnel available. The application of this principle is more difficult, but it is at least salutary to keep it in mind.

Another important principle, this one easier to apply, is the chess principle, applicable when alternative courses of action have to be selected. The chess principle says that a "bad" but thought-out move is better than a "better" move which is the result of a sudden inspiration. A different way of stating it is "a bird in the hand is worth two in the bush." A tried method, even if it is not very good, must not be replaced by another method that looks better, but has not been tested. Statistical systems benefit greatly from procedural continuity, and constant "tinkering" has a cost in terms of reducing this continuity. Clearly, one must not cling rigidly to unworkable procedures, and it is important to examine the effectiveness of study methods and systematically discard inadequate procedures in favor of better, more workable alternatives. This implies a program of ongoing methodological research.

Nevertheless, it is also true that an undertrained or undermotivated staff will often be too quick to classify a quite adequate procedure as unworkable. Because all procedures are essentially unworkable unless the staff has been given sufficient training and imbued with sufficient motivation, and because of the value of procedural continuity, it is usually better to improve existing procedures than to introduce new ones.

Footnotes

[1] If the sample design calls for an average cluster size of less than 200 structures, it may be advisable to drop one of the specified levels of organization. Whatever the method of organization, the same number of layers should be used in all sample areas. The occasional undersized sample areas or chunks can be handled without deviating from the standard method of organization by "subdividing" them into single chunks or blocks, respectively.

[2] Mapping procedures can be greatly simplified if small-scale maps are available from other programs. It is our understanding, for example, that maps produced for the WHO Malaria Eradication campaigns would be helpful. The use of aerial photography should also be considered.

[3] More generally, the professional standards of the three types of maps need not be anywhere close to the examples given in Figures 4.1(a) through 4.3(b). The maps may be much "scruffier" and still serve their purpose (after all, they are supposed to be living documents). What is important is that they be based on true topographic maps similar to Figures 4.1(a), 4.2(a), and 4.3(a).

[4] Given low density, there will be fewer structures per block because more of the interviewing officials' time will be spent traveling. That is to say, there will be fewer structures than in the example in the text. It would then be possible, and advisable, to use the first digit of the structure numbers in each block as a code for the block.

[5] In the initial stages of the PGE study, when sample areas are being defined, whitewash can be used to number structures. Later, however, the whitewashed numbers should be replaced.

[6] In some designs there is an intentional difference between the registration area and the enumeration area, see Chapter 7, Sections C and D.

[7] In the Pakistan PGE study, relative to the registration system, the survey obtained better reporting for the events of usual residents occurring away from the sample area than for events occurring to visitors in the area (Yusuf, 1968a).

[8] "Demographic analysis" refers to the group of techniques developed by Brass, Coale, Demeny, and others to estimate basic demographic variables (see glossary).

[9] The distinction between "demographic analysis" and "substantive tabulation" as used here is somewhat arbitrary. It is a useful distinction, however, in that it helps make clear the items needed to apply the Brass method and related techniques, and those that are needed for general analytical purposes.

[10] Using such a working definition will result in fewer events being classified as live births than if the World Health Organization's medical definition, which is based on the presence of any one of four vital signs, were used. No estimates of the extent of this difference are available. However, the undercount relative to the WHO definition if "breathing" and "respiratory effort" (rather than "crying") are the criteria for a live birth has been estimated in two studies of hospitalized deliveries as 0.4 percent (United Nations, 1955) and 2.6 percent (U.S. National Center for Health Statistics, 1972), respectively. For countries where few births are medically attended, the classification

of events reported by either a survey or a registration procedure is likely to be subject to substantially greater variability than these studies imply. For this reason, it is important that stillbirths be included in the initial stages of the matching process along with the live-birth reports.

[11] So major a departure from the registration ideal of covering events as they occur should be avoided in the main study, as it may teach the registrars (incorrectly) that missed contacts can be made up later. They can, but at the price of lower coverage rates and more out-of-scope reports.

[12] Some arbitrariness in the count of matching errors may arise because of the order in which reports are compared, particularly where the blocking units are small and when, for a given tolerance limit, the proportion of reports with unique identification codes is low. The arbitrary effect of order can be reduced by repeating single-characteristic matching a number of times for each tolerance limit, with the order in which the reports are compared randomized anew each time. The average number of erroneous matches and nonmatches obtained for any given tolerance limit can be used to identify the tolerance limit that produces minimum gross matching error.

[13] In a large, one-time study of civil registration completeness, the costs associated with high supervisory or field follow-up referral rates may be so great that these referral rates should be considered explicitly when the initial matching rules are developed.

[14] In theory, other characteristics of this type may exist; in practice, they appear to be rarely encountered. Fellegi in a personal communication to the authors has suggested a procedure for handling the matching operation when a number of such characteristics are available. In that situation, Fellegi recommends that, after ranking all the characteristics in terms of decreasing discriminating power, one expand the set of criteria by alternately taking a characteristic from the top and then the bottom of the list.

[15] This example also illustrates the disadvantage in terms of matching error of a redundant characteristic. While sex of baby cannot reduce the number of erroneous matches if agreement on full given name is required, because of carelessness in recording sex in either source the use of sex as a matching characteristic may add to the number of erroneous nonmatches and the gross error. Under these circumstances the level of net error will also rise because the number of erroneous matches remains constant and the number of erroneous nonmatches increases.

[16] A very simple alternative to the Soundex system for coding names that has been used successfully in some matching operations is to code only the first four or five consonants, ignoring all vowels. Although this procedure has the important advantage of simplicity, it may, in some languages and populations, involve too high a cost in terms of reduced discriminating power.

[17] Tribal names or names of villages may be coded by using some form of the Soundex system or by using a master list of tribes or villages.

[18] With small batches, it is possible for the matching clerks and others involved in office processing to count, physically, the number of vital events reports in each unit at the start and finish of their assignment. As batches get larger, it becomes increasingly likely that any instructions to this effect will be ignored in practice and that documents control will deteriorate accordingly.

[19] See CATEGORY in glossary.

[20] We emphasize that rotation of the population sample is meant, not rotation of registrars or enumerators.

[21] Note, however, that the estimate of the extent of completeness of the civil registration system is algebraically identical whether a one-way or two-way match has been made.

[22] In some cases, it may be possible to persuade the agency responsible for civil registration to add adequate identification to the birth and death certificates, but in many cases this will not be possible.

[23] Admittedly, clusters of this size are inefficient if sampling variance alone is considered. However, if total error (that is, mean square error) is used as a criterion, then large clusters may turn out to be less impractical. Large clusters often involve the use of a resident full-time registrar and closer supervisory control than can be achieved with a larger number of smaller sampling units.

[24] There may be exceptions to this rule. For example, two small hamlets distinctly separated may form one daily ration, but it is convenient for mapping purposes to call them two blocks. We then have one daily ration with two blocks.

[25] It is conceivable that the posting of the weekly report may require a whole day's trip to the nearest post office. Such a need should be allowed for in structuring the registrar's duties, and the use of one day out of five or six does not appear excessive for such a purpose. Especially in remote areas, it is particularly important for headquarters to keep in close touch with the registrar. However, should a trip to the nearest post office require two days' travel, then perhaps the weekly report should be changed to a fortnightly report. Alternatively, if messengers can be hired at rates lower than the pay of the registrar, the posting can be effected in this manner. However, experience tells us that hiring messengers opens the door for shunting the responsibility onto others and should, as a rule, be avoided.

[26] These informal sections are internal to the PGE unit or organization. In addition, the usual statistical office service units covering data processing, sampling, printing, and so on are required.

[27] Between 1969 and 1971 the Central Statistical Office of the Government of Pakistan used a dual system based on overlapping recall periods in its Population Growth Survey (PGS). Two different designs were tried: In half the sample areas, quarterly interviews were conducted with six-month recall periods; in the other half of the sample, interviewing was done semiannually with a 12-month recall period. In addition, an effort was made to ensure that the same interviewer did not interview the same household in successive survey rounds. Some matching work and field follow-up was carried out but no report on this matching experience was published. On the basis of fragmentary matching results (after follow-up) it appeared that either the overlap design was effective in detecting a considerable number of omitted events or that the matching yielded a number of erroneous nonmatches that remained undetected after field follow-up.

[28] As a first reaction one might say that, if there are no problems, PGE has no role to perform. However, good roads and smoothly functioning postal and telegraph services do not ensure civil registration system completeness so that there is a continuing need to evaluate the quality of registration work. Moreover, see Linder (1970), who urges that analysts even in developed countries should end their complacency and stop relying on the system of civil registration as their main, and often only, source of data on fertility and mortality.

Designing a PGE Study: A Case Study 5

A. *Introduction*

Whether or not one ends up with one of the three models described in Chapter 4, it is desirable in *planning* a PGE system to start with one of these alternatives. However, no one of the three alternatives will ever exactly fit the requirements of any given country. The heart of designing a PGE system is the process of adapting standard procedures and general principles to specific conditions and spelling out the *details* of sampling, data collection, matching, field follow-up, estimation, etc. In developing such adaptations and in making a choice among alternatives, the planner should be guided by the principles laid down in Chapter 3. We must, however, emphasize that standard procedures and principles of design, no matter how excellent they may be, do not eliminate the need for meticulous, detailed planning based on the *specifics* of the particular country involved. Although this process will never be identical in any two cases, it will be useful to examine a case history of how the principles described in the preceding chapters might be applied to the design of a specific PGE study.

In Chapter 5, we present a "case history" of the design of a PGE study in a hypothetical country. Those who have actually tried to design such a statistical system will recognize that a good deal more guesswork and a good deal less logic are involved in such an effort than in the somewhat "idealized" case history presented here. However, the situations described are based on real experiences and actual conditions, even though they represent combinations from different countries. Although a completely rational design procedure is probably an unattainable goal in the real world, progress comes by "inching oneself" in the direction of the "ideal."

The country described in this "case history" is called Pacifica. A fictitious country was purposely chosen to emphasize that the solutions suggested here are not applicable to any existing real situation. This chapter will be useful in illustrating the process of balancing the arguments "for" and "against" each aspect of design—a process that is necessary in arriving at usable solutions to PGE design problems. This process cannot safely be shortened by using ready-made formulae or recipes for success.

It should be emphasized also that the design of a statistical system for an entire country cannot be considered in isolation from political and administrative considerations. These are important "background variables" for the PGE system of Pacifica. The planners of that study wish to use modern social science to create a statistical information system of maximum social value. But, as realists, they must shape that system so that it is capable of surviving the storms and stresses of a real-life setting. For example, there may be considerable pressure to shape personnel selection in such a manner as to secure support from the currently dominant political party; yet if such short-run political considerations are given too much weight, the statistical system will be threatened by destruction at the next change of government. Thus although it is important that a PGE study conform to current political realities, it is even more important that the study serve the continuing need of the country for statistical information—a need that will outlast the current political situation. This type of reasoning is incorporated in the design decisions described below, even though it almost never appears as an explicit consideration.

B. Pacifica: Defining the Measurement Problem

B.1 THE POPULATION

Pacifica is primarily an agricultural country, with two staple crops, rice and cotton, accounting for over 80 percent of total agricultural production. About 40 percent of the cotton is exported, either in raw form or as fabrics. None of the rice is exported, and in years when the crop is poor, rice or other cereal grains must be imported.

According to the most recent census, conducted in 1961, the agricultural population, which accounts for about 70 percent of the total population, lives in villages varying in size from 200 to about 5,000 persons. Another 25 percent of the population are urban. About 15 percent of the total are concentrated in four metropolitan (industrial-commercial) centers each with a population of about 500,000, and about 10 percent are in 27 "trading center" towns of 10,000 to 100,000 population. The remaining 5 percent of Pacifica's population (and perhaps as much as 10 percent) live under very primitive conditions in sparsely settled jungle and mountain areas.

Depending upon the data source, the techniques used, and the assumptions made, the results of demographic analysis gave varying estimates of the current (1969) vital rates. Birth and death rates were estimated to be about the same for the rural and urban populations. The birth rate was estimated as being between 35 and 55 per 1,000 and the death rate as being between 10 and 22 per 1,000, although the official statistics (based on the civil registration system and the 1961 Census) were 25 per 1,000 for the birth rate and 7 per 1,000 for the death rate.

There is practically no information about the jungle or mountain people other than some very subjective estimates from anthropological studies. The 1961 Census did have an estimate of the total jungle and mountain population by sex and broad age groups (under 10, 11 to 49, 50 years and over), but it was based on very incomplete reports collected from tribal chiefs by traveling inspectors. The 1961 Census was reasonably complete for the remainder of the population (urban and rural agricultural), and another census is planned for next year.

As indicated earlier, Pacifica has a civil registration system for births and deaths. Parents are under a legal obligation to file reports of births at the local police station in rural areas and at the town or city hall in urban areas. Reports of death are to be filed in the same offices by the persons "responsible for burial" (next of kin, undertakers, or local officials). The civil registration law provides substantial fines for failure to report events, but no attempt has ever been made to collect these fines. Birth and death certificates are prepared in duplicate by local officials (police sergeants or clerks) on the basis of verbal reports by parents, relatives, or neighbors. One copy of the certificate is sent to the provincial office of the Ministry of the Interior and from there to the Central Bureau of Statistics (CBS). The other copy of the certificate is filed in the local registration office at the subject's usual place of residence. (Thus certificates for some events have to be sent from the local office at the place of occurrence to the office at the place of residence.)

The number of certificates received by the CBS is consistently short of the figures on certificates filed, published monthly by the Ministry of the Interior on the basis of summary reports from its local offices. The shortage varies from year to year and from province to province, averaging 5 percent nationally for both births and deaths with a range of from 2 to 20 percent for the number of certificates received annually. Because of irregularities in the receipt of certificates from the local registration offices, in the preparation of statistical summaries at the provincial offices, and in transmitting copies of the registration certificates to the CBS, monthly figures vary even more widely. In fact, in some months, the CBS receives more certificates than the Interior Ministry indicates have been registered.

Birth and death rates are published by the CBS for each province and for each town or city on a monthly basis. The rates are based on the civil registration and on the previous census figures, the latter adjusted each year for cumulative births and deaths in the area since the census. No adjustment of any kind is made for the discrepancy between the number of certificates received and the reported number filed.[1] As noted above, for the most recent year the "official" birth rate was 25 per 1,000 and the "official" death rate was 7 per 1,000 for the country as a whole (exclusive of the mountain and jungle areas). However, the registered urban birth rate was considerably higher and the rural birth rate somewhat lower (30 per 1,000 for urban versus 23 per 1,000 for rural) than that for the country as a whole. Urban death rates were also somewhat higher than those in rural areas (8.4 versus 6.6 per 1,000).

The difference in vital rates for urban and rural areas may have been due in part to differential reporting, but the statisticians doubt that urban reporting of births and deaths was appreciably better than rural. The major reason for the observed urban-rural differential was thought to be the very large migration from rural to urban areas during the past eight years. Since the census-based population estimates used to calculate birth and death rates are adjusted for births and deaths but not for migration, the urban population is generally underestimated while the rural population is overestimated. This, in turn, tends to bias the urban rates upward and the rural rates downward. The same kind of problem also accounts for much of the large observed variation in the registered vital rates among the provinces.

A number of special studies had been done on a sample survey basis for various urban and rural areas, using sample data for both the numerator and the denominator of birth and death rates. These studies showed very small differences (other than those due to sampling variance) in birth and death rates between rural and urban areas or between provinces. Overall, the most carefully done special studies using retrospective household surveys reported a birth rate of about 37 per 1,000 and a death rate of about 10 per 1,000. Attempts at dual system (PGE) estimation in one of the special studies (with somewhat limited geographic coverage) indicated a birth rate of 50 per 1,000 and a death rate of 18 per 1,000.

B.2 THE GOALS OF THE PGE STUDY

The CBS decided to undertake a PGE study with the assistance of Pacifica's National Planning Board in conjunction with the country's current Five Year Development Plan. About four years prior to the start of planning for the PGE study, some work on family planning had been initiated by the government. After two years the pilot program was scheduled to be expanded into a full-scale national family planning program. At that time, however, the civil registration figures indicated a slight *rise* in the birth rate—up two points to 25 per 1,000 from 23 per 1,000 at the start of the pilot program. Unfortunately, the registered death rate also rose during that period by one point, from 6 to 7 per 1,000, and as a result the estimated growth rate was up slightly over this period (from 1.7 to 1.8 percent). These figures were not considered usable by the administrators of the family planning program, who pointed to figures on IUD insertions and estimates of births averted as evidence of program gains. The figures from the special surveys cited earlier gave little information on demographic change; they suggested either no change or a very small decrease in birth rates for the two years, but all estimates were subject to a standard deviation of 10 to 20 per 1,000.

The National Planning Board and the central government were under tremendous pressure from both opponents and proponents of family planning. The "best guess" of the Planning Board staff, after extensive consultation with the CBS and other experts, was that the family planning program "had begun to catch on." That is, it had achieved some very small but encouraging success. It was not nearly as great a success as the proponents of family planning claimed, but not at all the total failure the program's opponents claimed. The Planning Board decided to continue the program for another two years, expanding it moderately, but not to the extent originally planned. The Board felt, however, that it had to have better data on which to base future decisions about the family planning program. Thus, the CBS was asked to prepare a program for obtaining figures on birth and death rates that would be "satisfactory" guides to future action.

The Bureau's first task was, of course, to make some educated guesses about what degree of accuracy and detail would be "satisfactory" and what size budget would be "adequate." After much discussion between the CBS and the Planning Board staff, it was agreed that:

(1) the reduction in the birth rate was not likely to exceed 5 per 1,000 in any one year and would average much less than that;

(2) with a reduction in the birth rate of 2 to 5 per 1,000 per year the Planning Board would want to continue the current family planning program;

(3) with a reduction in the birth rate of less than 0.2 per 1,000 per year the pressure on the Planning Board to drop or curtail the family planning program as a waste of resources would be great;

(4) with a reduction in the birth rate between 0.5 and 2 per 1,000 per year the Planning Board would want to consider an expansion and/or intensification of the family planning program;

(5) although the target of the current family planning program was to reduce the birth rate by about 10 per 1,000 over a five-year period, it was unlikely that an average reduction as large as 2 per 1,000 per year could actually be achieved;

(6) the Planning Board would want to know if the effectiveness of the family planning program in urban areas differed from that in rural areas. (For their purposes they wanted to be able to detect any urban-rural difference averaging more than 1 per 1,000 per year in the amount of change in the birth rate.)

On the basis of these specifications the CBS next prepared estimates of the cost of obtaining birth and death rates of the needed accuracy—that is, of measuring changes in the birth rate with an estimated total error[2] of 0.5 per 1,000 or less. It was immediately apparent that only a dual system estimate would yield anything even approaching the required accuracy. Moreover, some fairly elementary calculations indicated that it was very unlikely that birth rate estimates with a bias of less than 1 per 1,000 could be obtained even by spending $100,000 or more.[3]

These calculations indicated that an annual budget of $150,000 would produce estimates of birth rates whose variable error component (or standard error) would be about 1.5 per 1,000. The size of the nonvariable error component (or bias) would, of course, be unknown, but it was felt that $150,000 per year would allow procedures where the bias would not exceed the variable error. This would, then, give a total error of about 2.1 per 1,000 in the crude birth rate.[4] For an additional annual expenditure of $25,000, death rates could probably be obtained subject to approximately the same error. That meant a root mean square error of about 3 per 1,000 in estimates of the rate of natural increase and a .95 confidence band of *at best* 5 per 1,000.[5] (Since Pacifica's net international migration is quite small, the rate of natural increase and the population growth rate are equal.) As for separate urban and rural estimates, the errors in these rates would probably be about 40 to 60 percent higher—that is, each would have a .95 confidence band of 7 or 8 per 1,000. Moreover, doubling the expenditure would only reduce these errors by about 20 percent—that is, provide a .95 confidence band of about 4 per 1,000 for the population growth rate of the country as a whole.[6]

The Planning Board representatives took a very brief look at these estimates and quickly rejected them. They felt that the accuracy that could be obtained was inadequate and the expenditures involved were excessive in the context of decisions on the family planning program—that is, possible savings and improvements in the family planning program would not by themselves justify expenditures of this magnitude. A week later, however, a Board representative was involved in a discussion over the amount of government funds to be allocated for new school construction and teacher training. Estimates of the amount required per year varied from less than $20 million to over $50 million, depending largely upon whether the estimated birth rate was in the neighborhood of 25 per 1,000 (the "official estimate" based on the civil registration system results) or 50 per 1,000 (the PGE estimate based on the small dual system study). At about the same time the Planning Board staff also discovered that crucial questions in agricultural planning—notably the amount by which it would be necessary to increase total rice production over the next ten years to avoid substantial increases in grain imports—were very much dependent upon the outcome of those same arguments about the country's elusive birth rate.

In terms, then, of trying to pin down the population growth rate to a level that might permit rational planning for agriculture or education, an error of 4 or 5 per 1,000 was much more tolerable than the 25 per 1,000 difference between the "official" registered rate and the unofficial special study estimate over which the Planning Board was hopelessly bogged down. In this context an annual expenditure of $100,000 to $200,000 for improved population growth estimates began to seem entirely reasonable.

On this basis, the Planning Board decided to go ahead with the study and together with the CBS, set the following initial goals:

(1) a sampling error[7] of 2 per 1,000 (or less) for the national birth rate;
(2) sampling errors of not more than 3 per 1,000 for the urban and rural birth rates;
(3) biases no larger in magnitude than the sampling errors; and
(4) a budget of $150,000 per year for the first three years of the system.

Preliminary estimates indicated that a PGE system budgeted at $150,000 per year could produce the standard error of goal 1. As for goal 2, it was felt to impose no great restrictions not already included in producing goal 1, unless the CBS had grossly misjudged the situation. Goal 3 was, of course, a problem, since the exact magnitude of the biases was unknown. However, it was felt that goal 3 could be achieved with very careful planning and meticulous execution of the study.

It was also decided that estimates for provinces and for each of the four major cities were desirable, but not imperative, and should be attempted only if this could be done without exceeding the $150,000 budget and with standard errors of not more than 10 per 1,000 over a two-year period. It was also decided that although death rates should be published, if possible, their accuracy was not an issue—that is, the design would aim at the accuracy of the birth rate figures specified by goals 1 and 2 above and accept whatever this might imply for the accuracy of other estimates published by the PGE system.

There was also some discussion of the desirability and feasibility of extending the PGE system to the mountain and jungle areas. The major argument for doing this was that part of the country's Five Year Development Plan would involve attempts to extend the area of "settled agriculture" by terracing mountain areas to permit rice-growing and clearing jungle areas to allow for the cultivation of cotton and rice. However, the initial experiments in this direction would be on a small scale. It was therefore agreed to defer any consideration of PGE in the mountain and jungle areas until such time as a program for large-scale development in these areas might be launched.

The brief history of the origin of Pacifica's PGE Study given here illustrates the fact that the importance of the use of data does not necessarily correlate with the accuracy required. To be of any use at all for the family planning program of Pacifica, the PGE Study would have to be accurate within 1 per 1,000. But for the purposes of the country's educational and general economic planning, estimates with errors of as much as 4 or 5 per 1,000 would be of very great value. The accuracy required of a survey and the expenditure appropriate for it are, then, functions of the uses to be made of the results. Statistics that may be useless (or even misleading) for some purposes may be extremely valuable for other purposes—*provided the users are aware of the limitations and inaccuracies of the data.*

B.3   THE TIME SCHEDULE FOR THE PGE STUDY

The decision to proceed with the design of a PGE system was made in May 1969. The next population census of Pacifica was scheduled for March 1970. Since the PGE system would involve considerable sampling work, it would be preferable to base the sampling on the maps and counts of the 1970 Census rather than try to use maps and data from the old Census of November 1961. This, of course, would mean that field work could not start much before September 1970, and figures for the first year in which the PGE system was operational would not be available until early 1972.

The Planning Board was at first unhappy about waiting three years for "results." However, a more detailed consideration indicated that (1) the necessary funds and personnel for planning would not be available before 1 July 1969 and (2) at least nine months would be needed to design and test a PGE system capable of yielding data that would be a real improvement over the existing vital statistics. Thus, at most, six months might be saved by not waiting for the new census. Furthermore, starting data collection in March or April 1970 (while the census was going on) rather than in September or October would mean that few, if any, of the more experienced personnel of the CBS would be available to help get the PGE system underway.

Gradually, the Planning Board was made to see the realities of the situation and to appreciate that the design and operation of a good statistical system was not an undertaking that could be accomplished overnight. It was decided to lay out an operations timetable, assuming that sampling would be based on the 1970 Census. The initial schedule, drawn up in May 1969 and necessarily very general, was as follows:

(1) May 1969 to June 1969: Decide type of system to be used (survey, registration, etc.).

(2) July 1969 to November 1969: Design sample, questionnaires, procedures, etc.

(3) October 1969 to July 1970: Select and train supervisory staff and other professional personnel.

(4) December 1969 to July 1970: Pretest and revise questionnaires, procedures, etc.

(5) July 1970 to September 1970: Select sample.

(6) July 1970 to September 1970: Recruit and train interviewers and registrars.

(7) October 1970: Begin data collection.

(8) February 1971: Issue first quarterly PGE release.

(9) February 1972: Issue first annual PGE release.

By the end of August 1969, after it had been determined (see Section C below) that the PGE study should involve a dual system of special registration plus a periodic household survey in a sample of areas, a revised timetable containing a more detailed schedule for steps 2 through 5 was prepared. For example, steps 2 and 4 became:

(a) September 1969 to December 1969: Design sample.

(b) September 1969: Determine characteristics to be used for matching (names, dates of birth, location, etc.) and for tabulation (age, sex, occupation, etc.).[8]

(c) October 1969: Design special registration form and household questionnaire.

(d) October 1969 through December 1969: Pretest registration form and household questionnaire.

(e) November 1969 through January 1970: Perform matching and field follow-up to reconcile doubtful cases.

(f) February and March 1970: Revise questionnaire and certificate and pretest for second time.

(g) April through June 1970: Perform matching and field check for second pretest.

(h) July 1970: Complete final revision of questionnaires, certificates, and instructions to interviewers and registrars.

Before this revised timetable could be prepared, a series of basic decisions had had to be made about the nature of the system for estimating Pacifica's population growth. The major issue was whether the study should use a single or dual collection system. A related consideration was the extent to which the existing civil registration system could be used and what alternative collection systems were feasible. This decision-making process took about four months (from May to August) rather than the two months originally scheduled, but given the other demands on the CBS staff the delay was considered unavoidable.

C. *Selection of the Systems*

C.1 BACKGROUND

It was clear to the CBS staff as well as most demographers in Pacifica that the registration system as it then existed could not alone provide population growth estimates of the desired accuracy. There was some discussion of the possibility of using the $130,000 annual budget[9] to bring the civil registration system up to an acceptable level of accuracy. One possibility would be to hire special registrars who would devote themselves entirely to improving the registration of births and deaths. However, not only were there jurisdictional problems involved (the civil registration system was currently under the Ministry of the Interior), but the minimum wage for the lowest-paid government clerk was $400 per year at the time, so that a maximum of 325 special registrars could be hired—paying the minimum wage only and with no allowance for supervision, travel, or necessary improvements in communications or central office work.

Taking 250 as a more realistic figure for the number of special registrars who could be used, it was clear that a staff of this size could have little impact on the registration system of the entire country. It might, of course, be possible to use these special registrars to improve civil registration in a sample of areas. Alternatively, the same size staff might be used in a sample of areas to set up a special registration system (or periodic survey) entirely independent of the official civil registration system. This might simplify some of the jurisdictional problems.[10]

In spite of the possible advantages in terms of cost and simplicity of a single system for estimating population growth, it was decided that a dual system must be used. The primary reason for this decision was the increased control over the variability in completeness of reporting afforded by a PGE estimate based on a dual system. As pointed out in Chapter 3, the effect of variability in completeness of reporting on a single system estimate may be substantial. This was certainly true for the estimate produced by the civil registration system of Pacifica. The CBS staff felt, moreover, that attempts to improve the completeness of reporting by using a system of special registration (or a periodic household survey) alone might actually increase the short-term variability in the completeness of reporting.[11]

C.2 THE POSSIBILITY OF A DUAL SYSTEM USING THE CIVIL REGISTRATION SYSTEM

The variation in completeness of the civil registration was not, however, a bar to its use as one of the data sources in a dual system (in combination with a periodic household survey); and in view of the probable cost advantages of such a course, this was one of the first alternatives to be considered.

The primary considerations in determining the feasibility of such a system are matching biases and independence. Problems of maintaining independence were, in fact, the major reason for preferring a dual system combining the civil registration system with a periodic household survey rather than with a special registration system. The difference between a "special registration system" and a "periodic household survey" is partly a matter of definition. For the moment, we are using the term "special registration" to refer to a data collection system (see the outline of alternatives in Figure 3.1) which uses "continuous" reporting—that is, very frequent checks, weekly or more often (A.1), a local resident as registrar (B.1), active soliciting of reports (C.2), and all sources (D.1 through D.4) to locate vital events. The term "periodic household survey" refers to a system in which data are collected once a month or less frequently (A.2), "outside" reporters are used (B.2 or B.3), a full canvass is done of all households (C.3), and household sources only are used (D.1).

Special registration activities are more apt to affect civil registration results than is a periodic household survey because of the "continuous" nature of the reporting in any registration system. Over time, however, both a periodic household survey and special registration activities may tend to increase the completeness of reporting of the civil registration system, but only in the sample areas. As long as one is interested not in evaluating the completeness of the civil registration system, but in preparing measures of fertility and mortality, the PGE estimates based on two-way matching with the civil registration system for the sample areas alone are not biased by any improvements in the completeness of registration in these areas. However, identifying birth and death certificates by sample area for the purpose of two-way matching would be extremely difficult in Pacifica. In addition, the restriction of data collection to a sample in both sources would mean losing much of the reduction in sampling variance gained by using the entire civil registration system as one data source.

The other method for dealing with possible improvements in civil registration in the sample areas attributable to the existence of another data collection source in the same areas is to move frequently (once a year or more) to new sample areas. The costs of doing this will, however, be much higher for special registration systems using *local residents* as registrars than for periodic household surveys taken by "outside" interviewers.

As we saw in Chapter 4, a great advantage of the use of a one-way match of a periodic household survey to the civil registration system is the fact that geographic boundary problems are reduced and the effects of geographic out-of-scope errors can be practically eliminated. That is, the PGE estimate in this case is

$$\hat{n} = \frac{N_1}{w} , \qquad\qquad\qquad\qquad [5.1]$$

where

$$w = \frac{m}{n_2} ,$$

N_1 = number of births (or deaths) reported in the civil registration system,

n_2 = number of events reported by the household survey, and

m = number of household survey events matched in the civil registration system.

The value w in equation 5.1 is an estimate of the completeness of reporting in the civil registration system. If the matching of the household survey with the registration system ignores the sample area boundaries, w will not be biased by the survey interviewer's crossing these boundaries and reporting some geographically out-of-scope events—unless, of course, the completeness of the civil registration system near (poorly defined) area boundaries differs in a consistent direction from the completeness elsewhere (and differences of this type must be very large to have any appreciable biasing effect on the value of w).

Of course, the advantage of being able to ignore sample area boundaries in matching is offset by the disadvantage of the likelihood of increased erroneous nonmatches or increased matching costs. This disadvantage can be major or trivial. Given unique and invariant addresses that can be arranged systematically within some fairly large area, ignoring the boundaries of sample areas in matching will have little effect on either matching errors or costs. Actually, this will be the case even in a situation that falls somewhat short of the ideal where all streets bear unique and permanent names or numbers, every structure in a block is uniquely and permanently numbered along some street, and each dwelling unit within multiple-unit structures bears a unique and permanent number. Of course, provision must be made for this unique and permanent address information to be entered on *both* the civil registration certificates and the household survey questionnaire, but the difficulties in arranging this may be no greater than they would be if any other dual system were used.

On the other hand, the difficulties of matching the reports of another source against the civil registration system can be major in areas where large numbers of households have the same "address" or there is substantial duplication of names. This proved to be the case in most of the rural villages of Pacifica, which are not laid out in named streets. There are, in fact, usually no "streets" at all unless a highway runs through the village. There are no house numbers, there is a limited number of common names (about 50 for men and 75 for women), and in a village of 200 or more families, there may be only ten family names. In this situation one could mark unique and (hopefully) permanent numbers on each structure in a sample area and require the entry of these numbers on birth certificates, death certificates, and household survey forms. But doing this could theoretically introduce a "dependence bias" into the PGE estimate; that is, by singling out the villages in the sample survey one might conceivably increase the completeness of reporting in the civil registration system for these villages.

To explore the matching problems, a sample of ten rural and twenty urban areas was selected and a household canvass of vital events during the preceding year was carried out. The events reported in the household survey were then matched against the copies of the birth and death certificates on file with the CBS. The rural sample areas were villages, averaging about 2,000 people or about 300 families each (range of 30 to 600 families). The urban sample areas were city blocks and averaged about 1,000 people or 150 families (range also from 30 to 600 families). Unfortunately, none of the rural areas had any addresses below the village-name level and it was discovered that two of the villages shared names with another village in the same district. (Reports from these areas, however, could be distinguished by a Police Area number that appeared on most of the birth and death certificates.) For the urban sample areas, the civil registration certificates showed only the name of the town for the ten blocks in smaller cities. In the larger cities, there were house numbers and street names but only about half the certificates showed any address more specific than a "neighborhood" designation.

When matching was attempted in the rural areas, multiple matches (in which household survey birth reports matched equally well with two or more civil registration reports) were found for about 70 percent of all the household survey cases, single matches were found for 20 percent, and no matches were found for 10 percent (see Table 5.1).[12] In the urban areas, 60 percent of the survey reports were multiple matches, 30 percent were single matches, and 10 percent were non-matches. After field follow-up of the rural birth reports, 53 percent were classified as single matches, 25 percent as multiple matches, and 22 percent as nonmatches. Attempts at field follow-up in the urban areas were abandoned when only 10 percent of all cases could be resolved after two weeks of intensive searching. Rural matching and follow-up costs were about $1 per case. Urban matching and partial follow-up costs were about $2 per case up to the time follow-up was discontinued. The survey data collection costs averaged about $50 per village in rural areas and $35 per block in urban areas.

The experience from the test indicated that in urban areas the major cause of the matching difficulty was the meagerness of identifying information—particularly specific street addresses—on the birth and death certificates. Whereas most of the household survey birth reports had specific street addresses, such information was present on only about one-fourth of the registration certificates.

In order to determine if matching could be improved by recording complete address information on the forms of both sources, an independent reenumeration of ten of the urban blocks was conducted, using the same forms and instructions as in the original survey but with a different set of interviewers. The original survey reports were then compared with these new ones. (The results of this matching study are also given in Table 5.1.) Prior to field follow-up, 70 percent of the original survey reports were classified as matched with one report in the independent survey, 25 percent were nonmatches, and only 5 percent were matched with more than one report. After the follow-up, 78 percent of the reports were confirmed as single matches, while 22 percent remained unmatched. These improved figures, as well as the absence of any multiple matches, confirmed that the primary problem in the urban areas was, in fact, the recording of information and not the availability of it.

In the rural areas the primary obstacle to matching was also inadequate address information. In this case, however, neither the registration nor the household survey reports contained anything in

Table 5.1   Results of Matching Survey Birth Reports with the Civil Registration System and with an Independent Survey: Pacifica

Matching status before and after field follow-up	Rural sample areas		Urban sample areas			
	Civil registration test[1]		Civil registration test[2]		Independent survey[3]	
	Number	Percent	Number	Percent	Number	Percent
All survey birth reports	760	100	745	100	376	100
Multiple matches—total	532	70	447	60	19	5
Status after follow-up:						
Matched with one report	228	30	u	u	19	5
Not a match	114	15	u	u	0	0
Unresolved	190	25	u	u	0	0
Single matches—total	152	20	223	30	263	70
Status after follow-up:						
Confirmed match	114	15	u	u	255	68
Not a match	38	5	u	u	8	2
Nonmatches—total	76	10	75	10	94	25
Status after follow-up:						
Matched	61	8	u	u	19	5
Confirmed nonmatches	15	2	u	u	75	20

u = unavailable.

[1] Ten rural sample areas were used, each containing an average of 2,000 persons.

[2] Twenty urban sample areas were used, each containing an average of 1,000 persons. Field follow-up was not completed because of inability to resolve multiple matches and other doubtful cases.

[3] Ten of the urban sample areas were reenumerated using different interviewers but the same forms and instructions as in the original survey.

SOURCE: Hypothetical data from matching studies conducted in Pacifica.

the way of specific address information. The results of an earlier matching effort, which used unique numbers painted on each structure in sample rural areas, demonstrated that this method of identification permitted satisfactory matching without having an appreciable effect on the completeness of civil registration reporting.

It seemed, then, that provisions for getting house numbers on birth and death certificates—using existing numbers in urban areas and creating numbers in rural areas—would make it feasible to match survey reports with civil registration reports. The Ministry of the Interior (under pressure from the Planning Board) was willing to provide a space on the birth and death certificates for entering house numbers, but the CBS's experience in urban areas (where there were house numbers in existence and a space on the birth and death certificates for entering the address) indicated that this would not be sufficient. Some "policing" would be necessary to insure that house numbers would be entered. For this, the Ministry of the Interior lacked both the motivation and the personnel.

One solution would have been to transfer much of the responsibility for the civil registration system to the Ministry of Health. The senior staff at the Ministry were anxious to take over the registration function and felt (probably correctly) that it had personnel—local health officers, maternal and child health workers, and family planning staff—who would be able both to do the work at the local level and to improve birth and death registration by virtue of their special contacts and interests. Some problems, however, existed at the central level. The Ministry of Health wanted to take over all vital statistics tabulation and publication (particularly the *budgets* for these functions). The CBS was unenthusiastic about this prospect, although they agreed fully that it would be desirable for the Ministry of Health to assume responsibility for vital registration at the *local* level.

Some compromise could undoubtedly have been worked out between the CBS (backed by the Planning Board) and the Ministry of Health. A compromise was, in fact, emerging. However, an exploration of the political realities of the situation indicated that, although the Ministry of the Interior did not oppose the transfer, it was unwilling to actively support the proposal and, in consequence, the President's office was reluctant to recommend action. In fact, the Presidential staff was inclined to delay the proposal indefinitely. It was considered probable that the transfer proposal would go through eventually, but it looked like a four to five year effort. In the circumstances, the CBS decided to abandon, for the time being, the idea of using the civil registration system.

Although this case history is fictitious, several countries have gone through somewhat similar experiences. The major difference is that, in the example above, the CBS is depicted as trying very hard to develop a PGE system that would use the existing civil registration system. In many countries, this alternative has been dismissed on the basis of, at best, a very cursory inspection. We have pointed out before, and it should be emphasized again, that use of the civil registration system with one-way matching can greatly reduce or eliminate geographic out-of-scope errors. Furthermore, the use of civil registration reports in a dual system can be an important, even essential, first step toward establishing a satisfactory permanent system for measuring birth and death rates. In Pacifica, as in other countries, the attempt to use the civil registration system was abandoned for pragmatic rather than technical reasons.

C.3 THE PACIFICA SPECIAL REGISTRATION SYSTEM

Although attempts to use the civil registration system as one data source had to be abandoned, the initial explorations described above had given the CBS valuable experience in the design and operation of a periodic household survey. It was agreed, therefore, that the household survey should be retained as one source. It was hoped that eventually the civil registration system might serve as the other source; meanwhile, some interim substitute would be used as the second source. This other source, ultimately termed the "Pacifica Special Registration System," evolved slowly out of a series of initially informal discussions within the CBS and between the CBS and the Ministry of Health.

An argument developed at this point between the proponents of special registration and the proponents of overlapping household surveys; that is, a design providing for matching between the reports obtained in a survey and a special registration system (as described in Section D of Chapter 4) or a design providing for matching between the reports obtained in successive rounds in a multiround survey (as described in Section E of Chapter 4).

Those who favored a design using overlapping household surveys claimed that they would be both inexpensive and easy to administer, since similar forms and common personnel procedures could be employed. On closer inspection, however, it seemed as if the economies to be derived from using similar data sources might be considerably overestimated. For example, the savings on forms were mainly on their design. The savings on duplicating and processing costs were trivial, and there were no savings on distribution costs. Savings were also possible in training interviewers, but savings in the costs of hiring and of supervision depended more upon how *independent* the two sources were to be than on the nature of the sources. That is, one could save by having common hiring and supervision for all the field staff, whether they were all survey interviewers or whether half were survey interviewers and half were special registrars. On the other hand, it would be very desirable, in order to preserve the independence of the sources, to have different supervisors for two field workers who covered the same sample units, whether both of the workers were survey interviewers or one was an interviewer and the other a special registrar.

The main argument in favor of having a special registration system and a survey, rather than two overlapping surveys, was the greater independence achieved by using different methods of data collection. However, on closer inspection, this advantage of special registration plus a survey proved almost as illusory as the presumed cost advantage of overlapping surveys. The proponents of special registration plus a survey were thinking in terms of a resident registrar (a "local reporter"—B.1 in the classification system of Figure 3.1) and continuous registration (A.1). Survey interviewers would, in general, be from outside the area but have backgrounds similar to those of the registrars (B.2). However, a local resident doing continuous canvassing would have the effect of "sensitizing," to birth and death reporting, those sources with which he became familiar, thus making it more likely that they would report births and deaths to a subsequent household interviewer.[13] Of course, this "sensitizing" effect could be reduced by having a registrar who never became very well acquainted with any of the sources likely to be approached by the household interviewer, but this would mean sacrificing much of the advantage of continuous reporting.

Having a local registrar and continuous registration would also make it more difficult to prevent occasional accidental meetings between registrars and interviewers[14]; moreover, with local registrars one had to use either part-time registrars or large sample units. And both of these alternatives posed problems. The tentative budget for the PGE study would provide for at most 250 full-time field workers. Assuming half of these to be registrars, with each registrar limited to covering a single sample location, this meant a maximum of 125 sample locations. With part-time registrars one could, of course, have more registrars and more locations. But qualified *resident* part-time registrars were hard to come by in Pacifica. In some countries one can recruit part-time workers from among housewives with school-age children (who are free to work during school hours but cannot take full-time work) or among retired persons who are still able to work on a part-time basis. In the rural part of Pacifica, however, no such reserve of skilled labor was available.

Thus, the CBS had to consider whether the restriction to 125 sampling points, each with a full-time resident registrar, was desirable. A first question was whether this would yield the desired sampling precision, which had previously been established as an error of not more than 2 per 1,000 in the crude birth rate for the country as a whole.

The standard error of an estimated birth rate is given (approximately) by the formula

$$\sigma_{\bar{x}} = \frac{\sigma_r}{\sqrt{k}} , \qquad\qquad [5.2]$$

where

$\bar{x}$ = estimated birth rate,

$\sigma_{\bar{x}}$ = standard error of $\bar{x}$,

σ_r = standard deviation in the birth rate between sample areas, and

k = number of sample areas.

It was expected that full-time special registrars would, in most cases, be able to handle areas of about 5,000 population (about 900 families) reasonably well. This was close to the average size of the areas in the previous special study that used PGE estimation. For that study σ_r was approximately 22 per 1,000. Thus, a sample of 125 areas would be sufficient to give estimates of the overall national birth rate with a sampling error ($\sigma_{\bar{x}}$) of 2 per 1,000.

Even after the feasibility of achieving results of the desired precision with 125 special registrars had been established, however, there was considerable reluctance to use a permanent system of fixed sample areas covered by local registrars. Great difficulty was anticipated in securing competent personnel in some of the rural sampling points. With full-time workers, there would probably be an adequate supply of personnel for the country as a whole. However, in some of the more remote areas, it might be very difficult to find literate local residents to work as special registrars. Even if satisfactory local personnel could be found, the problems of training and supervising them would be substantial.

Even more important than the personnel problem was the difficulty of preserving independence while retaining a fixed sample of areas indefinitely. Over time, independence becomes increasingly threatened in an area where two sources are making repeated canvasses. Some rotation of the interviewers in the household survey might be feasible. However, any trading of assignments would probably be limited to two (or at most three) interviewers working in the same region, and would entail increased travel costs, since each interviewer would have to cover a larger area. In addition, if the sample areas were to be covered by two interviewers, there would be boundary difficulties, unless arrangements were made for coordinating the work (and the matching) to make sure assignments "dovetailed" with no overlapping or omissions.

Finally, although the idea of using the civil registration system had to be abandoned, it seemed desirable to use the special registration system as a pilot study for an improved civil registration system that would ultimately replace special registration. This suggested the possibility of using special registrars who would be under the Ministry of Health, while the survey interviewers would be under the CBS. Although there was initial resistance to this idea from *both* the Ministry of Health and the CBS, pressure and inducements, in the form of budget allocations that might otherwise not be available, finally produced a (somewhat reluctant) agreement.

This agreement, approved by the Minister of Health and the Minister of Planning (the latter was responsible for the affairs of the CBS), called for the establishment of the "Pacifica Population Growth Estimation Study" (PPGES), to be carried out jointly by the Ministry of Health and the CBS. The former agency would be responsible for the Pacifica Special Registration System, while the CBS would be responsible for the Household Survey and the matching, processing, and tabulation. Preliminary publications would be issued by the CBS and longer, more analytical reports prepared by either agency would be issued jointly. In order to coordinate planning and implementation of the program, an interagency committee including representatives from the CBS, the Ministry of Health, and the Planning Board was established and authorized to make all decisions necessary to carry out the study.

Once the agreement to establish the PPGES was reached, the staff of the CBS and the Ministry of Health were able to complete the design of the Special Registration System. The Ministry of Health suggested the use of its District Health Officers as part-time special registrars in rural areas. The Ministry had divided the rural areas of the country into 120 health districts. For each health district, there was supposed to be a health officer who was responsible for the Ministry's health program in the district. This was supposed to include infectious disease control (mostly malaria and typhus), maternal and child health care, and family planning. A few of the District Health Officers were physicians, and the rest were college graduates with training in administration and public health. Most of them had an assistant as well as public health nurses and/or public health "trainees" (usually high school graduates who were hoping to go on for university training in public health under a government scholarship program administered by the Ministry of Health). The health workers in a district worked out of a District Health Center. An attempt was made to have the health worker visit every village in the area at least once every three months to check the village water supply for pollution, check on mosquito control, hold classes in child care for mothers, train midwives, distribute diet supplements for infants and mothers, distribute family planning information and contraceptives, and arrange for insertions of IUDs (at the District Health Center by a local or visiting physician).

The plan was to have special registration areas in each health district. In general, these areas would be single villages, but the larger villages were to be divided and a few smaller villages combined to produce units of a more uniform size (about 1,000 population). The urban areas were to be divided in a similar manner into areas of approximately 1,000 population. The four metropolitan areas were each separate health districts. The "trading center" towns were each part of one of the health districts.

This sample design was largely dictated by the nature of the field operations of the Ministry of Health. The decision to use villages as sampling units was largely determined by the very uneven quality of the available maps of Pacifica, most of which had not been revised since the Census of 1961. It was difficult to find units smaller than the village with recognizable boundaries, although most of the larger villages were either strung out along a main road with houses on both sides or clustered around the intersection of two roads and these roads could be used to subdivide the village. Although the villages themselves seldom had well-defined boundaries, there was frequently an extensive area without dwellings surrounding them. Thus for purposes of a demographic study it was not necessary to define the village boundaries precisely. Moreover, while some persons lived outside compact village settlements, nearly all the available maps showed boundaries in terms of "revenue villages"; that is, the settled villages plus the lands associated with them for tax purposes. For sampling purposes, it was considered desirable to cover the entire revenue village, though it was recognized that coverage would be better in the more densely settled areas (both the village proper and major satellite clusters of structures).

The village was also a convenient work unit from the standpoint of the Ministry of Health, since District Health Officers were accustomed to scheduling their regular visits by village and the task of checking with local informants and visiting households for which a birth or death was reported was usually less than a day's work. Because most of the larger villages had been subdivided for sampling purposes anyway, a District Health Officer would rarely need more than one day to complete the special registration work in any village.

On the other hand, most of the villages, although compact, had more people than could be covered in one day by a household survey interviewer required to canvass every household in the village. Where the villages were small enough to be canvassed in one day, it seemed desirable from the standpoint of both sampling and the special registration system to combine them into larger units.

In each sample area, the District Health Officer was to arrange with one or more local residents to keep a register of births and deaths. These local residents were to be village chiefs, school teachers, or other local functionaries. The District Health Officer or his assistant would visit each sample area every three months, check the registers by visiting the households listed, and prepare birth and death certificates. The District Health Officer would also inquire about other births and deaths in the area, particularly infant deaths and delayed registrations. The local persons who kept registers were to be paid $0.50 for each *verified* birth or death certificate.

Initially, the sample areas in each health district were to be divided into three equal groups, and special registration for each group was to start in a different month. Since a periodic household survey was also to be taken in the sample areas, the scheduling of the survey and the special registration was to be arranged so that the District Health Officer would not make calls in any area during the month of the periodic household survey.

This plan was not arrived at without extended discussion, and its adoption was made possible largely by the presence of a small group of well-trained statisticians in the CBS. This group was able to persuade the Planning Board, as well as their colleagues in the CBS, of the critical importance of maintaining independence between the two data sources.

It took considerable self-restraint on the part of the CBS to accept a solution that meant sharing the available funds with another agency. However, once the responsible personnel became convinced of the desirability of involving another agency, it was logical to turn to the Ministry of Health, since it had a major interest in birth and death registration as well as personnel engaged in activities (family planning and maternal and child health care) closely related to such registration.

In terms of data collection from a national sample, the logical source of manpower for the Ministry of Health would be the District Health Officers. Any data collection not done through the health officers would involve hiring additional personnel to work only on vital registration. Although not completely out of the question, hiring additional personnel would go counter to the primary goal of using personnel from within the Ministry with experience that would facilitate vital registration. Furthermore, the Ministry of Health was concerned with using the funds allocated to it to strengthen its entire program by hiring personnel in those health districts which were undermanned, by moderate salary increases to improve the quality of personnel available, and by expansion of the training programs, particularly for personnel working at the village level. Since these improvements in the Ministry of Health programs would also contribute to the quality of vital events registration, the use of Ministry of Health field workers as part-time registrars was viewed as a more efficient use of available funds than the hiring of separate field workers as registrars only.

C.4   THE PACIFICA HOUSEHOLD SURVEY

The first step in designing the Pacifica Household Survey was to determine the basic procedure to be followed in an individual household—how frequently each sample household was to be visited, what questions were to be asked, what data were to be recorded. Basically, the Pacifica Special Registration System was a fairly straightforward adaptation of standard civil registration techniques; that is, the objective was continuous reporting of births and deaths, the recording of each event as soon as possible after it occurred, and the noting of "standard" demographic and identification data for each event. Some decisions were also necessary on the kind of supplementary data to be recorded (for example, occupation, racial background, parity), on sampling, and on *de jure* versus *de facto* reporting. Since these decisions were to be made jointly for both the Special Registration System and the Household Survey, they were necessarily preceded by a consideration of the basic Household Survey design.

The Household Survey design started with the assumption that the survey would involve a complete house-by-house canvass of a sample of areas. These areas would be identical with those for which births and deaths were to be reported by the Special Registration System. It was also assumed that the survey interviewers would, as a minimum, obtain a listing of the household members and of births and deaths for this household for some specified period preceding the visit.

The listing of household members could, of course, be *de jure* (all persons "who usually live here") or *de facto* (all persons "who stayed here last night"). Births or deaths could also be obtained according to either counting rule; that is, vital events associated with persons who usually live in the dwelling unit as opposed to events that occurred there. Whichever rule is adopted, there are the problems of "special cases" (for example, persons with no usual place of residence when *de jure* procedures are used, births and deaths that did not occur inside a dwelling unit when *de facto* procedures are used) and the problems of events not likely to be reported (for example, a death dissolving the household and leaving no household member to report it or the death of a transient who is not known in the area). Special rules and procedures are usually provided to minimize the error introduced by these cases. Even without such cases, however, there is likely to be considerable error due to poor reporting of events in the ordinary stable household—particularly failures to report events associated with individuals only marginally connected with the basic household.

Two techniques that have been used to reduce reporting error in surveys of vital events were considered. One method involved reducing the time period covered by the report on the grounds that (a) an event occurring recently (within, say, the past three months) is less likely to be forgotten than one more remote in time, (b) time distortions (that is, placing an event in the wrong month or the wrong year) are less likely for more recent events, and (c) it will be easier to locate persons with firsthand knowledge of more recent events. These assumptions were, in fact, advanced as arguments for preferring continuous registration to a periodic survey.

The other method of reducing reporting error considered involved the technique discussed in Chapter 3 of accounting for changes in household composition between two successive visits. The household-change technique requires, of course, more than one visit to the same household. There is an advantage in terms of cost, and for some purposes in terms of variance, to repeated interviews with the same household as opposed to interviews with different households in each survey round. Two important considerations in using the household-change technique are the number of times each household is to be interviewed and the interval between successive visits.

In general, this technique works best with fairly short intervals (three months or six months) between visits; the probability of a complete change in dwelling unit occupants is reduced, and one is less likely to miss pregnancies, infant deaths, etc. As mentioned above, with a short interval between visits, one is also less likely to miss events on direct questioning, since one is asking about a shorter time period and, therefore, more recent events.

As noted in Chapter 3, there are disadvantages to short intervals for reporting births and deaths, and to repeated visits to the same household. With a shorter reporting period the number of births and deaths reported by a given number of sample households is reduced, making the variance for estimated birth or death rates higher. The reduction in bias obtained by using a shorter reporting period must be weighed against this increase in variance (or against the costs of using a larger sample to reduce the variance).

The principal disadvantage of repeated visits to the same household is the possibility of an increase in correlation bias, since one source of this type of bias is the sensitizing of sample households interviewed in a survey to birth and death reporting, making them more likely to register births or deaths than comparable households that are missed by the household survey. Presumably, this sensitization would be increased by repeated interviews asking about vital events, particularly with very short intervals (three or six months) between interviews. Sensitizing may also manifest itself in another way: Respondents (and interviewers) bored by frequent visits may automatically indicate that "no change" in the household has occurred.

In the absence of hard data on the numerous methodological issues involved, the CBS staff had to make a largely intuitive guess as to the best way of proceeding. It was decided, after some discussion, to use the household-change technique with interviews every quarter and rotation of sample areas every two years. To initiate the rotation, the sample areas were divided into eight equal groups; at the end of each quarter the sample segments in one group would be replaced by new sample areas. The new sample areas were, in turn, to be replaced after eight visits (two years) by another area from the same health district. Urban areas would be replaced only by other urban areas, and rural areas only by other rural areas. No area would be eligible to be resampled until all areas of the same type (urban or rural) in the health district had been sampled.

Another feature of the rotation scheme, in addition to the reduction of sensitization, was that special tabulations for methodological purposes could be made using the survey results from each rotation group separately. The PPGES plans called for an analysis of the effects of the household-change technique and of repeated interviews by comparing "first visit" reports with "second, third, fourth, . . . eighth visit" reports for the same quarter. That is, in a given quarter, the sample areas which had been visited once, twice, and so on would represent equivalent random samples of all areas, and results for these areas would all have the same expected value except for the cumulative effects of repeated interviews and the fact that accounting for household changes would not affect the first visit reports. The CBS statisticians also hoped to study the effects of less frequent visits and of longer reporting periods by having subsamples of the areas visited semiannually and annually (instead of quarterly).

D. Aspects of Implementation

D.1 THE SIZE OF THE SAMPLE

An upper limit was placed on the sample size by the Ministry of Health's restriction that the average number of sampling units in nonmetropolitan health districts be six or less and not above four unless the funds tentatively allocated to the Ministry of Health were increased. These restrictions reflected the Ministry's plans for staffing and the rest of the health district workload not connected with vital statistics.

In determining sample size the range of alternatives was from 400 to 800 sample areas. Up to 800 units would have been feasible from the standpoint of the Ministry of Health, although it would probably have demanded some increase in funds if the sample included over 550 areas. In any case, it seemed likely that 400 units would give a satisfactory sampling error—that is, σ_r (in equation 5.2) would be about 26 per 1,000 for units with a population of 1,000, and this would mean a sampling error ($\sigma_{\bar{x}}$) of about 1.3 per 1,000 for the estimated birth rate.

As noted above, the budget for current work (apart from planning) was $130,000 per year. About $40,000 of this would go to the Ministry of Health for the Special Registration System. Matching, field follow-up, supervision, printing, tabulation, and other office expenditures would come to at least $50,000 per year. This left a maximum of $40,000 per year for the Household Survey field-work. To secure better personnel, the CBS decided to pay the household survey interviewers $550 per year. This meant that a maximum of 73 interviewers could be used, if no allowance was made for their travel expenses.

In the four metropolitan areas, interviewers could presumably live at home and reach the sample areas by public transportation. This would make their travel costs fairly low (about $30 per year), and they would require an average of about one and one-half hours per day in travel time. Taking travel time and the nature of interviewing in urban areas into account (the high "not at home" rate and the many call-backs needed), it was estimated that the metropolitan interviewers might be able to cover 15 to 20 households per day (or 4,000 to 5,000 interviews per year).[15]

Outside the metropolitan areas there usually would be one interviewer for two health districts. Even if the interviewer lived in one of the health districts to which he (or she)[16] was assigned, he might be able to use public transportation (mostly busses) for about half of his travel but would need to use other forms of transportation (possibly a bicycle, taxi, horse, or boat) to reach the remaining areas.

An allowance of $90 per year and three hours per day was made for this travel.[17] However, due to the lower call-back rate required in rural areas, these interviewers should also be able to do about 15 to 20 households per day.

With 60 nonmetropolitan area interviewers (each responsible for an average of two health districts) receiving an average annual payment, including travel expenses, of about $640 and ten metropolitan area interviewers receiving $580 each per year, the annual interviewing cost would be about $44,000. This was close enough to the preliminary allocation of $40,000 to be acceptable. If four visits a year were to be made to each sample household, each interviewer could cover between 1,000 and 1,200 households per year, and all of them together could cover a total of about 75,000 households. Since the sample areas would average about 180 households, about 420 sample areas could be covered (six areas per interviewer).

The sample areas were to be drawn systematically with equal probability. To insure a systematic selection, the areas within each health district were to be numbered in a serpentine pattern, numbering separately the urban and rural portions of a health district. A total of 423 units was selected, of which 62 were in the four metropolitan areas and 361 in the 120 nonmetropolitan health districts. No nonmetropolitan health district had more than eight sample areas nor less than one sample area.

D.2 MATCHING: GENERAL CONSIDERATIONS

The procedure for determining the initial matching rules for the PPGES was, in general, that described in Section F of Chapter 3 and Section B.6 of Chapter 4. The first step was to compile a list of all the characteristics that could be collected in both sources and used in the matching. It appeared feasible to collect information on those characteristics listed in Table 5.2—"feasible" meaning that a substantial proportion (20 percent or more) of the informants would be able to furnish information consistent with specified tolerance limits. A number of additional items such as race, eye color, birthplace of father, and birthplace of mother were considered and rejected because previous studies indicated that they had low discriminating power (race, eye color), were not reported consistently (parents' birthplaces for births), or were reported for less than 20 percent of the cases (parents' birthplaces for deaths). Accordingly, the birth form was designed to call for items 1 through 14 and the death form to call for items 1 through 8 and 15 through 20. The vital events report forms used for the Special Registration System and the Household Survey were the same in this regard but were otherwise quite different.

There had been several previous attempts at matching studies. For four of these (two vital registration-survey matches, one death registration-census match, one census-survey match), attempts had been made to obtain a "definitive" classification of cases as matched or unmatched by partial field follow-up and reconciliation. While final

Table 5.2   Availability of Information for Use in Matching Vital Events: Pacifica PGE Study

(Limited to characteristics of events for which 20 percent or more of the informants could supply "consistent" information. For further qualifications, see text.)

Characteristic	Probably available for	
	Births	Deaths
1. Name	Yes	Yes
2. Name of father	Yes	Yes
3. Maiden name of mother	Yes	Yes
4. Address	Yes	Yes
5. Date of birth	Yes	Yes
6. Place of occurrence	Yes	Yes
7. Sex	Yes	Yes
8. Religion	Yes	Yes
9. Age of mother	Yes	No
10. Age of father	Yes	No
11. Parity of mother	Yes	No
12. Occupation of father	Yes	No
13. Education of father	Yes	No
14. Name of doctor or midwife	Yes	No
15. Own occupation	No	Yes
16. Own education	No	Yes
17. Name of undertaker	No	Yes
18. Marital status	No	Yes
19. Name of spouse	No	Yes
20. Date of death	No	Yes

matching rules would have to await analysis of the data from the population growth study itself, preliminary rules were set up by studying the effects of applying different possible procedures to the somewhat fragmentary data of the four studies.

In addition to providing a rational basis for establishing initial matching rates, this analysis was particularly useful in suggesting instructions to the interviewers and health officers for filling out the forms. For example, handwriting differences caused difficulties in trying to match names. Intelligent matching clerks could make good decisions on the basis of partly illegible scrawls and their knowledge of what names and letter combinations were common in the various regions of Pacifica. However, the number of clerks competent to do this was small and the time required to match on this basis was long. Instructions for entering information on the birth and death forms specified, therefore, that block letters were to be used for all names. Of course, these instructions were not always followed (particularly during the first few months of the PPGES), but the exceptions could be referred to the matching supervisor for special handling.

D.3   TOLERANCE LIMITS IN MATCHING

The next step in establishing the matching rules was to determine the "optimum tolerance" for each of the possible characteristics in Table

5.2. Chapter 3 (Section F.5) suggests determining the number of errors for "zero tolerance" of a given characteristic and then increasing the tolerance until "the increase in erroneous matches begins to be greater than the decrease in erroneous nonmatches."[18] In somewhat simpler terms, this amounts to determining the total number of matching errors (erroneous matches plus erroneous nonmatches) for various tolerance levels and selecting the tolerance level that gives the minimum number of errors. Tables 5.3 and 5.4 show the results of doing this in Pacifica using the combined results of all four previous matching studies. Both tables refer to deaths only. Table 5.3 is based on the name of the deceased and Table 5.4 on the dead person's date of birth.

Table 5.3   Matching Status and Number of Matching Errors for Source 1 Reports, by Type of Tolerance Limit Used for Name of Deceased: Pacifica

(For qualifications, see text.)

Tolerance limit	Matching status[1]		Errors[2]		
	Matched in Source 2	Non-matched in Source 2	Erroneous match	Erroneous nonmatch	Gross matching errors
1. Exact agreement on family name and initial of given name and no inconsistency[3]	1,229	861	563	492	1,055
2. Exact agreement on family name and initial of given name	1,300	790	581	439	1,020
3. First six letters[4] of family name and initial of given name agree	1,503	587	652	307	959
4. First four letters[4] of family name and initial of given name agree	1,614	476	671	215	886
5. Agree on first four letters of family name	1,675	415	715	198	913
6. First four consonants of family name and initial of given name agree	1,443	647	584	299	883
7. Agree on initial of given name and on all of family name except for specified spelling differences[5]	1,684	406	707	181	888
8. Agree on family name except for specified spelling differences[5]	1,720	370	732	170	902
9. Agree on initial of first name, and family name is judged to sound alike	1,728	362	724	154	878
10. Family name is judged to sound alike	1,739	351	731	150	881

[1] Based on specified individual tolerance limit.

[2] Represents the difference between the classification of each report based on the specified individual tolerance limit and the presumably correct classification based on all available information.

[3] "Rustem Lee" and "Rostam C. Lee" are inconsistent entries for name, while "Rustem Lee" and "R. C. Lee" are consistent entries.

[4] If name contains less than the specified number of letters, agreement on letters present.

[5] Based on a list of alternative spellings common for names in Pacifica.

SOURCE: Hypothetical data from four matching studies conducted in Pacifica.

Table 5.4 Matching Status and Number of Matching Errors for Source 1 Reports, by Type of Tolerance Limit Used for Date of Birth of Deceased: Pacifica

(For qualifications, see text.)

Tolerance limit	Matching status[1]		Errors[2]		
	Matched in Source 2	Non-matched in Source 2	Erroneous match	Erroneous nonmatch	Gross match-ing errors
1. Agree exactly on month, day, and year	133	573	20	384	404
2. Agree within 30 days	260	446	75	312	387
3. Agree on month and day and within 1 year	226	480	67	340	407
4. Agree on month and day and within 5 years	296	410	125	326	451
5. Agree on day and year	308	398	108	297	405
6. Agree on month and day and within 1 year, or agree on day and year, or agree within 30 days[3]	325	381	113	205	318
7. Agreement on year	504	202	194	187	381
8. Agreement within 1 year	534	172	211	174	385

[1] Based on specified individual tolerance limit.
[2] Represents the difference between the classification of each report based on the specified individual tolerance limit and the presumably correct classification based on all available information.
[3] Where more than one source 1 report agreed with a given source 2 report, agreement on the month and day within one year was given first preference as a match and agreement within 30 days second preference.

SOURCE: Hypothetical data from four matching studies conducted in Pacifica.

Source 1 for Table 5.3 had a total of 2,090 death reports, of which 1,158 had been determined to be actually matched in source 2 on the basis of all the information available, and 932 were unmatched in source 2. (In each study, the source with the most reports was arbitrarily designated as source 1.) Source 2 had 1,597 reports, 439 of them not matched in source 1. The numbers in Tables 5.3 and 5.4 refer to the source 1 reports only, and for a given tolerance limit, a source 1 report was considered "matched" (with reference to the characteristic) if it agreed with one or more source 2 reports within the specified tolerance limits. Where a source 1 report agreed with more than one source 2 report, one of these was arbitrarily selected as its "match." Similarly, a given source 2 report could be assigned as a match only to a single report in source 1.

All matching was done within areas of about the same size (700 to 1,500 population) as those to be used in the PPGES. Table 5.4 shows data only for the 706 source 1 reports (497 true matches and 209 true nonmatches in source 2) that had entries for "Date of birth." Some of the 706 reports showed the year of birth only. These were therefore considered "unmatched" where agreement on the month and/or day of birth was required, but "matched" if they agreed with any source 2 report on the year of birth when the specification was "no inconsistency" in the month and/or day of birth.

An examination of Table 5.4 suggests that tolerance limit 6 ("Agree on month and day and within one year, or agree on day and year, or agree within 30 days") will be best for the deceased's date of birth. For Name (Table 5.3) tolerance limit 9 gives the lowest total error. However, tolerance limit 9 ("Family name judged to sound alike and agrees on initial of first name") depends heavily on the judgment of the matching clerks. Hence it was thought better to use some more mechanical rule for the initial classification, with a subsequent reexamination of erroneous nonmatches by the matching supervisors to determine whether any should be classified as "matched" or "doubtful" (with the "doubtful" cases to be resolved by field follow-up). On this basis, tolerance limit 6 ("First four consonants of family name and initial of first name agree") would be preferred. However, the difference between tolerance limit 4 ("Agrees on first four letters of family name and initial of given name") and tolerance limit 6 was trivial and, since limit 4 is simpler to apply and verify, limit 4 was adopted.

A similar process was used to develop tolerance limits for most of the other characteristics listed in Table 5.2. That is, the reports from the four previous studies that employed dual collection were rematched using only one characteristic at a time, and the matching errors associated with alternative tolerance limits for a characteristic were compared. The tolerance limit selected for each characteristic was the one that involved the minimum anticipated difficulty in use consistent with a level of gross matching error at, or near, the minimum. The tolerance limits set for each of the 14 characteristics originally considered for matching births in the PPGES are shown in Table 5.5. Comparable tolerance limits were set for the characteristics available for matching deaths.

Table 5.5   Tolerance Limit Set for Each Characteristic Likely to be Available for Matching Births: Pacifica

Characteristic	Tolerance limit
1. Name of infant	Same as Table 5.3, limit 4
2. Given (first) name of father	Agree on first five letters
3. Maiden name of mother	Agree on first five letters
4. Address	If structure number, exact agreement; otherwise no inconsistency
5. Date of birth	Same as Table 5.4, limit 2
6. Place of occurrence	Agree on city or district
7. Sex of infant	Exact agreement
8. Religion	Exact agreement
9. Age of mother	Agree within five years
10. Age of father	Agree within five years
11. Parity of mother	Agree within one birth
12. Occupation of father	No limit established
13. Education of father	Same broad education group
14. Name of doctor or midwife	Agree on first three letters

SOURCE: Hypothetical data from four matching studies conducted in Pacifica.

For two characteristics, Sex and Religion, no attempt was made to set the tolerance limits on the basis of the results of experimental matching. Zero tolerance (exact agreement required) was specified from the start.[19] In addition, no attempt was made to establish tolerance limits for Occupation of father (Characteristic 12) or Own occupation (Characteristic 15). The nature of the occupation entries was such that they could not be used for matching unless they were coded, and even if they were coded, occupation had very little discriminating power in the rural areas. It would appear that for Pacifica (and probably most other countries) occupation was not a very satisfactory characteristic for matching purposes. After a few preliminary tallies were made using Name of decedent's father (Characteristic 2) and Name of undertaker (Characteristic 17) in matching death reports, it became evident that because of the level of nonresponse and the illegibility of entries, these items would be of little use in matching. No tolerance limits, therefore, were set for either of these characteristics.

D.4 MATCHING CHARACTERISTICS

Having determined tolerance limits for each charactertistic separately, the PPGES staff's next step was to determine what combination of characteristics should be used. The procedure followed was that used by Srinivasan and Muthiah (reported in Section F.4 of Chapter 3). Essentially this involves arraying the individual characteristics in order of their discriminating power and, starting with the "most discriminating" characteristic, adding characteristics and determining the net and gross matching errors associated with each set of characteristics. The final set designated should yield near minimum net error, as well as satisfy the criteria of low gross error and operational feasibility. The concept of "operational feasibility," as it is used here, includes such factors as the cost and reliability (consistency) of clerical matching; the incidence, cost, and value of supervisory referrals; and the net value of any field follow-up procedure employed.

The proportion of source 1 reports with unique identification on a characteristic is used to rank the characteristics by discriminating power.[20] Unique identification on a characteristic means that no other report in the source and blocking unit has the same identification within the tolerance limit set for the characteristic. In computing the proportion of source 1 reports with unique identification, one includes in the numerator only those reports with unique and usable information on the characteristic, while the denominator consists of all source 1 reports. In other words, this measure of discriminating power depends not only on the heterogeneity of the population with respect to the characteristic being considered and the strictness of the tolerance limit used but also on the nonresponse rate for the characteristic. More homogeneity, wider tolerances, and higher item-nonresponse rates all tend to lower the discriminating power of a characteristic and the percentage of reports with unique identification.

Table 5.6 Matching Status and Matching Errors for Source 1 Birth Reports, by Combination of Matching Characteristics Used: Pacifica

(Match status and matching errors are expressed as a percentage of all source 1 birth reports.)

Matching characteristics used[1]	Matching status[2]		Errors[3]			
	Matched	Non-matched	Erroneous matches	Erroneous nonmatches	Net error	Gross error
1	85	15	34	9	25	43
1, 3	80	20	30	10	20	40
1, 3, 5	73	27	26	13	13	39
1, 3, 5, 4	66	34	22	16	6	38
1, 3, 5, 4, 2	62	38	21	19	2	40
1, 3, 5, 4, 2, 14	60	40	20	20	0	40
1, 3, 5, 4, 2, 14, 9	55	45	18	23	−5	41
1, 3, 5, 4, 2, 14, 9, 10	55	45	19	24	−5	43
1, 3, 5, 4, 2, 14, 9, 10, 11	55	45	19	24	−5	43
1, 3, 5, 4, 2, 14, 9, 10, 11, 13	54	46	19	25	−6	44
1, 3, 5, 4, 2, 14, 9, 10, 11, 13, 6	51	49	18	27	−9	45
1, 3, 5, 4, 2, 14, 9, 10, 11, 13, 6, 7	51	49	18	27	−9	45

[1] Numbers refer to characteristics listed in Table 5.2. However, Characteristic 2 as used here refers to the given name of the father, since the family name is already included in Characteristic 1.

[2] Based on the specified combination of matching characteristics using the fixed tolerance limits listed in Table 5.5.

[3] Refers to the percentage of all source 1 reports that are erroneously matched or nonmatched, according to the specified characteristics.

SOURCE: Hypothetical data from two matching studies conducted in Pacifica.

Table 5.6 shows the effect that increasing the number of characteristics used in matching birth reports has on net and gross matching errors. In a given line of this table, a source 1 report was classified as matched with a source 2 report if the two reports agreed, within tolerance limits, on all the specified characteristics for which both reports had a usable entry.[21] For example, for line 2 of Table 5.6, where Characteristics 1 and 3 were used in matching, if two birth reports agreed on Name and both had entries for Mother's maiden name (Characteristic 3) but disagreed, the reports were not to be considered matched. However, if Mother's maiden name was missing on one or both documents, they were classified as matched on Characteristics 1 and 3. As in the case of a single-characteristic match, a source 2 report could not be counted as matched to more than one source 1 report and vice versa.

As additional characteristics were used in matching, net matching error declined from 25 percent (using Name only) to zero (using Name, Mother's maiden name, Date of birth, Address, Father's name, and Name of doctor or midwife), and then increased, in absolute terms, to − 9 percent (using all the characteristics in Table 5.5 except Religion and Occupation of father). At the same time, gross matching error first declined from 43 percent (using Name only) to 38 percent (using Name, Mother's maiden name, Date of birth, and Address), and thereafter rose to 45 percent using either 11 or 12 specified characteristics.

In reviewing these results, the PPGES staff noted that the set of characteristics that produced minimum net error differed from that which yielded minimum gross error. On the other hand, neither set substantially increased the levels of net or gross error above their respective minimal values. Clearly, less effort was involved in a clerical comparison based on the four characteristics (1, 3, 5, 4) associated with minimum gross error than in one based on the six characteristics (1, 3, 5, 4, 2, 14) associated with minimum net error, but the difference was considered to be marginal. More important to the PPGES staff was the realization that the net errors shown in Table 5.6 were *estimates* which were subject to relatively large sampling errors when the estimates of gross error were large. There was little point in using additional characteristics (in this case, Father's name and Name of doctor or midwife) that increased the gross error unless they resulted in a very substantial decrease in estimated net error.

As indicated earlier, Characteristic 7 (Sex of infant) ranked very low in terms of discriminating power when considered by itself (the percentage of reports with unique identification on this characteristic being zero), and it was, therefore, the last characteristic introduced in Table 5.6. Nevertheless, this characteristic usually is very reliably reported, and in combination with other characteristics it will often increase the discriminating power of the set. Its use in matching can lower the erroneous match rate (or, at worst, leave it unchanged) without increasing the rate of erroneous nonmatches.[22] As a result, this characteristic can reduce the level of both net and gross error if it is introduced into a set of characteristics yielding more erroneous matches than erroneous nonmatches.

Acting on this principle, the PPGES staff tested the effect of adding Sex of infant to the set (Characteristics 1, 3, 5, 4) identified in Table 5.6 as producing minimum gross error. As anticipated, the inclusion of Characteristic 7 resulted in reductions in the percentages of both net and gross error, as the figures below show:

	Characteristics (1, 3, 5, 4)	Characteristics (1, 3, 5, 4, 7)
Match status		
Matched	66	61
Nonmatched	34	39
Match errors		
Erroneous matches	22	18
Erroneous nonmatches	16	16
Net error	6	2
Gross error	38	34

While the reduction in error achieved by using Sex of infant as a matching characteristic was not as great as the PPGES staff had hoped, it was considered substantial enough to warrant the inclusion of this characteristic.

On the basis of these results the set of characteristics adopted for matching birth reports in the initial rounds of the PPGES was:

1. Name,
3. Mother's maiden name,
5. Date of birth,
4. Address, and
7. Sex of infant.

A similar procedure was employed to designate the combination of characteristics to be used for the matching of death reports in the PPGES. Table 5.7 summarizes the outcome of the experimental re-matching of death reports, as Table 5.6 does for birth matching. Four of the sets of characteristics studied in Table 5.7 were selected for further scrutiny because they involved promising mixes of low levels of matching error and a small number of characteristics. These four sets are listed in Table 5.8, along with the errors obtained when Sex of decedent (Characteristic 7) was also included in each set. After reviewing the estimates of matching error given in Table 5.8 and attempting to anticipate the difficulties involved in the use of each set, the PPGES staff selected the following characteristics for use in the matching of death reports:

1. Name,
21. Name of spouse (if deceased ever married) or Name of mother (if deceased never married),
5. Date of birth,
4. Address, and
7. Sex.

Some further refinement of both the birth and death matching rules could have been achieved by manipulating the tolerance limits, by using combinations of characteristics not appearing in Tables 5.6, 5.7, and 5.8, or by doing both; but for a variety of reasons, the CBS decided against any attempt to improve the matching rules at this stage. Given the method used to set the tolerance limits, there was great reluctance to alter them. The experimental matching work already done, particularly that summarized in Table 5.8, suggested that simple recombinations of the available characteristics (using the previously specified tolerance limits) would not substantially reduce gross error. While more complicated rules (for example, "classify as matched those reports which agree on Characteristics 1, 3, 5, or 1, 4, 5, or 4, 5, 7, 9") could probably be found that would yield very low levels of matching error, such rules would necessarily be difficult for the matching clerks to apply. Furthermore, additional work on improving the matching rules would have required the allocation of limited funds and senior staff time to this task.

Underlying all these considerations was the awareness that the data available were not really good enough for fine tuning of the matching rules. After all, the matching errors given in Tables 5.6, 5.7, and 5.8 were estimates based on a fairly small number of reports

Table 5.7 Matching Status and Matching Errors for Source 1 Death Reports, by Combination of Matching Characteristics Used: Pacifica

(Matching status and matching errors are expressed as a percentage of all source 1 death reports.)

Matching characteristics used[1]	Matching status[2]		Errors[3]			
	Matched	Nonmatched	Erroneous matches	Erroneous nonmatches	Net error	Gross error
1	79	21	36	12	24	48
1, 21	71	29	31	15	16	46
1, 21, 5	64	36	27	18	9	45
1, 21, 5, 4	57	43	22	20	2	42
1, 21, 5, 4, 20	53	47	20	22	−2	42
1, 21, 5, 4, 20, 16	50	50	20	25	−5	45
1, 21, 5, 4, 20, 16, 18	49	51	19	25	−6	44
1, 21, 5, 4, 20, 16, 18, 6	45	55	18	28	−10	46
1, 21, 5, 4, 20, 16, 18, 6, 7	45	55	18	28	−10	46

[1] Numbers refer to characteristics listed in Table 5.2, together with the fixed tolerance limits developed for each characteristic. However, Characteristic 21 is a combination, substituted for 3 and 19, which uses, for married persons, the wife's maiden name (for husband) and the husband's family name (for wife) and, for unmarried persons, the mother's maiden name. Characteristic 1 refers to the husband's own name or the wife's maiden name.

[2] Based on the specified combination of matching characteristics.

[3] Refers to the percentage of all source 1 reports that are erroneously matched or nonmatched, according to the specified characteristics.

SOURCE: Hypothetical data from two matching studies conducted in Pacifica.

Table 5.8 Matching Errors for Source 1 Death Reports, by Whether or Not Decedent's Sex Is Used in Matching, for Four Specified Sets of Characteristics: Pacifica

(Matching errors refer to the percentage of source 1 death reports that are erroneously matched or nonmatched, according to the specified characteristics, expressed as a percentage of all source 1 death reports.)

Basic characteristics used for matching[1]	Without Characteristic 7[2]				With Characteristic 7[3]			
	Erroneous matches	Erroneous nonmatches	Net error	Gross error	Erroneous matches	Erroneous nonmatches	Net error	Gross error
1, 21	31	15	16	46	26	15	11	41
1, 21, 5	27	18	9	45	20	18	2	38
1, 21, 5, 4	22	20	2	42	19	20	−1	39
1, 21, 5, 4, 20	20	22	−2	42	[4]	[4]	[4]	[4]

[1] Numbers refer to characteristics listed in Table 5.2, together with fixed tolerance limits developed for each characteristic. However, Characteristic 21 is a combination, substituted for 3 and 19, which uses, for married persons, the wife's maiden name (for husband) and the husband's family name (for wife) and, for unmarried persons, mother's maiden name. Characteristic 1 refers to the husband's own name or the wife's maiden name.

[2] Matching errors obtained using specified basic characteristics; data taken from Table 5.7, lines 2 through 5 inclusive.

[3] Matching errors obtained using specified basic characteristics plus Characteristic 7.

[4] Not tested.

SOURCE: Hypothetical data from two matching studies conducted in Pacifica.

and were therefore subject to substantial sampling errors. Equally important, the CBS did not know at the time whether the overall quality of the PPGES data would be better, worse, or about the same as the quality of the data used in the experimental matching. For example, only one of the four studies used to examine the tolerance limits and matching characteristics for the PPGES assigned individual dwelling numbers as a regular part of the field operations. In consequence, Address ranked only fourth in discriminating power among the characteristics studied. It was anticipated that most reports in both sources would contain the PPGES structure number placed on each building by the Special Registration System staff. The widespread use of structure numbers would probably both reduce the level of erroneous matches and increase the level of erroneous nonmatches, relative to the estimates in Tables 5.6, 5.7, and 5.8. Other variations in quality were likely, but it was very difficult to anticipate what effect they would have. Related to these uncertainties was the inability of the PPGES to assess with precision variations in the extent, costs, and usefulness of supervisory referrals and field follow-up associated with the use of different matching rules.

In spite of these limitations, the procedures and data used to develop the initial matching rules for the PPGES were judged to be a better guide for this purpose than those which might be obtained by guesswork, and as good a guide as any that were available to the PPGES staff. It was decided, however, that revised matching rules would have to be developed on the basis of the PPGES data to deal with any remaining uncertainties. And it was agreed that, in the interim, the results of matching and field follow-up would be closely monitored to determine if the matching rules yielded error rates that differed radically from those anticipated.

D.5   FIELD FOLLOW-UP

As part of the continuing study of PPGES matching, it was decided to divide the matched and unmatched reports into four categories:

(1) Clearly matched—documents agree on all matching characteristics and there is no information that conflicts with the conclusion.

(2) Probably matched—meets the matching criteria but sufficient inconsistencies exist in other items to cast some doubt on the matching status; that is, the reports might be classified as a nonmatch if the matching rules were different.

(3) Probably unmatched—does not meet the matching criteria but sufficient evidence exists on the basis of other items to cast doubt on the matching status; that is, the report might be classified as a match if the matching rules were different.

(4) Clearly unmatched—documents contain discrepancies which point clearly to the conclusion that they could not refer to the same vital event.

Cases in Categories 2 and 3 ("Probably matched" and "Probably unmatched") would be reviewed on a judgmental basis by the matching supervisor(s), who would examine all available evidence and decide either (a) to shift reports from Categories 2 and 3 into Categories 1 or 4 or (b) to refer them for field follow-up and final decision.

Field follow-up would be used in an attempt to obtain additional evidence for resolving the classification of the doubtful reports (Categories 2 and 3) as matched or unmatched. Attention would also be given, both in the office work and the field follow-up, to determining whether any reports might be "out-of-scope."

As mentioned previously, reports may be out-of-scope geographically or temporally. Geographic out-of-scope errors are largely a function of sampling—that is, they arise from (a) difficulties with segment boundaries and (b) problems of associating the birth or death uniquely with a particular sample area. Either type of "geographic" problem can lead to erroneous inclusions in the sample of births or deaths. Temporal out-of-scope errors occur independently of sampling—that is, they exist even for a one-way match between a complete register and a census. Temporal out-of-scope errors in the survey should, however, be minimized with the use of the technique of accounting for household changes.

The PPGES staff considered it particularly important to check the unmatched reports for out-of-scope errors. (Other studies, such as the Pakistan Population Growth Estimation Study of 1962–1965, had field-checked all unmatched reports to determine whether they were unmatched because they were out-of-scope. On the other hand, there was a tendency to accept the matched reports as being in-scope without checking further.) It was decided that initially all unmatched reports (those in Category 4 as well as those in Category 3) would be sent to the field so that their status as out-of-scope or in-scope could be checked. First, however, all these unmatched reports were to be classified in the office as:

A. Clearly in-scope
B. Probably in-scope
C. Probably out-of-scope
D. Clearly out-of-scope

A sample of "Clearly matched" and all "Probably matched" reports were also to be checked for scope.

The office classification of a report as probably in-scope or probably out-of-scope would be on the basis of such evidence as:

(a) the geographic location of the household—whether it was near a boundary and whether its position relative to a boundary was indicated;
(b) disagreement on the exact date of birth or death;
(c) a date of birth or death near the boundary of the reference period;
(d) a conflict with birth dates of other members of the same household;
(e) an unknown birth or death date; and
(f) changes in household composition between two enumerations.

The stress in the field follow-up was to be on developing classification rules that would permit a reduction in the amount of field follow-up without loss of precision. For example, if the field follow-up during the initial period confirmed that virtually all the Category 4 reports classified as "clearly in-scope" actually were in-scope, it would not be necessary to follow up on these cases in later periods. Similarly, if after field follow-up the number of matched and probably matched cases was about the same as it had been before field follow-up (that is, if the number of Category 2 reports that became nonmatches or probable nonmatches as a result of field follow-up was about equal to the number of Category 3 reports that became matches or probable matches), it would be possible to reduce the proportion of matched reports sent for field follow-up. Nevertheless, some field follow-up might be continued to ensure the matching operation remained under control.

The amount of field follow-up required would also be reduced by improving the classification of reports, both with regard to matching (Categories 1, 2, 3, 4) and with regard to scope (Categories A, B, C, D). It might be possible to distinguish subgroups among the Category 2 and 3 reports that could be classified as matched or unmatched with very low probability that field follow-up would contribute much to altering this classification. Similarly, subgroups might be distinguished within Categories B and C which could be classified as in-scope or out-of-scope with low probability that the classification would be changed by field follow-up.

As previously indicated, a review of the matching rules on the basis of the first year of operation of PPGES was also planned. Basically this review would involve repeating the procedures for selecting "optimum tolerance limits" (see Tables 5.3 and 5.4) and for selecting "an optimum set of matching characteristics" (see Tables 5.6, 5.7, and 5.8), this time using data from the PPGES itself. Revised matching rules should presumably reduce the matching error and/or reduce the amount of field follow-up required for a given level of matching precision.

D.6   ESTIMATING THE BASE POPULATION

A heated controversy developed within the CBS over the choice of a population estimate to be used in computing birth and death rates. Two alternatives were possible: (a) an estimate of population from the Household Survey, supplemented by a count of the institutional population,[23] and (b) an estimate based on the 1970 Census updated by the PGE estimates of births, deaths, and net migration.

In general, the 1970 Census would give a better population estimate than the survey for 1970 and for two or three years thereafter. Over time, however, biases in the estimates of population growth (birth and death estimates) could result in a cumulative bias greater than the bias of a Household Survey. It was, therefore, agreed that, although it might be desirable to use the 1970 Census plus the estimated population growth as the base for 1971 and 1972 birth and death rates, these considerations would not apply for 1973 and later years.

There were, however, arguments that even for 1971 and 1972 the Household Survey (plus an estimate of the institutional population) was preferable to the Census as a base for birth and death rates. It was pointed out that if the Household Survey provided both the numerator and the denominator of the birth and death rates, the biases would tend to cancel. In particular, it was argued that there would be less need to be concerned about the sample areas always having well-defined boundaries since, whatever sampling biases occurred, the births or deaths reported would properly represent the births or deaths for the households actually included in the sample.

Those who favored the use of the adjusted 1970 Census as the population base agreed that the use of a population base derived from the sample would help in reducing coverage bias for a single system estimate of vital rates based on the Household Survey results only. However, they maintained that this advantage did not apply to a dual system estimate. Both sides agreed that use of a population estimate derived from the sample would tend to correct for bias due to the inclusion of geographically out-of-scope households, but it was argued that use of this population estimate introduced a coverage bias with respect to the vital rates for omitted in-scope households. That is, events for these households might be reported by the registration system and thus be included in the numerator of the vital rates (along with their contribution to the estimate of missed events), while the population of in-scope households omitted in the survey was excluded from the denominator of the rates. Because omissions were compensated for only in the numerator, it was claimed that the denominator would underestimate the base population, and vital rates computed from the PGE estimate of events and the survey estimate of the population would therefore be overestimates.

The proponents of a sample-derived population base were somewhat shaken by this argument that omission of geographically in-scope households in the population estimate would cause overestimates of the vital rates. However, they argued that this bias would be small and would be balanced by the reduced sampling variance resulting from the use of a "ratio estimate," with the numerator and denominator having a high positive correlation. This was felt to be particularly important since, despite all efforts to define sample areas of uniform size (180 households), the coefficient of variation for the size of the areas was likely to be at least 25 percent (a standard deviation of 45 households) and the resultant correlation would have a very marked effect in reducing the variance.

The advocates of using the adjusted Census as the population base suggested that the effects of variability in the size of the sample areas could be taken care of by inflating the sample results (which were to be "self-weighting") with the ratio of the 1970 Census population of the country to the 1970 Census population of the sample areas. Thus, the PGE estimate of the number of events (births or deaths) for Pacifica would be:

$$\hat{n} = \frac{Cn'}{c'} \, , \qquad\qquad\qquad [5.3]$$

where

C = 1970 Census population of Pacifica,

c' = 1970 Census population in the sample areas,

n' = PGE estimate of number of births or deaths in the sample areas, and

$\hat{n}$ = PGE estimate of total number of births or deaths for the entire country.

One could then divide by the independent estimate of the current population of Pacifica (D) to obtain the vital rate (r_1):

$$r_1 = \frac{\hat{n}}{D} = \frac{n'}{t_1 c'} \, , \qquad\qquad\qquad [5.4]$$

where

D = $t_1 C$ = independent estimate of the current population of Pacifica and

t_1 = independent estimate of ratio of the current population of Pacifica to the 1970 Census population (C).

This would compare with the vital rate (r_2) using the survey population estimate (d),

$$r_2 = \frac{\hat{n}}{d} = \frac{n'}{d'} \, , \qquad\qquad\qquad [5.5]$$

where

d = $\dfrac{Cd'}{c'}$ = estimate of the current population of Pacifica based on the Household Survey and

d' = current population from the Household Survey of the sample areas.

Equation 5.4 was developed by the leading advocate of an independent estimate for the population base, in an attempt to demonstrate that use of an independent estimate was superior to the use of an estimate derived from the Household Survey. However, by comparing r_1 with r_2, the statistician in question convinced himself that the use of an estimate derived from the Household Survey would, in fact, be preferable to the independent estimate he had previously advocated. The willingness of this man to examine the evidence in an open-minded, scientific manner did much to abate the heat of the discussion.

A comparison of equations 5.4 and 5.5 indicated that for 1971 and 1972 they probably would give practically identical results and that, to the extent that there were differences, these would be an argument in favor of the use of the population estimate derived from the sample. That is, the differences would reflect primarily changes since the Census in the sample areas. Of course, there would be some rotation of sample areas, and by the middle of 1972 the rotation could produce substantial differences between $t_1 c'$ and d' since t_1 would be derived from a different sample than d'.

Differences between $t_1 c'$ and d' would reflect either coverage bias differences between the Census and the PPGES Household Survey or sampling variance of the rate of population growth in the sample areas. Use of d' rather than $t_1 c'$ might not result in any marked reduction in the bias of the vital rate, but it was agreed that it probably would not increase the bias.

From the variance standpoint, deviations of the sample growth rate from that for the general population would be reflected in the numerators of the vital rates. It was desirable, therefore, to reflect them also in the denominators. For example, if the sample areas had, by chance, an unusually large amount of construction of new housing units or an unusually large amount of net in-migration, this would usually tend to affect the absolute number of births and deaths in the sample areas much more than it affected the birth and death *rates*. Almost certainly, the correlation between n' and d' would be higher than the correlation between n' and $t_1 c'$, while the coefficient of variation for $t_1 c'$ would not be much different from that for d'.

It was tentatively decided, then, to use the Household Survey estimate of population as the base of vital rates. However, obtained differences between $t_1 c'$ and d' were to be analyzed to see whether they indicated a need for changes in PPGES procedures. For the early periods of the study (that is, for 1970–1971), t_1 should be close to 1.0 and differences between d' and c' could be due to (a) extensive new construction or demolition or high migration rates in the sample areas; (b) defective Census coverage of the sample areas; or (c) defective Household Survey coverage of the sample areas. Analyses of the first two sources of difference would help in developing special procedures for identifying and sampling areas where new construction, demolition, or migration were major problems, or where Census coverage was exceptionally poor. Evidence of defective Household Survey coverage would, of course, indicate the need for changes in procedures.

To deal with the possible upward bias in the vital rate due to the omission of in-scope households, it was also decided to explore a method of estimation using the Household Survey estimate of population, and applying the PGE estimate of events to births and deaths associated with households included in the Household Survey. This procedure would require trying to determine if any of the unmatched registration certificates corresponded to a household included in the survey, by examining the address and the names of household members (see Section B of Chapter 7). With respect to names, this would involve primarily those of parents for births and of spouses for deaths.

Unmatched registration certificates that did not correspond to a household enumerated in the survey would not be used in the PGE estimate of events. This procedure would ensure that the events in the numerator of the vital rate corresponded more closely to the base population in the denominator.

In this phase of the PPGES, as in other phases, the emphasis was on using the original design as a means both of estimating vital rates and of collecting data that could be used to improve the design itself. Thus the original design, and any subsequent modification thereof, was conceived as *an adaptive model whose major goal was to produce its own replacement.*

Many aspects of the design and implementation of Pacifica's PGE study have not been included in this chapter. They were omitted not because they were unimportant, but because the purpose of this case study is to illustrate methods of solving design problems rather than to present specific solutions. Particularly as one moves on to the detailed problems of sampling, questionnaire design, supervision, processing, and tabulation, the illustrative value of Pacifica's solutions to its necessarily unique design problems diminishes. Even with regard to the more general questions that were discussed, such as the kind of collection methods to be employed, relatively minor changes in the situation in Pacifica might well have resulted in different decisions than those described here. In summary, the purpose of this chapter has been to illustrate the kind of thinking necessary in planning and carrying out a successful PGE study.

Footnotes

[1] The CBS believes that most of the discrepancy is due to the failure of the local, district, or provincial office to forward copies of all birth and death certificates. However, some of the discrepancy is probably clerical error and double counting of certificates—particularly those certificates sent to another office for filing.

[2] The "estimated total error" is equal to the square root of the mean square error as defined in Chapter 3, equation 3.4.

[3] It should not be assumed that these calculations were based on definite information about costs and sampling errors. The head of the Sampling Methods Unit of the CBS developed these rough estimates on the basis of data from a variety of other surveys conducted in Pacifica, and none of the figures were totally applicable to the contemplated PGE study.

[4] That is, $2.1 = \sqrt{(1.5)^2 + (1.5)^2}$, where "the bias [does] not exceed the variable error" (in other words, each about 1.5).

[5] That is, $3 = \sqrt{(2.1)^2 + (2.1)^2}$, where the crude birth and death rates have approximately the same estimated total error (2.1). Actually, this yields an overestimate. To the extent that the biases offset each other, one need only add the variable error components of the estimated total errors. The 5 per 1,000 confidence interval was based on the assumption that the biases of the crude birth and death rate estimates partially cancelled each other out.

[6] All figures in this paragraph are given to illustrate design considerations specific to the Pacifica PGE study and should not be assumed to apply to another sampling situation. An expert in survey sampling should be consulted to develop comparable figures for a particular design situation.

[7] This is the standard error (σ) of the birth rate and thus excludes the bias contribution to total error.

[8] The initial matching characteristics for the Pacifica PGE study were developed on the basis of previous matching experiences in Pacifica and not from the results of the small pilot study, see Sections D.3 and D.4.

[9] Of the $450,000 budgeted for the first three years, $60,000 was reserved for planning and experimentation, leaving an operating budget of $130,000 per year.

[10] Actually, the jurisdictional problems were not particularly serious. The Minister of Interior had absolutely no interest in retaining jurisdiction over birth and death registration. However, the red tape involved in a jurisdictional change was formidable and likely to be time-consuming.

[11] For a further discussion of a number of the issues raised here, see Sections B.4 and D.3 of Chapter 3.

[12] Figures on matching relate to births only. In general, matching reported deaths would give similar results.

[13] With "continuous" registration the registrar should have picked up all but the last week's or the last two week's births and deaths before the survey interviewer's visit.

[14] With any system, it is impossible to prevent meetings by collusion even with elaborate scheduling and continuous checking.

[15] While 15 to 20 households per day may seem to be a heavy workload for one interviewer, that number was possible because the questionnaire used in the Pacifica Household Survey was not extensively detailed.

[16] In parts of Pacifica female interviewers were routinely employed by the CBS for survey work. In fact, in the pilot study referred to earlier, female interviewers were noticeably better than male interviewers at obtaining interviews and birth reports from female respondents. Unfortunately, because of very poor facilities for lodging in the field, female interviewers could not be used routinely throughout the country.

[17] In estimating rural travel expenses and time, an allowance was made for the fact that in some cases it would be cheaper for interviewers to stay overnight than to make two round trips to a sample area.

[18] There are a few very reliably reported characteristics with only moderate discriminating power which, if used in matching, should be considered only in terms of zero tolerance. Sex of infant or of decedent is the most common characteristic of this type.

[19] In countries with extensive religious diversity, particularly where there are numerous religious sects and subsects, such an assumption for religion may not be warranted. In Pacifica, about 85 percent of the population belongs to the dominant

national religious group, and the religious minorities generally live in separate settlements. Therefore, though religion was very reliably reported, it had little discriminating power as a matching item either by itself or in conjunction with other items.

[20] Characteristics can also be ranked according to discriminating power by using either the number of erroneous matches or the average number of reports per identification code class. Both of these measures vary inversely with discriminating power, while the proportion of reports with unique identification varies directly with it.

[21] The tolerance limit associated with each characteristic considered for birth matching in the PPGES is listed in Table 5.5 and remains fixed throughout the study of matching characteristics illustrated in Table 5.6. For example, tolerance limit 4 (as defined in Table 5.3) is used for Name of infant (Characteristic 1) in all lines of Table 5.6.

[22] When Sex of infant (Characteristic 7) was introduced as last among the 12 characteristics in Table 5.6, it had no identifiable effect on matching error. In theory, the use of sex as a matching item could increase the erroneous nonmatch rate and, hence, the gross matching error when some other item used in matching (for example, infant's given name) also indicated the person's sex.

[23] The institutional population consists primarily of persons whose usual residence is a religious, educational, or penal institution plus the resident population of Pacifica's military installations. Figures for the latter were available from the Ministry of Defense. The remaining institutional population was small and could be estimated from the routine establishment data of various ministries. Procedures would, of course, have to be developed to prevent counting a person in both an institution and a regular household.

PGE Results and the Implications of Evaluation

6

A. Introduction

In the previous chapters of this handbook we were primarily concerned with questions of design. We described one method of measuring a major source of error in the collection of demographic data (dual collection) and suggested ways of constructing study procedures that, for given costs, tend to yield minimum error. We also attempted to help planners of studies with the difficult task of translating procedural ideals into operational realities. In this chapter the focus shifts from the design of studies to the rational assessment of their results. Our objective is the same as it was in earlier chapters—that is, to increase the "net value" of basic demographic data (see Chapter 3, Section A). However, we are now concerned with ways of examining estimates to identify their strengths and weaknesses, and with the implications that can be drawn from such evaluations.

Although evaluation can have numerous consequences, the discussion here will be divided into three basic actions that can follow from a systematic and rigorous examination of study results: (1) the adjustment of estimates to reduce the effect of errors; (2) the modification of the study design to improve future estimates; and (3) the development of a new study design when minor design modifications are no longer sufficient. There is an unavoidable arbitrariness in this division, particularly between the last two categories. From the viewpoint of an administrator of a statistical agency, however, it does represent a logical ordering of possible actions.

After a discussion of the philosophy behind evaluation and a careful review of the things that can go wrong in a PGE study, the chapter moves into a consideration of these three basic action categories. The discussion of the last category, involving the design of a new study, inevitably leads back to the core concerns of Chapter 3. Some of the material presented in this chapter deals with problems that are unique to the PGE technique. However, much of the chapter, in spite of its PGE orientation, presents a general approach to error that is relevant to the evaluation of any body of freshly collected demographic data.

B. Some General Principles for Evaluating Demographic Estimates

B.1   A RATIONAL ATTITUDE TOWARD ERROR

All human endeavors are subject to error. There is no reason to think that studies designed to obtain demographic estimates are an exception. Fortunately, most demographers and survey statisticians are aware of this basic fact of life. Furthermore, they have accepted the responsibility of trying to provide users of data with clear statements on the nature of the errors that a given set of data may contain and the likely effects of these errors.

Such statements on errors may produce varied reactions, depending on the familiarity of the reader with empirical data.[1] There appears to be a common road along which each data user (and producer) travels as he becomes familiar with study results. At first there is full confidence in the data collected and in each digit of the printed tabulations. The results are taken seriously and considered simply as a true picture of the phenomenon being measured. Results are often shown to several decimal places, and whatever small errors are acknowledged to have occurred, fortunately, "tend to cancel out." As experience accumulates, as a wide variety of empirical results are critically analyzed, and as reading deepens, there is often a swing to the opposite extreme. The presence of defects in data formerly considered perfect is interpreted as totally invalidating the data. Now everything is wrong, nothing can be trusted, all social data are useless, and common sense is the only guide. Finally, one reaches a point where one begins to achieve a balance between the value of data and the limitations imposed by errors and uncertainties. Now errors are acknowledged, but methods are sought to measure and adjust for them; and the effects of possible residual errors are considered in terms of the uses to which the data are to be put. At this point data evaluation becomes constructive rather than destructive or superfluous.

The measurement of error is of value both to the consumers of demographic data (that is, policy planners, program administrators, and social researchers) and to the data producers. Although we cannot measure error precisely, we can examine data rationally and use a variety of procedures to make approximations of error and to estimate the range within which the true value is likely to be. In this way we can reduce the inevitable blur of uncertainty that surrounds any empirical demographic estimate. Errors, once identified and measured, in large part cease to be liabilities. Instead they can help in providing adjustments to the demographic estimates and can serve as a starting point for making improvements in study procedures and design. An analysis of one's own mistakes is, in fact, a prerequisite to any constructive attempt to correct those mistakes.

The philosophy regarding error and estimation advocated here has four important consequences. First, the study design and overall budget must provide a means of evaluating the quality of the demographic estimates with a rigor appropriate to their intended use. In practical terms this means inserting line items for evaluation into statistical budgets and planning for evaluation from the start of a study, rather than letting it arise as an afterthought. Second, it means collecting data beyond the bare minimum needed to make basic demographic estimates. Such data may be obtained from the respondents, or refer to the collection process itself, or refer to the matching and other office work of the study. Furthermore, the collection of supplementary data for methodological purposes is wasted if the supplementary data are not tabulated and the results reviewed. Third, some action should follow from the results of error measurements. In other words, the results of evaluative studies must be taken into account in the preparation and analysis of current estimates, if at all possible, and in the collection of demographic data in the future. Finally, a rational attitude toward error implies a publication policy that provides the general user with a statement of major findings along with an honest and revealing assessment of the accuracy of the underlying data. It also provides the technical user with full information on procedures, error estimates, and any methodological studies conducted. (Such a policy is described in more detail in Section F, later in the chapter.)

B.2 ON LOOKING AT DATA

Having accepted the proposition that it is highly unlikely that any given set of demographic estimates for a real population is error-free and that there is a consequent need for evaluative studies, the question then becomes "how does one deal with new demographic estimates of uncertain quality?" There are two basic approaches to evaluating data. One focuses on the estimates themselves, and the other on the processes used to collect the data and to prepare the estimates.

The first approach involves examining the estimates for internal consistency or making comparisons with independently derived estimates. Eventually, any meaningful evaluation is limited by the availability of data; understandably, then, most of the evaluative effort goes into maximizing the use of either supplementary or external data. The second approach, which can also provide valuable insights into data quality, is based on a careful scrutiny of the processes used to obtain a given set of results rather than the results themselves. (To cite an extreme example, a birth rate chosen from the digits of a table of random numbers may or may not be correct. However, regardless of its correctness, one would want to question the process of estimation used.) A major advantage of this approach is that it can destroy the complacency created by superficial consistencies. Neither internal consistency nor agreement with external estimates guarantees that a given demographic estimate is correct or even nearly correct. Agreement and consistency are often the consequence of similar error processes or are simply fortuitous. Also, since terms such as "consistent" or "agree" are rarely defined in advance of tabulation and analysis, there is a real and understandable tendency to ignore any differences that do appear on the grounds that they are "minor" discrepancies. For these reasons, it is often useful to forget for a while the particular estimates being evaluated and think about how the data were generated.

One way of proceeding with this approach is to prepare a list of all the things that may have gone wrong in the study. Such a list of possible errors should include errors that are known or thought to have occurred, those that are rumored to have occurred, those that have occurred in other studies in the same country or in similar countries, and those suggested by the studies' critics. Because the list of possible errors will be a long one, it is best to compile it separately for each stage of study operations—sampling, registration data collection, survey data collection, matching, other office processing, field investigation, and tabulation.

An incomplete listing of possible errors for the sampling stage of a hypothetical study might look something like this:

(1) The Census list of rural revenue areas, which served as the frame for the second stage of sampling, is found in practice to have omissions and ambiguities.

(2) Maps used to form rural clusters at the last stage of sampling show boundaries quite imprecisely in sparsely settled regions.

(3) In one province, three villages and one "revenue village" (a group of villages with a common tax collector) all have the same name, and the one nearest the regional field office allegedly has been arbitrarily designated as the "sample area" by the director of the regional office.

(4) Two sampled villages in a region that is very difficult to enumerate are reported as "no longer existing" by the regional field office.

(5) Three pages of the district census report that was used as the frame for first-stage sampling have been found clipped together with a heavily rusted paper clip.

(6) According to the report of a visiting sampling expert, "the first-stage sample frame for the recently built-up areas at the edge of big cities is clearly inadequate."

(7) Maps for urban sample areas in slum neighborhoods frequently have very imprecise boundaries.

(8) The measures of size used in the final stage of sampling for many areas have been found to differ substantially from the field survey counts.

To be most useful, the list of potential errors must be as complete as possible.[2] One way of helping to ensure a complete listing is to keep a diary of mistakes and problems from the start of the study. Another useful source of information about possible errors is the comments of statisticians who visit the project, particularly those who go out into the field or spend time with the office processing staff. Although no list of possible errors will really ever be complete, the list is probably reasonably complete when neither the study managers nor a number of knowledgeable critics of the project can suggest any source of error that is not already listed. If the list is anywhere near as complete as it should be, it will be long and discouraging. However, it would be a mistake to yield to discouragement and leave the list half-finished, since the very act of having a comprehensive list of possible errors is an important step in the evaluation and analysis of the data.

Some of the errors listed, were they really to have occurred, would have a very great effect on a broad range of study results; other errors on the list would, by their very nature, have only limited consequences; and still others would have effects that could not be determined without more information. The next step in the analysis of the measurement process is to proceed through the list of possible errors, assuming provisionally that each has occurred, and make a rough assessment of the potential effect of each error on the study estimates. As before, this assessment should be done without reference to the actual demographic estimates of the study.

The consequences of specific errors can be looked at in terms of the direction of their potential effect (that is, whether they tend to bias estimates upward or downward), the magnitude of their effect (that is, whether they are likely to have a large or small effect on the estimates), the variability of their effect (that is, whether they tend to have a fixed, specific effect or whether their effect varies widely depending upon other factors), or the types of estimates that will be affected. Since a demographic study will produce many different statistics, one should concentrate initially on such basic measures as the rate of natural increase, the crude birth and death rates, and age-specific fertility and mortality.

This review of the list of possible study errors in terms of the direction, magnitude, and variability of their potential effect on the primary measurement objectives of the study provides a means of determining evaluation priorities. The rule to follow is clear and simple: Concentrate evaluation efforts on those sources of error whose effect on important statistics is or could be large. Those errors which, on the basis of this criterion, one decides not to evaluate specifically cannot be totally ignored. They must be discussed, or at least summarized, in the section of the study report on data limitations. Moreover, one should be alert to the possible *cumulative* effect of a series of errors, each "trivial" in itself.

A further ordering of evaluation priorities can be made when one turns from the review of the measurement process to the actual estimates of fertility and mortality produced by the study. Now one can take into account the direction of the potential effect on errors and formulate the following working rule: Concentrate evaluation efforts, initially, on errors that are the potential cause of unexpectedly high or low estimates of important variables or that result in differences that run counter to expectations—for example, higher fertility for women aged 30 years or over than for those aged 25 to 29 years. Note that this is a rule for establishing evaluation priorities, not for evaluation itself. An unexpected result is not necessarily wrong. It must certainly be looked at carefully, but the grounds for rejecting unexpected findings should be more substantial than one's own limited imagination. Furthermore, initial priorities established in this way do not preclude the possibility that, in the long run, it may be necessary to try to measure the net effect of two biases with opposite signs.

To some extent, initial evaluation priorities must be established in advance of the field work on the basis of theoretical considerations and past experience with comparable studies. This departure from the ideal of evaluation priorities tailored to the needs of a specific study is necessary so that the required evaluation procedures can be built into ongoing data collection and processing operations. Advance planning on the basis of a provisional assessment of priorities is particularly important in a study where the field work will be confined to a period of six months or less. Nevertheless, it is always useful to reassess the provisional priorities in light of the problems actually encountered.

Having established a provisional set of evaluation priorities, one can turn to the means available for carrying out the evaluation. This will include the basic estimates themselves, any supplementary data available, any ongoing evaluation built into the study (for example, dual collection and matching), and any supplementary evaluative studies that can be carried out. In the context of the present discussion, "evaluation" means measuring the extent to which specific kinds of errors affect the study estimates. Clearly, once the major sources of error in a specific study have been identified and even approximately measured, it is possible to take these errors into account in the analyses of the data and to improve the measurement process in the future.

In the rest of this chapter, we will be applying the principles discussed in this section specifically to the evaluation of PGE studies. We shall look first at what can go wrong in a PGE study, next at the potential effects of these errors, then at the methods available for measuring error, and finally at what can (and should) be done after the errors have been measured.

C. A Typology of Errors Affecting PGE Estimates

C.1 WHAT CAN GO WRONG

It is useful to begin the process of rationally reviewing the basic demographic estimates produced in a PGE study by considering each major source of error in terms of its effect on the PGE vital rate estimates. One such summary of the types of bias and variance affecting PGE estimates is presented in Figure 6.1. The principle underlying this figure is simple: All errors that bias the PGE estimates *upward* are listed in Part A, those that bias the PGE estimate *downward* are listed in Part B, and those that contribute to variance without themselves being a source of bias are listed in Part C. The sources of error listed in each part of the figure could be expanded almost indefinitely by listing increasingly specific factors relating to each phase of the study's design and execution. However, the detail shown in Figure 6.1 should be an adequate starting point for most studies.

While the individual sources of error listed in Figure 6.1 have a gross effect as shown in the figure, the error of a particular PGE estimate is the net result of all the relevant error processes that are operative in the study. For example, the existence of positive response correlation bias (factors B.2 and B.3 in Figure 6.1) would by itself (that is, if we ignored the effects of other possible sources of error) bias the PGE vital rate estimates downward. However, the study estimates may be too high, too low, or without net error as a consequence of bias or variance from other sources.

Since the use to which the PGE estimates are to be put determines the standards by which their quality should be judged, a phrase such as "without net error" does not have a fixed meaning. In one context, it may be sufficient to be reasonably certain that the crude vital rates fall somewhere within a range of ±20 percent of the obtained value (for example, a range between 16 and 24 for a crude death rate estimate of 20 per 1,000); in another context, one may want to be able to determine whether a decline of two points in the estimated crude birth rate can be considered an indication that the rate actually declined or must be attributed to the uncertainties of the measurement process.

The thought that the definition of "error-free" is flexible may at first seem disturbing. However, further reflection should make it evident that we often apply such a flexible definition in our everyday lives. (Few of us would insist upon measuring time by a stopwatch with a sweep second hand distinguishing between tenths of a second; on the other hand, we would hesitate to rely on an uncalibrated hourglass to get us to an airport on time. Yet stopwatches are often used in scientific measurements and at sporting events.) Clarifying and defining what is meant by "error-free" is particularly important once the question of cost is introduced. Very large errors can usually be detected relatively cheaply, but the accurate measurement of small errors tends to be quite expensive.

Most PGE studies have multiple objectives, and the full range of likely, or at least important, uses of the results should be considered (along with the constraints of cost and time) in shaping the evaluation effort of the data producer. Evaluation based on the quality standard implied by the least demanding use of the estimates, although the easiest to implement, is usually of the least value. Chapters 3 and 5 dealt to some extent with the process of clarifying the quality standard appropriate for a specific PGE study. To ensure an efficient study design, an operational definition of "free from error" should be developed long before data collection begins. In any case, for the purposes of the present discussion we will assume that such a definition already exists.

There is no system for automatically handling the work of evaluation. It is the nature of the problem that one is faced with uncertainty at every hand; yet the necessary relationships underlying Figure 6.1 can be employed to suggest a meaningful set of evaluation

Fig. 6.1   Sources of Error in PGE Vital Rate Estimates, by Nature of Gross Effect[1]

A. *Factors biasing PGE estimates upward:*
   1. Base population underestimated;
   2. Events reported in one system less likely to be reported in the other system than those that are not reported in the first system (negative response correlation bias);
   3. Events occurring in the wrong year or the wrong place or that never occurred (out-of-scope events) remaining among the (unmatched) reports of vital events, after the field follow-up;
   4. Errors or variability in the information used for matching, resulting in erroneous nonmatches;
   5. Large ratio bias (the expected number of matched reports is a very small number).

B. *Factors biasing PGE estimates downward:*
   1. Base population overestimated;
   2. Tendency of both systems to miss the same types of events (positive response correlation bias);
   3. Direct communication between collection systems leading to reporting in one system of events because they were reported in the other (positive response correlation bias);
   4. Characteristics used for matching have weak discriminating power, resulting in erroneous matches.

C. *Factors which contribute to variance without contributing to bias:*
   1. Small size of sample;
   2. Low completeness rate of either system;[2]
   3. Intraclass correlation of number of events and of reporting errors within sample units;
   4. Correlation between the completeness rates of the two sources and the total number of events within sample units.

---

[1]"Gross effect" refers to the effect of a given factor considered by itself; whether or not a specific PGE estimate is too low or too high is determined by the net effect of all sources of error operative in the study.
[2]With both very low completeness rates and very small samples, ratio bias may also arise.

priorities. If the estimated rates are too high, either the biasing factors listed in Part A must predominate over those listed in Part B or the results obtained must be a consequence of one of the kinds of variance listed in Part C; by contrast, if the estimates are too low, either the Part B biases must predominate over the Part A biases or the results must be attributable to the Part C variances. Of course, there is no certain way of knowing if the estimates are in fact too low or too high, but a working hypothesis about the direction of net error can often be formed on the basis of other estimates. Alternatively, the choice of the hypothesis about the direction of net error can be made with a view to testing some substantive hypothesis with respect to the level of or change in the vital rates. Whether one concentrates evaluation efforts on Part A or Part B biases depends upon the working hypothesis chosen; that is, whether one assumes a particular PGE estimate errs on the high or low side. (This recommendation for establishing evaluation priorities must be considered in the context of the entire evaluation process described in the preceding section.)

Before considering the individual sources of error listed in Figure 6.1 in somewhat more detail, a few words of caution are in order. The systematic discussion of the shortcomings of the PGE approach presented in this section should not lead one to the mistaken belief that the technique is a particularly error-prone procedure. It is our belief that a full discussion of error is necessary for the effective use of any statistical technique and the estimates it produces. The absence of a similar review of errors for most single-source estimation procedures does not mean that these procedures are not subject to major errors. Indeed, the main reason for using the PGE technique is that single data collection sources frequently produce quite unreliable estimates.

Another point one must keep in mind is that errors in the estimates of total births, deaths, or populations are not the only errors affecting demographic data. Although crude vital rates have a number of valuable uses, a demographer will require age- and sex-specific rates almost from the start, and subsequent analysis can involve an extensive list of variables. Unfortunately, each of these variables is also subject to biases and variances of its own. For example, the occupations recorded for half the labor force in recent United States Censuses were erroneous in the sense that when the occupations originally recorded were checked against relevant official records, a difference of some sort was found. Discrepancies between reports for the same individual are less frequent for sex (usually less than 1 percent). The consistency of age reporting varies markedly among countries, depending upon both basic cultural patterns and data collection procedures. Age reporting is usually less precise than sex reporting and more precise than occupation reporting for the nonagricultural labor force.

Reported age is of particular importance because of the central role age-specific rates play in demography. Many studies of the accuracy of age reporting illustrate the fragility of the base on which these age-specific rates are calculated (see, for example, van de Walle, 1968b).[3]

Age pyramids tend to look like Christmas trees, with branches protruding at ages ending with zeroes and shorter branches at ages ending with fives. What is less obvious is that such summary and global statements show only net errors. There are apparently much more serious gross errors (Hashmi and Alam, 1969).

Errors affecting the independent, or control, variables can have complex and unexpected consequences, depending not only upon the amount of error involved but also upon the nature of the analysis and the use to which the estimates will be put. Although we shall limit our discussion here to errors affecting overall birth and death aggregates and rates, errors affecting the other characteristics used in the analysis cannot be ignored. Characteristic-specific rates are subject to a more extensive list of errors than are crude rates; and because many of these errors are correlated with fertility or mortality, their effect may be complex, unpredictable, and analytically confusing (Coale and Zelnik, 1963; Bogue and Murphy, 1964; United Nations, 1967; and van de Walle, 1968a).

While characteristic-specific fertility and mortality rates, like the crude vital rates, are subject to all the sources of error listed in Figure 6.1, other types of PGE estimates are not affected by the full list of factors. For example, errors in the estimate of the base population will not alter the estimate of the number of births or deaths. The relevance of each of the biases listed in Parts A and B of Figure 6.1 for the estimation of vital rates, aggregates, and completeness rates is shown in Table 6.1.

We turn now to a discussion of the individual factors listed in Figure 6.1, looking first at the sources of upward bias, then at the downward biasing factors, and finally at sources of variance in the PGE estimate.[4]

C.2 FACTORS BIASING THE PGE ESTIMATES UPWARD

Factor A.1—Base Population Underestimated. Vital rate estimates are affected by errors both in the numerator (events) and in the denominator (population). The net relative error of an estimated rate (measured by the ratio of the observed value to the true value) is equal to the quotient of the net relative errors of its numerator and denominator. Thus, if both numerator and denominator are subject to equal relative errors, the vital rate estimate will be error-free. With single system estimates both the number of events and the base population are usually underestimated. Nevertheless, because the underreporting of vital events tends to be substantially greater than the underenumeration of the base population, the resulting vital rates are frequently too low. The same situation also occurs when vital rate estimates are calculated from survey or registration estimates of events and independent estimates of the base population. (Independent estimates are commonly based on the most recent census count updated for population change due to vital events and migration.) That is, the net relative

Table 6.1   Relevance of Specified Sources of Bias in PGE Estimation, by Type of Estimate

Source of bias[1]	Vital rate estimate	Estimated number of vital events	Estimated completeness or coverage rate
A.1 Population underestimated	Yes	No	No
A.2 Negative response correlation	Yes	Yes	Yes
A.3 Out-of-scope reports	Yes	Yes	Yes
A.4 Erroneous nonmatches	Yes	Yes	Yes
A.5 Ratio bias	Yes	Yes	No
B.1 Population overestimated	Yes	No	No
B.2 Positive response correlation	Yes	Yes	Yes
B.3 Positive response correlation	Yes	Yes	Yes
B.4 Erroneous matches	Yes	Yes	Yes

[1] See Figure 6.1 and the text for a fuller description of each source of bias.

error of such an independent estimate will usually be smaller than the single-source undercount of vital events.

With the PGE technique, however, the estimate of the number of vital events has been adjusted in an effort to eliminate the downward bias usually present in single-source reporting of events. Since no comparable adjustment is applied to the denominator, the estimated vital rates may be based on a numerator with fewer relative omissions than the denominator. If this is the case, the PGE rate estimate will be biased upward. However, the amount of net upward bias is likely to be smaller than the error of the comparable single-system estimate, because the population estimate is relatively much more complete than the uncorrected count of events. Moreover, the PGE correction for omitted events may be ineffective due to response correlation or to a marked excess of erroneous matches over erroneous nonmatches (factors B.2, B.3, and B.4). In this case, even if factor A.1 is operative, the net bias in the PGE vital rate estimate may be downward.

Assuming reasonably effective PGE corrections for the vital rate numerator, it is important to select a base population estimate that is as complete as possible. In most countries, censuses tend to be more complete than surveys taken at the same time, suggesting the use of an independent population estimate based on a recent census. However, as time goes on increasingly speculative adjustments for intervening population growth will be necessary, and this may make it desirable to use a base population estimated from the PGE survey. The decision must be based upon a consideration of the quality of the previous census, on the quality of the current survey, on the time that has elapsed since the census, on the population changes (due to both natural increase and migration) since the last census, and on the quality of the information about these changes. For a more complete discussion of the issues involved here, see Section J of Chapter 3 and Section F.1 of Chapter 4.

Factor A.2—Negative Response Correlation. All available evidence suggests that negative response correlation bias is not a frequent source of systematic error (see Chapter 2, Tables 2.13 and 2.14). Although situations in which events recorded by one source would have lower collection probabilities in the second source than events missed by the first source are conceivable, they are much less common than situations that give rise to positive response correlation bias (factors B.2 and B.3). For a general discussion of response correlation bias and procedures designed to encourage independence between the two systems, see Chapter 3, Section E, and Chapter 7, Section F.

Negative response correlation bias arises when the events reported by one system tend to be different from those reported by the other system. This may happen when there is a falsely conceived *esprit de corps* among field workers, based, for instance, on ethnic or religious prejudice. For example, negative response correlation will arise if the field workers of the two systems in many individual sample areas come from different ethnic or religious groups and tend to record the events of their own subgroup more completely than those of other subgroups. One can also imagine circumstances in which "professional" rivalry between the two systems would make the field workers of one system talk against the other system. Running the second system down might encourage or entice respondents to keep reporting events only to the field workers of the first system.[5]

A similar situation can arise when the field workers of one system have particularly good access to selected information on vital events (because of their prestige with local officials, frequent visits to barbers and tea shops, connections with midwives and gravediggers, and so on) and few or no contacts with other sources (for example, individual respondents), while the field workers of the other system have better rapport with individual respondents and little contact with local officials or other secondary sources. Finally, the respondents themselves may feel that they ought to report events only once, especially when the survey enumerators ask about events "since the last visit." The question refers, of course, to the last visit of the enumerator (say, six months ago), but the respondents may reply in terms of the last visit of the registrar (say, three weeks ago). Despite the plausibility of these hypothetical examples, negative response correlation bias has not been a major problem in studies using the PGE approach in the past.

Factor A.3—Unpurged Out-of-Scope Reports. Birth or death rates are defined in terms of time (for example, events occurring in 1968), place (either the place of occurrence of the event or the place of usual residence), and concept (that is, some agreed-upon definition of what constitutes a live birth or a death). Out-of-scope reports refer to events that did not occur within the proper time period, that occurred outside the study area (in the case of a *de facto* counting rule) or to persons whose usual residence was outside the study area (with a *de jure* rule), or that did not meet the agreed-upon definition of a live birth or a death (for example, the out-migration of an old man reported as a death or a stillbirth reported as a live birth followed by an infant death). A longer discussion of out-of-scope errors can be found in Section G of Chapter 3 on coverage bias.

Out-of-scope errors can arise as a result of the design of the two collection procedures used, because of reporting or recording errors in either of the collection systems, or because of processing errors. In practice, most out-of-scope reports arise during data collection as a result of poorly worded or otherwise badly designed questionnaires, or because of vague or unrealistic instructions to field workers. Temporal out-of-scope reports are most frequently associated with unbounded recall periods, with reference periods that do not run to the date of interview, with time references not commonly used by the population under study (for example, an unfamiliar calendar or an odd time interval, such as 18 months), and with information supplied by respondents only distantly associated with the event in question.

Geographic out-of-scope errors can arise with either a *de facto* or a *de jure* rule for counting events. If a *de facto* rule is used, they are particularly likely to occur when sample area boundaries are vague or have little meaning in the field (for example, boundaries based on arbitrary lines that are unrelated to the physical features of the countryside or that cut across a village or an urban neighborhood), when address systems are incomplete and many individual structures do not bear a single and unique house number, when maps are poor or outdated and do not show individual structures and individual structure numbers, or when the field workers of either source cannot or do not use maps. If a *de jure* counting rule is used, geographic out-of-scope reports are most commonly associated with confusion among the field staff and respondents about who is to be counted among the usual residents of a household. Studies conducted in countries in which informal adoption is widespread or where extended visits or absences for employment, schooling, or family reasons are common are particularly prone to confusion and out-of-scope reports. Regardless of which counting rule is used, substitute respondents or long recall periods are also likely to increase geographic out-of-scope reports. Moreover, as discussed in Chapter 4, Section B.4, household survey procedures using a *de facto* counting rule for events and registration procedures using a *de jure* rule tend to generate out-of-scope reports unless special steps are taken to prevent or eliminate them.

Less commonly, out-of-scope reports can be attributed to specific features of the study design (for example, a design in which each source uses a somewhat different definition of an in-scope event or different but overlapping sample areas) or to errors in the data processing operations. Data processing errors can affect individual reports (for example, a keypunching error can mean that a report for a stillbirth is erroneously tabulated as a live birth), but the processing errors that affect groups of reports are more serious. Lack of specific instructions to the data processing staff as to what is meant by "1974 events,"

"*de jure* events," or "births" can result in tabulations that contain many
out-of-scope reports or improperly exclude many in-scope reports (see
Chapter 4, Section B.7). Similarly, careless machine or computer room
practices can result in processing errors ranging from minor to glaring.
Most of these data processing problems can be avoided by the routine
use of control totals at each stage of processing and a rigid insistence
that any variation in the observed number of records be treated seriously
and investigated fully.

All the sources of out-of-scope reports just described, except
those directly attributable to the design of a dual collection system,
can affect either a single-source collection procedure or a PGE study.
In the case of single-source procedures, the effect of out-of-scope reports
is usually more than offset by the erroneous omissions of in-scope
events. In a successful PGE study, erroneous omissions are largely
eliminated as a source of error, so that out-of-scope reports may emerge
as a major source of error and a determinant of the net error of
the PGE estimate. Moreover, because out-of-scope reports are likely
to be unique to each collection source, an overwhelming number of
them will be nonmatches and thus will contribute disproportionately
to the PGE estimate.

Because of the importance of out-of-scope errors in PGE estimation, a variety of techniques aimed at controlling this source of error
are presented in the Handbook. A number of procedures for limiting
the occurrence of out-of-scope reports in PGE studies are mentioned
in Section G of Chapter 3. Field follow-up, an important technique
for eliminating out-of-scope reports once they have occurred, is described
in Chapter 3, Section I.1, and Chapter 5, Section D.5. Additional methods of minimizing or avoiding out-of-scope bias are presented in Chapter
7, Sections B and D.2.

Factor A.4—Erroneous Nonmatches. A large number of matching
errors of either type usually indicates that the matching rules being
used are not appropriate. This occurs most often when the rules were
either established arbitrarily or developed using improper procedures
or an unrepresentative group of vital events reports. However, even
well-designed matching rules may function poorly in a particular round
of matching due to normal variations in the nature of the events and
in the recording errors present in the reports. For this reason, the
evaluation of the matching operation should be adjusted to accord
with the initial effort that went into developing the matching rules.
Carefully developed rules should not be altered or abandoned too
quickly, particularly if a large number of vital events reports were
used in the experimental matching. On the other hand, when the
procedures used to develop the matching rules were clearly inadequate
or even questionable, high levels of either type of matching error
(identified either by field follow-up or by supervisory verification)
indicate the need for a prompt reconsideration of the adequacy of
the rules.

As seen in Chapter 3, Section F, and Chapter 4, Section B.6, the matching rules should be designed so as to minimize *net* matching error (erroneous matches minus erroneous nonmatches) at some low level of *gross* matching error (erroneous matches plus erroneous nonmatches). This means that one cannot consider erroneous nonmatches without also looking at factor B.4, erroneous matches. Which of the two factors will predominate in a particular study will depend upon the variability of the population with respect to the identifying characteristics used in matching, the quality of the field work, and the details of the matching procedure used. Among the studies reviewed in Section C of Chapter 2, examples can be found of studies in which erroneous matches were thought to predominate (the United States 1940 birth registration test) and those in which erroneous nonmatches seemed to be more common (the Pakistan PGE study).

Erroneous nonmatches result from variability in the identification items beyond the level allowed by the tolerance limits for matching the reports from the two sources.[6] No single feature of the matching rules used is entirely responsible for there being an excessive number of erroneous nonmatches. Although the number of such errors can usually be reduced by shortening the list of items used for matching, relaxing the tolerance limits for one or more items, or enlarging the blocking units employed, modifications of this kind should not be made without considering their impact on the rate of erroneous matches and the levels of net and gross matching error.

Regardless of the matching rules employed, inadequate instructions or questionnaires and sloppy or poorly supervised field work may produce documents in the two sources with different entries for the same event. (For example, the forms may leave insufficient space for writing names legibly, or parity may be systematically undercounted in one source because the field workers consider parity to mean the number of previous live births.) In processing, erroneous nonmatches can arise when errors are made in reading the documents (for example, when a poorly written "3" is interpreted as a "5" or an "a" as an "o") or in sorting, coding, or transcribing them. If matching is done by machine, keypunching or other processing errors can be an important source of erroneous nonmatches (see Chapter 3, Section I.2).

Particular attention must be given to controlling variability in name and address information, since these items usually have very high discriminating power and play a key role in matching. It is important that instructions for entering names and addresses be specific, unambiguous, and equivalent for both sources. Some of our suggestions on procedures that may aid in the consistent recording of these items appear in Sections B.1, B.2, B.5, and B.6 of Chapter 4.

A number of common sources of variability in the reporting of names and addresses, and thus likely sources of erroneous nonmatches, are shown in Figure 6.2. This listing is a partial one and is merely illustrative. In practice, one would want to develop a list that more fully reflected relevant local conditions and the procedures

Fig. 6.2   Some Major Sources of Variability in the Reporting of Names and Addresses in PGE Studies

---

A. *Sources of variations in names*

1. Variations in the spelling of names that sound alike (for example, "Li" and "Lee," "Jeanne" and "Gene").

2. Confusion due to minor variations in the pronunciation of names (for example, "Li" and "Ri," "Jeanne" and "Jane").

3. Multiple names not always shown in full. (For example, Mahmoud Abdul Aziz ibn Hamid appearing as "Mahmoud ibn Hamid," "Mahmoud Abdul Aziz," "Abdul Aziz ibn Hamid," "M. Abdul Aziz ibn Hamid.")

4. Use of nicknames.

5. Use of different scripts with no one-to-one correspondence in the spelling of names.

B. *Sources of variations in addresses*

1. Use of structure numbers, but with many numbers omitted.

2. Existence of more than one structure number system in the same area (for example, numbers assigned by the PGE study and a preexisting house numbering system used by the postal service, the Malaria Eradication Program, the last census, or a previous study).

3. Existence of more than one name or designation for roads, streets, villages, streams, etc.

4. No standard names for roads, streets, villages, streams, etc., and the method of designating them not standardized and identical for both collection sources.

5. Use of more than one numbering script with similar digits (for example, Arabic and Devanagri numbers used in the same area).

6. Designation of the sequential position or distance of structures used without a clear indication of the reference point.

7. Designation of direction (for example, "left," "right," "west," "east," "north," "south," "clockwise," or "counterclockwise") used without a clear indication of the reference point.

---

of a specific study.[7] The study schedules, instructions to field workers, and matching and other processing operations should be reviewed carefully to determine the relevance of the various types of errors listed in Figure 6.2. This review should be made in light of the tolerance limits adopted for name and address information.

Factor A.5—Ratio Bias. The PGE estimate ($\hat{n}$) is a ratio of two random variates (n_1 and w_1, or n_2 and w_2) where $w_1 = m/n_2$ and $w_2 = m/n_1$ (see Chapter 3, Section D.1). In other words, we divide the number of events reported in a source (n_1) by the estimated completeness of reporting for that source (w_1) to obtain an estimate of the number of reports corrected for underreporting. If reporting is independent between sources, w_1 will vary around the true completeness rate (P_1) and the expected value of w_1 will be P_1; that is, w_1 will be an unbiased estimate of P_1. However, because

$$E\left(\frac{1}{x}\right) > \frac{1}{E(x)} \quad ,$$

the PGE correction $1/w_1$ (that is, n_2/m) is biased upward; that is,

$$E\left(\frac{1}{w_1}\right) > \frac{1}{P_1} \quad .$$

The origin of this bias is discussed further in Chapter 3, Section E.2.

The upward bias in $1/w_1$ is called "ratio bias," and its size depends upon the relvariance of w_1.[8] That is, if the relvariance of w_1 is very small, then w_1/P_1 will always lie close to 1.0 and the PGE correction $1/w_1$ will be very near $1/P_1$. Thus, as the relvariance of w_1 approaches zero, ratio bias rapidly vanishes as a source of error in PGE estimation. The relvariance of w_1 (and of w_2) is very nearly the same as that for m, which is of the order of magnitude of $1/m'$, where m' is the number of matched reports in the sample prior to inflation of the estimate m.[9]

As indicated in Chapter 7, Section B.4, ratio bias is negligible if the coefficient of variation of w_1 or w_2 is less than 5 percent (that is, if $m' \geq 400$). Even where m' is substantially smaller (say, about 100 matched reports), ratio bias is not likely to be an important factor. However, as the coefficients of variation of the completeness estimates increase much beyond 10 percent and m' drops below 100, ratio bias can be an increasingly important source of error in PGE estimation. For example, when the coefficient of variation of w_1 or w_2 is in the neighborhood of 20 percent ($m' = 25$), PGE estimates of vital statistics (rates or aggregates) will be subject to a ratio bias of about 5 percent (see Table 7.1). (However, as noted in Table 6.1, a comparable ratio bias does not affect the PGE estimate of the completeness of reporting of either source.)

Because of the sample sizes typically employed in PGE studies, ratio bias will seldom be a significant consideration in national PGE estimates if these estimates are based upon all sample birth or death reports. On the other hand, it may be a source of substantial error in the case of estimates prepared for specific geographic areas or other population subgroups and then summed to give an estimate for an entire country or region. Although the relative variance of a set of ratio estimates is reduced by summing or averaging them, the relative bias is not. For example, if separate PGE estimates are made for seven age groups, each containing only 25 matched sample reports, and these estimates are then summed to give the final estimate, the ratio bias will be that appropriate to $m' = 25$ rather than to $m' = 175$. This suggests that the procedure for reducing response correlation bias by preparing separate PGE estimates for subgroups could, if inappropriately applied, substitute a large upward ratio bias for a substantially smaller downward correlation bias.

C.3 FACTORS BIASING THE PGE ESTIMATES DOWNWARD

Factor B.1—Base Population Overestimated. This factor is the complement to factor A.1, base population underestimated. As mentioned in the discussion of that factor in the preceding section, estimates of the base population, if in error, are usually underestimates; and if the PGE correction for omitted events is accurate, then the PGE estimates of vital rates will be too high. However, if the base population is overestimated (or if the PGE correction is not fully effective and the base population figure is accurate or only slightly underestimated), the PGE study estimates of crude birth and death rates will be too low.

Although overestimation of the base population is less common than underestimation, it can occur, for example, where the base population figure has been obtained from a faulty independent estimate, where a census or survey estimate of the base population has been overcorrected for estimated underenumeration, or where overlapping sampling frames have been employed in the enumeration process without sufficient effort to avoid duplication. This last problem frequently arises when there has been a failure to specify, or adequately control, whether persons are to be enumerated at their usual place of residence or at the place they are found at the time of enumeration. For example, in countries or regions where seasonal work causes substantial proportions of the population to be temporarily away from their homes, inadequate procedures that result in many persons being counted both at their place of usual residence and at temporary work camps can produce an overestimate of the base population.

If the base population estimate is based on a survey that serves as one of the two sources for vital events reporting, uncertainties and errors in the definition of the boundaries of the sample area are not usually a major source of error in the vital rate estimates, since both the numerator and the denominator are similarly affected. Sometimes, however, the information on vital events and population, although nominally from a single source, is in fact obtained from distinct field operations—for example, when the base population estimate is based on a special canvass by supervisory personnel of either source or on the enumeration results of one round of a multiround survey and the data on vital events come from other rounds. In these situations the differential impact of boundary errors on the numerator and the denominator of the estimated rates can be more serious.

Factor B.2—The Tendency for Both Systems to Miss the Same Kinds of Events (Positive Response Correlation Bias). While negative response correlation (factor A.2 in Section C.2) appears to make a relatively unimportant contribution to bias in PGE estimation, positive correlation is common enough to warrant a separate discussion of its two sources—the nature of the events and reporting systems (factor B.2) and the communication between the two sources (factor B.3).

Positive correlation attributable to both sources missing the same kinds of events has long been identified as a potential source of downward bias in PGE estimates as indicated in Chapter 2, Section C.[10] (The topic is also considered in detail in Section E of Chapter 3.) Usually, factor B.2 is more likely to be a problem when the procedures employed by the two sources are quite similar. This might be the case if both sources were household surveys or special registration systems, or if they both used common questionnaires. In addition, positive response correlation can occur if the personnel of both sources come from similar social or cultural backgrounds and if suspicion or hostility hinders data collection from persons with different backgrounds.

Some kinds of events will have a relatively low probability of being reported no matter what collection procedures or personnel are used—for example, out-of-hospital events (particularly deaths) occurring to strangers, itinerants, or others without regular ties in the sample area. In some countries illegitimate births tend to have low collection probabilities, except perhaps in the case of civil registration reports for hospitalized births. With the same exception, the underreporting of both births and deaths is quite common when the baby dies within the first few weeks of life.[11]

Although not generally as serious a problem as the situations just mentioned, low reporting probabilities may also obtain in cases where there is a difference between the place of occurrence of a vital event and the place of residence of the individuals involved (the decedent, mother, or infant). As mentioned in the discussion of factor A.3 in the preceding section, this kind of situation can lead to out-of-scope reporting—that is, reporting of the event at the place of residence in a *de facto* system or at the place of occurrence in a *de jure* system. It can also lead to omission of the event because of the same confusion about where it is supposed to be reported.

Positive response correlation should also be suspected as a source of bias where the obtained match rates are very high and other evidence indicates that the true completeness rate is considerably lower (see Chapter 3, Section E.5). Generally, bias attributable to factor B.2 can be reduced by changing the procedures and personnel of the two sources to make them more dissimilar, or by making special efforts to increase the coverage by either source of the kinds of events that have particularly low probabilities of collection.

Factor B.3—Communication Between the Collection Systems (Positive Response Correlation Bias). The most obvious type of communication is the conscious collusion between field personnel of the two systems. This kind of communication is relatively rare. It usually occurs either near the start of a PGE study because the field staff has been given insufficient training or unrealistic work loads or, as the study continues, because the pay, motivation, or supervision of the field workers is inadequate. Overt collusion is fairly easy to detect, but to correct it the PGE planning staff must recognize that basically the fault is theirs rather than that of the colluding personnel. If one pays field personnel very low wages, hires persons with unsuitable education, expects interviewers or registrars to cover unrealistically large assignments, and does not provide adequate training and supervision, one can only expect a shoddy performance.[12]

A number of other, more subtle forms of communication between the two systems are more difficult to deal with than direct collusion. Some of these may be planned, in the sense that they explicitly involve features of the study design or operating procedures (for example, the use by the two systems of a common set of maps, a common sample, and common definitions of an in-scope report); while others are not (for example, chance meetings between the two sets of field workers in the sample area, the regional office, or at headquarters). At least some planned communication is necessary if the matching is to be carried out successfully; but, wherever possible, procedures that contribute to communication and response correlation bias should be avoided.

A particularly troublesome type of communication between systems arises from the attempt to combine field supervision with PGE activities. For example, some countries have tried to use the field supervisors of a special registration system or a vital events survey as a second source. Even if the supervisors are not given, prior to their own canvass, the results obtained by the registrar or interviewer, their supervisory functions and data-gathering activities will be mutually conditioning. The use of supervisors to verify and improve the quality of field work is desirable. If necessary, they can also be used to do field checks for doubtful matches and, possibly, out-of-scope reports. They cannot, however, function effectively as supervisors *and* as data gatherers in an *independent* data collection system. Similarly, the procedures for updating the PGE maps and handling unnumbered structures are a potential, but avoidable, source of correlation bias (see Sections B.1 and B.2 of Chapter 4).

Communication between the two sources can also be introduced in the editing process, if the presence of a report for an event in one source becomes the basis for deciding whether or not an event is considered to be reported in the second source. For example, events reported in a registration source and not reported on the survey vital events forms, but implied by information contained in the survey household schedule, cannot be considered matched unless *all* such implied events on the household schedule are included in the reports of the survey. To do otherwise will mean that the probability of "reporting" an event in one system is increased by the presence of a report in the other source, thus introducing positive response correlation bias. It is perfectly acceptable to use either infants listed on the household schedule or births reported by the survey interviewer on a birth form in determining which births are considered as reported in the survey. However, the decision as to which rule will be used must be made before the birth reports of the other system are examined.

Accidental encounters between primary-level field workers are almost inevitable and may lead to an exchange of information without any thought of cheating or realization that such communication is undesirable. After all, an interviewer or a registrar may consider comparing lists of reported events with his counterpart in the other system simply a way of conscientiously carrying out his instructions to obtain reports of all events occurring in the sample area. Elaborate schemes for scheduling the itineraries of registrars and interviewers to prevent their being aware of each other's presence in the area will almost certainly break down of their own weight.

It is desirable, then, to instruct each set of field personnel about the importance of collecting information directly from the population, without either avoiding or stressing references to other data gathering operations in the area. The field workers of each system should be told which sources of data they may use and reminded that canvassing is restricted to these sources. Supervisors and senior staff members should reinforce these instructions both by word and by example.

Even more important are a study design and procedures that make the jobs of the primary-level field workers of each system as different as possible (see Section E.3 of Chapter 3 and Section F of Chapter 7). To this end, the layout of the questionnaires and forms, the items of information, the reference period for vital events reporting, and the persons contacted should be as unlike as possible while still providing the two sources with sufficient common identifying data for events to permit matching. Such a policy, as we have already noted, will also help to reduce the other source of positive response correlation bias (factor B.2).

Factor B.4—Erroneous Matches. This factor is symmetrical with factor A.4, "erroneous nonmatches." As discussed elsewhere in this handbook, the matching procedure should be designed to lower to a minimum the net error caused by factors A.4 and B.4. Thus, some erroneous matches may be expected even if there is no matching bias. Only when the number of erroneous matches is greater than the number of erroneous nonmatches will the PGE estimates of vital rates and aggregates be biased downward. Broadly speaking, an excess of erroneous matches indicates a design-problem, while an excess of erroneous nonmatches indicates errors in execution. However, execution and design problems interact; for example, anticipated high response variation in the identification items used for matching (producing erroneous nonmatches) may suggest the use of wide tolerance limits with a consequent reduction in discriminating power (producing erroneous matches).

Erroneous matches are associated with matching rules that employ too few items in matching, tolerance limits that are too broad, or blocking units that are too large. They also occur where the items available for matching have relatively low discriminating power—for example, where many events have the same name or address. In places where individual structure numbers are nonexistent or unknown, addresses will have little value for matching purposes. (At the extreme, all events in a given area would be identified by the same address, making the discriminating power of the item zero.) If a system of structure numbering exists but many structures are unnumbered, the discriminating power of address will also be reduced, roughly in proportion to the percentage of structures without numbers. An occasional use of the same number more than once is not a major source of concern; most matching procedures are robust enough for that. However, the use of the same number over and over again will substantially diminish the discriminating power of that number and reduce the average discriminating power of address information in the study.

Large blocking units can also be a source of erroneous matches, particularly if the matching procedure is developed on the basis of a relatively small number of reports or by using smaller blocking units than those used in the main study. For example, other things being equal, one would expect matching rules developed on the basis of reported events for a six-month period to produce a higher than optimum number of erroneously matched reports when applied to the reported events for a 12-month period.[13] A matching procedure using implicit rather than explicit rules (see Chapter 3, Section F.6) would also seem to be prone to the production of erroneous matches.

Matching problems and their solution are discussed at greater length in Chapter 3, Section F, in Chapter 4, Section B.6, and in Chapter 5, Sections D.2 to D.4. It should be noted that although a higher than expected match rate may be caused by a net excess of erroneous matches over erroneous nonmatches, high match rates may also indicate positive response correlation (factors B.2 or B.3).

C.4   THE VARIANCES OF PGE ESTIMATES

Because the variances of the estimates, unlike the biases, can be estimated directly from the sample results, a detailed analysis of the various factors affecting variance is usually unnecessary. Of course, variance estimates based on sample results are themselves subject to variance. Situations will exist, mostly as a result of unduly small sample sizes, where the estimates of variance should be viewed with suspicion. For example, if one uses subsampling for source 2 and estimates the completeness of source 1 from a subsample of 20 events, one may get a completeness estimate $(w_1 = m/n_2)$ that is very high and the estimated variance of this completeness rate may be very low—in fact it could be zero if all 20 source 2 events discovered are also reported in source 1. However, a variance estimate based on 20 cases is not likely to be very dependable, and this fact should be made clear to the users of the w_1 estimate and its variance. Unreliable variance estimates may also arise as a result of the concentration of all cases in a few (five or less) sample areas.

It is important that variance estimates properly reflect the actual sample, with respect to size, clustering, the correlations between number of events and completeness of reporting, and so on, rather than an inappropriate ideal. For example, the simple formulae for binomial samples do not apply to clustered samples. The formulae appropriate for estimating the variances of a typical PGE sample are given in Chapter

7, Sections A.6 to A.8. For PGE sample designs not covered by Section A in Chapter 7, appropriate variance estimation formulae can be developed along the lines outlined in Hansen, Hurwitz, and Madow (1953).

Although breakdowns of PGE variances by cause are not necessary in order to evaluate the reliability of PGE statistics, an examination of causal factors will be important in determining the action required to reduce the PGE variances. These causal factors are listed in Figure 6.1 as factors C.1 to C.4. A small sample size (factor C.1) is easily spotted. Moreover, it is relatively simple to calculate the variance reduction that would be obtained by increasing the sample size while maintaining the original cluster size and collection procedures for both sources.

The effects of completeness on variance estimates (factor C.2) are discussed in Section C.5 of Chapter 4. One of the factors involved in computing these effects is whether one is using the PGE estimate with sampling in one source ($\hat{N}$) or with sampling in both sources ($\hat{n}$). (For reasons of cost, the former design is almost always used in association with a one-way matching procedure and the latter design with a two-way procedure.) With either estimate, the variance increases as the estimated completeness rates w_1 and w_2 decrease, but this increase is more rapid with the one-way estimate, $\hat{N}$, than with the two-way estimate, $\hat{n}$. With high completeness rates, the variance of $\hat{N}$ will be lower than that of $\hat{n}$ because N_1, the number of vital events obtained by source 1 for the universe, has no sampling variance. As the completeness rate for source 1 drops below about 50 percent, however, the variance of $\hat{n}$ becomes less than that of $\hat{N}$ for a given set of completeness rates. Formulae for the variances of the PGE estimates $\hat{n}$ and $\hat{N}$, with simplifying assumptions, are given in Chapter 4, Section C.5. For a description of the more general case, and of methods of estimating variances from sample data, see Section A of Chapter 7.

The effects of intraclass correlation (factor C.3) can be estimated by computing the variance for a simple random (unclustered) sample and comparing this with the variance obtained using the estimating formulae given in Chapter 7, Sections A.6 through A.8. The increase in variance attributable to intraclass correlation can be estimated by the formula

$$(1 - \delta + \bar{n}\delta) = \frac{v_x^2}{\hat{v}_x^2} \quad , \qquad\qquad [6.1]$$

where

$$\delta \;\; = \;\; \text{intraclass correlation coefficient,}$$

$$v_x^2 \;\; = \;\; \text{estimated relvariance of } x \text{ in the sample actually used,}$$

$$\hat{v}_x^2 \;\; = \;\; \text{estimated relvariance of } x \text{ for a simple random sample,}$$

$$\bar{n} = \frac{\hat{n}}{k} \quad = \quad \text{estimated average true number of events}$$
per sample area,

$$\hat{n} = \frac{n_1 n_2}{m} \quad = \quad \text{PGE estimate, and}$$

$$k \quad = \quad \text{number of sample areas.}$$

If $(1 - \delta + \bar{n}\delta)$ is fairly large, it may be desirable to consider whether the number of sample areas is optimum—that is, whether a change in the number of sample areas with or without subsampling for one of the sources might produce a lower variance for the same cost of the sample. One would also want to consider whether or not a change in the size of the sample areas might reduce the value of $(1 - \delta + \bar{n}\delta)$, and consequently of v_x^2. For example, with very large sample areas, a reduction in size may mean an increase in δ that is proportionately smaller than the reduction in $(\bar{n} - 1)$. It may therefore be possible to reduce the variance by taking additional, smaller sample areas with no increase in cost. For very small sample areas, an increase in the size of sample units may increase the value of $(1 - \delta + \bar{n}\delta)$ proportionately less than it increases the unit costs (costs per sample area), and thus permit one to take a larger sample for the same total cost with a reduction in variance. As discussed in Chapter 3, one would want to weigh any gains with respect to variances against the possible losses in terms of bias for any contemplated design change.

Using data from the sample, one can also estimate factor C.4, the correlation between the completeness rate w_1 (or w_2) and its denominator n_2 (or n_1), by taking, for each sample area,

$$n_{1i} \quad = \quad \text{number of events reported in source 1}$$
for sample area i,

$$n_{2i} \quad = \quad \text{number of events reported in source 2}$$
for sample area i,

$$m_i \quad = \quad \text{number of events reported in both sources}$$
for sample area i,

$$w_{1i} = \frac{m_i}{n_{2i}} \quad = \quad \text{estimated completeness rate of source 1}$$
for sample area i, and

$$w_{2i} = \frac{m_i}{n_{1i}} \quad = \quad \text{estimated completeness rate of source 2}$$
for sample area i.

If there is *negative* correlation between w_1 and n_2 or between w_2 and n_1, this will act to increase the relvariance of $\hat{n}$. In such cases, it may be desirable to see whether coverage in the larger sample areas can be improved—possibly at the expense of coverage in the smaller areas—without a corresponding increase in overall costs or a decrease in overall completeness. Alternatively, it may be possible to decrease the variance in the size of sample units—that is, make the larger sample areas smaller and the smaller ones larger—without an increase in overall costs or a decrease in overall completeness. This will reduce the amount of negative correlation and thus the relvariance of $\hat{n}$.

D. Methods of Detecting and Measuring Error

There are two broad approaches to error detection and measurement in a PGE study. The first is to investigate the quality of the individual components of the measurement process that constitutes a PGE study. In many respects the component method of error detection and measurement resembles an audit of study results. Like a financial audit, this measurement audit tries to identify the aspects of study operations that are affected by carelessness, faulty procedures, waste, or deliberate falsification. Focusing on each component of the PGE study and the errors arising from it can enable one to make relatively strong statements about the quality of the resulting estimates. In addition, this type of evaluation provides a means of identifying the major sources of error and uncertainty in the PGE estimates and thus provides guidance about the comparative advantages of different corrective actions.

The second approach is to attempt to measure the total error in the PGE estimate, regardless of how the error arose. This is generally done by preparing independent fertility or mortality estimates and comparing them to the PGE estimates. Compared to the component method, this approach has a number of advantages. It generally involves the collection of a smaller amount of supplementary data and is thus less expensive. As long as the required analytical data are available, the work can be carried out by any data user, no matter how distant in time or space he is from the study operations. And, finally, the results relate directly to the substantive issue—the accuracy of the basic demographic estimates. The weakness of this approach lies in the fact that the measurement of total error is only as good as the independent estimate with which the PGE estimate is compared. In many instances this means that, instead of measuring error, one merely obtains a rough indication of the consistency of two estimates of uncertain quality. Despite this limitation, efforts at measuring total error are an important complement to the component approach to error measurement.

Needless to say, individual errors will also be identified in the course of regular supervisory activities. Section D.1 below contains a discussion of the supervisory and evaluative approaches to error detection; Sections D.2 and D.3 outline some specific procedures appropriate to the component and calibration approaches to error measurement, respectively; and Section D.4 deals with special studies conducted for evaluative, experimental, or methodological purposes.

D.1 DISTINGUISHING BETWEEN SUPERVISION AND EVALUATION

Supervision and evaluation have a common purpose—that of maintaining and, where necessary, improving the accuracy and utility of the study results. Because of this shared purpose there is frequently a tendency to confuse the two functions, and even to treat them as a single operation. This tendency is reinforced when there is a lack of funds or a shortage of properly qualified personnel for either function. However, supervision and evaluation are quite different and should be performed by different personnel at different operating levels. Supervisors must be in close day-to-day contact with the actual data collection or data processing operations, while those doing evaluative work must ordinarily be sufficiently insulated from daily operations to facilitate their making overall assessments about general kinds of errors rather than about the performance of particular enumerators, registrars, or clerks.

Both supervision and evaluation are concerned with the detection and correction of defective performance. Supervision is primarily concerned with the identification and correction of specific errors that occur in the implementation of the study. It also provides administrative and personal links between the organization and the individual staff members. In these latter capacities, the supervisor interprets the policies and rules of the organization to the staff, helps staff members overcome administrative difficulties, and in general tries to build staff morale without sanctioning the violation of administrative rules or study objectives.

The detection and control of error in the data collection operations can involve a number of distinct supervisory activities, including the work of field supervisors, the supervisory work of the headquarters staff, and supplementary training of the field staff. In general, the emphasis in supervision is on the detection of mistakes rather than the measurement of error, although some estimate of the magnitude of the errors that are found must be made to determine whether the cost of corrective action is justified. A supervisor may direct or do a recanvass of all or part of the work he deems defective. He may also replace the worker responsible for bad quality or retrain him when the difficulty is with the procedure rather than the personnel.

Quite commonly, the weakest link in many collection systems is the field supervisor. Supervisors should not be permitted to remain in the office and have the field workers visit them; rather, they should travel to the sample areas and meet with the registrars or interviewers there. Specific tour programs should be established for each supervisor, records of actual visits to sample areas should be maintained by the supervisors and approved by the regional director, and the services of supervisors who fail to carry out their assignment should be terminated. More positively, efforts should be made to get the supervisors to take a professional interest in their job by holding half-day review sessions, in which the technical problems of data collection in each system are discussed, from time to time. If this is attempted, supervisors associated with each source should be convened separately, so as to minimize unnecessary communication between the two systems.

The routine reports of each source, as well as the basic data collection forms, contain information that can be used to supplement the work of the field supervisors. The headquarters staff can make use of these important sources of information. For example, the individual birth and death reports can be tallied monthly by subunits of the sample areas, by date of occurrence, by date of registration (for an informant system of special registration), and so on. These tallies can answer such questions as "Are events reasonably spread over time and space, or are they highly clustered?" or "Are there reasonable numbers of early infant deaths?" Rapid and informed scrutiny of data as they come in from the field provides information about field problems so that corrections can be made before a situation gets out of hand. In situations where the performance of the field supervisor is not very good, this office review may be an important means of supervising and controlling the field operation.

It is important that the errors and misunderstandings of the field workers be corrected as promptly as possible. An excellent method of insuring that all members of the field staff learn the correct procedures is to bring them all together for a supplementary training session that concentrates on common problems, reviews procedures, and serves as a general morale booster. Other ways of getting feedback to the field workers are also possible—for example, by mail or through the supervisors—but a supplementary training session once or twice a year is a good way of achieving effective and standardized feedback. It also provides a good opportunity for the senior staff to hear the problems and complaints of enumerators and registrars.

Basically, evaluation should be directed at detecting major deficiencies in procedures and measuring the effects of these shortcomings on the study estimates. It should, for example, be concerned with detecting widespread collusion between interviewers and registrars rather than specific instances. Similarly, it should be concerned with detecting and correcting general types of matching defects, such as confusion about the kinds of numerals (the country's own or the "universal" Arabic numerals) to be used in recording addresses, that could lead to a high rate of erroneous nonmatches. Supervision, in contrast, should be concerned with correcting specific instances of failure on the part of the field workers to understand and use the prescribed numerals. Because evaluation is concerned with measuring and preventing general classes of failures, it should try to remedy specific defects only if this can be done cheaply and efficiently. Usually, however, this is not possible, and attempts to use the evaluation results for this purpose can be a waste of time and funds.

Rather than trying to correct the matching status of specific reports involved in matching errors, the evaluator should concentrate on correcting deficiencies in the matching procedures—for example, inadequate tolerance limits for some of the items used in matching, leading to a very high level of erroneous nonmatches. He may recommend changing the tolerance limits in the future. Alternatively, he may conclude that the necessary changes will lead to such low discriminating power that the erroneous match level will be unduly increased and that it is best to continue with the present matching procedures, making an allowance for the erroneous nonmatches in the estimates. In either case, the evaluator may want to recommend changes in future data collection—for example, improvements in recording information so that response variability is lowered or the addition of items to the vital events documents that could be used in matching.

Both evaluation and supervision must be handled in such a manner as not to impair the independence of the two sources. Evaluation results rarely lead directly to a reduction of independence, but there is some danger that specific results may be wrongly used in an administrative context to discipline staff. If this practice becomes common, many members of the staff will have a vested interest in the outcome of evaluation, and they may take steps to ensure a favorable result. In the case of supervision, independence is best maintained by having a separate set of supervisors for each source. If this is possible, the job of each set will be very like that of the supervisors in a single system study. As an added precaution, the supervisors of each source should be specifically instructed not to become involved with the problems, procedures, and results of the other source.

If one set of supervisors must be used for both sources, considerable care must be exercised to prevent the supervisors from introducing correlation bias. In particular, they must never use information about specific events obtained from supervising one source to influence the reporting of the same events in the other source. Moreover, the supervisors should be instructed not to use the reports of one source to criticize the workers of the other source, since this will only encourage the interviewers and registrars to collaborate behind the supervisors' backs. These points tend to be difficult for supervisors to grasp; thus their instructions in this regard must be clear and emphatic.

D.2   CHECKS AIMED AT SPECIFIC SOURCES OF ERROR

The measurement of error associated with every component of a PGE study is a technically demanding, time-consuming, expensive, and next-to-impossible task. For this reason, it will usually be necessary to allocate the limited resources available for evaluation according to a set of priorities established along the lines suggested in Sections B and C.1. Moreover, because one can rarely assess each component of a study and each potential source of error with adequate thoroughness, it is important to combine measurements of component error with estimates of total error (see Section D.3). Often the demographic analysis that forms an important part of such estimates of total error can be "subcontracted" to an experienced academic demographer outside the PGE organization, so that the PGE staff can concentrate its evaluation efforts on investigating specific sources of error. This division of labor is usually a good one, since the detection and measurement of many types of error that arise during data collection and matching must be done as promptly as possible by those with detailed knowledge of these operations.

The procedures available for identifying and measuring the individual sources of error that affect PGE study results include the replication of the operation in whole or in part, or the use of analytical models to estimate the consistency or accuracy of results. These procedures are similar to those available for evaluating the overall study estimates. In the present case, however, they involve the output of individual components of the measurement process rather than the final study estimates.

Errors in the estimated base population (factors A.1 and B.1 in Figure 6.1), which may contribute to bias in the PGE vital rate estimates, can often be identified by a post-enumeration quality-check survey (U.S. Bureau of the Census, 1964d; Marks and Waksberg, 1966) or by an independent estimate of the base population (Coale, 1955). In either case, one may be uncertain whether the result obtained by the new procedure is any closer to the "true value" of the population size than the original estimate. However, if a post-enumeration quality check is employed, one can use case-by-case matching to obtain direct evidence about the quality of both the original enumeration and the quality-check resurvey. Where case-by-case matching is not feasible, attempts to look directly at the individual components of change—births, deaths, in-migration, and out-migration since the last population census—either for the country as a whole or for each sample area, can often provide a suitable measure of the reliability of survey estimates of the base population.

The results themselves may contain information that will help to determine whether factors A.1 or B.1 are operative. Frequently, sharp, unexplained variations in population totals for individual sample areas, blocks, or other subgroups between survey rounds are an indication that the quality of the survey enumeration may be poor and that some further investigation of the population estimates is warranted. In assessing the final estimates, one should remember that both fertility and mortality rates are affected by base population errors. That is, if the base population is underestimated (factor A.1), both the fertility and mortality rates will tend to be too high; while if the population is overestimated (factor B.1), both will tend to be too low. Thus, in a given study, if the fertility rates seem to be too high and the mortality rates too low, or *vice versa*, one must begin to question the relative importance of base population errors in the study or the accuracy of one's expectations. This lack of parallelism in the direction of error can only be accounted for by other sources of error that, taken together, are larger than the errors affecting the base population estimate and have a quite different effect on the estimates of births and deaths.

The presence of response correlation bias (factors A.2, B.2, and B.3) can be suggested by calculating the correlation between w_{1i} and w_{2i}, the estimated source 1 and source 2 completeness rates for the sample area i. Although it is not really a very dependable indicator, a substantial correlation coefficient between completeness rates often signals the presence of response correlation bias, particularly if the sample consists of many relatively small clusters. Another, and perhaps no more effective, method of detecting response correlation bias is to compare the estimates based on the summed PGE estimates for subgroups with the corresponding unstratified PGE estimate. (See Chapter 2, Section D, Tables 2.13 and 2.14, and Chapter 3, Section E.2.)[14]

It should be remembered that these estimates of correlation bias are underestimates to the extent that correlation between the sources remains even after stratification. On the other hand, the use of very small strata in preparing subgroup estimates can lead to ratio bias (factor A.5) and either a possible overestimate of positive response correlation bias (factors B.2 and B.3) or a possible underestimate of negative response correlation bias (factor A.2).

Two related, but less complicated, procedures for detecting possible response correlation bias are available. Very high or very low match rates for *both* sources for the same subgroups often indicate the existence of positive or negative correlation, respectively. This is particularly true if the subgroups in question are individual sample areas or individual pairs of field workers for the two sources. Even with ungrouped data, if match rates for both sources are unexpectedly close to zero or one it is wise to check further for the presence of response correlation bias. Factor B.3 (positive correlation bias arising from communication between the two sources) can usually be detected by comparing the reports of the two systems using zero tolerance for an item with high reporting variability (for example, full name or date of birth of mother). Some variability in the reporting of names, dates, ages, and so on is to be expected, and if the two sources agree exactly on this information too frequently some form of communication between them should be suspected.

Out-of-scope reporting, or coverage bias (factor A.3), is commonly detected by field follow-up (see Section I.1 of Chapter 3). Out-of-scope reports are most often found among the nonmatched cases reported as occurring near the geographic boundaries of the sample areas, occurring near either end of the (time) reference period, or associated with a temporary or permanent change in residence status. Field follow-up will eventually be concentrated among these reports. However, the initial evaluation must also show that the prevalence of out-of-scope reports is indeed very low among the matched reports and those unmatched reports outside the high-risk groups.

Almost always, in the past, field follow-up has been used to identify and eliminate individual instances of out-of-scope reporting on a 100-percent basis; that is, all reports of a given type have been sent for field follow-up and those identified as referring to out-of-scope events on the basis of the follow-up have been removed prior to the preparation of the PGE estimates. An alternative approach, particularly worth considering once the data collection and matching operations have become stabilized, is to send out only a sample of reports for field follow-up and obtain estimates of coverage bias on the basis of this sample. The desirability of this approach should be decided on the basis of the cost, the timing, the reliability needed, and similar factors.

Out-of-scope bias can also be studied by observing whether the match rate is lower in either source for situations in which out-of-scope reports can be anticipated—near the boundaries of sample areas or near the beginning or end of the reference period, or when the place of residence of the parents or decedent differs from the place of occurrence of the event.

The detection of matching error (factors A.4 and B.4) involves, basically, repeating the matching operation using either more information, more care, or a more skillful staff. Field follow-up in one form (Shapiro, 1954) or another (Population Growth Estimation, 1968) has been used in an effort to detect erroneous nonmatches (factor A.4) in many PGE studies. A number of studies have also tried, along with field follow-up, having more experienced staff members concentrate on matching the residual nonmatches after the routine matching by the junior staff has been completed. The results of these "extra" efforts provide some measure of the level of erroneous nonmatches after the routine matching procedures have been carried out.

Attempts at identifying erroneous matches have generally involved a comparison of the outcomes of the regular matching operation with those obtained for the same group of reports by more senior staff members using all the information available in the reports of both sources (Shapiro, 1954; Yusuf and Turowicz, 1967). However, because the existence of some matching errors of both types is compatible with an accurate PGE estimate, only if efforts are made to detect and measure *both* erroneous matches (factor A.4) and erroneous nonmatches (factor B.4) can one determine which predominate.

If the matching rules were developed along the lines recommended in Chapters 3 and 4, some initial estimate of matching error will be available. The goal of the evaluation program should be to determine the extent to which this initial estimate of matching error is confirmed by subsequent experience. This task is considerably more difficult when the matching rules are developed more or less arbitrarily, without data on the matching errors associated with various criteria. Given a rationally developed matching procedure and a well-conducted field follow-up involving, at least in the initial matching rounds, both matched and nonmatched reports, satisfactory estimates of matching bias should be available.

Whether a particular PGE estimate is subject to ratio bias (factor A.5) depends upon the expected number of matched reports in the denominator of the PGE estimate. Table 7.1 or equation 7.93 can be used to obtain some indication of the extent to which a given PGE estimate may be affected by ratio bias. However, one cannot be certain of the amount of error introduced into any specific estimate by this factor because it is defined in terms of the "expected value" of the number of matched reports.

From this discussion, field follow-up emerges as a crucial element of any error detection and measurement effort in a PGE study. It is usually the major method of identifying matching and coverage biases—two of the most important sources of error in PGE estimation. However, if field follow-up is handled in a careless manner or if its independence and effectiveness is threatened by employing the supervisors of either source for this task, there is a real danger that its evaluative usefulness will be compromised. Field follow-up should be given sufficient priority to ensure that an independent and well-qualified staff is made responsible for its conduct. To pay for the special personnel needed, part of the costs of field follow-up can be charged to the funds set aside for evaluation.

D.3 CALIBRATING THE PGE ESTIMATES

Because the PGE approach is often offered as a method of calibration for single system estimates, there is a real question as to whether a higher standard exists against which PGE estimates may be compared. Although the procedures now available for assessing the overall accuracy of the PGE estimates for any given study are themselves subject to considerable variations in quality, a few methods do provide comparatively more certain estimates of overall error. However, these procedures only become available as a result of an appropriate international research program.

For example, in a country where most vital events occurred in hospitals and the civil registration system was virtually complete for many years one could use this known universe to evaluate the estimates of a PGE study consisting of a special registration system and a household survey. Although one might try to use the results of this three-way match to evaluate the two-way PGE results (see Chapter 7, Section D.1), this would be a costly procedure with errors of its own. If the civil registration system was obtaining reports for substantially all events, then an aggregative comparison between such a two-system PGE estimate and the civil registration results would probably be a more efficient method of calibration. This approach would be cheaper to carry out than a three-way match, and it would prevent the confounding of matching errors with the estimate of total error of the PGE estimates. The implicit assumption of this approach is that the net error of the civil registration results is small—both absolutely and in comparison with the net error introduced by a three-way matching operation.

Clearly, this calibration procedure, based as it is on firm knowledge about the number of events occurring, is suitable only in nations where PGE studies are *not* needed for vital statistics estimation. Unfortunately, many of the factors that make accurate survey work and demographic measurement more difficult, and a PGE study necessary, are largely absent in these countries. For this reason, the "set of general conditions" (see Hansen, Hurwitz, and Bershad, 1961) would almost certainly vary greatly between the PGE studies supplying calibration data and those using these results. Any measures of error obtained by this procedure could be generalized only with caution. Nevertheless, by suitably choosing the population to be studied and the collection procedures to be tested, one might obtain valuable insights into the likely accuracy of a PGE estimate under a variety of conditions.

Another type of calibration procedure in which the universe of events is assumed to be known is a computer simulation of the PGE measurement and estimation process (see Choi, 1970, for a specialized use of simulation in this context). A simulation approach to calibration gives the investigator wide latitude in specifying the population of events, the collection and matching procedures, relevant cost functions, the means by which error processes are introduced, and so on. However, for the results of such simulation experiments to have any practical value, great care must be exercised in specifying each component of the model. A well-designed simulation study can play an important role in measuring the overall reliability of the PGE approach and other methods of vital statistics estimation. On the other hand, a computer simulation study based on an inappropriate model can be just as wasteful and counterproductive as a poorly designed or executed field survey.

Short of these approaches to true calibration, one must rely on some form of relative calibration, such as: (1) the repeated application of the same PGE procedure in one country or region for a number of years; (2) the comparison of the PGE estimates with those obtained from the usual methods of demographic analysis; and (3) the comparison of the PGE estimates to standards developed by other means.

The first of these methods assumes that the vital rates are invariant over time or change by a known amount. Since this assumption hardly ever holds true, this is an extremely weak approach to the calibration problem. However, one is certainly justified in questioning the reliability of PGE estimates if they display a considerably greater year-to-year change than can be attributed to likely demographic trends or to chance and if the study procedures remain relatively unchanged.

In many parts of the Handbook we have mentioned the value of using the techniques of demographic analysis as part of a PGE study. The past decade has seen notable advances in the variety and sophistication of these analytical techniques. Some of these procedures can be used to obtain estimates of current fertility and/or mortality, and these estimates can be directly compared to the PGE results for evaluative purposes. More commonly, different analytical procedures will supply estimates—quite often somewhat conflicting—of different aspects of the demographic picture, and the evaluation process will consist of determining how well the PGE estimates fit the usually fuzzy picture obtained by analytical means. Of course, this kind of analysis can lead to a major research endeavor of its own (see, for example, Demeny and Shorter, 1968; Bean, Khan, and Rukanuddin, 1968; or van de Walle, 1968a).

The total number of analytical techniques available is large, but not all methods are appropriate in any particular situation. The United Nations' *Manual IV*, prepared by Ansley Coale and Paul Demeny, lists some 16 distinct circumstances involving differences in data available, in assumptions about population stability or quasi-stability, or in the types of estimates to be prepared (United Nations, 1967, pp. 2–3). Moreover, estimation techniques using data on own children classified by age and age of mother (Grabill and Cho, 1965; Cho, 1971) and pregnancy history analysis (Bogue and Bogue, 1967, 1970) are well documented in other publications.

We will not attempt to instruct the reader in these techniques or to assess in any detail their strengths and limitations. Suffice it to say that these analytical tools, though powerful, are not robust enough to assure that even a skilled user will always obtain a plausible estimate. A number of documents exist that provide discussions, in differing degrees of detail, of the underlying assumptions of one or more of the analytical procedures (Brass and Coale, 1968; Demeny, 1965; Brass, 1971b); information on data needs (Demeny, 1967; Population Council, 1970); instructions as to their use (United Nations, 1967); worked examples (United Nations, 1967; Brass *et al.*, 1968; Cho, 1971); or statements about the quality or comparative advantages of one approach or another (United Nations, 1967; Brass, 1969; Page, 1971).

Beyond these generally applied and widely known methods, a number of novel and ingenious approaches to the evaluation of vital statistics have been used in the past. For example, Arriaga (1967) developed an index of registration completeness using data on roads and registration offices, and Khan (1960) developed a rough estimate of the birth rate in West Pakistan on the basis of smallpox vaccination data. More widely known, but no less ingenious, were the estimates of registration completeness made by Whelpton (1934), using census data, and by Moriyama (1946), using data on hospitalized births (see Chapter 4, Section C.4). Such a procedure tends to have limited general validity but may be quite appropriate to a particular place and time. Certainly, if the result is correct, it can be used to measure the overall error of a PGE estimate for the same period and population.

Unfortunately, the correctness of an independent estimate is not easy to determine, and the very novelty of an approach may make it even more difficult to assess the estimate. This holds true both for newly developed techniques in the regular tradition of demographic analysis and for those new approaches that use data external to routine demographic scrutiny. Despite this important limitation, statisticians and demographers should be alert to the possible availability of some special data source that, if cleverly used, may provide independent demographic estimates suitable for at least a rough assessment of the PGE study results. Such procedures are particularly valuable if they employ data sources whose error structures are quite different from those of the survey, registration, or PGE procedures for vital statistics reporting.

All the procedures for estimating the extent of total error in the PGE estimates except those involving a known universe of events (for example, a computer simulation study) are essentially consistency checks. Note that inconsistencies, whether external or internal, may demonstrate the presence of errors in the data even though they do not necessarily indicate which of the figures being compared is in error and by how much. On the other hand, consistency in the figures cannot establish the absence of error. Two figures may be in agreement because they are affected by a common source of error or by errors from different sources that give coincidentally similar results; in either case both figures may be quite wrong.

Thus, even if the consistency checks and other analytical measures indicate no discrepancies in the data, it will be important to review the data collection and processing operations for evidence of major departures from the study design that might bias the results (see Section D.2). If discrepancies exist, a similar examination of the study procedures guided by specific hypotheses about the probable nature, direction, and magnitude of error, is in order. However, if a careful investigation of the study results cannot locate errors of sufficient magnitude to account for the observed discrepancies, it will also be necessary to question the accuracy of the analytically based estimates.

D.4 METHODOLOGICAL STUDIES AND EXPERIMENTAL WORK

PGE studies should be designed to provide for orderly, periodic changes in procedures (see Section E.2). At least in the initial phases, part of the provision for orderly change might well include experimentation to explore some of the questions the development of the initial design has raised but left unresolved. Also, as time goes on, defects are bound to appear. Changes suggested to deal with these defects are best tested on an experimental basis using a carefully designed "split sample" that permits an unbiased comparison between alternatives or between the results of current procedures and proposed modifications. A model for such an experimental design was developed by Fellegi (1971) for the Moroccan Poplab study. This design must, of course, be modified to accommodate the particular circumstances of each PGE study, but the principles on which it is based are generally applicable.

When providing for experimentation it is important to steer a middle course between an operating setup so rigid that useful experimental comparisons are very difficult and a setup with so much freedom for experimentation that the timely production of reliable demographic estimates is jeopardized. The solution is to build in a procedure for making changes on a periodic basis, for example, annually as described in Section E.2. There is a twin advantage to such an institutionalization of change: (a) the feeling of routine removes the atmosphere of crisis, and (b) having a fixed time for making changes prevents too many people from popping up with "bright" ideas at the last moment, in an *ad hoc* manner (see the discussion of the "chess principle" in Section F.2 of Chapter 4).

An experimental design such as the one cited above for the Moroccan Poplab study will provide adequate data on variances and at least some information on the differential biases of the alternatives under study. In addition, modern sampling theory and sound administrative practice require that cost be an integral part of all design considerations.

In spite of the importance of detailed cost information, good data in this area are few and far between. Furthermore, with a few exceptions, costs have not been the subject of experimental studies, although there are very few subjects on which experimental results are needed more urgently. For example, pay scales are still determined almost solely by administrative considerations rather than by any logical analysis of the effects of the pay scale adopted on the quality of output.

One reason for the paucity of good cost information is the very considerable difficulties experienced in setting up adequate cost records. The success of any methodological investigation depends critically upon the mode and nature of record keeping. The major prerequisites to good record keeping are an unshakable belief in the value of thorough and consistent records and the willpower and perseverance to ensure that such records are kept.

In addition to being consistent and complete, records must be analytically revealing. They should attempt to distinguish between costs that vary with the work load assigned and those that merely expand to fill the remaining time available. It is also desirable to identify situations in which costs are being reduced at the expense of quality—for example, when an excessive work load makes it necessary for the field workers to do only a very superficial job.

The results of research into costs can be used directly in making a number of basic decisions affecting the design of PGE studies. One such issue—critical to improving the designs of PGE studies—is that of the utility function appropriate for a PGE matching operation. Tepping (1971) has explored some of the theoretical properties of such a function, but more work is needed before the approach can be explicitly incorporated into the design of matching rules. A major part of this further research effort would have to be carried out within the context of an ongoing PGE study.

There are many other instances in which a PGE study provides a congenial setting for needed demographic and statistical research. Almost every aspect of design and its implementation is a fit subject for controlled experimentation: the sample design, the nature of the two sources, the data collection procedures employed by each source, the matching operation, the level and type of field follow-up needed, the type of estimates prepared, and so on. A PGE study provides an excellent opportunity for conducting such experiments because the PGE estimate can be used as a standard of comparison for estimates based on alternative procedures.

On the other hand, there is some danger that overloading the PGE study with too many experimental features will make the basic data collection and matching operations fall apart. Furthermore, it is quite difficult to set up large-scale field studies for the sole purpose of clarifying methodological issues. The need for substantive demographic estimates is generally so strongly felt that administrators will rarely sanction for long an "experimental" PGE study that is not responsive to national and international requests for demographic data, particularly if the sample is large and representative. Study managers with an initial commitment to methodological investigation and experimentation may find themselves frustrated by decisions that transform plans for an "experiment" into a basic source of national demographic data. They should not respond by attempting to stretch available resources to carry out both a full-scale substantive study and a large experimental program. In these altered circumstances, it would be far better to include a modest, and thus effectively monitored, experimental program that could supply definite answers to a few research questions within the basic study.

E. *Actions Resulting from Evaluation*

As noted before, the goal of evaluation is maintaining and, where necessary, improving the accuracy and utility of the vital statistics estimates. If evaluation indicates that the accuracy of the existing estimates is satisfactory, the main action to be taken will be to make sure that all information about errors and data limitations is presented to users in a simple and readily understandable form (see Section F, "Errors, Evaluation, and Publication Policy"). In such situations, there may also be some attempts to avoid a deterioration in the quality of the study or even to improve it at little or no cost. These will usually take the form of minor changes in questionnaires and procedures or of supplementary instructions alerting supervisors and other field personnel to some of the more common forms of error.

More often, the results of evaluation imply a less passive response. The simplest and least expensive action for countering defects in quality disclosed by evaluation is to adjust the estimates on the basis of existing data. More serious defects may require modifications in procedures, possibly radical or expensive ones. In extreme cases, the evaluation may disclose defects in basic procedures of such far-reaching proportions that it will be less wasteful of money and effort to start again with a fully redesigned study, rather than try to salvage the existing study by modifying the procedures.

E.1 ADJUSTING THE ESTIMATES

Adjustments may be used to deal with a variety of problems—item nonresponses, known defects in the collection procedures affecting one or both sources, errors in the sample frame, other sampling biases, and so on. Essentially, the PGE approach is a method of adjusting single system estimates of vital statistics to correct for the most common defect of collection—the failure to report many events at all. The desirability of this type of adjustment and its importance in evaluation are the major subject matter of this volume and require no additional elaboration here.[15] Some of the defects of PGE statistics, as well as those of single system estimates, can be removed or reduced by adjustments based on information obtained through the regular data collection effort, through field follow-up, or through some special methodological, experimental, or evaluative study. In addition, most adjustment procedures involve the use of assumptions about the population under study or the nature of reporting errors, or both.

On the other hand, one should avoid applying arbitrary adjustments to basic study estimates. Such adjustments, however well intentioned, can easily introduce larger errors than those in the original estimates and may expose the study managers to charges of "cooking" or "fudging" the data. Regardless of their nature, the very fact that arbitrary, or merely complex, adjustments are used at all may raise questions about the trustworthiness of study results. For example, more or less arbitrary adjustments introduced to convince potential study critics that the effects of likely sources of bias have been eliminated may be cited by the same critics as reasons for not trusting the results of the study. Rather than confounding the basic study estimates with essentially speculative adjustments, it would be better to introduce such adjustments in the technical and nontechnical portions of the study report dealing with data limitations.

One simple type of adjustment is that designed to correct for item nonresponse or other sources of omitted entries. Corrections for failure to report age are typical of this type of adjustment. For example, birth statistics can and should be published showing the number of births where the age of mother is not reported, and these may be paralleled by statistics showing the number of females in the base population for whom age was not reported. In computing age-specific fertility, one might omit births with mother's age not reported and females in the base population with unreported ages. Such a procedure would be acceptable if there were no other data available for estimating age and if at each age in the child-bearing years the proportion of omissions for recent mothers was approximately the same as it was for all women in the population.

However, the true age distribution of those not reporting age will be unknown and will often be quite different for mothers than it is for all women (or for decedents than it is for all persons). Over the past 30 years, an increasing number of national statistical offices have adjusted for failures to report age by "imputing" an age on the basis of other characteristics—marital status, age of spouse (if available), years of schooling, number of children living with the person, number of children ever born, and so on. The assumption is that a random assignment of age based on the distribution of reported ages in a specific group to which an individual belongs will be less biased than one based on the distribution for all persons reporting age.

Such adjustments for omitted entries are usually similar in principle to the adjustment for response correlation bias that involves making separate estimates for subgroups (see Chapter 3, Sections E and K). The effectiveness of the adjustment depends upon one's ability to identify subgroups of substantial size that do in fact differ markedly with respect to the biases considered. The desirability of this type of adjustment must also be weighed against costs and, when the subgroups are small, against the possibilities of ratio bias and increased variance.[16]

The effect of various types of biases and variances in sampling can be reduced by the use of ratio estimates or schemes for stratification after sampling (see Hansen, Hurwitz, and Madow, 1953). Adjustments designed to compensate for a biased sampling procedure usually involve an assumption that the fertility (or mortality) of the *sample* cases in population subgroup i is not very different from that for *all* cases in the subgroup. Since the adequacy of such an assumption can seldom be verified, adjustments based upon it are inevitably tainted. Moreover, intuition and common-sense judgments in this area often lead to incorrect decisions. There is a real danger that well-intentioned but naive "corrections" will introduce further error and confusion into the results. The only safe course if defects in the design or the implementation of the sample are discovered after data collection has begun is to consult an expert on the theory and practice of sampling. Adjustments, if any, to deal with sampling bias will then be based on a knowledgeable review of the seriousness of the problem and the methods recommended for dealing with it.

Errors in the data collection or processing operations of either source can also be reduced by using one or more adjustment factors. For example, in the Pakistan PGE study two kinds of adjustments of this nature were used. One compensated for the fact that the 12-month reference period used for gathering survey reports of vital events did not correspond exactly to the calendar year used for matching purposes. The other was used to counteract the effect of a presumed excess of erroneous nonmatches relative to erroneous matches (Population Growth Estimation, 1971, Chapter III). In general, such adjustments can be justified only when the nature of the error process involved is known and a reasonable estimate of its frequency and effect is available (for example, from field follow-up done in the current or previous matching rounds.)

Other adjustments may make use of known or presumed relationships between different substantive variables. These adjustments may range from those based on simple demographic patterns (for example, correcting the reported number of live births by imputing a sufficient number of births to bring an abnormal sex ratio at birth closer to the value usually observed [Cairo Demographic Centre, 1970]) to those based on more complex interrelationships between demographic variables (for example, see Coale and Zelnik, 1963; United Nations, 1967; and Brass *et al.*, 1968).

The division between demographic estimation and demographic analysis is not a definite one. Clearly, we do not suggest that it is never appropriate for the managers of a PGE study to make use of known demographic patterns in preparing adjusted estimates. However, the producer of demographic data should usually be hesitant to apply such adjustments.

There are a number of reasons for a policy of restraint in this regard. First, although data producers are in a unique position to develop adjustments based on field follow-up or other types of evaluative studies, they rarely have any special knowledge of the demographic processes on which analytical adjustments are based. Second, the time and skill needed to develop valid analytical adjustments may mean either delaying the publication of basic estimates or publishing estimates that incorporate ill-considered adjustments. Third, corrections made on the basis of one analytical procedure may not only be of limited value but may also preclude subsequent reanalysis using improved techniques. For example, the publication of a "smoothed" age distribution instead of the original age distribution will often destroy, or at least distort, a considerable amount of the substantive and methodological information. A policy of restraint in the use of analytical adjustments need not prevent the preparation and publication of estimates based on demographic analysis, although, as pointed out in Section D.3, this analytical work is often best done outside the PGE organization on a concurrent basis. We strongly caution that the senior staff of a PGE study should not become heavily involved in data analysis before the data gathering operations are functioning smoothly.

E.2   CHANGES IN PROCEDURES

In some cases the defects disclosed by evaluation can be properly corrected only by changes in study procedures. More frequently, at the same time that adjustments are applied to the data already collected, procedures for future data collection can be modified in an effort to make further adjustments unnecessary. The principles for deciding upon alterations in an ongoing study are essentially the same as those for planning a study, as discussed and illustrated in Chapters 3, 4, and 5. One should in fact view "study design" as a continuing process, not as something that ceases when data collection begins. Before data collection even starts, there must be a period of developing and testing procedures until an apparently workable design is achieved. At this point there will still be much that is unknown about accuracy and costs, and there is frequently a strong temptation to continue the developmental phase of the study in order to resolve these uncertainties. This temptation is often reinforced by an unwillingness to risk putting into the field a study that may require considerable future revision.

It is certainly unwise to put procedures that have not been subjected to some sort of testing into full-scale operation. One should have confidence that the procedures initially adopted will produce usable results without costing more than the available budget. On the other hand, there is no "perfect" procedure. Further tests will no doubt disclose inadequacies and, almost certainly, suggest possible improvements. The process of testing and developing improved procedures *can* go on indefinitely, and, indeed, it *should*—but not at the expense of postponing indefinitely the collection of data and the publication of usable results.

The solution to the need for further refinement of procedures and the need to produce useful results is to proceed with the study just as soon as workable techniques for data collection and matching exist *and* to develop improved procedures as one goes on. In general, it is wise to defer decisions on many features of a vital statistics system until evidence on costs and errors has accumulated from an actual operating system. Such evidence tends to be much more conclusive than that derived from a small-scale test. In particular, the introduction of some features that involve an increase in the total budget should often be deferred pending a demonstration of their value.

Given that some procedural changes over time are inevitable, PGE studies should be designed to provide for *orderly, periodic* change. On the other hand, overly frequent changes in procedures must be avoided. Field and office workers should be given sufficient experience with a procedure so that any initial roughness and uncertainty is "worked off." A procedure that seems awkward and unreliable initially may, with time, prove to be quite satisfactory. Conversely, a procedure that appears to give good results initially may, over time, encourage bad interviewing habits, provoke respondent resistance, or turn out to be based on a serious misinterpretation.

Although no fixed time period between changes is universally applicable, most procedures should be tried out for at least two survey rounds before changes are considered. Except for gross blunders in the design that require immediate correction, it is usually feasible and desirable to defer putting procedural changes into operation until enough of them have been accumulated—possibly once a year—to justify the cost of issuing new instructions and arranging training sessions. Although many changes will be so simple that they can be instituted without elaborate retraining of the personnel, all the personnel responsible for carrying out a procedure should be given an opportunity to raise questions about any points bothering them. An instruction that seems simple and unambiguous to the planners and supervisors may be totally incomprehensible or a source of utter confusion to most of the field staff.

Finally, changes in procedure should be carefully monitored during an initial period. This monitoring activity should be done primarily by the central office staff and should involve quantitative checks whenever possible because subjective impressions can be grossly misleading. Many reportedly "major" problems occur so infrequently and have such limited consequences that they can safely be ignored. On the other hand, many "trivial" problems occur so frequently that they become a major handicap to the project.

Another form of planned change is the rotation of sample clusters over time. Because of the expense of preparing maps, numbering houses, and developing contacts with the population, sample rotation should not be taken lightly or begun too quickly. Nevertheless, if the PGE study is to continue for more than three or four years, the need to keep up the morale of respondents and field workers, the sampling considerations, and the difficulty of maintaining independence with an unchanging set of sample areas all argue in favor of the use of some slow, systematic procedure for phasing out "old" sample areas and incorporating "new" areas into the study.

One argument quite justifiably used against frequent rotation of sample areas in PGE studies is that the resultant uncertainties about boundaries make increases in the reporting of out-of-scope reports more common. Uncertainties, ambiguities, and misunderstandings with respect to sample area boundaries have been an important source of out-of-scope reports and missed in-scope events in the past. These problems tend to diminish with time, as the understanding of the boundaries stabilizes and the grey area on both sides of the boundaries becomes narrower, but after a while further gains are trivial. For example, in the Pakistan PGE study the base population enumerated for the individual sample areas by the quarterly household survey fluctuated markedly during the first year or so of the study, reflecting initial uncertainty over boundaries. With time these fluctuations diminished, but even after four years of quarterly enumeration some uncertainty over boundaries remained.

Moreover, decreased uncertainty is not equivalent to increased accuracy. The PGE registrars in Pakistan and, with the passage of time, the enumerators also may have resolved doubts by excluding dwellings and households near the boundary. When out-of-scope vital events were erroneously included by only one of the two systems due to confusion about boundaries, field follow-up was usually able to detect this. When one system failed to report in-scope events near boundaries, often the other system rightly picked them up. However, it was rarely possible to detect cases where boundary questions were resolved identically, but wrongly, by both systems—that is, the omission by both systems of events inside the boundary or the probably rarer inclusion by both systems of events just outside the boundary.

E.3   THE REDESIGN OF A PGE STUDY

In most cases, careful design and step-by-step testing of procedures should produce a PGE study in which acceptable quality can be maintained by limited adjustments and procedural changes along the lines discussed in Sections E.1 and E.2. In some cases, initial mistakes in design may be so basic that no limited change will make any appreciable improvement. For example, an extended delay in implementing registration reforms or other difficulties might seriously affect the success of a PGE study that was designed on the assumption that the civil registration system would be a satisfactory source. A design optimized on the basis of one set of quality and cost assumptions may be quite unsatisfactory if these assumptions are no longer valid.

Similarly, a PGE study design based on the expectation that the supervisors of a special registration system could also constitute an independent, second data collection source may be found to be defective because the supervisors have given up all efforts at independent data gathering after a year of operation in a national sample. One way to deal with this problem might be to separate the supervisory and data gathering duties of the registration supervisors and hire separate personnel for each function, but such a change would mean additional costs. If additional funds were not forthcoming, the additional costs would have to be met by cutting costs in other parts of the study. Such cuts will almost always result in a study design that is less efficient (that is, produces lower accuracy for a given cost) than the initial design developed on the basis of a completely independent registration system and survey. Furthermore, the costs of retraining the study personnel may be almost as high as the original training costs and will still leave much of the staff with bad habits developed during their initial contacts with the project. Thus, if there is a major defect in the basic design of a PGE study, sometimes even the best that can be achieved through procedural changes may result in higher costs and poorer quality data than could be obtained by completely redesigning the study and using mostly new personnel. On the other hand, scrapping an ongoing study and starting afresh may involve substantial costs in terms of prestige and morale. In addition, laying off old personnel and hiring replacements is much simpler in nonbureaucratic theory than it is in bureaucratic reality.

The choice between attempting to correct design defects by procedural changes and correcting them by a new study design can be a very difficult one. However, the line between "extensive procedural modifications" and "a totally new design" is somewhat arbitrary. Frequently, the considerations involved are more "political" than "statistical" or "demographic." This is as it should be. A good study design must and should recognize political realities and be as meticulous in its handling of personnel and public relations as it is in the mathematics of sampling.

If a decision is made to start over again, the new design should be based on a reconsideration of the series of design choices originally presented in Chapter 3, an appraisal of the circumstances at hand, and an analysis of past experience. As appropriate, features of earlier studies should then be incorporated into the new study.

F. *Errors, Evaluation, and Publication Policy*

A legitimate dilemma arises as to the attitude a responsible statistician or statistical organization should have about the publication of results. On the one hand, the continual publication of many pages of data of poor quality, year after year, undermines confidence in the value of using statistics for decision making and research. For this reason, one might want to insist on a highly restrictive publication policy, publishing only those data for which all evaluation work has been completed and for which all doubts about quality and accuracy have been resolved. On the other hand, concern about evaluation and error can result in long publication delays if one insists that all possible sources of error be thoroughly examined before the study results are released. Such an objective, if too rigorously pursued, could end in the suppression of all statistical results, since absolute accuracy and certainty are unobtainable.

Whether or not administrators, planners, students, and other data users believe in the statistics they employ, they are required by the realities of public and academic life to find or make up large amounts of statistical data each year. Thus, unsophisticated producers and consumers of data, undeterred by concern or knowledge about error, will continue dealing with poor statistics regardless of the self-imposed embargoes on publication of the responsible data producer. Thus, a restrictive publication policy, however well motivated, may have the unintended consequence of giving free scope to poor data. And the wide circulation of such data, uncontradicted and unevaluated, may reinforce the naive belief that all statistical estimates are error-free, or the slightly less naive belief that all statistical estimates are worthless.

Overly restrictive publication policies have two further shortcomings. First, they invite the suppression of data for reasons of policy or administrative convenience, or because someone in a responsible position has irrationally rejected some aspect of the study results. A practice of promptly releasing data makes this type of suppression more difficult. Second, restrictive publication policies may delay methodological improvements and result in the costly repetition of mistakes. Only if statisticians and subject-matter specialists are clear about what was done and what was or was not achieved in earlier studies can they avoid the mistakes of the past and develop better procedures and designs in future studies.

In general, then, a rational publication policy should provide guidance primarily on *how, when, where,* and *in what form* basic results should be released, rather than on *whether* they should be published at all. Of course, a nonrestrictive policy does not mean that every available figure from each study must be released in published form. Here, as in other aspects of design, one must strike a balance between the costs and benefits of alternative courses of action. A large number of factors have to be considered in the formulation of a good publication policy, including the basic objectives of the study, the various ways in which the results will be used, the statistical sophistication of different kinds of data users, the anticipated quality of the data, and the existence and quality of other data on the topic being investigated. Moreover, though any publication policy must be developed within the context of administrative constraints (for example, costs and deadlines) and policy constraints (for example, unwillingness to publish data for "sensitive" topics such as ethnic group, mother tongue, or religion separately), these are not usually a major problem if the publication policy is agreed on before the substantive results of the study become available.

These general considerations apply equally to all types of social and economic statistics, including the demographic data supplied by a PGE study. The central objective of a PGE study will be either to produce estimates of the completeness of the vital statistics from the civil registration system or to produce basic estimates of population growth, fertility, and mortality. High priority should be given to the early and regular release of data that throw light on the core objectives of the PGE study, particularly if there is great uncertainty about the quality of the registration system or the levels of fertility and mortality. Lower priority should be given to estimates for population subgroups, analytical cross-tabulations involving variables other than age and sex, and the calculation of more refined demographic measures.

These recommendations as to priorities should be tempered by considerations of how the estimates will be used, who the users will be, and the availability of comparable demographic data for the same area. For example, unadjusted fertility or mortality estimates from either source in a dual collection system should not be released in advance of the PGE estimates without a thoughtful professional review of the situation. In general, unless such an estimate is noticeably different from those already available, advance publication will add little to knowledge about the population or to the understanding of the measurement problems involved.

One method of assuring a timely first release of data on fertility and mortality is to prepare and release a few estimates based on demographic analysis of the information collected in the first survey round. This approach is preferable to the publication of "quick count" estimates; that is, estimates based on cover sheet totals, telegraphic reports, unverified regional office summaries, or extrapolations from part-year data.

As soon as possible, estimates of sampling and nonsampling errors should be prepared and published with the basic estimates. The PGE estimates themselves are essentially demographic estimates adjusted to take into account the largest source of nonsampling error in most single systems—omission of in-scope births and deaths. Estimates of sampling error made by conventional methods as well as estimates of nonsampling error made using the PGE technique or other evaluation techniques are all subject to error. However, error estimates, even when the margins of error are relatively wide, are valuable to those using the data.

Unsophisticated users will also find such information helpful and instructive if the implications of the error estimates are clearly presented. Although technical appendices discussing in detail the limitations of the data are necessary, the text and tables of the basic report should also reflect known information on the shortcomings of the data. For example, tables may provide interval estimates in place of (or in addition to) point estimates; estimates from other sources can be presented for purposes of comparison; and table headnotes can contain a warning, such as "Estimates subject to substantial sampling and nonsampling error."

It is probably best to publish the comparable single source estimates unadjusted for omitted events along with the final PGE estimate. As Moser (1967, p. 143) has observed, "To many people, any adjusting or weighting of results denotes something shady and it is up to the researcher to allay such misgivings by a thorough explanation." Although it is unnecessary to show both estimates for every figure published (just as it is unnecessary to publish variance estimates for every statistic), one should try to be sure that some indication of the magnitude of the PGE adjustment is given somewhere in each report giving PGE results. The only problem that sometimes arises is that the proportion of events estimated as being in the "fourth category" may be wrongly used as a measure of the size of the PGE adjustment. As pointed out in Chapter 2, it is only the events in the "third category" and "fourth category" combined that fully reflects the contribution of the PGE procedure.

The tendency of users to ignore the cautions and qualifications that accompany statistical publications is a strong reason for publishing PGE estimates even when they may contain fairly large errors. Publication of the PGE estimates can usually be justified on the grounds that the figures are at least as good as any others available. Even where this is not the case, publication of PGE results will serve the useful function of forcing a reexamination of the statistics currently in use. For example, in 1968 a small PGE test was run in the Valdivia *comuna* of Chile (see Tacla, 1969, and Marks, 1970). This study showed a completeness rate of 80 percent for birth registration (with a standard error of 5.9 percent) and 85 percent for death registration (with a standard error of 8.1 percent). As noted by Marks (1970):

> There have been objections that the Valdivia results are based on a very small sample (a total of 214 births and 68 deaths were reported in the survey), are not representative of Chile as a whole, and are obtained by a biased methodology.

The point is not that the Valdivia results should be published because they offer a better estimate of birth and death rates than the civil registration statistics. They probably do *not,* but the publication of evaluative studies such as this one may stimulate a more critical attitude toward the existing vital statistics. Hopefully, this will lead to a more definitive study of civil registration completeness.

Insistence that the basic PGE estimates should be published in a form accessible to the general user does not mean that all the results should be published in this way. Many methodological studies can be published as technical articles in professional journals or in a technical series of the statistical office. Indeed, unless it is handled carefully, the inclusion of very detailed technical studies in the reports of substantive results can hamper the effective use of the basic PGE estimates by making these reports too bulky. What is very important is that the procedures and results of all methodological studies be preserved in such a manner that demographers and statisticians can refer to them in the future, and publication in some form is the best way of assuring this.

The dangers involved in preparing estimates for small or even moderate-sized population subgroups were discussed in Section K of Chapter 3. Despite initial good intentions, pressure may arise at the publication stage or even later to release subgroup estimates that are likely to have unacceptably large mean square errors. Two strategies are recommended for dealing with such pressures. The first is to adhere consistently to a predetermined set of publication standards. If each request is considered on an *ad hoc* basis, it is often difficult to say no. On the other hand, if all requests are examined in terms of a standard set of criteria, it is much easier for the statistical office to say that a particular table cannot be released and for the agency making the request to accept this decision. Second, if the pressure to release the data is impossible to resist (and one does not know this until one has first refused the request), one can present the required information in terms of an appropriate interval estimate using an estimated mean square error. It takes a very determined user to ignore the uncertainty of an estimate presented in the form "the chances are about 19 out of 20 that the crude birth rate of Little City in Minor Province lies somewhere between 22 and 58 per 1,000."

The words "release" and "publication" have been used somewhat interchangeably in this discussion, and intentionally so. It is an unwise and self-defeating policy to have one standard for publication and another for unofficially releasing data to users in and out of government. Either the subgroup estimates are usable and can be released, or they are subject to such large errors that the PGE study should avoid both preparing and releasing them. Of course, there are a number of instances when it is appropriate to release unpublished estimates. For example, particular subgroup estimates may be of such little general interest that publication is not warranted even though their quality is adequate for publication, or data may be released to particular users in advance of normal publication. However, in each of these situations the same quality standard is applied to both the published and unpublished estimates. Generally, requests for the release of data prior to their final publication are best handled by providing an advance publication format. In the long run, this leads to prompter and more widespread use of the study results than the *ad hoc* release of estimates to individual users. It also serves to reduce the errors and misunderstandings often associated with the informal release of data.

Even with a good publication policy, well-designed and well-labeled tables, and a text that deals adequately with data limitations, some users will ignore or evade the indicated qualifications to the data. This is no reason for abandoning interest in the production of data of high quality or in the preparation of reports that reflect high standards. Indeed, one should consider each published release of data from a PGE study both as answering specific needs for demographic data and as helping users to develop a more realistic attitude toward data and employ statistical information more effectively.

Footnotes

1. Errors affect all empirical data, and all scientific formulations must be compatible with the reality of measurement error. In this sense at least, the distinction between the "hard" data of natural sciences and the "soft" data of social sciences is arbitrary and misleading. For an introduction to the measurement problems in the natural sciences, see the U.S. National Bureau of Standards Series, *Precision Measurement and Calibration* (1969, Volume I).

2. It must be stressed that not all items listed actually result in errors in the study estimates, since the list includes known mistakes, reported problems, and suspicious indicators of problems. Upon investigation, a number of listed items may turn out to be based on false information. (For example, in the case of item 3 on the hypothetical list, careful investigation may reveal that the allegation was untrue and that the director of the regional office acted in a perfectly correct manner.) Or, they may prove to be of no consequence. (For example, in the case of item 5, a check of the sampling interval used may indicate that the first-stage units in the clipped pages were not excluded from the frame.)

3. Differential age misreporting in the numerator and denominator of age-specific rates has also been the source of significant distortions in mortality patterns in the United States (Hambright, 1969).

4. As used here, "bias" is the difference between the vital rate one is trying to estimate (the so called true value) and the average rate that would be obtained from a large number of hypothetical repetitions of the same measurement procedure carried out under the same general study conditions, whereas "variance" is a measure of the variability of the estimates over these repetitions. There is some arbitrariness in this division, since the repetitions are necessarily hypothetical and a phrase such as "the same general study conditions" may be interpreted in very different ways. Some of these issues are discussed in Chapter 3, Sections C and D, and in Hansen and Waksberg, 1970.

5. Such a situation can be invited when a prize is given for each proven case of an event not reported by the other system. Conceivably the prize could then be shared by the more "enterprising" field workers with the respondents, provided they did not reveal the event to the field workers of the other system.

6. As the discussion of matching errors in the previous chapters pointed out, erroneous matches and erroneous nonmatches arise from distinct, though related, problems. In general, the former can be considered as arising from the use of matching criteria that are too relaxed and the latter from errors (more accurately, variability) in the reporting and recording of identification information. Thus, although one type of matching error tends to decline as the other increases, this relationship is not perfectly symmetrical.

7. Problems with variations in the usage of multiple names (item A.3 in Figure 6.2) are particularly likely in Spanish-speaking areas where, in addition to the problems with given names common to other groups, there is variation in the use of the family names—father's family name, mother's family name, and husband's family name. Often the maternal family name is omitted or only the initial is used. In some countries, married women tend to use their husband's family name only for formal social occasions. Illegitimacy and common-law marriage increase the variation in family name usage. For example, a person whose parents were not formally married may use only his mother's family name, particularly if the mother did not live with the father when the person was a child. The reporting of names will also vary with the respondent. A son or daughter may give a different response from that given by the father or mother or a member of the father's or mother's family. A woman with the full name "Maria Rosario Hernandez Garcia de Sanchez" may have her given name reported as "Maria Rosario," "Maria R.," "Maria," "M. Rosario," or "Rosario" and her family name as "Hernandez Garcia de Sanchez" (rare), "Hernandez de Sanchez," "Hernandez Garcia," "Hernandez Sanchez," "Hernandez G." "Hernandez de S." "H. Sanchez," or "Sanchez." Some variants (for example, "Maria Rosario" vs. "Maria R." or "Rosario") permit an agreement on name *if* the matching procedures are set up properly, whereas others do not (for example, "Maria" vs. "Rosario").

8. Although ratio bias is presented here in terms of $1/w_1$, a comparable ratio bias affects $1/w_2$.

9. Actually, the relvariance of m will ordinarily be somewhat greater than $1/Em'$ because of intraclass correlation—that is, the tendency of the completeness rates to exhibit greater than binomial variation between clusters. However, the number of events reported per cluster is usually small enough so that the relvariance of m can be adequately approximated by $1/m'$.

10. Positive response correlation bias is a source of *downward* bias in the PGE estimates of vital rates or aggregates, which is equivalent to being a source of *upward* bias in the PGE estimate of completeness of reporting. Because positive response correlation was first identified as a potential source of bias in connection with civil registration completeness studies in North America, early references list it as an upward bias.

11. While the collection probabilities for events associated with early infant deaths are low, they tend to be even lower for stillbirths and other forms of fetal wastage. One would suspect, therefore, that factor B.2 would be a major source of error if an attempt were made to use the PGE approach to estimate stillbirths, abortions, and so on. Whether stratification procedures could be devised that would reduce the effect of this bias (see Chapter 3, Section E.2) remains to be investigated.

12. Using highly educated personnel in low-level field jobs may be as damaging as using poorly educated personnel. University graduates may accept work as interviewers not because they want to make survey work a career but merely because no work suited to their professional training and interests was available. Unless they are carefully supervised and motivated, overeducated interviewers and registrars may begin to cut corners and develop their own procedures, leading in extreme cases to fabrication of entire assignments. In addition, urban, university-trained personnel often do quite poorly in rural, traditional sample areas.

13. The degree to which the use of large blocking units increases the number of erroneous matches depends upon whether the characteristic used to form the blocking

unit is also used as one of the matching characteristics, the tolerance employed, and the accuracy of reporting for this characteristic.

14. More reliable estimates of correlation between two sources could be prepared on the basis of the results of a PGE study using three or more sources (see Chapter 7, Section D.1).

15. As we have pointed out at some length, dual system estimation has its own deficiencies, but it is our belief that they are less extreme and less erratic than those of single system estimation.

16. If this type of adjustment for omitted entries is not feasible or desirable, and if the proportion of omissions of data on age of mother for births differs from the proportion of omitted ages for all women, one should adjust age-specific rates to reflect the differential proportions with unknown ages in the numerator and the denominator. This can be done by multiplying the age-specific rates obtained from the reports with age recorded by a ratio equal to the percentage of all women with age recorded divided by the percentage of births with mother's age recorded. For example, if the omission rate for age among all women is 5 percent and that for birth reports is 15 percent, the total number of births with age reported should be multiplied by about 1.118 (that is, .95 ÷ .85) to obtain the age-specific birth rates adjusted for omissions in age. This adjustment assumes that the age-specific fertility rates for women with age unknown are identical to those for women whose age is known.

Special Topics 7

This chapter is divided into six sections, each dealing with a separate, unrelated topic. These topics were not covered in any detail in the earlier chapters either because they involve a novel idea insufficiently developed or tested, or because the detailed analysis involved in their presentation would have interrupted the flow of the main narrative.

Each section of this chapter is to be read independently of the others, and no effort has been made to standardize either the notation or the format within the chapter. Moreover, although we have tried to keep the notation clear, it departs in some sections from the notation used in the earlier chapters. Readers should therefore consult the notational definitions given in the individual sections, rather than relying on memory.

The topics covered are (A) variance derivations, (B) stratification, (C) subsampling, (D) unconventional design modifications, (E) institutional populations and other special population groups, and (F) independence. Sections A through D assume familiarity with basic sampling theory; Sections E and F do not.

A. Variances of PGE Estimates and Their Derivation

Section A provides formulae for the variances and estimated variances of PGE estimates. Although the basic model is based on a non-self-weighting cluster sample without stratification, the presentation also provides guidelines for self-weighting samples and stratified samples.

We assume that those using this section have had considerable prior experience with the theory of survey sampling applicable to complex, multistage designs. Indeed, those without this expertise may find much of the material difficult to use and open to misinterpretation. In any case, an expert in survey sampling should always be asked to review in advance the procedures (including tabulation plans and draft calculation sheets) proposed for use in any specific application of the theory presented in Section A.

The first of the eight parts of this section establishes the notation to be used throughout. In this section, as throughout the chapter, the notation is not necessarily consistent with the notation used earlier in the handbook. One notation used earlier and in this section is the use of capital letters (N, N_i, M, K, *etc.*) to refer to "population" (100-percent sample) values and lower-case letters (n, n_i, m, k, *etc.*) to refer to the corresponding sample values. The use of $\hat{n}$ for cases where both sources are covered by samples and $\hat{N}$ for cases where source 1 tries to cover the whole population (even though source 2 is a sample) involves a minor extension of this distinction between capital and lower-case symbols.

Some capitals and some lower-case letters (M, N_1, N_2, n, n_i, m, n_1, n_2, *etc.*) designate variables, whereas others (N, N_i, K, k, *etc.*) designate constants. The variables designated by capitals (M, N_1, N_2, N_{1i}, N_{2i}, M_i, *etc.*) are subject only to response variation, whereas the corresponding variables designated by small letters (m, n_1, n_2, n_{1i}, n_{2i}, m_i, *etc.*) involve sampling variation and, in some cases, response variation as well.

As usual, the notation $\Sigma_i^{k_1}$, $\Sigma_j^{N_i}$, etc. indicates the sum of k_1 values (for the k_1 areas in the source 1 sample) of whatever follows the summation sign or of N_i values (for the N_i vital events in population area i) of whatever follows the summation sign. The notation $\Sigma_{i \neq v}^{k_1}$ represents the sum of the $k_1 (k_1 - 1)$ values for which i is not equal to v. The notation $\doteq$ should be read as "is approximately equal to." For example, $A_i \doteq B_j$ indicates that A_i is approximately equal to B_j.

After the notation has been established in Section A.1, Sections A.2 through A.4 present derivations of the "true" variances of the PGE estimate $\hat{n}$ with sampling in both sources and the PGE estimate $\hat{N}$ using the entire population for one source, and a comparison of the two estimates. Section A.5 examines the effects on variances of correlations between the number of vital events in the sample area and the completeness of reporting. Sections A.6 through A.8 develop techniques for estimating variances from sample data, first for the general case, then for self-weighting samples, and finally for stratified samples.

A.1   NOTATION AND DEFINITIONS

The PGE estimate $\hat{n}$ involves sampling for both sources, usually where both sources try to cover all sample areas. In some cases, however, source 2 covers a subsample, k_2, of the k_1 areas covered by source 1. The general situation is, then, one in which source 1 covers k_1 areas and source 2 covers k_2 ($\leq k_1$) areas. For sample area i, there are n_i events (actual births or deaths), of which n_{1i} are reported in source 1 and n_{2i} are reported in source 2.

The estimate is

$$\hat{n} = \frac{n_1 n_2}{m} , \qquad\qquad [7.1]$$

where

$$n_1 = \frac{1}{k_1} \sum_i^{k_1} \frac{n_{1i}}{\pi_i} = \text{estimated number of vital events reported by source 1 for the universe,}$$

$$n_2 = \frac{1}{k_2} \sum_i^{k_2} \frac{n_{2i}}{\pi_i} = \text{estimated number of vital events reported by source 2 for the universe,}$$

$$m = \frac{1}{k_2} \sum_i^{k_2} \frac{m_i}{\pi_i} = \text{estimated number of vital events classified as matched for the universe,}$$

K = total number of sampling areas for the universe,

$$f_1 = \frac{k_1}{K} = \text{sampling rate for source 1,}$$

$$f_2 = \frac{k_2}{K} = \text{sampling rate for source 2,}$$

π_i = probability of selection for the ith area chosen for the sample, where i represents the order in which areas are selected (that is, $1 \leq i \leq k_1$ or k_2), and

Π_i = probability of area i in the universe being chosen on a given sample selection (that is, $1 \leq i \leq K$).

To clarify the distinction between π_i and Π_i, note that if the *third* area selected into the sample is "Area 7," whose selection probability is .04, then $\pi_3 = \Pi_7 = .04$. However, if the sample is self-weighting, then the π_i's and Π_i's are constants all equal to $1/K$. This is important to remember since it is assumed throughout the chapter that, where there is subsampling, each of the k_1 sample areas has an equal probability of being selected as one of the k_2 subsampling areas.

We also define, for use in Section A,

n_i = "true" number of vital events for sample area i—that is, the number of events that would be reported with complete reporting in the area;

$n \quad = \quad \dfrac{1}{k_1} \displaystyle\sum_{i}^{k_1} \dfrac{n_i}{\pi_i} \quad = \quad$ estimated "true" number of vital events for the universe with complete reporting;

$N_i \quad = \quad$ "true" number of vital events for area i in the universe;

$N \quad = \quad \displaystyle\sum_{i}^{K} N_i \qquad = \quad$ "true" number of vital events for the universe—that is, the value we are trying to estimate;

$N_{1i} \quad = \quad$ number of vital events that would be reported by source 1 for area i of the universe (if it were in the sample);

$N_1 \quad = \quad \displaystyle\sum_{i}^{K} N_{1i} \quad = \quad$ number of vital events that would be reported by source 1 in a 100-percent sample;

$N_{2i} \quad = \quad$ number of vital events that would be reported by source 2 for area i of the universe;

$N_2 \quad = \quad \displaystyle\sum_{i}^{K} N_{2i} \quad = \quad$ number of vital events that would be reported in source 2 in a 100-percent sample;

$M_i \quad = \quad$ number of vital events that would be classified as matched for area i of the universe;

$M \quad = \quad \displaystyle\sum_{i}^{K} M_i \qquad = \quad$ number of vital events that would be classified as matched in a 100-percent sample;

$P_{1ij} \quad = \quad$ probability of vital event j in area i of the universe being reported in source 1;

$P_{2ij} \quad = \quad$ probability of vital event j in area i of the universe being reported in source 2;

$P_{12ij} \quad = \quad$ probability of vital event j in area i of the universe being reported in both sources;

$P_{1i} \quad = \quad \dfrac{\displaystyle\sum_{j}^{N_i} P_{1ij}}{N_i} \quad = \quad$ average probability of vital events in area i of the universe being reported in source 1;

$$P_{2i} = \frac{\sum_{j}^{N_i} P_{2ij}}{N_i}$$ = average probability of vital events in area i of the universe being reported in source 2;

$$P_{12i} = \frac{\sum_{j}^{N_i} P_{12ij}}{N_i}$$ = average probability of vital events in area i of the universe being reported in both sources;

$$P_1 = \frac{\sum_{i}^{K} \sum_{j}^{N_i} P_{1ij}}{N} = \frac{\sum_{i}^{K} N_i P_{1i}}{N}$$ = probability of a vital event being reported in source 1;

$$P_2 = \frac{\sum_{i}^{K} \sum_{j}^{N_i} P_{2ij}}{N} = \frac{\sum_{i}^{K} N_i P_{2i}}{N}$$ = probability of a vital event being reported in source 2;

$$P_{12} = \frac{\sum_{i}^{K} \sum_{j}^{N_i} P_{12ij}}{N} = \frac{\sum_{i}^{K} N_i P_{12i}}{N}$$ = probability of a vital event being reported in both sources;

$$P_{1.2i} = \frac{P_{12i}}{P_{2i}}$$ = conditional probability that a vital event which is reported in source 2 in area i of the universe will also be reported in source 1;

$$P_{2.1i} = \frac{P_{12i}}{P_{1i}}$$ = conditional probability that a vital event which is reported in source 1 in area i of the universe will also be reported in source 2;

$$P_{1.2} = \frac{P_{12}}{P_2}$$ = conditional probability that a vital event which is reported in source 2 will also be reported in source 1;

$$P_{2.1} = \frac{P_{12}}{P_1}$$ = conditional probability that a vital event which is reported in source 1 will also be reported in source 2;

$$w_1 = \frac{m}{n_2}$$ = estimated completeness of source 1; and

$$w_2 \quad = \quad \frac{m}{n_1} \quad = \quad \text{estimated completeness of source 2.}$$

In the definitions of P_{12ij}, $P_{1.2i}$, $P_{1.2}$, etc., and later for m_{ij}, matching error is assumed to be zero for purposes of variance derivations. Matching error will have little or no effect on these variances and is allowed for in the variance estimates in Sections A.6 through A.8.

Based on the definitions given above, we can see that

$$En \quad = \quad E\left(\frac{n_i}{\pi_i}\right) = \sum_i^K \Pi_i \left(\frac{N_i}{\Pi_i}\right) = N \quad ;$$

$$En_1 \quad = \quad E\left(\frac{n_{1i}}{\pi_i}\right) = P_1 N = P_1 (En) \quad ;$$

$$En_2 \quad = \quad E\left(\frac{n_{2i}}{\pi_i}\right) = P_2 N = P_2 (En) \quad ; \text{and}$$

$$Em \quad = \quad E\left(\frac{m_i}{\pi_i}\right) = P_{12} N = P_{12} (En) \quad .$$

Thus,

$$E\hat{n} \quad \doteq \quad \frac{(En_1)(En_2)}{(Em)} = \left(\frac{P_1 P_2}{P_{12}}\right) N \quad .$$

The bias of $\hat{n}$ is

$$\beta \quad = \quad E\hat{n} - N \doteq \left(\frac{P_1 P_2 - P_{12}}{P_{12}}\right) N \quad , \qquad [7.2]$$

and the relative bias of $\hat{n}$ is

$$B \quad = \quad \frac{E\hat{n} - N}{N} \doteq \frac{P_1 P_2 - P_{12}}{P_{12}} \quad . \qquad [7.3]$$

A.2   VARIANCE WITH SAMPLING IN BOTH SOURCES ($\hat{n}$)

The relvariance (relative variance) can be separated into its components as follows:[1]

$$V_{\hat{n}}^2 \quad = \quad \frac{\sigma_{\hat{n}}^2}{(E\hat{n})^2} = V_{n_1}^2 + V_{n_2}^2 + V_m^2 + 2V_{n_1 n_2} - 2V_{n_1 m} - 2V_{n_2 m} \quad . \quad [7.4]$$

In order to estimate these components, we make use of the fact that the estimates n_1, n_2, and m are means of the sample values n_{1i}/π_i, n_{2i}/π_i, and m_i/π_i. For example, since

$$n_1^2 \quad = \quad \frac{\left(\sum_i^{k_1} \frac{n_{1i}}{\pi_i}\right)^2}{k_1^2} = \frac{\sum_i^{k_1} \left(\frac{n_{1i}}{\pi_i}\right)^2 + \sum_{i \neq v}^{k_1} \left(\frac{n_{1i}}{\pi_i}\right)\left(\frac{n_{1v}}{\pi_v}\right)}{k_1^2} \quad ,$$

then

$$E(n_1^2) \quad = \quad \frac{1}{k_1} E\left(\frac{n_{1i}}{\pi_i}\right)^2 + \frac{k_1 - 1}{k_1} E\left(\frac{n_{1i} n_{1v}}{\pi_i \pi_v}\right) \quad,$$

and, since $En_1 = E\left(\dfrac{n_{1i}}{\pi_i}\right)$,

$$\sigma_{n_1}^2 \quad = \quad E(n_1^2) - E(n_1)^2 = \frac{1}{k_1} E\left(\frac{n_{1i}}{\pi_i}\right)^2$$

$$+ \; E\left(\frac{n_{1i} n_{1v}}{\pi_i \pi_v}\right) - \frac{1}{k_1} E\left(\frac{n_{1i} n_{1v}}{\pi_i \pi_v}\right) - \left(E\frac{n_{1i}}{\pi_i}\right)^2 \quad .$$

For sampling with replacement,

$$E\left(\frac{n_{1i} n_{1v}}{\pi_i \pi_v}\right) \quad = \quad \left(E\frac{n_{1i}}{\pi_i}\right)\left(E\frac{n_{1v}}{\pi_v}\right) = \left(E\frac{n_{1i}}{\pi_i}\right)^2 \quad,$$

so that

$$\sigma_{n_1}^2 \quad = \quad \frac{1}{k_1}\left[E\left(\frac{n_{1i}}{\pi_i}\right)^2 - \left(E\frac{n_{1i}}{\pi_i}\right)^2\right] \quad,$$

and,

$$V_{n_1}^2 \quad = \quad \frac{\sigma_{(n_{1i}/\pi_i)}^2}{k_1\left(E\dfrac{n_{1i}}{\pi_i}\right)^2} = \frac{1}{k_1} V_{(n_{1i}/\pi_i)}^2 \quad . \qquad [7.5]$$

In a similar manner,

$$V_{n_2}^2 \quad = \quad \frac{1}{k_2} V_{(n_{2i}/\pi_i)}^2 \quad \text{and} \qquad\qquad [7.6]$$

$$V_m^2 \quad = \quad \frac{1}{k_2} V_{(m_i/\pi_i)}^2 \quad . \qquad\qquad [7.7]$$

To evaluate the covariances, starting with $n_1 m$, we note that

$$n_1 m \quad = \quad \frac{\left(\sum\limits_i^{k_1} \dfrac{n_{1i}}{\pi_i}\right)\left(\sum\limits_i^{k_2} \dfrac{m_i}{\pi_i}\right)}{k_1 k_2} = \frac{\sum\limits_i^{k_2} \dfrac{n_{1i} m_i}{\pi_i^2} + \sum\limits_{i\neq v}^{k_1 k_2 - k_2} \dfrac{n_{1i} m_v}{\pi_i \pi_v}}{k_1 k_2} \quad .$$

Thus,

$$E(n_1 m) \quad = \quad \frac{1}{k_1} E\left(\frac{n_{1i} m_i}{\pi_i^2}\right) + \frac{k_1 - 1}{k_1} E\left(\frac{n_{1i} m_v}{\pi_i \pi_v}\right) \quad,$$

and, for sampling with replacement,

$$E\left(\frac{n_{1i}m_v}{\pi_i\pi_v}\right) \ = \ \left(E\frac{n_{1i}}{\pi_i}\right)\left(E\frac{m_v}{\pi_v}\right) = (En_1)(Em) \quad.$$

By definition,

$$\sigma_{n_1 m} \ = \ E(n_1 m) - (En_1)(Em) \quad,$$

so that, for sampling with replacement,

$$\sigma_{n_1 m} \ = \ \frac{1}{k_1}\left[E\left(\frac{n_{1i}m_i}{\pi_i^2}\right) - \left(E\frac{n_{1i}}{\pi_i}\right)\left(E\frac{m_i}{\pi_i}\right)\right] \quad,$$

and

$$V_{n_1 m} \ = \ \frac{\sigma_{n_1 m}}{(En_1)(Em)} = \frac{1}{k_1}V_{(n_{1i}/\pi_i)(m_i/\pi_i)} \quad. \qquad [7.8]$$

Similarly,

$$V_{n_1 n_2} \ = \ \frac{1}{k_1}V_{(n_{1i}/\pi_i)(n_{2i}/\pi_i)} \qquad\qquad [7.9]$$

and

$$V_{n_2 m} \ = \ \frac{1}{k_2}V_{(n_{2i}/\pi_i)(m_i/\pi_i)} \quad. \qquad\qquad [7.10]$$

Substituting the values of equations 7.5 through 7.10 into equation 7.4, we have, for the general case of sampling with replacement,

$$V_{\hat{n}}^2 \ = \ \frac{1}{k_1}\left[V_{(n_{1i}/\pi_i)}^2 + 2V_{(n_{1i}/\pi_i)(n_{2i}/\pi_i)} - 2V_{(n_{1i}/\pi_i)(m_i/\pi_i)}\right]$$

$$+ \ \frac{1}{k_2}\left[V_{(n_{2i}/\pi_i)}^2 + V_{(m_i/\pi_i)}^2 - 2V_{(n_{2i}/\pi_i)(m_i/\pi_i)}\right] \quad. \qquad [7.11]$$

If the sample is self-weighting, with $\pi_i = 1/K$, we can obtain a somewhat simpler formula:

$$V_{(n_{1i}/\pi_i)}^2 \ = \ \frac{\sigma_{(n_{1i}/\pi_i)}^2}{\left(E\dfrac{n_{1i}}{\pi_i}\right)^2} = \frac{K^2\sigma_{n_{1i}}^2}{K^2(En_{1i})^2} = V_{n_{1i}}^2 \quad.$$

$$V_{(n_{1i}/\pi_i)(m_i/\pi_i)} \ = \ \frac{\sigma_{(n_{1i}/\pi_i)(m_i/\pi_i)}}{\left(E\dfrac{n_{1i}}{\pi_i}\right)\left(E\dfrac{m_i}{\pi_i}\right)} = \frac{K^2\sigma_{n_{1i}m_i}}{K^2(En_{1i})(Em_i)} = V_{n_{1i}m_i} \quad,$$

and similar expressions hold for the other variances and covariances. Thus, for $\pi_i = 1/K$ and sampling with replacement,

$$V_{\hat{n}}^2 \ = \ \frac{1}{k_1}\left[V_{n_{1i}}^2 + 2V_{n_{1i}n_{2i}} - 2V_{n_{1i}m_i}\right] + \frac{1}{k_2}\left[V_{n_{2i}}^2 + V_{m_i}^2 - 2V_{n_{2i}m_i}\right] \quad. \qquad [7.12]$$

For many, if not most purposes (including all general analytic uses), it is appropriate to consider the sample as being selected from an "infinite population." In this case, the formulas given above for sampling with replacement apply. A discussion of this issue appears in Deming, 1950, Chapter 7. To deal with sampling without replacement—the usual case in PGE studies—it is desirable to consider the individual sample elements composing sample area i. These can be defined either as persons or as events. With persons as the elements, a death can be considered to be a characteristic that takes the value 1 if the person dies during the period, zero if the person does not. Similarly, a birth is a characteristic with the value 1 if the person (the mother) gives birth to a live baby during the period, zero if she does not. At this point, however, it will be more convenient to consider our "elements" to be events, and

n_{1ij} $\quad$ = 1 if event j in area i is reported in source 1;

n_{1ij} $\quad$ = zero if event ij is not reported in source 1;

n_{2ij} $\quad$ = 1 if event ij is reported in source 2;

n_{2ij} $\quad$ = zero if event ij is not reported in source 2;

m_{ij} $\quad$ = 1 if event ij is reported in both sources; and

m_{ij} $\quad$ = zero if event ij is not reported in both sources.

Then

$$n_{1i} = \sum_{j}^{n_i} n_{1ij} \; ,$$

$$n_{2i} = \sum_{j}^{n_i} n_{2ij} \; , \text{and}$$

$$m_i = \sum_{j}^{n_i} m_{ij} \; .$$

Also,

$$\sum_{j}^{n_i} n_{1ij}^2 = \sum_{j}^{n_i} n_{1ij} = n_{1i} \; ,$$

$$\sum_{j}^{n_i} n_{2ij}^2 = \sum_{j}^{n_i} n_{2ij} = n_{2i} \; ,$$

$$\sum_{j}^{n_i} m_{ij}^2 = \sum_{j}^{n_i} m_{ij} = m_i \; , \text{and}$$

$$\sum_j^{n_i} n_{1ij} n_{2ij} \quad = \sum_j^{n_i} m_{ij} n_{1ij} = \sum_j^{n_i} m_{ij} n_{2ij} = \sum_j^{n_i} m_{ij} = m_i \quad .$$

We can divide the variances and covariances of equation 7.4 into two parts, one of which will include a "finite multiplier"—either $(1 - f_1)$ or $(1 - f_2)$—to account for the effect of sampling without replacement. To do this, we shall consider for simplicity a self-weighting sample containing a fixed number of events, n. For the case of a self-weighting sample with a variable number of events, the term V_n^2 must be added to the formulas for the relative variances and covariances $V_{n_1}^2$, $V_{n_2}^2$, V_m^2, and $V_{n_1 n_2}$. We also make use of the relationships developed in the discussion of sampling with replacement,

$$\sigma_{n_1}^2 \quad = \quad En_1^2 - (En_1)^2 = \frac{K^2}{k_1} En_{1i}^2 + \frac{K^2 (k_1 - 1)}{k_1} E(n_{1i} n_{1v}) - K^2 (En_{1i})^2$$

For the various expected values, we have

$$En_{1i} \quad = \quad \frac{\sum_i^K E(n_{1i} | i)}{K} \quad ,$$

where

$$E(n_{1i} | i) \quad = \quad \sum_j^{N_i} En_{1ij} = \text{expected value of } n_{1i} \text{ conditional upon } i\text{—that is, conditional upon the selection of a particular sample area—}$$

and

$$En_{1ij} \quad = \quad P_{1ij} \quad .$$

Thus,

$$En_{1i} \quad = \quad \frac{\sum_i^K \sum_j^{N_i} P_{1ij}}{K} = \frac{P_1 N}{K} = P_1 \bar{N} \quad ,$$

where

$$\bar{N} \quad = \quad \frac{N}{K} = \frac{1}{K} \sum_i^K N_i \quad .$$

Also,

$$En_{1i}^2 \quad = \quad \frac{\sum_i^K E(n_{1i}^2 | i)}{K} \quad ,$$

with

$$E(n_{1i}^2 \mid i) \quad = \sum_j^{N_i} E n_{1ij}^2 + \sum_{j \neq w}^{N_i} E(n_{1ij} n_{1iw})$$

$$= \sum_j^{N_i} P_{1ij} + \sum_{j \neq w}^{N_i} P_{1ij} P_{1iw} = \sum_j^{N_i} P_{1ij} + \left(\sum_j^{N_i} P_{1ij} \right)^2 - \sum_j^{N_i} P_{1ij}^2 \quad ,$$

so that

$$E n_{1i}^2 \quad = \frac{\displaystyle\sum_i^K \sum_j^{N_i} P_{1ij}(1 - P_{1ij})}{K} + \frac{\displaystyle\sum_i^K P_{1i}^2 N_i^2}{K} \quad ;$$

and

$$E(n_{1i} n_{1v}) \quad = \frac{\displaystyle\sum_{i \neq v}^K E(n_{1i} n_{1v} \mid i, v)}{K(K-1)}$$

$$= \frac{\displaystyle\sum_{i \neq v}^K P_{1i} N_i P_{1v} N_v}{K(K-1)} = \frac{\left(\displaystyle\sum_i^K P_{1i} N_i \right)^2 - \displaystyle\sum_i^K P_{1i}^2 N_i^2}{K(K-1)} \quad .$$

Thus,

$$\sigma_{n_1}^2 = \frac{K}{k_1} \sum_i^K \sum_j^{N_i} P_{1ij}(1 - P_{1ij})$$

$$+ \left(\frac{K}{k_1} \right) \left(\frac{K - k_1}{K - 1} \right) \sum_i^K P_{1i}^2 N_i^2 - \frac{K - k_1}{k_1(K-1)} \left(\sum_i^K P_{1i} N_i \right)^2 \quad ,$$

or, for sampling without replacement, and taking $\dfrac{K}{K-1} \doteq 1$,

$$\sigma_{n_1}^2 = \frac{K}{k_1} \left[\sum_i^K \sum_j^{N_i} P_{1ij}(1 - P_{1ij}) + (1 - f_1) \sum_i^K (P_{1i} N_i - P_1 \bar{N})^2 \right] \quad . \qquad [7.13]$$

Similarly, it can be shown that

$$\sigma_{n_2}^2 = \frac{K}{k_2} \left[\sum_i^K \sum_j^{N_i} P_{2ij}(1 - P_{2ij}) + (1 - f_2) \sum_i^K (P_{2i} N_i - P_2 \bar{N})^2 \right] \quad , \qquad [7.14]$$

and

$$\sigma_m^2 = \frac{K}{k_2} \left[\sum_i^K \sum_j^{N_i} P_{12ij}(1 - P_{12ij}) + (1 - f_2) \sum_i^K (P_{12i} N_i - P_{12} \bar{N})^2 \right] \quad . \qquad [7.15]$$

For the covariances, we have, starting with $\sigma_{n_1 m}$,

$$\sigma_{n_1 m} \quad = \frac{K^2}{k_1} E(n_{1i} m_i) + \frac{K^2 (k_1 - 1)}{k_1} E(n_{1i} m_v) - K^2 (E n_{1i})(E m_i) \quad .$$

$$E(n_{1i} m_i) = \frac{\sum_i^K E(n_{1i} m_i | i)}{K} \quad,$$

with

$$E(n_{1i} m_i | i) = \sum_j^{N_i} E(n_{1ij} m_{ij}) + \sum_{j \neq w}^{N_i} E(n_{1ij} m_{iw}) = \sum_j^{N_i} P_{12ij} + \sum_{j \neq w}^{N_i} P_{1ij} P_{12iw}$$

$$= \sum_j^{N_i} P_{12ij} + \left(\sum_j^{N_i} P_{1ij} \right) \left(\sum_j^{N_i} P_{12ij} \right) - \sum_j^{N_i} P_{1ij} P_{12ij} \quad;$$

and

$$E(n_{1i} m_v) = \frac{\sum_{i \neq v}^K E(n_{1i} m_v | i, v)}{K(K-1)} = \frac{\sum_{i \neq v}^K P_{1i} N_i P_{12v} N_v}{K(K-1)}$$

$$= \frac{\left(\sum_i^K P_{1i} N_i \right) \left(\sum_i^K P_{12i} N_i \right) - \sum_i^K P_{1i} P_{12i} N_i^2}{K(K-1)} \quad,$$

so that

$$\sigma_{n_1 m} = \frac{K}{k_1} \sum_i^K \sum_j^{N_i} P_{12ij} (1 - P_{1ij}) + \left(\frac{K}{k_1} \right) \left(\frac{K - k_1}{K - 1} \right) \sum_i^K P_{1i} P_{12i} N_i^2$$

$$- \frac{K - k_1}{k_1 (K - 1)} \left(\sum_i^K P_{1i} N_i \right) \left(\sum_i^K P_{12i} N_i \right) \quad,$$

or,

$$\sigma_{n_1 m} = \frac{K}{k_1} \left[\sum_i^K \sum_j^{N_i} P_{12ij} (1 - P_{1ij}) \right.$$

$$\left. + (1 - f_1) \sum_i^K (P_{12i} N_i - P_{12} \bar{N})(P_{1i} N_i - P_1 \bar{N}) \right] \quad. \qquad [7.16]$$

Similarly,

$$\sigma_{n_2 m} = \frac{K}{k_2} \left[\sum_i^K \sum_j^{N_i} P_{12ij} (1 - P_{2ij}) \right.$$

$$\left. + (1 - f_2) \sum_i^K (P_{12i} N_i - P_{12} \bar{N})(P_{2i} N_i - P_2 \bar{N}) \right] \quad. \qquad [7.17]$$

For $\sigma_{n_1 n_2}$, we have

$$\sigma_{n_1 n_2} = \frac{K^2}{k_1} E(n_{1i} n_{2i}) + \frac{K^2 (k_1 - 1)}{k_1} E(n_{1i} n_{2v}) - K^2 (En_{1i})(En_{2i}) \quad.$$

$$E(n_{1i} n_{2i}) = \frac{\sum_i^K E(n_{1i} n_{2i} | i)}{K} ,$$

with

$$E(n_{1i} n_{2i} | i) = \sum_j^{N_i} E(n_{1ij} n_{2ij}) + \sum_{j \neq w}^{N_i} E(n_{1ij} n_{2iw})$$

$$= \sum_j^{N_i} P_{12ij} + \left(\sum_j^{N_i} P_{1ij} \right) \left(\sum_j^{N_i} P_{2ij} \right) - \sum_j^{N_i} P_{1ij} P_{2ij} ,$$

so that

$$E(n_{1i} n_{2i}) = \frac{\sum_i^K \sum_j^{N_i} (P_{12ij} - P_{1ij} P_{2ij})}{K} + \frac{\sum_i^K P_{1i} P_{2i} N_i^2}{K} .$$

Also,

$$E(n_{1i} n_{2v}) = \frac{\sum_{i \neq v}^K P_{1i} N_i P_{2v} N_v}{K(K-1)} = \frac{\left(\sum_i^K P_{1i} N_i \right) \left(\sum_i^K P_{2i} N_i \right) - \sum_i^K P_{1i} P_{2i} N_i^2}{K(K-1)} .$$

Thus,

$$\sigma_{n_1 n_2} = \frac{K}{k_1} \left[\sum_i^K \sum_j^{N_i} (P_{12ij} - P_{1ij} P_{2ij}) \right.$$

$$\left. + (1 - f_1) \sum_i^K (P_{1i} N_i - P_1 \bar{N})(P_{2i} N_i - P_2 \bar{N}) \right] . \qquad [7.18]$$

In equations 7.13 through 7.18, the first term represents the effects of response variance or covariance *within* sample areas, and the second term represents the effects of variance or covariance *between* sample areas. Only the second term has the "finite multiplier," $(1 - f_1)$ or $(1 - f_2)$, since replacement of areas in sample selection has no effect on the variances and covariances within sample areas. The relative variances and covariances for sampling with replacement shown in equation 7.12 can be separated into within-area and between-area components which are identical with those of equations 7.13 through 7.18, except that the finite multiplier is omitted from the second term.

Although PGE sampling will almost necessarily be without replacement, the finite multiplier can usually be ignored and the variance formula for sampling with replacement of equation 7.12 used. That is, the sample rate f_1 is usually small (less than .02) and $f_2 \leq f_1$, so that $(1 - f_1)$ and $(1 - f_2)$ are usually close to 1.0. An exception is the case of PGE estimates of $\hat{N}$ in Section A.3 below, where

$f_1 = 1$. (For more detailed guidelines, see Hansen, Hurwitz, and Madow, 1953, p. 123.)

More precisely, the response variances and covariances in the first terms of equations 7.13 through 7.18 represent the variation *within individual events*. Since each source takes only one observation per vital event, the response variances are somewhat smaller than those which would be obtained without this restriction—that is, when the sample might include two or more observations for the same event by a given source. Algebraically, the relationships are

$$\sum_i^K \sum_j^{N_i} P_{1ij}(1 - P_{1ij}) \quad = \quad P_1(1 - P_1)N - \sum_i^K \sum_j^{N_i} (P_{1ij} - P_1)^2 \quad,$$

$$\sum_i^K \sum_j^{N_i} P_{2ij}(1 - P_{2ij}) \quad = \quad P_2(1 - P_2)N - \sum_i^K \sum_j^{N_i} (P_{2ij} - P_2)^2 \quad,$$

and

$$\sum_i^K \sum_j^{N_i} P_{12ij}(1 - P_{12ij}) \quad = \quad P_{12}(1 - P_{12})N - \sum_i^K \sum_j^{N_i} (P_{12ij} - P_{12})^2 \quad.$$

Similar relations obtain for the "response covariances":

$$\sum_i^K \sum_j^{N_i} P_{12ij}(1 - P_{1ij}) \quad = \quad P_{12}(1 - P_1)N - \sum_i^K \sum_j^{N_i} (P_{12ij} - P_{12})(P_{1ij} - P_1) \quad,$$

$$\sum_i^K \sum_j^{N_i} P_{12ij}(1 - P_{2ij}) \quad = \quad P_{12}(1 - P_2)N - \sum_i^K \sum_j^{N_i} (P_{12ij} - P_{12})(P_{2ij} - P_2) \quad,$$

and

$$\sum_i^K \sum_j^{N_i} (P_{12ij} - P_{1ij}P_{2ij}) \quad = \quad (P_{12} - P_1P_2)N - \sum_i^K \sum_j^{N_i} (P_{1ij} - P_1)(P_{2ij} - P_2) \quad.$$

The first term on the right is the variance or covariance of a sample of N observations, and the second term is the error involved in using this variance or covariance as an approximation to that for a sample of N events with one observation per event. Since the second term represents a sum of squared differences (or a sum of a product of differences) between two probabilities of the same order of magnitude, it will be small relative to the first term. For some purposes, the between-person variances and covariances are not negligible; but for others, such as that of comparing $V_{\hat{n}}^2$ with V_N^2, the approximations above will be quite satisfactory; that is, one can use $P_1(1 - P_1)N$ for

$$\sum_i^K \sum_j^{N_i} P_{1ij}(1 - P_{1ij}),$$

and so on.

Before we deal with the variances of $\hat{N}$, it is desirable to introduce a useful simplification of equations 7.4 and 7.12. We can write

$$m \quad = \quad w_2 n_1 = w_1 n_2 \quad ,$$

$$mn_1 \quad = \quad w_2 n_1^2 \quad , \text{and}$$

$$mn_2 \quad = \quad w_1 n_2^2 \quad .$$

Usually, $w_2 = m/n_1$ will be independent of n_1, and $w_1 = m/n_2$ will be independent of n_2. (But see Section 7.5 for cases for which this is not so.) Thus,

$$Em \quad = \quad (Ew_2)(En_1) = (Ew_1)(En_2) \quad ,$$

$$\sigma_{mn_1} \quad = \quad E(mn_1) - (Em)(En_1) = E(w_2 n_1^2) - E(w_2 n_1)(En_1)$$

$$= \quad (Ew_2)(En_1^2) - (Ew_2)(En_1)^2 = (Ew_2)\sigma_{n_1}^2 \quad ,$$

and

$$V_{mn_1} \quad = \quad \frac{\sigma_{mn_1}}{(Em)(En_1)} = \frac{(Ew_2)\sigma_{n_1}^2}{(Ew_2)(En_1)^2} = V_{n_1}^2 \quad . \qquad [7.19]$$

Similarly,

$$\sigma_{mn_2} \quad = \quad (Ew_1)(En_2^2) - (Ew_1)(En_2)^2 = (Ew_1)\sigma_{n_2}^2 \quad , \text{and}$$

$$V_{mn_2} \quad = \quad \frac{\sigma_{mn_2}}{(Em)(En_2)} = \frac{(Ew_1)\sigma_{n_2}^2}{(Ew_1)(En_2)^2} = V_{n_2}^2 \quad . \qquad [7.20]$$

This gives

$$V_{\hat{n}}^2 = 2V_{n_1 n_2} - V_{n_1}^2 + V_m^2 - V_{n_2}^2 \quad , \qquad [7.21]$$

or, for self-weighting samples in terms of n_{1i}, n_{2i}, and m_i,

$$V_{\hat{n}}^2 = \frac{1}{k_1}(2V_{n_{1i} n_{2i}} - V_{n_{1i}}^2) + \frac{1}{k_2}(V_{m_i}^2 - V_{n_{2i}}^2) \quad . \qquad [7.22]$$

A.3   VARIANCE WITH SAMPLING IN SOURCE 2 ONLY ($\hat{N}$)

The PGE estimate $\hat{N}$ involves a one-way match of the events reported by source 2 for the sample against the entire file of source 1 events for the universe. The estimate is

$$\hat{N} \quad = \quad \frac{N_1 n_2}{m} \quad , \qquad [7.23]$$

where (according to the definition in Section A.1)

$$N_1 \quad = \quad \sum_i^K N_{1i} \quad = \quad \text{number of events reported in source 1 in a 100-percent sample,}$$

$$N_{1i} \quad = \quad \text{number of events reported in source 1 for area } i \text{ of the universe,}$$

and n_2 and m are defined as in the derivation of the variance of $\hat{n}$. The equations

$$E\hat{N} \;=\; \frac{(EN_1)(En_2)}{(Em)} \;\;,$$

and

$$EN_1 \;=\; P_1 N = En_1$$

are analogous to the equations in Section A.2. As before,

$$En_2 \;=\; P_2 N \;\;,$$

and

$$Em \;=\; P_{12} N \;\;,$$

so that

$$E\hat{N} \;=\; \frac{P_1 P_2 N}{P_{12}} = E\hat{n} \;\;.$$

For the components of the variance of $\hat{N}$, we have

$$V_{\hat{N}}^2 = V_{N_1}^2 + V_{n_2}^2 + V_m^2 + 2 V_{N_1 n_2} - 2 V_{N_1 m} - 2 V_{n_2 m} \;\;. \tag{7.24}$$

In the following discussion, we shall assume that the sample areas were drawn from the universe with equal probability, $\Pi_i \equiv 1/K$, which is often the case. Assuming $\Pi_i \equiv 1/K$ also simplifies the variance estimation, since in this case the sampling design is a special case of a self-weighting sample of $k_1 = K$ areas covered by source 1 and k_2 areas subsampled from the k_1 areas with equal probability.

The expressions for the variances and covariances are analogous to those in equations 7.13 through 7.18 for the variance of $\hat{n}$ in a self-weighting sample selected without replacement. The factor $(1 - f_1)$ is equal to zero and, since f_2 is almost always small, $(1 - f_2)$ will be approximately 1. Thus, we have

$$V_{\hat{N}}^2 \;=\; \frac{1}{K} \left[V_{N_{1i}}^2 + 2 V_{N_{1i} n_{2i}} - 2 V_{N_{1i} m_i} \right] + \frac{1}{k_2} \left[V_{n_{2i}}^2 + V_{m_i}^2 - 2 V_{n_{2i} m_i} \right] \;\;, \tag{7.25}$$

where

$$V_{N_{1i}}^2 \;=\; \frac{\sigma_{N_{1i}}^2}{(EN_{1i})^2} = \frac{\displaystyle\sum_i^K \sum_j^{N_i} P_{1ij}(1 - P_{1ij})}{K P_1^2 \bar{N}^2} \;\;, \tag{7.26}$$

$$V_{N_{1i} n_{2i}} \;=\; \frac{\sigma_{N_{1i} n_{2i}}}{(EN_{1i})(En_{2i})} = \frac{\displaystyle\sum_i^K \sum_j^{N_i} (P_{12ij} - P_{1ij} P_{2ij})}{K P_1 P_2 \bar{N}^2} \;\;, \tag{7.27}$$

$$V_{N_{1i} m_i} \;=\; \frac{\sigma_{N_{1i} m_i}}{(EN_{1i})(Em_i)} = \frac{\displaystyle\sum_i^K \sum_j^{N_i} P_{12ij}(1 - P_{1ij})}{K P_1 P_{12} \bar{N}^2} \;\;, \tag{7.28}$$

$$V_{n_{2i}}^2 \quad = \quad \frac{\sigma_{n_{2i}}^2}{(En_{2i})^2} = \frac{\sum\limits_{i}^{K}\sum\limits_{j}^{N_i} P_{2ij}(1 - P_{2ij}) + \sum\limits_{i}^{K}(P_{2i}N_i - P_2\bar{N})^2}{K P_2^2 \bar{N}^2} \quad , \qquad [7.29]$$

$$V_{m_i}^2 \quad = \quad \frac{\sigma_{m_i}^2}{(Em_i)^2} = \frac{\sum\limits_{i}^{K}\sum\limits_{j}^{N_i} P_{12ij}(1 - P_{12ij}) + \sum\limits_{i}^{K}(P_{12i}N_i - P_{12}\bar{N})^2}{K P_{12}^2 \bar{N}^2} \quad , \qquad [7.30]$$

and

$$V_{n_{2i}m_i} \quad = \quad \frac{\sigma_{n_{2i}m_i}}{(En_{2i})(Em_i)}$$

$$= \quad \frac{\sum\limits_{i}^{K}\sum\limits_{j}^{N_i} P_{12ij}(1 - P_{2ij}) + \sum\limits_{i}^{K}(P_{2i}N_i - P_2\bar{N})(P_{12i}N_i - P_{12}\bar{N})}{K P_2 P_{12} \bar{N}^2} \quad . \qquad [7.31]$$

To derive forms of $V_{\bar{N}}^2$ analogous to those of $V_{\bar{n}}^2$ in equations 7.21 and 7.22, we assume that $w_2 = m/N_1$ is independent of N_1 and that $w_1 = m/n_2$ is independent of n_2. Thus, using the same reasoning as in deriving equations 7.19 and 7.20,

$$V_{N_1 m} \quad = \quad V_{N_1}^2 \quad ,$$

and

$$V_{n_2 m} \quad = \quad V_{n_2}^2 \quad ,$$

so that

$$V_{\bar{N}}^2 \quad = \quad 2V_{N_1 n_2} - V_{N_1}^2 + V_m^2 - V_{n_2}^2 \quad , \qquad [7.32]$$

or,

$$V_{\bar{N}}^2 \quad = \quad \frac{1}{K}(2V_{N_{1i}n_{2i}} - V_{N_i}^2) + \frac{1}{k_2}(V_{m_i}^2 - V_{n_{2i}}^2) \quad . \qquad [7.33]$$

If we use the approximation $P_1(1 - P_1) N$ for $\Sigma_i^K \Sigma_j^{N_i} P_{1ij}(1 - P_{1ij})$ in $V_{N_1}^2$ and $(P_{12} - P_1 P_2) N$ for $\Sigma_i^K \Sigma_j^{N_i}(P_{12ij} - P_{1ij}P_{2ij})$ in $V_{N_1 n_2}$, we get

$$V_{N_1}^2 \quad \doteq \quad \frac{1 - P_1}{P_1 N} = \frac{1}{P_1 N} - \frac{1}{N} \quad , \qquad [7.34]$$

and

$$V_{N_1 n_2} \quad \doteq \quad \frac{P_{12} - P_1 P_2}{P_1 P_2 N} = \frac{P_{12}}{N P_1 P_2} - \frac{1}{N} \quad . \qquad [7.35]$$

Thus,

$$2V_{N_1 n_2} - V_{N_1}^2 \quad = \quad \frac{2P_{12} - P_1 P_2 - P_2}{N P_1 P_2} \quad ,$$

and

$$V_{\hat{N}}^2 \qquad\qquad = \quad V_m^2 - V_{n_2}^2 + \frac{2P_{12} - P_1 P_2 - P_2}{N P_1 P_2} \quad , \qquad\qquad [7.36]$$

or,

$$V_{\hat{N}}^2 \qquad\qquad = \quad \frac{1}{k_2}(V_{m_i}^2 - V_{n_{2i}}^2) + \frac{2P_{12} - P_1 P_2 - P_2}{N P_1 P_2} \quad . \qquad [7.37]$$

A.4 A COMPARISON OF $V_{\hat{n}}^2$ AND $V_{\hat{N}}^2$

It is useful to compare the relvariance of $\hat{N}$ with that of the corresponding estimate $\hat{n}$, which is obtained by using two-way matching in the k_2 sample areas covered by source 2. That is, we consider $\hat{n}$ for

$$k_1 \quad = \quad k_2 = k \quad ,$$

$$n_1 \quad = \quad \frac{K}{k}\sum_i^k n_{1i} \quad ,$$

$$n_2 \quad = \quad \frac{K}{k}\sum_i^k n_{2i} \quad ,$$

$$m \quad = \quad \frac{K}{k}\sum_i^k m_i \quad , \text{and}$$

$$\hat{n} \quad = \quad \frac{n_1 n_2}{m} \quad .$$

In comparing $V_{\hat{N}}^2$ and $V_{\hat{n}}^2$, it is desirable to separate the response variance from the variance of n, where

$$n \qquad = \quad \frac{K}{k}\sum_i^k n_i \quad = \quad \text{estimate of the true number of vital events } N \text{ based on the } k \text{ sample areas only.}$$

To make this separation, we define the (unknown) sample statistics

$$p_1 \qquad = \quad \frac{n_1}{n} \qquad = \quad \text{estimated proportion of vital events reported in source 1—that is, the estimate of } P_1,$$

$$p_2 \qquad = \quad \frac{n_2}{n} \qquad = \quad \text{estimate of } P_2, \text{ the proportion of vital events reported in source 2, and}$$

$$p_{12} \qquad = \quad \frac{m}{n} \qquad = \quad \text{estimate of } P_{12}, \text{ the proportion of vital events reported in both sources.}$$

Since n is usually independent of p_1, p_2, and p_{12}, we have

$$V_m^2 \qquad = \quad V_{p_{12}}^2 + V_n^2 \quad , \qquad\qquad\qquad\qquad [7.38]$$

$$V^2_{n_1} \quad = \quad V^2_{p_1} + V^2_n \quad , \qquad\qquad\qquad\qquad [7.39]$$

$$V^2_{n_2} \quad = \quad V^2_{p_2} + V^2_n \quad , \text{and} \qquad\qquad\qquad [7.40]$$

$$V_{n_1 n_2} \quad = \quad V_{p_1 p_2} + V^2_{,n} \quad . \qquad\qquad\qquad\quad [7.41]$$

From equations 7.21 and 7.38 through 7.41, we obtain

$$V^2_{\hat{n}} \quad = \quad V^2_{p_{12}} - V^2_{p_2} + 2 V_{p_1 p_2} - V^2_{p_1} + V^2_n \quad . \qquad [7.42]$$

From equations 7.36, 7.38, and 7.40, we obtain

$$V^2_{\hat{N}} \quad = \quad V^2_{p_{12}} - V^2_{p_2} + \frac{2 P_{12} - P_1 P_2 - P_2}{N P_1 P_2} \quad . \qquad [7.43]$$

Note that equation 7.43 does not involve V^2_n at all. In general, the relvariance of n will be considerably greater than the response error variance, so that one would expect $V^2_{\hat{n}}$ to be larger than $V^2_{\hat{N}}$. We can indicate the extent of this difference more precisely if we assume no intraclass correlation and a self-weighting sample. With a self-weighting sample,

$$\pi_i \quad = \quad \frac{1}{K} \quad ,$$

$$f \quad = \quad \frac{k}{K} \quad ,$$

$$n \quad = \quad \frac{\sum\limits_i^k n_i}{f} \quad ,$$

$$n_1 \quad = \quad \frac{\sum\limits_i^k n_{1i}}{f} \quad ,$$

$$n_2 \quad = \quad \frac{\sum\limits_i^k n_{2i}}{f} \quad , \text{and}$$

$$m \quad = \quad \frac{\sum\limits_i^k m_i}{f} \quad .$$

If there is no intraclass correlation, we can consider p_1, p_2, and p_{12} as based on a sample of $fn = \Sigma^k_i n_i$ cases[2] selected at random from the entire N. Thus,

$$V^2_{p_1} \quad \doteq \quad \frac{1 - P_1}{f(En) P_1} = \frac{1 - P_1}{fN P_1} \quad ,$$

$$V_{p_2}^2 \doteq \frac{1 - P_2}{f(En)P_2} = \frac{1 - P_2}{fNP_2} \quad,$$

$$V_{p_{12}}^2 \doteq \frac{1 - P_{12}}{f(En)P_{12}} = \frac{1 - P_{12}}{fNP_{12}} \quad, \text{ and}$$

$$V_{p_1 p_2} \doteq \frac{P_{12} - P_1 P_2}{f(En)P_1 P_2} = \frac{P_{12} - P_1 P_2}{fNP_1 P_2} \quad.$$

Consequently,

$$V_{\hat{n}}^2 \doteq \frac{1}{fN}\left(\frac{1}{P_{12}} - \frac{1}{P_1} - \frac{1}{P_2} + \frac{2P_{12}}{P_1 P_2} - 1\right) + V_n^2 \quad, \tag{7.44}$$

and

$$V_{\hat{N}}^2 \doteq \frac{1}{fN}\left(\frac{1}{P_{12}} - \frac{1}{P_2}\right) + \frac{2P_{12} - P_1 P_2 - P_2}{NP_1 P_2} \quad, \tag{7.45}$$

so that

$$V_{\hat{n}}^2 - V_{\hat{N}}^2 \doteq V_n^2 - \frac{(1 - f)(P_2 + P_1 P_2 - 2P_{12})}{fNP_1 P_2} \quad. \tag{7.46}$$

If the reporting is independent between sources with $P_{12} = P_1 P_2$, then[3]

$$V_{\hat{n}}^2 - V_{\hat{N}}^2 \doteq V_n^2 - \frac{(1 - f)(1 - P_1)}{fNP_1} \quad. \tag{7.47}$$

As noted above, the sample elements can be considered to be persons or events. The variances and covariances of p_1, p_2, and p_{12} can be estimated—upon the assumption of independence between them and n—more easily in terms of a fixed sample of events. However, since n is actually a random variable, in determining its variance it is preferable to consider a sample of persons where the occurrence of an event is a binomial characteristic of the persons, having a probability equal to the vital rate. This probability is small ($<.06$), so that, for the large sample of persons used in PGE studies, the number of sample events fn is very nearly a Poisson variate, with

$$V_n^2 = V_{fn}^2 \doteq \frac{1}{f(En)} = \frac{1}{fN} \quad.$$

The effect of sampling areas rather than sampling individual persons (or households) is to increase V_n^2 and, since $(1 - f)$ is usually quite near 1 (usually f will be less than .02), it is reasonable to assume that, for independence between sources,

$$V_{\hat{n}}^2 - V_{\hat{N}}^2 \doteq \frac{1}{fN} - \frac{1 - P_1}{fNP_1} = \frac{1}{fN}\left(2 - \frac{1}{P_1}\right) \quad. \tag{7.48}$$

If P_1 is greater than about .5, $V_{\hat{n}}^2$ will be greater than $V_{\hat{N}}^2$. Thus, the use of N_1 for an entire civil register will be preferable to estimating N_1 from a sample, unless the completeness of the civil register is less than about 50 percent.

A.5 EFFECTS OF CORRELATION BETWEEN THE SIZE OF SAMPLE AREA AND THE COMPLETENESS OF REPORTING

Equations 7.19 and 7.20 assume that the ratio estimates w_1, w_2, p_1, p_2, and p_{12} are independent of their denominators (n_2, n_1, and n). This will usually be true or very nearly true—that is, there will usually be a zero or very small correlation between the ratios and their denominators. However, it is possible for the sampling units to be defined in such a way that correlations exist. For example, the sample areas with high death rates and, consequently, high values of n_{1i}, n_{2i}, and n_i may tend to have lower than average completeness rates $P_{1.2i}$, $P_{2.1i}$, P_{1i}, P_{2i}, and P_{12i}. The result will be a negative correlation between the ratio estimates and their denominators. For example, the assumption of independence enables us in equation 7.19 to use the relationship

$$\sigma_{mn_1} = Ew_2 n_1^2 - (Ew_2 n_1)(En_1) = (Ew_2)\sigma_{n_1}^2 = P_{2.1}\sigma_{n_1}^2 \quad,$$

which relies on the fact that, for fixed n_1,

$$E(m|n_1) = E(w_2 n_1|n_1) = n_1 E(w_2|n_1) \text{ and}$$

$$E(mn_1|n_1) = E(w_2 n_1^2|n_1) = n_1^2 E(w_2|n_1)$$

and assumes that, for *all* n_1,

$$E(w_2|n_1) \equiv Ew_2 = P_{2.1} \quad.$$

We may, however, have a situation where completeness of reporting tends to be worse in larger areas than in smaller areas or *vice versa*. Where reporting completeness is worse in the larger areas, then for high values of n_1, w_2 will tend to be smaller than $P_{2.1}$ and m will tend to be less than $(n_1 P_{2.1})$; whereas for low values of n_1, w_2 will tend to be greater than $P_{2.1}$ and m will tend to be greater than $(n_1 P_{2.1})$. In general, the effect of negative correlation of w_2 with n_1 and n_1^2, and of w_1 with n_2 and n_2^2, is such that

$$V_{mn_1} < V_{n_1}^2 \text{ and}$$

$$V_{mn_2} < V_{n_2}^2 \quad.$$

As a result, $V_{\hat{n}}^2$ will be underestimated by equation 7.21; also, the reverse will be true where reporting completeness tends to be worse in the smaller areas.

Similar correlation effects can be observed in the estimation of other percentages—for example, where a sample of households is used to estimate the proportion of the population employed. If the proportion of persons employed is the same for large households as it is for small households, there will be no correlation between the proportion and its denominator, so that the relvariance of the proportion x/y (where x equals the number of persons employed and y equals the number of persons in the sample) will be

$$V_{x/y}^2 = V_x^2 + V_y^2 - 2V_{xy} = V_x^2 - V_y^2 \quad .$$

However, larger families may contain more children and, therefore, a smaller proportion of employed persons, so that a negative correlation will exist between the proportion and its denominator. This, in turn, means that $V_{xy} < V_y^2$, and thus the relvariance of the proportion x/y will be greater than $(V_x^2 - V_y^2)$.

A.6   ESTIMATING VARIANCES FROM SAMPLE DATA

To estimate the variances of $\hat{n}$ and $\hat{N}$ from the data available in a PGE study, we can start with equations 7.4 and 7.24, which can be written as

$$\sigma_{\hat{n}}^2 = (E\hat{n})^2 \left[\frac{\sigma_{n_1}^2}{(En_1)^2} + \frac{\sigma_{n_2}^2}{(En_2)^2} + \frac{\sigma_m^2}{(Em)^2} + \frac{2\sigma_{n_1 n_2}}{(En_1)(En_2)} \right.$$
$$\left. - \frac{2\sigma_{n_1 m}}{(En_1)(Em)} - \frac{2\sigma_{n_2 m}}{(En_2)(Em)} \right] \quad , \text{and} \qquad [7.49]$$

$$\sigma_{\hat{N}}^2 = (E\hat{N})^2 \left[\frac{\sigma_{N_1}^2}{(EN_1)^2} + \frac{\sigma_{n_2}^2}{(En_2)^2} + \frac{\sigma_m^2}{(Em)^2} + \frac{2\sigma_{N_1 n_2}}{(EN_1)(En_2)} \right.$$
$$\left. - \frac{2\sigma_{N_1 m}}{(EN_1)(Em)} - \frac{2\sigma_{n_2 m}}{(En_2)(Em)} \right] \quad . \qquad [7.50]$$

We use $\hat{n}$, m, n_1, n_2, $\hat{N}$, and N_1, as estimates of their respective expected values.

We can illustrate the derivation of variance and covariance estimates by taking n_1 as an example. We assume sampling with replacement and let

$$x_i = \frac{n_{1i}}{\pi_i} \quad , \text{and}$$

$$\bar{x} = \frac{1}{k_1} \sum_i^{k_1} x_i = n_1 \quad .$$

Then

$$E\bar{x} = \frac{1}{k_1} \sum_i^{k_1} Ex_i = Ex_i \quad ,$$

and

$$E(\bar{x}^2) = \frac{1}{k_1^2} \sum_i^{k_1} E(x_i^2) + \frac{1}{k_1^2} \sum_{i \neq v}^{k_1} E(x_i x_v) = \frac{1}{k_1} E(x_i^2) + \frac{k_1 - 1}{k_1} E(x_i x_v) \quad .$$

For sampling with replacement,

$$E(x_i x_v) = (Ex_i)^2 \quad ,$$

so that

$$\sigma_{\bar{x}}^2 = E(\bar{x}^2) - (E\bar{x})^2 = \frac{1}{k_1}\left[E(x_i^2) - E(x_i x_v) \right] \quad . \qquad [7.51]$$

Since $(\Sigma_i^{k_1} x_i^2)/k_1$ is an unbiased estimate of Ex_i^2 and $(\Sigma_{i \neq v}^{k_1} x_i x_v)/k_1(k_1 - 1)$ is an unbiased estimate of $E(x_i x_v)$, we have, for an unbiased estimate of $\sigma_{\bar{x}}^2$,

$$
\begin{aligned}
s_{\bar{x}}^2 &= \frac{1}{k_1^2}\sum_i^{k_1} x_i^2 - \frac{1}{k_1^2(k_1 - 1)}\sum_{i \neq v}^{k_1} x_i x_v \\
&= \frac{\displaystyle\sum_i^{k_1} x_i^2}{k_1^2} - \frac{\left(\displaystyle\sum_i^{k_1} x_i\right)^2 - \displaystyle\sum_i^{k_1} x_i^2}{k_1^2(k_1 - 1)} = \frac{\displaystyle\sum_i^{k_1}(x_i - \bar{x})^2}{k_1(k_1 - 1)} \quad . \qquad [7.52]
\end{aligned}
$$

Substituting n_1 for $\bar{x}$ and n_{1i}/π_i for x_i,

$$s_{n_1}^2 = \frac{\displaystyle\sum_i^{k_1}\left(\frac{n_{1i}}{\pi_i} - n_1\right)^2}{k_1(k_1 - 1)} \quad . \qquad [7.53]$$

Similarly, it can be shown that

$$s_{n_2}^2 = \frac{\displaystyle\sum_i^{k_2}\left(\frac{n_{2i}}{\pi_i} - n_2\right)^2}{k_2(k_2 - 1)} \quad , \text{ and} \qquad [7.54]$$

$$s_m^2 = \frac{\displaystyle\sum_i^{k_2}\left(\frac{m_i}{\pi_i} - m\right)^2}{k_2(k_2 - 1)} \quad . \qquad [7.55]$$

For estimates of the covariances, we use the previous definitions of x_i, $\bar{x}$, and $E\bar{x}$, and let

$$n_1' = \frac{1}{k_2}\sum_i^{k_2}\left(\frac{n_{1i}}{\pi_i}\right) \quad ,$$

$$\bar{\bar{x}} = \frac{1}{k_2}\sum_i^{k_2} x_i = n_1' \quad ,$$

$$y_i = \frac{n_{2i}}{\pi_i} \quad ,$$

$$\bar{y} = \frac{1}{k_2}\sum_i^{k_2} y_i = n_2 \quad .$$

Then

$$E\bar{y} \quad = \quad Ey_i \quad \text{and}$$

using the same reasoning as in equation 7.52, it can be shown that

$$\sigma_{\bar{x}\bar{y}} = E(\bar{x}\bar{y}) - (E\bar{x})(E\bar{y}) = \frac{1}{k_1}\left[E(x_i y_i) - E(x_i y_v)\right] \quad , \qquad [7.56]$$

and that

$$s_{\bar{x}\bar{y}} = \frac{\displaystyle\sum_i^{k_2}(x_i y_i)}{k_1 k_2} - \frac{\displaystyle\sum_{i\neq v}^{k_2}(x_i y_v)}{k_1 k_2 (k_2 - 1)}$$

$$= \frac{\displaystyle\sum_i^{k_2}(x_i y_i)}{k_1 (k_2 - 1)} - \frac{k_2 \bar{\bar{x}}\bar{y}}{k_1 (k_2 - 1)} = \frac{\displaystyle\sum_i^{k_2}(x_i - \bar{\bar{x}})(y_i - \bar{y})}{k_1 (k_2 - 1)} \qquad [7.57]$$

is an unbiased estimate of $\sigma_{\bar{x}\bar{y}}$. Note that for $k_1 = k_2$, $\bar{\bar{x}} = \bar{x}$ and $n_1' = n_1$.

Substituting the appropriate variables in equation 7.57, we have

$$s_{n_1 n_2} \quad = \quad \frac{\displaystyle\sum_i^{k_2}\left(\frac{n_{1i}}{\pi_i} - n_1'\right)\left(\frac{n_{2i}}{\pi_i} - n_2\right)}{k_1 (k_2 - 1)} \quad , \qquad [7.58]$$

$$s_{n_1 m} \quad = \quad \frac{\displaystyle\sum_i^{k_2}\left(\frac{n_{1i}}{\pi_i} - n_1'\right)\left(\frac{m_i}{\pi_i} - m\right)}{k_1 (k_2 - 1)} \quad , \text{ and} \qquad [7.59]$$

$$s_{n_2 m} \quad = \quad \frac{\displaystyle\sum_i^{k_2}\left(\frac{n_{2i}}{\pi_i} - n_2\right)\left(\frac{m_i}{\pi_i} - m\right)}{k_2 (k_2 - 1)} \quad . \qquad [7.60]$$

We are now in a position to estimate $V_{\hat{n}}^2$ which is equivalent to

$$\frac{s_{\hat{n}}^2}{\hat{n}^2} = \frac{s_{n_1}^2}{n_1^2} + \frac{s_{n_2}^2}{n_2^2} + \frac{s_m^2}{m^2} + \frac{2s_{n_1 n_2}}{n_1 n_2} - \frac{2s_{n_1 m}}{n_1 m} - \frac{2s_{n_2 m}}{n_2 m} \quad , \qquad [7.61]$$

using equations 7.53, 7.54, 7.55, 7.58, 7.59, and 7.60 to find the estimated variances and covariances.

To estimate $V_{\hat{N}}^2$, we need estimates of $V_{N_1}^2$, $V_{N_1 n_2}$, and $V_{N_1 m}$. Equations 7.53, 7.58, and 7.59 cannot be used, because, with one-way matching, the values of n_{1i} for the individual sample areas are not determined. We can, however, estimate $V_{N_1}^2$ by substituting N_1 for its expected value, $P_1 N$, in equation 7.34 and using $w_1 = m/n_2$ as an estimate of P_1. This gives us

$$v_{N_1}^2 = \frac{1 - w_1}{N_1} \quad . \qquad [7.62]$$

It should be noted that the use of w_1 to estimate P_1 in equation 7.62 assumes independence between collection systems (that is, that $P_{12} = P_1 P_2$). This means that $V_{N_1 n_2} = 0$, which is, of course, the value obtained by using w_1 for P_1, m for $P_{12} N$, and n_2 for $P_2 N$ in equation 7.35.

Substituting $v_{N_1 n_2} = 0$ and the values from equations 7.54, 7.55, and 7.62 in equation 7.32 gives us

$$v_{\hat{N}}^2 = \frac{s_m^2}{m^2} - \frac{s_{n_2}^2}{n_2^2} - \frac{1 - w_1}{N_1} \quad . \qquad [7.63]$$

A.7 VARIANCE ESTIMATES FOR SELF-WEIGHTING SAMPLES

With self-weighting samples, we can simplify the calculations somewhat. Since $\pi_i = 1/K$, we have

$$n_1 = \frac{K \sum_i^{k_1} n_{1i}}{k_1} \quad ,$$

$$n_2 = \frac{K \sum_i^{k_2} n_{2i}}{k_2} \quad ,$$

$$m = \frac{K \sum_i^{k_2} m_i}{k_2} \quad ,$$

$$n = \frac{K \sum_i^{k_1} n_i}{k_1} \quad , \text{and}$$

$$n_1' = \frac{K \sum_i^{k_2} n_{1i}}{k_2} \quad .$$

We also define

$$\bar{n} = \frac{\sum_i^{k_1} n_i}{k_1} = \frac{n}{K} \quad ,$$

$$\bar{n}_1 = \frac{\sum_i^{k_1} n_{1i}}{k_1} = \frac{n_1}{K} \quad ,$$

$$\bar{n}_2 \quad = \frac{\sum_i^{k_2} n_{2i}}{k_2} = \frac{n_2}{K} \quad,$$

$$\bar{m} \quad = \frac{\sum_i^{k_2} m_i}{k_2} = \frac{m}{K} \quad, \text{ and}$$

$$\bar{n}_1' \quad = \frac{\sum_i^{k_2} n_{1i}}{k_2} = \frac{n_1'}{K} \quad.$$

Consequently, the estimates of the individual variances would be

$$s_{n_1}^2 \quad = \frac{K^2}{k_1} s_{n_{1i}}^2 \quad, \tag{7.64}$$

$$s_{n_2}^2 \quad = \frac{K^2}{k_2} s_{n_{2i}}^2 \quad, \tag{7.65}$$

$$s_m^2 \quad = \frac{K^2}{k_2} s_{m_i}^2 \quad, \tag{7.66}$$

$$s_{n_1 n_2} \quad = \frac{K^2}{k_1} s_{n_{1i} n_{2i}} \quad, \tag{7.67}$$

$$s_{n_1 m} \quad = \frac{K^2}{k_1} s_{n_{1i} m_i} \quad, \text{ and} \tag{7.68}$$

$$s_{n_2 m} \quad = \frac{K^2}{k_2} s_{n_{2i} m_i} \quad, \tag{7.69}$$

where

$$s_{n_{1i}}^2 \quad = \frac{\sum_i^{k_1} (n_{1i} - \bar{n}_1)^2}{k_1 - 1} \quad, \tag{7.70}$$

$$s_{n_{2i}}^2 \quad = \frac{\sum_i^{k_2} (n_{2i} - \bar{n}_2)^2}{k_2 - 1} \quad, \tag{7.71}$$

$$s_{m_i}^2 \quad = \frac{\sum_i^{k_2} (m_i - \bar{m})^2}{k_2 - 1} \quad, \tag{7.72}$$

$$s_{n_{1i} n_{2i}} \quad = \frac{1}{k_2 - 1} \sum_i^{k_2} (n_{1i} - \bar{n}_1')(n_{2i} - \bar{n}_2) \quad, \tag{7.73}$$

$$s_{n_{1i}m_i} = \frac{1}{k_2 - 1} \sum_i^{k_2} (n_{1i} - \bar{n}_1')(m_i - \bar{m}) \quad \text{, and} \qquad [7.74]$$

$$s_{n_{2i}m_i} = \frac{1}{k_2 - 1} \sum_i^{k_2} (n_{2i} - \bar{n}_2)(m_i - \bar{m}) \quad . \qquad [7.75]$$

This gives

$$s_{\hat{n}}^2 = \frac{\hat{n}^2}{k_1} \left[\frac{s_{n_{1i}}^2}{\bar{n}_1^2} + \frac{2 s_{n_{1i}n_{2i}}}{\bar{n}_1 \bar{n}_2} - \frac{2 s_{n_{1i}m_i}}{\bar{n}_1 \bar{m}} \right] + \frac{\hat{n}^2}{k_2} \left[\frac{s_{n_{2i}}^2}{\bar{n}_2^2} + \frac{s_{m_i}^2}{\bar{m}^2} - \frac{2 s_{n_{2i}m_i}}{\bar{n}_2 \bar{m}} \right] \quad . \qquad [7.76]$$

The variance of $\hat{N}$ corresponding to equation 7.63 is

$$s_{\hat{N}}^2 = \frac{\hat{N}^2}{k_2} \left[\frac{s_{m_i}^2}{\bar{m}^2} - \frac{s_{n_{2i}}^2}{\bar{n}_2^2} \right] - \frac{\hat{N}^2 (1 - w_1)}{N_1} \quad . \qquad [7.77]$$

A.8 VARIANCE ESTIMATES FOR STRATIFIED SAMPLES

The formulae presented thus far in section A apply when all k_1 sampling units are drawn from a single stratum. Modification of the variance estimation formulae to fit stratified sampling is fairly straightforward. We assume sampling with replacement and no subsampling, and let

π_{hi} = probability of a given area being selected as sample area i in stratum h,

n_{1hi} = number of vital events reported by source 1 for sample area i of stratum h,

n_{2hi} = number of vital events reported by source 2 for sample area i of stratum h,

m_{hi} = number of vital events classified as matched for sample area i of stratum h, and

k_h = number of sample areas from stratum h.

For stratum h, we have the following estimates of numbers of events reported in source 1, reported in source 2, and classified as matched:

$$n_{1h} = \frac{1}{k_h} \sum_i^{k_h} \frac{n_{1hi}}{\pi_{hi}} \quad ,$$

$$n_{2h} = \frac{1}{k_h} \sum_i^{k_h} \frac{n_{2hi}}{\pi_{hi}} \quad \text{, and}$$

$$m_h = \frac{1}{k_h} \sum_i^{k_h} \frac{m_{hi}}{\pi_{hi}} \quad .$$

For the entire universe of L strata, the corresponding estimates are

$$n_1 \quad = \sum_h^L n_{1h} \quad = \sum_h^L \frac{1}{k_h} \sum_i^{k_h} \frac{n_{1hi}}{\pi_{hi}} \quad , \qquad [7.78]$$

$$n_2 \quad = \sum_h^L n_{2h} \quad = \sum_h^L \frac{1}{k_h} \sum_i^{k_h} \frac{n_{2hi}}{\pi_{hi}} \quad , \text{ and} \qquad [7.79]$$

$$m \quad = \sum_h^L m_h \quad = \sum_h^L \frac{1}{k_h} \sum_i^{k_h} \frac{m_{hi}}{\pi_{hi}} \quad . \qquad [7.80]$$

Thus, corresponding to equations 7.53, 7.54, 7.55, 7.58, 7.59, and 7.60, we have the estimates

$$s_{n_1}^2 \quad = \sum_h^L \frac{1}{k_h(k_h-1)} \sum_i^{k_h} \left(\frac{n_{1hi}}{\pi_{hi}} - n_{1h} \right)^2 \quad , \qquad [7.81]$$

$$s_{n_2}^2 \quad = \sum_h^L \frac{1}{k_h(k_h-1)} \sum_i^{k_h} \left(\frac{n_{2hi}}{\pi_{hi}} - n_{2h} \right)^2 \quad , \qquad [7.82]$$

$$s_m^2 \quad = \sum_h^L \frac{1}{k_h(k_h-1)} \sum_i^{k_h} \left(\frac{m_{hi}}{\pi_{hi}} - m_h \right)^2 \quad , \qquad [7.83]$$

$$s_{n_1 n_2} \quad = \sum_h^L \frac{1}{k_h(k_h-1)} \sum_i^{k_h} \left(\frac{n_{1hi}}{\pi_{hi}} - n_{1h} \right)\left(\frac{n_{2hi}}{\pi_{hi}} - n_{2h} \right) \quad , \qquad [7.84]$$

$$s_{n_1 m} \quad = \sum_h^L \frac{1}{k_h(k_h-1)} \sum_i^{k_h} \left(\frac{n_{1hi}}{\pi_{hi}} - n_{1h} \right)\left(\frac{m_{hi}}{\pi_{hi}} - m_h \right) \quad , \text{ and} \qquad [7.85]$$

$$s_{n_2 m} \quad = \sum_h^L \frac{1}{k_h(k_h-1)} \sum_i^{k_h} \left(\frac{n_{2hi}}{\pi_{hi}} - n_{2h} \right)\left(\frac{m_{hi}}{\pi_{hi}} - m_h \right) \quad . \qquad [7.86]$$

These values and those of n_1, n_2, and m can be substituted directly into equation 7.61 to give $v_{\hat{n}}^2$.

With self-weighting stratified samples, we have the sampling fraction $f \equiv k_h \pi_{hi}$ and

$$n_1 \quad = \frac{1}{f} \sum_h^L \sum_i^{k_h} n_{1hi} \quad ,$$

$$n_2 \quad = \frac{1}{f} \sum_h^L \sum_i^{k_h} n_{2hi} \quad , \text{ and}$$

$$m \quad = \frac{1}{f} \sum_h^L \sum_i^{k_h} m_{hi} \quad .$$

Thus, for the variance estimates, we have

$$s_{n_1}^2 \quad = \frac{1}{f^2} \sum_h^L \frac{k_h}{k_h-1} \sum_i^{k_h} (n_{1hi} - \bar{n}_{1h})^2 \quad , \qquad [7.87]$$

$$s_{n_2}^2 \quad = \frac{1}{f^2} \sum_h^L \frac{k_h}{k_h-1} \sum_i^{k_h} (n_{2hi} - \bar{n}_{2h})^2 \quad , \qquad [7.88]$$

$$s_m^2 = \frac{1}{f^2} \sum_h^L \frac{k_h}{k_h - 1} \sum_i^{k_h} (m_{hi} - \bar{m}_h)^2 \quad , \qquad [7.89]$$

$$s_{n_1 n_2} = \frac{1}{f^2} \sum_h^L \frac{k_h}{k_h - 1} \sum_i^{k_h} (n_{1hi} - \bar{n}_{1h})(n_{2hi} - \bar{n}_{2h}) \quad , \qquad [7.90]$$

$$s_{n_1 m} = \frac{1}{f^2} \sum_h^L \frac{k_h}{k_h - 1} \sum_i^{k_h} (n_{1hi} - \bar{n}_{1h})(m_{hi} - \bar{m}_h) \quad , \text{ and} \qquad [7.91]$$

$$s_{n_2 m} = \frac{1}{f^2} \sum_h^L \frac{k_h}{k_h - 1} \sum_i^{k_h} (n_{2hi} - \bar{n}_{2h})(m_{hi} - \bar{m}_h) \quad , \qquad [7.92]$$

where

$$\bar{n}_{1h} = \frac{\sum_i^{k_h} n_{1hi}}{k_h} \quad ,$$

$$\bar{n}_{2h} = \frac{\sum_i^{k_h} n_{2hi}}{k_h} \quad , \text{ and}$$

$$\bar{m}_h = \frac{\sum_i^{k_h} m_{hi}}{k_h} \quad .$$

B. *Stratification*

The reduction of sampling variance by means of a sample design employing stratification is no different for PGE estimates than it is for single source estimates. In both situations, stratification is usually desirable when it can be accomplished at a small additional cost, but it is often of questionable value when complex and costly stratification techniques are used. Stratification of this type is dealt with in Section A. It involves distinguishing the strata prior to sample selection and selecting the sample separately for each stratum.

Another form of stratification involves the preparation of separate estimates for different population subgroups and combining these stratum estimates to produce an overall estimate. For this purpose one may use either strata that are established subsequent to sampling and data collection (a type of stratification sometimes referred to as "post-stratification") or the strata employed in sampling. This use of stratification is much more important for PGE studies than for single source studies. In this section, we shall deal with a number of such methods for improving the PGE estimates by stratification.

One form of stratification—the use of separate PGE estimates for subgroups to reduce correlation bias—is discussed in some detail in Chapter 3. This type of stratified estimate represents no great methodological departure from making one PGE estimate for the entire population; that is, the form of the estimate is identical for every stratum. The separate subgroup estimates operate to reduce the effect of correlation bias due to differences between strata in completeness of reporting.

Another type of stratification little used to date, either in PGE studies or elsewhere, involves the use of different forms of estimation in different strata. PGE estimation was originally introduced (and is strongly advocated in this handbook) to correct for the incompleteness of reporting that appears even with very highly developed and well-controlled single-source reporting systems. On the other hand, PGE estimation can exacerbate the effects of the erroneous inclusion of out-of-scope reports of vital events. With single-source estimation (from, say, source 1), erroneous inclusions lead to increasing n_1 by some amount $b_1 > 0$ (although, because of erroneous omissions, the total bias in a single-system estimate will usually be negative). With PGE estimation, b_1 is multiplied by $1/w_1$ (where $w_1 = m/n_2$) and since $1/w_1 > 1$, this leads to a PGE bias, $\hat{b} = b_1/w_1$, that is greater than b_1 even if the second source does not contain any erroneous inclusions. If n_2 also contains erroneous inclusions that are independent of and unmatched with those in the first source, w_1 will underestimate the erroneous underreporting in source 1 (that is, n_2 will be increased by the number of erroneous inclusions b_2), and this will further exaggerate the upward bias $\hat{b}$ of the PGE estimate. For some classes of vital events, the erroneous inclusions may approach or exceed the erroneous omissions. Where these latter classes can be identified with reasonable accuracy, it may be desirable to define them as separate strata and *not* subject them to the PGE correction for incomplete reporting.

The use of stratification in such circumstances involves establishing two strata: (1) cases with a low probability of out-of-scope error and (2) cases with a high probability of out-of-scope error. For the standard PGE estimate, only the first stratum would be used. For the second stratum, one should establish rules for classification such that the inclusion of out-of-scope events approximately balances the omission of in-scope events. To estimate the number of vital events in this stratum, either the more accurate of the two collection sources could be used in a single-source estimate, or an average of the two sources could be employed.

Note that the use of stratification requires that it be possible to assign events in *both* sources to the proper stratum. This may be quite difficult for some forms of stratification. For example, in the stratification for boundary problems discussed below, the stratum with a high probability of out-of-scope error includes events occurring near poorly defined geographic boundaries. For a survey, provision can be made in advance for identifying these events. In a registration system, the reports frequently will not indicate the address (of occurrence or residence), or if they do contain this information, it may be a quite laborious job to associate the address with the boundaries of the sample area.

B.1 STRATIFICATION FOR BOUNDARY PROBLEMS

One example of the application of this technique is its use in reducing the effects of boundary problems, both temporal and geographic. The first step is to establish the two strata. Stratum 2 will include events occurring near poorly defined geographic boundaries, as well as events reported as having occurred near the beginning or the end of the reference period. For example, events which occurred in a city block that was divided by the sampling unit boundary, events which occurred on the outskirts of a village used as a sampling unit, and events reported occurring in the first and last months of the study period might all be placed in stratum 2 for a particular study, while all other events were included in stratum 1.

The actual rules for inclusion of events in stratum 2 should be based on estimates of both the number of in-scope omissions and the number of out-of-scope inclusions, with the two strata defined to (approximately) equalize the two. Of course, it should be remembered that boundary problems, both temporal and geographic, cause in-scope omissions as well as out-of-scope inclusions, though not necessarily in the same proportions.

B.2 STRATIFICATION FOR *DE FACTO* VS. *DE JURE* DISCREPANCIES

A similar technique can be applied to the *de jure* vs. *de facto* problem. The two strata might consist of events where the *de jure* and *de facto* locations are the same, as well as events where they differ. This implies that both sources must identify both the *de facto* location and the *de jure* location for every event. If both locations are clearly identified, it is possible to eliminate out-of-scope events reported because of *de facto*/ *de jure* confusion—that is, eliminate events reported at the *de jure* location for a *de facto* PGE, or eliminate events reported at the *de facto* location for a *de jure* PGE. However, eliminating the out-of-scope events and doing a PGE estimate for the stratum where *de facto* and *de jure* locations differ may give a poorer estimate (one with a much higher variance and probably with a high ratio bias) than that obtained by using the better single system estimate or the average of the two single system estimates for this stratum.

B.3 STRATIFICATION FOR ESTIMATES USING A SAMPLE BASE POPULATION

Stratification is particularly important where birth and death rates are computed by dividing the PGE estimates of births and deaths by a population estimate derived from the same sample. Section J.1 of

Chapter 3 discusses the problem of overestimation in PGE studies that use a survey-derived base population. That is, the PGE estimate of the number of vital events includes a correction for omitted events, but the base population will be underestimated because of omitted persons; consequently the birth or death rates may be overestimated.

With a base population estimate derived from the sample, the bias due to omitted persons can be reduced by applying the dual system estimation procedure only to births and deaths associated with households included in the household survey. This procedure would require trying to determine which of the unmatched registration forms (assuming a dual system involving registration and a household survey) corresponded to a household included in the survey, by trying to match on the basis of the address and the names of household members. With respect to names, matching would involve primarily parents' names for births and name of spouse for deaths. Note that this is equivalent to assuming the same birth and death rates for the two strata, which may or may not be the case. This may be misleading if the households not included are a large proportion of the population and differ substantially in fertility and mortality from the households covered. If an estimate is to be made of the absolute number of events, it should be done in the usual PGE manner, ignoring stratification.

B.4 STRATIFICATION AND RATIO BIAS

When any type of statification is used, one should guard against the possibility of substantial ratio bias. As noted in Chapter 3, Section K.3, ratio bias is likely to result from using separate PGE estimates for small subgroups with very low completeness rates. Some idea of the likely sizes of ratio biases may be obtained from Table 7.1.[4]

The biases in Table 7.1 apply to PGE estimates $\hat{n}$ or $\hat{N}$ in the form

$$\hat{n} = n_1 / w_1$$

or

$$\hat{N} = N_1 / w_1 \quad ,$$

where $w_1 = m / n_2$.[5] If w_1 and n_1 (or N_1) are assumed to be independent, the relative bias of $\hat{n}$ or $\hat{N}$ will be the same as that of $1/w_1$.

PGE studies are usually designed to give at least 1,000 vital events estimated from the entire sample as the base for w_1, which almost always means a coefficient of variation for w_1 of .05 or less. At this level, the relative ratio bias of $\hat{n}$ or $\hat{N}$ will be only 0.3 percent—for example, a bias of .03 per 1,000 in an estimated death rate of 10 per 1,000 as opposed to a standard deviation of .5 per 1,000.

For a subgroup or stratum estimate of $\hat{n}$ (or $\hat{N}$), n_2 may be as small as 25 vital events. Even with an expected value for w_1 of .6

Table 7.1 **Relative Bias of $1/w$ for Specified Coefficients of Variation of w, Assuming Zero Intraclass Correlation.**

Coefficient of variation of w	Relative bias of $1/w$
.025	.001
.05	.003
.10	.010
.15	.024
.20	.046
.25	.08
.30	.14
.35	.24
.40	.35
.45	.47

and negligible intraclass correlation effects, the coefficient of variation of w_1 would be .16 and the relative ratio bias of $\hat{n}$ or $\hat{N}$ would be about .025. Of course, the biases for these small groups will have only a small effect on an estimate for the entire sample. Note also that the upward ratio bias (2.5 percent) of the PGE estimate is likely to be less than the downward bias (40 percent with $E(w_1) = .6$) of the single system estimate. On the other hand, a small intraclass correlation might double the coefficient of variation of w_1 and increase the ratio bias to about .15, which would make it well to consider whether the gains from stratification are as great as the losses from the resultant ratio bias.

In connection with the capture-tag-recapture technique used in estimating the size of animal populations (see Chapter 2, Section E), a number of modifications of the basic estimation equation have been proposed that adjust, approximately, for ratio bias. For example, Bailey (1951, p. 296) proposes to overcome the effects of ratio bias by using

$$\check{n} = \frac{(n_1)(n_2 + 1)}{(m + 1)} , \qquad\qquad [7.93]$$

in place of the basic estimate

$$\hat{n} = \frac{n_1 n_2}{m} ,$$

where the notation has been transformed into the standard notation of this handbook. Such a modified estimate can also be used to reduce the ratio bias of a PGE estimate for small subgroups. However, the technique has appreciable effect only for very small values of m and n_2. Even then, although the reductions in the coefficient of variation of w and the bias of $\hat{n}$ are considerable, the residual variance and bias may still result in an unacceptably large mean square error.

C. One Source as a Subsample of the Other Source

In the past, most PGE studies have used the same sample for both collection systems. This is not necessarily the optimum design in terms of cost and variance. In some situations, there may be substantial cost and/or variance advantages to making the sample for one collection system a subsample of the sample for the other system.

As a matter of fact, the nature of data collection in the two sources is usually so different that a sample design which is optimal for one source will almost always be less than optimal for the other source. For example, the use of full-time resident registrars in a special registration system will probably imply larger clusters than would be optimal for a household survey, and the size of the sampling unit for a civil registration system is generally based on administrative considerations that have little to do with sampling efficiency. Ideally, subsampling will allow the use of designs that are optimal for both sources.

In spite of its enticingly lower costs and apparent logic, a design involving subsampling should not be attempted without a very careful review of *all* the factors involved. Unfortunately, subsampling can easily become an example of the tendency to overelaboration and oversophistication readers were warned against in Chapter 4. The problems associated with its use may be many, and the gains may be illusive. To begin with, the costs and completeness rates used in determining the optimum subsampling rates, which must be estimated before data collection begins, are at best approximations and may in fact be found to be seriously wrong after the study gets under way. Second, subsampling itself has costs, both direct (the cost of establishing additional boundaries, mapping, consulting time, and so on) and indirect (the confusion it introduces into the study). Finally, although the following discussion is put first in terms of cost and variance, the most important consequence of subsampling is the bias it may introduce. This can be controlled, but only at a price that rapidly reduces the apparent savings from subsampling.

The difficulties of subsampling are not unique. Similar problems occur in decisions on other design features—for example, matching rules and procedures—and one should not concentrate on the difficulties of subsampling to the exclusion of the possible advantages. In particular, the fact that cost and administrative considerations dictate using very large sampling units for special registration (as, for example, in the Pakistan PGE study) should not automatically mean adopting these large (and probably inefficient) units for the survey as well.

In determining the desirability of subsampling, the problem of dealing with the interplay between cost and variance is complex. PGE estimation imposes limitations such that one cannot merely split the budget between the two collection sources, and still optimally design each within that budgetary limitation. For one thing, there is the question of how to split the budget between the two sources. There is also the fact that a change in the sample which reduces the variance of n_1 or n_2, or even both, may increase the variance of $\hat{n}$. The question, then, is what design yields minimum error for a fixed total expenditure.

To simplify the problem somewhat, we shall consider the desirability of subsampling first in terms of costs and the effects on the variance of $\hat{n}$, and later in terms of the bias of $\hat{n}$. More specifically, we shall limit ourselves to a situation where

(a) a single PGE estimate is made on the basis of all sample reports of vital events;

(b) the source 2 sample is identical to, or is a subsample of, the source 1 sample—that is, all source 2 sample areas are also to be covered by source 1;

(c) the source 1 sample consists of k_1 sample areas selected independently and with equal probability from a total of K areas of approximately equal population; each of the k_1 sample areas is covered completely by source 1; and

(d) source 2 consists of k_2 sample areas ($k_2 \leq k_1$), and either covers each sample area completely or covers h out of H ($1 \leq h \leq H$) subareas in each sample area. The h subareas are of appproximately equal population and are selected with equal probability.

Subject to these limitations, the subsampling for source 2 can be carried out in one of two ways. Either a subsample of k_2 units can be drawn directly from k_1 primary sampling units, or one can derive the source 2 sample by subdividing the primary sampling units and drawing one or more subunits from each primary unit.

With the above sample design, we can classify PGE costs as

(a) fixed costs for general direction, planning, sample selection, result publication, and so on;

(b) costs varying with $k_1 H$ for source 1 data collection and data processing (including the costs of recruiting, training, and supervising field personnel); and

(c) costs varying with $k_2 h$ for source 2 data collection and matching.[6]

The fixed costs will be the same regardless of the PGE sample design; they will, in fact, also be almost the same for a single system design with the same total of variable expenditures. The variable expenditures can be expressed as

$$ C \quad = \quad c_1 k_1 H + c_2 k_2 h \quad , \qquad\qquad [7.94] $$

where

c_1 = variable cost per subsampling unit included in source 1, and

c_2 = variable cost per subsampling unit included in source 2 (and in the matching operation).

C.1   SUBSAMPLING ENTIRE PRIMARY SAMPLING UNITS

We shall consider first the case in which $h = H$—that is, source 2 covers each of the k_2 sample areas completely (Figure 7.1). Here a sample of $k_1 = 5$ sample areas has been drawn for the household survey, of which $k_2 = 1$ were subsampled for the special registration system. The rationale for this design is that, given higher unit costs for the special registration system than for the household survey, money can be saved by using fewer of the expensive registration areas.

We first approach this problem from the variance standpoint, starting with the relvariance of $\hat{n}$, as developed in Section A,

$$V_{\hat{n}}^2 = 2V_{n_1 n_2} - V_{n_1}^2 - V_{n_2}^2 + V_m^2 \quad . \tag{7.95}$$

This can be expressed as [7]

$$V_{\hat{n}}^2 = \frac{1}{k_1}(2V_{Bn_1 n_2} - V_{Bn_1}^2) + \frac{1}{k_2}(V_{Bm}^2 - V_{Bn_2}^2) \tag{7.96}$$

where

$$V_{Bn_1}^2 = \frac{\sigma_{Bn_1}^2}{(En_1)^2} \quad = \quad \text{relvariance of } n_{1i} \text{ between primary units,}$$

$$V_{Bn_2}^2 = \frac{\sigma_{Bn_2}^2}{(En_2)^2} \quad = \quad \text{relvariance of } n_{2i} \text{ between primary units,}$$

$$V_{Bm}^2 = \frac{\sigma_{Bm}^2}{(Em)^2} \quad = \quad \text{relvariance of } m_i \text{ between primary units,}$$

$$V_{Bn_1 n_2} = \frac{\sigma_{Bn_1 n_2}}{(En_1)(En_2)} \quad = \quad \text{relative covariance of } n_{1i} \text{ and } n_{2i} \text{ between primary units.}$$

Figure 7.1   Illustrative Sample Design for Subsampling Entire Primary Units, Using a Household Survey (S) and a Special Registration (R)

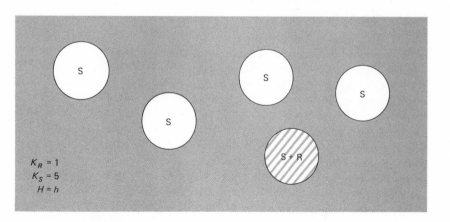

SOURCE: Hypothetical.

Assuming the same intraclass correlation within primary sampling units for n_1, n_2, and m, we have

$$V_{\hat{n}}^2 = \frac{1}{k_1 \bar{N}}(1 - \delta + \bar{N}\delta)(2\hat{V}_{n_1 n_2} - \hat{V}_{n_1}^2) + \frac{1}{k_2 \bar{N}}(1 - \delta + \bar{N}\delta)(\hat{V}_m^2 - \hat{V}_{n_2}^2) \quad , \qquad [7.97]$$

where $\bar{N}$ is the mean number of events per primary sampling unit, δ is the intraclass correlation between elementary units within primary sampling units, and $\hat{V}_{n_1 n_2}$, $\hat{V}_{n_1}^2$, $\hat{V}_{n_2}^2$, $\hat{V}_m^2$ are the relative covariance and variances between elementary units of the population.[8]

Assuming that the number of true events in the sample or subsample is a Poisson variate with expected values $k_1 \bar{N}$, and $k_2 \bar{N}$, respectively, equation 7.97 becomes

$$V_{\hat{n}}^2 = \frac{A}{k_1} + \frac{B}{k_2} \quad , \qquad [7.98]$$

where

$$A \doteq \frac{(1 - \delta + \bar{N}\delta)(2P_{12} - P_2)}{\bar{N} P_1 P_2} \quad , \text{ and}$$

$$B \doteq \frac{(1 - \delta + \bar{N}\delta)(P_2 - P_{12})}{\bar{N} P_2 P_{12}} \quad .$$

If we assume costs as in equation 7.94 and independence $(P_{12} = P_1 P_2)$,

$$\frac{B}{A} = \frac{1 - P_1}{2 P_1 P_2 - P_2} \quad ,$$

and the optimum subsampling rate is given by

$$f = \frac{k_2}{k_1} = \sqrt{\frac{c_1 B}{c_2 A}}$$

$$= \sqrt{\frac{c_1 (1 - P_1)}{c_2 (2 P_1 P_2 - P_2)}} \quad , \text{ where } k_2 \leq k_1 \quad . \qquad [7.99]$$

That is, the optimum subsampling rate k_2 / k_1 varies directly with the unit cost of source 1 and inversely with the unit cost of source 2. In other words, the greater the unit cost for a given source, the smaller the sample for that source that the study can afford. On the other hand, the lower the variance for a given source, the smaller will be the number of areas needed to reduce error. Since for a particular source, lower costs usually mean poorer coverage, which in turn means higher variance for that source, the unit cost and variance factors usually, though not always, will operate in the same direction.

If the optimum subsampling ratio k_2 / k_1 is greater than .5, there is probably no justification for subsampling, due to the uncertainties, costs, and, above all, the biases associated with the procedure (see Section C.3 below). If the ratio is substantially less than .5, subsampling may well be worth looking into. In general, the justification for subsampling is that c_2 is greater than c_1. However, for P_1 between $1/2$ and $2/3$, B/A will be greater than 1.0, and subsampling will be desirable only if c_2 is much higher than c_1—for example, if source 1 is the civil registration. If $P_1 < .5$, the optimum subsampling ratio becomes imaginary, suggesting that source 1 should not be used at all.

On the other hand, if completeness rates in both sources are very high, subsampling may be justified. For example, if P_1 and P_2 are both greater than .8, $\sqrt{B/A}$ will be less than .65 and, with c_2 greater than c_1, there may be advantages to subsampling. In countries with highly developed national statistics systems, such an approach may be warranted; in the absence of developed systems, it is unwise to assume such high completeness rates.

Even when the unit cost differences justify subsampling, it is easy to overestimate the gains from very drastic subsampling. Planners are easily impressed by the high costs of one of the systems and often push for reductions in the sample size for that source. When the cheaper source has a low completeness rate (about .5 or less), achieving some of the savings by cutting the sample for this source may be more nearly optimal, but this tends to be overlooked because making drastic cuts in the sample for the cheaper source yields only moderate savings.

An example may help to illustrate how these factors may operate in practice. Consider a PGE design calling for a household survey in 150 sample areas, with an intensive special registration system in 30 of these areas. If we assume a completeness rate for the household survey of $P_1 = .7$ and a completeness rate for the special registration system of $P_2 = .8$, then for $k_1 = 150$ and $k_2 = 30$, we would have

$$A \quad = \quad \frac{.32\,(1 - \delta + \bar{N}\delta)}{.56\bar{N}} \quad ,$$

$$B \quad = \quad \frac{.24\,(1 - \delta + \bar{N}\delta)}{.448\bar{N}} \quad , \text{and}$$

$$V_{\hat{n}}^2 \quad = \quad \frac{1 - \delta + \bar{N}\delta}{\bar{N}} \left(\frac{.32}{(.56)(150)} + \frac{.24}{(.448)(30)} \right) \quad .$$

A value of $k_1 = k_2 = 51$ will give the same value of $V_{\hat{n}}^2$ without any of the problems introduced by subsampling. Thus the proposed design would be worth considering only if it cost substantially less than a design calling for 51 sample areas, each covered by the household survey and the special registration system, with no subsampling. Equation 7.99 indicates that $k_1 = 150$ and $k_2 = 30$ would be optimum for $P_1 = .7$ and $P_2 = .8$ only if $c_2 = 23.4\,c_1$. Other likely combinations of P_1 and P_2 yield similarly unlikely cost ratios in this equation, leading to the conclusion that a subsampling ratio of $30/150$ could rarely be justified. This is similar to the conclusion reached by Hansen (1965) in commenting on an identical subsampling scheme for a PGE study.

C.2   SUBSAMPLING WITHIN PRIMARY SAMPLING UNITS

The second type of subsampling, illustrated by Figure 7.2, involves dividing each of the primary units to be used in the first source into subunits and subsampling one or more of these subunits for the second source. In Figure 7.2, each of the primary sample areas is covered completely by a registration system, but has been divided into five subareas, of which only one is sampled and enumerated in the survey. (The dotted lines in the area at the upper left are a reminder that before subsampling one must first, of course, define the subclusters.) In this case, $k_1 = k_2 = 5$, while $H = 5$ and $h = 1$.

As previously noted, special registration usually implies sampling units larger than might be desirable on the basis of cost and sampling variance alone. The problem is with the "continuous" and "active" features of special registration, which are the two main advantages of such a system. The continuity reduces the memory and time-boundary problems of periodic data collection, while the active checking on births and deaths produces a more complete coverage than passive registration, thereby reducing the response correlation bias for the "hard-to-cover" cases. Unfortunately, continuous and active registration is fairly expensive and also difficult to control. To reduce travel costs and to make training and supervision more effective, special registration systems are usually set up to use *full-time, resident* registrars. This means that the registrar's assignment must be concentrated in a single large sampling unit. For example, in the Pakistan PGE Study the sampling units contained approximately 5,000 persons, this being judged to be the work load necessary to provide full-time work for a special registrar.

The use of such large sampling areas makes it possible to use only a small number of areas (because of the cost), and this, in turn,

Figure 7.2   Illustrative Sample Design for Subsampling Within Primary Units, Using a Household Survey (S) and a Special Registration (R)

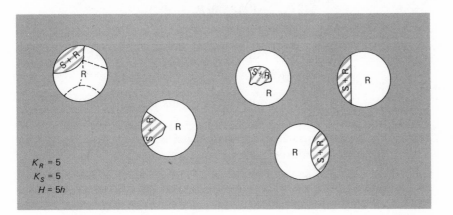

SOURCE: Hypothetical.

increases the variance. Given, then, that one must use full-time resident registrars covering a small number of large sampling units, the question arises whether the survey should use the same size sampling units. It can be argued that reducing the size of the survey areas may save a good deal of money with a relatively small increase in variance; this would make it possible for more registration units to be used, thus reducing the variance for a given expenditure, or conversely, reducing the expenditure for a given variance.

For example, Ivan Fellegi of Statistics Canada has suggested a system in which a total of k large clusters are selected for the registration and are divided into H subclusters; in each of the k large clusters 1 of the H subclusters is selected for the household survey.[9] For this sample design and making the same assumptions as above—that is, (a) the independence of w_2 $(= m/n_1)$ and n_1, and w_1 $(= m/n_2)$ and n_2; (b) the independence of n and p_1, p_2, and p_{12}; (c) equal intraclass correlations for n_1, n_2, and m; and (d) that n is a Poisson variate —the relvariance of $\hat{n}$ is

$$V_{\hat{n}}^2 \doteq \frac{A}{k\bar{N}} + \frac{B}{k\bar{n}} + \frac{D}{k} ,$$
[7.100]

where

$$f \quad = \frac{\bar{n}}{\bar{N}} \quad = \text{subsampling rate,}$$

H = number of subclusters per primary cluster,

$$A \quad \doteq \frac{(1 - \Delta)(2P_{12} - P_2)}{P_1 P_2} ,$$

$$B \quad \doteq \frac{(1 - \delta)(P_2 - P_{12})}{P_2 P_{12}} ,$$

$$D \quad \doteq \frac{\Delta(2P_{12} - P_2)}{P_1 P_2} + \frac{\delta(P_2 - P_{12})}{P_2 P_{12}} ,$$

$\bar{N}$ = average number of vital events per primary cluster,

$$\bar{n} \quad = \frac{\bar{N}}{H} \quad = \text{average number of events per subcluster,}$$

Δ = intraclass correlation (of n_{1ij}, n_{2ij}, m_{ij}) within primary clusters,[10] and

δ = intraclass correlation (of n_{1ij}, n_{2ij}, m_{ij}) within subclusters.

For this situation, we use the cost equation

$$C \quad = c_1 k\bar{N} + c_2 k\bar{n} + c_3 k$$
[7.101]

where

c_1 = variable cost per event for source 1,

c_2 = variable cost per event for source 2, and

c_3 = variable cost per primary sampling unit (for mapping, training, subsampling, and so on).

Then the optimum subsampling rate is

$$f = \frac{\bar{n}}{\bar{N}} = \sqrt{\frac{c_1 B}{c_2 A}} = \sqrt{\frac{c_1 (1 - \delta) P_1 (P_2 - P_{12})}{c_2 (1 - \Delta) P_{12} (2P_{12} - P_2)}} \quad . \qquad [7.102]$$

For the case $\Delta = \delta = 0$ and $P_{12} = P_1 P_2$, equation 7.102 gives the same value as equation 7.99; that is

$$f = \sqrt{\frac{c_1 (1 - P_1)}{c_2 (2P_1 P_2 - P_2)}} \quad . \qquad [7.103]$$

The unit costs c_1 and c_2 will vary depending upon local conditions and the study design. In general, a special registration system will require more person-hours per year, whereas a survey system will require higher-paid interviewers. Since a registrar does not have to visit all the households personally, he can cover an area in less time than a survey interviewer, but he must visit the area frequently to ensure "continuous" registration. He might be expected to visit each daily ration, consisting of perhaps 100 households, once every two weeks. The survey interviewer would require about five days to cover these 100 households, doing an average of two and one-half households per hour. At this rate it would take him about ten weeks to cover the registrar's entire area once. With quarterly enumeration, then, the survey interviewer would require about 40 weeks to cover what the registrar covers in a year; with semiannual enumeration, he would need only about 20 weeks. On the one hand, survey interviewers are usually trained personnel who are paid big-city wages and are in full-time travel status. Full-time special registrars, on the other hand, are typically people of moderate education and status who are paid in accordance with rural wage levels and reside in the area. Hence survey costs per hour are likely to be somewhat higher than special registration costs per hour. On balance, we would not usually expect survey unit costs to be more than 20 percent higher than special registration costs. Since c_2 also includes the unit costs for matching, we might have a value of $c_2 = 1.67 c_1$. Assuming $h = 1$, $\Delta = \delta = 0$, and $P_1 = P_2 = .8$, we have, from equation 7.103,

$$f = \frac{\bar{n}}{\bar{N}} = \sqrt{\frac{.2}{(1.67)(.48)}} \doteq .5 \quad .$$

Thus one might use in the survey subclusters about half the size of the primary sampling units used in the special registration.

On the other hand, Hansen (1965) notes that registration costs can run higher (even considerably higher) than survey costs.[11] Thus, if $P_1 = .8$ and $P_2 = .75$, but $c_1 = 1.5c_2$, we have

$$f = \sqrt{\frac{.3}{.45}} \doteq .8 \quad .$$

Or, reversing the sources—that is, taking the survey as source 1 and the registration as source 2—we have

$$f = \sqrt{\frac{.25}{.6}} \doteq .65 \quad .$$

In either case, subsampling would be hard to justify. These examples are, of course, selective and the equations presented are approximate. There may be other circumstances where subsampling has great advantages.

However, the preceding discussion is based on the assumption that full-time, resident registrars are to be used in the special registration system. This is often desirable for several reasons, discussed more fully in Chapter 4, Section D.1—reasons such as control, independence, and coverage. It may not, however, be necessary, depending upon local conditions. If it is not, the special registrar may either be a full-time employee in travel status, covering several small areas, or a part-time local resident, covering a single small area. In either case, more registration areas can be covered at the same cost, thereby lowering variance. First, then, one may want to reconsider the necessity of full-time, resident registrars.

In addition, the savings in cost from subsampling may not, in fact, be very great. After all, one only saves part of the collection costs for one source, and the savings in matching and processing are small. These factors must be weighed against the costs, in both cash and confusion, of subsampling.

Also, as mentioned before, one must estimate the values of the factors involved before the study begins, so that the calculation of the optimum subsampling rate will of necessity be a rough approximation. It will be especially difficult to get an *a priori* idea of the magnitude of intraclass correlation.

Finally, and most important, are the considerations involving bias.

C.3   BIAS CONSIDERATIONS IN SUBSAMPLING

The major bias problem associated with subsampling is that, over time, the completeness of source 1 in the subsample areas tends to become better than the completeness in the areas which are not in the subsample, even when there is no response correlation bias in the usual sense. That is, the presence of two vital statistics systems in the same area will tend to improve the coverage of both systems, though they continue to be independent. This problem of "respondent conditioning" applies generally to one-way matching. An example may help to clarify how "conditioning bias" can operate even with two independent systems.

Suppose we have a special registration system (source 1) operating in k clusters. Each cluster is divided into four subclusters, and one of these subclusters is covered by the survey (source 2). The PGE estimate that makes use of the registration reports from all four subclusters of the k clusters and the survey reports from the subsample of k subclusters is

$$\hat{n}_A = \frac{n_{A1} n_2}{m} ,$$

where

$$n_{A1} = \frac{K}{k} \sum_i^k n_{1i} = \frac{K}{k} \sum_i^k \sum_j^4 n_{1ij} ,$$

$$n_2 = \frac{4K}{k} \sum_i^k n_{2i} = \frac{4K}{k} \sum_i^k \sum_j^1 n_{2ij} , \text{ and}$$

$$m = \frac{4K}{k} \sum_i^k m_i = \frac{4K}{k} \sum_i^k \sum_j^1 m_{ij} .$$

Alternatively, we could have the PGE estimate that uses registration reports only from the subclusters covered by the survey. That is,

$$\hat{n}_B = \frac{n_{B1} n_2}{m} ,$$

where

$$n_{B1} = \frac{4K}{k} \sum_i^k n_{1i} = \frac{4K}{k} \sum_i^k \sum_j^1 n_{1ij} .$$

The estimate $\hat{n}_B$ would use one sample for both sources with two-way matching in the selected subclusters. Since n_{B1} is based on fewer sample cases than n_{A1}, it and $\hat{n}_B$ will have a higher variance than n_{A1} and $\hat{n}_A$.

Suppose further that, in the first year, the registration and the survey are both getting 70 percent completeness. In the second year, the registration and survey improve to 80 percent completeness in the subclusters covered by both sources, and the registration coverage improves to 76 percent in the remaining subclusters. The registration and survey are independent in both years—that is, in the first year the probability of an event being reported by both sources is $P_1 P_2 = .7 \times .7 = .49$, and in the second year it is $P_1 P_2 = .8 \times .8 = .64$. We assume that the true number of events (N) will be the same for both years.

Expected values for the various estimates are shown in Table 7.2. In the first year, both $E\hat{n}_A$ and $E\hat{n}_B$ are unbiased, but in the second year a 4-percent bias has crept into $E\hat{n}_A$. This bias results from the fact that although the numerator $(n_{A1} n_2)$ reflects the difference in registration coverage between the subclusters covered by both sources and those not covered by the survey, the denominator (m) does not, since it is based only on reports from areas covered by both systems. Of course, the bias of $\hat{n}_A$ must be weighed against the higher variance of $\hat{n}_B$.

As Hansen (1965) points out,

> A way to avoid this bias would be to redraw another random subsample of 30 villages from the original 150, and carry out the intensive registration activity and final supervisors survey in this new sample of 30, and a similar rotation of subsampled villages might take place in each subsequent year.

In the example treated above, we could, in the second year, reselect the subsample from each of the original k clusters ($4k$ subclusters).

Table 7.2   Expected Values of the Estimated Number of Source 1, Source 2, and Matched Reports and the PGE Estimate, for Three Designs with Subsampling: Hypothetical Example, Year 1 and Year 2

Design used and type of estimate	Expected value in terms of the true number of events, N	
	1st year	2nd year
Design A (source 1 uses 4k subclusters, source 2 uses k subclusters; no rotation)		
En_{A1}—source 1 estimate	.70N	.77N
En_2—source 2 estimate	.70N	.80N
Em—estimate of events reported by both sources	.49N	.64N
$E\hat{n}_A$—PGE estimate	N	.96N
Design B (source 1 and source 2 use k subclusters; no rotation)		
En_{B1}—source 1 estimate	.70N	.80N
En_2—source 2 estimate	.70N	.80N
Em—estimate of events reported by both sources	.49N	.64N
$E\hat{n}_B$—PGE estimate	N	N
Design C (source 1 uses 4k subclusters, source 2 uses k subclusters independently selected each year)		
En_{A1}—source 1 estimate	.70N	.77N
En_{C2}—source 2 estimate	—	.725N
Em_C—estimate of events reported by both sources	—	.559N
$E\hat{n}_C$—PGE estimate	—	.9987N

NOTE: Estimates based on the assumptions that for year 1, $P_1 = P_2 = .7$; that for year 2 in the k subclusters covered by both sources, $P_1 = P_2 = .8$, while in the remaining $3k$ subclusters $P_1 = .76$; that in each year $P_{12} = P_1 P_2$; and that N is the same for both years. For further details, see text.

The subclusters used in the first year would be eligible to be subsampled again in the second year, and we would expect one-fourth of the second-year subsample areas to be the same as in the first year. Thus the completeness rate for the survey in the second year would be 70 percent for three-fourths of the subsample and 80 percent for one-fourth of the subsample. We would have second-year estimates n_{C2} and m_C based on the second-year subsample and would use as the PGE estimate

$$\hat{n}_C = \frac{n_{A1} n_{C2}}{m_C} \quad .$$

Expected values of n_{C2}, m_C, and $\hat{n}_C$ also appear in Table 7.2. Here the rotation has removed practically all the bias—that is, $E\hat{n}_C = .9987N$.

Note that, because both sources cover the same area, $\hat{n}_B$ is an unbiased estimate even though experience with vital events reporting in the first year led to improved coverage of both systems in the second year. With no subsampling and two-way matching to give estimates like $\hat{n}_B$, frequent rotation is less necessary than with subsampling or one-way matching. Nevertheless, some rotation is desirable over time, since the improvement in coverage is not likely to be uniform over the whole sample, and this will ultimately result in a response correlation bias.

Although rotation can eliminate much of the bias of $\hat{n}_A$, it is a costly procedure and it should not be undertaken without regard for the dislocations it may cause. Mapping, lodging, liaison, and so on, have to be arranged anew each time the subsample is rotated. New sources of confusion are introduced into the handling and processing of data. Problems of boundary definition, which can be reduced over a period of time, are much more difficult to handle with a frequently rotated subsample.

On the whole, we feel that a PGE study is complicated enough in its simplest form. With a study design calling for subsampling and frequent rotation, maintaining the tight control necessary for a successful study will be a very difficult task. Particularly when subsampling is introduced in order to use full-time resident registrars in large registration areas, one should consider whether the biases from using part-time registrars are greater than the subsampling biases.

C.4 SUBSAMPLING AND ONE-WAY MATCHING

Regardless of the study design used, it is always possible to use either a one-way or a two-way match to determine the number of matched reports. The difference lies only in whether one explicitly determines the match status of each report in both sources, or of each report in only one source. In general, two-way matching has the advantage of improving control over the matching process, while one-way matching of a smaller file of vital event reports against a larger file reduces costs and may reduce out-of-scope error. In practice, the basic sample design will usually involve practical factors that will dictate whether a one-way or a two-way match is used. If both sources use the same sample, one-way matching causes no reduction in out-of-scope error, so that two-way matching will nearly always be preferable, unless the blocking units are very large and a one-way match is preferable on the grounds of cost. If subsampling is used (including the case where one source covers the entire population), it will often be impossible to determine accurately which reports in the larger source refer to events occurring in the sample for the smaller source. In such a situation two-way matching would be undesirable.

With the study design leading to the estimate $\hat{n}_A$ in the preceding section, either a one-way or a two-way match might have been feasible. Here each of the k sample areas in a special registration system was divided into four subareas, one of which was selected for the household survey sample. If the special registration system could have been designed to provide adequate geographic identification for each reported event, it might well have been possible to determine which registration reports referred to events in the survey sample areas, thus permitting the improved control over the matching process provided by two-way matching. On the other hand, a one-way match of the household survey reports against the larger file of registration reports might have been justified in terms of reduced out-of-scope bias where the geographic identification was inadequate.

Given a study design that calls for a sample of special registration areas subsampled for the household survey, the gains from one-way matching (the cost savings and reduction of out-of-scope bias) may outweigh those from two-way matching (better control over the matching process). The advantages, however, would rarely be enough to overcome the disadvantages of the basic subsampling design, which have been described in the previous subsections. In considering the desirability of one-way matching of a household survey subsample against a special registration sample, the costs and mean square error should always be checked against the best alternative using a two-way match, but no subsampling.

Although cost considerations play a relatively minor role in determining whether a one-way or a two-way match will be used with a special registration system, matching costs can be a crucial factor when the civil registration system is used as one of the sources. The critical feature here is whether the geographic classification of the civil registration system identifies the vital events with reasonably small geographic areas. A civil registration file that distinguishes areas of 10,000 population will be much easier to search than one in which the smallest geographic grouping has a population of 100,000. The former might contain between 100 and 500 vital events, the latter between 1,000 and 5,000.

D. Special-Purpose and Unconventional Design Modifications

D.1   MATCHING AND ESTIMATION WITH MORE THAN TWO COLLECTION SYSTEMS

The basis of PGE estimation is the use of two independent sources, the idea being that if one system fails to report a vital event the other system will still have a chance of picking it up. Of course, it is impossible to achieve complete independence. It has been argued that independence is not important, that the real contribution of a PGE estimate is in adding the unmatched reports of the second source to the source 1 reports. Consequently, some have advocated that one ignore z (the number of reports not reported in either source) and use an estimate

$$n' = m + u_1 + u_2 \quad , \qquad\qquad [7.104]$$

where

m = number of matched cases,
u_1 = number of source 1 cases unmatched in source 2, and
u_2 = number of source 2 cases unmatched in source 1.

That is, $n' = \hat{n} - \hat{z}$. This is in contrast to the usual two-way PGE estimate,

$$\hat{n} = m + u_1 + u_2 + \frac{u_1 u_2}{m} \quad , \qquad\qquad [7.105]$$

where

$$\hat{z} = \frac{u_1 u_2}{m} = \text{estimated number of cases not reported in either source.}$$

The Indian Sample Registration uses the estimate n' of equation 7.104. As described by Ramabhadran (1971), considerable thought and much careful experimentation went into the design of the Indian SRS. Ramabhadran explains that "the analytical method of Chandrasekaran-Deming is not being applied as the conditions for its application are not fully met by SRS. Further, since the number of events recorded by one method and missed by the other is small . . . the contribution of the C-D formula is less than 1 percent."

The difficulty with the Indian SRS is that much still remains to be done to reduce the correlation between the two sources. The argument for using n' is that z is not estimated correctly because of the correlation between the sources and that n' is therefore a more accurate estimate. This argument is not valid, since the expected value of the PGE estimate $\hat{n}$ is almost always nearer to the true value than that of n'. It is true that n' has somewhat lower variance than $\hat{n}$ but this would only outweigh the bias caused by omitting $\hat{z}$ in situations where u_1 or u_2 is so small that $\hat{n}$ has no advantage over (that is, has about the same mean square error as) the single system estimate, n_1 or n_2.

In any case, the advantage of a dual system is dependent upon one system picking up some cases that were missed by the other system.

As a result, it is sometimes suggested that *more* than two systems be used in order to reduce the number of events not reported in any source. For example, with three sources we would have the reporting model illustrated in Figure 7.3. This reporting model involves eight basic reporting statuses corresponding to the eight possible combinations of three things, each of which has two possible outcomes.

Thus, we have

$$
\begin{aligned}
m_{123} &= \text{events reported in all three sources,} \\
m_{023} &= \text{events reported in sources 2 and 3,} \\
m_{120} &= \text{events reported in sources 1 and 2,} \\
m_{103} &= \text{events reported in sources 1 and 3,} \\
m_{100} &= \text{events reported in source 1 only,} \\
m_{020} &= \text{events reported in source 2 only,} \\
m_{003} &= \text{events reported in source 3 only, and} \\
m_{000} &= \text{events not reported in any source.}
\end{aligned}
$$

These eight categories are the eight internal (nonmarginal) cells of Figure 7.3. In terms of our three-source model, the two-source statistics m, u_1, u_2, and z (see Figure 3.2 in Chapter 3) become

Figure 7.3 Reporting Model for a Three-Source PGE Study

(Events reported by a given source are indicated by an appropriate numerical subscript; a zero subscript means the event was not reported; a period (.) subscript indicates all events regardless of their reporting status in given source.)

Source 2 and source 3 reporting status	Reported in source 1	Not reported in source 1	Total regardless of source 1 reporting status
Reported in source 2: Reported in source 3	m_{123}	m_{023}	$m_{.23}$
Not reported in source 3	m_{120}	m_{020}	$m_{.20}$
Total reported in source 2	$m_{12.} = m$	$m_{02.} = u_2$	$m_{.2.} = n_2$
Not reported in source 2: Reported in source 3	m_{103}	m_{003}	$m_{.03}$
Not reported in source 3	m_{100}	m_{000}	$m_{.00}$
Total not reported in source 2	$m_{10.} = u_1$	$m_{00.} = z$	$m_{.0.}$
All events regardless of source 2 reporting status: Reported in source 3	$m_{1.3}$	$m_{0.3}$	$m_{..3} = n_3$
Not reported in source 3	$m_{1.0}$	$m_{0.0}$	$m_{..0}$
Total regardless of source 2 and source 3 reporting status	$m_{1..} = n_1$	$m_{0..}$	$m_{...} = n$

$$m \quad = \quad m_{12.} \quad = \quad m_{123} + m_{120} \quad ,$$

$$u_1 \quad = \quad m_{10.} \quad = \quad m_{103} + m_{100} \quad ,$$

$$u_2 \quad = \quad m_{02.} \quad = \quad m_{023} + m_{020} \quad ; \text{ and}$$

$$z \quad = \quad m_{00.} \quad = \quad m_{003} + m_{000} \quad .$$

There are a number of possible estimates of $\hat{n}$ from a three-source match system. There is, for example, the average of the three dual system estimates,

$$\hat{n} = 1/3 \left(\frac{n_1 n_2}{m_{12.}} + \frac{n_1 n_3}{m_{1.3}} + \frac{n_2 n_3}{m_{.23}} \right) \quad ; \qquad [7.106]$$

or, to reduce ratio bias, a preferable estimate,

$$\hat{n} = \frac{n_1 n_2 + n_1 n_3 + n_2 n_3}{m_{12.} + m_{1.3} + m_{.23}} \quad . \qquad [7.107]$$

The estimates of equations 7.106 and 7.107 do not use the information given by the three-way match. They can, in fact, give a lower value than that obtained by adding the values in the seven known cells; that is,

$$\hat{n} = m_{123} + m_{023} + m_{120} + m_{103} + m_{100} + m_{020} + m_{003} \quad . \qquad [7.108]$$

For example, consider a situation in which half the events are in a stratum that has a probability .9 of an event being reported in any one source, the other half of the events are in a stratum that has a probability .6 of an event being reported, and there is independence between sources *within* the two strata. Here the expected values will be

$$E(n_1) \quad = \quad E(n_2) = E(n_3) = \frac{.9 + .6}{2} N = .75N \quad ,$$

$$E(m_{12.}) \quad = \quad E(m_{1.3}) = E(m_{.23}) = \frac{.81 + .36}{2} N = .585N \quad ,$$

$$E(m_{123}) \quad = \quad \frac{.729 + .216}{2} N = .4725N \quad ,$$

$$E(m_{120}) \quad = \quad E(m_{103}) = E(m_{023}) = \frac{.081 + .144}{2} N = .1125N \quad ,$$

$$E(m_{100}) \quad = \quad E(m_{020}) = E(m_{003}) = \frac{.009 + .096}{2} N = .0525N \quad , \text{ and}$$

$$E(m_{000}) \quad = \quad \frac{.001 + .064}{2} N = .0325N \quad .$$

For this example, equations 7.106 and 7.107 give an estimate with the expected value

$$E(\hat{n}) \doteq \frac{.5625 N^2}{.585 N} = .9615 N \quad ,$$

whereas equation 7.108 gives $E(\hat{n}) = .9675 N$.

Das Gupta (1964) gives a formula for the "maximum likelihood estimator" of the total number of events N based on matching among k independent sources. For $k = 2$, the maximum likelihood estimator is the usual dual system estimate

$$\hat{n} = \frac{n_1 n_2}{m} \quad .$$

For $k = 3$ (using the notation above), Das Gupta's formula becomes

$$\hat{n} \quad = \frac{b + \sqrt{b^2 - 4 n_1 n_2 n_3 a}}{2a} \quad , \qquad\qquad [7.109]$$

where

$$a \quad = \quad m_{120} + m_{103} + m_{023} + 2 m_{123} = m_{12.} + m_{1.3} + m_{.23} - m_{123} \text{ and}$$

$$b \quad = \quad n_1 n_2 + n_1 n_3 + n_2 n_3 \quad .$$

For the example cited above, the value given by equation 7.109 is

$$E(a) \quad = \quad 3(.1125) N + 2(.4725) N = 1.2825 N \quad ,$$

$$E(b) \quad = \quad 3(.75 N)^2 = 1.6875 N^2 \quad , \text{and}$$

$$E(\hat{n}) \quad \doteq \quad \frac{1.6875 N^2 + N^2 \sqrt{(1.6875)^2 - 4(.75)^3 (1.2825)}}{2(1.2825) N} \quad ,$$

or

$$E(\hat{n}) \quad \doteq \quad .9802 N \quad .$$

The maximum likelihood estimator of equation 7.109 is unbiased (except for ratio bias) if the three sources are independent. That is, with independence,

$$E(b) \quad = \quad N^2 (P_1 P_2 + P_1 P_3 + P_2 P_3) = N^2 \bar{b} \quad , \text{and}$$

$$E(a) \quad = \quad N(P_1 P_2 + P_1 P_3 + P_2 P_3 - P_1 P_2 P_3) = N\bar{b} - N P_1 P_2 P_3 \quad ,$$

with

$$E(n_1 n_2 n_3) \quad = \quad P_1 P_2 P_3 N^3 \quad ,$$

so that

$$E(\hat{n}) \quad \doteq \quad N \left[\frac{\bar{b} + \sqrt{\bar{b}^2 - 4 \bar{b} P_1 P_2 P_3 + 4 P_1^2 P_2^2 P_3^2}}{2 \bar{b} - 2 P_1 P_2 P_3} \right]$$

$$E(\hat{n}) \quad \doteq \quad N \left[\frac{\bar{b} + \bar{b} - 2 P_1 P_2 P_3}{2 \bar{b} - 2 P_1 P_2 P_3} \right] = N \quad .$$

However, the estimate of equation 7.109 does not take into account the information about the correlation furnished by a three-way match. That is, equation 7.109 yields an estimate that maximizes the probability of obtaining the specified results on the assumption that the three sources are independent (ignoring any relationship of the method of estimation to the effects of matching or out-of-scope errors).

Where there is appreciable correlation of reporting error among the sources, it may be better to accept the obtained values in the seven cells as the best estimates for those cells and to estimate only m_{000}—either on an assumption of independence or on some other assumption about the correlations among sources.

Assuming independence, we can have estimates of m_{000} of the form

$$m_{000} = \frac{m_{100}\,m_{020}}{m_{120}}\,, \qquad\qquad [7.110]$$

$$m_{000} = \frac{m_{100}\,m_{003}}{m_{103}}\,, \text{ and} \qquad\qquad [7.111]$$

$$m_{000} = \frac{m_{020}\,m_{003}}{m_{023}}\,. \qquad\qquad [7.112]$$

We can also have estimates of the form

$$m_{000} = \frac{m_{120}\,m_{003}}{m_{123}}\,, \qquad\qquad [7.113]$$

$$m_{000} = \frac{m_{103}\,m_{020}}{m_{123}}\,, \text{ and} \qquad\qquad [7.114]$$

$$m_{000} = \frac{m_{023}\,m_{100}}{m_{123}}\,. \qquad\qquad [7.115]$$

Combining the six estimates above gives[12]

$$\hat{m}_{000} = \frac{m_{100}\,m_{020} + m_{100}\,m_{003} + m_{020}\,m_{003} + m_{120}\,m_{003} + m_{103}\,m_{020} + m_{023}\,m_{100}}{m_{120} + m_{103} + m_{023} + 3m_{123}}\,,$$

$$[7.116]$$

so that we can now estimate $\hat{n}$ by adding the eight cells: that is,

$$\hat{n} = m_{123} + m_{120} + m_{103} + m_{023} + m_{100} + m_{020} + m_{003} + \hat{m}_{000}\,. \quad [7.117]$$

For the example above, the estimates of equations 7.116 and 7.117 would have expected values of $.0148\,N$ for m_{000} and $.9823\,N$ for $\hat{n}$. This bias is slightly smaller than that of the maximum likelihood estimator. However, the estimate of equation 7.117 will have a slightly higher variance.

In general, the estimates of equations 7.110 through 7.112 tend to have less correlation bias than those of equations 7.113 through

7.115. That is, in equations 7.110 through 7.112, the estimate will be unbiased if there is independence of reporting between two of the sources for those cases *not* reported in the third source. Such independence is more likely to hold, since we are dealing with cases that are likely to be omitted from at least one source. Thus, where there is appreciable correlation bias, a better estimate of m_{000} may be

$$\hat{m}_{000} = \frac{m_{100}m_{020} + m_{100}m_{003} + m_{020}m_{003}}{m_{120} + m_{103} + m_{023}} \ . \qquad\qquad [7.118]$$

For the example, the estimate of m_{000} in equation 7.118 has an expected value of .0245 N. Using this value in equation 7.117 gives an estimate of $\hat{n}$ with an expected value of .992 N.

Although the m_{000} estimate given by equation 7.118 will tend to have a lower bias than the estimate given by equation 7.116, it will have a higher variance and also may have an appreciable ratio bias because only those cases omitted from one of the sources appear in the denominator of the ratio. The number of such cases may be quite small if reporting coverage is good (.8 or above) in all three sources.

Rather than basing our estimate of m_{000} on an assumption of independence—either overall for equation 7.116 or within the class of events omitted from one of the sources for equation 7.118—we can assume that the correlation within the class of events omitted from one of the sources is the same as the correlation within the class of events included in that source. That is, we can set up the equations

$$r_{12|3} = r_{12|\bar{3}} \ , \qquad\qquad [7.119]$$

$$r_{13|2} = r_{13|\bar{2}} \ , \text{ and} \qquad\qquad [7.120]$$

$$r_{23|1} = r_{23|\bar{1}} \ , \qquad\qquad [7.121]$$

where

$r_{12|3}$ = correlation between source 1 and source 2 reporting for cases reported in source 3,

$r_{12|\bar{3}}$ = correlation between source 1 and source 2 reporting for cases *not* reported in source 3,

$r_{13|2}$ and $r_{23|1}$ are defined in a manner analogous to $r_{12|3}$, and

$r_{13|\bar{2}}$ and $r_{23|\bar{1}}$ are defined in a manner analogous to $r_{12|\bar{3}}$.

Equations 7.119 through 7.121 are quadratic equations in the unknown m_{000}. They can each be solved to yield an estimate of m_{000}, and these three estimates can be averaged. The formulae for $r_{12|3}$ and $r_{12|\bar{3}}$ are

$$r_{12|3} = \frac{m_{123}m_{003} - m_{103}m_{023}}{\sqrt{(m_{123} + m_{103})(m_{123} + m_{023})(m_{003} + m_{103})(m_{003} + m_{023})}} \qquad [7.122]$$

and

$$r_{12|\bar{3}} = \frac{m_{120} m_{000} - m_{100} m_{020}}{\sqrt{(m_{120} + m_{100})(m_{120} + m_{020})(m_{000} + m_{100})(m_{000} + m_{020})}} \ . \qquad [7.123]$$

For the example above, the expected value of $r_{12|3}$ (and of $r_{13|2}$ and $r_{23|1}$) is .126. The expected value of $r_{12|\bar{3}}$ (and of $r_{13|\bar{2}}$ and $r_{23|\bar{1}}$) is .064—about halfway between $r_{12|3}$ and the value of zero assumed for equation 7.118. Since m_{000} will not be available from the sample data, it can be estimated by using the obtained value of $r_{12|3}$ for $r_{12|\bar{3}}$ in equation 7.123 and solving for m_{000}. Similar estimates of m_{000} can be obtained from equations 7.120 and 7.121, and the average of these three estimates can be added to the sum of the other seven cells (see equation 7.108) to estimate $\hat{n}$. In terms of the expected values, equation 7.119 then becomes

$$r_{12|3} \doteq .126 = \frac{(.1125\ N)(E\hat{m}_{000}) - (.0525\ N)^2}{(.165\ N)(E\hat{m}_{000} + .0525\ N)} \ .$$

Solving this equation gives an $E\hat{m}_{000} = .0420\ N$. In this case, the solutions to equations 7.120 and 7.121 would have identical expected values; thus the expected value of $\hat{n}$ would be 1.01 N. This has about the same bias upward as the equation 7.118 estimate has downward. Usually, the estimate based on equations 7.119 to 7.121 has no appreciable advantage over equation 7.118 and is much harder to compute.

There may, of course, be cases in which the correlation bias is considerably greater and where, in fact, $r_{12|\bar{3}}$ is much closer to being equal to $r_{12|3}$, with a correspondingly better approximation to equality for equations 7.120 and 7.121. In such cases, the "equal partial correlation" estimate may be preferable to that of equation 7.118. However, in such cases there is a serious question of the advisability of using the three-way system rather than devoting one's efforts to establishing a dual system with substantial independence between the sources.

In general, the preferable estimate for three-way matching will be that using $\hat{m}_{000}$ as given by equation 7.118. This estimate will tend to have a lower bias than the two-way estimate given by equation 7.105 if there is an appreciable reporting correlation between sources. On the other hand, the variance of the three-way estimate for a given sample size will be somewhat greater than the variance of the two-way estimate. Thus, the reduction in mean square error obtained by using three sources will usually be small. Of course, even a small reduction in error is desirable if it can be achieved at zero cost. Almost inevitably, however, this is not the case. In general, the marginal cost for source 3 is of the same order of magnitude as that for source 2. In addition, matching costs are bound to be double to triple those of two-way matching. Thus, three-way matching will usually mean either very greatly increased costs or, if the sample size is cut to cover these costs, a considerable increase in variance.

Adding a fourth and fifth source results in an even smaller reduction in bias and even larger increases in costs and/or variance.

These facts pretty effectively rule out any possibility of gaining anything by using more than three sources. There is a need, however, for a further exploration of the gains from a three-way match. It is possible for a three-way match to give gains over a two-way match when the third source adds little to the cost of the survey—for example, when a civil registration system is added to a dual system consisting of a survey and a special registration system. For a civil registration system, the only "out-of-pocket" costs are for matching, and it may be possible (with a well-organized file) to keep these very low. However, in such cases, one must also see whether the three-way match has net advantages over a two-way match of the survey or the special register with the civil registration. If not, the savings through eliminating one source could be used to improve independence, reduce matching and out-of-scope error, and increase sample size in the two-source system.

One line of further research is suggested by the review of the capture-tag-recapture (CTR) literature in Section E of Chapter 2. A common refinement of the basic technique is to sample and tag repeatedly the population under study and estimate the total population in part on the basis of the number of tagged individuals found in each recapture sample. This multiple sampling version may have a number of advantages over the basic technique in estimating the size of animal populations and corresponds closely to the use of more than two collection systems in PGE estimation.

A major advantage of multiple sampling approaches is that they permit one to control for the fact that the population being studied is not a closed one. In other words, if any births, deaths, or in- or out-migration occur between the capture and recapture rounds of a simple CTR study, the resulting estimates of population size will almost certainly contain an upward bias (analogous to out-of-scope bias) of an unknown amount. With multiple capture rounds it is often possible to estimate, and hence control for, this type of bias (Dowdeswell, Fisher, and Ford, 1940; Bailey, 1951).

Since biases in CTR estimates arising from the departure from the closed population assumption are similar in nature to out-of-scope biases in PGE estimation, there may be some gain from suitably adapting the theory and procedures developed for CTR studies with multiple round sampling designs to the PGE measurement situation. For example, some of the procedures discussed by Bailey (1951, Section 5) would seem to be applicable to a three-source PGE study. If such an adaptation were successful, one might be able to justify the cost of the third collection system in a PGE study—not so much in terms of response correlation bias, but rather because one could now deal more effectively with out-of-scope bias.

D.2 THE USE OF A *DE FACTO* REGISTRATION WITH A *DE JURE* SURVEY

As noted in Chapters 3 and 4, PGE estimation requires that the same sample be used by both sources. This means that one must ordinarily use a *de facto* definition for both sources or a *de jure* definition for both sources. Thus, one of the sources will almost always be covered using a definition which is not optimal for that source. That is, for registration or some other form of reporting near the time of occurrence, a *de facto* definition is simpler and less likely to produce incomplete reporting or misunderstandings about which events are to be included. For surveys or other procedures in which there is a substantial time lapse between the occurrence of the event and the reporting of it, a *de jure* definition is less likely to produce confusion and omissions about events occurring to visitors or transients who have long since left the sample area—sometimes without leaving any discernible traces of their passage through the area.

The need to use the same definition of events to be included in the sample arises from the matching requirement. In order for the match rates to estimate completeness of reporting correctly, there must be a pool of vital events common to both systems from which the reported events can be drawn. This pool will be slightly different with a *de jure* concept than with a *de facto* one. The problem of matching between *de jure* and *de facto* reporting can be minimized if one of the collection systems obtains enough information so that either concept can be used. Thus, it may be possible to do a one-way match from a *de jure* household survey to a *de facto* civil registration system if the reports of both sources contain a sufficient number of identification items in common to permit accurate matching at reasonable cost. Usually this means that the survey reports the place of occurrence of the events in enough detail and with enough accuracy to permit searching for the event in the civil register at the locality where the event occurred. In other words, the survey sample would be on a *de jure* basis but would be used to estimate the completeness of the *de facto* civil registration by identifying the survey reports that were not registered at the location at which they occurred. Poor identification of place of occurrence in the survey or serious misclassification (filing) errors in the civil registration are the major problems with this technique. Both will operate to increase the number of erroneous nonmatches and reduce the match rate, leading to an upward bias in the PGE estimate.

The two-way matching of a *de jure* survey with a *de facto* registration system is likely to lead to a gross overestimate unless, as suggested in Section B of this chapter, some form of a two-stratum estimate is used. For example, registration could be on a *de facto* basis, but the certificates would have to indicate the place of usual residence; the survey reports would be on a *de jure* basis, but they would also show the place of occurrence. Two-way matching and PGE estimation would be restricted to stratum 1, events for which place of occurrence and place of residence were the same—that is, to registrations where the decedent or infant lived in the sample area and to survey reports of events that occurred in the sample area. For stratum 2 (events for which place of residence and place of occurrence were different), one might use either the more accurate of the two single system estimates or their average if there is no satisfactory way of determining which estimate is more accurate.

It is preferable to make a PGE estimate for stratum 2 by applying the completeness rate estimated for stratum 1 to the single system estimate for stratum 2. This will probably improve the single system estimate. However, since the reporting of stratum 2 events will usually be less complete than the reporting of stratum 1 events, the stratum 2 events will still be underestimated.

A case can sometimes be made for using different sampling frames in the two sources for a one-way match between a *de facto* civil registration system and a *de jure* survey. Admittedly there are costs involved in determining where each of the survey events occurred and in searching for some registration certificates in portions of the file not related to any PGE sample area. This will mean maintaining an adequately indexed central file of registered events or doing the searches in local registration offices, and either alternative may mean a substantial added expense.

These higher costs, however, may be justified by the improved completeness of the survey results and, even more important, by a reduction in correlation bias. That is, there will be a number of events whose chances of being reported when a *de facto* rule is used are very low, even when attempts are made to register the event shortly after its occurrence. This will be true, for example, of most accidental deaths and of those where the person is suddenly taken ill and dies before he can be brought to his home. The probability of such an event being reported in a survey taken some time later at the place of occurrence is even smaller than the probability of its being registered at the time of occurrence. On the other hand, many such events will have an excellent chance of being reported some months later when a *de jure* rule is used. For example, the fact that an older member of the household died while returning from town will not appreciably affect the chances of the death being reported in a *de jure* survey.

Although increased accuracy and independence may sometimes justify the additional data collection and matching costs of using a *de jure* survey in a one-way match with a *de facto* registration, the decision to follow such a course should be based on a careful examination of the facts of the specific situation. The presence of an ongoing *de jure* household survey and a *de facto* civil registration system in a country does not necessarily mean that it will be cheaper and easier to use the existing frames in a proposed PGE study, particularly with two-way matching. At times, the pressure to combine the two concepts reflects an unwillingness to consider the merits of new alternatives.

For example, the ongoing survey may be collecting population information on a *de jure* basis for other purposes (frequently for labor force estimates) and may not be collecting any data on vital events. One might add questions about births and deaths to this ongoing survey, but such questions can just as well relate to births and deaths that occurred in the segment as births and deaths of residents. The canvass of population can and frequently should be of residents living in the sample areas at the time of the survey, but this has nothing to do with whether birth and death reporting should be *de jure* or *de facto*.

The decedents are, in any event, not included in the *de jure* current population regardless of the basis of reporting, and many of the persons involved in *de jure* births will no longer be resident in the sample area by the time of the survey.

If the existing survey is already collecting vital events information on a *de jure* basis, changing to a *de facto* concept will be largely a matter of changing the questionnaire and retraining interviewers. The costs of this must be weighed against the losses entailed in using a single system estimate or a dual system estimate based on the completeness of stratum 1 reporting for stratum 2. Alternatively, one could consider replacing the civil registration system, for purposes of PGE estimation, with another data collection source set up on a *de jure* basis, for example, a special registration system. Of course, one may decide that a one-way match from the *de jure* survey to a *de facto* civil registration source is justified in terms of accuracy and costs. In general, however, the use of a different sampling frame for the survey and the registration system is desirable only as the lesser of two evils.

On occasion one may be impelled by circumstances to consider dual sampling frames other than the combination of a *de facto* registration and a *de jure* survey. For example, in Korea civil registration is based on a "legal" or "family" residence concept. Births and deaths are registered at the legal seat of the (extended) family, which is often a place in which the decedent or the parents of the infant have not in fact lived or have not visited for many years, if ever. For civil registration purposes the system works moderately well, but an attempt to get events reported in a household survey on the basis of this legal family residence is bound to introduce endless complications of definition and coverage, complications that will frequently be resolved by sacrificing independence between the systems. Here, the use of a "legal residence" civil registration is justified by the low costs involved, and the use of a regular *de jure* or *de facto* survey is justified as the best alternative that both preserves independence and permits reasonably unbiased one-way matching and a standard PGE estimate.

D.3 PGE AND IMPROVING CIVIL REGISTRATION

An important use of the PGE technique is as a way of improving civil registration. This was one of the earlier uses of the method in the United States (in connection with the development of birth and death registration) and elsewhere. It is also likely to be the major use in countries that already have well-developed civil registration systems. In many such countries there is a tendency to assume that officially published civil registration statistics "must" be accurate, and arguments for setting up alternative systems get short shrift from the government bodies responsible for budget allocation. Experience in such countries shows that even suggestions for measuring the accuracy of the civil registration statistics will be dismissed as a waste of government funds. One can, in fact, run into opposition from trained demographers, who dismiss evidence of gross underregistration as unbelievable at the same time that they are developing elaborate methods for "correcting" the inconsistencies in fertility and mortality rates derived from the civil registration system.

Even countries with presumably complete and accurate current vital statistics should occasionally (for example, in connection with a national census of population) do a PGE study to check whether the quality of the system is holding up over time. The cost will be attractively low, since both collection systems are funded independently of the PGE study; the only major expenses will be for matching, tabulation, and publication. Such studies can be particularly valuable in rapidly developing countries where migration of the rural population to the crowded lower-class areas of large cities makes a large proportion of the population very difficult to enumerate in a survey or list in a registration. In such a situation, even with improvements in the quality of survey or registration techniques, the overall coverage may actually deteriorate. This may be one factor in the unexpectedly low estimates of intercensal growth shown by several recent population censuses in Latin America and Asia.

In any case, when a country is able and willing to attempt to improve its civil registration system, it is desirable to devote some proportion of the available funds to measuring the amount of improvement actually achieved in various areas. For this purpose, PGE estimation is an essential feature. Some of the issues involved here are discussed in a proposal for improving registration in Korea that suggests using "registration promoters" in a sample of areas (Korea, Republic of, 1971). To measure the effectiveness of the registration promoters and to determine the desirability of extending the system to the rest of the country, four techniques were suggested:

(1) time trend analysis in the demonstration areas,
(2) comparison of the demonstration areas with control areas,
(3) obtaining reports from the personnel engaged in promoting vital registration,
(4) matching with demographic surveys that would collect reports of vital events for the same area.

The third technique (reports by the registration personnel) can yield very valuable information, but not, of course, any satisfactory measurement of effectiveness. With respect to the first two techniques, the Korean proposal and an unpublished critique of it have this to say:

"Time trend analysis" (the first technique) is based on the assumption that "neither birth nor death rates are likely to increase over the next few years"; thus "any increase in registered births or deaths would be attributable to the promoter input rather than to an actual rise in fertility or mortality." The critique notes that "time trend analysis in the demonstration areas will not be very helpful, unless you have a very peculiar sample with zero net migration in and out of the sample E.D.'s." The critique notes further that, even if birth or death rates remain constant in the major urban areas, the populations (and therefore the number of vital events) are likely to increase drastically. The critique also suggests that, in other parts of the country, apparently decreased birth and/or death rates resulting from failure to measure net emigration may make it look as if the special promotion is not accomplishing anything.

In connection with the second technique of measuring the effectiveness of the registration promoters, the proposal suggests a "comparison between the demonstration areas and a carefully selected matched set of promoterless control areas," with "registration levels before and after the assumption of duties by the promoters" considered. The critique notes that, although this technique is unbiased, the variance for a sample of 25 demonstration areas will "be enormous when there is no way of distinguishing between changes in completeness of registration and changes in the population or in the birth and death rates."

It is suggested instead, in line with the fourth technique mentioned earlier, that proposed improvements in vital registration be set up on an experimental basis, with a sample of areas in which the improvements are introduced and a sample of comparable control areas with no changes. (Alternatively, more than one method of improving registration might be studied, and these methods could be tried in comparable samples of areas, with or without a sample of "control" areas with no changes.) In each experimental and control sample area, vital events would also be collected by a household survey and matched to the civil registration. This would yield PGE estimates of completeness rates (and, possibly, changes in completeness rates). The completeness rates could be used, in conjunction with relative cost data from the experiment, in deciding whether to extend the experimental treatment to all areas. A comparison of the effects of different techniques for improving registration on completeness rates and an analysis of the relationships between completeness rates and other factors could be used to determine the most efficient ways of improving civil registration.

D.4   "HYBRID" PGE DESIGNS

In some situations, it may be desirable to use different kinds of collection systems for different strata or areas of the country. For example, civil registration in the national capital and other major urban centers of a country frequently develops well ahead of that in the more remote rural areas. To set up a special registration system in sample areas with a good civil registration system would mean a duplication of existing data; and even if the special registration were superior to the civil registration in some respects, the improvements might not justify the additional costs involved. In other areas, however, civil registration may not exist or may be so bad that it is worthless for PGE purposes. The solution is to set up a stratified PGE sample. In both strata, one would do a household survey. However, in the stratum with good civil registration the survey reports would be matched to civil registration certificates; in the other areas, the survey reports would be matched with a special registration record. Separate PGE estimates would be prepared for the two subuniverses and averaged—with weighting to reflect any differences in sampling rates in the different strata—to give the final estimates.

This method may also be applied to the technique of improving civil registration by "registration promoters" described in the preceding section. Here the experimental areas are covered by a system rather similar to special registration, while the control areas are covered by a standard civil registration system. Assuming that the experimental and control areas are from the same population, one PGE estimate can be prepared using the "registration promotion" scheme and the household survey, and another matching the survey with the standard civil registration system.

E.   Vital Events in Institutions and Other Special Population Groups

E.1   SOME TYPES OF SPECIAL POPULATION GROUPS

There are certain population groups that cannot be covered very efficiently using a study design based on dual collection of vital events in family dwellings and households. The events of these groups can be placed into two categories: nonhousehold vital events, of which by far the largest number occur in institutions, and events occurring in groups or areas that are difficult to cover with standard PGE collection sources.

Institutional populations are generally understood to be those groups in the society—a small minority—who live under nonhousehold arrangements such as prisons, hospitals, army barracks, students' or workers' dormitories, monasteries or convents, large boarding houses, large hotels, and so on. Such populations usually inhabit structures (see Glossary), although some may live in the open without the benefit of such shelter.

Some institutions will have birth or death rates substantially higher or lower than those for the population at large. For example, both fertility and mortality are likely to be high in general hospitals, whereas homes for the aged or special-purpose hospitals (other than maternity hospitals) are likely to have high death rates but very low birth rates. Except in wartime, a military encampment is likely to have very low birth and death rates. On the other hand, refugee camps or camps for disaster victims are apt to have higher than average mortality and average fertility. Thus in considering the problems posed by the institutional population, one must look not only at its total size but also at the prevalence of various types of institutions in a country.

The institutional problem, which will occupy the bulk of this section, is part of the more general problem of "nonfamily vital events." In addition to vital events occurring in institutions, these include births where the mother gave birth while traveling, deaths of homeless people, and the like. However, these other nonfamily vital events are considerably less important than the institutional events and will not require any modification in the sample design. Some will be picked up from the institutions where the mother or the victim was temporarily accommodated (for example, a police station, hospital, or mortuary). Some should be picked up from village officials and other sources of village gossip during the PGE registrar's "routine rounds," particularly during the calls allotted specifically to nonhousehold sources of "first intelligence" (see Section D.2 of Chapter 4). Like institutional events, these events are quite unlikely to be picked up by a survey that depends on a canvass of dwelling units for its reports.

A number of countries have populations living in desert, jungle, or mountain areas that are out of touch with persons outside their own village or tribe and not covered or very poorly covered by normal data gathering procedures. These may be nomadic tribes or simply groups of people living in sparsely populated or hard-to-reach areas. The central statistics office of the country will frequently exclude these areas from the national census coverage, or it may send a few agents into the area to try to contact the tribal chiefs and obtain some rough estimate of the numbers of tribe members, possibly with some breakdown by sex and age. In other cases, these isolated populations may be sufficiently large to warrant attempts to cover them in censuses, but the population figures will be published separately and with big question marks.

Trying to cover nomadic populations twice and independently is extremely difficult. Where the decision is made to attempt vital events coverage of these populations, there may be advantages to independent household (tribal) surveys with overlapping recall periods. For example, a tribe might be canvassed quarterly for events that occurred during the preceding six months, with the two surveys doing independent canvasses in alternate quarters. The sampling unit must be the tribe regardless of its momentary geographic location, and births and deaths must be covered in *de jure* terms—that is, births and deaths of members of the tribe must be covered regardless of the place of occurrence. If the main study is conducted on a *de facto* basis, care must be taken to avoid double coverage.

Developing a sampling frame for nomadic groups can be a major problem. The areas to be covered are typically vast and sparsely inhabited. One device that has been used successfully with seasonal migrants is to sample the migration routes and subsample time periods—that is, to sample the tribes passing point A on route B during week C. The method is applicable to nomadic groups whose movements are nonseasonal, provided the routes followed can be mapped and segmented for sampling purposes. In this case the sample would cover any tribe encountered between point A and point B of route C during a specified time period.

With dual system estimation, locating the same nomadic tribe at two different points in time is a problem. Usually, however, the tribe has a standard routing, and the times at which it will reach specified points are predictable within limits. Of course, the migration schedule may be accelerated, and the route may have to be extended in bad seasons when pasture is sparse and more ground must be covered to obtain adequate food for the herds. Handling this type of coverage requires considerable mobility on the part of the study personnel and can be quite expensive. Considerable difficulties may also be involved in controlling the movements of two enumeration teams so that they encounter the same tribes at different points in time, but do *not* encounter each other at any point in time!

Often there are remote desert, jungle, or mountain populations living in villages that can be sampled in the same manner as other village populations. The main problem is the cost of getting to the sample village and returning with usable data. In addition, there may be little usable information available at the beginning of the study for mapping or estimating the base population. If the population is small relative to the total population of the country (even though the land area involved is substantial), it is usually best to exclude such nomadic and remote population groups from the frame of the study. Attempts to deal with data collection problems in these areas will take funds and staff time better spent collecting information from the remaining 99 percent of the population. If the number of people involved is substantial, it may be unwise to ignore the problem, but prohibitively expensive to treat it within the basic study design. In such situations, the wisest course may be single system coverage with a careful household survey in a relatively small sample of these areas and acceptance of the error involved.

E.2   INSTITUTIONAL VITAL EVENTS: DESIGN CONSIDERATIONS

The usual PGE technique will be ineffective for improving estimates of the number of vital events in institutions, at least if *de facto* counting rules are used in both sources. There are three problems with respect to institutional events that may require special attention in setting up a PGE study. The first is the sampling problem, which is one of cluster size and variability; the second is the difficulty of access to respondents in many types of institutions; the third is that many institutional inmates are transients. From the sampling viewpoint, each large institution can be considered a separate cluster. Because the noninstitutional PGE areas are also apt to be large, the fact that some institutional clusters could contain up to 1,000 or more persons does not in and of itself contribute to variance. On the other hand, the fact that some institutions have fertility and mortality markedly different from that of the population at large may.

Actually, institutions that have very low birth or death rates pose no special problem. However, the variance in estimated deaths contributed by large hospitals and other institutions likely to have high death rates may be substantial, as may be the variance in the estimated number of births contributed by maternity hospitals and homes for unmarried mothers. For example, one large hospital could have upward of 400 births and 200 deaths in a year.

It should be noted that the problem of clusters with exceptionally high death rates is not exclusively institutional. There are areas within the larger cities of many countries to which the homeless, jobless, hopeless poor gravitate after they have tried unsuccessfully to find work and/or shelter elsewhere. These derelicts have no family ties, or at least none that are known to the police or anyone else in the area. Many are old or ill, and deaths among them are common. Coverage of such deaths can often be achieved by providing for reporting at the place where the body is taken—the morgue, mortuary, or hospital. However, in many cases, such an *ex post facto* reporting rule is unworkable or undesirable for other reasons and it is necessary to rely upon *de facto* reporting of the death in the area in which it occurs. In such cases, it will be desirable for sampling purposes to put these areas in the stratum of clusters with high death rates and sample them along with the institutions having high death rates. For other purposes—data collection, matching, and estimation—these areas should be treated in the same way as areas of family residence, even though a large part of the population of the area has no known family to report the death.

The other two distinctive problems in gathering data on the institutional population are (1) the difficulties in obtaining free access to respondents in military camps, in prisons, in hospitals, in monasteries and nunneries, and even in students' or workers' dormitories, and (2) the fact that in some institutions—hospitals, jails or other places for temporary detention, and hotels—a high proportion of the clientele is transient. Because of the latter problem a survey interviewer is not likely to encounter anyone who had direct knowledge of the event, and a registrar calling even a few days later is unlikely to encounter the mother of an infant or the next of kin of a decedent or, in an institution of any size, to be able to locate a staff member who has *personal* knowledge of the birth or death.

The first important question in counting vital events in a transient population is whether the events are to be counted on a *de jure* or a *de facto* basis. For purposes of estimating the population base, the survey can solve the difficulties of interviewing a transient population either way—by conducting interviews with the *de facto* population staying in the institution at the time of the interviewer's call or by enumerating people on a *de jure* basis at their place of usual residence. The latter procedure reduces the problem in hospitals and hotels to one of estimating the population of the resident staff, permanent guests or patients with chronic ailments, or patients and guests with no usual residence elsewhere.

The use of a *de facto* definition, however, provides no real solution to interviewing transients about *vital events* that occurred in the past. A *de jure* definition is also unsatisfactory for transient populations, at least with respect to enumerating deaths. First, there is the problem of persons with no usual place of residence—particularly in the general hospitals of large urban centers which act as ports of final call for the homeless dying of the cities, as well as in dormitories or shelters that, for a few pennies, provide a place where the indigent can sleep. An even more serious objection to using a *de jure* definition for determining where to count deaths of transients is that it avoids, without solving it, the problem of large numbers of cases that are unlikely to be reported at the usual residence of the decedent.

On balance, it will usually be desirable, in the case of institutional events, to stick to a *de facto* definition. Certainly, a *de facto* procedure is desirable for the registration source. That is, it is better to complete the death report on a *de facto* basis at the institution and, where appropriate, transmit the report (or a copy) to the decedent's place of residence than to incur the high risk that the death will not be reported at all under *de jure* reporting rules. The superiority of *de facto* reporting for deaths of transients also applies to surveys, although here the difference between the completeness of *de facto* and *de jure* death reporting may be small unless some method is developed for using institutional records. Moreover, a survey using a *de jure* rule may provide reasonably good coverage for live births occurring in hospitals.

As indicated elsewhere, the population in institutions can be enumerated on either a *de facto* or a *de jure* basis. In either case, the population enumerated as transients in institutions will rarely be associated with the reported vital events occurring at the institution.

Various ways of dealing with the problems posed by institutional events are possible. In most cases, the first step is to isolate the institutional events in a separate stratum. If institutional events are relatively rare, it may be possible to do nothing—that is, to measure only noninstitutional events. Alternatively, one can do nothing for a while and then, once the data collection and matching for the noninstitutional population is well under control, attempt to prepare independent estimates for the institutional stratum. At the other extreme, one may provide procedures for sampling and measuring institutional events from the start. Which course of action is appropriate in a given situation depends upon bias, variance, and cost considerations that, in turn, depend largely upon the proportion of events that occur in institutions. For example, in the Pakistan PGE study it was initially assumed that institutional events represented a tiny fraction of all events. Accordingly, in the initial two years of the study no attempt was made to deal with this stratum, and efforts were concentrated on establishing workable procedures for the noninstitutional population. Subsequently, it was possible to prepare estimates for the institutional stratum by contacting hospitals and other institutions directly. On the basis of this study the original assumption was confirmed—that is, only trivial biases in the crude rates were introduced by ignoring institutional events (Afzal, 1966).

For most situations, we recommend making a listing of all institutions likely to have very high birth rates and one of all institutions likely to have very high death rates, regardless of how one expects to handle institutional events. Although it is not necessary to make a precise determination of the number of births or deaths for these institutions, it is necessary to make some kind of listing in order to ascertain whether they in fact account for only a small proportion of vital events. If these strata are such that the expected number of sample areas to be selected from them for a self-weighting sample is less than 0.5, it may be better to sample them with higher probabilities and weight the sample obervations *down* or, if this is not feasible from a cost standpoint, to accept the bias caused by omitting these clusters entirely rather than the variance that would result from sampling them with the same probabilities as the regular (family-type) clusters.

In practice, the "do nothing" approach also involves accepting the bias that results from omitting clusters with very high numbers of deaths or births, rather than using a variance which includes them in the sample estimate. However, with the "do nothing" approach the decision will have to be made only if one of these clusters happens to be selected for the sample. Of course, this saves the cost of identifying all the clusters with high birth or death rates and setting up separate strata for them. However, if the institutions to be omitted from the PGE coverage account for a very small proportion of all vital events, listing them as a separate stratum should be a very inexpensive operation; that is, there will be only a few institutions in the institutional strata, and these will stand out like sore thumbs.

If an attempt is made to measure fertility and mortality for the institutional strata, both the difficulty of access to individual institutional respondents and the problem of reporting births and deaths of transients emphasize the desirability of basing vital events reporting at institutions on institutional records. This will be true whether the institutions are included in the regular sample strata or are set up as separate strata, and whether reporting is on a *de facto* or a *de jure* basis. Large institutions (those with 100 or more persons), and particularly large institutions for transients, must almost of necessity maintain some type of records for administrative purposes. These may not be very suitable for purposes of vital events reporting, but at least a basis for such reporting exists. For small institutions, the problem of access to respondents is likely to be less severe, as is the problem of locating staff members with personal knowledge of (recent) vital events. Coverage of small institutions, whether for transients or longer-term residents, can best be handled by the sampling and reporting procedures applicable to the noninstitutional population. Some special modifications of the canvassing and reporting procedures may be desirable, but these are usually easier to make and more likely to be workable if they are formulated on an *ad hoc* basis.

Regardless of whether institutional records are available, there are likely to be problems in the matching operation. If the records of the institution are not used, there will usually be a high rate of erroneous nonmatches. For small institutions the overall impact of these errors will be minor and can in most cases be handled adequately by the regular matching procedures. For institutions with a large number of births or deaths, out-of-scope events and erroneous nonmatches for reports not based on institutional records can be a serious problem; and the inclusion of even one such institution in the sample may substantially affect the coverage and matching errors. If hospital records are used for reporting vital events, the only out-of-scope and matching errors will be those due to seriously faulty transcription, and these can be practically eliminated by rigorous supervision of the transcriptions. On the other hand, the use of hospital records will result in no gain from matching in institutions. That is, if events are erroneously omitted from the institutional records, either intentionally or inadvertently, these omissions will affect both sources, and the reporting error correlation between sources will be close to 1.0.

If institutional records are used, PGE estimation will usually be undesirable. That is, if both sources for the PGE estimate are based on the institutional records, the reports will be identical except for matching and transcription errors, so that dual system estimation will add to the cost, but not the accuracy, of the estimate. If only one source is based on institutional records, the events reported in the other source either will be a subset of those in the record-based source or will contribute a high proportion of out-of-scope events and/or erroneous nonmatches. This assumes, of course, that the institutional records are an integral part of the institutions' operations and hence are essentially complete. If institutional records are incomplete or lacking, it will be desirable to use two sources with matching on the same basis as for noninstitutional events.

If institutional records are used without matching, the institutional events should be added to the PGE estimate without any adjustment for completeness of reporting. That is, it is usually better to treat the recorded institutional events as if reporting were complete than to apply to them completeness rates based on the noninstitutional reporting.

E.3 INSTITUTIONAL VITAL EVENTS: SOME OPERATIONAL PROBLEMS

Although it is usually desirable to set up separate strata for clusters likely to have very high death and birth rates, this will not solve the sampling problem where the number of such clusters is small but not zero. The problem is familiar to samplers. It occurs when a small number of sampling units have frequencies of occurrence for the characteristic under observation that are several times the average frequencies. If these clusters are sampled from the same stratum with the same probability of selection as other clusters, the probability of such a cluster being selected for the sample is small; but when it is selected, it inflates the estimate unduly.

The problem can be illustrated with an example. Suppose that we wish to estimate the number of deaths in a given year for a country of 16 million population which has been divided into 16,000 clusters for sampling purposes, each having an average (*de facto*) population of 1,000 persons and an annual average of 20 deaths. Two of the 16,000 clusters are the two wings of a large hospital in the country's big metropolitan center. This hospital averages about 2,000 patients at any one time—about half in each wing. Because the hospital is a receiving station for accident cases and others found near death, the number of deaths is very high—approximately 1,350 a year for each of the two clusters, with almost complete registration. For the other clusters, death registration is only 80-percent complete. In these clusters, the average number of deaths reported per cluster is about 16, with a standard deviation of about 6.

If we select 80 sample clusters from the 16,000 with equal probability, the samples that do not include either of the two special hospital clusters will average 16 sample deaths reported, with a standard deviation of about 0.75, or between 1,100 and 1,500 registered deaths for the entire sample. The inclusion of either one of the special hospital clusters will double the reported number of deaths in the sample, to between about 2,300 and 2,900, and bring about a corresponding increase in the death rate estimates. It is true there is less than a .01 probability of selecting a sample that includes one of the two hospital clusters. However, the standard deviation of the estimated number of deaths is nearly quadrupled by including these two clusters in the same stratum as the others. Furthermore, the PGE death rate estimate of 31 to 36 per 1,000 for any sample that included one of the special clusters would be completely unacceptable. The statistical office would be forced, at the very least, to drop the hospital segment results from the sample estimate.

Both retaining and rejecting extreme observations in data from an unstratified sample are undesirable options, but when faced with such a dilemma after the data have been collected, the study manager must do one or the other. A preferable course is to arrange the sampling so that the retention of extreme observations does not distort the results. This involves doing what we suggested previously—putting the extreme observations in one stratum that can be sampled separately. Frequently this can be done using about the same probability for sampling the high death rate clusters as for the normal death rate clusters. For example, if there were 200 high death rate clusters and 15,800 normal death rate clusters, one could select one cluster from the 200 and 79 from the 15,800, using the same sampling rate (1/200) in both strata. Since all the sample clusters would have the same probability of selection, the sample would be self-weighting.

If there are only a few high death rate clusters, it is desirable to select clusters from the different strata with different probabilities—for example, 1/2 for a high death rate stratum with two clusters and 1/200 for the other stratum. This means weighting down the results from the sample cluster with the high death rate, which may be a somewhat expensive procedure. Data collection may cost about as much for this cluster from the high death rate stratum, which has the very small weight of .01, as for one of the clusters from the other stratum, which has a weight of 1. One may again be faced with a choice between accepting the bias that results from eliminating the cluster or paying a high cost for retaining it. Here, the magnitude of the bias must be weighed against costs rather than against a variance. Here, also, the decision to eliminate the observation must always be viewed with suspicion and only adopted if there is strong evidence that the bias is so small that spending the money elsewhere is clearly preferable.

Actually, the cost of oversampling the strata of institutions with high death or birth rates may be fairly reasonable. For one thing, if there is to be no matching of institutional vital events it may be feasible to subsample within institutions. This might be done by subdividing them by wards or some other physical units and sampling only one of the wards. Another possibility would be "time sampling"—for example, taking only the deaths for every 13th week or for every 30th day. Although such subsampling may not produce a self-weighting sample, it may reduce the cost of oversampling to more palatable dimensions.

Another factor affecting the cost of data collection for sample institutions will be the feasibility and cost of using records. As mentioned above, if records cannot be used in institutions with largely transient populations, one may have to spend a very large amount for very inferior data—data that are grossly incomplete and also quite unusable in matching to correct their incompleteness. Of course, one could station a special registrar at the institution continuously and have an interviewer do a daily canvass so that matching could be done. But even if the registrar and interviewer could obtain permission to talk to respondents (and to talk to them independently), the cost is likely to be prohibitive. On the other hand, it may be possible to induce all institutions, or at least all large institutions, to prepare birth and death certificates for events occurring there as part of their own record-keeping activities. The cost to the PGE study would then be reduced to that of monitoring the institution's activities to make sure the certificates were filled out and explaining the procedures for preparing certificates to the personnel of the institution.

In some cases, the cooperation of an institution can be obtained and the quality of the data supplied greatly enhanced by a small payment either to the institution or, preferably, directly to the personnel preparing the data. Such payments can be quite effective even though they are only a fraction of the cost of sending a registrar or an interviewer to obtain the data. Although payments should be adjusted according to the work load of a given institution, there are pros and cons to paying on a per certificate basis. On the "pro" side is the fact that the institution can link the fee directly to the work performed—that is, the fee is clearly a "fee for service" rather than a general income supplement. Also, a payment per event reported may reduce the tendency to omit events through haste or carelessness. On the "con" side is the possibility of events being "manufactured" or reported more than once in order to increase the payments and of attention being given to the quantity of the reports at the expense of their quality.

Probably, the method of payment and, within limits, the size of the fee are less important than the care with which an institution's reporting is monitored, the attention given to simplifying reporting forms and making sure the reporting requirements and procedures are clear and are well understood by the personnel involved, and the extent to which requests for information not readily available are kept to a minimum. For example, a requirement that the cause of death be reported may be a substantial obstacle to the prompt completion of death certificates.

The alternative to having the institution extract the data needed by the PGE study from its records is to send in study personnel (registrars or interviewers) to do the job. This may be necessary if the institution does not have any personnel to assign to vital statistics tasks or is unwilling to make such assignments. It may be *desirable* to use PGE study personnel when the personnel an institution is able and willing to assign to PGE tasks are so incompetent or uncooperative as to cast doubt on the validity of any information supplied by them. That is, it may be easier and cheaper to have study personnel do the job than to "police" data transcription done by the institution's own personnel.

Regardless of whether data are extracted from the institution's records by study personnel or by institutional personnel, steps must be taken to see that the institution's records contain the requisite data and that its files are such as to make vital statistics reporting feasible at a reasonable cost. A distinction is necessary here between the reporting of the population for the vital rate base and the reporting of vital events. Most institutions (except hospitals, where deaths, and in some cases births, are basic administrative data) will not have any standard record-keeping procedures for vital events. On the other hand, almost all institutions of any size—whether prisons, hospitals, military barracks, schools, hotels, or flophouses—must, as an administrative necessity, maintain some continuous record of their *de facto* population. An institution with fewer than 30 occupants may be able to operate without a written roster of current occupants but, where the number exceeds that level, some current listing is almost certain to exist, even if the institution does not maintain any records of past occupancy.

Hospitals will usually keep fairly complete records of vital events, showing age, sex, marital status, and place of residence for the decedent or mother. Their records may also contain considerable additional data—for example, age of spouse or father and education and occupation. However, the demographic detail may vary considerably from hospital to hospital within the same city. Most other institutions will keep no vital events records other than a notation on their rosters of deaths of occupants (and, in rarer cases, of births).

If institutional records of vital events are incomplete, lack adequate detail, or are difficult and expensive to use for statistical purposes, it is desirable to use two sources with matching. In general, a survey should not be used in institutions, even if one is used elsewhere. Interviews with the occupants or staff after a lapse of time will usually be unsatisfactory. Neither the surviving occupants nor the staff members are likely to be able to supply more complete information about decedents than appears in the institutional records.

For institutions whose records are incomplete or difficult to use, a special registration based on reports of the responsible institutional staff members matched to the institution's records as the other source may prove reasonably efficient. If the institution's records are voluminous and expensive to use, a sample of records may be selected for matching against a complete registration.

If institutional records are unavailable or completely unusable, it will probably be necessary to rely on a single system estimate derived from some form of registration and accept the bias due to incomplete coverage. If this is the only feasible recourse, the primary emphasis should be on getting as complete coverage as possible.

We should point out that all the statements above apply only to large institutions—say, those with at least five staff members. Small institutions can be covered in the same way as regular households. True, there will be problems in obtaining vital events information when the institutional occupants are largely transients, but these problems will be no worse than the problem of obtaining information on noninstitutional transients. In fact, better information may be available where institutions are involved, since the staff will often ascertain data on age, place of residence, and so on at the time a patient or inmate is admitted.

E.4   POPULATION BASE ESTIMATES FOR INSTITUTIONS

Population base estimates may be obtained, quite independently of the vital events reporting, from the sample institutions or from a special reporting system set up for all institutions of a given class—for example, for reporting by the military of the numbers and demographic characteristics of men and women living in camps or barracks. If the population base reporting is restricted to sample institutions, the correlation of the population estimate with the number of vital events will be higher and the variance of the birth or death rate estimate will be lower than for a population estimate using all institutions. Also, the *de facto* population of a hospital, jail, or other transient quarters at any point in time during the reporting period will be more highly correlated than the *de jure* population with the number of deaths in the institution during the period, even though there is no one-to-one correspondence between the events and the people. However, institutions for transients will usually have only a small effect on either the correlation or the variance of the rate; and, for other institutions, any differences between the *de facto* and the *de jure* population is primarily a matter of definition. That is, if soldiers in barracks, students in dormitories, prisoners, and so on are considered residents of the institution rather than of their original homes, the differences between *de facto* and *de jure* counts will be less than the variation in either total during the reporting period.

These remarks apply, however, only to large institutions. In defining "large institutions" it is not necessary to have a precise cutoff on size or a particularly rigorous definition of "institution." Nor is it either necessary or desirable for the sampling and the reporting treatment of a given institution to be consistent. For example, there may be no need to put prisons in a separate stratum for sampling purposes. However, it will be desirable (or even imperative) to rely on the prison records for a report of persons and events, but to exclude the prison from the matching and the PGE completeness adjustment. Similarly, a 20-bed hospital may come into the sample as part of a cluster of otherwise noninstitutional units, and it may be desirable to base reporting of the vital events on the hospital records but to exclude them from the matching and the PGE adjustment.

F. *Features Contributing to Independence Between the Two Systems*

The point has been made repeatedly in this handbook that the supervision of the field work of either collection system and the statistical evaluation of the two systems are distinct operations. Since one key to an accurate statistical evaluation of the coverage of the collection systems is the independence of the two systems, some discussion of the factors affecting this independence is in order. On the other hand, independence cannot be considered in isolation from other aspects of design. In particular, if the principle of independence is carried beyond reason, matching and out-of-scope problems will tend to adversely affect the result. However, in the early history of the use of the PGE approach the problem nearly always was too little independence rather than too much. Even in a number of recent PGE studies, the failure to give sufficient attention to the problem of independence has seriously affected the results.

Lack of independence can arise either because of communication, planned or unplanned, between the two collection systems or because the same kinds of events are missed by both systems. This leads directly to two operational principles: (1) the opportunities for overt collusion must be minimized, and (2) the systems must be as separate and unlike each other as possible. Fortunately, many of the techniques for preserving independence contribute to both objectives; by and large, the more dissimilar the systems, the fewer the opportunities for cooperation, and *vice versa*.

Many of the problems relating to independence result from overzealous pursuit of the goal, praiseworthy in itself, of improving coverage. It will occur to many PGE employees that one obvious way of improving coverage in one system is to use the results of the other system to augment or supervise the first. It should be understood by all responsible officials of the PGE study that any attempt at this sort of thing is misguided; the individual reports of one collection system should never be used to improve coverage in the other. Similarly, the field results from one system should never be used in supervisory checks of the field results from the other system. Required supervision should come from other channels.

Moreover, any field follow-up done after the office matching should be performed by a third party specially appointed for that purpose and should involve a third document. Those doing the follow-up should not flaunt the document produced by the enumerator or, for that matter, any other vital event record, in front of the registrar's eyes. The less there is of an investigatorial air about the proceedings, the better. Otherwise, the interviewers and registrars involved may try the next time to collaborate in preparing their reports in a manner that will prevent an unpleasant auditing. It is natural to react defensively to the inquisitiveness of auditors. The workers hired for the field follow-up should be sufficiently well trained and mature not to go to either of the two field workers and try to train them, or commiserate with them, or taunt them by referring to specific errors found during the checking process.

Each of the two systems should have an organization and a supervisory staff of its own. Ideally, the first supervisor they have in common should be the highest-ranking manager of the whole study, the boss at the top. This is not always possible because of administrative control or budgetary reasons. Sometimes local supervisory and coordinating arrangements are inherited from prior administrative undertakings. In practice, a common supervisory staff for the two systems can often be avoided at the level of the registrars and enumerators, but occurs at the regional level. It is essential for regional directors, if they do serve as a common link, to be aware of the importance of maintaining the independence of the two systems and to restrain themselves from "correcting" either system on the basis of knowledge of individual cases obtained from the other system. They must be subtle enough to abdicate this managerial function without giving up others.

The principle of avoiding unnecessary cooperation between the critical parts of the organization must be carried over into the work of the study director. The preparation of a consolidated list of vital events and a system of rewards and punishments tied to the knowledge obtained from the other system are techniques to be avoided because of their subversive effect on independence, however attractive they appear to personnel management. The organizers themselves should strive to view the population in all its probabilistic aspects as a pond of fish into which one net is thrown from one direction and a second is thrown from another direction quite independently of the first. Whatever the nets do, they do; and no interference is necessary to bring them into any specific relationship with regard to each other.

A number of clerical arrangements can lessen somewhat the possibility of collusion between the two systems. One can make the content of the questionnaires for the two systems different in as many ways as possible without compromising the demographic and methodological purposes of the study. One can rearrange the order of the items on one questionnaire so that a quick comparison with the other questionnaire is difficult. Or, one can use a different size and format for each questionnaire so that not even visual comparisons can be easily made. (One way of moving in this direction is to combine, in one of the two systems, all the questionnaire entries for both types of vital events on one recording form. Several items are common to births and deaths and can therefore be conveniently arranged in columns on the same form.)

It is also possible to arrange the collection of documents from the field in such a manner that the opportunities for the registrar to view the work of the enumerator, and for the enumerator to view the work of the registrar, are limited. The registrar's opportunities can be limited by having his area covered by more than one enumerator, and the situation can be further improved by also giving each of the enumerators an area outside the registration area. In such circumstances any copying or comparisons by the registrar would be a very cumbersome procedure. Enumeration by a team is thus advantageous from the point of view of strengthening independence.

If all copies of the registration documents are taken from the registrar and sent to headquarters as soon as possible, the enumerator is deprived of the opportunity of consulting them to any appreciable extent. On the other hand, if copies of the registration documents are removed too quickly, duplicate registrations are likely to occur (for example, when the same birth is reported to the registrar by the father and the mother's brother). Assuming a registrar need have with him data for no more than the last two months, a book of death registration forms, when filled, should contain about 25 registrations for a population of 8,000 persons that has a death rate of 20 per 1,000 population per annum. On the average, then, the enumerator would be able to consult the death registrations for one month or, say, 13 deaths out of the 160 deaths he should record in a year.

Although typically a registrar has time on his hands, it would be inviting collusion if he were to spend it providing himself and headquarters with a list of the population by household and changes therein. Soon he would be passing this information on to the enumerator. The same argument cannot be made against the enumerator, because he is in the area for only a short time. He gets in, lists the households, and walks on. He has no reason to linger over the lists or to make duplicate copies.

Another possible method of reducing the opportunity for communication between the special registrars and the survey field staff is to withdraw the special registrars from the sample areas during the enumeration period for training or other administrative purposes. This procedure, untested as far as we know, would seem not to be practicable for a survey conducted more frequently than once a year or where the enumeration in any sample area took more than two weeks per round.

The instruction manuals for the field workers of the two systems should contain no admonitions about the impropriety of consulting the documents of the field workers of the other system. The matter should not be made one of grave import. The less said about it the better, so as not to call undue attention to the existence and purposes of the other system.

The potential or real dangers to independence arising out of the requirements of matching will have an important influence on a number of organizational features. One source of conflict is the desire for frequent and early matching, resulting in early field follow-up, special investigations, and so on to resolve questions that have arisen during the matching. It will soon become apparent to the field staff that the annoyance caused by these efforts has arisen because of discrepancies between the records of the registrar and enumerator, and they may well begin to think, "Why not ensure avoiding the inconsistency from the very beginning?" With matching and field follow-up somewhat delayed, such subversive ideas are unlikely to arise.

The requirements of matching must not become the tail that wags the dog of the PGE. After all, one could have perfect matching with perfect collusion, but that would not be very good for the central purposes of the experiment. Nor, on the other hand, must complete independence become the only objective, before which all other aspects of good design—reasonable costs, complete coverage, short recall periods, and prompt field follow-up—are sacrificed. The achievement of the best balance between the conflicting claims of the various relevant considerations is the ultimate art of a successful PGE study and is a frequently recurring theme in this handbook.

Footnotes

1. The derivation of equation 7.4 is closely related to the derivation of the variance of the ratio of two random variates given in Volume II of Hansen, Hurwitz, and Madow (1953, pp. 107–109). These derivations are based on a Taylor series approximation that ignores all relative moments higher than the second. In general, the error introduced by such an approximation is trivial unless the coefficient of variation is quite large. In the present case it is the higher relative moments of m that are principally involved. Assuming m to be a normal variate with a coefficient of variation less than 1.0, all its odd moments are zero and the even moments are less than or equal to three times the fourth power of the coefficient of variation. For example, with a coefficient of variation of 10 percent, the largest term ignored is less than or equal to .0003, that is $3(.1)^4$.

2. Note the difference between fn, the number of events in the sample, and

$$n = \frac{K}{k} \sum_i^n n_i \quad ,$$

which, like n_1, n_2, or m, is a sample estimate of the number of events in the population.

3. Under these circumstances, equation 7.44 simplifies to

$$V_{\hat{n}}^2 \doteq V_n^2 + \frac{(1 - P_1)(1 - P_2)}{f P_1 P_2 N} \quad .$$

This is similar to the formula originally given by Chandrasekaran and Deming (1949), who treated the case where both sources covered the entire population. Their formula is the one given above for the case $f = 1$ so that $V_n^2 = 0$; that is,

$$V_{\hat{n}}^2 = \frac{(1 - P_1)(1 - P_2)}{P_1 P_2 N} \quad .$$

4. In computing a ratio estimate, one must, of course, exclude cases where the denominator is zero. The relative biases of $1/w$ in Table 7.1 are computed from normal distributions that have been truncated to reject very small values of w, specifically cases where $w < (0.1)\,(Ew)$.

Where the coefficient of variation is small, values of w of this magnitude have essentially a zero probability of occurrence. For example, for a coefficient of variation of $w = .10$, a value of $w < (.01)\,(Ew)$ would be at least 9.9σ below Ew. However, for large coefficients of variation, $w < (.01)\,(Ew)$ is quite likely. For example, with a coefficient of variation of $w = .45$, the quantity $(.01)\,(Ew)$ would correspond to a value 2.2σ below the mean; and values this small or smaller have a probability of occurring of about .01.

Actually the biases for the larger coefficients of variation tend to be understated in Table 7.1. Often, the coefficient of variation of w_1 or w_2 will be approximately the same as that of m. For a simple random sample, m would be a Poisson variate with a coefficient of variation equal to $1/Em$. The use of a clustered sample increases this coefficient of variation of m but usually has little effect on that of w_1 and w_2. For small coefficients of variation, the distributions of m, w_1, and w_2 will be closely approximated by a normal distribution. The larger coefficients of variation will mean smaller expected values of m, n_1, and n_2. For such cases, the normal distribution will be a poor approximation, and the actual distributions of m, w_1, and w_2 will be skewed toward the lower values, thus giving probabilities for very large values of $1/w$ greater than those that would be obtained with a normal distribution of w and the same coefficient of variation.

5. In general, w_1 is an unbiased estimate of $P_{1.2}$. That is, the completeness rates w_1 and w_2 are usually not correlated with their denominators, n_2 and n_1, so that $Ew_1 = P_{12}/P_2 = P_{1.2}$ and $Ew_2 = P_{12}/P_1 = P_{2.1}$. The situation where w_1 is a biased estimate due to correlation of the completeness rates in the same areas with the number of events in the areas is discussed in Section A.5 of this chapter.

6. The fact that matching costs have been included (arbitrarily) in source 2 is a relatively small source of error. The cost of collecting reports of vital events is generally substantially larger than the cost of matching them. The costs of collection are related to the size of the entire population in the sample (both persons with and without events), whereas the costs of matching are related to the actual number of events reported (Seltzer, 1971a). The only exception is the case of a civil registration, when the matching costs, which in this case are a substantial part of the costs associated with source 1, should be evenly divided between the two sources.

7. Since f is usually very small ($< .02$) in PGE studies, we have ignored the "finite population multiplier" $(1 - f)$ in this section.

8. The intraclass correlation within sampling units for the variance of x or the covariance of xy is defined as:

$$\delta_{xx} = \frac{\sigma_{Bx}^2 - \sigma_{Wx}^2/(\bar{N} - 1)}{\hat{\sigma}_x^2}$$

or $\qquad \delta_{xy} \qquad = \qquad \dfrac{\sigma_{Bxy} - \sigma_{Wxy}/(\bar{N}-1)}{\hat{\sigma}_{xy}}$

where

$\qquad \sigma_{Bx}^2 \qquad =$ variance between sampling units,

$\qquad \sigma_{Wx}^2 \qquad =$ variance between elements within sampling units,

$\qquad \hat{\sigma}_x^2 \qquad = \quad \sigma_{Bx}^2 + \sigma_{Wx}^2 \qquad =$ variance between elements over the entire population, and

σ_{Bxy}, σ_{Wxy}, and $\hat{\sigma}_{xy}$ are the corresponding covariances. From the above, σ_{Bx}^2 or σ_{Bxy} can be expressed in terms of δ_{xx} and $\hat{\sigma}_x^2$ or δ_{xy} and $\hat{\sigma}_{xy}$ as

$\qquad \sigma_{Bx}^2 \qquad = \qquad \dfrac{\hat{\sigma}_x^2}{\bar{N}}(1 - \delta_{xx} + \bar{N}\delta_{xx}) \quad ,$

$\qquad \sigma_{Bxy} \qquad = \qquad \dfrac{\hat{\sigma}_{xy}}{\bar{N}}(1 - \delta_{xy} + \bar{N}\delta_{xy}) \quad ;$

or, in terms of relative variances and covariances as

$\qquad V_{Bx}^2 \qquad = \qquad \dfrac{\hat{V}_x^2}{\bar{N}}(1 - \delta_{xx} + \bar{N}\delta_{xx}) \quad ,$

$\qquad V_{Bxy} \qquad = \qquad \dfrac{\hat{V}_{xy}}{\bar{N}}(1 - \delta_{xy} + \bar{N}\delta_{xy}) \quad .$

Equation 7.97 is derived using these last relationships to substitute for $V_{Bn_1}^2$, $V_{Bn_2}^2$, V_{Bm}^2, and $V_{Bn_1 n_2}$ in equation 7.96, taking all the δ's as equal.

     9. Fellegi's suggestions, with supporting arguments, are contained in an unpublished paper entitled "Some Aspects of the Survey Design for the Moroccan Population Growth Experiment."

     10. Note that Δ in Section C.2 is equivalent to δ in Section C.1.

     11. If the field workers of both sources are paid at approximately the same wage rates, the registration field costs are likely to be substantially higher than the survey costs, particularly if the survey travel costs are low and the enumeration rounds are limited to two or less per year.

     12. An estimate given by Deming and Keyfitz (1967) is related to equation 7.116, but differs by using only an apparently arbitrary subset of the terms. Readers are cautioned that some of the formulae in that paper as published contain typographical errors.

A Glossary
of Technical Terms and Concepts

A successful PGE study requires a cooperative effort by persons with widely different backgrounds: administration, data processing, demography, statistics, and so on. Each of these fields has a technical vocabulary that is largely unknown to those in other fields. Our purpose in providing this glossary is to ease somewhat the task of interdisciplinary learning and communication by providing working definitions of some 125 technical terms used in the handbook and elsewhere in the PGE literature.

This list of terms is not intended to be comprehensive: Some terms have been included because they are basic and others because they have been the source of much confusion in the past. Nor do we pretend that the individual definitions are rigorous and complete. We hope that the omissions and errors are minor and that readers will find a helpful entry most of the time when they turn to the glossary for assistance. Extensive cross-referencing (indicated by capital letters) has been used within the glossary to clarify individual definitions and to facilitate instructive browsing.

ACCOUNTING FOR HOUSEHOLD CHANGES TECHNIQUE
See **HOUSEHOLD CHANGE TECHNIQUE**.

ADAPTIVE SYSTEM
A system set up so that feedback of information is compared with previously anticipated results, with observed discrepancies then leading to ongoing modification of the existing model to bring it into line with the total information available at any given point in time.

AGE-SPECIFIC FERTILITY (RATE)

> The level of fertility experienced by women of a given age, expressed as a rate. More precisely, the number of live births occurring in one year to women of a given age in some well-defined population divided by the number of women of that age in the population at midyear. For convenience, this rate is frequently multiplied by 1,000. Age-specific fertility can also be expressed in terms of the fertility of women in five-year age groups, usually the six five-year age groups from 15–19 to 40–44 or the seven groups ending in 45–49. The sum of the age-specific fertility rates for five-year age groups multipled by five is the **TOTAL FERTILITY RATE.**

AGE-SPECIFIC MORTALITY (RATE)

> The level of mortality experienced by persons of a given age, expressed as a rate. More precisely, the number of deaths occurring in one year to persons of a given age in some well-defined population divided by the number of persons of that age in the population at midyear. For convenience, this rate is usually multiplied by 1,000. Frequently age-specific mortality rates are also sex-specific; that is, they are computed separately for males and females.

AMENDMENT

> A formalized procedure aiming at an orderly correction and updating of a set of identical procedural **MANUALS** in active use in an organization. The basic problem which the amendment process must overcome is that all the manuals cannot be withdrawn from use at the same time and corrected at once.

ANALYSIS UNIT

> The unit whose characteristics are tabulated or aggregated to produce statistical results—for example, an individual person, a household, an establishment, or a single birth or death.

BASE POPULATION

> The number of people in a given area (such as a nation, province, city, or sample area) to which a specific vital rate applies—for example, the denominator .of the **CRUDE BIRTH RATE** or the **CRUDE DEATH RATE.**

BIAS   A measure of the **ERROR** associated with a particular method of data collection over the long run. More precisely, the bias of a particular method or procedure is equal to the difference between the **EXPECTED VALUE** of the population characteristic being measured obtained from the repeated use of the procedure and the **TRUE VALUE** of the characteristic. See also **SAMPLING ERROR** and **VARIANCE.**

BLOCK   A convenient subdivision of a **CHUNK** in a **PGE AREA,** usually consisting of from 50 to 100 dwellings, or about 200 to 500 residents—approximately the size of a small census enumeration district. In urban areas a PGE block corresponds to one or more urban blocks.

BLOCKING

> A concept used in technical literature on **MATCHING** to describe the separation of documents, usually on the basis of geographic variables, in order to lower the quantity of documents to be matched at any one time.

CALIBRATION

The process of establishing the level of **ERROR** associated with a measurement process and of providing quantitative corrections in terms of either specific adjustments or ranges of uncertainty.

CATEGORY

In the PGE literature, sometimes used without further qualification to refer to one, some, or all of the four cells of the two-by-two contingency table used to demonstrate how PGE estimates are developed. By convention, when **DUAL COLLECTION** is being used, the "first" category refers to **VITAL EVENTS** caught by both systems, the "second" category consists of events caught by the first system but missed by the second system, the "third" category consists of events missed by the first system but caught by the second system, and the "fourth" category consists of events missed by both systems. This model is directly applicable only in the case of a **TWO-WAY MATCH.** The term "category" is also used to mean a population **SUBGROUP.**

CBR   See **CRUDE BIRTH RATE.**

CDR   See **CRUDE DEATH RATE.**

CENTRAL RATE

Any of several rates such as **AGE-SPECIFIC FERTILITY, AGE-SPECIFIC MORTALITY,** the **CRUDE BIRTH RATE,** and the **CRUDE DEATH RATE.** A central rate is calculated using annual vital events as the numerator and the midyear population as the denominator.

CHILDREN EVER BORN

A measure of the fertility over time since puberty of a group of women. More precisely, the total number of live births occurring to a group of women (often of a given age) since the start of their reproductive life, divided by the number of women in the group. It is often based on the fertility experience of ever-married women only and expressed as a rate per 1,000 ever-married women. Comparisons of this rate for different age groups are affected by differences in fertility between those who survive and those who die before reporting their fertility performance, and by differential forgetfulness by age.

CHILDREN SURVIVING

A measure obtained and calculated in conjunction with **CHILDREN EVER BORN.** It is based only on the number of live-born babies that remain alive at the time to which the rate refers.

CHUNK   A division of a **PGE AREA,** consisting of several **BLOCKS,** roughly corresponding to a village or subward.

CIVIL REGISTRATION

The traditional method of registration of births and deaths, intended to be continuous and comprehensive. A civil registration system provides both legal documentation of each **VITAL EVENT** and statistical **RECORDS** for the compilation of vital statistics. It must be supplemented by information on the **BASE POPULATION** so that the necessary vital rates can be calculated. A registration system created specifically for PGE purposes is called **SPECIAL REGISTRATION.**

CLASSIFICATION BIAS

A form of **BIAS** arising from the failure to classify a specific person or vital event as belonging to the correct population **SUBGROUP.** Classification errors may arise at the time of data collection as reporting or recording errors or during processing because of editing, coding, punching, or matching errors.

CLUSTER A group of related **ANALYSIS UNITS** used as a **SAMPLING UNIT**—for example, the households in a given city block. If all analysis units in a cluster are to be in the sample, it is referred to as an "ultimate cluster."

CODING The translation of entries in words on a questionnaire or some other document into a numeric or alphanumeric code to facilitate further processing. The codes can be entered onto special coding sheets or in a specially provided space on the original questionnaire or document. When a coded answer is entered by the person completing the document (for example, when the interviewer enters the last two digits of the year of birth or darkens one circle out of four circles provided for marital status), this is called "self-coding."

COMPARISON CLASS

A group of matching pairs having the same or similar **COMPARISON FUNC-TION** values—that is, whose degree of agreement on **IDENTIFICATION CODE** is approximately the same. Operationally, the comparison class is used to estimate the probability of matching value $P(M)$, and all pairs in the class are treated alike in determining the **MATCHING STATUS** to be assigned.

COMPARISON FUNCTION

A statement indicating the kind and degree of correspondence between two **IDENTIFICATION CODES** that are being compared to determine whether they **MATCH.** This function can be expressed either as a scalar or a vector. For example, the statement that two codes "agree on initial of first name and/or last name and last name is unusual; agree on street name and disagree on house number, but the disagreement is in an inversion of two adjacent digits; agree within one year on age" may be a comparison vector.

COMPLETENESS

The proportion of all live births or deaths actually occurring in a population that is recorded by some data collection system (for example, **ENUMERATION** or **REGISTRATION**). One method of estimating completeness is by **DUAL COLLECTION** and **MATCHING.** When this technique is employed, the **MATCH RATE** of one system equals the estimated completeness of the other system. Completeness is also sometimes called **COVERAGE.**

CORRELATION BIAS

See **RESPONSE CORRELATION BIAS.**

COVERAGE

In vital statistics literature, a term that describes the geographic area in which a **CIVIL REGISTRATION** system functions effectively. In PGE literature, coverage is often used to mean **COMPLETENESS.**

COVERAGE BIAS

In a PGE study, the **BIAS** arising from undetected **OUT-OF-SCOPE** reports.

If, as is usually the case, such reports are primarily **NONMATCHES,** they will give a downward bias to the **MATCH RATE.** Another form of coverage bias, which the **PGE TECHNIQUE** is designed to correct, is caused by the failure to report all **IN-SCOPE** events.

CRUDE BIRTH RATE

A summary measure of fertility in a population (abbreviated as CBR); that is, the total live births occurring to a given population in a year divided by the corresponding population at midyear, usually expressed as a rate per 1,000 population.

CRUDE DEATH RATE

A summary measure of mortality in a population (abbreviated as CDR); that is, the total deaths occurring in a given population in a year divided by the corresponding population at midyear, usually expressed as a rate per 1,000 population.

DAILY RATION

A daily assignment that corresponds to the part of the **PGE AREA** to be visited on a given day of a week by the PGE special registrar active in **SPECIAL REGISTRATION.** There is one daily ration for each day of a week, and there are as many multiples of five daily rations as there are **WEEKLY RATIONS.** With a system of daily rations, the inspecting official will always know where a registrar will be working on a given day.

DE FACTO

Implying an actual presence (of a person) or occurrence (of an event) within an area.

DE JURE Implying a formal belonging to an area by virtue of residence.

DEMOGRAPHIC ANALYSIS

As used in this handbook, a general term for a group of techniques for estimating basic demographic variables from census or **HOUSEHOLD SURVEY** data on the basis of assumptions about either the nature of the population being studied or the expected relationships in the reporting of certain kinds of information. While these techniques have roots deep in the history of demography, they have been improved markedly in recent years by the technical advances associated with the work of Brass, Coale, and Demeny.

DEPENDENCE BIAS

See **RESPONSE CORRELATION BIAS.**

DISCRIMINATING POWER

The ability of a characteristic, or of a category within a characteristic, to distinguish **RECORDS** that are actually different. For example, marital status has less discriminating power than five-year age groups. In the case of names, common ones such as Khan (in Pakistan), Kim (in Korea), Lopez (in Mexico), or Smith (in the United States) have less discriminating power than other, less common names in these countries. There are various ways of measuring discriminating power and its characteristics—for example, by "the percentage of unique categories" or "the average number of entries per category in a characteristic."

DOCUMENTS CONTROL

Procedures established to ensure that the appropriate blank schedules are available for use where needed and that all completed schedules are received for processing. Such procedures must be simple enough to permit the rapid flow of documents, yet specific enough to account for the whereabouts of all classes of documents. A major goal of documents control is to prevent completed schedules from being lost or misplaced. An adequate system of documents control also facilitates the routine assembly of data on the progress of field and office work. See **OPERATIONS CONTROL.**

DUAL COLLECTION

The simultaneous collection of **REPORTS OF VITAL EVENTS** or other occurrences by two data gathering operations that, ideally, are independent of each other. See **INDEPENDENCE.**

DWELLING

Any inhabited **STRUCTURE** such as a house, hut, or tent where one or more households are living. A dwelling usually has one main entrance from the outside.

DWELLING UNIT

That part of a **DWELLING** inhabited by one **HOUSEHOLD.** In the case of one-household dwellings the dwelling and the dwelling unit are the same. Strictly speaking, a dwelling unit refers to a physical place where people live, whereas a household refers to the social unit that inhabits a dwelling unit. The value of this distinction varies from country to country and is largely ignored in the PGE literature.

EDITING

An office review of documents either before or after **CODING,** in order to detect omissions, obvious errors, and ambiguous classifications that might otherwise delay the production of tabulations or lead to serious **ERROR** in the tabulated results. Editing may lead, in particularly difficult cases, to field inquiries. It is commonly done by **MANUAL** means, but a computer or a mechanical method can be used.

ENUMERATION

A method of obtaining data on the **BASE POPULATION** and **VITAL EVENTS** in a census or **HOUSEHOLD SURVEY** by using interviews to collect information systematically from each household in a defined area. Enumeration is often one of the two methods used for obtaining **REPORTS OF VITAL EVENTS** in a PGE study.

ENUMERATION DISTRICT

The geographic area assigned to a single enumerator in a census, as a single assignment. One enumerator is expected to obtain the required information for all **ANALYSIS UNITS** in an enumeration district.

ERRONEOUS MATCH

A form of **MATCHING ERROR** in which a **REPORT OF A VITAL EVENT** in one collection system is classified as a **MATCH,** but does not correspond to *any* report in the other system. (For PGE purposes, **MISMATCHES** are not counted as erroneous matches.) The number of erroneous matches is calculated separately for each collection system and may be different for each system, although **NET MATCHING ERROR** will be the same for both. Erroneous matches arise when the **MATCHING ITEMS** used lack sufficient **DISCRIMINATING POWER.**

ERRONEOUS NONMATCH

A form of **MATCHING ERROR** in which a **REPORT OF A VITAL EVENT** in one collection system is classified as a **NONMATCH** but does in fact correspond to some report in the other source. Like **ERRONEOUS MATCHES,** erroneous nonmatches are counted separately for each collection system; again, the number may differ between systems, although **NET MATCHING ERROR** will be the same for both. Erroneous nonmatches arise because of data errors in particular **MATCHING ITEMS** that exceed the specified **TOLERANCE LIMITS.**

ERROR In an ideal sense, any departure from "what is true." In practical terms, a departure from "what is true" equal to or greater than some explicit or implicit standard. Departures from "what is true" less than this standard are then treated as trivial and effectively ignored. The determination of this standard is an important aspect of designing any measurement system. As the standard approaches the **TRUE VALUE,** measurement costs tend to increase, while the likelihood of making incorrect decisions (and incurring the consequent costs) tends to decrease. Thus, errors have meaning only in the context of the intended uses of a set of measurements. See also **TOTAL ERROR** and its components, **BIAS** and **VARIANCE.**

EXPECTED VALUE

In sampling literature, used as a synonym for "mathematical expectation." Simply put, it is the mean (average) value of all possible outcomes of a random process. See also **BIAS.**

FIELD FOLLOW-UP

A field procedure carried out as part of the **MATCHING** operation and designed to investigate the nonmatched reports further, to identify the **OUT-OF-SCOPE** reports, and, in the case of a **TWO-WAY MATCH,** to match correctly some of the nonmatched reports with each other. Field follow-up should always be conducted by workers not used by either of the two systems—that is, by a third party. Other purposes of a field investigation are to establish the best **MATCHING RULES** at the early stages of the experiment, to check the **BASE POPULATION,** and to check doubtful matches. It is not the purpose of a field follow-up to discover more vital events.

FIELD INSPECTOR

In a **SPECIAL REGISTRATION** system, the person who is the immediate supervisor of the registrars. He is required to inspect the work of the registrars carefully, to correct any errors they may have been making, and to set a high standard of accuracy. His job requires constant travel to PGE areas.

FIELD WORKERS

A general term covering the entire field staff used to collect information on vital events and the base population—that is, the registrars and the enumerators.

FIRST INTELLIGENCE

The initial indication, sometimes in the form of mere hint, that a **VITAL**

EVENT has taken place. Even if the information is very complete, it must be followed up by a visit to the household most directly concerned.

FOURTH CATEGORY
See **CATEGORY.**

GEOGRAPHIC OUT-OF-SCOPE
REPORTS OF VITAL EVENTS that occurred (1) to persons whose usual residence is outside the **PGE AREA** in a **DE JURE** system or (2) outside the PGE area in a **DE FACTO** system. See **OUT-OF-SCOPE.**

GROSS MATCHING ERROR
A measure of **MATCHING ERROR** equal to the sum of **ERRONEOUS MATCHES** and **ERRONEOUS NONMATCHES.** Gross matching error is the major component of the **VARIANCE** of the estimate of **NET MATCHING ERROR.** However, it has no direct effect on the variance or the **BIAS** of the **MATCH RATE.**

HOUSEHOLD
For the purposes of **ENUMERATION,** a household is defined as one or more persons interviewed as one unit on a single household schedule. The definition used may refer to persons related by blood, marriage, or adoption, or to persons living together and eating their main meals from the same kitchen. The particular definition used will depend upon local circumstances. Whatever rule is used, it must permit each member of the population to be unambiguously classified, first, as to whether or not he or she is a member of any household, and second, as to which household he or she belongs. The definition used will thus make adequate provision for guests, servants, lodgers, and casual visitors. It will exclude the **INSTITUTIONAL POPULATION.** See also **DWELLING UNIT** and **STRUCTURE.**

HOUSEHOLD CHANGE TECHNIQUE
A method of enumerating **VITAL EVENTS** in a **MULTI-ROUND SURVEY** by comparing the lists of **HOUSEHOLD** members obtained in successive survey rounds and accounting for changes in the persons listed as members in terms of vital events or migration. Not all events can be covered by this technique (for example, the births and deaths of infants who are born and die between survey rounds will be missed); those missed by this procedure must be covered using **RETROSPECTIVE QUESTIONS.**

HOUSEHOLD SURVEY
A method of data collection using interviews with designated **HOUSEHOLDS** to obtain and record responses to a specified list of questions. A household survey may involve a single interview with a given household or repeated interviews over an extended period of time. It differs from a census, the other method of **ENUMERATION,** in that only a sample of households is interviewed. In a PGE study, a household survey is often one of the methods of **DUAL COLLECTION** used to obtain information on **VITAL EVENTS** and the **BASE POPULATION.**

IDENTIFICATION CODE
The characteristics (that is, the **MATCHING ITEMS**) and **TOLERANCE**

LIMITS used to identify or label each report in **MATCHING.** For example, an identification code for Frederick William Parsons, Jr., using the first four consonants of the last name, the initial letter of the first name, and the date of birth within one month might read "PRSN,F.,April-May-June 1944."

INDEPENDENCE

A statistical term used in PGE literature to mean that the probability of a given **VITAL EVENT** being reported in one data source in a dual collection system is the same whether or not that event is reported in the other data source. Lack of independence leads to **RESPONSE CORRELATION BIAS.**

IN-SCOPE

A term used to describe **REPORTS OF VITAL EVENTS** that are properly recorded by some data collection procedure with respect to the fact, time, and place of occurrence. See also **OUT-OF-SCOPE.**

INFANT MORTALITY RATE

A measure of mortality during the first year of life, usually expressed as a rate per 1,000 live births. It is commonly obtained by dividing the number of deaths of all babies under one year of age occurring in a 12-month period by the number of babies born during the same period. Sometimes abbreviated as IMR.

INFLATION FACTOR

An alternate expression for **RAISING FACTOR.**

INSTITUTIONAL POPULATION

Persons living under arrangements that exclude them from membership in ordinary family **HOUSEHOLDS.** The institutional population usually consists of the inhabitants of hospitals, prisons, military establishments, boarding schools, hotels, larger boarding houses, and the like. Provision must be made for borderline cases such as caretakers or other staff who may live with their families on the grounds of an institution. The institutional population is usually excluded from the **SAMPLING FRAME** of a **HOUSEHOLD SURVEY.**

INTRACLASS CORRELATION COEFFICIENT

As used in sampling, a measure of the homogeneity of the population with respect to some characteristic within the **CLUSTERS** of a sample, and as such an indication of the extent to which the use of a cluster sample increases the **SAMPLING ERROR** of an estimate. In other words, it reflects the degree to which total **VARIANCE** can be accounted for by between-cluster variance. The value of the intraclass correlation coefficient (δ) varies depending upon the population sampled, the variable under study, and the size and nature of the clusters. When the elementary units within clusters are very similar to each other with respect to some characteristic, δ will approach $+1$. On the other hand, if the elementary units within clusters are relatively heterogeneous with respect to the characteristic, δ will approach zero or, occasionally, be a negative value.

LIFE TABLE POPULATION

See **STATIONARY POPULATION.**

LINKAGE
> See **MATCHING.**

LIVE-BIRTH ORDER
> See **PARITY.**

MANUAL This term has two quite different meanings. First, it can be used to refer to a book or pamphlet of instructions—for example, "Has the amendment to the coding *manual* been given to the clerks?" Second, it can refer to any process carried out directly by human beings rather than by machines—for example, "*Manual* matching is sometimes quicker than matching done on an electronic computer."

MATCH   In one sense, the **MATCHING STATUS** of two **RECORDS** that are linked under a given set of **MATCHING RULES** by the identification information contained in each, and are therefore, presumed to refer to the same event. In another sense, two records which, in fact, correspond to the same event and are known as a **TRUE MATCH,** although they may not be classified as a match under the particular set of rules applied.

MATCHING
> In a PGE study, the process of establishing whether two **REPORTS OF VITAL EVENTS,** each obtained by one part of a **DUAL COLLECTION** procedure, refer to the same or different **VITAL EVENTS.** The determination of whether or not any two reports are a **MATCH** is based on a set of **MATCHING RULES.** The application of these rules in any given instance may lead to a correct match or to one or more different kinds of **MATCHING ERRORS.** The process can involve an attempt to match either all the reports of one of the two systems (see **ONE-WAY MATCH**) or all the reports of both systems (see **TWO-WAY MATCH**).

MATCHING CHARACTERISTIC
> See **MATCHING ITEM.**

MATCHING CRITERIA
> See **MATCHING RULES.**

MATCHING ERRORS
> The incorrect outcomes of a **MATCHING** process. Specifically, either a failure to **MATCH** two reports that, in fact, refer to the same vital event (an **ERRONEOUS NONMATCH**) or the incorrect linkage of two reports which, in fact, refer to different vital events (an **ERRONEOUS MATCH**). A **MIS-MATCH,** however, is not considered to be a matching error for PGE purposes. See also **GROSS MATCHING ERROR** and **NET MATCHING ERROR.**

MATCHING ITEM
> Any one of the items in a **RECORD** that is part of the **IDENTIFICATION CODE** used to determine whether or not two records **MATCH.** Matching items must be present on the records of both systems. In conjunction with the **TOLERANCE LIMITS** employed, individual matching items have **DIS-CRIMINATING POWER.** However, in most situations it is advisable to use a combination of matching items in the identification code. Also called a "matching characteristic."

MATCHING MODE

The physical means of comparing two **REPORTS OF VITAL EVENTS** to determine whether or not they **MATCH. MATCHING** may be done by human beings, by mechanical punchcard equipment, or by an electronic computer.

MATCHING RULES

A set of criteria, sometimes explicit and sometimes implicit, used to determine whether or not two **RECORDS** are a **MATCH**—that is, whether they are to be treated as referring to the same person or event. As an intermediate step in the application of matching rules, pairs of records may be classified as doubtful matches pending further processing or **FIELD FOLLOW-UP** (see also **COMPARISON FUNCTION**). Matching rules, and their application, also give rise to **ERRONEOUS MATCHES** and **ERRONEOUS NONMATCHES.** Also called "matching criteria."

MATCHING STATUS

The classification of a **RECORD** in relation to the final outcome of a **MATCHING** process—that is, whether a particular record is a **MATCH** or a **NONMATCH.** In a **TWO-WAY MATCH,** the matching status of all records from both systems is determined, yielding the following final categories: matched (events reported by both systems), nonmatched in the first system (events reported by the first system and missed by the second system), and nonmatched in the second system (events reported by the second system and missed by the first system). In a **ONE-WAY MATCH,** the matching status of all the records of only one of the systems is determined. See also **CATEGORY** and **MATCH RATE.**

MATCH RATE

The proportion of **RECORDS** from a given data collection system that are found to **MATCH** the records of another system. Given an independent **DUAL COLLECTION SYSTEM,** the absence of **RATIO BIAS** and of **OUT-OF-SCOPE** reports, and zero **NET MATCHING ERROR,** the match rate of either system is an unbiased estimate of the **COMPLETENESS** of the other system. The match rate should not be confused with the proportion of events reported by both systems (that is, the "first **CATEGORY**"), which has the same numerator but a different denominator. In the case of the match rate, the denominator is the sum of the matched and nonmatched reports of a particular collection system; the proper denominator for the other proportion is *all* events, whether or not they were reported in either system.

MEAN SQUARE ERROR

A measure of **TOTAL ERROR** equal to the sum of the **VARIANCE** and the square of the **BIAS.** In many applications the square root of the mean square error is used and is referred to as the **ROOT MEAN SQUARE ERROR,** abbreviated as RMSE.

MISMATCH

The linkage of a **RECORD** from one system that has a partner in the other system (and thus should be classified as a **MATCH**) with the *wrong* record in the second system. For the purposes of a PGE study a mismatch is not considered a **MATCHING ERROR.**

MULTI-ROUND SURVEY

One of the two types of **HOUSEHOLD SURVEY,** the other being a one-time or single-visit survey. In a multi-round survey the same panel of **SAMPLING UNITS** are reinterviewed one or more times; either the **HOUSEHOLD CHANGE TECHNIQUE** or **RETROSPECTIVE QUESTIONS** can be used to obtain reports of the vital events that occurred between each survey round. Only the latter method can be used in a single-visit survey or in the first round of a multi-round survey.

NET MATCHING ERROR

A measure of **MATCHING ERROR** equal to the difference between the number of **ERRONEOUS MATCHES** and **ERRONEOUS NONMATCHES;** by convention, erroneous matches minus erroneous nonmatches. Positive net matching error, undetected, causes an upward **BIAS** in the **MATCH RATE** and a downward bias in the **PGE ESTIMATE;** negative net matching error, undetected, causes a downward bias in the match rate and an upward bias in the PGE estimate. See also **GROSS MATCHING ERROR.**

NONMATCH

In one sense, any pair of data **RECORDS,** presumably referring to different persons or events, that do not **MATCH.** In another sense, any individual data record that, at the end of a **MATCHING** process, has not been linked with another record. See also **MATCHING STATUS.**

ONE-WAY MATCH

A **MATCHING** operation that is concluded when the **MATCHING STATUS** of all the **RECORDS** (or a probability sample thereof) of one of the two systems has been determined. A one-way match yields only one **MATCH RATE** (for the system in which each record has a known matching status) and, hence, only one **COMPLETENESS** estimate (for the other system). See also **TWO-WAY MATCH** and **WRONG-WAY MATCH.**

OPERATIONS CONTROL

The group of procedures used by the study managers to actively direct and coordinate a PGE study or other data gathering operation so as to best achieve the project's objectives in terms of the quality, quantity, and timeliness of results, on the basis of the resources available for their production. The major purpose of operations control is the early identification of system malfunctions so that they can be corrected before they become major problems. To achieve this end, the study managers must set up ways for keeping themselves routinely informed about the quantity and quality of work being done in the various parts of the study. On the basis of such information the study managers take any necessary corrective action. See **ADAPTIVE SYSTEM, DOCUMENTS CONTROL, OPERATIONS TIMETABLE, QUALITY CONTROL, SUPERVISION,** and **TRAINING.**

OPERATIONS TIMETABLE

A chronological listing of the various tasks that need to be performed, together with a reasonable estimate of the starting and completion date of each. Such a timetable is essential for the realistic planning of any complex study and valuable as one of the tools of **OPERATIONS CONTROL.** In line with the concept of an **ADAPTIVE SYSTEM,** unrealistic timetables must be replaced by more realistic ones.

OUT-OF-SCOPE

A term used to describe those **REPORTS OF VITAL EVENTS** which should not be included in a given estimate because they refer to events that took place outside the time period being studied **(TEMPORAL OUT-OF-SCOPE)**, events not in the sample **(GEOGRAPHIC OUT-OF-SCOPE),** or events that did not occur. Out-of-scope reports are often detected by **FIELD FOLLOW-UP;** undetected, they lead to **COVERAGE BIAS.** See also **IN-SCOPE.**

PARITY The number of live births a woman has had. If a woman has had no live births, her parity is zero; if she has had one live birth, her parity is one, and so on. Strictly speaking, parity is a characteristic of a woman and "live-birth order" is the equivalent characteristic of a child. Less rigorously the terms are used interchangeably.

PES See **POST-ENUMERATION SURVEY.**

PGE AREA

The **SAMPLING UNIT** used in a PGE study. If **SPECIAL REGISTRATION** is one of the collection methods, each PGE area may be an ultimate **CLUSTER** with a population of approximately 5,000 or 10,000—providing an adequate work load for a full-time special registrar. Other designs may call for somewhat smaller areas.

PGE ESTIMATE

An estimate made using the **PGE TECHNIQUE.**

PGE TECHNIQUE

A method of preparing estimates of vital statistics adjusted for omitted **VITAL EVENTS** or of estimating the completeness of reporting of the collection systems used to gather vital data. The PGE technique has three basic features: **DUAL COLLECTION, MATCHING,** and the use of the **MATCH RATE** to prepare **COMPLETENESS** estimates. It also frequently involves the collection of data on a sample basis.

P(M) The probability that a pair of **RECORDS** randomly selected from a given **COMPARISON CLASS** will be a **TRUE MATCH**—that is, will correspond to the same event.

POST-ENUMERATION SURVEY

A special-purpose **HOUSEHOLD SURVEY** conducted after a main **ENUMERATION** activity in order to assess the quality of the original enumeration. Often abbreviated as PES.

PROBABLE MATCH

An interim **MATCHING STATUS** assigned to a pair of **RECORDS** during a **MATCHING** process. It indicates that the validity of the match might be investigated should **FIELD FOLLOW-UP** be done for some other reason. In the absence of such a follow-up the probable match is accepted as a correct match. This classification is used most often during the early stages of a PGE study when the **MATCHING RULES** are being established.

PSU   A common abbreviation for "primary sampling unit." PSUs are the **SAMPLING UNITS** selected in the first stage of a multistage sample design. They are, in turn, the **SAMPLING FRAME** for the next stage of sampling—that is, further sampling is confined to within each PSU.

QUALITY CONTROL

A variety of methods used to monitor any process, including a measurement process, to ensure that it does not go out of control; that is, produce results that contain unacceptable **ERRORS.** In a PGE study, information that can be used in quality control procedures arises routinely from such project activities as **SUPERVISION, DOCUMENTS CONTROL,** and **MATCHING,** or from special activities such as a **POST-ENUMERATION SURVEY.** See also **OPERATIONS CONTROL.**

QUASI-STABLE POPULATION

A model population generated, in the absence of external migration, by an assumed fixed schedule of **AGE-SPECIFIC FERTILITY** and steadily changing **AGE-SPECIFIC MORTALITY.** The smaller and slower the changes in mortality, the closer the quasi-stable population is to the **STABLE POPULATION.** The proportionate age distributions of many populations in underdeveloped countries are likely to be of the quasi-stable kind, and therefore approximate the proportionate age distribution of the theoretical stable population. See also **DEMOGRAPHIC ANALYSIS.**

RAISING FACTOR

The number by which sample values for a given **PGE AREA** are multiplied to inflate them to represent the **STRATUM** from which the PGE area was selected. The raising factor should be approximately equal to the reciprocal of the **SAMPLING FRACTION.** The terms **WEIGHT** and **INFLATION FACTOR** mean the same as raising factor.

RATE OF NATURAL INCREASE

A measure of the change in the total population of a nation, or other area, due to factors other than migration. Specifically, the difference between the number of live births and the number of deaths occurring in a year (that is, the natural increase), divided by the midyear population. It is also equal to the difference between the **CRUDE BIRTH RATE** and the **CRUDE DEATH RATE.** The rate of natural increase is often abbreviated as RNI and is usually expressed as a percentage. In those countries or subnational areas where net migration is small relative to natural increase, the rate of natural increase is approximately equal to the population growth rate.

RATIO BIAS

In PGE estimation, a source of **BIAS** that may lead to **ERROR** in making estimates if the number of matched reports is very small. In such a situation the reciprocal of the **MATCH RATE** can become very large, yielding a **PGE ESTIMATE** with an upward bias. Ratio bias occurs most often when estimates are prepared separately for small population **SUBGROUPS.**

RECALL PERIOD

The length of time between the data of **ENUMERATION** and the earliest date for which information is requested in a **RETROSPECTIVE QUESTION.**

For example, for a survey conducted during July that asks about births since the start of the year, both the recall period and the **REFERENCE PERIOD** are approximately six and one-half months. On the other hand, a survey conducted during August and using the first six months of the year as the reference period for questions about births would have a recall period of about seven and one-half months.

RECONCILIATION

A field procedure carried out by a registrar or an enumerator, or an immediate supervisor of either, to determine the correctness of conflicting entries. Even though it may be done in connection with a study using the **PGE TECHNIQUE,** reconciliation is basically different from **FIELD FOLLOW-UP** (which is conducted by a "third party") because of the probable loss of independence between the two systems during a reconciliation.

RECORD(S)

All the information for an individual **ANALYSIS UNIT** reported in one collection system as it exists at any given stage of processing—for example, a line from a census schedule referring to one person, or a birth certificate for one live birth, or the punchcard or the portion of a computer tape prepared from these documents. In vital statistics estimation, the records used in the **MATCHING** operation are **REPORTS OF VITAL EVENTS.**

REFERENCE PERIOD

Depending upon the context, either the interval of time about which information is sought in a **RETROSPECTIVE QUESTION** or the time interval for which results are processed. Used in the first sense, the reference period is often identical to the **RECALL PERIOD** in length, occasionally shorter, and never longer. However, reference periods that do not continue to the date of **ENUMERATION** generally should be avoided. Reference periods are said to "overlap" when, in a multi-round survey, the frequency of the rounds and the length of the reference period are such that information is sought about the same time interval in two or more rounds.

REGISTRATION

A method of gathering information on **VITAL EVENTS** shortly after they occur, either through a **CIVIL REGISTRATION** system or by means of **SPECIAL REGISTRATION.** Registration is usually one of the two methods used to obtain **REPORTS OF VITAL EVENTS** in a PGE study.

RELATIVE BIAS

A measure of the relative **ERROR** of a measurement process attributable to systematic error; that is, the **BIAS** of a process divided by the **TRUE VALUE** of the quantity being measured.

RELVARIANCE

A shortened form of the term "relative variance"; that is, the **VARIANCE** of an estimate divided by the square of its **EXPECTED VALUE.** The relvariance of an estimate is also equal to the coefficient of variation squared.

REPORT(S) OF VITAL EVENT(S)

The document or portion of a document arising from **ENUMERATION** or

REGISTRATION indicating, correctly or incorrectly, that a **VITAL EVENT** has taken place. In the **PGE TECHNIQUE** it is these reports that are used in **MATCHING.** Since they may refer to nonexistent or otherwise **OUT-OF-SCOPE** events, procedures such as **FIELD FOLLOW-UP** must be developed to exclude such reports from the final estimates. **IN-SCOPE** reports, on the other hand, should be retained.

RESPONSE CORRELATION BIAS

A source of **BIAS** in a **DUAL COLLECTION** procedure arising from a failure to maintain **INDEPENDENCE** between the two collection systems in the reporting of vital events. In other words, a failure to meet the condition that the probability of an event being reported by either system if it is covered by the other system is equal to the probability that it will be reported by the first system if it is omitted by the second. Response correlation may be due either to the nature of the population or to undue communication between the two systems. It is almost always positive, giving an upward bias to the **MATCH RATE** and a downward bias to the **PGE ESTIMATE.** Also called "correlation bias" or "dependence bias."

RESPONSE ERROR VARIANCE

A form of variable **ERROR** arising from variation in the reporting of the same **VITAL EVENTS,** or some other characteristic, for a given household observed in repeated applications of the same measurement process. It can be defined as the **VARIANCE** of the individual observations made by the same collection process operating under the same general survey conditions around the **EXPECTED VALUE** of these observations taken over a large number of conceived repetitions.

RESPONSE VARIANCE

See **RESPONSE ERROR VARIANCE.**

RETROSPECTIVE QUESTION(S)

A type of question, used primarily in **ENUMERATION,** seeking information about past actions or events rather than about the present status of the respondent and his family. Responses to retrospective questions are affected by two distinct error processes: "forgetting," a general tendency for respondents to omit more events as the **REFERENCE PERIOD** is extended further into the past; and "telescoping," the tendency for events that occurred prior to the start of the reference period to be brought forward in time and thus reported as occurring in the period.

RMSE   See **ROOT MEAN SQUARE ERROR.**

RNI   See **RATE OF NATURAL INCREASE.**

ROOT MEAN SQUARE ERROR

The square root of the **MEAN SQUARE ERROR** and, like it, a measure of **TOTAL ERROR.** Abbreviated as RMSE.

ROUTINE ROUND CONTACT

A term used in some **SPECIAL REGISTRATION** systems. The routine round is an arrangement by which each sector (consisting of approximately ten households) in a **PGE AREA** is visited once in the course of every one to four weeks by the registrar. Every routine round contact (appointed informally from among the residents of each sector by the registrar) is contacted once during a routine round. He is expected to furnish information on any **VITAL EVENTS** that may have occurred in the sector since the registrar's last visit.

SAMPLING ERROR

That part of the **TOTAL ERROR** of an estimate attributable to the fact that a measurement is based on a sample of observations rather than on all the observations. The sampling error of an estimate is measured in terms of the sampling **VARIANCE** or its square root, the "standard error."

SAMPLING FRACTION

The rate at which **SAMPLING UNITS** are selected from a population. It may vary from **STRATUM** to stratum. Depending upon the adequacy of the **SAMPLING FRAME** and the vagaries of field work, the actual sampling fraction may differ from the fraction that was intended. In general, the reciprocal of the actual sampling fraction should approximately equal the **RAISING FACTOR** used. Changing the sampling fraction usually has very little effect on the **SAMPLING ERROR.**

SAMPLING FRAME

An actual or conceptual arrangement of all the **ANALYSIS UNITS** in a population in terms of **SAMPLING UNITS,** in such a manner that each unit has a fixed (and known) probability of being in the sample. A sampling frame is used to facilitate the design and selection of a sample. For example, the country might be divided into areas (PSUs) and sampling an area would constitute selection of all the analysis units associated, in some unique manner, with the area. When an area is sampled: (1) all analysis units in it may be considered to be in the sample; (2) the analysis units may be listed and sampled; or (3) the area may be divided into smaller areas and these smaller units sampled (and the process repeated on them). A sampling frame can be a complete listing of individual analysis units or of groups of individual units—for example, the names of all the tribes making up the population of the country, regardless of the geographic location of the individual tribal members.

SAMPLING UNIT(S)

Individual **ANALYSIS UNITS** or **CLUSTERS** of analysis units, one or more of which is selected at any given stage of sampling—for example, individual persons selected from a census listing of all persons in the country or villages selected from a list of all villages in a given district. In general, the absolute number of sampling units in the sample, particularly the number of PSUs, plays a crucial role in the determination of **SAMPLING ERROR.**

SEGMENT

A small geographic area used as a **CLUSTER,** often an ultimate cluster.

SEX RATIO

The number of males in a population divided by the number of females, generally expressed as a ratio per 100 or 1,000.

SLIPPAGE

The effective loss of **REGISTRATION** reports after they have been prepared by the registrar, but prior to their inclusion in the tabulated vital statistics.

This phenomenon is particularly common in **CIVIL REGISTRATION** systems lacking adequate **DOCUMENTS CONTROL** procedures.

SOUNDEX CODE

A common system for **CODING** names, designed to minimize the effects of mispronunciation, mishearing, and alternative spellings on **MATCHING**.

SOURCE OF FIRST INTELLIGENCE

A term sometimes used in **SPECIAL REGISTRATION** to indicate how the special registrar received his **FIRST INTELLIGENCE** of a particular **VITAL EVENT**.

SOURCE OF REPORT

In a **DUAL COLLECTION** system, an identification item on each **RECORD** indicating which system supplied a particular report.

SPURIOUS

See **OUT-OF-SCOPE.**

SPECIAL REGISTRATION

A system of registration of **VITAL EVENTS** established independently of, or as a supplement to, **CIVIL REGISTRATION** for the purposes of a PGE study. A special registration system employs full-time or part-time special registrars and may issue certificates to respondents, but these have no statutory standing. The primary purpose of special registration is the collection of statistical data. Unlike civil registrars, special registrars actively seek out vital events.

STABLE POPULATION

A theoretical population generated, in the absence of external migration, by a fixed schedule of **AGE-SPECIFIC FERTILITY** and **AGE-SPECIFIC MOR-TALITY.** A stable population has a constant proportionate age distribution. It is a useful tool of **DEMOGRAPHIC ANALYSIS** in developing countries because age distributions are determined primarily by fertility and fertility, in turn, can be deduced from the proportionate age distribution. See also **QUASI-STABLE POPULATION.**

STATIONARY POPULATION

A special case of the **STABLE POPULATION** in which births have been equal to deaths for a long time; that is, a stable population whose growth rate is zero.

STRATUM

One of two or more groups of **ANALYSIS UNITS** into which a population may be divided to facilitate sampling. Other things being equal, the division should be done so as to maximize the differences between strata and minimize those within each stratum. The use of strata can reduce **SAMPLING ERROR** when the **SAMPLING FRACTION** within each stratum is varied in proportion to the variability of the characteristic being estimated. Furthermore, different sampling methods or **SAMPLING FRAMES** can, if necessary, be used in each stratum.

STRUCTURE

Any inhabited or inhabitable building, shack, tent, or similar construction that can provide permanent or semipermanent shelter for **HOUSEHOLDS.** If it is actually inhabited at the time of determination, it is a **DWELLING,** which may consist of one or more **DWELLING UNITS.** If it is inhabitable, but not inhabited at the time of determination, it is *vacant.* There are difficulties of definition and application at the borderline—when, for example, a road bridge over a dry river is sometimes inhabited or at least could be made inhabitable.

STRUCTURE NUMBER

An identifying number, unique within a given **PGE AREA,** assigned to each **STRUCTURE** for the purposes of the PGE study, whether or not the structure is occupied. Structure numbers are used when other possible **MATCHING ITEMS,** such as names or street addresses, cannot be relied on to provide **UNIQUE IDENTIFICATION.** Like a house number, a structure number is most useful when it is clearly visible as one approaches the structure from the front.

SUBGROUP

Any division of a population or sample with a characteristic or set of characteristics of analytical or methodological interest to the investigator.

SUPERVISION

A set of procedures used to help control the quantity and quality of work done by office and field staff. To be most effective, supervision must be frequent and continuing; in the case of the field staff this may mean extensive travel. Supervisors, in addition to ensuring that the staff is following all the appropriate technical and administrative instructions, must be attentive to staff needs and should play a role in staff **TRAINING.** See also **FIELD INSPECTOR.**

TELESCOPING

See **RETROSPECTIVE QUESTIONS.**

TEMPORAL OUT-OF-SCOPE

A term used to describe **REPORTS OF VITAL EVENTS** that did not occur during the time period under study. See **OUT-OF-SCOPE.**

TOLERANCE LIMITS

In **MATCHING,** the range of values for a part of an **IDENTIFICATION CODE** within which variation is disregarded—for example, considering all first names of identical origin regardless of spelling variations as the same or treating all ages in any five-year age interval as the same.

TOTAL ERROR

The difference between the estimate from a particular sample and the **TRUE VALUE** of the same characteristic. In other words, the sum of all the sources of **ERROR** affecting such an estimate. For analytical purposes, total error is often divided into two components: variable error (**VARIANCE**) and fixed error (**BIAS**). For other purposes, some other division may be more appropriate. **MEAN SQUARE ERROR** and its square root, **ROOT MEAN SQUARE ERROR,** are often used as measures of total error.

TOTAL FERTILITY RATE

See **AGE-SPECIFIC FERTILITY.**

TRAINING

The instructions and explanations given to the field and office staff so that they can carry out their assigned tasks effectively. It refers both to the initial training given to the staff on joining the project and to subsequent "refresher" training given individually or collectively. Training may take many forms: required readings in instruction **MANUALS,** formal lectures, self-study exercises, pretend interviews with the instructor and other trainees (often called "mock interviews"), practice interviews conducted in real households outside the sample, comparable practice for the office staff, and informal conversations with supervisors. Training is an important tool in implementing a program of **OPERATIONS CONTROL.** See also **ADAPTIVE SYSTEM.**

TRUE VALUE

The correct value of a given population characteristic. Alternatively, the "target" value of an ideal procedure designed to measure this characteristic, or the value of this characteristic measured without **ERROR.**

TWO-WAY MATCH

A **MATCHING** operation that is continued until the **MATCHING STATUS** of all the **RECORDS** in both the systems has been determined. A two-way match yields two **MATCH RATES** and two **COMPLETENESS** estimates. PGE studies using **SPECIAL REGISTRATION** and a **HOUSEHOLD SURVEY** frequently employ two-way matching. See also **CATEGORY, ONE-WAY MATCH,** and **WRONG-WAY MATCH.**

UNIQUE IDENTIFICATION

The situation in which a given **RECORD** from a single source is the only item with a particular **IDENTIFICATION CODE.** The probability of an **ERRONEOUS MATCH** is a decreasing function of the proportion of records with unique identification.

VARIANCE

As sampling variance, a measure of the average difference between a sample estimate and its **EXPECTED VALUE** for samples of a given size. As population variance, a measure of the variability of a population about its mean.

VITAL EVENTS

In the PGE literature this term refers to live births and deaths, and occasionally to stillbirths. Strictly speaking, the term also includes all other types of fetal wastage, and marriages and divorces. See also **REPORTS OF VITAL EVENTS.**

VITAL EVENTS REPORTS

See **REPORT(S) OF VITAL EVENT(S).**

WEEKLY RATION

In a **SPECIAL REGISTRATION** system, that part of a **PGE AREA** scheduled to be visited by a special registrar during a given week. See also **DAILY RATION.**

WEIGHT

An alternate expression for **RAISING FACTOR.**

WRONG-WAY MATCH

A **ONE-WAY MATCH** that yields a **MATCH RATE** and **COMPLETENESS** estimate irrelevant to the question being studied—for example, an attempt to estimate the completeness of birth registration by taking a 10-percent sample of registered births and matching these reports with the enumeration records for all infants included in a recent census. Such a one-way match yields an estimate of the census's coverage of infants.

References

Abernathy, J. R., and A. S. Lunde, 1970
> "Dual Record Systems: A Review of Population Surveys in Developing Countries." Background paper for the First Poplab Planning Conference, University of North Carolina, Chapel Hill.
————, 1972
> *Subject Matter Coverage in the Dual-Report Systems of India, Pakistan, Turkey, and Liberia.* Scientific Series No. 3, Chapel Hill, N.C.: Laboratories for Population Statistics.

Acheson, E. D. (ed.), 1968
> *Record Linkage in Medicine: Proceedings of the International Symposium, Oxford, July 1967.* Baltimore: Williams and Wilkins Co.

Afzal, M., 1966
> *Estimation of Institutional Births and Deaths in West Pakistan.* PGE Special Research Study No. 2, Population Growth Estimation, Karachi.

Agrawal, B. L., 1969
> "Sample Registration in India." *Population Studies* 23, no. 3 (November): 379–94.

Ahmed, N., and K. J. Krotki, 1963
> "Simultaneous Estimations of Population Growth—the Pakistan Experiment." *Pakistan Development Review* 3, no. 1 (Spring): 37–65.

Andrewartha, H. G., 1961
> *Introduction to the Study of Animal Populations.* Chicago: University of Chicago Press.

Arriaga, E. E., 1967
> "Rural-Urban Mortality in Developing Countries: An Index for Detecting Rural Underregistration." *Demography* 4, no. 1 (1967): 98–107.

Bahri, M. A., 1969
> "Enquête démographique par sondage en Algérie, 1969–70." Paper presented at the United Nations Interregional Workshop on the Methodology of Demographic Sample Surveys, Copenhagen, Denmark.

Bailey, N. T. J., 1951
> "On Estimating the Size of Mobile Populations from Recapture Data." *Biometrika* 38: 293–306.

Barclay, G. W., 1958
> *Techniques of Population Analysis.* New York: Wiley.

Bean, L., Masihur Rahman Khan, and A. Razzaque Rukanuddin, 1968
> *Population Projections for Pakistan: 1960–2000.* Monographs in the Economics of Development, No. 17. Karachi: Pakistan Institute of Development Economics.

Blacker, J., n.d.
> "Report on Malawi Population Change Survey." Mimeographed.

Bogue, D. J., and E. J. Bogue, 1967
> "The Pregnancy History Approach to Measurement of Fertility Change." In *Proceedings of the Social Statistics Section, 1967.* Washington, D.C.: American Statistical Association, pp. 212–31.

————, 1970
> *Technique of Pregnancy History Analysis.* Family Planning Evaluation Manual Number 4, Community and Family Study Center. Chicago: University of Chicago.

Bogue, D. J., and E. M. Murphy, 1964
> "The Effect of Classification Errors upon Statistical Inference: A Case Analysis with Census Data." *Demography* 1, no. 1 (1964): 42–55.

Boyarski, A. and P. Shusherin, 1951
> *Demograficheskaya Statistika* [Demographic Statistics]. Moscow.

Brass, W., 1969
> "Disciplining Demographic Data." *International Population Conference, London, 1969* vol. 1, Liege: International Union for the Scientific Study of Population, 1971, pp. 183–204.

————, 1971a
> "A Critique of Methods for Estimating Population Growth in Countries with Limited Data." *Bulletin of the International Statistical Institute* 44, part 1, Washington, D.C., pp. 397–412.

————, 1971b
> "On the Scale of Mortality." In *Biological Aspects of Demography.* Edited by W. Brass. Symposia of the Society for the Study of Human Biology, vol. 10. London: Taylor and Francis Ltd.

Brass, W., and A. J. Coale, 1968
> "Methods of Analysis and Estimation." In *The Demography of Tropical Africa.* By W. Brass *et al.*, Princeton: Princeton University Press, pp. 88–150.

Brass, W., *et al.*, 1968
> *The Demography of Tropical Africa.* Princeton: Princeton University Press.

Byrne, J., 1966
> "Completeness of Birth Registration in the Commonwealth Caribbean." Revised copy of a paper presented at the First Conference of Commonwealth Caribbean Government Statisticians, Trinidad.

Bystrova, V. A., 1967
> "The Anamnestic Method of Studying Demographic Processes." In *Proceedings of the World Population Conference, Belgrade, 30 August–10 September, 1965,* vol. 3. New York: United Nations, pp. 131–36.

Cairo Demographic Centre, 1970
> *Demographic Measures and Population Growth in Arab Countries.* Research Mono-
> graph Series 1. Cairo: S.O.P. Press.

Ceylon, Government of, 1953
> *Post Enumeration Survey 1953,* Monograph No. 1. Columbo, Ceylon: Department
> of Census and Statistics.

Chandrasekaran, C., and W. E. Deming, 1949
> "On a Method of Estimating Birth and Death Rates and the Extent of
> Registration." *Journal of the American Statistical Association* 44, no. 245 (March):
> 101–15. Also available as Reprint Series No. 1, Laboratories for Population
> Statistics. Chapel Hill: University of North Carolina, May 1971.

Chapman, D. C., 1954
> "The Estimation of Biological Populations." *Annals of Mathematical Statistics*
> 25: 1–15.

Charbonneau, H., Y. Lavoie, and J. Légaré, 1970
> "Recensements et registres paroissiaux du Canada durant la période 1665–1668."
> *Population* 25, no. 1 (Jan.–Feb.): 97–124.

Cho, Lee-Jay, 1971
> "On Estimating Annual Birth Rates from Census Data on Children." In
> *Proceedings of the Social Statistics Section, 1971.* Washington, D.C.: American
> Statistical Association, pp. 86–96.

Choe, Ehn Hyun, 1967
> *Problems and Adequacy of Vital Statistics in Korea.* The Population Studies Center,
> Publication Series No. 1. Seoul: Seoul National University, April.

Choi, Chi-Hoon, 1970
> "A Bayesian Estimation of Unobserved Vital Events." Ph.D. dissertation, Univer-
> sity of Michigan.

Coale, A. J., 1955
> "The Population of the United States in 1950 Classified by Age, Sex, and
> Color—A Revision of Census Figures." *Journal of the American Statistical Associa-
> tion* 50 (March): 16–54.

——————, 1961
> "The Design of an Experimental Procedure for Obtaining Accurate Vital
> Statistics." *International Population Conference, New York, 1961* vol. 2. London:
> International Union for the Scientific Study of Population, 1963, pp. 372–75.

Coale, A. J., and M. Zelnik, 1963
> *New Estimates of Fertility and Population in the United States from 1855 to 1960
> and of Completeness of Enumeration in the Censuses from 1880 to 1960.* Princeton:
> Princeton University Press.

Colombia, Republic of, Departmento Administrativo Nacional de Estadistica, 1971
> "Country Report, Colombia." Paper prepared for the Second International
> Poplab Conference, University of North Carolina, Chapel Hill.

Cooke, D. S., 1971
> *Mapping and House Numbering.* Manual Series No. 1. Chapel Hill, N.C.:
> Laboratories for Population Statistics.

Dalkey, N. C., 1971
> "Group Judgment and Statistics." Paper presented at the 131st annual meeting
> of the American Statistical Association, Ft. Collins, Colorado.

Das Gupta, Pr., 1964
> "On the Estimation of the Total Number of Events and of the Probabilities
> of Detecting an Event from Information Supplied by Several Agencies." *Calcutta
> Statistical Association Bulletin* 13, nos. 49 and 50, pp. 89–100.

Demeny, P., 1965
  "Estimation of Vital Rates for Populations in the Process of Destabilization."
  Demography 2: 516–30.
———, 1967
  "A Minimum Program for the Estimation of Basic Fertility Measures from
  Censuses of Population in Asian Countries with Inadequate Demographic
  Statistics." In *International Union for the Scientific Study of Population: Contributed
  Papers, Sydney Conference, Australia, 21–25 August 1967*, pp. 818–25.
Demeny, P., and F. C. Shorter, 1968
  Estimating Turkish Mortality, Fertility and Age Structure. Institute of Statistics,
  Faculty of Economics, Publication No. 218, University of Istanbul, Istanbul,
  in English and Turkish.
Deming, W. E., 1950
  Some Theory of Sampling. New York: Wiley.
Deming, W. E., and N. Keyfitz, 1967
  "Theory of Surveys to Estimate Total Population." In *Proceedings of the World
  Population Conference, Belgrade, 30 August–10 September, 1965* vol. 3, New York:
  United Nations, pp. 141–44.
Dmitrieva, R. M., 1969
  "Sampling in Demographic Studies in the USSR." Paper presented at the United
  Nations Interregional Workshop on the Methodology of Demographic Sample
  Surveys, Copenhagen, Denmark.
Dowdeswell, W. H., R. A. Fisher, and E. P. Ford, 1940
  "The Quantitative Study of Populations in the Lepidoptera." *Annals of Eugenics*
  10 (1940): 123–36.
Dunn, H., 1936
  "Vital Statistics Collected by the Government." *Annals of the American Academy
  of Political and Social Science* 188 (November): 340–50.
Fellegi, I. P., 1971
  "Report on the Survey Design for the Moroccan Population Growth Experiment
  (CERED)." Unpublished.
Fellegi, I. P., and A. B. Sunter, 1969
  "A Theory for Record Linkage." *Journal of the American Statistical Association*
  64, no. 328 (December): 1183–1210.
Feller, W., 1968
  Introduction to Probability Theory and Its Applications, Vol. 1. 3rd ed. New York:
  Wiley.
Ferber, R., 1965
  "The Reliability of Consumer Surveys of Financial Holdings: Time-Deposits."
  Journal of the American Statistical Association 60, no. 309 (March): 148–63.
Goldberg, D., and A. Adlakha, 1968
  "Infant Mortality Estimates Based on Small Surveys in the Ankara Area." In
  *Turkish Demography: Proceedings of a Conference Sponsored by the Institute of
  Population Studies, Hacettepe University, Izmir, February 21–24, 1968.* Edited by
  F. C. Shorter and B. Guvenc. Ankara: Hacettepe University Institute of
  Population Studies, pp. 133–45.
Goodman, L. A., 1953
  "Sequential Sampling Tagging for Population Size Problems." *Annals of Mathe-
  matical Statistics* 24 (1953): 59–69.
Grabill, W. H., and Lee-Jay Cho, 1965
  "Methodology for the Measurement of Current Fertility from Population Data
  on Young Children." *Demography* 2 (1965): 50–74.

Grove, R. D., 1943
  "Studies in the Completeness of Birth Registration: Part I. Completeness of Birth Registration in the United States, December 1, 1939 to March 31, 1940." *Vital Statistics—Special Reports* 17, no. 18 (April 1943): 224–30.

Gutman, R., 1959
  Birth and Death Registration in Massachusetts, 1639–1900. New York: Milbank Memorial Fund. Reprinted from *The Milbank Memorial Fund Quarterly* 36 (January and October 1958) and 37 (July and October 1959).

Hambright, T. Z., 1969
  "Comparison of Information on Death Certificates and Matching 1960 Census Records: Age, Marital Status, Race, Nativity and Country of Origin." *Demography* 6, no. 4 (November 1969): 413–23.

Hansen, M. H., 1965
  Personal communication to Dr. Calvert L. Dedrick regarding the Turkish Demographic Survey, 1 September.

Hansen, M. H., W. N. Hurwitz, and M. A. Bershad, 1961
  "Measurement Errors in Censuses and Surveys." *Bulletin of the International Statistical Institute* 38, part 2, Tokyo: International Statistical Institute.

Hansen, M. H., W. N. Hurwitz, and W. G. Madow, 1953
  Sample Survey Methods and Theory. New York: Wiley.

Hansen, M. H., and J. Waksberg, 1970
  "Research on Non-sampling Errors in Censuses and Surveys." *Review of the International Statistical Institute* 38, no. 3: 317–32.

Hashmi, S. S., and I. Alam, 1969
  "The Problem of Obtaining Age Data in Pakistan: A Study of Age Reporting of a Panel of Ever Married Females in Yearly Enumerations: 1962–65." Paper prepared for the Conference of the International Union for the Scientific Study of Population, London.

Hedrich, A. W., J. Collinson, and F. D. Rhoads, 1939
  "Comparison of Birth Tests by Several Methods in Georgia and Maryland." *Vital Statistics—Special Reports* 7, no. 60 (November 1939): 679–95.

Horvitz, D. G., 1966
  "Problems in Designing Interview Surveys to Measure Population Growth." In *Proceedings of the Social Statistics Section, 1966.* Washington, D.C.: American Statistical Association, pp. 245–49.

Hubbard, M. R., and J. E. Fisher, 1968
  "A Computer System for Medical Record Linkage." In *Record Linkage in Medicine: Proceedings of the International Symposium, Oxford, July 1967.* Edited by E. D. Acheson. Baltimore: Williams and Wilkins Co.

India, Government of, 1969
  Sample Registration in India: Report on Pilot Studies in Urban Areas, 1964–67. New Delhi: Office of the Registrar General.

————, 1970
  Sample Registration of Births–Deaths in India: Rural, 1965–68. New Delhi: Office of the Registrar General.

Indonesia, Government of, 1968
  "A Study of the Completeness of Birth and Death Statistics in Indonesia." Paper prepared for the ECAFE Seminar on Civil Registration and Vital Statistics, Copenhagen, Denmark.

Jabine, T. B., 1969
  "Collection of Data on Population Growth and Fertility Within the Framework of the Atlantida Program." Paper presented at the Interregional Workshop on the Methodology of Demographic Sample Surveys at Copenhagen, Denmark.

Jabine, T. B., and M. A. Bershad, 1968
    "Some Comments on the Chandrasekaran-Deming Technique for the Measure-
    ment of Population Change." Paper prepared for the CENTO Symposium
    on Demographic Statistics, Karachi, Pakistan.

Jackson, C. H. N., 1933
    "On the Time Density of Tsetse Flies." *Journal of Animal Ecology* 2: 204–09.

Kahn, R. L., and C. F. Cannell, 1957
    The Dynamics of Interviewing: Theory, Technique, and Cases. New York: Wiley.

Kerala, 1967
    "Report No. 1 for the Period 1965–66." Trivandrum: Kerala State Bureau
    of Economics and Statistics. November.

——————, 1968
    "Report No. 2 for the Period 1966–67." Trivandrum: Kerala State Bureau
    of Economics and Statistics. August.

Khan, M. K. H., 1960
    "Assessment of Birth Rate in West Pakistan from the Statistics of Primary
    Vaccination Against Smallpox." In *Summary Report of a Seminar on Population
    Growth and Economic Development.* Karachi: Institute of Development Economics.

Kish, L., 1965
    Survey Sampling. New York: Wiley.

Koons, D. A., 1971
    "Estimates of Completeness of Birth Registration, 1964–1968." U.S. Bureau
    of the Census, Response Research Branch Report No. 71-8, E14, no. 17 (April
    16). Processed.

Korea, Republic of, 1971
    "Proposal for a System of Special Health Statistics Promoters to Improve Vital
    Registration in Korea." Seoul: Ministry of Health and Social Affairs. Unpublished
    paper.

Krotki, K. J., 1967
    "The Problems of Estimating Vital Rates in Pakistan." In *Proceedings of the
    World Population Conference, Belgrade, 30 August–10 September, 1965* vol. 3.,
    New York: United Nations, pp. 154–58.

Krotki, K. J., and N. Ahmed, 1964
    "Vital Rates in East and West Pakistan: Tentative Results from the PGE
    Experiment." *Pakistan Development Review* 4, no. 4 (Winter): 734–59.

Lauriat, P., 1966
    "Field Experiences in Estimating Population Growth." In *Proceedings of the Social
    Statistics Section, 1966,* Washington, D.C.: American Statistical Association, pp.
    250–62.

Liberia, Republic of, 1971a
    "Selected Demographic Indices, 1970." *Bulletin of the Population Growth Survey*
    (February).

——————, 1971b
    "Patterns of Natality." *Demographic Annual of the Population Growth Survey,* Series
    N–1. Monrovia: Department of Planning and Economic Affairs, August.

——————, 1971c
    "Patterns of Mortality." *Demographic Annual of the Population Growth Survey,*
    Series D–1. Monrovia: Department of Planning and Economic Affairs, August.

Lincoln, F. C., 1930
    "Calculating Waterfowl Abundance on the Basis of Banding Returns." U.S.
    Dept. of Agriculture Circular no. 118 (May).

Linder, F., 1970
    "A Proposed New Vital Event Numeration Unitary System for Developed

Countries." *The Milbank Memorial Fund Quarterly* 48, no. 4, part 2 (October): 77–87.

Lininger, C. A., and D. P. Warwick, 1967
    Introduction to Survey Research. SERH, Ministeriode Trabajo, Lima (also in Spanish).

Losee, G. J., 1970
    "Design Elements of CIMED's Research Methods in Measuring Population Change." Unpublished working paper, December.

Madigan, F. C., 1973
    The Mindanao Center for Population Studies: A Philippine POPLAB Report. Scientific Series No. 8, Chapel Hill, N.C.: Laboratories for Population Statistics, July.

Marks, E. S., 1958
    "Probability and Automation in Clerical Operations." Technical Series No. 5. Philadelphia: National Analysts, Inc. April.

————, 1970
    "Measurement of Population Growth Through Household Sample Surveys." Paper presented at the Second Symposium on Household Surveys in Latin America, Rio de Janeiro.

Marks, E. S., and J. Waksberg, 1966
    "Evaluation of Coverage in the 1960 Census of Population Through Case-by-Case Checking." In *Proceedings of the Social Statistics Section, 1966.* Washington, D.C.: American Statistical Association, pp. 62–70.

Mauldin, W. P., 1966
    "Estimating Rates of Population Growth." In *Family Planning and Population Programs.* Edited by B. Berelson *et al.* Chicago: University of Chicago Press, pp. 635–53.

Mauldin, W. P., and L. L. Bean, 1969
    "Current Status of Family Planning Research and Evaluation." In *Proceedings of the Pakistan International Family Planning Conference at Dacca, January 28 to February 4, 1969.* Lahore: Sweden-Pakistan Family Welfare Project, pp. 542–50.

Mauldin, W. P., O. K. Sagen, and F. F. Stephan, 1964
    Report to the Managing Committee of the Population Growth Experiment. Pakistan, December 11. Mimeographed.

Mehta, D. C., 1967a
    Report on Under-Registration Study (Pilot), Urban Vaso Project, Gujarat. Gujarat, Amedabad: State Bureau of Health Intelligence, Directorate of Health and Medical Services (Health).

————, 1967b
    Report on Matching: Under-Registration Study (Pilot), Urban Vaso Project. Report Series No. 3, Kaira Sample Registration Research Project, KSRRP (Urban)-KU(9)-2. Gujarat, Ahmedabad: Directorate of Health and Medical Services.

————, 1969
    "Sample Registration in Gujarat, India." *Demography* 6, no. 4 (November): 403–11.

Mehta, D. C., and M. H. Shah, 1966
    Report on Sample Registration Scheme (Pilot), Rural Gujarat. Gujarat, Ahmedabad: Directorate of Health and Medical Services (Health).

————, 1968
    Report on Sample Registration, Rural Gujarat, October 1965 to September 1966. Gujarat, Ahmedabad: Directorate of Health and Medical Services (Health).

Moriyama, I. M., 1946
    "Estimated Completeness of Birth Registration: United States, 1935 to 1944."

Vital Statistics—Special Reports 23, no. 10 (September): 222–40.

Moser, C. A., 1967
Survey Methods in Social Investigation. London: Heinemann. First published in 1958.

Murty, D. V. R., and P. K. Jain, 1967
"Report on Pilot Sample Registration Scheme in Five Villages in Mehrauli Block, South Delhi: December 1, 1963–November 30, 1966." New Delhi: Central Family Planning Institute, February. Mimeographed report, labeled "Preliminary."

Naeem, J., 1969
"Estimation of Vital Rates of Lulliani by the Chandra-Deming Method." Paper prepared for the Conference of the International Union for the Scientific Study of Population, London.

Nathan, G., 1964
"On Optimal Matching Processes." Ph.D. disseration, Case Institute of Technology.

————, 1967
"Outcome Probabilities for a Record Matching Process with Complete Invariant Information." *Journal of the American Statistical Association* 62, no. 318 (June): 454–69.

Neter, J., and J. Waksberg, 1965
Response Errors in Collection of Expenditures Data by Household Interviews: An Experimental Study. Technical Paper No. 11, U.S. Bureau of the Census. Washington, D.C.: U.S. Government Printing Office.

Newcombe, H. B., 1965
"Record Linkage: Concepts and Potentialities." In *Mathematics and Computer Science in Biology and Medicine.* London: Medical Research Council—H.M. Stationary Office, pp. 43–49.

————, 1966
"Present State and Long-Term Objectives of the British Columbia Population Study." In *Proceedings of the Third International Congress of Human Genetics.* Baltimore: Johns Hopkins Press, pp. 291–313.

Nitzberg, D. M., and H. Sardy, 1965
"The Methodology of Computer Linkage of Health and Vital Records." In *Proceedings of the Social Statistics Section, 1965.* Washington, D.C.: American Statistical Association, pp. 100–06.

Oppenheim, A. N., 1966
Questionnaire Design and Attitude Measurement. New York: Basic Books.

Page, H. J., 1971
"Fertility and Mortality Estimation from Single-Round Survey Data." In *Proceedings of the Social Statistics Section, 1971.* Washington, D.C.: American Statistical Association, pp. 75–80.

Perkins, W. M., and C. D. Jones, 1965
"Matching for Census Coverage Checks." In *Proceedings of the Social Statistics Section, 1965.* Washington, D.C.: American Statistical Association, pp. 122–39.

Population Council, 1970
A Manual for Surveys of Fertility and Family Planning: Knowledge, Attitudes, and Practice. New York: The Population Council.

Population Growth Estimation, 1968
Report of the Population Growth Estimation Experiment: Description and Some Results for 1962 and 1963. Karachi: Pakistan Institute of Development Economics. Special publication.

————, 1971
>Final Report of the Population Growth Estimation Experiment, 1962–1965.* Dacca: Pakistan Institute of Development Economics.

Rachidi, M., 1973
"Discussion of Preliminary Results from the Moroccan PGE/ERAD Study," presented at the first meeting of the International Association of Survey Statisticians, Vienna.

Ramabhadran, V. K., 1971
"Experience and Problems in the Creation of the Sample Registration System in India." Paper delivered at the International Symposium on Statistical Problems in Population Research, The East-West Center, Honolulu.

Richardson, S. A., B. S. Dohrenwend, and D. Klein, 1965
Interviewing: Its Forms and Functions. New York: Basic Books.

Robinson, W. C., W. Seltzer, and S. S. Hashmi, 1965
"Quasi-Stable Estimates of the Vital Rates of Pakistan." *The Pakistan Development Review* V, no. 4 (Winter), Karachi: Pakistan Institute of Development Economics, 638–58.

Rumford, J. C., 1970
"Use of the Chandrasekar-Deming Technique in the Liberian Fertility Study." *Public Health Reports* 85, no. 11 (November): 965–73.

————, 1971
"Enumeration, Enumerator and Vital Event Characteristics Which Affect Case Finding in the Liberian Fertility Survey." Unpublished manuscript.

Rumford, J. C., Y. Heperkan, and N. Fincancioglu, 1968
"The Principles and Preliminary Results of the Turkish Demographic Survey." *Public Health Reports* 83, no. 7 (July): 573–82.

Samuel, E., 1969
"Comparison of Sequential Rules for Estimation of the Size of a Population." *Biometrics* 25, no. 3 (September): 517–27.

Sarma, R. S. S., 1964
"Use of Birth Registration Records to Estimate Resident Births in an Action Area for Family Planning Research in Greater Bombay." Demographic Training and Research Center, Chumbur, Bombay, (unpublished).

Schnabel, Z. E., 1938
"The Estimation of the Total Fish Population of a Lake." *American Mathematical Monthly* 45: 348–52.

Scott, C., 1967
"Sampling for Demographic and Morbidity Surveys in Africa." *Review of the International Statistical Institute* 35, no. 2: 154–71.

————, 1968
"Vital Rate Surveys in Tropical Africa: Some New Data Relevant to Sample Design." In *The Population of Tropical Africa.* Edited by J. C. Caldwell and C. Okonjo. London: Longmans, Green.

Scott, C., and J. B. Coker, 1969
"Sample Design in Time and Space for Vital Rate Surveys in Africa." *International Population Conference, London, 1969* vol. 1, Liege: International Union for the Scientific Study of Population, 1971, pp. 248–56.

Seber, G. A. F., 1970
"The Effects of Trap Response on Tag Recapture Estimates." *Biometrics* 26, no. 1 (March): 13–22.

Seltzer, W., 1968
"Benchmark Demographic Data for Pakistan: A Review of Summary Estimates

Derived from the PGE Experiment." Research Report No. 66, Pakistan Institute of Development Economics, Karachi, March.

_____, 1969

"Some Results from Asian Population Growth Studies." *Population Studies* 23, no. 3 (November): 395–406.

_____, 1971a

"PGE Studies: Cost and Effectiveness." In *Proceedings of the Social Statistics Section, 1971,* Washington, D.C.: American Statistical Association, pp. 97–105.

_____, 1971b

"Report and Recommendations with Respect to ERED/POPLAB Research Study." December. Mimeographed paper.

Seltzer, W., and A. Adlakha, 1969

"On the Effect of Errors in the Application of the Chandrasekar-Deming Technique." Paper prepared for the Population Council Seminar on The Chandrasekar-Deming Technique: Theory and Application, New York.

Shapiro, S., 1950a

"Development of Birth Registration and Birth Statistics in the United States." *Population Studies* 4, no. 1 (June): 86–111.

_____, 1950b

"Estimating Birth Registration Completeness." *Journal of the American Statistical Association* 45, no. 250 (June): 261–64.

_____, 1954

"Recent Testing of Birth Registration Completeness in the United States." *Population Studies* 8, no. 1 (July): 3–21.

Shapiro, S., and J. Schachter, 1952

"Methodology and Summary of the 1950 Birth Registration Test in the United States." *Estadistica* 10, no. 37: 688–99.

_____, 1954

"Birth Registration Completeness in the United States and Geographic Areas; Part I: Data for Each State." *Vital Statistics—Special Reports* 39, no. 2 (September): 37–70.

Simmons, W. R., 1972

Operational Control of Sample Surveys. Manual Series No. 2. Chapel Hill, N.C.: Laboratories for Population Statistics.

Sirken, M. G., 1972

Designing Forms for Demographic Surveys. Manual Series No. 3. Chapel Hill, N.C.: Laboratories for Population Statistics.

Sirken, M. G., and P. N. Royston, 1971

"Reasons Deaths are Missed in Household Surveys of Population Change." In *Proceedings of the Social Statistics Session, 1970.* Washington, D.C.: American Statistical Association, pp. 361–64.

Som, R. K., 1959

"On Recall Lapse in Demographic Studies." In *International Population Conference, Vienna, 1959.* Vienna: Christoph Reisser's Söhne, pp. 50–61.

_____, 1973

Recall Lapse in Demographic Enquiries. New York: Asia Publishing House.

Srinivasan, Shri K., and Shri A. Muthiah, 1968

"Problems of Matching Births Identified from Two Independent Sources." *The Journal of Family Welfare* 14, no. 4 (June): 13–22.

Sunter, A. B., and I. P. Fellegi, 1967

An Optimal Theory of Record Linkage. Ottawa, Canada: Dominion Bureau of Statistics.

Tacla, O., 1969

"Experiencia de Chile en materia de encuestas demograficas por muestreo." Paper prepared for the Interregional Workshop on the Methodology of Demographic Sample Surveys, Copenhagen, Denmark.

Tepping, B. J., 1955

Study of Matching Techniques for Subscription Fulfillment. Philadelphia: National Analysts, Inc., August.

————, 1960

Progress Report on the 1959 Matching Study. Philadelphia: National Analysts, Inc., Opinions Research Group, January.

————, 1968

"A Model for Optimal Linkage of Records." *Journal of the American Statistical Association* 63, no. 324 (December): 1321–32.

————, 1971

"The Application of a Linkage Model to the Chandrasekar-Deming Technique for Estimating Vital Events." U.S. Bureau of the Census, Technical Notes No. 4, Washington, D.C.

Thailand, Government of, National Statistical Office, 1969a

Report of the Survey of Population Change: 1964–67. Publication series E-SuR-No. 3-69. Bangkok: Office of the Prime Minister.

————, 1969b

Final Report: The Survey of Population Changes: Supplementary Survey on Knowledge of Attitude Toward, and Practice Concerning, Official Registration of Births and Deaths, March 21–April 22, 1966. Publication Series E-SuR-No. 4-69. Bangkok: Office of the Prime Minister.

Tracey, W. R., 1941

"Fertility of the Population of Canada." Reprinted from Dominion of Canada, Dominion Bureau of Statistics, *Seventh Census of Canada, 1931,* vol. 2, Census Monograph no. 3. Ottawa: Cloutier.

Turkish Demographic Survey, 1967

Vital Statistics from the Turkish Demographic Survey, 1965–66. Ankara: School of Public Health, Ministry of Health and Social Welfare, Republic of Turkey.

————, 1970

Vital Statistics from the Turkish Demographic Survey, 1966–67. Ankara: School of Public Health, Ministry of Health and Social Welfare, Republic of Turkey.

Tuthill, D. D., 1945

"Completeness of Birth Registration in Urban and Rural Areas: United States and Each State, December 1, 1939 to March 31, 1940." *Vital Statistics—Special Reports* 13, no. 6 (November): 99–115.

————, 1946

"Completeness of Registration of Births Occurring in Institutions and of Births Not Occurring in Institutions: United States, December 1, 1939 to March 31, 1940." *Vital Statistics—Special Reports* 23, no. 8 (August): 169–98.

United Nations, 1955

Handbook of Vital Statistics Methods. Studies in Methods, Series F, no. 7. New York: U.N. Department of Economic and Social Affairs.

————, 1961

The Mysore Population Study. Population Studies, no. 34. New York: U.N. Department of Economic and Social Affairs.

————, 1964a

Guanabara Demographic Pilot Survey: A Joint Project of the United Nations and the Government of Brazil. Population Studies, no. 35. New York: U.N. Department of Economic and Social Affairs.

————, 1964b

Handbook of Household Surveys: A Practical Guide for Inquiries on Levels of Living. Studies in Methods, Series F, no. 10. New York: U.N. Department of Economic and Social Affairs.

————, 1967

Manual IV: Methods of Estimating Basic Demographic Measures from Incomplete Data. Population Studies, no. 42. New York: U.N. Department of Economic and Social Affairs.

————, 1971

Methodology of Demographic Sample Surveys. Statistical Papers, Series M, no. 51. New York: U.N. Department of Economic and Social Affairs.

U.N. Advisory Mission to India, 1969

An Evaluation of the Family Planning Programme of the Government of India. New York: Department of Economic and Social Affairs, November.

U.N. Economic and Social Council, Statistical Office of the United Nations, 1969

Sources and Quality of Demographic Data and Measures Being Taken and Current Steps for Improvement for Purposes of Application to Development Planning. Paper presented at the International Seminar on the Application of Demographic Data and Studies to Development Planning, Kiev.

U.N. Economic Commission for Africa, 1971

Manual on Demographic Sample Surveys in Africa. Joint ECA/UNESCO document distributed at Seventh Session of the Conference of African Statisticians, Dakar.

U.S. Bureau of the Census, 1953

Infant Enumeration Study 1950. Procedural Studies of the 1950 Censuses, no. 1. Washington, D.C.: U.S. Government Printing Office.

————, 1960

The Post-Enumeration Survey, 1950: An Evaluation Study of the 1950 Censuses of Population and Housing. Technical Paper no. 4. Washington, D.C.

————, 1964a

Evaluation and Research Program of the U.S. Censuses of Population and Housing, 1960: Accuracy of Data on Population Characteristics as Measured by CPS-Census Match. Series ER60, no. 5. Washington, D.C.

————, 1964b

Evaluation and Research Program of the U.S. Censuses of Population and Housing, 1960: Accuracy of Data on Population Characteristics as Measured by Reinterviews. Series ER60, no. 4. Washington, D.C.

————, 1964c

Evaluation and Research Program of the U.S. Censuses of Population and Housing, 1960: Background, Procedures, and Forms. Series ER60, no. 1. Washington, D.C.

————, 1964d

Evaluation and Research Program of the U.S. Censuses of Population and Housing, 1960: Record Check Studies of Population Coverage. Series ER60, no. 2. Washington, D.C.

————, 1964e

Enterprise Statistics: 1958—Part 3 Link of Census Establishment and IRS Corporation Data. Series ES-3. Washington D.C.

————, 1965–7

Atlantida: A Case Study in Household Sample Surveys. Series ISPO 1, published in 14 separate booklets. Washington, D.C.: various dates between 1965 and 1967.

————, 1965a

Atlantida: A Case Study in Household Sample Surveys, Unit I: Survey Objectives and Description of Country. Series ISPO 1, no. 1-B. Washington, D.C.

————, 1965b
>   *Atlantida: A Case Study in Household Sample Surveys, Unit II. Content and Design of Household Surveys.* Series ISPO-1, no. 1-C. Washington, D.C.

————, 1967
>   *Atlantida: A Case Study in Household Sample Surveys, Unit VIII. Tabulation Processes.* Series ISPO 1, no. 1-J. Washington, D.C.

U.S. Census Office, 1872
>   *Ninth Census of the United States, 1870.* vol. 2, *Vital Statistics,* Washington, D.C.: U.S. Government Printing Office.

U.S. National Bureau of Standards, 1969
>   *Precision Measurement and Calibration: Statistical Concepts and Procedures.* Special Publication 300, vol. 1. Washington, D.C.

U.S. National Center for Health Statistics, 1969
>   *Comparison of the Classification of Place of Residence on Death Certificates and Matching Census Records, United States, May–August 1960.* Vital and Health Statistics, PHS Pub. no. 1000, Series 2, no. 30. Washington, D.C.: Public Health Service, January.

————, 1970
>   *A Study of Infant Mortality from Linked Records: Method of Study and Registration Aspects.* Pub. no. 1000, Series 20, no. 7. Washington, D.C.: Public Health Service.

————, 1972
>   *Vital Signs Present at Birth.* Vital and Health Statistics, DHEW Pub. no. (HSM) 72-1043, Series 2, no. 46, Rockville, Md., February.

Vallin, J., 1971
>   "L'enquête nationale démographique tunisienne." *Population,* Special Issue (March): 205–66.

van de Walle, E., 1968a
>   "Characteristics of African Demographic Data." In *The Demography of Tropical Africa.* By W. Brass *et al.* Princeton: Princeton University Press, pp. 12–87.

————, 1968b
>   "Note on the Effect of Age Misreporting." In *The Demography of Tropical Africa.* By W. Brass *et al.* Princeton: Princeton University Press, pp. 143–50.

Vincent, P. E., 1955
>   "Une méthode préconisée en URSS pour apprécier la qualité de statistiques démographiques." *Proceedings of the World Population Conference, 1954* vol. 4. New York: United Nations, pp. 241–47.

Vostrikova, A. M., 1963
>   *Sample Surveys in Demographic Statistics.* Report prepared for a meeting of developing countries, Moscow.

Wagner, G., and H. B. Newcombe, 1970
>   "Record Linkage—Its Methodology and Application in Medical Data Processing." *Methods of Information in Medicine* IX, no. 2 (April): 121–38.

Wells, H. B., 1971
>   "Dual Record Systems for Measurement of Fertility Change." Working paper no. 13. Honolulu: East-West Population Institute, April.

Wells, H. B., and B. L. Agrawal, 1967
>   "Sample Registration in India." *Demography* 4, no. 1: 374–87.

Wells, H. B., and D. G. Horvitz, 1973
>   "The State of the Art in Dual Record Systems for Measuring Population Change." Paper presented at the first meeting of the International Association of Survey Statisticians, Vienna.

Whelpton, P. K., 1934

"The Completeness of Birth Registration in the United States." *Journal of the American Statistical Association* 29, no. 186 (June): 125–36.

————, 1938

Needed Population Research. Lancaster, Pa.: The Science Press Printing Co.

Wishik, S. M., 1968

"Evaluation of National Family Planning Programs Through Group-Specific Fertility Patterns." In *Proceedings of the American Statistical Association, 1968.* Washington, D.C.: American Statistical Association, pp. 181–87.

Yusuf, F., 1968a

"Population Growth Estimation: Studies in Methodology I: Matching of Vital Events." Research Report No. 67. Karachi: Pakistan Institute of Development Economics.

————, 1968b

"Population Growth Estimation: Studies in Methodology II: Sample Design, Estimation Procedures and Reliability of Estimates." Research Report No. 76. Karachi: Pakistan Institute of Development Economics.

Yusuf, F., and A. Turowicz, 1967

A Comparison of Matched Reports of Vital Events Caught by the Two Systems of Data Collection in the PGE Experiment. Paper presented at the Seventh All Pakistan Statistical Conference, Dacca. Mimeographed.

Index

Accurate counts, problems of, 3
Action set:
  example of, 109
  in matching operations, 105, 108, 114
  in PGE approach, 106, 110–114
Active data collection methods, 72–73
Adaptive system, defined, 431 (*see also under* Information)
Addresses of structures:
  ambiguity of, in matching, 273
  correcting and updating, 177
  determination of, 185, 193
  discriminating power of, 210–211, 296, 325–326
  enumeration of unnumbered, 177, 185
  marking of, 176
  matching factors in, 193, 202, 273–275
  numbering procedures for, 173, 176–177, 213, 259*n*.5
  reporting errors in, 317
  reporting under *de facto* rule, 185 (*see also* Rules of enumeration)
  in rural areas, 274–276
  in sampling units, 173–177
  structure numbers defined, 449
  variations in, 320
Adjustments, to estimate defects, 342–344, 350
Administrative factors: (*see also* Project administration; Supervision)
  in adjustment policies, 344
  in civil registry utilization, 227–228
  in demographic analysis, 344
  in independence of sources, 425–426
  in political relationships, 227, 347
  publication policy, 348–352 (*see also under* Publication; Publication policy)
  in response correlation bias reduction, 97
  in sampling unit size, 130–132

Administrative section, in special registration, 249
African nations, population studies in, 46–49, 55–59
Age classification bias, 150–151
Age data:
  characteristic tabulations of, 225–226
  discrepancies in reports of, 80, 313–314
Age-specific fertility rate:
  adjustments for omissions of, 342–343, 354*n*.16
  definition of, 432
  and regression technique, 151
Age-specific vital rate estimation, 80
Agreement, weighting comparisons in terms of, 106–107
Alberta, birth registration results, 20
Algeria, demographic survey in, 48
Analysis unit, 432 (*see also* Cluster)
Area canvassing, 73–74, 83
Arkansas, 54
Asian nations:
  population studies in, 35–45, 53–54, 59
  urban migration and low estimates in, 411
Atlantida program, 180

Bailey, N. T. J., on formula to overcome ratio bias effects, 387
  on multiple round sampling, 408
Bangalore City (Mysore, India), 38
Bangladesh, 10*n*
Barbados, 49–50, 54
Base population: (*see also* Base population estimation)
  census coverage of, 143
  definition of, 432
  tabulations, 225–226
Base population estimation, 142–149, 233, 298–302 (*see also* PGE estimates)

Base population estimation *continued*
  calculations for, 299–302
  census-based computation, 76, 254
  control totals in, 222
  errors in, 88, 254–256, 314, 321–322, 333 (*see also* Errors)
  independent, 146–147, 333
  for institutions, 424–425
  migration in, 255, 322
  post-enumeration quality check, 333
  single-source biases in, 88, 143
  sources for deriving, 142–143, 254
  stratification in, 385–386
  variances in, 145–146
Base population section, in special registration, 248–249
Between-area components, of variance and covariance, 367
Bias: (*see also* Classification bias; Response correlation bias; Relative bias)
  in base population estimates, 143
  —overestimates, 321–322
  —underestimates, 256, 314–315
  calculations to reduce, 70
  in capture-tag-recapture, 60, 408
  components of, 69–70, 79, 81–82
  definition of, 432
  in dual systems approach, 87–93
  elimination by sample rotation, 398–399
  enumerator as source of, 81
  errors resulting in, 311–314
  factors affecting, downward, 321–326; upward, 314–321
  from households newly formed, 181
  with lack of independence, 87, 95, 144, 160*n*.5
  matching error in, 88, 101
  measurement and balancing of, 119, 143
  miscounting error as, 140
  in multiple-source studies, 407